Contemporary Authors®

Contemporary

Authors®

A Bio-Bibliographical Guide to
Current Writers in Fiction, General Nonfiction,
Poetry, Journalism, Drama, Motion Pictures,
Television, and Other Fields

volume 225

THOMSON

GALE

Detroit • New York • San Francisco • San Diego • New Haven, Conn. • Waterville, Maine • London • Munich

Contemporary Authors, Vol. 225

Project Editor
Lisa Kumar

Editorial
Katy Balcer, Sara Constantakis, Michelle Kazensky, Julie Keppen, Joshua Kondek, Mary Ruby, Lemma Shomali, Susan Strickland, Maikue Vang, Tracey Watson

Permissions
Denise Buckley

Imaging and Multimedia
Lezlie Light, Kelly A. Quin

Composition and Electronic Capture
Carolyn Roney

Manufacturing
Lori Kessler

LIBRARY OF CONGRESS CATALOG CARD NUMBER 62-52046

ISBN 0-7876-6705-6
ISSN 0010-7468

Printed in the United States of America
10 9 8 7 6 5 4 3 2 1

Contents

Preface vii

Product Advisory Board...xi

International Advisory Board...xii

CA Numbering System and
Volume Update Chart xiii

Authors and Media People
Featured in This Volume..xv

Acknowledgments xvii

Author Listings...1

Indexing note: All *Contemporary Authors* entries are indexed in the *Contemporary Authors* cumulative index, which is published separately and distributed twice a year.

As always, the most recent Contemporary Authors cumulative index continues to be the user's guide to the location of an individual author's listing.

Preface

Contemporary Authors (*CA*) provides information on approximately 115,000 writers in a wide range of media, including:

- Current writers of fiction, nonfiction, poetry, and drama whose works have been issued by commercial publishers, risk publishers, or university presses (authors whose books have been published only by known vanity or author-subsidized firms are ordinarily not included)

- Prominent print and broadcast journalists, editors, photojournalists, syndicated cartoonists, graphic novelists, screenwriters, television scriptwriters, and other media people

- Notable international authors

- Literary greats of the early twentieth century whose works are popular in today's high school and college curriculums and continue to elicit critical attention

A *CA* listing entails no charge or obligation. Authors are included on the basis of the above criteria and their interest to *CA* users. Sources of potential listees include trade periodicals, publishers' catalogs, librarians, and other users of the series.

How to Get the Most out of *CA*: Use the Index

The key to locating an author's most recent entry is the *CA* cumulative index, which is published separately and distributed twice a year. It provides access to *all* entries in *CA* and *Contemporary Authors New Revision Series* (*CANR*). Always consult the latest index to find an author's most recent entry.

For the convenience of users, the *CA* cumulative index also includes references to all entries in these Thomson Gale literary series: *Authors and Artists for Young Adults, Authors in the News, Bestsellers, Black Literature Criticism, Black Literature Criticism Supplement, Black Writers, Children's Literature Review, Concise Dictionary of American Literary Biography, Concise Dictionary of British Literary Biography, Contemporary Authors Autobiography Series, Contemporary Authors Bibliographical Series, Contemporary Dramatists, Contemporary Literary Criticism, Contemporary Novelists, Contemporary Poets, Contemporary Popular Writers, Contemporary Southern Writers, Contemporary Women Poets, Dictionary of Literary Biography, Dictionary of Literary Biography Documentary Series, Dictionary of Literary Biography Yearbook, DISCovering Authors, DISCovering Authors: British, DISCovering Authors: Canadian, DISCovering Authors: Modules* (including modules for Dramatists, Most-Studied Authors, Multicultural Authors, Novelists, Poets, and Popular/Genre Authors), *DISCovering Authors 3.0, Drama Criticism, Drama for Students, Feminist Writers, Hispanic Literature Criticism, Hispanic Writers, Junior DISCovering Authors, Major Authors and Illustrators for Children and Young Adults, Major 20th-Century Writers, Native North American Literature, Novels for Students, Poetry Criticism, Poetry for Students, Short Stories for Students, Short Story Criticism, Something about the Author, Something about the Author Autobiography Series, St. James Guide to Children's Writers, St. James Guide to Crime & Mystery Writers, St. James Guide to Fantasy Writers, St. James Guide to Horror, Ghost & Gothic Writers, St. James Guide to Science Fiction Writers, St. James Guide to Young Adult Writers, Twentieth-Century Literary Criticism, 20th Century Romance and Historical Writers, World Literature Criticism,* and *Yesterday's Authors of Books for Children.*

A Sample Index Entry:

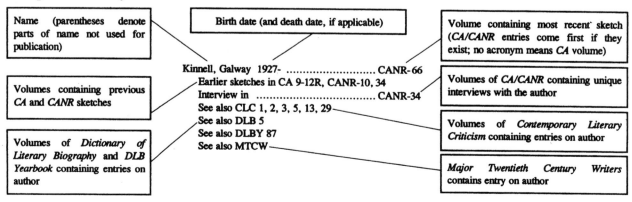

Name (parentheses denote parts of name not used for publication)

Birth date (and death date, if applicable)

Volume containing most recent sketch (*CA/CANR* entries come first if they exist; no acronym means *CA* volume)

Volumes containing previous *CA* and *CANR* sketches

Volumes of *Dictionary of Literary Biography* and *DLB Yearbook* containing entries on author

Kinnell, Galway 1927- CANR-66
Earlier sketches in CA 9-12R, CANR-10, 34
Interview in CANR-34
See also CLC 1, 2, 3, 5, 13, 29
See also DLB 5
See also DLBY 87
See also MTCW

Volumes of *CA/CANR* containing unique interviews with the author

Volumes of *Contemporary Literary Criticism* containing entries on author

Major Twentieth Century Writers contains entry on author

How Are Entries Compiled?

The editors make every effort to secure new information directly from the authors; listees' responses to our questionnaires and query letters provide most of the information featured in *CA*. For deceased writers, or those who fail to reply to requests for data, we consult other reliable biographical sources, such as those indexed in Thomson Gale's *Biography and Genealogy Master Index,* and bibliographical sources, including *National Union Catalog, LC MARC,* and *British National Bibliography.* Further details come from published interviews, feature stories, and book reviews, as well as information supplied by the authors' publishers and agents.

An asterisk (*) at the end of a sketch indicates that the listing has been compiled from secondary sources believed to be reliable but has not been personally verified for this edition by the author sketched.

What Kinds of Information Does An Entry Provide?

Sketches in *CA* contain the following biographical and bibliographical information:

- **Entry heading:** the most complete form of author's name, plus any pseudonyms or name variations used for writing

- **Personal information:** author's date and place of birth, family data, ethnicity, educational background, political and religious affiliations, and hobbies and leisure interests

- **Addresses:** author's home, office, or agent's addresses, plus e-mail and fax numbers, as available

- **Career summary:** name of employer, position, and dates held for each career post; resume of other vocational achievements; military service

- **Membership information:** professional, civic, and other association memberships and any official posts held

- **Awards and honors:** military and civic citations, major prizes and nominations, fellowships, grants, and honorary degrees

- **Writings:** a comprehensive, chronological list of titles, publishers, dates of original publication and revised editions, and production information for plays, television scripts, and screenplays

- **Adaptations:** a list of films, plays, and other media which have been adapted from the author's work

- **Work in progress:** current or planned projects, with dates of completion and/or publication, and expected publisher, when known

- **Sidelights:** a biographical portrait of the author's development; information about the critical reception of the author's works; revealing comments, often by the author, on personal interests, aspirations, motivations, and thoughts on writing

- **Interview:** a one-on-one discussion with authors conducted especially for *CA*, offering insight into authors' thoughts about their craft

- **Autobiographical essay:** an original essay written by noted authors for *CA*, a forum in which writers may present themselves, on their own terms, to their audience

- **Photographs:** portraits and personal photographs of notable authors

- **Biographical and critical sources:** a list of books and periodicals in which additional information on an author's life and/or writings appears

- **Obituary Notices** in *CA* provide date and place of birth as well as death information about authors whose full-length sketches appeared in the series before their deaths. The entries also summarize the authors' careers and writings and list other sources of biographical and death information.

Related Titles in the *CA* Series

Contemporary Authors Autobiography Series complements *CA* original and revised volumes with specially commissioned autobiographical essays by important current authors, illustrated with personal photographs they provide. Common topics include their motivations for writing, the people and experiences that shaped their careers, the rewards they derive from their work, and their impressions of the current literary scene.

Contemporary Authors Bibliographical Series surveys writings by and about important American authors since World War II. Each volume concentrates on a specific genre and features approximately ten writers; entries list works written by and about the author and contain a bibliographical essay discussing the merits and deficiencies of major critical and scholarly studies in detail.

Available in Electronic Formats

GaleNet. *CA* is available on a subscription basis through GaleNet, an online information resource that features an easy-to-use end-user interface, powerful search capabilities, and ease of access through the World-Wide Web. For more information, call 1-800-877-GALE.

Licensing. *CA* is available for licensing. The complete database is provided in a fielded format and is deliverable on such media as disk, CD-ROM, or tape. For more information, contact Thomson Gale's Business Development Group at 1-800-877-GALE, or visit us on our website at www.galegroup.com/bizdev.

Suggestions Are Welcome

The editors welcome comments and suggestions from users on any aspect of the *CA* series. If readers would like to recommend authors for inclusion in future volumes of the series, they are cordially invited to write the Editors at *Contemporary Authors*, Thomson Gale, 27500 Drake Rd., Farmington Hills, MI 48331-3535; or call at 1-248-699-4253; or fax at 1-248-699-8054.

Contemporary Authors Product Advisory Board

The editors of *Contemporary Authors* are dedicated to maintaining a high standard of excellence by publishing comprehensive, accurate, and highly readable entries on a wide array of writers. In addition to the quality of the content, the editors take pride in the graphic design of the series, which is intended to be orderly yet inviting, allowing readers to utilize the pages of *CA* easily and with efficiency. Despite the longevity of the *CA* print series, and the success of its format, we are mindful that the vitality of a literary reference product is dependent on its ability to serve its users over time. As literature, and attitudes about literature, constantly evolve, so do the reference needs of students, teachers, scholars, journalists, researchers, and book club members. To be certain that we continue to keep pace with the expectations of our customers, the editors of *CA* listen carefully to their comments regarding the value, utility, and quality of the series. Librarians, who have firsthand knowledge of the needs of library users, are a valuable resource for us. The *Contemporary Authors* Product Advisory Board, made up of school, public, and academic librarians, is a forum to promote focused feedback about *CA* on a regular basis. The six-member advisory board includes the following individuals, whom the editors wish to thank for sharing their expertise:

- **Anne M. Christensen,** Librarian II, Phoenix Public Library, Phoenix, Arizona.

- **Barbara C. Chumard,** Reference/Adult Services Librarian, Middletown Thrall Library, Middletown, New York.

- **Eva M. Davis,** Youth Department Manager, Ann Arbor District Library, Ann Arbor, Michigan.

- **Adam Janowski, Jr.,** Library Media Specialist, Naples High School Library Media Center, Naples, Florida.

- **Robert Reginald,** Head of Technical Services and Collection Development, California State University, San Bernadino, California.

- **Stephen Weiner,** Director, Maynard Public Library, Maynard, Massachusetts.

International Advisory Board

Well-represented among the 115,000 author entries published in *Contemporary Authors* are sketches on notable writers from many non-English-speaking countries. The primary criteria for inclusion of such authors has traditionally been the publication of at least one title in English, either as an original work or as a translation. However, the editors of *Contemporary Authors* came to observe that many important international writers were being overlooked due to a strict adherence to our inclusion criteria. In addition, writers who were publishing in languages other than English were not being covered in the traditional sources we used for identifying new listees. Intent on increasing our coverage of international authors, including those who write only in their native language and have not been translated into English, the editors enlisted the aid of a board of advisors, each of whom is an expert on the literature of a particular country or region. Among the countries we focused attention on are Mexico, Puerto Rico, Germany, Luxembourg, Belgium, the Netherlands, Norway, Sweden, Denmark, Finland, Taiwan, Singapore, Spain, Italy, South Africa, Israel, and Japan, as well as England, Scotland, Wales, Ireland, Australia, and New Zealand. The sixteen-member advisory board includes the following individuals, whom the editors wish to thank for sharing their expertise:

- **Lowell A. Bangerter,** Professor of German, University of Wyoming, Laramie, Wyoming.

- **Nancy E. Berg,** Associate Professor of Hebrew and Comparative Literature, Washington University, St. Louis, Missouri.

- **Frances Devlin-Glass,** Associate Professor, School of Literary and Communication Studies, Deakin University, Burwood, Victoria, Australia.

- **David William Foster,** Regent's Professor of Spanish, Interdisciplinary Humanities, and Women's Studies, Arizona State University, Tempe, Arizona.

- **Hosea Hirata,** Director of the Japanese Program, Associate Professor of Japanese, Tufts University, Medford, Massachusetts.

- **Jack Kolbert,** Professor Emeritus of French Literature, Susquehanna University, Selinsgrove, Pennsylvania.

- **Mark Libin,** Professor, University of Manitoba, Winnipeg, Manitoba, Canada.

- **C. S. Lim,** Professor, University of Malaya, Kuala Lumpur, Malaysia.

- **Eloy E. Merino,** Assistant Professor of Spanish, Northern Illinois University, DeKalb, Illinois.

- **Linda M. Rodríguez Guglielmoni,** Associate Professor, University of Puerto Rico—Mayagüez, Puerto Rico.

- **Sven Hakon Rossel,** Professor and Chair of Scandinavian Studies, University of Vienna, Vienna, Austria.

- **Steven R. Serafin,** Director, Writing Center, Hunter College of the City University of New York, New York City.

- **David Smyth,** Lecturer in Thai, School of Oriental and African Studies, University of London, England.

- **Ismail S. Talib,** Senior Lecturer, Department of English Language and Literature, National University of Singapore, Singapore.

- **Dionisio Viscarri,** Assistant Professor, Ohio State University, Columbus, Ohio.

- **Mark Williams,** Associate Professor, English Department, University of Canterbury, Christchurch, New Zealand.

CA Numbering System and Volume Update Chart

Occasionally questions arise about the *CA* numbering system and which volumes, if any, can be discarded. Despite numbers like " 29-32R," " 97-100" and "224," the entire *CA* print series consists of only 276 physical volumes with the publication of *CA* Volume 225. The following charts note changes in the numbering system and cover design, and indicate which volumes are essential for the most complete, up-to-date coverage.

CA **First Revision**
- 1-4R through 41-44R (11 books)
  Cover: Brown with black and gold trim.
  There will be no further First Revision volumes because revised entries are now being handled exclusively through the more efficient *New Revision Series* mentioned below.

CA **Original Volumes**
- 45-48 through 97-100 (14 books)
  Cover: Brown with black and gold trim.
  101 through 225 (125 books)
  Cover: Blue and black with orange bands.
  The same as previous *CA* original volumes but with a new, simplified numbering system and new cover design.

CA **Permanent Series**
- *CAP*-1 and *CAP*-2 (2 books)
  Cover: Brown with red and gold trim.
  There will be no further Permanent Series volumes because revised entries are now being handled exclusively through the more efficient *New Revision Series* mentioned below.

CA **New Revision Series**
- CANR-1 through CANR-131 (131 books)
  Cover: Blue and black with green bands.
  Includes only sketches requiring significant changes; **sketches are taken from any previously published CA, CAP, or CANR volume.**

If You Have:	You May Discard:
CA First Revision Volumes 1-4R through 41-44R and *CA Permanent Series* Volumes 1 and 2	*CA* Original Volumes 1, 2, 3, 4 Volumes 5-6 through 41-44
CA Original Volumes 45-48 through 97-100 and 101 through 225	**NONE:** These volumes will not be superseded by corresponding revised volumes. Individual entries from these and all other volumes appearing in the left column of this chart may be revised and included in the various volumes of the *New Revision Series*.
CA New Revision Series Volumes *CANR*-1 through *CANR*-131	**NONE:** The *New Revision Series* does not replace any single volume of *CA*. Instead, volumes of *CANR* include entries from many previous *CA* series volumes. All *New Revision Series* volumes must be retained for full coverage.

A Sampling of Authors and Media People
Featured in This Volume

Alfred Brendel

Brendel is one of the world's most celebrated classical pianists. Largely self-taught, he learned how to play piano by attending concerts in Vienna and listening to the masters. He has performed throughout Europe and America, released a number of recordings, including a 25-CD set, and published several books, including *Musical Thoughts and Afterthoughts,* published in the U.S. in 1977, *Music Sounded Out: Essays, Lectures, Interviews, Afterthoughts,* published in 1991, and *Alfred Brendel on Music: Collected Essays,* published in 2002. Among his many awards are the Franz Liszt Prize, the Royal Philharmonic Society prize, the Cannes Award, the Edison Award, and the Beethoven Ring award. He has also been named an honorary Knight Commander of the British Empire.

Robin Hathaway

Hathaway is the author of the "Andrew Fenimore Mystery" series, which features an old-fashioned cardiologist who works out of his house in Philadelphia. In plots revolving around his patients, and which also provide some "jargon-free medical lore," according to a critic for *Publishers Weekly,* Fenimore has solved such mysteries as why an Indian girl's body was buried in a local city park and how a little girl's toy dollhouse figures into a string of poisonings. Hathaway received an Agatha Award in 1998 for her novel *The Doctor Digs a Grave.*

Mat Hoffman

Hoffman is one of the greatest vert-ramp bicycle riders today. In addition to winning numerous free-style bicycle championships, Hoffman has created and named more than 100 of aerial stunt biking's flips, turns, and moves. He also is the star of two video games devoted to the sport and runs two companies, Hoffman Promotions and Hoffman Bikes. In 2002 he won the Action Sports Lifetime Achievement Award from ESPN. In 2003 Hoffman published *The Ride of My Life,* an account of his athletic career.

Joe Kubert

Kubert is a comic book illustrator and graphic novelist who served as director of publications for DC Comics from 1967 to 1976. Since 1976, he has run the Joe Kubert School of Cartoon and Graphic Art. Kubert is especially known for his realistic war comics, including the *Sgt. Rock* and *Enemy Ace* series, and for the graphic novels *Fax from Sarajevo: A Story of Survival* and *Yossel: April 19, 1943.* He has received the Will Eisner Award, the Harvey Award, the Jack Kirby Award, and the Ignatz Award, as well as two awards from the National Cartoonists Society.

Patrick McDonnell

McDonnell is the creator of the popular comic strip "Mutts," which appears in hundreds of newspapers throughout the United States. Featuring a dog named Earl and a cat named Mooch who live next door to each other, the comic strip focuses on the real-life concerns of everyday characters. Collections of the "Mutts" comic strip include *More Shtuff, Mutts: Sunday Mornings,* and *Mutts: The Art of Patrick McDonnell.* "Mutts" was named the Best Comic Strip of the Year by the National Cartoonists Society in 1998, while McDonnell has won five Harvey Awards for best syndicated strip.

Felice Picano

Picano is a leading figure in American gay literature as a novelist, publisher, and poet. After writing several mainstream literary works, Picano decided in the mid-1970s to write openly about the gay scene and his own life. Among his most popular works are *Ambidextrous: The Secret Lives of Children, Men Who Loved Me: A Memoir in the Form of a Novel,* and *Like People in History.* Picano also cowrote *The New Joy of Gay Sex.* He has won awards from the American Library Association, the Poetry Society of America, and *Gay Times of England,* as well as the Ferro-Grumley Award. An autobiographical essay by Picano is included in this volume of *CA.*

Mary Anne Stewart

Stewart, an Englishwoman who wrote travel books and short stories under her married name of Mary Anne Barker, is best remembered for her books describing British colonial life during the nineteenth century. Barker ran a sheep farm in New Zealand with her second husband. Her popular *Station Life in New Zealand* was based on her letters home to her sister. *A Year's Housekeeping in South Africa* recounts her experiences when her husband was made colonial secretary in that colony. Other books include *Holiday Stories for Boys and Girls* and the memoir *Colonial Memories.*

Nirmal Verma

A noted Hindi author and a leading member of India's "New Story" movement, Verma has published numerous novels, collections of short stories, and essays. Focusing on characters in modern India, Verma often portrays the loneliness and emptiness of contemporary life. Among Verma's books translated into English are *The Crows of Deliverance, The World Elsewhere and Other Stories,* and *India and Europe: Selected Essays.* In 1999 Verma was awarded the Jnanpith Award for outstanding contribution to the enrichment of Indian literature.

Acknowledgments

Grateful acknowledgment is made to those publishers, photographers, and artists whose work appear with these authors's essays. Following is a list of the copyright holders who have granted us permission to reproduce material in this volume of *CA*. Every effort has been made to trace copyright, but if omissions have been made, please let us know.

Photographs/Art

Glancy, Diane: Most photographs reproduced by permission of Diane Glancy. One photograph courtesy of Wayne Gilbert.

Picano, Felice: Most photographs reproduced by permission of Felice Picano. One photograph courtesy of Edgar B. Anderson. One water portrait courtesy of Don Bachardy. Lowe, Bob, photograph, reproduced by permission of Felice Picano.

A

ACKMANN, Martha (A.) 1951-

PERSONAL: Born February 11, 1951, in MO; father worked for Department of Defense in mapmaking. *Education:* Lindenwood College, B.A.; Middlebury College, M.A.; University of Massachusetts, Ph.D.; attended Oxford University.

ADDRESSES: Office—Porter Hall, Room 122, Mount Holyoke College, 50 College St., South Hadley, MA 01075-1426; fax: 413-538-2082. *E-mail*—mackmann@mtholyoke.edu.

CAREER: Educator, journalist, and author. Mount Holyoke College, South Hadley, MA, lecturer in women's studies, 1987—, director of Community-Based Learning Program, Weissman Center for Leadership. Founding editor, *LEGACY: A Journal of American Women Writers,* University of Nebraska Press.

AWARDS, HONORS: Corecipient of the Amelia Earhart Research Scholars Grant, the Ninety-Nines.

WRITINGS:

The Mercury Thirteen: The Untold Story of Thirteen American Women and the Dream of Space Flight, Random House (New York, NY), 2003.

Contributor to periodicals, including the *New York Times, Chicago Tribune, Washington Post, Los Angeles Times,* and *Salon.com.*

SIDELIGHTS: Martha Ackmann is an educator and author whose writings range from the discrepancy in prize money awarded to male versus female Wimbledon champions to President Clinton's relationship with Monica Lewinsky. She has also written extensively about the poet Emily Dickinson for an academic audience. In a *Library Journal* review of her first book, *The Mercury Thirteen: The Untold Story of Thirteen American Women and the Dream of Space Flight,* Jeffrey Beall referred to the work as "a feminist perspective on the space program." The book recounts the little-known tale of the women who tested during the early 1960s in hopes of becoming astronauts. In 1961 Randolph Lovelace II, head of NASA's Life Sciences Committee, gathered the nation's best female pilots in Albuquerque, New Mexico, to determine if women were capable of handling the rigors of space travel. These pilots underwent the same grueling physical and psychological exams as their male counterparts. The women's results were equal to those of the men, and in some cases even superior. However, when it came time for flight simulations and further training at the U.S. Naval School of Aviation Medicine in Pensacola, Florida, NASA pulled the plug on Lovelace's experiment, denying the women advancement into the astronaut program. The decision led to the United States forfeiting its chance to launch the first woman into space, an honor that went to the Russians in 1963, twenty years ahead of American astronaut Sally Ride. While noting the difficulty in wading through the large amount of details, Alice Kessler-Harris from *Women's Review of Books* pointed out that Ackmann relates how many of the women involved with the program ultimately realized that "NASA's dismissal of the women was part of a larger system of social bias that restricted women's opportunity in nearly every aspect of American life." *Booklist* contributor Carol Haggas agreed stating that *The Mercury Thirteen* "delivers both a stinging indictment of an intolerant society and a stirring endorsement of women whose valor and dedication remain inspirational."

BIOGRAPHICAL AND CRITICAL SOURCES:

PERIODICALS

American Scientist, January-February, 2004, Volume 92, issue 1, Kathryn D. Sullivan, "Ad Astra per Aspera," p. 74.

Astronomy, December, 2003, Volume 31, issue 12, Mae Jemison, "The Right Stuff," p. 102.

Booklist, June 1, 2003, Carol Haggas, review of *The Mercury Thirteen: The Untold Story of Thirteen American Women and the Dream of Space Flight,* p. 1733.

Kirkus Reviews, April 1, 2003, review of *The Mercury Thirteen,* p. 513.

Library Journal, June 1, 2003, Jeffrey Beall, review of *The Mercury Thirteen,* p. 158.

Miami Herald, June 25, 2003, Anne Bartlett, review of *The Mercury Thirteen.*

Newsday, July 6, 2003, Wendy Smith, "Reaching for the Stars," p. 30.

Publishers Weekly, April 21, 2003, Natalie Danford, "Babes in NASA-land: PW Talks with Martha Ackmann," p. 46; review of *The Mercury Thirteen,* p. 46.

School Library Journal, November, 2003, Christine C. Menefee, review of *The Mercury Thirteen,* p. 172.

Time, June 2, 2003, Lev Grossman, "Barred from Heaven," p. 32.

Times (Seattle), August 25, 2003, "In the Space Program's Infancy, Thirteen Female Pilots Were Grounded by Sexism."

USA Today, June 26, 2003, "Mercury Boldly Goes into Forgotten History," p. 6.

Women's Review of Books, July, 2003, Volume 20, issue 10/11, Alice Kessler-Harris, "Into the Blue."

ONLINE

Mount Holyoke Web site, http://www.mtholyoke.edu/ (November 7, 2003), faculty profile.

Philadelphia City Paper Web site, http://citypaper.net/ (November 7, 2003), A. D. Amorosi, review of *The Mercury Thirteen.*

Racerchicks Web site, http://www.racerchicks.com/ (November 7, 2003), review of *The Mercury Thirteen.*

OTHER

"Interview: Martha Ackmann Discusses Her New Book 'The Mercury Thirteen'" (radio interview), *All Things Considered,* National Public Radio, June 17, 2003.

"Mercury Thirteen Project Helped Pave the Way for Female Astronauts" (government custom wire), Military and Government Collection, April 8, 2004.*

*   *   *

AFFINITO, Alfonso G. 1930-

PERSONAL: Born November 1, 1930, in New Haven, CT. *Politics:* Democrat. *Religion:* "Religious Science." *Hobbies and other interests:* Opera.

ADDRESSES: Home—576 Forest Rd., West Haven, CT 06516. *E-mail*—gioman2@aol.com.

CAREER: Playwright.

MEMBER: Dramatists Guild of America, Authors League of America.

AWARDS, HONORS: Winner of Mark Twain Playwriting Competition, Mark Twain Masquers, 1987, for *Second Sunday in May,* 1986, for *Dinner at Armand's,* and 1988, for *On Golden Wings.*

WRITINGS:

PLAYS

On Golden Wings, Yale University (New Haven, CT), 1997.

Second Sunday in May, Warner Studio Theater (Torrington, CT), 1998.

Agrippina, Studio Theatre, Inc. (New York, NY), 2000. *Dinner at Dario's,* Studio Theater, Inc. (New York, NY), 2003.

Also author of the play *Dinner at Armand's.* Author of a poem published in an anthology by International Library of Poetry.

WORK IN PROGRESS: Yesterday's Cakes, a play dealing with the problems of aging homosexuals.

SIDELIGHTS: Alfonso G. Affinito told *CA:* "I began to write plays as an experiment after being, for many years, passionate and exhilarated by the great classics and contemporary masterpieces. It is an outlet to express reactions to social, emotional, and universal problems which surround the human condition. I feel that we are all common denominators in one way or another and that there is always identification found, and truth felt, in drama and comedy. The writing process differs for each play and is peculiar to each work; at least it is in my case."

*   *   *

AIZLEY, Harlyn

PERSONAL: Female. *Education:* Brandeis University; Harvard University, M.A. (education).

ADDRESSES: Agent—c/o Author Mail, Alyson Books, 6922 Hollywood Blvd., Ste. 1000, Los Angeles, CA 90028. *E-mail*—buyingdad@aol.com.

CAREER: Author.

WRITINGS:

Buying Dad: One Woman's Search for the Perfect Sperm Donor, Alyson Books (Los Angeles, CA), 2003.

Contributor of fiction and poetry to numerous magazines and journals, including *Berkeley Fiction Review, Caffeine, Cups, Dialogue, Inside, Sierra Nevada College Review,* and *South Carolina Review* and the

anthologies *Beginnings, Love Shook my Heart,* and *Scream When You Burn.* Contributor of nonfiction articles to *Boston Magazine,* and the anthologies *The Best American Neurotica,* and *Mondo Barbie Redux.*

SIDELIGHTS: In her first book, *Buying Dad: One Woman's Search for the Perfect Sperm Donor,* writer Harlyn Aizley chronicles the story of her decision to begin a family with her partner, Faith. After weighing their options, they decide that Aizley, who at near forty is the older of the two, should try to conceive their first child through artificial insemination using donor sperm. In this memoir, Aizley details with humor the specifics of the process, including their choice to use an unknown donor rather than a friend, their struggles with the decisions involved in the selection process, such as the donor's race (Aizley and her partner are both Jewish), height, and a multitude of other characteristics, the insemination process itself, and Aizley's subsequent pregnancy. While attempting to conceive, Aizley also learns that her mother has cancer. This leads her to explore her feelings about parenthood more broadly, and she examines both her thoughts about becoming a mother and about losing one.

Margaret Cardwell in *Library Journal* noted that there are not many books dealing with the topic of lesbians who choose to become parents through artificial insemination, and she found Aizley's book to be a "thoroughly captivating read about the foibles of a twenty-first-century family." She also praised the humor with which Aizley tackles a number of complex and emotional topics, and observed that "rather than presenting a dry, tedious, and depressing narrative, she leaves the reader laughing out loud." Julia Query, in "Women's Review of Books" also praised Aizley's humorous approach and openness, and noted that while Aizley "presents herself as a stereotypical Jewish, neurotic, mildly self-hating lesbian...she doesn't stay two dimensional for long." She commented that Aizley "is that wondrous type of humor writer who dares to be vulnerable and open without losing her timing." Query felt that while the book holds appeal for those who, like Aizley, have been through the process of trying to conceive using donor sperm, it is also a "fun introduction to the topic" for those with little knowledge of the subject. A reviewer for *Publishers Weekly* also commented on the book's widespread appeal, noting that once the process of trying to conceive begins, "Aizley's tale reads like any woman's: failed insemination procedures, fears of fertility treatments and huge doses of self-doubt." Whitney Scott, writing for *Booklist* concluded that "perhaps anyone who has contemplated a baby will smile, chuckle, even laugh out loud at Aizley's story."

BIOGRAPHICAL AND CRITICAL SOURCES:

PERIODICALS

Booklist, June 1, 2003, Whitney Scott, review of *Buying Dad: One Woman's Search for the Perfect Sperm Donor,* p. 1715.
Curve, August, 2003, Rachel Pepper, review of *Buying Dad,* p. 44.
Kirkus Reviews, May 15, 2003, review of *Buying Dad,* p. 723.
Library Journal, June 1, 2003, Margaret Cardwell, review of *Buying Dad,* p. 146.
Publishers Weekly, April 21, 2003, review of *Buying Dad,* pp. 45-46.
Women's Review of Books, December, 2003, Julia Query, "Creating 'gay-bies,'" pp. 17-19.

ONLINE

Harlyn Aizley Home Page, http://www.buyingdad.com (March 6, 2004).*

*   *   *

ALTERMAN, Glenn 1946-

PERSONAL: Born November 18, 1946, in Brooklyn, NY; son of Harold Alterman (a bar owner). *Education:* Emerson College, B.S.

ADDRESSES: Home—400 West 43rd St., No. 7G, New York, NY 10036; fax: 212-967-8930 *E-mail*—glennalt@rcn.com.

CAREER: Actor and writer.

AWARDS, HONORS: Winner of Three Genres Playwrights Contest, with *Coulda, Woulda, Shoulda;* winner of Bloomington National Playwrights Project competition, with *Nobody's Flood.*

WRITINGS:

Street Talk: Character Monologues for Actors, Smith & Kraus (Newbury, VT), 1991.
Uptown: Original Monologues, Smith & Kraus (Newbury, VT), 1992.
Two Minutes and Under: Original Character Monologues for Actors, Smith & Kraus (Newbury, VT), 1993.
(Editor) *What to Give Your Agent for Christmas: And 100 Other Suggestions for the Working Actor,* Smith & Kraus (Lyme, NY), 1995.
Beginnings: Monologues of the Stars, Smith & Kraus (Lyme, NH), 1996.
Promoting Your Acting Career, Allworth Press (New York, NY), 1998.
Two-Minute Monologs: Original Audition Scenes for Professional Actors, Meriwether Publishing (Colorado Springs, CO), 1998.
Creating Your Own Monologue, Allworth Press (New York, NY), 1999.
An Actor's Guide: Making It in New York, Allworth Press (New York, NY), 2002.
More Two Minutes and Under: Character Monologues for Actors, Smith & Kraus (Hanover, NH), 2002.
The Perfect Audition Monologue, Smith & Kraus (Hanover, NH), 2003.

Other books include *The Job Book: 100 Acting Jobs for Actors* and *The Job Book II: 100 Day Jobs for Actors,* both published by Smith & Kraus. Work represented in anthologies, including *The Best Women's Monologues of 1992.* Also author of film scripts.

Also author of the plays including, *Coulda, Woulda, Shoulda* (one-act; performed in a staged reading in New York, NY, at Primary Stages Theater), published in *The Three Genres* (college textbook), Prentice-Hall (Tappan, NJ), 6th and 7th editions; *The Danger of Strangers,* produced at West Bank Café Theater and by Circle Repertory Laboratory in Pittsburgh, PA, at Pittsburgh New Works Festival; *Dirty Prayers,* produced at West Bank Café Theater; *Fifty, with Mickey,* performed in a staged reading by American Myth Project in New York, NY, at Primary Stages Theater, produced at West Bank Café Theater; *God in Bed,* produced by Laboratory Theater Company at West Bank Café Theater; *Goin' 'round on Rock Solid Ground,* produced by Circle Repertory Laboratory at West Bank Café Theater; *Heartstrings* (musical), produced on tour of U.S. cities; *Kiss Me When It's Over* (musical), produced in New York, NY, at La Mama Experimental Theater Club; *Nobody's Flood,* produced by Bloomington Playwrights Project; *Once in a Blue Moon,* produced by Circle Repertory Laboratory at Turnip Festival; *The Pain in the Poetry,* produced at West Bank Café Downstairs Theater; *Spilt Milk,* performed by Emerging Artists Theater Company, New York, NY; *Tourists of the Mindfield,* produced at West Bank Café Theater and Second Stage, Playwrights Horizons Theater, New York, NY; *Toxic Redemption,* produced in a staged reading in New York, NY, at Primary Stages Theater; and *Unfamiliar Faces,* performed in a staged reading by New York Project in New York, NY, at Primary Stages Theater, produced at West Bank Café Theater, and in New York, NY, at Circle in the Square Downtown.

SIDELIGHTS: Glenn Alterman told *CA:* "Most of the books I write are theater-related books. I write primarily for actors and those in the entertainment industry. I was an award-winning actor for twenty-five years, working in film, television, and theater. Many of my insights come from my own experience.

"I've written five books of original monologues. I very much enjoy the monologue form. I even wrote a book for actors wanting to write their own monologues. Aside from the books, I've written both plays and films.

"My main intent now is writing for theater and film. I plan to take the next couple of years off from book writing and focus on plays and films."

BIOGRAPHICAL AND CRITICAL SOURCES:

PERIODICALS

Library Journal, February 15, 2000, Howard E. Miller, review of *Creating Your Own Monologue,* p. 174.

ONLINE

Glenn Alterman Studio, http://www.glennalterman.com (December 10, 2003).

ALTSCHULER, Glenn C. 1950-

PERSONAL: Born 1950. *Education:* Cornell University, Ph.D. (American history), 1976.

ADDRESSES: Home—Ithaca, NY. *Office*—B-20 Day Hall, Cornell University, Ithaca, NY 14853. *E-mail*—gca1@cornell.edu.

CAREER: Administrator, educator, and author. Cornell University, Ithaca, NY, 1981—, currently Thomas and Dorothy Litwin Professor of American Studies, School of Continuing Education and Summer Sessions, dean, 1991—.

Regular panelist on national and international affairs for "The Ivory Tower Half-Hour," WCNY Television; formerly columnist for "Education Life" section of the *New York Times.*

AWARDS, HONORS: Clark Teaching Award, Donna and Robert Paul Award for excellence in faculty advising, and Kendall S. Carpenter Award for outstanding advising, all from Cornell University.

WRITINGS:

Andrew D. White: Educator, Historian, Diplomat, Cornell University Press (Ithaca, NY), 1979.
Race, Ethnicity, and Class in American Social Thought, 1865-1919, Harlan Davidson (Arlington Heights, IL), 1982.
(With Jan M. Saltzgaber) *Revivalism, Social Conscience, and Community in the Burned-over District: The Trial of Rohad Bement,* Cornell University Press (Ithaca, NY), 1983.
Better Than Second Best: Love and Work in the Life of Helen Magill, University of Illinois Press (Urbana, IL), 1990.
(With David I. Grossvogel) *Changing Channels: America in TV Guide,* University of Illinois Press (Urbana, IL), 1992.
(With Stuart M. Blumin) *Rude Republic: Americans and Their Politics in the Nineteenth Century,* Princeton University Press (Princeton, NJ), 2000.
All Shook Up: How Rock 'n Roll Changed America, Oxford University Press (New York, NY), 2003.

(With Isaac Kramnick and R. Laurence Moore) *The 100 Most Notable Cornellians,* Cornell University Press (Ithaca, NY), 2004.

Also contributor of articles to the *New York Times* and to academic journals, including the *New England Quarterly, Journal of Social History,* and *Cross Currents.*

SIDELIGHTS: A longtime faculty member at Cornell University and dean of its School of Continuing Education, Glenn C. Altschuler is a professor and one of the driving forces in the growing American Studies department. His course in American popular culture remains one of Cornell's most well-liked classes. His books, covering revivalism, television, and rock-and-roll, among other subjects, reflect his interest in popular culture and mass movements.

Altschuler's first book, however, deals with the career of a man from the upper reaches of society whose sense of noblesse oblige led him to pioneering reforms in a number of areas. *Andrew D. White: Educator, Historian, Diplomat* tells the story of Cornell's first president, whose efforts to create a coeducational, nonsectarian institution that would provide a progressive, practical education to its students made him a controversial figure in his day, and a hero in the annals of educational reform. Altschuler's portrayal of White is not entirely flattering, as Geoffrey Blodgett explained in the *American Historical Review:* "The portrait emerges of a self-serving, disingenuous administrator who shunned authentic female equality, championed didactic Christianity, was guilty of occasional intellectual dishonesty, and tolerated crimes against freedom." As for White's other careers, Altschuler finds him overly opinionated and moralistic as a historian, and naive and inept in his posts as ambassador to Germany. Some reviewers found the biography a bit unfair. "Altschuler's research is thorough, but his book goes far in demonstrating that the New Left may possess inappropriate tools for understanding such men as White," maintained Anne Hummel Sherrill in *Historian.* While acknowledging that "Altschuler does tend to underestimate the power of forces arrayed against White," *Journal of American History* contributor Benjamin G. Rader found it "a superb biography that adds significantly to our knowledge of nineteenth-century reformers."

In *Revivalism, Social Conscience, and Community in the Burned-over District: The Trial of Rhoda Bement* Altschuler and Jan M. Saltzgaber tell the tale of another would-be reformer from the nineteenth century, but one operating in the very different social setting of Seneca Falls, New York. When Presbyterian parishioner Rhoda Bement began to press the church leadership on abolition and temperance, she found herself brought up before an ecclesiastical tribunal. The book, which includes essays by each author and a transcript of the trial, "demonstrates once more how well a case study in local history can explore and illuminate regional and national issues," according to *Church History* contributor John Opie. The authors "argue persuasively that Bement's trial on the charges of 'unchristian' and 'unladylike behavior' sheds light on the inner dynamics of church and community life in the pre-Civil War period," observed Clifford E. Clark in *History: Reviews of New Books.* The result, according to a *Choice* reviewer, is a "superb example of the method of document case study."

Altschuler creates something of a hybrid of both these books in *Better Than Second Best: Love and Work in the Life of Helen Magill,* a biography of America's first female Ph.D. recipient, the assertive, unconventional woman who went on to marry Andrew D. White. "In writing about McGill, Altschuler not only helps us appreciate the achievements of a driven life but also makes us wonder about the society that consistently managed to put a woman who was 'better than second best' in second place," explained Eugenia Kaledin in *American Historical Review.* Born in 1853, Helen Magill was the first female to attend Boston Latin School, where her father taught, but unlike the rest of her class, she was denied admittance to Harvard. Instead, she earned a place in Boston University's Ph.D. program and later studied at Cambridge, but she still could not gain a decent position when she graduated. Seeking intellectual companionship, she married Andrew White but soon realized that she was "second best" in his eyes, compared to his devoted first wife, Angel. "It is not an altogether pleasant experience to feel a part of Helen Magill White's life through all its vicissitudes, but it is a very engrossing one," commented Jane Lewis in the *Journal of American History.*

Altschuler and coauthor Stuart M. Blumin provide a broader view of the antebellum period in *Rude Republic: Americans and Their Politics in the Nineteenth Century.* Focusing on small towns, the authors "examine the sustained participation of a few and the apparent indifference of the many," reported *Booklist* reviewer Vernon Ford. Through diaries, letters, novels, and newspapers, the authors trace the growing importance of politics in the lives of ordinary citizen as the nation approached the Civil War and its aftermath. The result, according to a *Publishers Weekly* reviewer, is a "rich and entertaining study."

Much of Glenn C. Altschuler's work has focused on nineteenth-century history, but he has also become known for studies of two ubiquitous, modern influences that would have amazed, and probably appalled, the generation of Andrew D. White and Helen Magill. In *Changing Channels: America in TV Guide,* Altschuler and coauthor David I. Grossvogel "look beyond the local listings of the magazine and serve up a comprehensive analysis of the articles themselves," explained Robert Thompson in the *Journal of Popular Culture.* Often dismissed as fluff, *TV Guide* did at one time include serious analysis of news, entertainment, and the impact of this hugely popular medium, with articles from the likes of Margaret Mead, John F. Kennedy, John Updike, and Betty Friedan. Through such articles, the authors are able to trace the magazine's, and the medium's, changing attitudes toward African Americans and women, and the way those attitudes mirror the wider society.

All Shook Up: How Rock 'n Roll Changed America looks at the only cultural phenomenon more omnipresent, and possibly even more influential, than television. Altschuler concentrates on the 1950s and early 1960s, when rock music sent parents into a panic and psychologists were called upon to analyze the music's dark tribal undertones, but there is also a chapter on rock's continuing influence. Throughout, Altschuler notes the ways that the music reflected the racial, sexual, and political conflicts that surrounded it. While there have been serious biographies of rock's legendary performers and cultural critiques of its style and musical importance, Altschuler "is one of the first to do rock-and-roll the significant service of locating it within the cultural and political maelstrom it helped to create," noted Eric Alterman in a review for the *Atlantic Monthly.*

BIOGRAPHICAL AND CRITICAL SOURCES:

PERIODICALS

American Historical Review, February, 1980, Geoffrey Blodgett, review of *Andrew D. White: Educator, Historian, Diplomat,* p. 226; February, 1984, Ed-

win S. Gaustad, review of *Revivalism, Social Conscience, and Community in the Burned-over District: The Trial of Rohad Bement,* p. 204; October, 1991, Eugenia Kaledin, review of *Better Than Second Best: Love and Work in the Life of Helen Magill,* p. 1294; October, 2001, Tyler Anbinder, review of *Rude Republic: Americans and Their Politics in the Nineteenth Century,* p. 1355.

Atlantic Monthly, July-August, 2003, Eric Alterman, "Rock On," pp. 143-144.

Booklist, April 1, 2000, Vernon Ford, review of *Rude Republic,* p. 1416.

Choice, July-August, 1983, review of *Revivalism, Social Conscience, and Community in the Burned-over District,* p. 1613; October, 1992, W. E. Colman, review of *Changing Channels: America in TV Guide,* p. 290; November, 2000, review of *Rude Republic,* p. 591.

Christian Century, May 11, 1983, review of *Revivalism, Social Conscience, and Community in the Burned-over District,* p. 466.

Church History, September, 1984, John Opie, review of *Revivalism, Social Conscience, and Community in the Burned-over District,* pp. 409-410.

Civil War History, June, 2001, Michael F. Holt, review of *Rude Republic,* p. 164.

Historian, November, 1980, Anne Hummel Sherrill, review of *Andrew D. White,* pp. 152-153.

History: Reviews of New Books, October, 1982, Clarke A. Chambers, review of *Race, Ethnicity, and Class in American Social Thought, 1865-1919,* pp. 6-7; October, 1983, Clifford E. Clark, review of *Revivalism, Social Conscience, and Community in the Burned-over District,* p. 7; spring, 1991, Sylvia D. Hoffert, review of *Better Than Second Best,* p. 136.

Journal of American History, March, 1980, Benjamin G. Rader, review of *Andrew D. White,* p. 958; March, 1991, Jane Lewis, review of *Better Than Second Best,* p. 1380; September, 1993, James Baughman, review of *Changing Channels,* p. 749; September, 2001, Philip J. Ethington, review of *Rude Republic,* p. 644.

Journal of Higher Education, January, 1981, Mark Beach, review of *Andrew D. White,* pp. 109-110.

Journal of Popular Culture, spring, 1994, Robert Thompson, review of *Changing Channels,* p. 220.

Journal of the West, fall, 2001, William M. Gray, review of *Rude Republic,* p. 111.

Kirkus Reviews, February 15, 1992, review of *Changing Channels,* p. 223.

Library Journal, April 1, 2000, Edward G. McCormack, review of *Rude Republic,* p. 114; July, 2003,

James E. Perone, review of *All Shook Up: How Rock 'n Roll Changed America,* p. 84.

Publishers Weekly, March 27, 2000, review of *Rude Republic,* p. 62; June 9, 2003, review of *All Shook Up,* p. 46.

Reviews in American History, December, 2000, Sven Beckert, review of *Rude Republic,* p. 560.

ONLINE

Cornell University Web site, http://www.cornell.edu/ (July 12, 2004), "Glenn C. Altschuler."*

*   *   *

AMSDEN, David 1980-

PERSONAL: Born 1980.

ADDRESSES: Agent—c/o Author Mail, William Morrow/HarperCollins, 10 E. 53rd Street, 7th Floor, New York, NY 10022.

CAREER: Author, journalist.

WRITINGS:

Important Things That Don't Matter, William Morrow (New York, NY), 2003.

Contributor to *New York* magazine.

SIDELIGHTS: A magazine contributor by the age of nineteen, David Amsden became a published novelist at age twenty-three with *Important Things That Don't Matter.* A former intern at the *New Yorker* and a regular contributor to *New York* magazine, Amsden fits easily into the city's hipster literary scene, but he felt a certain dissatisfaction with its literature. "Enough with this uber-neurotic fiction where nothing really happens! I can't relate to any of the stuff! I just wanted something that felt really raw and honest," he told *Gawker.com* editor Elizabeth Spiers in an interview for *Salon.com.* At the same time, Amsden wanted to correct another flaw he saw in a number of stories he came across. As he told Spiers, "'I was reading stories

from the '70s and '80s about couples [that are having problems]'. . . . *Important Things That Don't Matter,* he explains, reverses the traditional model and tells the story from the child's point of view."

In the book, the unnamed boy-narrator tells of his parents' divorce and his subsequent relationship with his cocaine-addicted father, who goes through an assortment of dead-end jobs and relationships, while treating his young son to trips to the local pub. "The narrator's voice is a likable mixture of bewilderment and tentative black humor, and some of the scenes . . . are well cast and darkly ironic, but the book as a whole doesn't gather much momentum," concluded a *Publishers Weekly* reviewer. *Onion A.V. Club* reviewer Tasha Robinson found that "These may be the most important things that ever happened to the narrator, but he doesn't know why or how they shaped him. Because he never leaves his own well-insulated head, they don't particularly matter to anyone else." For a *Kirkus Reviews* contributor, "The problem about Amsden's gum-chewing, childishly sarcastic vernacular is that it works only while the narrator's quirky, self-deprecating personality keeps the reader's interest. . . . The 'Me and Dad' anecdotes are good for a few laughs before we yearn for more substantial fare."

Other reviewers were more impressed with the story, and with the young narrator telling it. "The narrator's resentment only comes out in spurts . . . but when his anger appears, it is powerful and heartbreaking," wrote *Booklist* reviewer Kristine Huntley. "The kid in Amsden's book tells us an honest, open story. Make no mistake, he's talking directly to you. You suffer and laugh with him, and believe me, you'll be embarrassed as you recognize yourself," noted *PopMatters* contributor Valerie MacEwan. She concluded, "As a reviewer, I'll tell you—Get this book. Enjoy it. It's fun. It's quick. But be warned. There's a larger story here than appears on the surface. I suspect David Amsden has a lot more in store for us and I can't wait."

BIOGRAPHICAL AND CRITICAL SOURCES:

PERIODICALS

Booklist, March 1, 2003, Kristine Huntley, review of *Important Things That Don't Matter,* p. 1145.

Kirkus Reviews, January 15, 2003, review of *Important Things That Don't Matter,* p. 101.

Publishers Weekly, December 29, 2002, review of *Important Things That Don't Matter,* p. 58.

ONLINE

Onion A.V. Club, http://www.theonionavclub.com/ (January 29, 2003), Tasha Robinson, review of *Important Things That Don't Matter.*

PopMatters, http://www.popmatters.com/ (April 2, 2003), Valerie MacEwan, review of *Important Things That Don't Matter.*

Salon.com, http://www.salon.com/ (May 12, 2003), Elizabeth Spiers, "Don't Hate David Amsden because He's Brilliant, Celebrated and Twenty-three."*

*   *   *

ANDREWS, Andy 1959-

PERSONAL: Born May 22, 1959, in Birmingham, AL.

ADDRESSES: Agent—c/o Author Mail, Thomas Nelson, Inc., P.O. Box 141000, Nashville, TN 37214.

CAREER: Comedian, motivational speaker.

AWARDS, HONORS: Comedian of the Year, National Association of Campus Activities (NACA); Entertainer of the Year, NACA.

WRITINGS:

Andy Andrews Live at Caesars, Tahoe (sound recording), First Image (Nashville, TN), 1988.

Storms of Perfection, Lightning Crown Publishers (Nashville, TN), Volume 1: *In Their Own Words,* 1991, Volume 2: *Letters from the Heart,* 1994, Volume 3: *A Pathway to Personal Achievement,* 1996, Volume 4: *Letters from the Past,* 1997.

Andy Andrews' Tales from Sawyerton Springs, Lightning Crown Publishers (Nashville, TN), 1995.

The Traveler's Gift: Seven Decisions that Determine Personal Success, Thomas Nelson (Nashville, TN), 2002.

The Lost Choice: A Legend of Personal Discovery, Thomas Nelson (Nashville, TN), 2004.

SIDELIGHTS: A successful comedian and motivational speaker, Andy Andrews actually began his career on a dare, when his friends challenged him to try out his jokes at a local Pizza Hut. The brief stint doing stand-up next to the salad bar earned him some free pizzas, and convinced him that he had the talent to succeed in more professional settings. Before long, he was playing on the college circuit, where he earned the title Comedian of the Year from the National Association of Campus Activities. He went on to become a Las Vegas fixture, where his distinctly clean, family-friendly humor set him apart, garnering raves from radio host Paul Harvey and invitations to appear before Presidents Reagan and Bush, Sr.

In addition to comedy and motivational speaking, Andrews has also sought to reach audiences through inspirational writings. In the four volumes of *Storms of Perfection,* he compiles his correspondence with some of the world's most successful people to reveal the critical turning points and decisions that allowed them to overcome trials, failures, and even tragedy and to emerge victorious. In the fourth volume of the series, *Letters from the Past,* he imagines similar correspondence with historical figures such as Abraham Lincoln, Helen Keller, and Albert Einstein, who all had to overcome painful obstacles and setbacks to reach their goals.

Andrews followed this up with another fictional self-help title, *The Traveler's Gift: Seven Decisions that Determine Personal Success.* In the story, David Ponder must struggle back from the brink after losing his job and with it his confidence, and then gets into a car accident that leaves him unconscious. In the Capra-esque tale, Ponder finds himself transported through time to meet figures such as King Solomon, Christopher Columbus, and Harry Truman, who each impart to him a particular gift of wisdom. He awakens in a hospital bed, clutching letters given to him by his mentors. "At book's end, there is a strong element of faith, but Andrews uses a light touch," concluded *Library Journal* contributor Douglas Lord. "Some astute thinkers may be put off by the simplistic story line, but Andrews does an exemplary job at providing positive suggestions for overcoming life's obstacles," concluded a *Publishers Weekly* contributor.

BIOGRAPHICAL AND CRITICAL SOURCES:

PERIODICALS

Library Journal, September 15, 2002, Douglas Lord, review of *The Traveler's Gift: Seven Decisions that Determine Personal Success,* p. 80.
Publishers Weekly, October 21, 2002, review of *The Traveler's Gift,* p. 69.

ONLINE

Andy Andrews Home Page, http://www.andyandrews. com (March 18, 2004).*

*   *   *

APPY, Christian G.

PERSONAL: Married; children: two sons. *Education:* Amherst College, B.A. (American studies), c. 1970; Harvard University, Ph.D. (History of American Civilization).

ADDRESSES: Home—11 Walter Griffin Rd., Sharon, MA 02067. *E-mail*—Chrisappy@aol.com.

CAREER: Writer. Harvard University, Cambridge, MA, taught undergraduate history and literature; Massachusetts Institute of Technology, Cambridge, MA, associate professor of history.

AWARDS, HONORS: Best Dissertation, American Studies Association, for his dissertation on American combat soldiers in the Vietnam War.

WRITINGS:

(With Thomas V. DiBacco and Lorna C. Mason) *History of the United States,* Houghton Mifflin (Boston, MA), 1991.

Working-Class War: American Combat Soldiers and Vietnam, University of North Carolina Press (Chapel Hill, NC), 1993.
(Editor and contributor) *Cold War Constructions: The Political Culture of United States Imperialism,* University of Massachusetts Press (Amherst, MA), 2000.
Patriots: The Vietnam War Remembered from All Sides, Viking (New York, NY), 2003.

SIDELIGHTS: Christian G. Appy began his academic career in the 1970s at Amherst College where he received his B.A. in American studies. There he was inspired by new trends in scholarship that looked at the roles of poor and working-class people throughout history. He went on to Harvard where he received his Ph.D. in the History of American Civilization. He wrote his dissertation on American combat soldiers in the Vietnam War which earned him the award for the year's best dissertation from the American Studies Association. Appy continued on at Harvard teaching undergraduate history and literature for four years. He then went to the Massachusetts Institute of Technology where he was an associate professor of history for eight years. He left in 1999 to write full time. He lives in Sharon, Massachusetts with his wife and two sons.

Appy's first book, *Working-Class War: American Combat Soldiers and Vietnam,* is a continuation of the work he had done on his thesis at Harvard. In this work Appy discusses how nearly eighty percent of those who participated in the Vietnam War came from blue collar families, and explores how wealthier youths were overlooked by draft boards. To compile some of the first hand data for the book Appy attended a Vietnam Veterans group for seven years. G. David Curry of *Armed Forces and Society* explained, "*Working-Class War* is a contribution to what has been a slowly, but steadily, building debate about the equity of service in the military and in combat during the Vietnam War." He went on to praise Appy by stating, "The author's ability to weave together the content of his published sources with the words of his interviewees results in an absorbing narrative." John F. Guilmartin Jr. of *Reviews in American History* found that education was a more important factor than class in deciding who went to Vietnam and believed that "*Working-Class War* thus stands on shaky assumptions." A reviewer for the *Economist* concluded, "The flaw of Mr. Appy's chilling story is that he sees nothing to mitigate the undeniable horror of the war."

While Murray Polner of *Commonweal* called the work a "definitive and engrossing study of combat veterans and their economic class."

In his next work, *Cold War Constructions: The Political Culture of United States Imperialism*, Appy took on the role of editor in this collection of fifteen essays focusing on the United States and the Cold War. Appy included his own essay on Eisenhower and the invasion on Guatemala in the collection. A reviewer for *Reference and Research Book News* commented, "Appy . . . brings together the work of political, diplomatic, and cultural historians in order to foster an understanding of the complex interaction between culture and policy." Robert Griffith of *Reviews in American History* found the book to "deepen and extend our knowledge of the Cold War." John Earl Haynes commended Appy's work as editor in *American Historical Review,* "Most of the essays are remarkably innovative; some are true eye-openers," and found the book to be "a stimulating and welcome survey of how far cultural studies of U.S. foreign relations have come."

For his next work Appy returned to the familiar topic of Vietnam in *Patriots: The Vietnam War Remembered from All Sides*. In this oral history Appy presents the viewpoints of 135 vastly different people who were directly effected by the events of Vietnam. He talks with people on both sides of the struggle, from a variety of occupations, diverse in age, power, and prestige. The stories are edited and framed by Appy, but told from each person's point of view. It covers the entire history of the conflict starting in 1945 and ending in 1975. David Myer of *Anniston Star* wrote, "Simply by telling their stories, Appy's subjects teach truths about Vietnam that transcend the mere historical fact. But by framing their stories in the context of his own subjective history of the conflict, Appy at times suggests conclusions that readers could better reach on their own." A reviewer for *Publishers Weekly* called it "a solid contribution to the primary source background of the longest and most controversial overseas war in American History." A contributor for *Kirkus Reviews* described it as "An excellent addition to the literature of the Vietnam War, instructive and moving—but also likely to reopen old wounds." Karl Helicher of *Library Journal* felt that "this superb volume is quite possibly the best in a crowded field."

BIOGRAPHICAL AND CRITICAL SOURCES:

PERIODICALS

American Historical Review, April, 2001, John Earl Haynes, review of *Cold War Constructions: The Political Culture of United States Imperialism,* p. 599.

Armed Forces and Society, summer, 1994, G. David Curry, review of *Working-Class War: American Combat Soldiers and Vietnam,* p.648.

Commonweal, April 23, 1993, Murray Polner, review of *Working-Class War,* p. 29.

Economist, March 20, 1993, review of *Working-Class War,* p. 98.

Kirkus Reviews, April 1, 2003, review of *Patriots: The Vietnam War Remembered From All Sides,* p. 514.

Library Journal, May 1, 2003, Karl Helicher, review of *Patriots,* p. 133.

Publishers Weekly, April 21, 2003, review of *Patriots,* p. 54.

Reference and Research Book News, August, 2000, review of *Cold War Constructions,* p. 52.

Reviews in American History, June, 1994, John F. Guilmartin Jr., review of *Working-Class War,* p. 322; March, 2001, Robert Griffith, "The Cultural Turn in Cold War Studies," pp. 150-157.

ONLINE

Anniston Star, http://www.dailyhome.com/ (October 22, 2003), David Myer, "Looking Back at Vietnam, from Varied Angles."

BookPage.com, http://www.bookpage.com/ (October 22, 2003), Edward Morris, "A Divisive Conflict Remembered."

Christian G. Appy Home Page, http://www.chrisappy. com (October 22, 2003).*

* * *

ASSUNÇÃO, Leilah 1943-

PERSONAL: Born 1943, in Botucatu, São Paulo, Brazil. *Education:* University of São Paulo, B.S.

ADDRESSES: Agent—c/o Author Mail, Host Publications, 2717 Wooldridge Dr., Austin, TX 78703.

CAREER: Playwright, actress, and author. Associated with Theatro Oficina, Brazil. Actress on stage, appearing in *A vereda da slavação,* 1963, and *The Three-Penny Opera,* 1964. Formerly employed as a fashion model. Participant at International Women Playwrights conferences in Buffalo, NY, 1988, and Toronto, Ontario, Canada, 1991.

AWARDS, HONORS: Molière Prize, 1969, for *Fala baixo senão eu grito;* Sociedade Brasileira de Autores Teatraise Award, 1973; Ondas Award (Spain), for television work.

WRITINGS:

PLAYS

Da fala ao grito (includes *Fala baixo senão eu grito* [title means "Speak Softly, or I Shall Scream,"] 1969, *Jorginho, o machão,* 1970, and *Amélia ou Roda cor de roda* [title means "Amelia, or, Color Wheel,"] 1973), Símbolo (São Paulo, Brazil), 1977.

A kuka de Kamaiorá (title means "The Kuka of Kamaiorá"; produced 1978), Ministério de Educação e Cultura (Rio de Janeiro, Brazil), 1978, portions translated by Dawn Jordan published as *The Secret of the Golden Soul* and produced in Buffalo, NY, c. 1987.

(With others) *Feira brasileira de opinião* (includes *Sobrevividos*), Global Editora (São Paulo, Brazil), 1978.

Vejo um vulto na janela, me acudam que eu sou donzela, produced in Brazil, 1979.

Boca molhada de paixão calada, produced 1980, published in *Brasil: nunca mas,* Editora Vozes, 1985, translation published as *Moist Lips, Quiet Passion* in *Three Contemporary Brazilian Plays* (bilingual edition), edited by Elzbieta Szoka and Joe W. Bratcher III, Host Publications (Austin, TX), 1988.

Lua nua, Scipione (São Paulo, Brazil), 1990, 3rd edition, 1993.

Diz que ue fui pra Maiamum (title means "Say That I Went to Mayamoom"), produced in a reading off-Broadway, 1990.

O grande momento de Guta de Mello Santos, produced 1991.

Also author of *Use Pó de arroz Bijou,* 1968, *Feira* (title means "Fair"), 1967, *Da fala ao grito,* 1977, *Seda pura e alfinetadas,* 1981, and *Quem matou a baronesa?,* 1992. Author of television scripts for *Windmills* and *Avenida Paulista.* Contributor of short fiction to periodicals, including *Status Literatura.*

SIDELIGHTS: Brazilian-born playwright Leilah Assunção made a name for herself as part of a group of dramatists that in the late 1960s were referred to as the Teatro Novo. Often censored by Brazil's military dictatorship through the late 1970s, her plays, which include *Fala baixo senão eu grito, Lua Nua,* and *Diz que eu fui pra Maiamum,* focus on psychological rather than political themes, and often explore oppression and censorship as expressed through interpersonal and sexual relationships. Often this oppression and censorship is directed toward women. As she commented during conference proceedings published as *International Women Playwrights: Voices of Identity and Transformation,* "'What are you doing young lady! Pull your skirt down!' That's the first bit of censorship I got in life. Censorship is eternal, and it's been exercised by the man, the government, the Whites or the nation in power at any given time in history."

Assunção's first three plays immediately signaled to Brazilian audiences that she had broken with the mold of earlier, proletarian playwrights; *Fala baixo senão eu grito, Jorginho, o machão,* and *Roda cor de roda* focus on the world of the Brazilian middle class, painting a portrait of what Margo Milleret in *Luso-Brazilian Review* described as "a suffocating, decadent social structure where traditional sex roles cannot be altered and conformity to the status quo is required." Noting that Assunção's early works are "pessimistic" in portraying the lives of "characters . . . trapped in a stagnant social environment with no chance for escape or improvement," Milleret argued that the playwright intimates that such conditions are not unwanted; "members of the middle class cooperate in the perpetuation of these conditions and through cooperation legitimize them as 'tradition' or 'custom'," the critic noted.

Assunção's most overtly political play, *Boca molhada de paixão calada* focuses on her country's 1964-1979 dictatorship; it was produced on stage only after Amnesty Laws had lifted censorship restrictions imposed on the country's artistic communities. Written in 1980, the play focuses on a married couple, Mila and Antonio, who "come into conflict over the values of the social classes to which they belong," according to Milleret in an essay published in *Discurso Literario*. On the surface working out problems faced in their marriage, Assunção's characters on a deeper level "relive and rethink their sexual histories and their ties to the dictatorship as a means of freeing themselves," Milleret explained. In exile during the decades when Brazil was under military control, Mila and Antonio now "realize that as victims of the regime they have been dominated by fear, and that such constant fear has immobilized them. . . . [from making] commitments to people or ideals. . . . Through their new-found passion they find the strength to forgive the errors and concessions of the past and to reinforce their commitment to each other."

Although many of Assunção's plays focus on female characters trapped in subordinate roles in home or career, she does not willingly submit to the label of "feminist playwright." As Judith Bissett noted in an essay published in *Latin-American Women Dramatists: Theater, Texts, and Theories* "Assunção has rejected the idea that her approach is feminist. Instead, she emphasizes the very human, social and political nature of her plays. Although she began by focusing on the role of women in society, in an attempt to define their social identity, Assunção believes that she is much more involved in an investigation of what constitutes the essence of a Brazilian national identity." One of her nation's most successful playwrights, Assunção has managed to dedicate herself to her writing through her successful career as a television scriptwriter.

BIOGRAPHICAL AND CRITICAL SOURCES:

BOOKS

International Women Playwrights: Voices of Identity and Transformation, edited by Anna Kay France and P. J. Corso, Scarecrow Press (Metuchen, NJ), 1993, pp. 144, 147-148.
Latin-American Women Dramatists: Theater, Texts, and Theories, edited by Catherine Larson and Margarita Vargas, Indiana University Press (Bloomington, IN), 1998.

PERIODICALS

Dactylus, 1988-1989, pp. 15.
Discurso Literario, Volume VII, number 1, 1990, Margo Milleret, "(Re)Playing the Brazilian Dictatorship," pp. 213-224.

Latin-American Theatre Review, spring, 1976, Alcides João de Barros, "A situação social de Mulher no teatro de Consuelo de Castro e Leilah Assunção," pp. 13-20.
Luso-Brazilian Review, summer, 1984, Margo Milleret, "Entrapment and Flights of Fantasy in Three Plays by Leilah Assunção," pp. 49-56.*

*　　*　　*

ASTELL, Ann W.

PERSONAL: Female. *Education:* University of Wisconsin, received degree; Marquette University, received degree; University of Wisconsin—Madison, Ph.D. (medieval literature), 1987.

ADDRESSES: Home—West Lafayette, IN. *Office*—Purdue University, Department of English, 500 Oval Dr., West Lafayette, IN 47907; fax: 765-494-3780. *E-mail*—astell@purdue.edu.

CAREER: Purdue University, West Lafayette, IN, currently professor of English.

MEMBER: Secular Institute of the Schoenstatt Sisters of Mary.

AWARDS, HONORS: John Simon Guggenheim Memorial Fellowship in religion, 2001-2002.

WRITINGS:

The Song of Songs in the Middle Ages, Cornell University Press (Ithaca, NY), 1990.
Job, Boethius, and Epic Truth, Cornell University Press (Ithaca, NY), 1994.
Divine Representations: Postmodernism and Spirituality, Paulist Press (Ithaca, NY), 1994.
Chaucer and the Universe of Learning, Cornell University Press (Ithaca, NY), 1996.
Political Allegory in Late Medieval England, Cornell University Press (Ithaca, NY), 1999.
(Editor, with Bonnie Wheeler) *Lay Sanctity, Medieval and Modern: A Search for Models,* University of Notre Dame Press (Notre Dame, IN), 2000.

Joan of Arc and Spirituality, Palgrave Macmillan (New York, NY), 2003.

Joan of Arc and Sacrificial Authorship, University of Notre Dame Press (Notre Dame, IN), 2003.

SIDELIGHTS: Ann W. Astell is a professor of English at Purdue University who specializes in Middle English language and literature, medieval rhetoric and politics, St. Joan of Arc, Marian cult and women mystics, medieval theo-aesthetics, and the works of Geoffrey Chaucer. Her first book, *The Song of Songs in the Middle Ages,* is an "informative and readable study" on the famous epic love poem from the Old Testament, remarked Elizabeth Archibald in the *Times Literary Supplement.* The book's subject, the "Song of Songs," has long been a puzzling anomaly; clearly an erotic love poem, it has caused considerable debate among scholars and clerics. "The *Song of Songs* posed a particularly troubling challenge to early Christians," Archibald further remarked. "What is this erotic lyric without any explicit reference to God doing in the Old Testament, and how could it be interpreted so as to be acceptable?" Astell's book explores, in depth and from a Jungian perspective, a number of allegorical interpretations of the "Song of Songs" put forth by both literary and religious writers during the Middle Ages. Among the relevant works studied are those by Origen, an early Christian commentator, who asserted that the "Song" must be interpreted in allegorical terms as a mystical union, as between the church, as Bride, and clergy. Other works examined include sermons, religious lyrics, medieval literary works such as *Pearl,* and plays. "Astell analyzes closely a number of selected texts, and she proves herself to be a very good close reader," concluded Lawrence Besserman in *Speculum.*

In *Job, Boethius, and Epic Truth* Astell argues that the literary genre of heroic epic poetry, often thought to have not existed in the Middle Ages, continued without pause from ancient times to the Renaissance. Astell uses the biblical book of Job and Boethius's *Consultation of Philosophy* as examples of epic tradition persisting through the Middle Ages. Her theory is that "despite the formal discontinuities between classical epic and medieval romance, an allegorical core of epic truth survived into the Middle Ages through the influence of the 'heroic' Book of Job" and Boethius's work, which also encouraged "patient struggle against hostile fortune," wrote Mishtooni Bose in *Medium Aevum.* Astell's work claims that "medieval readers knowingly associated Boethius and Job as heroic figures" of the

type found in epics, commented Seth Lerer in *Speculum.* M. S. Stephenson, reviewing the book in *Choice,* also remarked, "The scholarship is prodigious, the argument convincing, and the Christian stance congenial to the subject." Bose concluded that Astell has "made an original, erudite, and admirably clear contribution to the study of medieval genre theory" with her work. And Lerer called *Job, Boethius, and Epic Truth* "a rarity in academic criticism: a study of great learning and great belief, whose arguments are voiced without the slightest tinge of pedantry or condescension." Marcia A. Dalbey, writing in *Journal of English and Germanic Philology,* concluded that the book is "a valuable study of the influence of classical and biblical literature on medieval vernacular texts."

Astell's *Chaucer and the Universe of Learning* analyzes whether or not "the ordering of the fragments of the *Canterbury Tales* in the Ellesmere Manuscripts reflects Chaucer's intent for his work, or results merely from the hand of an editor," reported John B. Friedman in the *Journal of English and Germanic Philology.* For the author, the Ellesmere order of the *Canterbury Tales* serves as an encyclopedia-like *compilato* "uniting, like Dante's *Paradiso,* a philosophical journey of the soul through planetary spheres with a topical survey of the divisions of knowledge" outlined by John Gower, wrote Karla Taylor in *Modern Philology.* Further, Astell argues that Chaucer's intent was to pass on academic and esoteric knowledge to a varied audience of vernacular readers, particularly other lay clerks like himself. By placing Chaucer in such a context, "Astell both accounts for his learning and argues that the *Canterbury Tales* is a social and philosophical encyclopedia thoroughly indebted to academic culture for both structure and meaning," Taylor remarked. "Whether one finds the overall scheme Astell has adduced to explain the Ellesmere ordering fully convincing or not, there is much of profit and pleasure to be found in this learned and ingenious book," Friedman concluded.

The book on Chaucer was followed by *Political Allegory in Late Medieval England,* which is a "learned and lucid study of political allegory" in the time period, according to Gerald Morgan in *Modern Philology.* Authors of allegories "are constructed as artful dodgers; using every kind of narrative sleight of hand safely to encode political commentary for those in the know which would be blithely ignored by those not skilled to see," commented Helen Barr in *Medium*

Aevum. Astell analyzes a number of medieval political allegories in this context, including works such as *Piers Plowman, Sir Gawain and the Green Knight,* and Ovid's *Fasti.* "Many of the political allegories unearthed here are forced," Barr commented. Although Morgan stated that problems with the book arise from "the simple absence of secure historical knowledge" and "the lack of detailed correspondence in the political analogies proposed," he found much to admire about the book, commenting that the first chapter, exploring the "importance of invention for a theorist such as Geoffrey of Vinsauf," will "prove to be of permanent value."

With *Lay Sanctity, Medieval and Modern: A Search for Models,* edited by Astell and Bonnie Wheeler, a number of contributing scholars examine "with academic reverence the lives of some holy lay people, how some became saints and why others of dazzling virtue didn't," commented Clarence Thomson in *National Catholic Reporter.* Since medieval times, "the most unspoken but persuasive criterion for saints is that they be as like monks as possible," Thompson observed. But laypeople are not participants in the monastic lifestyle. There are no requirements among them for miracles; obedience to a church or an order is immaterial; and there is no institutional background leading toward sainthood. But the book's contributors argue that saintliness is not always measured strictly by the ways in which sanctity is traditionally interpreted—good works, professional competence, dedication to a cause, and sincere spiritual practices can sometimes be enough. "This is inspiring reading," Thompson concluded.

BIOGRAPHICAL AND CRITICAL SOURCES:

PERIODICALS

Belles Lettres, spring, 1991, review of *The Song of Songs in the Middle Ages,* p. 55.

Choice, October, 1994, M. S. Stephenson, review of *Job, Boethius, and Epic Truth,* p. 276.

Journal of English and Germanic Philology, January, 1996, Marcia A. Dalbey, review of *Job, Boethius, and Epic Truth,* pp. 104-107; April, 2000, John B. Friedman, review of *Chaucer and the Universe of Learning,* p. 255.

Journal of Religion, April, 1992, Bernard McGinn, review of *The Song of Songs in the Middle Ages,* pp. 269-275.

Medium Aevum, fall, 1995, Mishtooni Bose, review of *Job, Boethius, and Epic Truth,* p. 297; fall, 1997, Norm Klassen, review of *Chaucer and the Universe of Learning,* pp. 39-41; Volume 69, number 2, 2000, Helen Barr, review of *Political Allegory in Late Medieval England,* pp. 305-306.

Modern Philology, February, 2000, Karla Taylor, review of *Chaucer and the Universe of Learning,* p. 445; August, 2001, Gerald Morgan, review of *Political Allegory in Late Medieval England,* p. 78.

National Catholic Reporter, June 2, 2000, Clarence Thomson, review of *Lay Sanctity, Medieval and Modern: A Search for Models,* p. 12.

Religious Studies, December, 1995, review of *Divine Representations: Postmodernism and Spirituality.*

Review of English Studies, November, 1992, Marjory Rigby, review of *The Song of Songs in the Middle Ages,* pp. 543-544.

Speculum, April, 1992, Lawrence Besserman, review of *The Song of Songs in the Middle Ages,* pp. 367-371; October, 1995, Seth Lerer, review of *Job, Boethius, and Epic Truth,* pp. 869-871.

Times Literary Supplement, April 3, 1992, Elizabeth Archibald, "Of Love and Custom," pp. 6-7.

Virginia Quarterly Review, spring, 1997, review of *Chaucer and the Universe of Learning,* p. 48.

ONLINE

Purdue University School of Liberal Arts Web site, http://www.sla.purdue.edu/ (January 30, 2001), profile of Ann W. Astell.

Theology Today Web site, http://theologytoday.ptsem. edu/ (January 30, 2004), biography of Ann W. Astell.*

*　　*　　*

AUERBACH, John 1922-2002

PERSONAL: Born 1922, in Warsaw, Poland; died 2002, in Israel; married second wife, Nola Chilton Auerbach (theater director); children: Adam (deceased, 1973). *Religion:* Jewish.

CAREER: Polish Army, beginning of the Second World War, soldier; served as a stoker on a German ship; served on Swedish ships after the war; Mossad

Aliyah Bet, transported refugees to Israel; worked as skipper on fishing boats; Israeli Merchant Marines, Chief Engineer, until 1973.

AWARDS, HONORS: PEN/UNESCO Award, 1993, for "The Owl."

WRITINGS:

Tales of Grabowski: Transformation, Escape, and Other Stories, TOBY Press (New Milford, CT), 2003.
The Owl and Other Stories, TOBY Press (New Milford, CT), 2003.

SIDELIGHTS: John Auerbach was born in Warsaw, Poland in 1922 and he served as a soldier in the Polish army during the beginning of World War II. He was placed in a Warsaw Ghetto during the German occupation of Poland, but escaped to work as a stoker on a German ship under a false identity. While trying to escape to Sweden in a stolen boat, Auerbach was captured and sent to the Stutthof concentration camp. It was after the war when he joined Mossad Aliyah Bet, a ship where he helped transport refugees to Israel. After three years he was captured by the British and held at a Cyprus camp for two years. After his release he lived at Kibbutz Sdot Yam in Israel where he worked as a skipper on a fishing boat. He completed officer training and served in the Israeli Merchant Marines as a Chief Engineer for fifteen years. In 1973 his son was killed in the Yom Kippur War and Auerbach left the marines and returned to live on the kibbutz where he worked on his writing. Though it is not his native language Auerbach does all of his writing in English, and it is often translated into Hebrew.

Both of Auerbach's major works were published after his death. *Tales of Grabowski: Transformation, Escape and Other Stories* is a story of one man's struggles during World War II and is based greatly on Auerbach's own ordeals. The book is comprised of two novellas, *Transformations* and *Escape,* which, together with several short stories, tell the story of David Gordon. Gordon, like Auerbach, is a Warsaw Jew serving in the Polish Army during WWII when he is forced to live in a Ghetto. He escapes and takes on a false identity, that of a Polish gentile killed earlier in the war named Wladyslaw Grabowski, and becomes a stoker on a German ship. Gordon struggles with his double identity, and issues of guilt surrounding his situation. He is given the opportunity to leak out information to an Argentinean spy, which helps him reconcile his guilt in that he is working against the Germans. Gordon tries to escape to Sweden but is captured and held in a concentration camp. He escapes and, like Auerbach, goes to live on a kibbutz where he tries to make sense of what has happened to him.

A reviewer in *Library Journal* stated "*Transformations* and *Escape* are undiscovered masterpieces of twentieth-century writing." Hazel Rochman of *Booklist* commented, "With stark immediacy, these interconnected, autobiographical stories by a recently discovered Jewish writer add a new dimension to Holocaust survival literature." A contributor for *Kirkus Reviews* found "Auerbach's prose has a raw, spare quality that is both the best and worst aspect of the collection." Cecilia H. Rothschild of *Aufbau* praised Auerbach, "His ingenious use of such ancient story-telling devices as disguise, trickery, role reversal and irony allow him to examine illusions of existence and the evils which thrive on social norms."

Published the same year as *Tales of Grabowski* was the collection *The Owl and Other Stories.* Auerbach received the first PEN/UNESCO award in 1993 for the title story of this collection. These stories also draw from Auerbach's own experiences and relate to times he spent out at sea and on the kibbutz. "The Owl" is the story of an Israeli merchant ship and the disruption of the crew when a large owl lands on top of their mast. "The Black Madonna" is the tale of a sailor who gives a locket containing the portrait of the Madonna to a woman at a mysterious port empty of men. "Cohen" is the story of two Polish Jewish sailors who find their connection to a Warsaw Ghetto in the hold of an Israeli steamer off the coast of Ireland. Hazel Rochman of *Booklist* conceded that all the stories are not of the same caliber "but the best of them speak with terse drama about the pain and power of being alone."

BIOGRAPHICAL AND CRITICAL SOURCES:

PERIODICALS

Booklist, June 1, 2003, Hazel Rochman, review of *Tales of Grabowski: Transformation, Escape, and Other Stories,* p. 1739; September 15, 2003, Hazel Rochman, review of *The Owl and Other Stories,* p. 208.
Kirkus Reviews, May 15, 2003, review of *Tales of Grabowski,* p. 692.

Library Journal, June 15, 2003, Edward Cone, review of *Tales of Grabowski,* p. 98; July, 2003, review of *The Owl and Other Stoires* and *Tales of Grabowski,* p. SS28.

Publishers Weekly, May 26, 2003, review of *Tales of Grabowski,* p. 47.

ONLINE

Aufbau, http://www.aufbauonline.com/ (October 22, 2003), Cecilia H. Rothschild,"Tales of Auerbach."*

B

BACHER, John 1954-

PERSONAL: Born November 25, 1954, in St. Catharines, Ontario, Canada; son of Winfred (a teacher) and Mary (Graham) Bacher; married Mary Lou Greeson (a labour ministry clerk), September 29, 2001 *Education:* Brock University, B.A. (with honors), 1979; McMaster University, M.A., 1980, Ph.D., 1985. *Politics:* New Democratic Party. *Religion:* Anglican. *Hobbies and other interests:* Cycling, hiking, bird watching.

ADDRESSES: Home and office—134 Church St., St. Catharines, Ontario, Canada L2R 3E4. *E-mail*—pals@ becon.org.

CAREER: Researcher, educator, and writer. Instructor in environmental topics at McMaster University and University of Toronto, Toronto, Ontario, Canada. Ontario Drainage Tribunal, hearing officer, 1991-97; Preservation of Agricultural Lands Society, researcher. Member, Niagara River Restoration Council; political candidate for federal office, 2000; lecturer, presenter at conferences and freelance writer.

MEMBER: Preservation of Agricultural Lands Society, Niagara Falls Nature Club, Friends of the Twelve.

AWARDS, HONORS: Friend of the Great Lakes Award, Environment Ministers of Ontario and Canada, 1996.

WRITINGS:

(With others) *Niagara Conservation Strategy,* Preservation of Agricultural Lands Society (Ontario, Canada), 1988.

Keeping to the Marketplace: The Evolution of Canadian Housing Policy, 1900-1990, McGill-Queen's University Press (Montreal, Quebec, Canada), 1993.

(With Wayne Roberts and Brian Nelson) *Get a Life,* privately published, 1994.

Petrotyranny, Science for Peace/Dundurn Press (Toronto, Ontario, Canada), 2000.

Contributor of articles and reviews to periodicals, including *Activist, Now, Urban History Review, Journal of Canadian Studies, Ecumenist, Acadiaensis, Toronto Star,* and *Peace Magazine.*

WORK IN PROGRESS: Pleistocene Park, a novel for Pindurn Press; *No Terror,* for Dundurn Press.

SIDELIGHTS: Canadian educator and environmental advocate John Bacher is the author of *Petrotyranny,* an exposé that focuses on the tendency for elite governments in control of vast amounts of wealth to resort to fundamentalist ideologies. As Meir Amor noted in a review of Bacher's book for *Peace* magazine, the book puts forth the argument that "the stability and governability of democracies, their respect for human rights and social diversity, and their tendency to resolve conflicts nonviolently, are rooted partly in their political economy. Likewise, fundamentalism, belligerency, and corruption, the characteristics of oil-producing countries, are also rooted in their political economy." Noting that Bacher's work is a "clear departure from the conventional wisdom on the consequences of the world's massive reliance on oil energy," *Choice* contributor R. H. Dekmejian called *Petrotyranny* "timely and provocative."

Bacher told *CA:* "My passion for writing is sparked by an ambition to show how relatively simple, rational, and workable measures can do an enormous amount of good in fostering the connected concerns of peace, human rights, social justice, and the protection of the environment. This strong missionary approach pervades my writing, which is continually refreshed from deep involvement in environmental issues, and from nature observation activities such as hiking, cycling, and bird-watching.

"*Petrotyranny* emerged out of my long involvement in the peace movement and in teaching peace studies at McMaster University and the University of Toronto. My involvement in the peace movement was heavily influenced by the example of the remarkable British historian E. P. Thompson. His writings on the relationship between peace and human rights encouraged me to meet in Moscow in 1985 with the independent persecuted peace group, the Moscow Trust Group. I have also been inspired by the great American prophet of nonviolent resistence to dictatorship, Gene Sharp, and have tried to popularize his work through my university courses and writings.

"I am working on a new book, *No Terror,* to further develop the insights of *Petrotyranny,* which does illustrate how the problem of terrorism, particularly the then relatively obscure threats posed by Osama bin Laden, were caused by the misuse of great oil wealth. This new book seeks to further probe the origins and cures for terrorism by examining how Canada was able to overcome the terrorist threat posed by the Front de Liberation de Quebec and the Mohawk Warriors Society. I will examine how Canada's pattern of multicultural compromise and maintaining the rule of law was largely responsible for its escape from the terror trap, and how such a tolerant 'Canadization' can address the problem of terrorism in other countries. In developing this analysis I was heavily influenced by the writings of retired Canadian General Dan Loomis and the brave investigative reporter and former intelligence agent Jim Moses.

"In advising young environmental writers, I would urge them to listen carefully to the earth around them and develop friendships with other people who share these values of respect. Show patience and build bridges, and if you keep diligently pursuing your goal of being a writer who fosters better public attitudes and policies toward the environment, you will succeed.

Avoid momentary fashionable extremist fads that legitimate violence and focus on what native American elders term the good mind of working nonviolently for peace, human rights, and the protection of the environment.

"Every community is full of exciting environmental issues which have evolved over thousands of years of human habitation and which can provide the basis for exciting and provocative writing. There are no shortage of inspiring stories to tell, making be believe that writers block must be some figment of the imagination. Consider, for instance, the struggles to obtain parks in your community, the history of its transit system, the impact of automobiles, and the role of aboriginal peoples. Try to discover and promote unappreciated heros of environmental protection and restoration. When the outlook appears bleak, attempt to create bold visualizations such as a world without car or the restoration of free-ranging bison to the great plains."

BIOGRAPHICAL AND CRITICAL SOURCES:

PERIODICALS

Canadian Historical Review, December, 1994, Albert Rose, review of *Keeping to the Marketplace: The Evolution of Canadian Housing Policy, 1900-1990,* p. 646.
Choice, March, 2001, R. H. Dekmejian, review of *Petrotyranny,* p. 1314.
International Journal of Urban and Regional Research, September, 1994, Pierre Filion, review of *Keeping to the Market Place.*
Peace, April-June, 2002, Meir Amor, review of *Petrotyranny,* pp. 26-28.
Ploughshares Monitor, March, 2001, review of *Petrotyranny,* p. 17.

*   *   *

BAKAL, Carl 1918-2004

OBITUARY NOTICE—See index for *CA* sketch: Born January 11, 1918, in New York, NY; died of a heart attack March 18, 2004, in Manhattan, NY. Editor, photographer, and author. Bakal is best remembered for his anti-gun stance, which he argued for in his

1966 book, *The Right to Bear Arms.* A graduate of City College (now of the City University of New York), where he earned a B.S. in 1939, he began his career as editor of *Fotoshop Almanac* and as associate and contributing editor to *U.S. Camera.* When America joined the war effort in 1942, Bakal enlisted in the Army Signal Corps and became a first lieutenant. After the war, he worked for the military government in Germany, where he produced documentary films, and he later did the same in Japan. In 1947, he returned to civilian life as a writer for the *New York Mirror,* and, during the early 1950s, as an associate editor for *Coronet* magazine. A brief time as a freelance photographer was followed by a year editing *Real* and *See* magazines. Then, in the early 1960s, Bakal was a public affairs consultant to the U.S. Department of Commerce and a senior associate for Howard Chase Associates in New York City. Two years as director of the magazine department at Carl Byoir & Associates then led to a long period as account supervisor for Anna M. Rosenberg Associates from 1968 to 1984. Continuing to move up the business officer ladder, Bakal became senior vice president of Jack Raymond & Company in 1984, during which time he was also a travel editor for *Sylvia Porter's Personal Finance* magazine, and then he headed his own company, Carl Bakal Associates, beginning in 1986. Bakal's first two books, the technical *Filter Manual* (1951) and *How to Shoot for Glamour* (1955), involved photography; a skilled photographer whose pictures appeared in such national publications as *Life, Esquire, Holiday,* and *Cosmopolitan,* he won the international *Popular Photography* competition in 1956. It was not until the 1960s that Bakal began publishing books on various issues, and his *The Right to Bear Arms* (revised in 1968 as *No Right to Bear Arms*) stirred much controversy about the effect of increased gun ownership in America on the level of violence in this country. In 1979 he also published *Charity U.S.A.: An Investigation into the Hidden World of the Multi-Billion Dollar Charity Industry,* in which he argued for more nonprofit organization accountability to governments.

OBITUARIES AND OTHER SOURCES:

PERIODICALS

Chicago Tribune, April 5, 2004, Section 4, p. 8.
Los Angeles Times, April 5, 2004, p. B9.
New York Times, April 3, 2004, p. A25.
Washington Post, April 12, 2004, p. B4.

BALLARD, Jane
  See GORMAN, Carol

*   *   *

BARBER, William Henry 1918-2004

OBITUARY NOTICE—See index for *CA* sketch: Born April 15, 1918, in Hove, Sussex, England; died February 22, 2004. Educator and author. Barber was a longtime professor at the University of London, and was best known as a Voltaire scholar. Graduating from St. John's College, Oxford, in 1940, he declared himself a conscientious objector during the war and was therefore assigned as an ambulance driver for the Royal Army Medical Corps. When the war ended, he taught German and French at the College of the Rhine Army, returning home to St. John's College to complete his master's degree in 1946 and a D.Phil. in 1950. Taking a job as a lecturer in French at the University College of North Wales in 1947, he later joined the faculty at Birkbeck College at the University of London in 1955, where he would remain for the rest of his career. Beginning there as a reader in French, he became a professor of French in 1968 and vice master of the college in 1979. Barber took on other administrative roles as well, including serving as chair of the council of governors at the School of Slavonic and East European Studies from 1983 to 1989 and as a member of the management committee for the British Institute in Paris. But his colleagues are most often grateful to Barber for his role as joint secretary and, later, general editor of the *Complete Works* of Voltaire, an immense series of critical editions of Voltaire's works that includes over two hundred volumes. In addition to being the general editor of the series, he coedited two of the books, *Traite de metaphysique* and *Elements de la philosophie de Newton,* both with R. L. Waters. Barber was also the author of the books *Leibniz in France: From Arnauld to Voltaire* (1955) and *Voltaire: Candide* (1960), and the editor of books such as Racine's *Britannicus* (1967). In 1993, Barber was made honorary president of the Voltaire Foundation, and in 2003 a volume of the Voltaire series was dedicated to him.

OBITUARIES AND OTHER SOURCES:

PERIODICALS

Times (London, England), April 30, 2004, p. 39.

BARDWELL, Leland 1928(?)-

PERSONAL: Born c. 1928, in India; *Education:* Attended Alexandra College.

ADDRESSES: Agent—c/o Author Mail, Blackstaff Press, 4c Heron Wharf, Sydenham Business Pk., Belfast BT3 9LE, Ireland.

CAREER: Poet, novelist, and playwright. *Cyphers,* coeditor and founder; *Force 10,* poetry editor.

MEMBER: Aosdana.

AWARDS, HONORS: Martin Toonder Award for Literature, 1992.

WRITINGS:

The Mad Cyclist, New Writers Press (Dublin, Ireland), 1970.

Girl on a Bicycle: A Novel, Irish Writers Co-operative (Dublin, Ireland), 1977.

That London Winter, Co-Op Books (Dublin, Ireland), 1981.

(Editor) *The Anthology,* Co-Op Books (Dublin, Ireland), 1982.

The Fly and the Bedbug, Beaver Row Press (Dublin, Ireland), 1984.

The House, Kerry, Brandon (Dingle, CO), 1984.

Different Kinds of Love (short stories), Attic Press (Dublin, Ireland), 1987.

There We Have Been, Attic Press (Dublin, Ireland), 1989.

Dostoevsky's Grave: Selected Poems, Dedalus (Dublin, Ireland), 1991.

The White Beach: New and Selected Poems 1960-1998, Salmon Publishing (Cliffs of Moher, County Clare, Ireland), 1998.

Pagan at the White Table, 1998.

Mother to a Stranger, Blackstaff Press (Belfast, Ireland), 2002.

Also author of the plays *Thursday* and *Open Ended Prescription;* the radio plays *The Revenge of Constance* and *Just Another Killing;* and the musical *Edith Piaf.*

SIDELIGHTS: Leland Bardwell was born in India around 1928. Her parents were from Ireland and they returned there when she was two. She grew up Leixlip, County Kildare and was educated in Lucan, Alexandra College, in Dublin, Ireland. Starting in 1970 she began publishing poems, novels, and stories, and has had plays produced. She is the coeditor and founder of a literary magazine, *Cyphers,* and the poetry editor of the Sligo literary journal *Force 10.*

Bardwell has published a number of books of poetry and fiction, including a collection of stories called *Different Kinds of Love,* released in 1987. In the ten stories of this volume Bardwell focuses on marginalized characters dealing with different and often difficult issues of love. Audrey S. Eyler of the *Irish Literary Supplement* wrote, "Most of the love in these stories mixes with delusions, cynicism, cruelty, violence, and pain." Roz Cowman of *Women's Review of Books* commended Bardwell because "she maintains a constantly distinguished style and a wonderful ear for dialogue which moves the stories along." Patricia Roth Schwartz of *Belles Lettres* concluded, "This deft combination of metaphor and voice permeates all of the tales in this book, as women deal with the small and large betrayals of the body and the heart—birth, battering, incest, illness—in a world they must live in but did not make."

In 1989, Bardwell published *There We Have Been.* The book is a novella framed by two chapters and the story is told through the main character's diaries with the bookend chapters natrrated from two other key characters' points of view. Bardwell tells the story of Dilligence Strong who after traveling returns to the family farm where her brother lives. The book deals with the past and present relationship between the siblings and challenges ideas of truth. Patricia Roth Schwartz of *Belles Lettres* noted that "there is a primal and archetypal feel to this story, a kind of moral agony of souls gone wrong." In *Irish Literary Supplement* John Dunne wrote that "this subtle, demanding book achieves a vast emotional range." He continued, "In its portrayal of complex relationships and dark family secrets, the writing frequently approaches the brooding power of William Faulkner, while certain episodes are as gripping as any thriller."

In 1998 Bardwell published a book of poetry, *The White Beach: New and Selected Poems 1960-1998.* This work illustrates her growth and development as a poet throughout four decades. Thomas Korthals of *Local Ireland* praised the collections diversity, stating that Bardwell "manages to mix autobiography with love poetry, to fuse the different states of Ireland from the sixties to the nineties with her own development, and still not to lose her sense of humor."

Mother to a Stranger, released in 2002, is the story of Nan and Jim, a middle-aged, successful couple with no children whose world is turned upside down with the emergence of the child Nan gave up for adoption long before she met her husband. Jim has never been told of the pregnancy and must learn to deal with the truth and the addition of a new person to their lives. Pauline Ferrie of *Bookview Ireland* observed, "The author has woven a story of anger and betrayal, of apathy and withdrawal, a descent into depression and the unlikely bonding of the three protagonists, and all against a background of continuing life in the Irish countryside." A contributor for *Kirkus Reviews* stated that Bardwell's "marriage tale displays and understated fervor that deserves attention. Tough-minded and moving."

BIOGRAPHICAL AND CRITICAL SOURCES:

PERIODICALS

Belles Lettres, spring, 1990, Patricia Roth Schwartz, "Bitterness and Truth," p. 3; spring, 1991, Patricia Roth Schwartz, "From the Other Side," p. 30.
Irish Literary Supplement, spring, 1988, Audrey S. Eyler, "Not even Greek to Us," p. 29; fall, 1990, John Dunne, "The Wisdom of the Novel," p. 22.
Kirkus Reviews, May 1, 2003, review of *Mother to a Stranger,* p. 621.
New Statesman and Society, January 5, 1990, Brian McAvera, "Forks of Frown." p. 38.
Women's Review of Books, July, 1988, Roz Cowman, "Lost Souls," p. 38.

ONLINE

Bookview Ireland, http://www.bookciewireland.ie/ (October 22, 2003), Pauline Ferrie, review of *Mother to a Stranger.*
Emigrant Online, http://www.emigarnt.ie/ (October 22, 2003), short bio.
Irish Writers Online, http://www.irishwriters-online. com/ (October 22, 2003), short biography.

Local Ireland, http://www.local.ie/ (October 22, 2003), Thomas Korthals, review of *The White Beach: New and Selected Poems 1960-1998.*
Salmon Poetry, http://www.salmonpoetry.com/ (October 22, 2003), synopsis of *The White Beach* and short bio.
Writer's Centre, http://www.writerscentre.ie/ (October 22, 2003), short biography.*

*   *   *

BARKER, Mary Anne
    See STEWART, Mary Anne

*   *   *

BARTH, Gunther 1925-2004

OBITUARY NOTICE—See index for *CA* sketch: Born January 10, 1925, near Düsseldorf, Germany; died January 7, 2004, in Berkeley, CA. Educator and author. Barth was a historian and former professor at the University of California at Berkeley. Before emigrating to the United States in 1951, he had a difficult life in Germany that included being drafted into the army when he was just fifteen years old, fighting in Italy during World War II, being wounded, and surviving as a prisoner of war for two years. After the war, Barth attended the University of Cologne, becoming interested in history when he got involved in rescuing pieces of Chinese art that had been damaged by Allied bombers. A fellowship from the U.S. State Department allowed him to travel to the University of Oregon in 1949, and in 1951 he returned to America permanently, receiving a B.A. from the University of Oregon in 1955, an M.A. in American history in 1957, and, in 1962, he completed a Ph.D. at Harvard. That year, Barth joined the faculty at the University of California at Berkeley as an instructor. He was promoted to full professor of history in 1971, retiring in 1995. A beloved teacher while at Berkeley, Barth was the author of half a dozen books, including *All Quiet on the Yamhill* (1959), *Instant Cities* (1975), and, with Christian Heeb, *California* (1996).

OBITUARIES AND OTHER SOURCES:

BOOKS

Directory of American Scholars, tenth edition, Gale (Detroit, MI), 2002.

PERIODICALS

Los Angeles Times, January 15, 2004, p. B12.
San Francisco Chronicle, January 22, 2004, p. A17.

*   *   *

BATTLES, Matthew

PERSONAL: Male. *Education:* University of Chicago, A.B., 1992; Boston University Graduate School of Arts and Sciences, 1996.

ADDRESSES: Home—12 Rocky Nook Ter., Jamaica Plain, MA 02130-2902. *Office*—Houghton Library, Harvard University, Cambridge, MA 02138. *E-mail*—mbattles@fas.harvard.edu.

CAREER: Widener Library, selector of the HD Push Project; Houghton Library, librarian; Harvard Library Bulletin at Houghton Library, coordinating editor.

WRITINGS:

Library: An Unquiet History, W.W. Norton (New York, NY), 2003.

Contributor to *Harper's Magazine, Boston Book Review, London Review of Books* and other publications.

SIDELIGHTS: Matthew Battles received his A.B. from the University of Chicago in 1992, and graduated from Boston University's Graduate School of Arts and Sciences in 1996. He worked as a selector of the HD Push Project at Widener Library and currently works as the coordinating editor for the Harvard Library Bulletin at Houghton Library, the rare books library at Harvard University. He is a contributor to *Harper's Magazine, Boston Book Review, London Review of Books* and other publications. He is the author of one book, *Library: An Unquiet History,* published in 2003, and is currently working on two others, one on the history of Widener Library and the other on the history of writing.

Battles first addressed the topic of libraries and their history in an article he wrote for *Harper's Magazine* in January 2000 titled "Lost in the Stacks: The Decline and Fall of the Universal Library." Battles was planning to expand the work into a book when contacted by a literary agent interested in the project; he completed the work in two years. In *Library* Battles looks at the early roles of libraries and how they have changed and evolved over time. He illustrates how libraries have either strove to exalt knowledge as in the Vatican Library by the Renaissance popes and the French *Bibliothèque Nationale* during the Age of Enlightenment, or strove to control it as in the destructions of books that took place during China's Quing Dynasty and in Hitler's Germany. He also looks at the progress made by libraries, from Julius Caesar's creation of the public library, to Antonio Panizzi's work in transforming the British Library catalog, to Melvil Dewey's creation of the Dewey Decimal system. He also discusses libraries today as they deal with space problems and implementing new technology. Alberto Manguel of *Spectator* called the book "an erudite, companionable, joyful book ideally suited for these gloomy times." Mary Ellen Quinn of *Booklist* commended Battles's effort, "The book is less a formal history than an exploration of the concept of library and how it evolved. Battles writes in an engaging way, and his book will be appreciated by librarians and book lovers." Tim Daniels of *Library Journal* wrote, "This is a great read, flowing over many time periods and geographic regions, from the great library at Alexandria to the war-ravaged libraries of Bosnia." A reviewer for *Publishers Weekly* stated that Battles "offers a distinguished portrait of the library, its endurance and destruction throughout history."

Battles told *CA:* "It was reading that first got me interested in writing. My most significant influence as a writer is the probably the 1957 edition of the *World Book Encyclopedia,* which my parents kept in the glass bookcase behind the yellow armchair. My writing process is entirely a flight from secular responsibilities.

"The most surprising thing I've learned as a writer is that I want to keep doing it. I've only written one book so far, so my favorite, I'd have to say, is the next one. I hope my book[s] will compel and abet readers to an intoxicated curiosity."

BIOGRAPHICAL AND CRITICAL SOURCES:

PERIODICALS

American Libraries, August, 2003, review of *Library: An Unquiet History,* p. 97.

Booklist, May 15, 2003, Mary Ellen Quinn, review of *Library,* p. 1620.

Kirkus Reviews, April 15, 2003, review of *Library,* p. 580.

Library Journal, May 1, 2003, Tim Daniels, "A Tumultous History," p. 161.

New York Times, August 24, 2003, Sherie Posesorski, review of *Library.*

Publishers Weekly, April 28, 2003, review of *Library,* p. 58.

Spectator, December 13, 2003, Alberto Manguel, "The Precious Core of Civilization," p. 68.

ONLINE

Book House of Stuyvesant Plaza, http://www.bhny. com/ (October 22, 2003), synopsis of *Library* and short biography.

BookPage.com, http://www.bookpage.com/ (October 22, 2003), Robert Weibezahl, "Exploring the Library's Colorful Past."

Bostonia, http://www.bu.edu/ (February 25, 2004), "Alumni Books."

Harvard University Gazette, http://www.news.harvard. edu/ (October 22, 2003), Paula Carter, "Writer Battles' Unusual Muse in a Library."

Hermenaut, http://www.hermenaut.com/ (February 15, 2004), short biography.

Houghton Library Web site, http://hcl.harvard.edu/ (October 22, 2003), contact information for Mathew Battles and Houghton Library.

*   *   *

BAUER, Erwin A(dam) 1919-2004

OBITUARY NOTICE—See index for *CA* sketch: Born August 22, 1919, in Cincinnati, OH; died of bone marrow failure February 19, 2004, in Sequim, WA. Photographer and author. Bauer was widely recognized as a leading outdoors writer and wildlife photographer. Initially, he studied engineering at the University of Cincinnati from 1935 to 1938, but it was an area that he did not enjoy and he did not complete a degree. Nevertheless, he joined the U.S. Army Corps of Engineers in 1939, later becoming a captain in the army and seeing action in North Africa and Italy. He was awarded a Purple Heart and Croix de Guerre. Bauer then began a career as an outdoor writer and photographer, contributing to such magazines as *Field & Stream* and *Outdoor Life.* He also wrote columns about the outdoors for the *Ironton Tribune* in Ohio. After serving in the army again during the Korean War, Bauer began publishing books on the outdoors, many of which he also illustrated with his own photographs. A prolific writer and editor, he completed over fifty books during his lifetime, many of which were in collaboration with his second wife, Peggy. Among these works are *The Bass Fisherman's Bible* (1961; third edition revised by Mark Hicks, 1989), *My Adventures with African Animals* (1968), *Hunting with a Camera: A World Guide to Wildlife Photography* (1974), *Wildlife Adventures with a Camera* (1984), *Yellowstone* (1999), *The Alaska Highway: A Portrait of the Ultimate Road Trip* (2003), and *The Last Big Cats: An Untamed Spirit* (2003). Bauer's extensive experience with wildlife naturally led to his desire to preserve the world's vanishing species and wild places; he belonged to a number of conservation organizations and recently opposed the environmental policies of the George W. Bush administration. Bauer was the recipient of several writing and photography awards from the Ohio Outdoor Writers Association and also won Gold and Silver awards from the Society of American Travel Writers in 1991 and 1992. In 2000, he and his wife were presented with the Lifetime Achievement Award from the North American Nature Photography Association.

OBITUARIES AND OTHER SOURCES:

ONLINE

Joseph Van Os Photo Safaris, http://www.photosafaris. com/ (April 28, 2004).

Peninsula Daily News, http://www.peninsuladailynews. com/ (February 22, 2004).

*   *   *

BAUER, Jutta 1955-

PERSONAL: Born 1955, in Hamburg, Germany. *Education:* Studied illustration at Fachhochschule für Gestaltung, Hamburg, Germany.

ADDRESSES: Agent—c/o author correspondence, Kane/Miller Book Publishers, P.O. Box 8515, La Jolla, CA 92038.

CAREER: Cartoonist, book illustrator, filmmaker and author. Films for children include *Julie und das Monster,* 1996, *Die Königin der Farben* (*The Queen of Colors*), 1997, and *Grandpa's Angel,* 2003.

AWARDS, HONORS: Numerous awards and honors in Germany for books, for illustration work on German children's books and for German language films for children. Selected awards include Troisdorfer Bilderbuchpreis, 1985, for *Gottfried, das fliegende Schwein;* Chicago International Children's Film Festival Award, 1997, for *Die Königin der Farben* (*The Queen of Colors*); Prix Danube, 2003, for *Grandpa's Angel.*

WRITINGS:

Die Königin der Farben, Beltz & Gelberg (Weinheim, Germany), 1998.
Ein Engel trägt meinen Hinkelstein, Lappan (Oldenburg, Germany), 1999.
Schreimutter, Beltz & Gelberg (Heinheim, Germany), 2000.
Selma, Lappan (Oldenburg, Germany), 2000, Kane/ Miller Book Publishers (La Jolla, CA), 2003.
Opas Engel, Carlsen (Hamburg, Germany), 2001.
Ich sitze hier im Abendlicht: Briefe gesammelt und illustriert von Jutta Bauer, Gerstenberg Verlag (Hildesheim, Germany), 2003.

Illustrator of numerous books published in Germany, including *Gottfried, das fliegende Schwein,* by Waldrun Behnecke, *Das Herz des Piraten,* by Benno Pludra, and *Kein Tag für Juli,* by Kirsten Boie.

SIDELIGHTS: Although she is relatively unknown on American shores, Jutta Bauer is a popular children's writer and illustrator in Germany who also makes films for youngsters. Bauer's lack of recognition in English-speaking nations is somewhat the unfortunate result of the language barrier. Only one of her titles, *Selma,* has been translated into English. *Selma* was a huge hit in Germany, selling more than 200,000 copies in its author's native language. Since then English-speaking audiences have received their first glimpse of the popular Bauer's work. *Selma* is not intended solely for a juvenile audience. Its theme of self-sufficiency and satisfaction in the small pleasures of life resonates as well with older readers, and it is this theme—as well as Bauer's whimsical line drawings—that assured the book's commercial appeal.

Selma the ewe possesses the key to happiness. In the morning she eats a little grass. Then she plays with her children, enjoys her lunch, and spends her afternoon rambling in the pasture. When asked what she would change about her life if she had more time or money, she cannot think of a single item that would enhance her contentment. Bauer charts Selma's blithe passage through a day using cartoon-like pen and ink drawings with a wash of watercolor. A *Publishers Weekly* reviewer felt that Selma's penchant for living in the here and now, and her unhurried, pleasurable daily schedule, provide a "charming antidote to the clamor of consumerism."

BIOGRAPHICAL AND CRITICAL SOURCES:

PERIODICALS

Publishers Weekly, August 11, 2003, review of *Selma,* p. 277.

*   *   *

BECK, Emily M(orison) 1915-2004

OBITUARY NOTICE—See index for *CA* sketch: Born October 25, 1915, in Boston, MA; died of kidney failure March 28, 2004, in Canton, MA. Editor and author. Beck is most often remembered as the editor of several editions of *Bartlett's Quotations.* After attending Radcliffe College, where she earned a B.A. in 1937, she studied for a year at Newnham College, Cambridge, returning to New York City to work as an editor for Harper & Brothers. During the 1940s, she was an editor for the publisher Alfred A. Knopf, and this was followed by two years as a reviewer for the Book-of-the-Month Club. From 1956 to 1975, Beck was an editor at Atlantic Monthly Press, serving as associate editor of "Atlantic Brief Lives" from 1967 to 1971. Her association with *Bartlett's Quotations* began in 1952, when her employers at Atlantic Monthly granted her a leave to help edit the 1955 centennial edition of the famous quotations reference. Her excellent work on the edition was duly noted, and she was rewarded by being made editor of the fourteenth edition, published in 1968. Beck would go on to edit the 1980 edition, as well. As editor of *Bartlett's* she was noted for adding more popular quotations, such as from films and movies, as well as for including, for the first time, quotes from such figures as Franz Kafka, Albert Camus, Sigmund Freud, and modern poets like Robert Lowell. Sometimes she was criticized for editorial choices by those who felt her guidelines were too inclusive, but others praised her boldness in including a wide spectrum of sources. In addition to her work on *Bartlett's,* Beck edited *Sailor Historian: The Best of Samuel Eliot Morison* (1977) and wrote an introduction to the new edition of her father's *The Story of Mount Desert Island* (2001).

OBITUARIES AND OTHER SOURCES:

PERIODICALS

Chicago Tribune, April 1, 2004, Section 3, p. 9.
Los Angeles Times, April 4, 2004, p. B16.
New York Times, March 31, 2004, p. C13.
Times (London, England), April 14, 2004, p. 26.
Washington Post, April 3, 2004, p. B6.

*   *   *

BELLOW, Adam 1957-

PERSONAL: Born 1957; son of Saul (an author) and Alexandra Bellow. *Education:* Princeton University, B.A., (Renaissance studies), 1980; completed postgraduate study at the University of Chicago.

ADDRESSES: Home—64 Grand St., New York, NY 10013.

CAREER: Doubleday Press, New York, NY, editor-at-large, 1997—. Editorial director, Free Press.

WRITINGS:

In Praise of Nepotism: A Natural History, Doubleday (New York, NY), 2003.

SIDELIGHTS: Adam Bellow began life as the son of the famous author Saul Bellow and his second wife Alexandra. As David Remnick chronicles in a January, 1995, interview in the *New Yorker,* after earning his

bachelor's degree from Princeton University in 1980 and several career changes, Bellow entered the Committee on Social Thought's Ph.D. program at the University of Chicago at his father's suggestion. He later became the editorial director at the Free Press, a conservative publishing house, where he edited the books *The Real Anita Hill* and *The Bell Curve,* among many others.

Adam Bellow enjoyed a successful career as the publisher of some of the most famous and controversial texts of his day at the Free Press. However, in his first major work, *In Praise of Nepotism: A Natural History,* he raises the issue of how much of this success was the result of his famous father: "My employers . . . undoubtedly assumed not only that I had the 'right stuff' to be an editor by virtue of my parentage, but that my name and social background would be useful in my publishing career." "Nor is it likely," he continued, "that I could have written and published this book without the added value that my name brings to the project."

Bellow's assertion that nepotism has played a major role in his life is a positive one. His book makes the case that nepotism is a concept deeply rooted in American history and culture, and often plays a positive role in society. He questioned the suspicion that nepotism engenders in American culture, and the hypocrisy with which we view it as a bad practice but utilize it to our benefit. In the first chapter of his book, which was published as an article in the *Atlantic Monthly,* Bellow envisions a "new nepotism" that combines "the privileges of birth with the iron rule of merit in a way that is much less offensive to democratic sensibilities."

Critical response to Bellow's book was varied. Scott McLemee, writing in *Newsday,* observed that "the image of a silver spoon on the cover of *In Praise of Nepotism* is an awfully cute touch, but to someone born without one, it looks like a weapon." *New Statesman* reviewer Richard Reeves commented, "It is tempting to dismiss Bellow Jr's arguments as a load of self-serving tosh. And given that he writes in a nation where the late Senator Strom Thurmond prevailed upon George W. Bush to appoint his twenty-eight-year-old son as U.S. attorney for South Carolina, this is a temptation to which we should succumb." Other reviewers responded positively to the book's assertions. Steve Sailer, in *National Interest,* argued that

Americans' insistence on achievement through merit alone put the nation at a disadvantage in foreign affairs. "Americans tend to be willfully blind to the crucial subject of nepotism," he pointed out. "We disapprove of it, so we feel we ought not to think about it—a dangerous illusion as we pursue a more activist foreign policy that brings us in touch with cultures that approach the topic quite differently." In the *National Review,* Paul Johnson questioned, "And why should not hereditary skills be rewarded? All the public really demands is fairness. I doubt whether that can be enforced by regulators and law."

A few reviewers felt that the book's premise was undermined by Bellow's redefinition of the term "nepotism." Writing in *New Criterion,* Anthony Daniels remarked that Bellow "does not really define nepotism very clearly, so that favoritism and cronyism come to be equated with it. But they are surely rather different phenomena." A contributor to *Publishers Weekly* also noted that "at times he casts such a wide net that he risks blurring nepotism with the entirety of human history," but felt that Bellow's "analysis of the flexibility and complexity of nepotism's forms is utterly enthralling and stimulating."

Nathan Glazer in a review for *Commentary* addressed the criticism, both positive and negative, that surrounded Bellow's first work: "This is a book whose provenance may well overshadow any serious discussion of its merits." He concluded that "Bellow deserves credit for having placed the issue on the table, and I hope it will not be held against him that he has a personal interest in the matter."

BIOGRAPHICAL AND CRITICAL SOURCES:

PERIODICALS

Booklist, July, 2003, David Siegfried, review of *In Praise of Nepotism: A Natural History,* p. 1842.
Commentary, September, 2003, Nathan Glazer, review of *In Praise of Nepotism,* pp. 61-63.
Esquire, August, 2003, David Updike, review of *In Praise of Nepotism,* p. 24.
Inc., September 1, 2003, Adam Hanft, review of *In Praise of Nepotism.*
Kirkus Reviews, May 15, 2003, review of *In Praise of Nepotism,* pp. 724-725.

Library Journal, July, 2003, Janet Ingraham Dwyer, review of *In Praise of Nepotism,* p. 110.
National Interest, winter, 2003, Steve Sailor, review of *In Praise of Nepotism,* pp. 149-144.
National Review, August 11, 2003, Paul Johnson, review of *In Praise of Nepotism.*
New Criterion, September, 2003, Anthony Daniels, review of *In Praise of Nepotism,* pp. 65-68.
Newsday, August 3, 2003, review of *In Praise of Nepotism.*
New Statesman, September 29, 2003, Richard Reeves, review of *In Praise of Nepotism,* pp. 22-24.
New Yorker, January 16, 1995, David Remnick, author interview, pp. 27-28.
New York Times, June 21, 2003, Emily Eakin, review of *In Praise of Nepotism,* p. B9.
Publishers Weekly, June 23, 2003, review of *In Praise of Nepotism,* and author interview, pp. 60-61.
U.S. News & World Report, July 21, 2003, review of *In Praise of Nepotism,* p. 54.

ONLINE

New York Metro, http://www.newyorkmetro.com/ (October 22, 2003), John Homans, review of *In Praise of Nepotism.*
Sacramento Bee Online, http://www.sacbee.com/ (October 22, 2003), Merle Rubin, review of *In Praise of Nepotism.**

*   *   *

BIEN, Thomas (H.) 1953-

PERSONAL: Surname is pronounced like "bean;" born June 2, 1953, in Summit, NJ; son of Frank John and Arlene LaVerne (Gokey; later surname, Pyle) Bien; married June 24, 1995; wife's name, Beverly (an executive and writer); children: Joshua. *Ethnicity:* "Caucasian." *Education:* Attended University of Bonn, 1973-74; Rutgers University, B.A. (summa cum laude), 1975; Princeton Theological Seminary, M.Div., 1978; University of New Mexico, M.S. (with distinction), 1990, Ph.D., 1992. *Politics:* "Liberal Democrat."

ADDRESSES: Home—12517 Conejo N.E., Albuquerque, NM 87123. *Office*—2501 San Pedro N.E., Suite 205, Albuquerque, NM 87110. *Agent*—Meredith Bernstein, 2112 Broadway, Suite 503A, New York, NY 10023.

CAREER: United Methodist minister, 1978-86; Veterans Administration Medical Center, Albuquerque, NM, clinical trainee, 1987; private practice of psychology, 1988-92; Health Psychology Associates, postdoctoral intern, 1992-93; Samaritan Counseling Center, psychotherapist, 1993-94; Health Psychology Associates, clinical psychologist, 1994-96; private practice of clinical psychology, Albuquerque, NM, 1996—. Veterans Administration Medical Center, therapist, 1993-94. Teacher of classes at University of New Mexico, 1988-90, 1993-94, and Albuquerque Technical-Vocational Institute, beginning 1992; presenter of seminars.

MEMBER: New Mexico Psychological Association, Phi Delta Kappa, Phi Kappa Phi.

AWARDS, HONORS: Scholarship for Germany, Federation of German-American Clubs, 1972.

WRITINGS:

(With Beverly Bien) *Mindful Recovery: A Spiritual Path to Healing from Addiction,* Wiley Publishing Group (New York, NY), 2002.

(With Beverly Bien) *Finding the Center Within: The Healing Way of Mindfulness Meditation,* Wiley Publishing Group (New York, NY), 2003.

Author of a booklet, "Helping People You Love to Change" RHD Associates (Sacramento, CA), 1992. Contributor to books, including *Psychotherapy and Substance Abuse: A Practitioner's Handbook,* edited by A. Washton, Guilford Press (New York, NY), 1995; and *Handbook of Alcoholism Treatment Approaches: Effective Alternatives,* edited by R. K. Hester and W. R. Miller, Allyn & Bacon (Needham Heights, MA), 2nd edition, 1995. Contributor to periodicals, including *International Journal of the Addictions, Behavioural and Cognitive Psychotherapy,* and *In Session: Journal of Clinical Psychology.*

WORK IN PROGRESS: Mindful Therapy: Psychotherapy as Spiritual Path, completion expected in 2005.

BIOGRAPHICAL AND CRITICAL SOURCES:

PERIODICALS

Library Journal, July, 2002, Antoinette Brinkman, review of *Mindful Recovery: A Spiritual Path to Healing from Addiction,* p. 103.

ONLINE

Mindful Psychology, http://www.mindfulpsychology. com/ (December 10, 2003).

*   *   *

BOISEN, Anton T(heophilus) 1876-1965

PERSONAL: Born October 29, 1876, in Bloomington, IN; died October 1, 1965, in Elgin, IL; son of Hermann Balthazar (a professor of languages and botany) and Louise (Wylie) Boisen. *Education:* Indiana University—Bloomington, graduated, 1897; studied forestry at Yale University; Union Theological Seminary, New York, NY, graduated, 1911; studied at Episcopal Theological Seminary and Andover Theological Seminary; additional graduate study at Harvard University.

CAREER: Ordained Presbyterian minister, 1911; Presbyterian Board of Home Missions, member of a rural survey in Tennessee and Missouri, 1911-12; pastor for five years at rural churches in Iowa, Kansas, and Maine; Young Men's Christian Association, overseas worker in France for nearly two years; Interchurch World Movement, director of a rural survey in North Dakota, prior to 1920; Boston Psychopathic Hospital, Boston, MA, social worker; Worcester State Hospital, Worcester, MA, chaplain, 1924-30; Elgin State Hospital, Elgin, IL, chaplain and trainer in clinical pastoral education, 1932-35, 1942-45. Chicago Theological Seminary, instructor, beginning 1924, resident, 1938-42. Teacher of clinical pastoral education classes in Boston as early as 1925; Council for the Clinical Training of Theological Students, founder, 1930.

WRITINGS:

Lift up Your Hearts, Pilgrim Press (Boston, MA), 1926, revised edition published as a booklet, "Hymns of Hope and Courage, with Services, Prayers, and Readings for Public and Private Worship," edited by Cecil Michener Smith, 1931.

My Own Case Record (memoir), 1928, revised edition published as *Out of the Depths: An Autobiographical Study of Mental Disorder and Religious Experience,* Harper (New York, NY), 1960.

The Exploration of the Inner World: A Study of Mental Disorder and Religious Experience, Willett, Clark and Co. (Chicago, IL), 1936.

Problems in Religion and Life: A Manual for Pastors, with Outlines for the Co-operative Study of Personal Experience in Social Situations, Abingdon-Cokesbury Press (New York, NY), 1946.

Religion in Crisis and Custom: A Sociological and Psychological Study, Harper (New York, NY), 1955.

Author of shorter works, including coauthor of a forestry bulletin and a church report of a rural survey in Missouri. Contributor of about forty articles to religious magazines and scientific journals.

The Boisen Files reside in the Boisen Room of the library, Chicago Theological Seminary, Chicago, IL; other manuscripts are stored in the archives of the Menninger Foundation, Topeka, KS.

BIOGRAPHICAL AND CRITICAL SOURCES:

BOOKS

Boisen, Anton T., *Out of the Depths: An Autobiographical Study of Mental Disorder and Religious Experience,* Harper (New York, NY), 1960.

PERIODICALS

Pastoral Psychology, September, 1968, Henri J. M. Nouwen, "Anton T. Boisen and the Study of Theology through 'Living Human Documents'."

Psychiatry, November, 1977, "Anton T. Boisen's 'Psychiatric Examination: Content of Thought' (c. 1925-31): An Attempt to Grasp the Meaning of Mental Disorder."*

*   *   *

BOLES, Philana Marie

PERSONAL: Born in Toledo, OH. *Education:* Bowling Green State University, B.F.A.

ADDRESSES: Agent—c/o Author Mail, Random House, 1745 Broadway, New York, NY 10019.

CAREER: Worked at 40 Acres & A Mule Filmworks and *Glamour* magazine; playwright.

WRITINGS:

Blame It on Eve: A Novel, Ballantine Books (New York, NY), 2002.

WORK IN PROGRESS: A second novel and a children's book.

SIDELIGHTS: In her debut novel *Blame It on Eve* Philana Marie Boles tells the story of Shawni Kaye Baldwin, a spoiled, naive model. Shawni turns down a great modeling job with a top designer to get engaged to her boyfriend Bo Delaney, a rich entertainment attorney. Bo spoils Shawni by buying her everything she wants, including a New York apartment and a brand new Lexus. At the last minute Shawni's brother, a music promoter, asks her to take a job as a stylist for a new music group. While working with the group she falls in love with Zin, the lead singer. Shawni starts to examine her relationship with Bo, and realizes she doesn't want to be his trophy wife, especially after she suspects Bo is cheating on her. Shawni is confused about what she wants in a man, in her career, and out of life, but is eventually able to put it all in perspective. A *Book Remarks* contributor praised the book as "an engaging and impressive read." *Booklist* writer Lillian Lewis concluded that "teen girls will identify with the young woman who thinks she knows what she want but doesn't."

BIOGRAPHICAL AND CRITICAL SOURCES:

PERIODICALS

Booklist, September 1, 2002, Lillian Lewis, review of *Blame It on Eve: A Novel,* p. 54.

Kirkus Reviews, July 15, 2002, review of *Blame It on Eve,* p. 971.

Library Journal, November 1, 2002, Ann Burns, review of *Blame It on Eve,* p. 110.

Publishers Weekly, September 2, 2002, review of *Blame It on Eve,* p. 54.

ONLINE

Ballantine Books, http://www.randomhouse.com/ (March 28, 2003), description of *Blame It on Eve.*
Book Remarks, http://www.book-remarks.com/ (March 28, 2003), "Featured Author: Philana Marie Boles."*

* * *

BOOKER, Cedella Marley 1926-

PERSONAL: Original name, Cedella Malcolm; born 1926, in Nine Miles, Jamaica; married Norval Marley, 1944 (deceased, 1962); companion of Toddy Livingstone (relationship ended); married Richard Booker; children: (with Marley) Robert Nesta Marley (deceased); (with Livingstone) Pearl; (with Booker) Anthony (deceased), Richard.

ADDRESSES: Office—2809 Bird Ave., Ste. 146, Coconut Grove, FL 33126. *E-mail*—cmbe@msn.com.

CAREER: Writer, musician, artist and sculptor; Bob Marley Festival, Miami, FL, founder, 1994.

WRITINGS:

(With Gerald Hausman) *56 Thoughts from 56 Hope Road: The Sayings and Psalms of Bob Marley,* Tuff Gong Books (Miami, FL), 2002.
(With Gerald Hausman) *The Boy from Nine Miles: The Early Life of Bob Marley,* illustrated by Mariah Fox, Hampton Roads (Charlottesville, VA), 2002.
(With Anthony C. Winkler) *Bob Marley, My Son,* Taylor (Lanham, MD), 2003.

SOUND RECORDINGS

Awake Zion, Rykodisc (Nashville, TN), 1991.
Smilin' Island of Song, Music for the Little People (Redway, CA), 1992.

SIDELIGHTS: Cedella Marley Booker is the mother of one of the most famous Jamaicans in history—the late Bob Marley. Booker has written books about the life of her son and is also a musician in her own right. She records reggae and gospel music. She is also the founder of the Bob Marley Festival, held annually in Miami, Florida. The festival was started in 1994 and features reggae and world music. Much of the proceeds go directly to charity. Booker told Piccoli in the *Sun-Sentinel,* "I am committed to do certain things to keep up his [Marley's] legacy because it was his desire." She went on to say, "there is a message that he left that people are feeding on." She feels that the festival will continue for as long as the people have a need for Bob Marley's message of peace and love.

Booker collaborated with Anthony C. Winkler to write her 2003 book, *Bob Marley, My Son.* The book explores the special relationship between Booker and Marley, and focuses more on Marley as a person than a famous musician. Bill Walker, a reviewer for *Library Journal,* stated that the book offers "many personal details that make Marley seem more like a complex, flawed human being than a mythical prophet." "Booker has much of value to say about her son's personal life," wrote Mike Tribby for *Booklist.*

BIOGRAPHICAL AND CRITICAL SOURCES:

PERIODICALS

Booklist, May 1, 2003, Mike Tribby, review of *Bob Marley, My Son,* p. 1563.
Consumers' Research Magazine, June, 1993, Robert Henschen, review of *Smilin' Island of Song,* p. 33.
Library Journal, May 1, 2003, Bill Walker, review of *Bob Marley, My Son,* p. 115.
Publishers Weekly, October 5, 1992, review of *Smilin' Island of Song,* p. 34.
School Library Journal, May, 1993, Abbey-jo Rehling, review of *Smilin' Island of Song,* p. 71.

ONLINE

Bob Marley Movement, http://www.bobmarley movement.com/ (February 25, 2004).
Sun-Suntinel.com, Sean Piccoli, http://www.sun-sentinel.com/ (February 6, 2004), interview with Cedella Marley Booker.*

* * *

BOROWITZ, Andy (Seth) 1958-

PERSONAL: Born January 4, 1958, in Cleveland, OH; son of Albert Ira and Helen Blanche (Osterman) Borowitz. *Education:* Harvard, B.A., 1980.

ADDRESSES: Agent—Bruce Vinokour, Creative Artists Agency, 9830 Wilshire Blvd., Beverly Hillls, CA 90212. *E-mail*—andy@borowitzreport.com.

CAREER: Writer, humorist, film and television producer. Regularly appears on CNN's *American Morning* and National Public Radio's *Weekend Edition.* Executive producer and creator of *The Fresh Prince of Bel Air,* National Broadcasting Company (NBC), 1990-96. Producer of motion pictures, including *Pleasantville,* New Line Cinema, 1998.

MEMBER: Writers Guild, Harvard Club, Friar's Club, Screen Actors Guild, Players Club.

AWARDS, HONORS: Jacob Wendell scholar, Harvard University, 1977; NAACP Image Award for *The Fresh Prince of Bel Air.* Winner of five *About.com* Political Dot-Comedy awards.

WRITINGS:

(With Henry Beard and John Boswell) *Rationalizations to Live By,* illustrated by Roz Chast, Workman (New York, NY), 2000.

The Trillionaire Next Door: The Greedy Investor's Guide to Day Trading, HarperBusiness (New York, NY), 2000.

Who Moved My Soap?: The CEO's Guide to Surviving in Prison, Simon & Schuster (New York, NY), 2003.

Governor Arnold: A Photodiary of His First 100 Days in Office, Simon & Schuster (New York, NY), 2004.

The Borowitz Report: The Big Book of Shockers, Simon & Schuster (New York, NY), 2004.

Contributor to periodicals including *Newsweek.com, New Yorker, New York Times,* and *Vanity Fair.* Writer for television shows including *Square Pegs,* Central Broadcasting Company (CBS), 1982 and *The Fresh Prince of Bel Air,* NBC, 1990.

SIDELIGHTS: Andy Borowitz is known as a powerful Hollywood producer, a leading comic voice, a prolific screenwriter, and a gifted comedic writing teacher. According to the *Greater Talent Network Web site,* Borowitz began his career in show business at the age

of thirteen. While studying at Harvard he wrote the *Hasty Pudding Show* and was president of the *Harvard Lampoon.* Borowitz has a long list of credentials including writing a daily column for his Web site, the *Borowitz Report.* He told an interviewer for *Zulkey,* "the great (or terrible) thing about the *Borowitz Report* is that through some insanity of my own I've committed myself to writing it five days a week." Borowitz is also the creator and executive producer of *The Fresh Prince of Bel Air* television sitcom, which ran from 1990-1996.

Borowitz has written three books of humor and has cowritten *Rationalizations to Live By* with Henry Beard and John Boswell. *The Trillionaire Next Door: The Greedy Investor's Guide to Day Trading* is a book poking fun at day-trading and dedicated to Oprah. The book features such advice as "when to buy, when to sell, and when to call Domino's." Borowitz illustrates the rules of becoming a trillionaire and each rule is followed by a real quote from a day trader. A reviewer for *Publishers Weekly* called *The Trillionaire Next Door* "an entertaining diversion."

According to a reviewer for *Bookreporter.com, Who Moved My Soap?: The CEO's Guide to Surviving in Prison* "is intended as a satirical guide for the CEO who finds himself going to prison." The book includes helpful hints such as "The Seven Habits of Highly Effective Prisoners." A reviewer for *Publishers Weekly* observed, "Borowitz offers a Zagat-like guide to prison food" and claims "this slim but very funny release riffs on the inexhaustible genre of business books." Borowitz's 2004 release is *Governor Arnold: A Photodiary of His First 100 Days in Office,* a book of pictures with fictious captions featuring the governor of California.

BIOGRAPHICAL AND CRITICAL SOURCES:

PERIODICALS

Publishers Weekly, June 5, 2000, review of *The Trillionaire Next Door: The Greedy Investor's Guide to Day Trading,* p. 82; May 12, 2003, review of *Who Moved My Soap?: The CEO's Guide to Surviving in Prison,* p 57.

ONLINE

Bookreporter.com, http://www.bookreporter.com/ (October 23, 2003), review of *Who Moved My Soap?: The CEO's Guide to Surviving Prison.*

Borowitz Report, http://www.borowitzreport.com (March 10, 2004).

Business Report, http://www.abc.net.au/rn/talks/ (October 23, 2003), Elizabeth Jackson, review of *Who Moved My Soap?*.

Greater Talent Network Web site, http://www. greatertalent.com/ (March 10, 2004).

Zulkey, http://www.zulkey.com/ (March 10, 2004), author interview.

*   *   *

BOUWSMA, William J. 1923-2004

OBITUARY NOTICE—See index for *CA* sketch: Born November 22, 1923, in Ann Arbor, MI; died of complications from an aneurysm, March 2, 2004, in Berkeley, CA. Educator, historian, and author. Bouwsma was a professor emeritus at the University of California at Berkeley, where he became well known as an authority on the Renaissance. After completing undergraduate studies at Harvard in 1943, he served in the Army Air Forces during World War II. He then returned to Harvard to complete his Ph.D. in 1950. While Bouwsma spent his first six years in academia teaching at the University of Illinois, when he joined the UC Berkeley faculty in 1956 it was to become his permanent home as a scholar. Starting out as an associate professor of history, he became a full professor in 1969 and was named Sather Professor of History in 1971. Bouwsma was also chair of the history department from 1966 to 1967, and again from 1981 to 1983, and he was vice chancellor for academic affairs from 1967 to 1969. While serving as vice chancellor, Bouwsma played an important part in adding studies in religious and ethnic history to the UC Berkeley curriculum. A highly respected author, he published several important studies on the Renaissance, including *Venice and the Defense of Republican Liberty: Renaissance Values in the Age of the Counter Reformation* (1968), *John Calvin: A Sixteenth-Century Portrait,* which won the Book of the Year Award from the Evangelical Publishers' Association, and his last publication, *The Waning of the Renaissance, ca. 1500-1640* (2000). A former president of the Society for Italian Historical Studies and the American Historical Association, Bouwsma retired from teaching in 1991.

OBITUARIES AND OTHER SOURCES:

PERIODICALS

Chicago Tribune, March 16, 2004, Section 2, p. 12.

Los Angeles Times, March 13, 2004, p. B21.
San Francisco Chronicle, March 8, 2004, p. B4.

ONLINE

UC Berkeley Press, http://www.berkeley.edu/news/ (March 5, 2004).

*   *   *

BOYD, Nan Alamilla

PERSONAL: Female. *Education:* University of California, B.A., 1986; M.A., 1989; Brown University, Ph.D., 1995.

ADDRESSES: Office—1801 E. Colati Ave., 51 Rachel Carson Hall, Rohnert Park, CA 94928. *E-mail*—nan. alamilla.boyd@sonoma.edu.

CAREER: Writer. University of Colorado, Boulder, assistant professor of women's studies, 1999-2003; Sonoma State University, assistant professor, 2003—.

WRITINGS:

Wide-Open Town: A History of Queer San Francisco to 1965, University of California Press (Berkley, CA), 2003.

SIDELIGHTS: Nan Alamilla Boyd is a professor of women's and gender studies. *Wide-Open Town: A History of Queer San Francisco to 1965* explores the history of gay men and women in San Francisco from 1900-1965. Boyd uses oral interviews, police and court records, tourist information, and manuscript collections to weave together the history of gay and lesbian culutre in San Francisco. *Wide-Open Town* is titled as such because San Francisco has a known reputation of a town where "anything goes." Critics have applauded *Wide-Open Town* as being surprizingly the first academic, comprehensive history of gay and lesbian activity in San Francisco. A reviewer for *Publisher's Weekly* stated, "Boyd has a keen ear for distinctive details, and it is this . . . that drives this welcome study."

BIOGRAPHICAL AND CRITICAL SOURCES:

PERIODICALS

Library Journal, May 1, 2003, Richard J. Violette, review of *Wide-Open Town: A History of Queer San Francisco to 1965,* pp. 140-141.
Publishers Weekly, May 19, 2003, review of *Wide-Open Town,* pp. 65-66.

ONLINE

Gay Today, http://www.gaytoday.com/ (October 23, 2003), review of *Wide-Open Town.**

*   *   *

BOYKIN, J. Robert III 1944-

PERSONAL: Born July 8, 1944, in Wilson, NC; son of J. Robert, Jr. and Geraldine (Dillon) Boykin; married Susan Mewborn, June 30, 1984; children: Robert Clark, George Barnes, Eleanor Williams, Dillon Alexander. *Ethnicity:* "Caucasian." *Education:* Barton College, B.A.; East Carolina University, M.A.Ed.; also attended University of North Carolina—Chapel Hill. *Religion:* Episcopalian.

ADDRESSES: Home—2112 Canal Dr., Wilson, NC 27896, *Office*—Boykin Antiques and Appraisals, Inc., P.O. Box 7440, Wilson, NC 27895; fax: 252-237-2314. *E-mail*—boykinappraisals@coastalnet.com.

CAREER: Boykin Antiques and Appraisals, Inc., Wilson, NC, owner, 1980—. International Society of Appraisers, certified appraiser of personal property, 1984. Indiana University, instructor in appraisal, 1986-92; public speaker. Wilson-Greene Mental Health Center, vice chair of board of trustees, 1973-2001; Arts Council of Wilson, president, 1973-75; Wilson City Council, council member, 1976-78, 1978-80; Friends of Wilson County Public Library, president, 1979-81; Wilson Historic Properties Commission, chair, 1984-86; Wilson County Chamber of Commerce, member of board of directors, 1997-99, vice president, 1999; Wilson Education Partnership, member of board of directors, 1999-2001. Historic

Preservation Foundation of North Carolina, member of board of advisors, 1984—; member of Claims Prevention and Procedures Council, Inc., North Carolina Museum of History, North Carolina Museum of Art, and National Trust for Historic Preservation.

MEMBER: International Society of Appraisers (member of board of directors, 1990-95, 2000-03), American Society of Appraisers (senior member; president of North Carolina chapter, 1993-94), North Carolina Antique Dealers Association, North Carolina Genealogical Society, Wilson County Antique Dealers Association (president, 1983-84; member of board of directors, 1989-98).

AWARDS, HONORS: Community Service Award, Heart of Wilson Associates, 1985; Leadership Award, Wilson Historic Properties Commission, 1987; Lester P. Rose Membership Award, Wilson County Chamber of Commerce, 1989.

WRITINGS:

1880 Census of Wilson County, North Carolina, privately printed, 1984.
Marriages of Wilson County, North Carolina, 1855-1899, privately printed, 1988.
Wills of Wilson County, North Carolina, 1855-1899, privately printed, 1992.
Historic Wilson in Vintage Postcards, Arcadia Publishing (Charleston, SC), 2003.

Contributor to professional journals.

SIDELIGHTS: J. Robert Boykin III told *CA:* "My motivation for writing is a love and passion for southern history, particularly eastern North Carolina history. My work has been influenced by Professor Hugh B. Johnston, Jr. of Barton College and Dr. William S. Powell of the University of North Carolina at Chapel Hill."

*   *   *

BRANDON-COX, Hugh 1917-2003

OBITUARY NOTICE—See index for *CA* sketch: Born June 14, 1917, in Elmstead Market, Essex, England; died December 3, 2003. Artist, photographer, filmmaker, and author. Brandon-Cox was known for his love of the natural landscapes and wildlife of such northern places as Norway, the Arctic Circle, and the countryside of Norfolk, England, which he captured in his books, paintings, films, and photographs. His early life was a tragic one, including his father's death during the South African Zulu uprising before he was born, the death of his mother from tuberculosis when he was just five years old, the death of his grandmother, who had been raising him, when he was nine, and the subsequent deaths of his aunt and uncle in a motorcycle accident. He was able to find some solace in the countryside, which his grandmother had encouraged him to explore, and decided to follow in his father's footsteps as a naturalist and explorer. With a love of Scandinavia, Brandon-Cox learned to speak Swedish; thus, with the onset of World War II, he was recruited by the military to serve in the special forces in that region. Here he helped Swede refugees to escape from the Germans and make their way to England. When the war was over, he founded the magazine *West Countryman* and later became a correspondent and photographer for magazines, recording stories about nature and wildlife. His love for photographs turned into a film career with the British Broadcasting Corp. for which he created such documentaries as *The Trail of the Arctic Nomads* (1969) and *In Summer of a Million Wings* (1974). He also began writing and publishing self-illustrated books, including *Hovran: Swedish Bird Lake* (1968), *A Longing to Explore* (1976), and books based on his films or that preceded his films. In the 1970s, Brandon-Cox took up painting and became a skilled wildlife and landscape artist while continuing to write books and articles for various magazines. Also the author of *Country Pageant* (1947), among Brandon-Cox's last publications are *Mud on My Boots: The Estuaries and Countryside of the Norfolk Heritage Coast* (2002) and *Softly Wakes the Dawn* (2003).

OBITUARIES AND OTHER SOURCES:

PERIODICALS

Daily Telegraph (London, England), February 6, 2004.
Times (London, England), March 4, 2004.

*   *   *

BRENDEL, Alfred 1931-

PERSONAL: Born January 5, 1931, in Wiesenberg, Moravia (now part of the Czech Republic); son of Albert (an architect, businessman, and theater manager), and Ida (Wieltschnig) Brendel; married Iris Heymann-Gonzala, 1960 (divorced, 1972); married Irene Semler, 1975; children: (first marriage) Doris; (second marriage) one son, one daughter. *Education:* Graz Academy of Music, diploma, 1947; studied under Sofija Dezelic, Ludovika V. Kaan, Edwin Fischer, Paul Baumgartner, and Eduard Steuermann.

ADDRESSES: Agent—Colbert Artists Management, Inc., 111 West 57th St., New York, NY 10019-2211.

CAREER: Concert pianist. Debut recital, Graz, Austria, 1948; U.S. debut, 1963.

MEMBER: American Academy of Arts and Sciences (honorary), Royal Academy of Music (honorary).

AWARDS, HONORS: Premio Citta de Bolzano Concorso Busoni, 1949; Grand Prix du Disque, 1965, 1984; Edison Prize, 1973, 1981, 1984, 1987; British Music Trade Association award, 1973, 1978, 1981; Grand Prix des Disquaires de France, 1975; Deutscher Schallplattenpreis, 1976-77, 1981-82, 1984; Wiender Flotenuhr, 1976-77, 1979, 1982, 1984, 1987; Japanese Grand Prix award, 1977-78, 1980, 1982, 1984, 1987; Gramophone Award, 1978, 1980, 1982, 1984; Franz Liszt Prize, 1979-80, 1982-83, 1987; Frankfurt Music award, 1984; named honorary member of the Vienna Philharmonic, 1998; Busoni Foundation award, 1990; Orden pour le Merite fur Wissenschaften und Kunste, 1991; Diapason D'Or award, Preis der deutschen Schallplatten-Kritik, and Hans von Bülow Medal, Berlin Philharmonic, all 1992; Royal Philharmonic Society prize, for *Music Sounded Out: Essays, Lectures, Interviews, Afterthoughts;* Cannes Award, Edison Award, Netherlands, and Beethoven Ring award, University of the Performing Arts, Vienna, all 2001; recipient of the Leonie Sonning Prize, the Furtwaengler Prize for musical interpretation, the South Bank Award, and Robert Schumann Prize. Honorary doctorates from the University of London, 1978, Sussex University, 1981, Oxford University, 1983, Warwick University, 1991, and Yale University, 1992. Appointed an honorary Knight Commander of the British Empire by Queen Elizabeth II, 1989, for outstanding services to music in Britain.

WRITINGS:

Musical Thoughts and Afterthoughts, Robson Books (London, England), 1976, Princeton University Press (Princeton, NJ), 1977.

Music Sounded Out: Essays, Lectures, Interviews, Afterthoughts, Robson Books (London, England), 1990, Farrar, Straus & Giroux (New York, NY), 1991.

Störendes lachen während des Jaworts: neue texte (title means "Annoying Laughter while Saying 'I Do'"), Carl Hanser (Munich, Germany), 1997.

One Finger Too Many (poems), translated by Brendel and Richard Stokes, Random House (New York, NY), 1998.

Kleine teufel: neue gedichte (poems; title means "Little Devils"), C. Hanser (Munich, Germany), 1999.

On Music, translated by Brendel and others, Robson Books (London, England), 2001, published as *Alfred Brendel on Music: Collected Essays,* Chicago Review Press (Chicago, IL), 2002.

Ausgerechnet ich (interview), Carl Hanser (Munich Germany), 2001, translated by Richard Stokes as *Me of All People: Alfred Brendel in Conversation with Martin Meyer,* Cornell University Press (Ithaca, NY), 2002, published in England as *The Veil of Order: Conversations with Martin Meyer,* Faber (London, England), 2002.

Also author of *Fingerzeig* (title means "Finger Pointing"). Contributor to periodicals, including *New York Review of Books.* Credited with numerous classical recordings. *The Art of Alfred Brendel,* a five-box set, was released in honor of his sixty-fifth birthday in 1996, and includes twenty-five CDs featuring the works of Haydn and Mozart, Beethoven, Schubert, Liszt, and Brahms and Schumann; work represented in Philips's "Great Pianists of the Twentieth Century" series.

SIDELIGHTS: Pianist Alfred Brendel has been called "the world's greatest classical player" by the *New Yorker,* and few would dispute this fact. He has played with the finest orchestras and musicians of his time in countries around the world. Brendel was the first pianist to have recorded all of Beethoven's piano compositions and one of the few to have recorded all of Mozart's piano concertos.

The author of a biography of Brendel that appears on the Pittsburgh Symphony Web site noted "Alfred Brendel, praised as a supreme master of his art who is always searching for new perspectives, is recognized by audiences the world over for his legendary ability to convey the emotional and intellectual development of the music he performs. His accomplishments as an interpreter of the great composers have earned him a place among the most revered musicians of our time."

Brendel was born in Moravia to a family of German, Austrian, Slavic, and Italian heritage. Because his father changed jobs frequently, the young Brendel traveled continuously, and he spent his early childhood in Croatia, on the Adriatic island of Krk, where his parents ran a hotel. Brendel took his first lessons at the age of six and studied formally only until the age of sixteen. The family moved from Zagreb, Yugoslavia to Graz, Austria in 1943. Brendel dug ditches for the war effort but was returned to his family after suffering frostbite. He earned a diploma from a state school, and like young musicians of his time, he also studied composition and conducting, and he was soon composing his own music. At the time of his debut at the age of seventeen, a one-man exhibition of his watercolors was being held in a Graz gallery.

Brendel is largely self-taught. He attended concerts in Vienna and learned from the masters. He began his international career after winning a prize in the 1949 Concorso Busoni competition and alternated between touring and taking classes with the preeminent musicians of the day, including Paul Baumgartner, Eduard Steuermann, and Edwin Fischer. He later said Fischer had the greatest impact on his style, and Brendel traveled to Lucerne, Switzerland to study with Fischer from 1949 to 1951.

Success did not come immediately to Brendel. His was not a flamboyant style, but rather a restrained concentration on interpreting the music as he felt the composers intended. In addition to playing, he also held master classes in Vienna from 1960 until the early 1970s, when he moved to London. With success came a schedule that was brutal. During the 1982-83 season, for example, he played seventy-seven recitals in eleven cities in France, Great Britain, the United States, Austria, Germany, Switzerland, and the Netherlands, all to sold-out audiences.

Brendel is also a student of architecture, literature, language, and film. He is an author and poet, and at times he has combined his poetry with his music, as he did in 1999 at Carnegie Hall and in many other performances. In that year, when Brendel was sixty-eight, *Time* contributor Helen Gibson wrote of his love of Beethoven, and remarked that "Brendel's playing is distinguished by its heightened intellectual and emotional intensity, by his ability to energize details while sustaining taut lines, by his infallible grasp of musical architecture and by his extraordinary empathy with composers. His performances often achieve a sense of inevitability. Surely, a listener feels, this is what the composer intended."

Brendel followed his twenty-five-CD album, *The Art of Alfred Brendel,* released on the occasion of his sixty-fifth birthday, with a number of other CDs featuring Beethoven's bagatelles, the fantasy and the piano concerto by Schumann (with Kurt Sanderling and the Philharmonia Orchestra), the Beethoven concertos (with Simon Rattle and the Vienna Philharmonic), Mozart concertos and sonatas, and a special live recording of Schubert sonatas released on the occasion of Brendel's seventieth birthday. The pianist also celebrated by performing in London, Paris, Vienna, Tokyo, Cologne, Amsterdam, Brussels, and Frankfurt. The following year found him in the United States and Japan, as well as at the Lucerne Festival in Switzerland.

Brendel compiled sixteen essays for *Musical Thoughts and Afterthoughts,* in which he discusses the compositions of Beethoven, Schubert, and particularly Liszt, for whom Brendel is a champion. In reviewing the book in the *Times Literary Supplement,* Samuel Lipman wrote that "it is plain that the significance of Mr. Brendel's literary efforts is the same as his reason for writing at all: to justify and perhaps even expand the individual role permitted to an interpreter by our present guardians of musical virtue. He makes clear, for instance, the insurmountable difficulties which lie in the way of the perfect recapture of original performance styles." Lipman continued, saying that "it is precisely because Mr. Brendel, in addition to his high pianistic skills and his dedication to the music he plays, is so conscious of himself and of his own role in his work that he may be counted as a fruitful force in bringing new life to music which may have begun to seem to many both overplayed and overfamiliar."

In *Music Sounded Out: Essays, Lectures, Interviews, Afterthoughts,* Brendel expresses his ideas about music, the state of musical performance, and the musicians he admires, including Beethoven, Liszt, Busoni, Mozart, Schumann, Bach, Schubert, and others. In writing about Schubert, Brendel demonstrates that the composer's sonatas are not failed attempts at mimicking Beethoven's, but rather original works that have suffered in comparison to the powerful Beethoven.

Calum MacDonald wrote in the *Times Literary Supplement* that "Brendel's thought proceeds from his repertoire, but is hardly limited by it. Few musicians are both articulate and literate; far fewer can boast such a high level of culture in the arts and literatures of several languages."

An *Economist* reviewer called Brendel "the antithesis of the smooth, jetsetting personality. To see him at the piano is to witness a man in the throes of recreation, trying to convey every nuance and implication of the work at hand as he pursues its central mystery. Indeed, he once compared a Beethoven sonata to a detective story, and his performances always convey the sense of a dramatic quest. These splendid essays have something of that same quality."

Many of the essays contained in the first two collections were reprinted, along with seven previously uncollected pieces, as *Alfred Brendel On Music: Collected Essays. American Record Guide*'s David Mulbury noted that "this is not a book for light reading. Rather it is an approach to music on an advanced, sophisticated level. The reader needs to peruse carefully, taking the time to digest the concepts Brendel introduces." Philip Hensher commented in the London *Observer* that "performing musicians needn't be intelligent, but it's nice when they are."

Brendel writes in both German and English, and his German-language book of poems titled *Kleine teufel: neue gedichte* was reviewed in *World Literature Today* by Richard Exner, who called it "delightful, witty, and sophisticated." Exner observed that Brendel "presents poems among whose godfathers we might wish to count Lewis Carroll and Christian Morgenstern."

With translator Richard Stokes, Brendel published *One Finger Too Many,* a collection of poems in which music is the central theme. In one, Brendel is mistaken for Woody Allen. In others, composers are called up and transformed into sometimes unsavory characters. The title poem is about a pianist with an extra index finger. A *Kirkus Reviews* contributor wrote, "A moralist and fabulist, Brendel displays his good taste and breeding everywhere in these sometimes absurdist little narratives" and described the volume as "celebrity verse for high-brow concertgoers, who will be properly amused."

The London *Observer*'s John Kinsella wrote that "viewed as a whole, the collection is a hybrid—both in the movement between literary and musical cultures, and in its being a work of apparent clarity while also innovative in its focus, voice, and, to a certain extent, structure."

Me of All People: Alfred Brendel in Conversation with Martin Meyer, published in England as *The Veil of Order: Conversations with Martin Meyer,* is a book-length interview in which Brendel talks about his life and career, the composers he reveres and those he does not. He says that he never plays the Russian composers Tchaikovsky or Rachmaninoff and that he prefers the English language over German.

Richard Coles commented in the *Times Literary Supplement* that Brendel "is not perhaps a man to whom comedy comes naturally (or intentionally)—indeed, I can't think of a more serious musician—but, as old age approaches, Brendel has become more and more fascinated by the comic." Coles noted that Brendel had once read everything by Agatha Christie and that "in Zagreb, Brendel acquired the *Dada Almanach* with a moustachioed Beethoven, like Duchamp's 'Mona Lisa,' bristling on the cover. And what of it? 'If I had to choose between sense and nonsense, I personally would prefer nonsense,' he says. 'Not in piano playing, where one hopes for performances that do not maltreat masterpieces, but elsewhere.'" Brendel is also fond of the work of Gary Larson ("The Far Side").

Donald R. Vroon reviewed the volume in *American Record Guide,* saying that "a touch of irony and some wit are present in most of what Alfred Brendel has to say, and that makes this entertaining and thought-provoking."

BIOGRAPHICAL AND CRITICAL SOURCES:

BOOKS

Brendel, Alfred, *Ausgerechnet ich* Carl Hanser (Munich Germany), 2001, translation by Richard Stokes published as *Me of All People: Alfred Brendel in Conversation with Martin Meyer,* Cornell University Press (Ithaca, NY), 2002.

Contemporary Musicians, Volume 23, Gale (Detroit, MI), 1999, pp. 50-53.

PERIODICALS

American Music Teacher, December, 2003, Richard Bobo, review of *Me of All People,* p. 62.

American Record Guide, March, 2002, David Mulbury, review of *Alfred Brendel on Music: Collected Essays,* p. 253; January-February, 2003, Donald R. Vroon, review of *Me of All People,* p. 252.

American Spectator, August, 1991, R. J. Stove, reviews of *Music Sounded Out: Essays, Lectures, Interviews, Afterthoughts* and *Musical Thoughts and Afterthoughts,* p. 40.

Booklist, December 1, 2002, Ray Olson, review of *Me of All People,* p. 640.

Economist, December 22, 1990, review of *Music Sounded Out,* p. 119.

Guardian (London, England), January 5, 1996, Andrew Clements, "Music: The perfect player—Alfred Brendel," p. 10.

Kirkus Reviews, May 1, 1999, review of *One Finger Too Many,* p. 668.

Los Angeles Times, March 31, 2002, Chris Pasles, "Performing Arts: The Touch of the Poet" (interview), p. F-10.

Observer (London, England), October 4, 1998, John Kinsella, review of *One Finger Too Many* and interview, p. 15, February 4, 2001, Philip Hensher, review of *On Music,* p. 15.

Sewanee Review, spring, 1994, Robert Miles, reviews of *Music Sounded Out* and *Musical Thoughts and Afterthoughts,* pp. R51-R53.

Time, May 24, 1999, Helen Gibson, "Back with Beethoven: No one loves the composer's piano concertos more—or plays them better—than Alfred Brendel," p. 83.

Times Literary Supplement, June 24, 1977, Samuel Lipman, review of *Musical Thoughts and Afterthoughts,* pp. 777-778; January 25, 1991, Calum MacDonald, review of *Music Sounded Out,* p. 18; October 23, 1998, David Wheatley, review of *One Finger Too Many,* p. 26; November 15, 2002, Richard Coles, review of *The Veil of Order: Conversations with Martin Meyer,* pp. 8-9.

World Literature Today, summer, 2000, Richard Exner, review of *Kleine teufel: neue gedichte,* p. 643.

ONLINE

Alfred Brendel Home Page, http://www.alfredbrendel.com (March 19, 2004).

Munich Philharmonic Web site, http://www.muenchner
philharmoniker.de/ (August 14, 2003).
Pittsburgh Symphony Web site, http://www.pittsburgh
symphony.org/ (August 14, 2003).

OTHER

Alfred Brendel: Man and Mask (documentary), British
Broadcasting Corporation, 2002.*

*   *   *

BRODSKY, Alyn 1928-

PERSONAL: Born 1928. *Education:* University of
Miami, B.A. (music and history), Sorbonne, Ph.D.
(history).

ADDRESSES: Home—1500 Bay Rd., Miami Beach,
FL 33139-3252. *Agent*—c/o Author Mail, St. Martin's
Press, 175 Fifth Ave., New York, NY 10010.

CAREER: Writer, historian, and lecturer on history
and classical music. Former combat correspondent in
Korea and features writer in Tokyo for *Stars & Stripes,*
press attaché for the U.S. Embassy in Paraguay, editor
of weekly newspapers, editorial director of encyclope-
dias, book critic and columnist for U.S. newspapers.

WRITINGS:

*The Kings Depart: A Saga of the Empire Judah Mac-
cabee Created and His Heirs Destroyed,* Harper &
Row (New York, NY), 1974.
*Madame Lynch and Friend: The True Account of an
Irish Adventuress and the Dictator of Paraguay,
Who Destroyed That American Nation,* Harper &
Row (New York, NY), 1975.
*Imperial Charade: A Biography of Emperor Napoleon
III and Empress Eugénie, Nineteenth-Century
Europe's Most Successful Adventurers,* Bobbs-
Merrill (Indianapolis, IN), 1978.
Grover Cleveland: A Study in Character, St. Martin's
Press (New York, NY), 2000.
*The Great Mayor: Fiorello La Guardia and the Mak-
ing of the City of New York,* St. Martin's Press
(New York, NY), 2003.
Benjamin Rush: Patriot and Physician, St. Martin's
Press (New York, NY), 2004.

SIDELIGHTS: A keen and witty eye for history is a
distinctive element of Alyn Brodsky's writings. The
Newark, New Jersey, native graduated from the
University of Miami with degrees in history and music.
After college, Brodsky was a war correspondent in
Korea and wrote in Japan. Later in his career, Brodsky
was a press attachée in Paraguay and worked as an
editor in the Midwest before moving to New York in
the 1950s. His unique combination of career moves is
captured in Brodsky's books.

In *The Kings Depart: A Saga of the Empire Judah
Maccabee Created and His Heirs Destroyed,* Brodsky
examines the rise and fall of the second Jewish commonwealth following their return from exile in 538
B.C. Forming a view that the Maccabees sought to Ju-
daize Palestine in addition to gain independence, Brodsky injects everything from personal opinion to humor
in defending his case. While delivering a history lesson on the past, Brodsky brings perspective to current
issues in the Middle East. The reviewer in *Booklist*
recognized that "the political, social, and military
events that shaped the era, the rise of dominant opposition leaders, as well as the divergence of religious
observation in the combatant countries are accorded
careful if critical attention to clarify roles each played
in the outcome whose implications remain viable to
the present."

Brodsky's past work in Paraguay adds an element of
interest to *Madame Lynch and Friend: The True Account of an Irish Adventuress and the Dictator of
Paraguay, Who Destroyed That American Nation.* It is
a story of the late nineteenth century in which an Irish
courtesan, Eliza Lynch, enters a marriage at age fifteen
with a French officer. It did not last, and Lynch eventually becomes the mistress to the heir of the throne of
Paraguay, the dictator Francisco Solane López. Both
cursed by enormous egos, the duo virtually decimates
Paraguay's populace with a devastating six-year war
against neighboring countries Brazil, Argentina, and
Uruguay. Lynch leaves the country upon the death of
the dictator, and she dies in poverty in France. Malcolm Deas of the *Times Literary Supplement* felt the
book's "scant and unreliable evidence is relentlessly
interpreted to show the dictator and Madame Lynch in
the worst light, from the nasty title to the mean-spirited
epilogue."

Other infamous rulers are examined in *Imperial
Charade: A Biography of Emperor Napoleon and
Empress Eugénie, Nineteenth-Century Europe's Most*

Successful Adventurers. Napoleon III and Empress Eugénie are a mismatched couple united by the desire to restore the Bonaparte legacy to France. The Empress survives Napoleon after years of corrupt rule, many years featuring incompetent influence by Eugénie when the last Emperor of France falls ill. She lives her final years in exile in England with her friend, Queen Victoria. The contributor from *Booklist* noted "Brodsky, holder of a doctorate in history from the Sorbonne, is sardonic but shrewdly insightful as he explains how the pair (considering their characters) implausibly came to occupy such exalted positions."

Brodsky looks toward the United States in *Grover Cleveland: A Study in Character,* a biography of America's only president to serve two nonconsecutive terms in office. While being a leader who held true to his ethics and resisted corruption, Cleveland also bore the stigma of being a father to an illegitimate child and marrying someone nearly thirty years younger than himself. He also bought his way out of service during the Civil War. Jay Freeman of *Booklist* felt the weight of the many details. "This is a rather solemn, slow-moving biography that frequently gets bogged down in irrelevant details. In his zeal to illustrate Cleveland's virtues, Brodsky is a bit too eager to stress his 'positive' accomplishments." As the lone Democrat to be president between the Civil War and World War I, Cleveland's tenure was marked by his challenging of monopolies and the struggle against land-grabbing elements in the railroad, cattle, and timber industries. The *Publishers Weekly* reviewer wrote, "The author justifiably praises our twenty-second/twenty-fourth president as an anti-imperialist who refused to recognize a Hawaiian government set up largely by U.S. planters, yet he concedes that, in foreign affairs, Cleveland's achievements were insignificant." Brodsky makes the argument that Cleveland was the nation's best president in the era between Abraham Lincoln and Theodore Roosevelt. A contributor from *Kirkus Reviews* concluded the biography was "engaging and persuasively argued . . . serves both as an excellent introduction to Cleveland and his world, and as a worthy supplement to the scholarship already in existence."

Narrowing his American scope even further, Brodsky focuses on one of the nation's most highly regarded mayors in *The Great Mayor: Fiorello La Guardia and the Making of the City of New York.* Known primarily as the mayor of New York and the namesake of the city's famous airport, La Guardia also is seen in a long look at the years leading up to his election in 1933. It took eighteen months for Brodsky to write the biography, which includes details about La Guardia's early life as an army brat and a consul in Europe. La Guardia even took time off from being a congressman to serve as a commander of United States air forces during World War I. Sam Roberts of the *New York Times* recognized the depth of information about La Guardia's experiences before his election as mayor, "The emphasis on the early years is valuable because it helps explain what shaped La Guardia's philosophy." With popularity rivaling that of President Franklin Roosevelt, La Guardia shaped the city of New York through three four-year terms served after spending seven terms in Congress while representing Greenwich Village and East Harlem. La Guardia expanded social services, cleared the slums, constructed parks, and created roads and bridges to completely reshape the look of the city. Through his support of Roosevelt's New Deal, La Guardia, also known as "the Little Flower," was able to secure federal support of the city's continuing financial needs during the Depression. The reviewer for *Publishers Weekly* commented "Brodsky's admiration for his subject—to whom, he says, New York City owes its present greatness—remains intact, despite the mayor's increasingly authoritarian nature as he consolidated power." *The Great Mayor* also is critical of La Guardia, however, especially during his difficult third term of office after his national aspirations were derailed. He also was known to disregard civil liberties and to occasionally bully and brag. In *Library Journal,* William D. Pederson noted "except for an occasional negative comparison to some recent contemporary presidents, this account is balanced, readable, and worthwhile."

BIOGRAPHICAL AND CRITICAL SOURCES:

PERIODICALS

Booklist, December 1, 1974, review of *The Kings Depart: A Saga of the Empire Judah Maccabee Created and His Heirs Destroyed,* p. 355; December 1, 1978, review of *Imperial Charade: A Biography of Emperor Napoleon III and Empress Eugénie, Nineteenth-Century Europe's Most Successful Adventurers,* p. 596; September 1, 2000, Jay Freeman, review of *Grover Cleveland: A Study in Character,* p. 60; April 15, 2003, George Cohen, review of *The Great Mayor: Fiorello La Guardia and the Making of the City of New York,* p. 1444.

Choice, October, 1975, review of *The Kings Depart,* p. 1019; February 1976, review of *Madame Lynch and Friend: The True Account of an Irish Adventuress and the Dictator of Paraguay, Who Destroyed That American Nation,* p. 1621; February, 1979, review of *Imperial Charade,* p. 1712.

Kirkus Reviews, September 1, 1974, review of *The Kings Depart,* p. 973; August 15, 1975, review of *Madame Lynch and Friend,* 950; August 15, 1978, review of *Imperial Charade,* p. 912; August 1, 2000, review of *Grover Cleveland,* p. 1089; March 15, 2003, review of *The Great Mayor,* pp. 436-437.

Library Journal, October 1, 1974, review of *The Kings Depart,* p. 2475; August, 2000, William D. Pederson, review of *Grover Cleveland,* p. 118; May 1, 2003, William D. Pederson, review of *The Great Mayor,* pp.128-129.

New York Times Book Review, June 29, 2003, Sam Roberts, review of *The Great Mayor.*

Publishers Weekly, September 15, 1975, review of *Madame Lynch and Friend,* p. 48; August 14, 1978, review of *Imperial Charade,* p. 58; July 17, 2000, review of *Grover Cleveland,* p. 185; March 31, 2003, review of *The Great Mayor,* p. 49.

Times Literary Supplement, May 6, 1977, Malcolm Deas, review of *Madame Lynch and Friend,* p. 544.

ONLINE

Book House of Stuyvesant Plaza, http://www.bhny.com/ (October 24, 2003), book description for *The Great Mayor.*

Miami Herald Online, http://www.bayarea.com/ (September 18, 2003), book press for *The Great Mayor.**

*   *   *

BROOKS, Kevin M. 1959-

PERSONAL: Born March 30, 1959, in Exeter, England; married, wife's name Susan (an editor). *Education:* Attended Aston University, 1980; North East London Polytechnic, B.A., 1983.

ADDRESSES: Home—Manningtree, Essex, England. *Agent*—c/o Author Mail, Scholastic, Inc., 524 Broadway, New York, NY 10012.

CAREER: Worked various jobs in England, including musician, gasoline station attendant, crematorium handyman, civil service clerk, hot dog vendor at the London Zoo, post office clerk, and railway ticket office clerk. Writer.

AWARDS, HONORS: White Raven Award, Branford Boase Award, Sheffield Children's Book Award, Lancashire Children's Book Award, South Lanarkshire Book Award, and Carnegie medal shortlist, all 2003, all for *Martyn Pig;* Guardian Children's Book Award and Teenage Booktrust Prize shortlists, 2003, for *Lucas;* Salford Children's Book Award, 2004, for *Martyn Pig.*

WRITINGS:

Martyn Pig, Scholastic (New York, NY), 2002.
Lucas, Scholastic (New York, NY), 2003.
Kissing the Rain, Scholastic (New York, NY), 2004.

SIDELIGHTS: After a long apprenticeship in which he taught himself the discipline to write, Kevin M. Brooks has achieved international success with his young adult novels. A poet and musician, Brooks pays careful attention to the prose in his stories, but he also crafts tight plots with a nod to the dark themes of American detective fiction. Brooks won Britain's prestigious Branford Boase Award for his first novel, *Martyn Pig,* and his subsequent books have earned warm reviews on both sides of the Atlantic. As for Brooks, being a full-time writer is a dream come true. In an online interview with *Push,* he remarked: "Being a writer is absolutely wonderful. I love writing, it's what I DO—thinking, writing, creating new worlds, it's fantastic."

Brooks drifted through a number of less-than-ideal jobs in his early post-college years. He sieved ashes in a crematorium and sold stamps in a post office, all the while trying to break through as a musician or artist. Brooks also wrote poetry and read widely, especially enjoying the works of American detective novelists such as Raymond Chandler and Lawrence Block. With age came discipline, not only to write novels but also to persist in trying to sell them. *Martyn Pig,* the author's first published work, is actually the third novel he wrote. Since shortly before it was published, Brooks has been a full-time writer, working six or more hours a day on his fiction.

The hero of *Martyn Pig* faces more than just the dilemma of going through life with a ghastly name. Over Christmas holiday, Martyn witnesses the accidental death of his alcoholic, abusive father—and then, for a multitude of reasons, tries to keep the death secret. He seeks help from a would-be girlfriend named Alex, and together they craft a plan to dispose of the corpse. Despite its grisly subject matter, *Martyn Pig* abounds in humor, as the young narrator tries to come to terms with the strange twists his life takes.

Brooks placed *Martyn Pig* with Chicken House Publishers, a British firm with ties to Scholastic. The novel was released in England and America in 2002 and drew critical praise for its poetic language, darkly funny plot, and engaging hero. *School Library Journal* correspondent Connie Tyrrell Burns felt that the book would have "tremendous teen appeal" due to its unconventional subject matter and Martyn's "distinctive voice." A *Publishers Weekly* reviewer praised Brooks's "self-assured debut" as "at once hard-boiled . . . and . . . laugh-aloud funny."

Lucas is set on fictitious Hale Island, a small community separated from the mainland by a causeway that sometimes floods at high tide. The story's narrator, Caitlin McCann, recalls a previous summer when a strange, almost mystical loner named Lucas wanders onto the island. Adèle Geras described Lucas in a review for *The Guardian*: "He is wild. He is gifted. He is enigmatic. Also, he is deeply hated by the boorish, drug-fuelled, bored and jealous oafs in the community and their unpleasant and sinister female sidekicks." Unjustly accused of assaulting a girl, Lucas finds himself falling victim to vigilante justice, even as Caitlin sees his ultimate goodness and falls in love with him.

Geras called *Lucas* "the sort of novel that prize-awarding juries like, but which will also appeal to readers." Other critics offered similar praise. Awarding the work a starred review, a *Publishers Weekly* contributor concluded: "Its powerful combination of big ideas and forthright narrative make this novel likely to linger in readers' minds." *Booklist* correspondent Ilene Cooper liked the "purity" of Brooks's style, calling the narrative "by turns sweet, taut, and terrifying." In *School Library Journal*, Sharon Rawlins likewise observed that the writing "is extraordinarily lyrical" and that *Lucas* is "a powerful book to be savored."

In an interview with a writer for *Push*, Brooks said: "I am interested in asking the questions which we think about a lot as kids, but get so used to when we grow up that we stop asking them. As adults we forget about the sky, and where we come from, and time, and pain, and all of those things; we just accept them. . . . Sometimes I get problems with American publishers who say they don't want to include this kind of thing because children aren't used to it or they won't understand it. But if you just keep avoiding difficult questions children won't learn to understand them."

BIOGRAPHICAL AND CRITICAL SOURCES:

PERIODICALS

Booklist, May 1, 2003, Ilene Cooper, review of *Lucas,* p. 1595.
Guardian, January 11, 2003, Adèle Geras, "Stand and Deliver."
Horn Book, March-April, 2003, Lauren Adams, review of *Lucas,* p. 210.
Publishers Weekly, May 27, 2002, review of *Martyn Pig,* p. 61; June 24, 2002, "Flying Tarts: Four First-Time Authors and Illustrators Talk about Their Spring Debuts," p. 27; February 10, 2003, review of *Lucas,* p. 188.
School Library Journal, May, 2002, Connie Tyrrell Burns, review of *Martyn Pig,* p. 147; May, 2003, Sharon Rawlins, review of *Lucas,* p. 148.

ONLINE

Guardian Online, http://books.guardian.co.uk/ (June 26, 2003), interview with Brooks, information about Branford Boase Award, link to review of *Lucas.*
Jubilee Books, http://www.jubileebooks.co.uk/ (December 3, 2003), fact file and interview with Brooks.
Push, http://www.thisispush.com/ (June 3, 2004), "An Interview with Kevin Brooks."

*   *   *

BURGES, Dennis

PERSONAL: Married; wife's name Jená. *Education:* B.A. (English and social studies); graduate degree (linguistics).

ADDRESSES: Office—Longwood University, Department of English and Modern Languages, 201 High St., Farmville, VA 23909. *Agent*—Jeff Gerecke, JCA Literary Agent, 27 West 20th St., Ste. 1103, New York, NY 10011. *E-mail*—burges7@earthlink.net; dburges@longwood.edu.

CAREER: Educator and writer. Longwood University, Farmville, VA, English professor. Worked as a teacher in AZ, carpenter, musician, and guitar builder.

WRITINGS:

Graves Gate, Carroll & Graf (New York, NY), 2003.

WORK IN PROGRESS: Unspeakable, another historic mystery novel featuring Baker and Wallace.

SIDELIGHTS: As a writer of mystery thriller novels, Dennis Burges draws from his varied background as a carpenter, soldier, musician, and teacher. Mostly, though, Burges's linguistic and historical knowledge forms the basis of his works. Inspiration starts at home in Arizona, where Burges taught for a decade while taking note of the contrast between modern life and the mysterious geography of the canyons. Burges may be an Arizona native but he traces his roots to colonial Virginia, where Burges continues a family tradition of teaching through his English professorship at Longwood University. His heartfelt interest in history shows in his novel *Graves Gate.*

Graves Gate is the post-World War I story of American reporter Charles Baker, a former spy who is hired by famed British writer Arthur Conan Doyle to investigate an intriguing situation. Through the entire book, Burges paints a realistic picture of the era. Reviewer D. L. Browne noted the historical accuracy in *I Love A Mystery Newsletter,* commenting that "*Graves Gate* very nearly reads as though it were written in the 1920s, and that's about as high praise as I can give a historical novel." In the book, Doyle, recently the subject of public criticism for his beliefs in spiritualism, has received a letter from someone claiming to be the late Dr. Bernard Gussmann, the same psychiatrist who treated Doyle's father years before. Doyle leans toward believing the letter is authentic because it includes information only the doctor would know. In the letter, Doyle is offered the opportunity to communicate with the dead if he agrees to bring one of three people to a prison to visit a woman about to be executed. Fearing more public ridicule if he pursues the spiritual challenge, Doyle hires Baker to investigate. Another associate of Doyle's is the beautiful Adrianna Wallace. Together, Wallace and Baker put together the pieces of the puzzle. All three people had connections to the Morton Graves Voluntary Hospital, the London asylum where Gussmann died. The journey becomes dangerous and eerie as the three subjects suffer from blackouts and mood swings, suggesting Gussmann might be controlling them with his mind. In the midst of the mystery, a romance develops between Baker and Wallace. A reviewer from *Publishers Weekly* found *Graves Gate* disappointing, but a *Kirkus Reviews* contributor wrote that "Burges offers fine Conan Doyle atmosphere and plotting without the old gasbag in the deerstalker hat."

BIOGRAPHICAL AND CRITICAL SOURCES:

PERIODICALS

Kirkus Reviews, May 1, 2003, review of *Graves Gate,* p. 623.
Publishers Weekly, June 23, 2003, review of *Graves Gate,* pp. 47-48.

ONLINE

Dennis Burges Home Page, http://www.dennisburges.com (October 24, 2003).
I Love A Mystery Newsletter, http://www.iloveamysterynewsletter.com/ (October 24, 2003), D. L. Browne, review of *Graves Gate.*

C

CAMPAGNA, Palmiro 1954-

PERSONAL: Born November 4, 1954, in Toronto, Ontario, Canada; son of Gilbert (a tailor) and Paolina (a homemaker and laborer; maiden name, Cardoni) Campagna; married Jane Elizabeth Maxwell (a teacher of English as a second language and homemaker), October 6, 1990; children: James Gilbert, Adrian Phillip, Katia Marie. *Ethnicity:* "Italian." *Education:* University of Guelph, B.Sc., 1977; Queen's University, Kingston, Ontario, Canada, B.A.Sc., 1981. *Hobbies and other interests:* Investigative archival research.

ADDRESSES: Home—Ottawa, Ontario, Canada. *Office*—Department of National Defence, 101 Colonel By Dr., Ottawa, Ontario, Canada K1A 0K2. *E-mail*—maxcam@storm.ca.

CAREER: Department of National Defence, Ottawa, Ontario, Canada, engineer and internal auditor, 1981—. CFRB-Radio, contributor to the weekly program *Strange Days Indeed.*

MEMBER: Professional Engineers of Ontario.

WRITINGS:

Storms of Controversy: The Secret Avro Arrow Files Revealed, Stoddart Publishing (Toronto, Ontario, Canada), 1992, 3rd edition, 1998.
The UFO Files: The Canadian Connection Exposed, Stoddart Publishing (Toronto, Ontario, Canada), 1997.

Requiem for a Giant: A. V. Roe Canada and the Avro Arrow, Dundurn Press (Toronto, Ontario, Canada), 2003.

Contributor to periodicals, including *Engineering Dimensions, CASI Log, UFO,* and *Airforce.*

WORK IN PROGRESS: Continuing archival research on unidentified flying objects (UFOs) and Avro.

SIDELIGHTS: Palmiro Campagna told *CA:* "The Avro Arrow interceptor was a project canceled under peculiar circumstances back in 1959. With almost no explanation, in one afternoon, over 25,000 people were fired. Subsequently, five flying aircraft plus thirty-two others in various stages of assembly were blow-torched into scrap, along with almost all technical data. The company itself, one of the largest in Canada at the time, closed its doors in 1962. A clear explanation was never provided. By 1978, the issue was still so sensitive that a television documentary on the subject was postponed because it was felt that it could have a significant impact on the upcoming Canadian election.

"Prior to the documentary, there was very little written on the subject. Historians included the Arrow saga in their history books and, in 1983, in a military history of Canada, the allegation was made that the Arrow was canceled because it was too costly and suffered from technical flaws. As an engineer myself, I found this difficult to believe. I was aware that many of the top engineers provided a significant boost to the space program of the National Aeronautics and Space Administration. In fact, after cancellation, twenty-five top engineers went there in key positions and helped to put the United States in space and on the moon. Many were awarded medals of merit. How then could these engineers design something that was technically flawed?

"This is what lit the fire under me. I embarked on a quest to discover the truth. I did what no other researcher or historian had done; I approached the United States, specifically the Eisenhower Library. I obtained documents which began shedding new light on the subject. I also proved the historians were incorrect with respect to technical flaws. This was documented in my article in *Engineering Dimensions* in 1988. In a subsequent issue, historian Desmond Morton blamed the work of a graduate student for having gotten the facts wrong.

"Shortly after this article was published, I began finding more information at the National Archives of Canada. Unlike other researchers, I did not ask for documents on the Arrow, but rather on anything related to the Royal Canadian Air Force and National Defence between 1950 and 1960. I ended up going through a mountain of information and found many answers. I approached the directorate of history at National Defence and found more.

"I was doing the work as a hobby, but friends urged me to prepare a book. I did, when I found the paper trail outlining the reasoning behind the blow-torching of the aircraft and documents. In fact, many documents in the form of memoranda had not been destroyed, and I was able to find carbon copies in the files of other government departments outside National Defence.

"I sent my manuscript to several publishers only to have it returned. It seems I needed an agent. Instead I asked a published author, and one who I knew had an interest in the Arrow, if he would write a foreword for the book. Naturally he asked to see the manuscript. When he read it, he suggested I get it published and advised me I could use him as a reference. Soon afterward I had a publisher for *Storms of Controversy: The Secret Avro Arrow Files Revealed*. The book became a Canadian best-seller and went into a third edition before the publisher when bankrupt due to external pressures on the Canadian publishing industry.

"I wrote about the Arrow because it was canceled under mysterious circumstances, but also because I always had an interest in aircraft. From an engineering perspective I could not believe the claims being made by the historians. I noted that they did not list their sources. In my books I list all sources and even reproduce key documents in the appendices.

"I have also had an interest in UFOs since 1966. As it turns out, Avro was building a flying saucer for the American government at the same time it was building the Arrow. In my Arrow research, I uncovered a significant amount on the saucer. With my prior interest in UFOs, I researched this topic in earnest and uncovered numerous documents in the archives. My UFO book covers the history of the phenomena in Canada from the 1900s to the present, using documents from the Department of National Defence, the Royal Canadian Mounted Police, and the National Research Council, as well as interviews and other sources.

"All my books maintain an objectivity with the intention of allowing the reader to draw his/her own conclusions, though I do offer my opinion. However, I am careful to point out when I am speculating and when I am using the documented record.

"I have not changed my writing. Perhaps to my detriment, I am not given to flowery prose, but rather I stick to the facts. My works are extremely detailed, but I feel I must do this in order to prove the historians and those who would make unfounded, sweeping statements incorrect. I have been successful. Articles written about me have indicated that I have done my homework, whereas the historians have not. My works have created no end of controversy and discussion in historical circles."

BIOGRAPHICAL AND CRITICAL SOURCES:

PERIODICALS

Alberta Report, September 15, 1997, review of *The UFO Files: The Canadian Connection Exposed,* p. 39.
Canadian Forum, September, 1997, Geoff Pevere, review of *The UFO Files,* p. 29.
Maclean's, May 12, 1997, review of *The UFO Files,* p. 13.
Quill & Quire, January, 1993, review of *Storms of Controversy: The Secret Avro Arrow Files Revealed,* p. 21.
Western Report, September 15, 1997, review of *The UFO Files,* p. 39.

CARROLL, Francis M(artin) 1938-

PERSONAL: Born January 31, 1938, in the United States; son of Martin F. (in sales) and Virginia C. (Johnson) Carroll; married Janet Foster, August 24, 1963; children: Charles Murray Howard. *Education:* Carleton College, B.A., 1960; University of Minnesota, M.A., 1962; Trinity College, Dublin, Ireland, Ph.D., 1969. *Hobbies and other interests:* Sailing.

ADDRESSES: Home—601 Wardlaw Ave., Winnipeg, Manitoba, Canada R3L 0M3. *Office*—St. John's College, University of Manitoba, 92 Dysart Rd., Winnipeg, Manitoba, Canada R3T 2M5. *E-mail*—fcarrol@cc.umanitoba.ca.

CAREER: South Dakota State University, faculty member, 1962-64; Kalamazoo College, Kalamazoo, MI, faculty member, 1967-68; University of Manitoba, Winnipeg, Manitoba, Canada, member of history faculty, 1969-98, senior scholar, 1999—, professor emeritus, 2002—. Dean of studies at St. John's College, 1976-78, acting warden, 1985-86, chair of assembly, 1989-90. Columbia University, visiting scholar in international law, 1980; National University of Ireland, University College, Dublin, Ireland, Mary Ball Washington Professor of American History, 1984-85; South Dakota State University, F. O. Butler Lecturer, 1988; University of Nottingham, guest lecturer, 1994; University of London, John Adams fellow at Institute of United States Studies, 1994-95; University of St. Thomas, visiting Irish historian, 2000.

MEMBER: Canadian Association for Irish Studies, American Historical Association, Organization of American Historians, Society of Historians of American Foreign Relations, American Conference of Irish Historians, Forest History Society, Minnesota Historical Society.

AWARDS, HONORS: Bicentennial fellow of British Council, Department of Education for Northern Ireland, Public Record Office of Northern Ireland, and Office of the American Consulate General, Belfast, Northern Ireland, 1998; honorary visiting fellow at Institute of Irish Studies, Queen's University, Belfast, Northern Ireland, 1998; John Wesley Dafoe Book Prize, 2001, for *A Good and Wise Measure: The Search for the Canadian-American Boundary, 1783-1842.*

WRITINGS:

American Opinion and the Irish Question, 1910-23, St. Martin's Press (New York, NY), 1978.

(Editor) *The American Commission on Irish Independence, 1919: The Diary, Correspondence, and Report,* Irish Manuscripts Commission (Dublin, Ireland), 1985.

Crossroads in Time: A History of Carlton County, Minnesota, Carlton County Historical Society (Cloquet, MN), 1988.

(With Franklin R. Raiter) *The Fires of Autumn: The Cloquet-Moose Lake Disaster of 1918,* Minnesota Historical Society Press (St. Paul, MN), 1990.

(With Marlene Wisuri) *Reflections of Our Past: A Pictorial History of Carlton County,* Donning Co. (Virginia Beach, VA), 1997.

A Good and Wise Measure: The Search for the Canadian-American Boundary, 1783-1842, University of Toronto Press (Toronto, Ontario, Canada), 2001.

Money for Ireland: Finance, Diplomacy, Politics, and the First Dáil Éireann Loans, 1919-1936, Praeger Publishers (Westport, CT), 2002.

Contributor to books, including *The DeVal-Erá in Ireland,* edited by Sidney Poger, Northeastern University (Boston, MA), 1984; *Irish Studies: The Irish in America* Volume 4, edited by J. P. Drudy, Cambridge University Press (New York, NY), 1984; and *James Joyce and His Contemporaries,* edited by Diana A. Ben-Merre and Maureen Murphy, Greenwood Press (Westport, CT), 1989. Contributor of articles and reviews to academic journals, including *New England Quarterly, Prologue, Eire-Ireland, International History Review, Irish Studies in International Affairs, Journal of Forest History, Canadian Journal of Irish Studies,* and *Minnesota History.*

WORK IN PROGRESS: Bridges across the Atlantic: The United States Consulate General and the American Presence in Ulster, 1796 to 1996.

SIDELIGHTS: Francis M. Carroll told *CA:* "I am fortunate to have been able to enjoy a career as a historian. Both teaching and research have enabled me to pursue many topics and issues that struck me as being of interest and importance. Much of my writing, both past and current, has grown out of my studies and research in Ireland and England. I wanted to understand the process through which Ireland became a self-governing and independent nation, and particularly the role of Great Britain and the United States on that process. My teaching at the University of Manitoba led me to consider a similar triangular relationship between Canada, the United States, and Great Britain, leading to my work on the Canadian-American boundary. I also began to develop an interest in the history of the region in which I had grown up—northern Minnesota—and the realization that northern Minnesota had also played a significant role in Canadian-American relations and even Irish migration to the upper Midwest.

"In writing history I have been drawn to topics that have not been extensively studied by other historians, or at least have not been examined in recent years. I find a particular pleasure in attempting to explain a topic on which no one else has written. I also enjoy archival and manuscript research. There is a sense of immediacy in working with the original historical documents, and there is also something of the element of the thrill of the hunt. Converting the notes to a narrative is always laborious, but reshaping the material through revising the drafts provides its own satisfaction. I have found writing and research to be a great help in my teaching, and publishing to be a way in which to maintain a place within the historical profession and also to reach out to the reading public."

*   *   *

CARSON, Mary Kay 1964-

PERSONAL: Born November 18, 1964, in Everett, WA; daughter of George Arthur (an industrial hygiene engineer) and Vicky Sue (a social worker; maiden name, Long) Carson; married Thomas Mark Uhlman (a photographer), March 4, 2003. *Education:* University of Kansas, B.S., 1987; attended Science and Environmental Reporting Program, New York University, 1990.

ADDRESSES: Home and office—3916 Tappan Ave., Cincinnati, OH 45223. *E-mail*—mkc@fuse.net; mkcarson@nasw.org.

CAREER: Freelance writer of books, articles and teaching materials for Newbridge, *Science World,* Scholastic, Inc., National Audubon Society, Kids-

Books, Chicago Review Press, and other educational companies, 1994—. *SuperScience,* New York, NY, associate editor and writer, 1991-94; Don Bosco Center, Kansas City, MO, and Delta School, Astillero, Spain, teacher of English as a second language, 1993-96. Served as a U.S. Peace Corps volunteer in La Peñita Arriba, Dominican Republic, 1987-89; worked as a National Marine Fisheries Service observer in Seattle, Washington, 1990.

WRITINGS:

Epilepsy, Enslow (Berkeley Heights, NJ), 1998.
The Creepiest, Scariest, Weirdest Creatures Ever!, Kidsbooks (Boston, MA), 2002.
The Wright Brothers for Kids: How They Invented the Airplane, Chicago Review Press (Chicago, IL), 2003.
Mars, Chelsea House (New York, NY), 2003.
In the Deep, Chelsea House (New York, NY), 2003.
The Underground Railroad for Kids, Chicago Review Press (Chicago, IL), 2004.

LEVELED READERS

Cool Science Jobs, Scholastic (New York, NY), 2003.
Gross Body Facts, Scholastic (New York, NY), 2003.
Driving on Mars, Houghton Mifflin (Boston, MA), 2004.
The Bald Eagle Is Back, Houghton Mifflin (Boston, MA), 2004.
The Greatest Electrician in the World, Houghton Mifflin (Boston, MA), 2004.
The Return of Wild Whoopers, Houghton Mifflin (Boston, MA), 2004.

PROFESSIONAL TITLES FOR TEACHERS

Space: Hands-On Activities, the Latest Information &, a Colorful Learning Poster, Scholastic (New York, NY), 1996.
Colonial America: A Complete Theme Unit Developed in Cooperation with the Colonial Williamsburg Foundation, Scholastic (New York, NY), 1999.
The Wow's and Why's of Weather, Scholastic (New York, NY), 2000.

Great Weather Activities: All the Background Info and How To's You Need for Teaching about the Wonders of Weather, Scholastic (New York, NY), 2000.

Space: Quick & Easy Internet Activities for the One-Computer Classroom, Scholastic (New York, NY), 2001.

Weather: Quick & Easy Activities for the One-Computer Classroom, Scholastic (New York, NY), 2002.

Easy Science Activity Journals, Scholastic (New York, NY), 2003.

Author of educational titles for the Newbridge Discovery Links, Newbridge *Ranger Rick* Science Program, and Newbridge Social Studies Links. Contributor to magazines, including *Ohio Magazine, Audubon Adventures, SuperScience, Ranger Rick, Missouri Conservationist for Kids,* and *Science World.*

SIDELIGHTS: Mary Kay Carson is the author of *The Wright Brothers for Kids: How They Invented the Airplane.* The book includes not only a history of the Wright Brothers' work, but also a collection of hands-on projects for kids, designed to demonstrate some of the challenges the inventors had to overcome to get the first airplane off the ground. A *Publishers Weekly* contributor praised the book for its "detailed and invigorating history of the Wright Brothers' work." In a review for *School Library Journal,* Harriett Fargnoli noted that "the narrative flows easily and is complemented by numerous photographs that give a sense of history and this event."

Carson once commented: "As a young person, I had no interest in being a writer. Becoming a biologist seemed like the obvious career for me. I've had a fascination with animals since early childhood. I likely inherited it from my mother's family—they're 'animal people.' Stuffed animal toys were soon replaced by a menagerie of pets—goldfish, guppies, gerbils, rats, rabbits, turtles, a ferret, as well as a parade of cats and dogs. I'd spend hours in the basement waiting for our mother cat to once again give birth. Then I'd watch her bring four—it was always four—blind furry kittens into the world. My parents were incredibly tolerant and let me keep nearly any animal I wanted as long as I took care of it. I even raised a couple of rescued baby possums. These pets were often playmates for me, especially after we moved to the country when I was nine. My sister and I would dress the current batch of kittens in baby clothes and 'invite' them to tea and mud pie parties. My little brother and I would race rabbits in the fenced-in dog run. There were no neighbor kids within walking distance, and we siblings quickly grew tired of each other's company during summer vacations. So I spent a lot of my time exploring the nearby hickory oak forest, violet-filled clearings, and shale creeks with a dog or two in tow. Surely my life-long love and awe of the natural world was sown during those long summer days.

"I never liked school much—too much monotonous routine—though I was a good student. But I did learn to like science, thanks to my engineer dad and a number of dedicated teachers. I have a vivid memory of doing a hands-on science activity in fourth grade that made a real impression on me! I took lots of biology classes in high school and also attended a year of special vocational high school at the Cincinnati Zoo. We worked with the zookeepers caring for the animals in the morning and had regular classes in the afternoon. I studied biology in college, as well, choosing the Systematics and Ecology Record Exam to get into where I wanted to go. I'd have to wait an entire year before retaking them, and there was little work for those with biology undergraduate degrees in 1987. The U.S. Peace Corps, on the other hand, was actively recruiting science majors. I'd never had the money to study abroad or travel much. At twenty-two I'd never been off the North American continent and had only flown in an airliner once as a first grader. I signed up and shipped out—well, flew actually—to the Dominican Republic the fall after graduation.

"The two plus years I spent working as a freshwater fisheries extension agent in the Peace Corps dramatically changed the direction of my life. It was while living in a rural peasant village without telephones, electricity, or running water that I discovered writing. I was the only English speaker in the village. I spoke decent Spanish, but I couldn't make myself understood as completely in Spanish as I could in English. Writing letters became an important outlet for me. They were a way to express myself freely. Luckily I had lots of family and friends to write! I also wrote a few stories and experienced that 'losing track of time' or 'being in the zone' feeling that I think a lot of writers become addicted to! Once out of the Peace Corps in 1989, I looked into graduate school programs for science writing. Writing about science seemed like the perfect union of an old and new love. I was accepted into New York University's Science and Environmental Reporting Program (SERP) for the fall of 1990. I got a job working on a fishing boat in Alaska that summer to save up money. I moved to New York City in time to start NYU. I attended the SERP program that fall but dropped out a year shy of finishing. I'd run out of money and needed to work full time if I wanted to stay in New York. I cobbled together a bunch of part-time jobs doing research for an author, typing letters for a literary agent, working temp jobs, and doing an internship at a National Audubon Society publication.

"Once set on the course of science writing, I hadn't really planned on writing for young people. But I landed a full-time job writing news and feature articles for a science magazine at Scholastic—a science magazine for 4th-6th graders. The creativity of the job forever hooked me on writing for kids. Within the first few months on the job I'd interviewed scientists, written and sketched out a four-paneled cartoon that explained center of mass, helped choose photos to accompany a feature article, traveled to school to interview kids measuring champion trees, came up with story ideas, and assisted the hands-on activities editor in tinkering with experiments set up in the hallway. What a fun place to work!

"Writing for kids allows for a lot more creativity than writing for adults, I think. Plus, it allows you to be forever a generalist. Most of the science writers for adults I know have become very specialized. Focusing on the developments in a narrow scientific field— biomedical engineering or material sciences for example—is how you build credibility with sources and readers as a science journalist. But I really like the diversity of being a generalist, and that's much more acceptable in children's writing. At any given time I might be writing about volcanoes, rhinos, and the Underground Railroad. I often don't know that much about a topic before I start doing research for the book. The process of discovery through research is part of what I like about writing. I'm always learning something new and interesting.

"I really like the process of writing science for kids, too. You have to research and understand your topic extremely well. You can't assume that kids know things, like you can with adults. After you've taken the information apart to understand it completely, you have to put it back together in a way that kids will understand. The fun part is putting it together in an interesting way that kids will want to read.

"After a couple of years at Scholastic, I caught the travel bug again. I went to Spain and got certified to teach English, traveled around for the summer, and then taught English in northern Spain for a school year. After a bit more travel, I came back to New York and filled in for a temporarily absent staffer at Scholastic for a month, made some good contacts, and decided to try freelancing. I knew it'd be hard to make a living freelancing in New York because it's an expensive place to live. So I went back to where my family was living in Kansas City. A friend had hooked me up with a job teaching English to immigrants and refugees three nights a week, so I'd have some steady income while I got my freelancing career off the ground. That was 1994, and I've been freelancing ever since! I mostly wrote magazine articles and teaching materials for the first few years. My first book was published in 1996. *Space: Hands-On Activities* is a book for teachers with reproducible pages for students, one of many I've since written. The first trade book I wrote for kids was *Epilepsy,* published in 1998. I moved to Cincinnati in 1997 and now mostly write books for kids, though I do write a few adult magazine articles now and again.

"I've been a self-employed writer who works out of a home office for nearly ten years. It's not for everybody! Many freelancers eventually trade in being able to work in their pajamas for the structure, regular salary, and companionship of an office job. People often ask me how I can have enough self-discipline to work as a home-based freelancer. But I don't believe the key is self-discipline—it's organization. I'm afraid that goofy saying, 'Fail to plan . . . Plan to fail' is very true for me!

"Writing *The Wright Brothers for Kids* was a chance to explore a topic in much more depth than I usually get a chance to. The 160-page book is a lot more than just an explanation of the science behind getting an airplane to fly. The book also includes lots of human flight history, a sense of the times in which the Wright brothers lived, fun activities, and the amazing human story of a family that made history. The topic also appealed to me because Wilbur and Orville lived and built their Wright Flyers just north of me in Dayton, Ohio. It was great to be able to visit the nearby places and where they once worked together and lived. *The Wright Brothers for Kids* also offered my husband and me the chance to work together on a larger project. (We'd already done some magazine articles together.) My husband, Tom Uhlman, is a freelance photographer and stringer for the Associated Press. Similar reasons led me to write my . . . book *The Underground Railroad for Kids*. Ohio was heavily traveled by runaways fleeing on the Underground Railroad.

"I hope that my books about animals, nature, and space foster a sense of wonder in kids and give kids a feeling of connection to the natural world. Every one of us is made up of the same stuff that goes into trees, rocks, and stars! I think it's becoming harder and harder for kids to experience that wonder and connection in their daily life. We all spend so much time indoors and at 'scheduled activities.' Books can be a great way to take a little trip someplace completely different, like Mars. Books can also show you something familiar in a new way, like seeing what lives under a log in the forest.

"I also hope that my books make science fun, interesting, and accessible to kids. We live in a world and time where science and technology drive changes affecting our daily lives and the lives of future generations. I feel that it's important for everyday people to understand the basic science behind the technologies we use and the ecosystem we're a part of. Otherwise, we'll all become beholden to 'experts' to make decisions for us about everything from environmental protection, medical ethics, and food safety to the space program."

BIOGRAPHICAL AND CRITICAL SOURCES:

PERIODICALS

Daily News (Dayton, OH), April 7, 2003, "Things to Read and Wright."
Publishers Weekly, March 24, 2003, "Wright Books at the Wright Time," p. 77.
School Library Journal, September, 1998, Christine A. Moesch, review of *Epilepsy,* p. 214; June, 2003, Harriett Fargnoli, review of *The Wright Brothers for Kids: How They Invented the Airplane,* p. 156.
Science News, May 31, 2003, review of *The Wright Brothers for Kids,* p. 351.
Washington Post Book World, May 11, 2003, "The Wright Stuff."

ONLINE

Mary Kay Carson Home Page, http://wwwmarykay carson.com (January 12, 2004).

* * *

CARTER, Warren 1955-

PERSONAL: Born June 1, 1955, in Palmerston North, New Zealand. *Education:* Victoria University of Wellington, B.A. (with honors), 1976; Melbourne College of Divinity, B.D., 1985, Th.M. (with first class honors), 1986; Princeton Theological Seminary, Ph.D., 1991.

ADDRESSES: Office—Saint Paul School of Theology, 5123 Truman Rd., Kansas City, MO 64127; fax: 816-483-9605. *E-mail*—wcarter@spst.edu.

CAREER: Saint Paul School of Theology, Kansas City, MO, instructor, 1990-91, assistant professor, 1991-95, associate professor, 1995-2000, Lindsey P. Pherigo Professor of New Testament, 2000—.

MEMBER: Society of Biblical Literature (cochair of Matthew Section, 1999-2004).

AWARDS, HONORS: National Regional Scholar Award, Society of Biblical Literature, 1995; Lilly faculty fellowship, Association of Theological Schools, 1998-99.

WRITINGS:

What Are They Saying about Matthew's Sermon on the Mount?, Paulist Press (Mahwah, NJ), 1994.
Discipleship and Households: A Study of Matthew 19-20, Sheffield Academic Press (Sheffield, England), 1994.
Matthew: Storyteller, Interpreter, Evangelist, Hendrickson (Peabody, MA), 1996.
(With J. P. Heil) *Matthew's Parables: Audience-Oriented Perspectives,* Catholic Biblical Association of America (Washington, DC), 1998.
Matthew and the Margins: A Religious and Socio-Political Reading, Orbis Books (Maryknoll, NY), 2000.

Matthew and Empire: Initial Explorations, Trinity Press International (Harrisburg, PA), 2001.

(With D. Jacobson, C. J. Dempsey, and J. P. Heil) *New Proclamation: Year A, 2001-2002,* Fortress Press (Minneapolis, MN), 2002.

Pontius Pilate: Portraits of a Roman Governor, Liturgical Press (Collegeville, MN), 2003.

Got Life? John: Storyteller, Interpreter, Evangelist, Hendrickson (Peabody, MA), in press.

Contributor to *Westminster Discipleship Study Bible,* Westminster John Knox (Louisville, KY), 2003; and *New Interpreter's Study Bible,* Abingdon (Nashville, TN), 2003. Contributor to scholarly journals and religious magazines, including *Journal for the Study of the New Testament.* Associate editor, *Catholic Biblical Quarterly,* 2003—; member of editorial board, *Journal of Biblical Literature,* 1998—.

SIDELIGHTS: Warren Carter told *CA:* "I write for various audiences. Some work is technical scholarly writing for other scholars working in the history and literature of the early Christian movement. Some writing is for clergy and for lay members of various Christian denominations. These pieces often translate more technical scholarship into more accessible formats for these audiences.

"I am especially interested in exploring the place of early Christian writings like the gospels of Matthew or John in relation to the Roman imperial world. While much scholarship has explored this literature in relation to other religious groups and traditions, not much work has investigated their place in relation to the societal structures, values, and commitments of the Roman imperial world. In this Roman context, the traditions about Jesus are often presented as contesting dominant cultural norms and injustices, while offering a counter-narrative that envisions very different societal relationships as expressions of God's just and merciful purposes."

BIOGRAPHICAL AND CRITICAL SOURCES:

PERIODICALS

Interpretation, October, 1997, Mark Allan Powell, review of *Matthew: Storyteller, Interpreter, Evangelist,* p. 432; July, 2002, Earl S. Johnson, Jr., review of *Matthew and Empire: Initial Explorations,* p. 332.

National Catholic Reporter, October 28, 1994, William Graham, review of *What Are They Saying about Matthew's Sermon on the Mount?,* p. 20.

Other Side, July-August, 2002, review of *Matthew and Empire,* p. 29.

*   *   *

CASE, Shirley Jackson 1872-1947

PERSONAL: Born September 28, 1872, in Hatfield Point, New Brunswick, Canada; immigrated to the United States, 1897; died December 5, 1947, in Lakeland, FL; son of George F. (a farmer and carriage builder) and Maria (Jackson) Case; married Evelyn Hill, June 29, 1899. *Education:* Acadia University, B.A., 1893, M.A., 1896; Yale University, B.D. (summa cum laude), 1904, Ph.D., 1906, D.D., 1917. *Hobbies and other interests:* Woodworking.

CAREER: St. Martin's Seminary and Horton Collegiate Academy, New Brunswick, Canada, teacher of mathematics, 1896-97; New Hampton Literary Institute, New Hampshire, teacher of Greek, 1897-1901; Yale University, New Haven, CT, instructor in Greek for one year; pastor of a Congregational church in Bethany, CT, 1902-03; pastor of a church in Beacon Falls, CT, 1903-06; Bates College, Lewiston, ME, teacher of history and philosophy of religion, 1906-08; University of Chicago, Chicago, IL, scholar at Divinity School, 1908, assistant professor, 1908-13, associate professor, 1913-15, professor of New Testament, 1915-38, professor of church history, 1917-38, professor of the history of early Christianity, 1925-38, department chair, beginning 1923, dean of Divinity School, 1933-38; Bexley Hall, Gambier, OH, special lecturer in New Testament, 1938-39; Florida Southern College, Lakeland, FL, professor of religion and dean of Florida School of Religion, 1940-47. Colgate-Rochester Divinity School, Rauschenbusch Memorial Lecturer, 1933.

MEMBER: American Society of Church History (president, 1924), Society of Biblical Literature and Exegesis (now Society of Biblical Literature (president, 1926); Chicago Society of Biblical Research (president, 1925).

WRITINGS:

The Historicity of Jesus, University of Chicago Press (Chicago, IL), 1912.

The Evolution of Early Christianity: A Genetic Study of First Century Christianity in Relation to Its Religious Environment, University of Chicago Press (Chicago, IL), 1914.

The Book of Revelation, University of Chicago Press (Chicago, IL), 1918.

The Millennial Hope: A Phase of War-time Thinking, University of Chicago Press (Chicago, IL), 1918.

The Revelation of John: A Historical Interpretation, University of Chicago Press (Chicago, IL), 1919.

The Social Origins of Christianity, University of Chicago Press (Chicago, IL), 1923.

Jesus: A New Biography, University of Chicago Press (Chicago, IL), 1927.

(Editor) *Studies in Early Christianity,* Century Co. (New York, NY), 1928.

Experience with the Supernatural in Early Christian Times, Century Co. (New York, NY), 1929.

(Editor) *A Bibliographical Guide to the History of Christianity,* University of Chicago Press (Chicago, IL), 1931.

Jesus through the Centuries, University of Chicago Press (Chicago, IL), 1932.

The Social Triumph of the Ancient Church, Harper & Brothers (New York, NY), 1933.

Makers of Christianity: From Jesus to Charlemagne, 1934, Kennikat Press (Port Washington, NY), 1971.

Divinity 301 (Divinity Education), University of Chicago Press (Chicago, IL), 1935.

Highways of Christian Doctrine, Willett, Clark & Co. (Chicago, IL), 1936.

Environmental Factors in Christian History, Kennikat Press (Port Washington, NY), 1939.

Christianity in a Changing World, Harper & Brothers (New York, NY), 1941.

The Christian Philosophy of History, University of Chicago Press (Chicago, IL), 1943.

The Origins of Christian Supernaturalism, University of Chicago Press (Chicago, IL), 1946.

Contributor to books, including *Contemporary American Theology,* edited by Vergilius Ferm, 1932. Contributor to periodicals, including *Crozer Quarterly.* Editor, *Journal of Religion,* beginning 1927.

BIOGRAPHICAL AND CRITICAL SOURCES:

BOOKS

Jennings, Louis B., *The Bibliography and Biography of Shirley Jackson Case,* University of Chicago Press (Chicago, IL), 1949.

Jennings, Louis B., *Shirley Jackson Case: A Study in Methodology,* (Chicago, IL), 1964.

PERIODICALS

Chronicle, July, 1948, Louis B. Jennings, "Shirley Jackson Case."

Crozer Quarterly, Volume 21, 1944, Shirley Jackson Case, "Education in Liberalism;" Volume 22, 1945, Shirley Jackson Case, "Living in the Garden of Eden."*

*   *   *

CASEY, Barbara (Louise) 1944-

PERSONAL: Born July 11, 1944, in Carrollton, IL; daughter of George Dallas (a retired Marine officer) and Charlotte Louise (a homemaker; maiden name, Guildander) Woods; married Willis Robert Casey (died, June 14, 1992); married Al Ferraro (a marketing director); children: Carlotta Love Brown-Harvard, Rene Louise Matthews. *Education:* Attended University of North Carolina—Chapel Hill, and North Carolina State University—Raleigh; North Carolina Wesleyan College, B.A. (summa cum laude). *Hobbies and other interests:* Reading, traveling, gardening.

ADDRESSES: Office—11924 West Forest Hill Blvd., Ste. 22, Box 346, Wellington, FL 33414. *E-mail*—barcafer@aol.com.

CAREER: Writer, editor, and literary agent. North Carolina Wesleyan College, director of alumni and public relations, 1975-77; North Carolina State University, department of athletics, 1977-79; full-time writer, 1989—. Guest author and panelist at BookFest of the Palm Beaches, 1993-2000; judge for the Pathfinder Literary Awards, 1994—; founded own editorial consulting business and literary agency; editorial consultant, Jamaican Writers Circle. Publisher of *Publishers Update,* a directory of children's publishers and literary agents.

MEMBER: Society of Children's Book Writers and Illustrators (regional advisor for the State of Florida, 1992-2003), Florida Freelance Writers, Poets of the Palm Beaches Society, North Carolina Writers Network.

AWARDS, HONORS: Award of Literary Merit, Palm Beach County Cultural Council, 2002, and Independent Publisher Book Award, 2003, both for *Shyla's Initia-*

tive; American Association of University Women Award, Society of Children's Book Writers and Illustrators Golden Kite Award nominee and Sir Walter Raleigh Literary Award nomination, for *Leilani Zan* and *Grandma Jock and Christabelle;* Southeastern Booksellers Association Award nominee, for *The Coach's Wife;* PEN Robert Bingham Fellowship for Writers nominee, 2004; special recognition for her editorial work on the English translations of Albanian children's stories.

WRITINGS:

Leilani Zan, Winston-Derek Publishers (Nashville, TN), 1992.

Grandma Jock and Christabelle, Winston-Derek Publishers (Nashville, TN), 1994.

Shyla's Initiative, CrossTIME (Santa Fe, NM), 2002.

The Coach's Wife, Benoy Publishing (Wilmington, NC), 2003.

The Airs of Tillie, Benoy Publishing (Wilmington, NC), 2004.

Slightest in the House, Benoy Publishing (Wilmington, NC), 2004.

The House of Kane, Benoy Publishing (Wilmington, NC), 2004.

Just Like a Family, Benoy Publishing (Wilmington, NC), 2004.

Also writer of a thirty-minute television special for WRAL-TV, Raleigh, NC. Contributor to periodicals, including *North Carolina Christian Advocate, New East, Chrysalis Reader, Raleigh News and Observer, Dog Fancy, ByLine, True Story, Christian Record,* and *Rocky Mount Sunday Telegram.* Contributor to books and anthologies, including *American Poetry Anthology, Sparrowgrass Poetry Forum, The Cosmic Unicorn,* and *A Cup of Comfort.*

SIDELIGHTS: Writer Barbara Casey has published novels for adults, middle readers, and children. A former public relations director, Casey left that job to pursue writing full time. She is also the founder and owner of her own editorial service and literary agency.

Casey once told *CA:* "I was born in Illinois, but because my father was a career officer in the U.S. Marine Corps, I lived in various and numerous places during my 'informative years.' As a child, no matter where I was, I always reserved a few moments before bedtime to record the day's events, what people I saw, which flowers were in bloom, what events took place, and so forth in my journal. My love for travel and seeing new places and writing about them has continued throughout my life, and I have now visited all fifty states as well as fifteen foreign countries.

"I began writing full-time in 1989, and my writing now includes novels, articles, and short stories, as well as poetry. Whenever I am not doing editorial or agent work, I guard that time in which I actually write (usually the early morning hours) as much as possible from interruptions and distractions. Once I have completed a project, I give myself a week or so off to dig in my flower garden or perhaps take a trip, and to just generally get recharged. But usually after a week I am ready to get back to what I most enjoy—writing.

"When my grandmother was ninety-two, she wrote a family history, something she had always wanted to do but never had the time. Apparently, the love for writing runs in my family. I am most proud of my two daughters, however: one is a lawyer and the other is an engineer. And now there is a new granddaughter on the scene, and I feel certain she shares my love for writing.

"Before I started my editorial service and literary agency, I would try to write every day except around holidays or big events when I have to force myself to concentrate on not burning turkeys or serving liquid Jell-O. Now, a good deal of my time is spent in helping others get published.

"I started out working as Director of Public Relations for a college in North Carolina." Casey later added. "Among other things, I was in charge of everything that was written and published at the college used for outside consumption. I also did freelance editorial work. At some point I realized that I had an overwhelming desire to write creatively. A story was forming in my mind. When that story became all I could think about, I decided to give myself a year to write it and try to get it published. That was the beginning of my writing career. . . . Four middle-grade/young adult novels, five adult novels, a picture book, and several award-winning poems and stories later, I continue to write. In addition to my own editorial consulting business and literary agency, I publish a bimonthly directory of children's publishers which details editorial changes and publishers' needs.

"I do editorial work and represent writers because I love it! I write because not to would make me feel incomplete."

*　　*　　*

CASIL, Amy Sterling 1962-
(Robert Sterling)

PERSONAL: Born March 10, 1962, in Los Angeles, CA; daughter of Eugene (an owner of a janitor service) and Sterling (an animator and art director; maiden name, Sturtevant) Glasband; married Michael Casil (divorced); children: Meredith Sterling. *Education:* Scripps College, B.A., 1983; attended Michigan State University, 1984; Chapman University, M.F.A. (with honors), 1999. *Religion:* American Baptist.

ADDRESSES: Office—Saddleback College, 20800 Marguerite Parkway, Mission Viejo, CA 92692. *E-mail*—ASterling@aol.com.

CAREER: Family Service Association, Redlands, CA, executive director, 1988-97; Chapman University, Orange, CA, instructor in English, 1997-2000; Saddleback College, Mission Viejo, CA, instructor in English, 2000—. Pierce College, faculty member. Wildside Press, worked in marketing and publicity. Associates of Redlands Bowl, member, 1990-95. Founding member and officer for Volunteer Center of Inland Empire and San Bernardino County Homeless Coalition, 1992-95.

MEMBER: Science Fiction Writers of America, Soroptimist Club of Redlands (president, 1994).

AWARDS, HONORS: Winner of Writers of the Future competition, 1999; Nebula Award nomination, Science Fiction Writers of America, 2002, for the short story "To Kiss the Star."

WRITINGS:

Without Absolution (short stories and poetry), Wildside Press (Holicong, PA), 2000.
Imago (science fiction novel), Wildside Press (Holicong, PA), 2002.
Choosing a Career in Aircraft Maintenance (textbook), Rosen Publishing Group (New York, NY), 2002.
B-1 Lancer (nonfiction), Rosen Publishing Group (New York, NY), 2003.
Coping with Terrorism (young adult nonfiction), Rosen Publishing Group (New York, NY), 2003.
Trinity (science fiction novel), Wildside Press (Holicong, PA), 2004.

Author of other nonfiction titles published by Rosen Publishing Group (New York, NY). Contributor of short stories to periodicals, including *Magazine of Fantasy and Science Fiction.* Some writings appear under the pseudonym Robert Sterling.

WORK IN PROGRESS: Research on the Middle East, early twentieth-century American communism, nineteenth-century romanticism, Russian mysticism, bio-anthropology, the science of complexity, and political disenfranchisement and marginalized populations in the late twentieth century.

SIDELIGHTS: Amy Sterling Casil told *CA:* "When I was in college in Claremont, California, I became the first female editor and publisher of the five-college newspaper and served in an internship at the *Los Angeles Times Book Review,* working for Art Seidenbaum, who was a great mentor. I twice won the Crombie Allen Award, which was the fiction/poetry award at Scripps College. I was a double major—British/American literature and studio art. I did most of the covers for the *Collage,* which was magazine-style, and started out as the art reviewer. But from age six, I wanted to be a writer. After college I began to work in community service, first as a fund-raiser for the United Way, then for ten years as the director of the Family Service Association in my hometown of Redlands, California. I had attended the Clarion Science Fiction Writers Workshop at Michigan State University in 1984, inspired by a story by Octavia Butler and an article written by Algis Budrys. At that time, I met and became friendly with Budrys and with Harlan Ellison, who were two of the instructors.

"At Clarion, although it was and is a type of 'boot camp' for aspiring science fiction/fantasy writers, I was from a wholly literary background, although steeped in science fiction as a reader since childhood. Like many, I was first inspired by Madeleine L'Engle's

A Wrinkle in Time, which my aunt gave me when I was about ten, and a bit later by Ray Bradbury's books, particularly *Dandelion Wine* and *The Martian Chronicles.*

"Painting, writing, and partying my way through college, I did a bit of student leadership as well as professional artwork and layout for political campaigns. After that, I married, went to Clarion, came home, and kept working. I wrote a great deal for the Family Service Association and local newspapers or charitable publications, but nothing for myself.

"When my daughter was small, never having forgotten my dream of being a writer, I started writing again, science fiction, just as I had wanted all along. I eventually entered the master's of fine arts program at Chapman University where, with the help of many friends and even later colleagues, wonderful writers and scholars, received my degree in 1999. My goal was to teach and to write, which is what I do today. I am deeply committed to my students.

"I am a Southern California science fiction writer. I write novels, short fiction, poetry, and I also enjoy the nonfiction books I have written for the opportunities they give for my learning and growth, as well as to help other."

BIOGRAPHICAL AND CRITICAL SOURCES:

PERIODICALS

Publishers Weekly, January 21, 2002, review of *Imago,* p. 69.

*   *   *

CERAMI, Charles A.

PERSONAL: Male. *Education:* Georgetown University, graduated 1942.

ADDRESSES: Home—4201 Massachusetts Ave. NW, Washington, DC, 20016-4725. *Agent*—c/o Author Mail, Sourcebooks, 1935 Brookdale Road, Suite 139, Naperville, IL 60563.

CAREER: Economist. Kiplinger Washington Publications, Washington, DC, former editor.

WRITINGS:

Successful Leadership in Business, Prentice-Hall (New York, NY), 1955.
How to Solve Management Problems, Prentice-Hall (Englewood Cliffs, NJ), 1957.
Stop Hiding from Success, Prentice-Hall (Englewood Cliffs, NJ), 1958.
Crisis, the Loss of Europe, Harcourt Brace Jovanovich (New York, NY), 1975.
More Profit, Less Risk: Your New Financial Strategy, McGraw-Hill (New York, NY), 1982.
(Editor) *A Marshall Plan for the 1990s: An International Roundtable on World Economic Development,* Praeger (New York, NY), 1989.
Real Estate for Profit: New Trends & Strategies for the '90s, Institute of Business Management (New York, NY), 1990.
Benjamin Banneker: Surveyor, Astronomer, Publisher, Patriot, J. Wiley (New York, NY), 2002.
Jefferson's Great Gamble: The Remarkable Story of Jefferson, Napoleon, and the Men Behind the Louisiana Purchase, Sourcebooks (Naperville, IL), 2003.

Contributor of articles to periodicals, including *Atlantic Monthly, New York Times, Playboy, Foreign Policy, Spectator,* and *Swiss Review of World Affairs.*

SIDELIGHTS: Charles A. Cerami is an economist and former editor at Kiplinger Washington Publications.

He served as the editor of *A Marshall Plan for the 1990s: An International Roundtable on World Economic Development.* The book includes twenty-one essays from various contributors, each describing a plan that would help the unemployment problem in the world.

In *Benjamin Banneker: Surveyor, Astronomer, Publisher, Patriot,* Cerami provides a biography of Benjamin Banneker, who is best known for being the surveyor of the city that eventually became known as Washington, D.C. Cerami notes that Banneker would have been more well-known, but because he was a black man, his accomplishments were kept from the public by Thomas Jefferson and other early leaders. *Sky and Telescope* contributor Gregg Dinderman noted, "Cerami's biography of Banneker is a heartfelt attempt to reconsider this amazing man."

In *Jefferson's Great Gamble: The Remarkable Story of Jefferson, Napoleon, and the Men Behind the Louisiana Purchase,* Cerami retells the why and how of the Louisiana Purchase. He focuses on the main players in the transaction, including Jefferson and Napoleon, but also discusses the involvement of less famous individuals, including Robert Livingston, Louis-Andre Pichon, and others. *Booklist* contributor Gilbert Taylor commented that "history buffs will find satisfying new nuggets in Cerami's synthesis."

BIOGRAPHICAL AND CRITICAL SOURCES:

PERIODICALS

America, April 26, 1975, Vincent S. Kearney, review of *Crisis, the Loss of Europe,* pp. 327-328.

Booklist, March 1, 2003, Gilbert Taylor, review of *Jefferson's Great Gamble: The Remarkable Story of Jefferson, Napoleon, and the Men Behind the Louisiana Purchase,* p. 1137.

Campaigns & Elections, June, 2003, review of *Jefferson's Great Gamble,* p. 14.

Choice, October, 1989, G.T. Potter, review of *A Marshall Plan for the 1990s: An International Roundtable on World Economic Development,* p. 360; December, 1991, George T. Potter, review of *A Marshall Plan for the 1990s,* p. 556.

Journal of Economic Literature, March, 1990, review of *A Marshall Plan for the 1990s,* p. 158.

Kirkus Reviews, September 1, 1982, review of *More Profit, Less Risk: Your New Financial Strategy,* p. 1029.

Library Journal, February 15, 1975, Jean Deuss, review of *Crisis, the Loss of Europe,* p. 381; November 1, 1982, Joseph Barth, review of *More Profit, Less Risk,* pp. 2092-2093; May 1, 2003, Michael F. Russo, review of *Jefferson's Great Gamble,* p. 14.

New York Times, October 17, 1982, Karen Arenson, review of *More Profit, Less Risk,* p. 18.

Publishers Weekly, January 27, 2003, review of *Jefferson's Great Gamble,* p. 245.

Reference & Research Book News, May, 2002, review of *Benjamin Banneker: Surveyor, Astronomer, Publisher, Patriot,* p. 219.

Sky and Telescope, January, 2003, Gregg Dinderman, review of *Benjamin Banneker,* pp. 68-69.

Times Literary Supplement, May 31, 2002, Adam I.P. Smith, review of *Benjamin Banneker,* p. 30.

ONLINE

Nathaniel Turner, http://www.nathanielturner.com/ (February 13, 2004), Winfield Swanson, "Foiling the Arsonists."

Sourcebooks, http://www.sourcebooks.com/ (October 24, 2003), review of *Jefferson's Great Gamble.*

Wiley Canada, http://www.wileycanada.com/ (October 24, 2003), review of *Benjamin Banneker.**

*   *   *

CHILSON, Peter 1961-

PERSONAL: Born July 3, 1961, in Detroit, MI. *Education:* Syracuse University, B.A. (international relations and journalism), 1984; Pennsylvania State University, M.F.A. (creative writing), 1994.

ADDRESSES: Home—Moscow, ID. *Office*—Department of English, Washington State University, Pullman, WA 99164-5020. *E-mail*—pchilson@mail.wsu.edu

CAREER: Essayist, journalist, and educator. Peace Corps volunteer, Niger, Africa, 1985-87; Associated Press, freelance reporter, West Africa; *High Country News,* Paonia, CO, associate editor, 1997-98; Washington State University, Pullman, assistant professor of English, 1998—.

WRITINGS:

Riding the Demon (nonfiction), University of Georgia Press (Athens, GA), 1999.

Also author of short fiction, essays, and reports for several magazines and newspapers, including the *London Daily Telegraph, Audubon, West Africa Magazine,* and *North American Review.*

SIDELIGHTS: After completing his undergraduate education in 1984, Peter Chilson volunteered for the Peace Corps and spent two years in the West African country of Niger. He then remained for a time in West Africa as a freelance reporter. In 1992 Chilson returned to Niger and traveled that country's rural roads via the notoriously unreliable bush taxi to explore the country and get an insider's view of its society. The result is *Riding the Demon,* a travel book that depicts the extremely dangerous and superstitious road culture of West Africa.

The book's title comes from the superstitious belief in demons by many of the bush taxi drivers and their passengers as they travel at speeds of up to one hundred miles per hour in the typical Peugeot 504 station wagon. Sometimes filled to the brim with up to ten passengers, these bush taxis are notoriously unreliable and pieced together haphazardly with bald tires, wire, and anything else available that will keep the taxis running. As these pieced-together cars speed down the roads, the drivers and their passengers routinely witness catastrophic accidents—that is, if they're lucky enough not to be in one.

In the book's opening scene, Chilson describes one such accident in which a station wagon and a gasoline tanker collide and leave behind only the charred shells of the vehicles and the remains of the dead passengers. In addition to the harrowing driving and fatal accidents, Chilson also describes how the drivers and their passengers routinely face hostile soldiers who often stop the taxis to collect bribes and harass the drivers and passengers. These soldiers have also been known to rape and kill women passengers. "Little wonder that a fatalistic belief in the 'demons' of the road dominates the drivers—a set of beliefs that also draws in the author, whose own fear is assuaged by amulets and, on occasion, numb withdrawal," commented a contributor to *Publishers Weekly.* Guided by his bush taxi driver, Issoufou Garba, Chilson spends most of his time in Niger but also makes forays into neighboring Nigeria, Burkina Faso, and the Ivory Coast. For Chilson, the bush taxi and its drivers are a metaphor that represents Africa's struggles for a more stable and prosperous society, and bush cabbie Issoufou enables Chilson to enter a world that few outsiders ever see.

Writing in the *New York Times Book Review,* Adam Goodheart commented, "There's almost a flavor of science fiction to the scenes Chilson describes, as though he were giving us a glimpse into a twenty-first-century dystopia of mad egoism and hurtling hulks of metal." Goodheart went on to note, "And Chilson's book, as vivid in places as a nightmare, has all the revelatory power of the early explorers' narratives, with their shreds of myth and rumor snatched from the borders of terra incognita." The *Publishers Weekly* contributor called *Riding the Demon* a "vivid exploration of road culture." *Booklist* contributor Joe Collins noted that "Chilson is expert at getting readers to shake their heads in disbelief."

BIOGRAPHICAL AND CRITICAL SOURCES:

PERIODICALS

Booklist, March, 1999, Joe Collins, review of *Riding the Demon,* p. 1146.
Library Journal, April 1, 1999, Mark L. Grover, review of *Riding the Demon,* p. 120.
New York Times Book Review, June 6, 1999, Adam Goodheart, review of *Riding the Demon,* p. 7.
Publishers Weekly, February 22, 1999, review of *Riding the Demon,* p. 77.
Times Literary Supplement (London, England), July 30, 1999, Deborah L. Manzolillo, review of *Riding the Demon,* p. 9.

ONLINE

Peter Chilson Home Page, http://www.wsu.edu/~pchilson (January 20, 2004).*

*   *   *

CHRISTIAN, Jeffrey E. 1956-

PERSONAL: Born 1956.

ADDRESSES: Home—Cleveland, OH. *Office*—Christian & Timbers, One Corporate Exchange, 25825 Science Park Drive, Suite 400, Cleveland, OH 44122. *E-mail*—Jchristian@ctnet.com.

CAREER: Christian & Timbers, Cleveland, OH, founder, chairman, and chief executive officer, 1980—. Commentator on employment issues for CNBC-TV and periodicals, including *Wall Street Journal, Forbes, Business Week, USA Today, New York Times,* and *Fortune.*

AWARDS, HONORS: "Midas List" citations, *Forbes* magazine, 2002 and 2003, for being one of the top fifty most influential deal makers in America.

WRITINGS:

Headhunter Confidential: How to Get the Best Jobs and the Best People—Exclusive Tips from One of the Top Headhunters in the Business, Random House (New York, NY), 2002.

SIDELIGHTS: As chairman and chief executive officer of Christian & Timbers, Jeffrey E. Christian presides over one of the nation's top executive placement firms. Christian has found top executives for such corporations as Adobe, General Electric, Microsoft, and Hewlett-Packard and has discussed his headhunting techniques in the press and on television. In 2002 he published *Headhunter Confidential: How to Get the Best Jobs and the Best People—Exclusive Tips from One of the Top Headhunters in the Business,* a book that delineates his techniques and demonstrates how he developed them over his own career. Part memoir, part advice tome, *Headhunter Confidential* explores strategies for finding, interviewing, hiring, and retaining valuable employees. As Mary Whaley put it in *Booklist,* Christian "aims to help readers find the smartest, most creative, and hardest-working talent available." Lucy Heckman in *Library Journal* described *Headhunter Confidential* as a "practical and highly informative guide."

BIOGRAPHICAL AND CRITICAL SOURCES:

PERIODICALS

Booklist, August, 2002, Mary Whaley, review of *Headhunter Confidential: How to Get the Best Jobs and the Best People—Exclusive Tips from One of the Top Headhunters in the Business,* p. 1900.
Library Journal, October 1, 2002, Lucy Heckman, review of *Headhunter Confidential,* p. 109.
Publishers Weekly, June 10, 2002, review of *Headhunter Confidential,* p. 48.

ONLINE

Christian & Timbers, http://www.ctnet.com/ (April 29, 2003), company Web site, includes brief biography of Christian.*

CLARK, Mary Jane Behrends

PERSONAL: Female. *Education:* Graduate of the University of Rhode Island.

ADDRESSES: Agent—Laura Dail Literary Agency, 80 Fifth Avenue, Suite 1503, New York, NY 10011. *E-mail*—maryjaneclark@maryjaneclark.com.

CAREER: Writer. Columbia Broadcasting System, Inc., New York, NY, news writer and producer.

WRITINGS:

The Commonwealth of Independent States (juvenile; part of "Headliners" series), Millbrook Press (Brookfield, CT), 1992.
Do You Want to Know a Secret? St. Martin's Press (New York, NY), 1998.
Do You Promise Not to Tell? St. Martin's Press (New York, NY), 1999.
Let Me Whisper in Your Ear, St. Martin's Press (New York, NY), 2000.
Close to You, St. Martin's Press (New York, NY), 2001.
Nobody Knows, St. Martin's Press (New York, NY), 2002.
Nowhere to Run, St. Martin's Press (New York, NY), 2003.

ADAPTATIONS: Nobody Knows was adapted for audio (unabridged; four cassettes), read by Fran Tunno, Audio Renaissance, 2002.

SIDELIGHTS: Mary Jane Behrends Clark's first book is a history written for readers in the middle grades. As a news writer and producer, she was well-qualified to write *The Commonwealth of Independent States,* in which she discusses the Russian Revolution, the formation of the Soviet Union, its breakup, and the former Soviet countries that chose to form the Commonwealth of Independent States. Of these republics, the founding members of Russia, the Ukraine, and Belarus, get the most coverage of their historical, political, and cultural backgrounds. Separate chapters discuss the region's environmental disasters, the role of the grandmother in the Russian household, the dispute between Armenians and Azeris, the "selling" of Russian scientists, and Gorbachev after the coup. Included are color photographs and maps.

A *Kirkus Reviews* contributor called "particularly interesting" the discussion of Asian republics with their sixty million Muslims and dependence on cotton. The reviewer called the volume "lucid, sympathetic, well-organized, and effectively detailed: a book that gives a real sense of these diverse lands." *School Library Journal* reviewer Pamela K. Bomboy called the book "a precisely written, well-organized presentation."

Like her well-known former mother-in-law, Mary Higgins Clark, Clark has written a growing list of mysteries, and her first, *Do You Want to Know a Secret?* benefits from her experience as a television writer and producer. The protagonist is morning coanchor Eliza Blake, a widow and mother who is finding success at KEY-TV in New York when the evening anchor is found dead. As she finds herself sharing his assignments, others are killed, and Eliza fears for the safety of her child and herself. A *Publishers Weekly* reviewer felt that "the few stereotyped minor characters . . . don't detract from Clark's refreshing surprise ending, a very nineties version of 'the butler did it.'"

Farrell Slater, a producer at KEY news, is burned out, and her career is dangerously close to being ended in *Do You Promise Not to Tell?*. She feels that one big story could change that outcome, and her chance comes when Farrell discovers that the Faberge Moon Egg recently sold at auction for six million is a fake. As Farrell and her cameraman become involved in the hunt for the authentic Romanov treasure, with an FBI agent close behind, the meet a Russian woman who insists that she has the real egg in her possession. An artisan is killed in his shop in Little Odessa, and other murders soon follow. Farrell discovers more than she'd hoped for in seeking out the story as secrets of murder, romance, scandal, and intrigue surface. A *Publishers Weekly* contributor wrote that "the suspense never flags, and the killer's identity remains a secret long into the tale."

Let Me Whisper in Your Ear features KEY reporter Laura Walsh, who becomes suspect when her obituaries of high-profile celebrities are ready to air before their bodies have cooled. Eliza Blake returns in *Close to You*, and has left her apartment for a house in the suburbs. The new home for Eliza and her daughter proves not to be a safe haven when Eliza begins receiving telephone threats and hate mail, some from stalkers who are genuinely dangerous. A *Publishers Weekly* contributor called this novel "an excellent psychological thriller that will keep readers pleasantly bound to the page."

Nobody Knows features Cassie Sheridan, KEY's Washington correspondent, who under pressure to produce a newsworthy story, reveals more than she should about a manhunt for a serial rapist who dresses as a clown. One of the three victims is the daughter of the FBI director, and when Cassie reveals her identity, the young woman commits suicide. Cassie is banished to report on the weather in Sarasota, Florida, and her husband, tired of playing second fiddle to Cassie's career, files for divorce. Nothing can revive Cassie's career unless the clown-rapist, nicknamed "Emmett Doe," strikes again.

The next victim is porn star Merilee Quinones, who is not raped but is killed when she surprises the murderer in his clown makeup. Cassie becomes reconnected to the case when she meets Vincent Baylor, a boy who finds Merilee's severed hand on the beach and who has removed a ruby ring from a finger in order to use it to help his poor family, thereby putting him, them, and eventually Cassie in great danger. Among the things that nobody knows is the strength of the hurricane that is bearing down on the area and how it will change the course of the investigation. A *Publishers Weekly* contributor who reviewed *Nobody Knows* noted Clark's "compelling characters and intricate plotting."

BIOGRAPHICAL AND CRITICAL SOURCES:

PERIODICALS

Booklist, February 15, 1993, Janice Del Negro, review of *The Commonwealth of Independent States*, p. 1046; October 15, 1998, Diana Tixier Herald, review of *Do You Want to Know a Secret?* p. 407; July, 1999, Emily Melton, review of *Do You Promise Not to Tell?* p. 1926; August, 2002, Melanie Duncan, review of *Nobody Knows*, p. 1929; June 1, 2003, Mary Frances Wilkens, review of *Nowhere to Run*, p. 1709.

Kirkus Reviews, December 15, 1992, review of *The Commonwealth of Independent States*, p. 1569; July 15, 2002, review of *Nobody Knows*, p. 973; June 15, 2003, review of *Nowhere to Run*, p. 819.

Library Journal, August, 2003, Jo Ann Vicarel, review of *Nowhere to Run,* p. 128.

Publishers Weekly, September 7, 1998, review of *Do You Want to Know a Secret?* p. 81; June 28, 1999, review of *Do You Promise Not to Tell?* p. 52; July 1, 2002, review of *Nobody Knows,* p. 54; November 4, 2002, review of *Nobody Knows* (audio) p. 23; July 28, 2003, review of *Nowhere to Run,* p. 79.

School Library Journal, January, 1993, Pamela K. Bomboy, review of *The Commonwealth of Independent States,* p. 110.

ONLINE

Mary Jane Clark Home Page, http://www.maryjaneclark.com (June 2, 2003).*

*   *   *

CLARKE, Alison (Jane)

PERSONAL: Female. *Education:* Manchester Metropolitan University, B.A. (design history); Royal College of Art, M.A. (design history); University College London, Ph.D. (social anthropology).

ADDRESSES: Agent—c/o Author Mail, Smithsonian Institution Press, 750 Ninth St. NW, Suite 4300, Washington, DC 20560. *E-mail*—Alison.Clarke@rca.ac.uk

CAREER: Winchester School of Art, University of Southampton, former senior lecturer; University of Brighton, former senior lecturer; Royal College of Art, senior tutor. Visiting professor in design history and theory, University of Applied Arts, Vienna, Austria.

WRITINGS:

Tupperware: The Promise of Plastic in 1950s America, Smithsonian Institution Press (Washington, DC), 1999.

Member of editorial board, *Journal of Visual Culture* and *Journal of Consumer Culture.*

SIDELIGHTS: Drawing from an extensive academic career in consumer culture and product design, Alison Clarke wrote *Tupperware: The Promise of Plastic in 1950s America,* which explores the higher function of those celebrated plastic containers in a context that reflects gender roles and consumerism in the mid-twentieth century.

Tupperware follows the career of Earl Silas Tupper, a plastics innovator who patented the tight-fitting lidded bowls in the late 1940s. Product sales for his creations were bleak until a Detroit single mother named Brownie Wise revolutionized 1950s consumerism with the advent of the Tupperware party, a lucrative in-home sales vehicle that offered extra income and regular social interaction to millions of American women. Reviewer Susan Vincent said in the *Canadian Review of Sociology and Anthropology* that Clarke's neofeminist take on Tupperware asserts that "the Tupperware experience is a valid part of women's history, disputing the mainstream feminist understanding of party sales as exploiting homemakers and promoting an image of subordinate domestic femininity." Clarke instead holds that Tupperware liberated suburban housewives via the sales experience and income it provided at a time when conventional workplaces were seldom realistic or available for women.

Chicago Sun-Times contributor Rachel Hartigan called *Tupperware* "a heavily academic cultural critique of Tupperware as a symbol of 'modernity,' an 'artifact' of consumerism and a facilitator of suburban 'social networks.'" Certainly, Clarke suggests that the Tupperware phenomenon was vital to the development of American consumer culture at the time—much larger than the sum of its injection-molded plastic parts, and surely a symbol of middle-class modernity and aesthetics. Jonathan Groner wrote in his *Salon.com* assessment, "Clarke's work is a significant addition to the reconsideration of that misunderstood decade."

BIOGRAPHICAL AND CRITICAL SOURCES:

PERIODICALS

Canadian Review of Sociology and Anthropology, August, 2001, Susan Vincent, review of *Tupperware: The Promise of Plastic in 1950s America,* p. 357.

Chicago Sun-Times, December 26, 1999, Rachel Hartigan, "Pop This One in the Fridge: The Story of Tupperware," p. 20.

Guardian (London, England), December 4, 1999, Veronica Horwell, review of *Tupperware,* p. 9.

Houston Chronicle, January 4, 2000, Kathleen Purvis, review of *Tupperware,* p. 3.

Journal of Women's History, summer, 2001, Andrea Friedman, review of *Tupperware,* p. 159.

Publishers Weekly, August 2, 1999, review of *Tupperware,* p. 60.

Women's Review of Books, March, 2000, Susan Porter Benson, "The Life of the Party," p. 6.

ONLINE

Royal College of Art Web site, http://www.rca.ac.uk/ (January 30, 2004).

Salon.com, http://www.salon.com/ (November 10, 1999), Jonathan Groner, review of *Tupperware.**

*   *   *

COLLINGS, Matthew 1955-

PERSONAL: Born 1955, in England. *Education:* Attended art school, mid-1970s.

ADDRESSES: Office—c/o Author Mail, Harry N. Abrams, 100 Fifth Ave., New York, NY 10011.

CAREER: Art critic and artist. Former editor of *Artscribe* magazine; art critic, British Broadcasting Corp. (BBC), 1988-97.

WRITINGS:

Blimey! From Bohemia to Britpop: The London Artworld from Francis Bacon to Damien Hirst, 2nd edition, 21 Publishing (Cambridge, England), 1997, 3rd edition, 1997.

It Hurts: New York Art from Warhol to Now, photographs by Ian MacMillan, 21 Publishing (Cambridge, England), 1998.

(With Neal Brown and Sarah Kent) *Tracey Emin. I Need Art Like I Need God* (exhibition catalog), Jay Jopling (London, England), 1998.

This Is Modern Art, edited by Sarah Fass, Weidenfeld & Nicholson (London, England), 1999, Watson-Guptill Publications (New York, NY), 2000.

(Author of introduction) *British Abstract Painting 2001* (exhibition catalog), Momentum (London, England), 2001.

Art Crazy Nation: The Post-Blimey! Art World, 21 Publishing (Cambridge, England), 2001.

Sarah Lucas, Abrams (New York, NY), 2003.

Author of scripts for television series *This Is Modern Art* and *Hello Culture.*

WORK IN PROGRESS: Another television series about art.

SIDELIGHTS: Matthew Collings is a British artist who has gained considerable attention in recent years as a modern art critic, both through his books and his British television shows. Described by *New York Times Book Review* writer Deborah Solomon as a "smart and clever British blabbermouth," Collings has a chatty, desultory writing style that is often contemptuous of the contemporary art scene, while he is still good-humored enough to find self-important artists entertaining. With the exception of some artists, such as Sarah Lucas, Tracy Emin, and Damien Hurst, Collings feels that many of today's artists are more interested in fame and fortune than producing genuine art. "Of course, I believe in art," he told Richard Marshall in *3AM Magazine,* "in the sense of some kind of tradition and history which includes modernism and to some extent contemporary art; but I believe it's a slightly stupid age for art right now. It's probably the worst age there's ever been. . . . Ever since I started this critical enquiry, whatever it is, the theme has always been the same. Why is art like this? Whose fault is it? Is it the audience's? Is it the art's? Is it inevitable? There are no easy answers to those questions."

Collings's first book, *Blimey! From Bohemia to Britpop: The London Artworld from Francis Bacon to Damien Hirst* looks into the young British artists movement using "stream-of-consciousness prose served up in sound bites to provide an insider's no-holds-barred multigenerational portrait of everyone who counts in London's contemporary art world," as *Art Journal* reviewer Alexandra Anderson-Spivy described it. Collings creates a mix of art criticism and personal accounts of artists he has met, writing it all down "with intelligence and humor," according to Carol J. Binkowski in *Library Journal.* Lisa Liebmann, writing in *Artforum International,* similarly called *Blimey!* "funny, fragmented, and sharp." Not only does the work relate some of what is happening in the modern world of British art, but it also "debunks some ideological trappings," wrote Binkowski, including the notion that young British artists evolved their style as a reaction to Thatcherism. Many reviewers particularly enjoyed the author's writing style, which Grady T. Turner described in *NY Arts* magazine as "faux-naive." The book, Turner concluded, provides "an irreverent primer for anyone who want[s] to make sense of a diverse group of artists being marketed as a cogent movement."

Turner, however, rewarded Collings with a much less flattering review of his next book, *It Hurts: New York Art from Warhol to Now.* Switching from the London to the New York City art scene, the book takes on an "irritating . . . cheeky style" that Turner felt does not cover up that Collings "did not do the research required to fulfill the role of an amusing curmudgeon." As with his first book, much of *It Hurts* includes Collings's encounters with famous artists. However, Turner contended that the author gets in the way of the interviews and seems "incapable, or unwilling, to let his subjects speak for themselves." Solomon, on the other hand, was more receptive to this second book. Although she noted that Collings overlooks some important artists on the New York scene and that "there are too many cheap shots and adolescent tantrums," she asserted that "one of the strengths of Collings's book is that it captures precisely the looping and sometimes loopy feeling of art-world conversations. His glancing, deliberately slight tone is true to the spirit of artists' shop talk, which typically abounds with the kind of information that textbook authors prefer to keep to themselves." Collings himself admitted to Marshall that *It Hurts!* "wasn't very good," believing that the problem was that he wrote the book too quickly. "Now when I read that one through," he confessed, ". . . it's the one that gives me the most pain."

This Is Modern Art, which is based on one of Collings's BBC programs, fared much better critically and helped to establish his reputation as a writer. "With *This Is Modern Art* I was recognized a bit," he told Marshall, "and that was when it became apparent to

me that a lot of people saw me as a populariser of a difficult subject, which I really thought myself as being." Complimented for taking neither himself nor his subject too seriously, Collings offers biographies of important artists and personalized trips through studios, galleries, and museums that put modern art in perspective with artists of the past. Collings, observed Marina Warner in a *London Review of Books* article, "feels easy with numbness and dumbness and 'shock horror' [of modern art]; he doesn't vituperate against vacuousness and lack of affect; he likes being made to feel 'glidey' and 'nice'; he's funny about the artists' self-mythologising and bad behaviour, and irony for him is natural."

As its title implies, *Art Crazy Nation: The Post-Blimey! Art World* is a continuation of Collings's first book in which he offers more wry observations and "breezy irreverence," as Binkowski described it in *Library Journal,* on the current state of modern art and art culture. Binkowski called the book "singularly witty and insightful," and added that anyone who is interested in what is going on in contemporary art "will thoroughly enjoy this unusual book."

Devoted to the history and idea of art, yet doubtful of the relevance of what today's artists are producing, Collings has become a populariser despite himself. "The weird thing about it is," he told Marshall, "that I either have never thought about it at all—making art popular—or else I've positively hated the popularisation of contemporary art. When I'm being extreme, I'm capable of thinking that frankly the whole art scene is made up of a bunch of idiots. And I have no desire to get millions of ordinary people to queue up to look at that stuff. Why should they? It's got nothing much to do with them." He lamented that many artists today get into art "for commercial reasons" and that much of the work either has no heart or just reflects current politically correct ideals. Furthermore, this situation will only get worse, he asserted: "It's going to be streamlined, fake, goo, pseudo-art that'll lie on the land for years and years. That's my vision of it. I think the only hope for anything creative or genuinely expressive, is that there has to be some sort of cultural underground. Because if something is only in the spotlight or striving to be in it, then inevitably it'll be hollow."

Still, writing about art and discussing it in his television programs remains important to him. As he told Sarah Vowell in *Salon.com,* "I really am interested in art. I do see the contemporary art world as a continuation of art history and I take art history very seriously. It's a source of values to me and a source of meaning. It makes sense out of life. But my drive is to be as intense and realistic and creative and imaginative about that as I can. So that causes me to write like this." Struggling somewhat with whether he wishes to focus on his own art or on his writings, he admitted to Marshall, "It's difficult to do serious painting and write as well. At least, that's my excuse, my reason why I haven't advanced as a painter. . . . But I want to do more painting. I'm going to find out in the next twenty-five years if it's possible to do both."

BIOGRAPHICAL AND CRITICAL SOURCES:

PERIODICALS

Artforum International, November, 1997, Lisa Liebmann, review of *Blimey! From Bohemia to Britpop: The London Artworld from Francis Bacon to Damien Hirst,* p. S3; May, 1999, David Rimanelli, review of *It Hurts: New York Art from Warhol to Now,* p. 35.
Art in America, June, 1998, Peter Plagens, review of *Blimey!,* p. 37; February, 2000, "Books for the Collector's Library," p. 65.
Art Journal, fall, 1998, Alexandra Anderson-Spivy, review of *Blimey!,* p. 88.
Library Journal, June 1, 1998, Carol J. Binkowski, review of *Blimey!,* p. 104; October 1, 2002, Carol J. Binkowski, review of *Art Crazy Nation: The Post-Blimey! Art World,* p. 86.
London Review of Books, April 13, 2000, Marina Warner, "A New Twist in the Long Tradition of the Grotesque," p. 24.
New Statesman, June 14, 1999, Andrew Gillen, review of *This Is Modern Art,* p. 40.
New York Times Book Review, September 26, 1999, Deborah Solomon, "It's Not Pretty, and It's Not Art," Section 7, p. 18.
School Arts, December, 2000, Kent Anderson, review of *This Is Modern Art,* p. 61.
Times Literary Supplement, February 26, 1999, Simon Grant, review of *It Hurts: New York Art from Warhol to Now,* p. 32; January 11, 2002, William Feaver, "Ambassadors of Awesome," p. 18.

ONLINE

3AM, http://www.3ammagazine.com/ (April 29, 2003), Richard Marshall, "Richard Marshall Interviews Matthew Collings."

NY Arts, http://www.nyartsmagazine.com/ (April 29, 2003), Grady T. Turner, "It Hurts: 'It Sucks.'"
Salon.com, http://www.salon.com/ (December 1, 1999), Sarah Vowell, "I'm a Pure Insider."
Web Studies, http://www.newmediastudies.com/ (March 21, 2004), "Matthew Collings."*

*   *   *

COLLINS, Mary Clementine 1846-1920

PERSONAL: Born April 18, 1846, in Alton, IL; died May 25, 1920, in Alton, IL. *Education:* Attended public schools in Alton, IL.

CAREER: Congregational Church, American Board of Commissioners for Foreign Missions, missionary among the Lakota Sioux Indians, beginning 1875, missionary and physician, 1884-1910. Ordained minister, 1899. Lecturer and advocate of Indian rights in East Coast cities.

WRITINGS:

Author of *How I Became a Missionary,* (New York, NY); and *Winona: The Autobiography of Mary C. Collins,* (New York, NY).

BIOGRAPHICAL AND CRITICAL SOURCES:

BOOKS

Religious Leaders of America, 2nd edition, Gale (Detroit, MI), 1999.

PERIODICALS

North Dakota History, Volume 19, 1952, Louise P. Olson, "Mary Clementine Collins: Decotah Missionary," pp. 59-81.
South Dakota Historical Collections, Volume 41, 1982, L. Richmond, "Autobiography of Mary C. Collins, Missionary to the Western Sioux," pp. 1-66.*

*   *   *

COLSTON, Fifi E. 1960-

PERSONAL: Born May 7, 1960, in York, England; married Adrian Parkyn (an advertising account director), December 2, 1983; children: Haley, Rory. *Education:* Massey University, diploma, 1980; Victoria

University, M.A., 1983. *Hobbies and other interests:* Painting, swimming.

ADDRESSES: *Home*—32 Konini Rd., Hataitai, Wellington, New Zealand. *E-mail*—fificolston@paradise. net.nz.

CAREER: Freelance illustrator, 1981-2003; Weta Workshop, Wellington, New Zealand, staff writer, 2003—.

MEMBER: New Zealand Illustrators' Guild (president, 1998-2001), New Zealand Writers Guild, New Zealand Society of Authors.

WRITINGS:

(Self-illustrated) *Fifi's Crafty Arts,* two volumes, Scholastic (New Zealand), 1995.
(Self-illustrated) *Fifi's Festive Fun,* Scholastic (New Zealand), 1996.
Fifi Verses the World, Steele Roberts (New Zealand), 1999.
Verity's Truth (novel), Scholastic (New Zealand), 2003.

ILLUSTRATOR

Anthony Holcroft, *The Old Man and the Cat,* Whitcoulls (New Zealand), 1984.
Anthony Holcroft, *The Oldest Garden in China,* Whitcoulls (New Zealand), 1985.
Ruth Corrin, *Not without Randolph,* Scholastic (New Zealand), 1993.
Diana Noonan, *Dear Tom,* Lands End (New Zealand), 1995.
Ruth Corrin, *Get Real Paddy Manson,* HarperCollins (New Zealand), 1996.
Brosie Browne, *This Tail,* Lands End (New Zealand), 1996.
Diana Noonan, *It's My Bread,* Learning Media (New Zealand), 1997.
Anna Kenna, *Brother Trouble,* Learning Media (New Zealand), 2001.
Wiremu Grace, *Nga Taonga O Te Kaitiora,* Huia Publishing (New Zealand), 2002.

Author of comedic poetry column, *Next* magazine, 1994-2002; author of humor page for *About Kids* magazine. Illustrator of New Zealand children's titles, including Janet Slater-Redhead, *Mr. Magee Comes Home for His Tea,* Scholastic (New Zealand); Barbara Hill, *Rain,* Scholastic (New Zealand); Elizabeth Pulford, *Midnight Feast,* Scholastic (New Zealand); John Parsons, *Mystery Valley,* Nelson ITP (New Zealand); Quentin Flynn, *The Great Egg Problem,* Nelson ITP (New Zealand); Margaret Cahill, *Going Places,* Learning Media (New Zealand); *The Great New Zealand Activity Book,* New Zealand Illustrators's Guild (Wellington, New Zealand); Hannah Rainforth, *Toroa (The Albatross),* Huia Publishing (New Zealand); *Te Takaro Rama Whaita,* Huia Publishing (New Zealand); Chelsea Wharepapa, *Te Wahi Ahuahanga,* Huia Publishing (New Zealand); and Te Waari Carkeek, *Panui Pangarau,* Huia Publishing (New Zealand). Contributor of articles and illustrations to school journals, popular magazines, and early reading books.

WORK IN PROGRESS: A children's television series, *Wild Cards,* for broadcast in New Zealand; a novel for children.

SIDELIGHTS: New Zealand-based author and illustrator Fifi E. Colston once commented: "Writing is a relatively recent career for me. I have spent my years since graduating from design school as an illustrator. After twenty years drawing blueberries and motorcycle helmets for the advertising world, I felt inspired to write. My tentative foray onto the keyboard ended up in winning a national competition, and *Verity's Truth* is the result. Looking for a structure within which to write and buoyed up by my success, I applied for Victoria University's M.A. in scriptwriting. I and nine others were accepted and I have been immersed in reading, writing, research, film, television, and theatre ever since. I have managed in the course of avoiding some of my study to write another kids' novel, create an art piece for New Zealand's fantastic yearly Wearable Art Show (mine is a Bodice-Ripper—a wearable novel) and work part time at the Weta Workshop on a writing team. Weta is the digital and special effects production company for Peter Jackson's "Lord of the Rings" trilogy and . . . *King Kong.*

"I love to write humour, without forgetting that you can have something to say—other than a series of one liners. Having kids myself and being immersed in their worlds for the past fifteen years, I find writing for this age group a satisfying and fascinating thing to do. It gives me a chance to be any twelve-year-old I want to be! I endlessly milk my kids for information, news, views and dialogue. One day they'll forgive me."

*   *   *

COOK, Roger F. 1948-

PERSONAL: Born September 14, 1948, in Little Rock, AR; son of James D. and Hazel (Copeland) Cook; married, October, 2002; wife's name Nada; children: Stephen Dawson, Darren Anthony. *Ethnicity:* "Caucasian." *Education:* Washington and Lee University, B.A., 1970; University of Freiburg, M.A., 1978; University of California—Berkeley, Ph.D., 1986. *Hobbies and other interests:* Tennis, backpacking.

ADDRESSES: Home—206 Spring Valley Rd., Columbia, MO 65203. *Office*—Department of German and Russian Studies, 451 GCB, University of Missouri—Columbia, Columbia, MO 65211. *E-mail*—cookrf@ missouri.edu.

CAREER: University of Missouri—Columbia, Columbia, MO, professor of German and chair of Department of German and Russian Studies, 1986—.

MEMBER: North American Heine Society (president), Modern Language Association of America, German Studies Association, American Association of Teachers of German.

WRITINGS:

The Demise of the Author: Autonomy and the German Writer, 1770-1848, Peter Lang (New York, NY), 1993.
The Cinema of Wim Wenders: Image, Narrative, and the Postmodern Condition, Wayne State University Press (Detroit, MI), 1996.
By the Rivers of Babylon: Heinrich Heine's Late Songs and Reflections, Wayne State University Press (Detroit, MI), 1998.
(Editor) *A Companion to the Works of Heinrich Heine,* Camden House, 2002.

WORK IN PROGRESS: Research on German-Jewish conceptions of history in the nineteenth century.

BIOGRAPHICAL AND CRITICAL SOURCES:

PERIODICALS

Choice, April, 1999, E. L. Vines, review of *By the Rivers of Babylon: Heinrich Heine's Late Songs and Reflections,* p. 1461.
Journal of English and Germanic Philology, January, 2000, Jeffrey L. Sammons, review of *By the Rivers of Babylon,* p. 106.
Modern Language Review, April, 2001, Jefferson S. Chase, review of *By the Rivers of Babylon,* p. 571.

*   *   *

COOKE, (Alfred) Alistair 1908-2004

OBITUARY NOTICE—See index for *CA* sketch: Born November 20, 1908, in Manchester, England; died March 30, 2004, in Manhattan, NY. Journalist, broadcaster, and author. Cooke, who was fascinated throughout his life with American culture though he was a born Brit, was well known as an erudite and entertaining narrator and host of such programs as *Letter from America, Masterpiece Theater,* and *Omnibus.* Originally entertaining thoughts of becoming a teacher or being involved in the theater, he attended Jesus College, Cambridge, on a scholarship; it was there that he changed his name from Alfred to Alistair and transformed himself into a popular socialite. He edited the college's literary magazine and was involved in theater, cofounding the Cambridge Mummers. He earned a B.A. in 1930 and a diploma in education the next year. A theater fellowship allowed him to travel to the United States in 1932, where he attended Yale University's School of Drama, visited jazz clubs, and even played piano, recording a jazz album for Columbia Records. The next year, he went to Harvard University, where he studied history and English and met H. L. Mencken, with whom Cooke would become friends. This trip caused his fascination for America and Americans, an interest he had fostered since World War I, when his family housed some U.S. troops, to blossom. Though he returned to England in 1934 to work as a film critic for the BBC, he would be back in the United States by 1937, gaining U.S. citizenship in 1941. Making his home in New York City, Cooke maintained ties to England, nevertheless, as a correspondent for the *London Times, London*

Daily Herald, and then the Manchester *Guardian,* for which he served as a United Nations correspondent for three years and worked as the *Guardian*'s U.S. correspondent until 1972. In 1946, Cooke began hosting *Letter from America,* a thirteen-minute program for the BBC in which he delved behind the headlines to offer his British audience insights into American life, culture, and politics. The program, which Cooke confessed he did not believe would last very long, remained on the air until illness finally led him to retire in 2004; selections from the broadcasts were published in *Letters from America* (1951), *Talk about America* (1968), and *The Americans: Fifty Talks on Our Life and Times* (1979). Cooke was also the host of the program *Omnibus,* a show about the arts that ran from 1952 until 1961 and for which he won an Emmy Award. In the United States, however, he is most often remembered as the host of *Masterpiece Theater,* a role he began in 1971. Though sometimes he was spoofed for this part in shows ranging from *Saturday Night Live* to *Sesame Street,* his work on the program was highly regarded. Cooke also won a second Emmy in 1973 for his part in the history miniseries *America.* In addition to his broadcasting work, though, Cooke was critically acclaimed for his books, most especially for his *A Generation on Trial: U.S.A. v. Alger Hiss* (1950; second enlarged edition, 1968). Honored with a Peabody Award for International News Reporting in 1952, and named a Knight Commander of the Order of the British Empire in 1973, Cooke was the author of numerous other books, including *Douglas Fairbanks: The Making of a Screen Character* (1940), *Alistair Cooke's America* (1973), *Six Men* (1977), *Masterpieces: A Decade of Masterpiece Theatre* (1981), *America Observed* (1988), and *Memories of the Great & the Good* (2000).

OBITUARIES AND OTHER SOURCES:

PERIODICALS

Chicago Tribune, March 31, 2004, Section 3, p. 9.
Los Angeles Times, March 31, 2004, p. B9.
New York Times, March 31, 2004, p. C12.
Times (London, England), March 31, 2004, p. 29.
Washington Post, March 31, 2004, p. B7.

*   *   *

COPELAND, Pala 1950-

PERSONAL: Born 1950; partner of Al Link; children: six. *Education:* University of Toronto, B.A.

ADDRESSES: Home—Allumette Island, Ontario, Canada. *Office*—4 Freedoms Tantra, P.O. Box 144, Pembroke, Ontario K8A 6X1, Canada. *E-mail*—4freedoms@tantraloving.com.

CAREER: Lecturer, writer, and teacher, 1997—.

WRITINGS:

(With Al Link) *Soul Sex: Tantra for Two,* New Page Books (Franklin Lakes, NJ), 2003.

Contributor to newspapers and magazines, including *Toronto Star, Queen's University Journal, Ottawa Citizen, Globe & Mail, Wall Street Journal, City Woman, Ladies Home Journal, Tone, Urban Male, Toronto Fashion, Flare, Tone, Above and Beyond.*

SIDELIGHTS: Pala Copeland has been practicing Tantra since 1987 and teaching others about the practice since 1997. In their seminars, Copeland and her patner Al Link emphasize the practice of Tantra in a committed, monogamous relationship. Their book *Soul Sex: Tantra for Two,* illustrates how to create a loving relationship using Tantra as the base. Tantra is the ancient Eastern practice of prolonged sexual experience and sexual unity.

The couple coauthored *Soul Sex: Tantra for Two.* In *Soul Sex* Copeland and Link offer techniques and information on Tantra and how to make relationships more spiritual and loving. *Library Journal* contributor Martha Cornog noted, "Their book concentrates on heterosexual relationships and making sexuality a focus in one's partnership."

BIOGRAPHICAL AND CRITICAL SOURCES:

PERIODICALS

Library Journal, May 1, 2003, Martha Cornog, review of *Soul Sex: Tantra for Two,* pp. 139-140.

ONLINE

Four Freedoms Relationship Tantra, http://www.tantra-sex.com/ (February 10, 2004), "About Tantra Teachers Al and Pala."
New Page Books, http://www.newpagebooks.com/ (October 26, 2003), review of *Soul Sex.**

CORMAN, Cid
See CORMAN, Sidney

*   *   *

CORMAN, Sidney 1924-2004
(Cid Corman)

OBITUARY NOTICE—See index for *CA* sketch: Born June 29, 1924, in Roxbury, MA; died March 12, 2004, in Kyoto, Japan. Editor, translator, publisher, and author. A prolific poet in his own right, Corman was well known for helping other poets get their works published through his Origin Press and was a highly influential figure among the Beat and Black Mountain poets. Ineligible for military service because of his health, he attended Tufts College (now University) during World War II, completing a B.A. in 1945 and continuing on to graduate study at the University of Michigan, where he won the Hopwood Prize for poetry in 1947, and University of North Carolina. Later, in the mid-1950s, he also attended the Sorbonne. Leaving university in 1947, Corman embarked on a across America and writing poetry, years before Jack Kerouac made such adventures famous in his own writings. Settling for a time in Boston in 1948, he started a radio program on WMEX in which the works of such writers as Archibald MacLeish and Stephen Spender were read without commercial interruption. Believing radio was an ideal medium for poetry, Corman thus had a powerful influence on what would become performance poetry in later years. At the same time, Corman prolifically penned poetry, hundreds of his verses being published in small magazines. Despite this success, Corman seemed even more interested in bringing the poems of others to the public light. He thus founded the poetry magazine *Origin* and Origin Press in 1951, featuring the works of such now-renowned figures as Robert Duncan and Denise Levertov. Enamored by the simple power of Japanese poetry, Corman moved to Kyoto, where he found work as a private teacher, married a Japanese woman, continued his work with Origin Press, and founded C.C.'s, a coffee and dessert shop that also provided a venue for poetry readings. In the 1950s, Corman also began having his poetry collections published on a yearly basis, mostly through Origin Press, with early collections including *A Thanksgiving Eclogue from Theocritus* (1954), *A Table in Provence* (1959), *For Instance* (1962), and *In Good Time* (1964). Fluent in Japanese, Corman began translating the works of such poets as Matsuo Basho and Shimpei Kusano. His own poems have, in fact, been likened to those of the Japanese masters, with their simple construction lulling readers into startling revelations and imagery. Financial problems led Corman to return to Boston in 1970, but in the early 1980s he returned to Japan, where he would remain the rest of his life. While continuing to publish poetry collections and translations, Corman wrote so much that, at the time of his death, some eighty thousand poems remained unpublished. One of his most ambitious works is called *Of,* a multi-volume series with the first two books being published in 1990. By 2004, five volumes had been published, and a sixth is to appear posthumously. Among his many, many other collections, which he published under the name Cid Corman, are *Stead* (1966), *Of the Breath Of* (1970), *So Far* (1973), *For the Asking* (1976), *Identities* (1981), *And the Word* (1987), *How Now: Poems* (1995), and *For Crying Out Loud* (2002); he also edited books by such authors as Franco Beltrametti and Lorine Niedecker, and published essay collections, such as *At Their Word: Essays on the Art of Language* (1978). Suffering a heart attack in Kyoto, Corman fell into a coma in 2004 and soon passed away.

OBITUARIES AND OTHER SOURCES:

BOOKS

Contemporary Poets, seventh edition, St. James Press (Detroit, MI), 2001.
Dictionary of Literary Biography, Volume 193: *American Poets since World War II, Sixth Series,* Gale (Detroit, MI), 1998.

PERIODICALS

Los Angeles Times, March 18, 2004, p. B12.
New York Times, March 16, 2004, p. C19.
Times (London, England), March 29, 2004, p. 26.

*   *   *

CRAIG, Colleen

PERSONAL: Female. *Education:* University of British Columbia, B.A. (creative writing and English).

ADDRESSES: Office—Pilates on the Ball Studio, 315 Albany Avenue, Toronto, Ontario M5R 3E2, Canada. *E-mail*—info@pilatesontheball.com.

CAREER: Writer for stage and film; Stott pilates trainer, Toronto, Ontario, Canada.

MEMBER: Playwrights Union of Canada.

WRITINGS:

Pilates on the Ball: The World's Most Popular Workout Using the Exercise Ball, Healing Arts (Rochester, VT), 2001.
Abs on the Ball: A Pilates Approach to Building Abdominals, Healing Arts (Rochester, VT), 2003.

Producer of *Colleen Craig's On the Ball* videotape.

SIDELIGHTS: Colleen Craig, a pilates trainer, is the author of two books that combine pilates movements with an exercise ball. In her first book, *Pilates on the Ball: The World's Most Popular Workout Using the Exercise Ball,* Craig provides an instructional guide on how to perform pilates exercises with the use of an exercise ball. In her second book *Abs on the Ball: A Pilates Approach to Building Abdominals,* Craig concentrates on the abdominal muscles. *Abs on the Ball* provides step by step instructions and illustrations on how to properly tone the abdominals using pilates and an exercise ball. The text is "full of sound guidance," noted Deborah Anne Broocker in a *Library Journal* review.

BIOGRAPHICAL AND CRITICAL SOURCES:

PERIODICALS

Library Journal, May 1, 2002, review of *Pilates on the Ball: The World's Most Popular Workout Using the Exercise Ball,* p. S5; May 1, 2003, Deborah Anne Broocker, review of *Abs on the Ball: A Pilates Approach to Building Abdominals,* pp. 146-147.
School Library Journal, June, 2003, review of *Pilates on the Ball,* p. S55.

ONLINE

Colleen Craig's Pilates on the Ball, http://www.pilatesontheball.com (October 26, 2003).

*   *   *

CRAWFORD, Isabel (Alice Hartley) 1865-1961

PERSONAL: Born May 26, 1865, in Cheltenham, Ontario, Canada; died November 18, 1961, in Winona, NY (some sources say Canada); buried in Saddle Mountain Mission cemetery, Saddle Mountain, OK; daughter of a Baptist minister. *Education:* Attended Baptist Missionary Training School, Chicago, IL.

CAREER: Worked as a missionary in Chicago, IL; American Baptist Home Missionary Society, missionary to Kiowa Indians in Elk Creek, OK, 1893-95, and Saddle Mountain, OK, 1895-1905; traveling lecturer, 1905-18.

WRITINGS:

Kiowa: The History of a Blanket Indian Mission, Fleming H. Revell (New York, NY), 1915, published as *Kiowa: A Woman Missionary in Indian Territory,* introduction by Clyde Ellis, University of Nebraska Press (Lincoln, NE), 1998.
Joyful Journey: Highlights of the High Way; An Autobiography, Judson Press (Philadelphia, PA), 1951.
A Jolly Journal (autobiography), Fleming H. Revell (New York, NY), 1932.

BIOGRAPHICAL AND CRITICAL SOURCES:

BOOKS

Crawford, Isabel, *Kiowa: The History of a Blanket Indian Mission,* Fleming H. Revell (New York, NY), 1915, published as *Kiowa: A Woman Missionary in Indian Territory,* introduction by Clyde Ellis, University of Nebraska Press (Lincoln, NE), 1998.

Crawford, Isabel, *Joyful Journey: Highlights of the High Way; An Autobiography* Judson Press (Philadelphia, PA), 1951.

Crawford, Isabel, *A Jolly Journal* (autobiography), Fleming H. Revell (New York, NY), 1932.

Religious Leaders of America, 2nd edition, Gale (Detroit, MI), 1999.

PERIODICALS

American Indian Quarterly, fall, 1998, Luke E. Lassiter, review of *Kiowa: A Woman Missionary in Indian Territory,* p. 498.

Foundations, October, 1978, Salvadore Mondello, "Isabel Crawford: The Making of a Missionary."*

*   *   *

CUNNINGHAM, Valentine 1944-

PERSONAL: Born October 28, 1944; son of Valentine (a reverend) and Alma Lillian (Alexander) Cunningham; married Carol Ann Shaw, August 6, 1966; children: Joseph, Willoughby. *Education:* Keble College, Oxford, M.A.; St. Johns College, Oxford, D.Phil. *Hobbies and other interests:* Jazz trumpet, piano.

ADDRESSES: Office—Corpus Christi College, Oxford, OX1 4JF, England. *E-mail*—valentine.cunningham@ccc.ox.ac.uk.

CAREER: Professor, author. St. John's College, Oxford, junior resident fellow, 1969-72; University of Oxford, lecturer in English, 1972—, chairman of English faculty, 1984-87, professor of English language and literature, 1996—; Corpus Christi College, Oxford, England, fellow and tutor in English, beginning 1972, dean, 1980-91; senior tutor, 1991-94; professor of English, fellow. University of Konstanz, Germany, visiting professor; BBC broadcaster. Judge for literary prizes, including Booker Prize, 1992, 1998, and Commonwealth Writers Prize, 2000-01.

WRITINGS:

Everywhere Spoken Against: Dissent in the Victorian Novel, Clarendon Press (Oxford, England), 1975.

British Writers of the Thirties, Oxford University Press (New York, NY), 1988.

In the Reading Gaol: Postmodernity, Texts, and History, Blackwell (Cambridge, MA), 1994.

Reading after Theory ("Blackwell Manifestos" series), Blackwell (Malden, MA), 2002.

EDITOR

The Penguin Book of Spanish Civil War Verse ("Penguin Poets" series), Penguin Books (Hardmondsworth, England), 1980.

Spanish Front: Writers on the Civil War, Oxford University Press (New York, NY), 1986.

Adam Bede/George Eliot ("The World's Classics" series), Oxford University Press (New York, NY), 1996.

The Victorians: An Anthology of Poetry and Poetics ("Blackwell Anthologies" series), Blackwell (Malden, MA), 2000.

Contributor to journals and newspapers in England and the United States, and to books, including *Literacy Is Not Enough: Essays on the Importance of Reading,* edited by Brian Cox, Manchester University Press (Manchester, England), 1998.

SIDELIGHTS: Valentine Cunningham is a professor of English whose interests include nineteenth-and twentieth-century fiction, the Victorian novel, Victorian poetry and poetics, and religion and literature.

His first book, *Everywhere Spoken Against: Dissent in the Victorian Novel* is a study of religious dissent as considered by such novelists as the Brontës, George Eliot, Charles Dickens, Mrs. Gaskell, Mrs. Oliphant, and William Hale White. Marghanita Laski commented in *Listener* that Cunningham's "sociological and historical detail is splendidly informative: on the relevant varieties of Dissent, on its association largely with the cities, its social standing, and its links—by no means inevitable—with radicalism. It is when he moves on to examination of specific novelists that the differing approaches—deriving, no doubt, from initial work for separate occasions—make the book as a whole less valuable than it might have been."

Roy Foster wrote in the *Times Literary Supplement* that in this volume, "the issues of politics, religion and Dissent come together and enlighten the whole nineteenth-century framework. It is a good measure both of the value of Victorian fiction in contributing to a holistic approach to the age, and of the value of Mr. Cunningham's work in his area of scholarship."

For *Spanish Front: Writers on the Civil War* Cunningham collected more than 100 poems, memoirs, articles, and stories by writers, most of whom were British writers of the left, who took a position on that struggle.

Lisa M. Schwerdt remarked in *Modern Fiction Studies* that *British Writers of the Thirties,* in which Cunningham describes and interprets the writings of an era, "is superb in its coverage—but perhaps an instance of when less would be more." The volume encompasses all that was written—not only the literature, but also films, detective stories, political tracts, and travel guides, and includes lists of trends seen in the writing, like the frequency of specific words in titles and text. Schwerdt noted that "there is much here to admire, however, and there are new emphases, if not insights. The book is useful, for instance, in drawing attention to social/historical backgrounds of various period symbols, icons, and metaphors." Cunningham studies the gay and lesbian writers of the period and how heterosexuality, family, and women's interests were often ignored in favor of the emphasis on males, anti-family sentiment, and the importance of school ties. He notes writers who were at school together.

Louis Menand commented in the *Times Literary Supplement* that Cunningham "connects images of physical violence with examples of surrealistic violence to language and the rhetorical violence of 1930s criticism. He discovers networks of tendencies: the habit among 1930s writers of modifying or replacing their given names, which connects with the notion of literary intellectuals 'going over' to the working class, with Auden's attachment to the charade as a literary form and with the trouble many 1930s texts have with the first-person pronoun."

The *Spectator*'s David Wright noted Cunningham's use of "lavish quotations, mainly from books that have long been unobtainable or undeservedly forgotten." Edward Mendelson wrote in the *London Review of Books* that the volume "marshals everything there is to know about the literary Thirties into an extraordinary and indispensable resource."

In *In the Reading Gaol: Postmodernity, Texts, and History,* Cunningham focuses on the "relationship of word and world" and references a slip in the diary of Virginia Woolf, wherein the word "underword" was mistakenly entered for the word "underworld." He writes that the "amalgamation of word and world is the condition not just of Virginia Woolf's writing but of all writing," and further says that it indicates the "persistent duality of language—made of both wordy and worldly things and not absolutely either the one or the other."

Also in *In the Reading Gaol,* Cunningham studies a number of fictional works, including *Jane Eyre, Emma, Hard Times,* and *Middlemarch.* Tony Tanner observed in the *Times Literary Supplement* that "the close and detailed readings of these works (and others) is often brilliantly perceptive and original."

In a *Review of English Studies* article, Robert Crawford wrote that Cunningham "has been infected by his reading. . . . So, spending much energy on a Huntley and Palmer's biscuit tin (from Reading) that appears in *Heart of Darkness,* Cunningham tells us how such biscuit tins carried empire and other biscuits to the ends of the imperial dominions, and he cites an array of texts giving documentation on the travels and uses of the tins."

In referring to some of Cunningham's puns, Tanner noted that "this rich book is undeniably clever, at times it is wearyingly 'clever'-clever. . . . Still, let me end by commending, and recommending this book. It gives an impressively clear and comprehensive account of the various theoretical issues raised during the past twenty years; it is full of intelligence and insight; and there is some exemplary close reading." *Choice* reviewer W. B. Warde, Jr. called the volume a "well-written (even manifesting a graceful, ludic spirit) and incisive study of 'postmodern' literary theory and practice."

Cunningham wrote *Reading after Theory* for the "Blackwell Manifestos" series, a collection that explores contemporary ideas. *Library Journal*'s Francisca Goldsmith stated that Cunningham "is stellar in his honing to that theme." He explores the concepts of the reader, the text, and the act of reading in the "post-theory" era.

John Kerrigan, who reviewed the volume in the *London Review of Books* called it a "survey of the strengths and drawbacks of Theory as it has influenced literary study in the last few decades. The settling of accounts may be timely, given that so many 'new approaches' have run out of steam. But the real test of the book comes in the chapter called 'Touching Reading,' which goes beyond the survey mode and argues for a style of criticism that is alert to touch and tact. The chapter raises fascinating questions." Goldsmith concluded by calling *Reading after Theory* "fun, involving, and inviting as both a social book-discussion subject and an important text."

BIOGRAPHICAL AND CRITICAL SOURCES:

PERIODICALS

Choice, March, 1995, W. B. Warde, Jr., review of *In the Reading Gaol: Postmodernity, Texts, and History,* p. 1108.

Library Journal, February 1, 2002, Francisca Goldsmith, review of *Reading after Theory,* p. 104.

Listener, March 4, 1976, Marghanita Laski, review of *Everywhere Spoken Against: Dissent in the Victorian Novel,* pp. 283-284.

London Review of Books, October 9, 1986, Michael Church, review of *Spanish Front: Writers on the Civil War,* pp. 16-17; June 23, 1988, Edward Mendelson, review of *British Writers of the Thirties,* pp. 12-14; September, 2002, John Kerrigan, review of *Reading after Theory,* pp. 19-20.

Modern Fiction Studies, winter, 1988, Lisa M. Schwerdt, review of *British Writers of the Thirties,* pp. 700-701.

Modern Language Review, January, 1978, T. J. Winnifrith, review of *Everywhere Spoken Against,* pp. 171-172.

Review of English Studies, February, 1996, Robert Crawford, review of *In the Reading Gaol,* p. 125.

Spectator, February 6, 1988, David Wright, review of *British Writers of the Thirties,* pp. 26-27.

Times Literary Supplement, February 27, 1976, Roy Foster, review of *Everywhere Spoken Against,* p. 229; June 10, 1988, Louis Menand, review of *British Writers of the Thirties,* p. 651; July 15, 1994, Tony Tanner, review of *In the Reading Gaol,* p. 6.*

D

DARBY, Mary Ann 1954-

PERSONAL: Born February 28, 1954, in Inglewood, CA; daughter of Lou (a roofing and building contractor and fiddle-player) and Nadia (a homemaker) Ritchey; married Creg Darby (a scientist), December 21, 1985; children: Patrick and John (twins). *Ethnicity:* "White." *Education:* Whitman College, B.A., 1976; San Jose State University, M.A., 2001. *Hobbies and other interests:* Reading.

ADDRESSES: Home—2233 Rockcreek Trail, Hoover, AL 35226. *E-mail*—bkwoman2@yahoo.com.

CAREER: High school teacher of English and social studies, Corvallis, MT, 1976-77, Klamath Falls, OR, 1978-82, and Seattle, WA, 1982-88; middle-school teacher of language arts, Renton, WA, 1993-98, and Los Altos, CA, beginning 1998; Jefferson State Community College, Birmingham, AL, English teacher. University of Washington, Seattle, guest lecturer, 1997. City of Bellevue, part-time employee, 1990-92.

MEMBER: National Council of Teachers of English, Assembly on Literature for Adolescents.

AWARDS, HONORS: Teacher Recognition Award, Johns Hopkins University; Renton Rotary Teacher of the Month Award; Books for Kids grant.

WRITINGS:

(With Miki Pryne) *Hearing All the Voices: Multicultural Books for Adolescents,* Scarecrow Press (Lanham, MD), 2002.

Contributor of articles and reviews to periodicals, including *Washington English Journal, International Journal for Teachers of English Writing Skills,* and *English International.*

WORK IN PROGRESS: Updating *Hearing All the Voices: Multicultural Books for Adolescents;* a project on science fiction, fantasy, and women in young adult literature.

SIDELIGHTS: Mary Ann Darby told *CA:* "After teaching English for twelve years at the high school level, I took some time off to be at home after the birth of our twins. When I went back to teaching, I ended up at a middle school, and my first thought was, 'What good books are out there for middle school students?' That started me on a quest that I am still following: finding good books for all students. I've read hundreds of books for young adults in the past eight years and have been continually amazed and delighted at the breadth of good writing and good literature on so many topics for middle and high school students. When my colleague and best friend, Miki Pryne Willa, discovered my interest, she countered with the idea that students want to find someone like themselves in books, so we needed to look for books that represented every culture. At that point, we started to consider our own ideas about what culture means: students who grow up in a non-traditional family, living with mom and grandma, certainly have a culture; students who have a physical challenge in their lives certainly have a culture. So the quest grew to find, not only wonderful books, but wonderful books representing as many cultures as we could locate and read. I gradually gained a reputation with teachers and students as someone who read a lot and loved to talk about books. At the last school where I taught, students whom I didn't know would walk into my room before and after school and during breaks to ask me for book recommendations. I always started by asking two questions. 'What is one book that you really enjoyed reading? What interests do you have?' By asking those questions, I could usually pull a half-dozen titles or so off my shelves to hand to the student, or I could give him or her a list to take to the library. I love putting books into the hands of young adults. I love even more having them come back asking please, could they have another good book. Engendering the love of reading is my goal. It makes me happy.

"So where is the writing in all of this? Miki and I went out to conferences with our message of finding books for every student and found receptive audiences. One woman approached us and asked us to write an article for her magazine. We agreed and embarked on writing one of our first articles together. Miki and I can finish each other's sentences when we talk and are close to that in our writing as well. The article made us do a lot of thinking, and many drafts exchanged between us before we were satisfied with our first article. After a number of conferences, we were asked why we hadn't written a book dealing with our ideas and book recommendations. Thus, repeated requests from colleagues and the thought of getting all these exciting and wonderful books into the hands of many students were our primary motivators for writing *Hearing All the Voices: Multicultural Books for Adolescents.* Even though by then I had moved to a different state and no longer saw Miki every day, we e-mailed our ideas back and forth and had goals and chapter ideas for our books, as well as a good start on our annotated bibliography, which was to be the heart of the book. Meanwhile I had applied to review books for *Voice of Youth Advocates* (*VOYA*) and in my biography, I mentioned I was working on a book about books for those who work with young adults. Amazingly enough, *VOYA* put me in touch with their parent company, Scarecrow Press. Soon thereafter, I told Miki we had a publisher interested in our idea, and we needed to work up a formal proposal now!

"All of the book was written while Miki and I were working full-time in middle schools in different states. We each wrote chapters, then we edited each other's work. We each wrote annotations and then exchanged annotations in order to add or fine-tune each other's

ideas. I loved coming home after teaching all day and sitting down to the computer to work on our book. (Cook dinner? Whoops! Just let me finish this page. . . .) There was immense satisfaction in seeing a dream of seven years actually taking form! I used my lunch breaks at school to look up publication information on the Library of Congress Web site, for, although I had long ago started a note card system for the books I read, I had not even dreamed of needing extra data like publication information, or of using them for anything beyond my own reference. I would wake up in the middle of the night and mentally sort books into a new 'literary circle' category. Someone would mention an idea at a staff meeting, and I would be off mentally creating another cross-curricular use for the books we were touting. One of my personal writing lessons dealt with indices. Somehow, I thought they were magically created by book publishers. I was fairly sure there were wands and potions involved. When I learned we would need to create any indices that we wanted, I volunteered for the task and, sans wand, tried to decide logically what would work. That was a challenge!

"Because Miki and I had been talking about our ideas for so long and had read over 500 books already, our book came together in roughly six months. Writing out the ideas was a joy! One of the hardest parts was drawing the line on other books to include in the annotated bibliography section. Writing had cut into our reading time (and both of us were also in graduate programs along with our jobs), but when Angela Johnson or Chris Crutcher or one of our dozens of other favorite authors wrote a new book, how could we ignore it? Actually, it was formatting the indices that made me finally throw up the red flag. I just didn't want to mess with that huge database any more!

"We deliberately kept the tone of our book fairly informal, which has garnered some criticism from a source or two. But we wanted our book to be user-friendly, and the whole undertaking was so personal to us that we wrote it in our own voices, as though we were talking to our colleagues or parents of students. We truly want every student to be able to find a book to enjoy, in which he or she can discover someone who has similar struggles or similar questions, a book with a character who has a life that touches the reader in some way, a book that shows young adults everywhere the joy of reading. One of my colleagues has copies of *Hearing All the Voices* in her classroom, and she told me that her students come up and say, 'I need to see that book—the one that talks about books!' Students are looking at something I created to get ideas for what to read. Is that exciting? Incredibly so.

"What now? I am continuing to keep a card for every young adult book I read. It's a habit. I am trying to spend more time writing, whether it is in my journal or at the computer, and I have paper and computer files started for any and all writing ideas I have. Seeing one dream come to life makes me believe others are possible, too. I hope to collaborate with Miki on more projects. Living life, working, and writing, too, are a lot to juggle. But when you write a book, other people can pick it up and read it. Is that cool or WHAT?"

BIOGRAPHICAL AND CRITICAL SOURCES:

PERIODICALS

Booklist, September 1, 2002, Sharon Cohen, review of *Hearing All the Voices: Multicultural Books for Adolescents,* p. 172.

*   *   *

D'AVENI, Richard

PERSONAL: Male. *Education:* Cornell University, A.B., 1975; Suffolk University, J.D., 1979; Boston University, M.B.A., 1979; Columbia University, Ph.D., 1987

ADDRESSES: Office—Tuck School of Business at Dartmouth, 100 Tuck Hall, Hanover, NH 03755. *E-mail*—richard.a.daveni@dartmouth.edu.

CAREER: Educator and author. University of North Carolina at Chapel Hill, assistant professor of business, 1986-88; Amos Tuck School of Business Administration, Dartmouth College, Hanover, NH, professor of strategic management, 1988—; CEO and founder, RadStrat.com. Consultant to *Fortune* 500 corporations; regular speaker at executive education programs, including Wharton School of Business.

AWARDS, HONORS: Fellowships from the World Economic Forum, the Richard D. Irwin Foundation, and the Sol E. Snider Entrepreneurial Center at the Wharton School of Business; A. T. Kearney Award.

WRITINGS:

(With Richard E. Gunther) *Hypercompetition: Managing the Dynamics of Strategic Maneuvering,* Free Press (New York, NY), 1994.

Hypercompetitive Rivalries, Free Press (New York, NY), 1995.

(With Robert E. Gunther and Joni Cole) *Strategic Supremacy: How Industry Leaders Create Growth, Wealth, and Power through Spheres of Influence,* Free Press (New York, NY), 2001.

Contributor to journals, including *Organization Science, Sloan Management Review,* and *Harvard Business Review.* Member of editorial board, *Academy of Management Journal,* 1991-96, *Organization Science,* 1992-2002, *Strategic Management Journal,* 1994-95, and *Administrative Science Quarterly,* 1995-96.

SIDELIGHTS: A professor of business strategy at Dartmouth College's Tuck School of Business, Richard D'Aveni also works extensively with strategic planners at large corporations, advising them on how to make their companies revolutionary within their fields. Additionally, he advises others on how to create order out of the chaos brought about by these corporate revolutionaries.

In *Strategic Supremacy: How Industry Leaders Create Growth, Wealth, and Power through Spheres of Influence,* D'Aveni and coauthors Robert E. Gunther and Joni Cole define strategic supremacy as "the ability to continually create, use, share, distribute, redistribute, preserve, stabilize, counter, circumvent and direct the pattern of power" within a particular business sector. They then caution that if companies do not gain strategic supremacy in their markets, others will. D'Aveni advises global giants that they will probably never become the elephant that learns to dance, thereby making it crucial that they build strategies around their massive resources. To leverage their weight, global firms will need to establish a sphere of influence, beat back the forces of competitive compression surrounding their spheres, and develop strategies for routing resources within their sphere to absorb, shape, hedge, or dampen the revolutionaries.

Reviewing D'Aveni and Gunther's *Hypercompetition: Managing the Dynamics of Strategic Maneuvering,* Cindy Tursman noted in a *Business Credit* appraisal that the authors are not blindly optimistic. In contrast, the strategies offered include "disrupting opponents so they experience constant psychological defeats, performance declines, and paralysis or bankruptcy, [and] it means 'that chivalry is dead' and cooperation is out." Tursman went on to observe that D'Aveni distrusts alliances between companies serving similar customers, noting that he believes "In an environment in which every advantage rapidly erodes, cooperative agreements are inherently unsustainable." A *Publishers Weekly* contributor maintained that the book has a limited scope: "Examples of companies that have followed these strategies, even unknowingly, are few, and the ones D'Aveni includes are unconvincing. If a reader is not in the upper ranks of a multibillion-dollar multinational company, it is difficult to translate his theory into reality. Presumably even tiny firms could follow this strategy, but they will be hard-pressed to learn how, given D'Aveni's abstract, academic approach." J. C. Thompson, writing in *Choice,* however, praised the book highly, concluding that *Hypercompetition* "deserves serious attention to its striking revelations about both problems and responses to the fast-paced changes in the business world."

BIOGRAPHICAL AND CRITICAL SOURCES:

PERIODICALS

Booklist, December 15, 2001, Mary Whaley, review of *Strategic Supremacy: How Industry Leaders Create Growth, Wealth, and Power through Spheres of Influence,* p. 693.

Business Credit, April, 1995, Cindy Tursman, review of *Hypercompetition: Managing the Dynamics of Strategic Maneuvering,* p. 40.

Business Ethics Quarterly, April, 1996, Noreen Dorenburg, review of *Hypercompetition,* p. 233.

Choice, October, 1994, J. C. Thompson, review of *Hypercompetition,* p. 330.

Kirkus Reviews, March 1, 1994, review of *Hypercompetition,* p. 263.

Library Journal, December, 2001, Susan C. Awe, review of *Strategic Supremacy,* p. 140.

New York Times, March 21, 1989.

Publishers Weekly, November 5, 2001, review of *Strategic Supremacy,* p. 55.

Site Selection, August ,1996, Jack Lyne, excerpted talk by D'Aveni.

ONLINE

Bookwatch.com, http://www.bookwatch.com/ (April 4, 2002), review of *Hypercompetition: Managing the Dynamics of Strategic Maneuvering.*

Tuck School of Business Web site, http://oracle-www. dartmouth.edu/ (February 21, 2004).*

*   *   *

DAVIS, Anita (Grey) P(rice) 1943-

PERSONAL: Born March 8, 1943, in Shelby, NC; daughter of Arthur Fred and Nell (a deputy sheriff and registrar of deeds; later surname, Burns) Price; married Buren Lee Davis (a postal employee), December 15, 1962; children: Robert Eric. *Ethnicity:* "Caucasian." *Education:* Appalachian State University, B.A. (cum laude), 1963, M.A., 1965; Duke University, Ed.D., 1971; Ohio State University, postdoctoral study, 1977-79. *Politics:* Democrat. *Religion:* Christian. *Hobbies and other interests:* Family activities, reading, church, pets.

ADDRESSES: Home—205 Mansfield Dr., Spartanburg, SC 29307. *Office*—Converse College, 580 East Main St., Spartanburg, SC 29302; fax: 864-596-9526. *E-mail*—anita13@charter.net.

CAREER: Teacher at public schools in Shelby, NC, 1963-67, and Browns Mills, NJ, 1967-68; Converse College, Spartanburg, SC, instructor, 1969-72, assistant professor, 1972-76, associate professor, 1976-83, professor, 1983-88, Charles A. Dana Professor of Education, 1988—, department chair, 1978-83, 1986-2000. Rutherford County Historical Committee, chair, 2003. Public speaker; workshop presenter; guest on media programs.

MEMBER: International Reading Association (president of Spartanburg County Council, 1982-83, 1994-95), Women's Historical Society of the South, Rutherford County Historical Society, Friends of the Library of Spartanburg County, Kappa Delta Pi, Pi Gamma Mu, Alpha Chi (charter member).

AWARDS, HONORS: Kathryne Amelia Brown Award for Distinguished Teaching, 1986; member of National Women's Hall of Fame, 1999; Parents' Choice Award for an article, "Finger Print Art;" certificate of appreciation, Michigan Council of the Social Studies.

WRITINGS:

HISTORY AND BIOGRAPHY MATERIALS

The South in the American Revolutionary War, Eastern National Park and Creative Publications (OH), 1993.

(With others) *Harriet Quimby: An Activity Book for Children,* Honoribus Press (Spartanburg, SC), 1993.

Harriet Quimby: America's First Lady of the Air—A Biography for Intermediate Readers, Honoribus Press (Spartanburg, SC), 1998.

Walnut Grove Plantation: A Fun and Learn Book, Walnut Grove Plantation (Roebuck, SC), 2000.

Real Heroes: Rutherford County Men Who Made the Supreme Sacrifice during World War II, Honoribus Press (Spartanburg, SC), 2002.

(With Barry Hambright) *Chimney Rock and Rutherford County,* Arcadia Publications (Charleston, SC), 2002.

North Carolina during the Great Depression: A Documentary Portrait of a Decade, McFarland and Co. (Jefferson, NC), 2003.

Rutherford County, North Carolina, in World War II, Arcadia Publications (Charleston, SC), 2003.

Contributor to periodicals, including *Inflight.*

EDUCATION AND TEST PREPARATION MATERIALS

(With others) *The Graduate Management Admission Test: The Best and Most Comprehensive in Test Preparation,* Research and Education Association (Piscataway, NJ), 1990, 3rd edition published as *The Graduate Management Admission Test: The Best and Most Comprehensive in Test Preparation,* 1997.

(With others) *The Best Test Preparation for the Graduate Record Examination,* Research and Education Association (Piscataway, NJ), 1990, 2nd edition, 1992.

(With others) *The Best Test Preparation for the Scholastic Aptitude Test,* Research and Education Association (Piscataway, NJ), 1990, 2nd edition published as *The Best Test Preparation for the New Scholastic Aptitude Test,,* 1993.

(With others) *The Best Test Preparation for the NTE Core Battery (and Tests of Professional Knowledge),* Research and Education Association (Piscataway, NJ), 1991.

(With others) *The Best Test Preparation for the Medical College Admission Test,* Research and Education Association (Piscataway, NJ), 1991.

(With others) *The Best Test Preparation for the Law School Admissions Test,* R & E Publishing (Piscataway, NJ), 1992, revised edition, 1992.

(With others) *Verbal Skill Builder,* Research and Education Association (Piscataway, NJ), 1992.

(With others) *The Best Test Preparation for the New PSAT/NMSQT: The Preliminary SAT/National Merit Scholarship Qualifying Test,* Research and Education Association (Piscataway, NJ), 1994.

Max Notes: To Kill a Mockingbird, Research and Education Association (Piscataway, NJ), 1994.

Max Notes: I Know Why the Caged Bird Sings, Research and Education Association (Piscataway, NJ), 1994.

(With others) *Focus on Women,* Teacher Created Materials (Westminster, CA), 1995.

Max Notes: The Inferno, Research and Education Association (Piscataway, NJ), 1995.

(With others) *The Best Test Preparation for the ACT Test,* Research and Education Association (Piscataway, NJ), 1995.

(With Katharine Preston) *Discoveries,* Butte Publications (Hillsboro, OR), 1996.

(With others) *The Best Test Preparation for the CLEP Exam,* Research and Education Association (Piscataway, NJ), 1996.

Reading Instruction Essentials, American Press (Boston, MA), 1996, 2nd edition, 1998.

(With others) *SAT I,* Research and Education Association (Piscataway, NJ), 1997.

(With others) *The Best CLEP Review,* Research and Education Association (Piscataway, NJ), 1997.

(With others) *Regents Test for Reading in the Elementary School,* 1997.

Max Notes: Sula, Research and Education Association (Piscataway, NJ), 1998.

The Best Test Preparation for the High School Proficiency Test, Research and Education Association (Piscataway, NJ), 1999.

(Author of revision) *NTE Study Guide,* Research and Education Association (Piscataway, NJ), 1999.

(Author of revision) *LSAT Study Guide,* Research and Education Association (Piscataway, NJ), 1999.

(Editor) *Max Notes: Tar Baby,* Research and Education Association (Piscataway, NJ), 1999.

Florida Teacher Certification Exam Study Guide, Research and Education Association (Piscataway, NJ), 1999.

Children's Literature Essentials, 2000.

The Best Test Preparation for the PRAXIS II, 2000.

(With others) *The Best Test Preparation for the Cooperative Admissions Examination and the High School Placement Test,* 2001.

The Best Teachers' Test Preparation for the PRAXIS PLT Test: K-6, Research and Education Association (Piscataway, NJ), 2002.

(Editor, with others, and contributor) *ACT Assessment: The Very Best Coaching and Study Course for the ACT,* with CD-ROM, Research and Education Association (Piscataway, NJ), 2002.

(Editor, with others, and contributor) *CLEP General Examinations: The Best Review for the College Level Examination Program General Examinations,* Research and Education Association (Piscataway, NJ), 2002.

(Editor, with others, and contributor) *FCTE: The Best Test Preparation for the Florida Teacher Certification Examination,* Research and Education Association (Piscataway, NJ), 2002.

(Editor, with others, and contributor) *GMAT CAT: The Best Test Preparation for the Graduate Management Admission Test, Computer-Adaptive Testing,* with CD-ROM, Research and Education Association (Piscataway, NJ), 2002.

The Best Teachers' Test Preparation for the PRAXIS PLT Test: 5-9, Research and Education Association (Piscataway, NJ), 2002.

The Best Teachers' Test Preparation for the PRAXIS PLT Test: 7-12, Research and Education Association (Piscataway, NJ), 2002.

(Editor, with others, and contributor) *LSAT with CD-ROM: The Very Best Test Preparation for the Law School Admission Test,* Research and Education Association (Piscataway, NJ), 2002.

(Editor, with others, and contributor) *MCAT with CD-ROM: The Very Best Test Preparation for the Medical College Admission Test,* Research and Education Association (Piscataway, NJ), 2002.

The Best Test Preparation for the COOP and HSPT, Research and Education Association (Piscataway, NJ), 2002.

(Editor, with others, and contributor) *PSAT/NMSQT Assessment: The Best Coaching and Study Course for the Preliminary Scholastic Test/National Merit Scholarship Qualifying Test,* Research and Education Association (Piscataway, NJ), 2002.

Author of instructional materials related to historic U.S. battlegrounds. Contributor to books, including *Education and Management of Children and Adolescents with Learning Disabilities,* edited by Sheryl Langer, Macmillan (New York, NY), 1993. Contributor of articles and reviews to periodicals, including *Education World, Hopscotch, South Carolina Women, Journal of School Health, Journal of Reading, Instructor, Reading Teacher,* and *Prim-Aid.* Member of editorial board, *Reading Matters,* 2001, and *Perspectives: Literacy.*

SIDELIGHTS: Anita P. Davis told *CA:* "I write about that which I know—and love! *Real Heroes: Rutherford County Men Who Made the Supreme Sacrifice during World War II* is a biography of 149 men from Rutherford County, North Carolina; it is dedicated to my dad who was killed at the Battle of the Bulge. *North Carolina during the Great Depression: A Documentary Portrait of a Decade* is dedicated to my mother. *Chimney Rock and Rutherford County* is dedicated to my stepfather; it is part of the 'Images of America' series of Arcadia Publishers. *Rutherford County, North Carolina, in World War II* is dedicated to my grandparents, who had sons and sons-in-law in service."

*   *   *

DAVIS, Olivia (Anne Carr) 1922-2004

OBITUARY NOTICE—See index for *CA* sketch: Born December 4, 1922, in Leeds, Yorkshire, England; died of respiratory failure March 10, 2004, in Alexandria, VA. Actress and author. Davis was a novelist and short story writer who also cofounded the Springfield Community Theater. After attending school in London and being privately tutored, she served in British Intelligence as a translator in Oxford. It was during the war that she met her husband, Tom, and they married and settled in Virginia after the war. Davis had been active in theater since acting with the London Theatre Arts Club in the mid-1940s; she also was part of the Anglo-American Little Theatre troop in Frankfurt, Germany. In 1956, she and her husband helped found the Springfield Footlighters, which later became the Springfield Community Theater, in Virginia. Davis, however, is often more recognized as an author of the novels *The Last of the Greeks* (1968) and *The Steps of the Sun* (1972), as well as the short story collection *The Scent of Apples* (1973); many of her stories also appeared in anthologies and magazines, and her fiction has been translated into twenty-six languages.

OBITUARIES AND OTHER SOURCES:

PERIODICALS

Washington Post, March 30, 2004, p. B7.

ONLINE

Springfield Community Theatre, http://sctonline.org/ (April 27, 2004).

*   *   *

DELSOHN, Gary 1952-

PERSONAL: Born April 23, 1952. *Education:* University of Illinois, Springfield, M.A. (public affairs journalism).

ADDRESSES: Agent—c/o Author Mail, Dutton, 375 Hudson St., New York, NY 10014. *E-mail*—gdelsohn@ sacbee.com.

CAREER: Writer. *Denver Post,* Denver, CO, reporter; *Sacramento Bee,* Sacramento, CA, senior writer, 1989—.

AWARDS, HONORS: Knight fellowship, Stanford University; Alicia Patterson Foundation fellowship; Pulitzer Prize nomination.

WRITINGS:

(With Alex English) *The English Language,* Contemporary Books (Chicago, IL), 1986.
The Prosecutors: A Year in the Life of a District Attorney's Office, Dutton (New York, NY), 2003.

Contributor to periodicals and Web sites, including *Denver Post, Rocky Mountain News* (Denver, CO), and *Salon.com.*

SIDELIGHTS: Gary Delsohn, whose first book is a coauthored autobiography of basketball player Alex English, took a year's leave from his job at the *Sacramento Bee* to observe the day-to-day activities within the offices of Sacramento County district attorney Jan Scully. Delsohn had covered criminal justice issues as a journalist, but his year of close observance was an eye-opener, as he observed the inner workings of an office that prosecuted more than 13,000 felonies a year. He concludes that although the system is not perfect, in nearly all cases justice is done.

Delsohn does document an instance where prosecutor Mark Curry won a murder verdict against a man who was later proved innocent when an informant came forward with the truth. He studies the impact of John Matthew O'Mara, the prosecutor in charge of homicide cases. The cases Delsohn describes involve gruesome murders, rapes, and a decades-old Symbionese Liberation Army (SLA) bank robbery/murder case that involved heiress Patty Hearst.

Delsohn spells out the toll that criminal investigations exact on the men and women inside the district attorney's office, describes courtroom dramas that never made the papers, and comments on interdepartmental politics. Writing for *Newsreview.com,* Cosmo Garvin noted that the book "is more true-crime novel than exposé. The closest thing to a bombshell is Delsohn's account of a scandal in the public defender's office involving a defense attorney who allegedly was having a romantic affair with a Sacramento jail inmate accused of a brutal murder." Delsohn recounts how the couple had phone sex, even though they knew all calls in and out of the jail are recorded. "Densely written, the text reads like a mix of early *Law and Order* scripts and old-school urban history," commented a *Kirkus Reviews* critic.

Oregonian reviewer David Reinhard wrote that Delsohn "does not waste the eye-popping access he was granted. . . . This is a gripping insider account—the good, the bad and ugly, the ambitious, the all-too-human, and the gossipy." Reinhard said that "it's tempting to write that Delsohn was fortunate to have fascinating cases to follow in 200 . . . but luck has a habit of finding talented writers, prosecutors, and others who work hard." *Seattle Times* critic Steve Weinberg concluded that *The Prosecutors* is a "remarkable book."

BIOGRAPHICAL AND CRITICAL SOURCES:

PERIODICALS

Kirkus Reviews, May 15, 2003, review of *The Prosecutors: A Year in the Life of a District Attorney's Office,* p. 726.
Library Journal, May 1, 2003, Harry Charles, review of *The Prosecutors,* p. 138.
Newsday, November 20, 1986, Buddy Martin, review of *The English Language,* p. 171.
Oregonian, August 10, 2003, David Reinhard, review of *The Prosecutors,* p. D7.
Publishers Weekly, June 2, 2003, review of *The Prosecutors,* p. 43.
Seattle Times, August 10, 2003, Steve Weinberg, review of *The Prosecutors,* p. K10.

ONLINE

Newsreview.com, http://www.newsreview.com/ (February 26, 2004), Cosmo Garvin, review of *The Prosecutors.**

* * *

den HARTOG, Kristen 1965-

PERSONAL: Born 1965, in Deep River, Ontario, Canada.

ADDRESSES: Home—Toronto, Ontario, Canada. *Agent*—c/o Author Mail, MacAdam/Cage Publishing, 1900 Wazee St., Suite 210, Denver, CO 80202.

CAREER: Author, florist.

WRITINGS:

Water Wings (novel), Knopf Canada (Toronto, Ontario, Canada), 2001, MacAdam/Cage (San Francisco, CA), 2003.
The Perpetual Ending (novel), MacAdam/Cage (San Francisco, CA), 2002.

Work represented in anthologies, including *The Journey Prize Anthology* and *The Turn of the Story: Canadian Short Fiction on the Eve of the Millennium.* Contributor to periodicals, including *Canadian House and Home.*

SIDELIGHTS: Canadian author Kristen den Hartog's *Water Wings* was reviewed by *Quill & Quire* critic Padma Viswanathan, who wrote that this "dark, tender first novel reveals her as a sort of literary younger sister to Alice Munro, plumbing the landscape of small town southern Ontario to turn up stories of sexual discontent and childhood secrets."

The story begins with the return of adult sisters Vivian and Hannah to the place where they grew up and where their mother, the beautiful and seductive Darlene Oelpke, is marrying her second husband, shoe store man Reg Sinclair. Vivian, who is five years older than Hannah, was a teen when their father, Mick, was killed in a boating accident. She had tried to keep his memory alive for her younger sister, whose own recollections are not nearly as clear. Den Hartog uses flashbacks to recall Darlene and Mick's breakup and a cast of characters that includes Darlene's string of boyfriends. Significant to the story is Darlene's sister, Angie, and her only daughter, Wren, a child born with webbed hands and a love of insects who is also sensitive to the similarities between the relationships of humans and the natural world.

Books in Canada reviewer W. P. Kinsella noted that the childhoods of the three narrators are recalled in "long flashbacks," but as to the present "we know far too little." However, Kinsella added that the writing is "strong, and the plethora of detail makes for interesting characterizations." *Booklist* critic Ellen Loughran wrote that the end "of this impressive novel artfully refers back to the book's beginnings, provides no easy answers, and closes the story with hope."

Den Hartog's second novel, *The Perpetual Ending,* is set in present-day Vancouver and is the story of Jane Ingram, whose mirror-image and completely opposite twin, Eugenie, has been long-dead. Jane, the serious twin, now calls herself the "twinless twin," so important was the identity she had shared with her carefree sister. In flashbacks, den Hartog reveals that the twins' parents had a volatile marriage. Their alcoholic father, David, berated their mother, Lucy, and her art, and she finally flees with the girls to Toronto. The girls miss their father, however, and when he comes to take them home with him, the tragedy upon which the story turns occurs: an automobile accident kills Eugenie. Now an adult, Jane, who inherited her mother's gift of storytelling, writes fairy tales that are illustrated by her lover, Simon, who does not realize that the stories hold clues to Jane's past and its unspeakable secrets.

Herizons reviewer Bev Greenberg wrote that not only does *The Perpetual Ending* "celebrate a young woman's resiliency in overcoming a difficult childhood, but it also attests to the transformational power of the imagination as a means of coping." *Globe & Mail* reviewer Fiona Foster called the fables that are interspersed throughout the novel "the really good parts ... the fables in which Jane exorcises her demons. Her heroines are horned, telepathic, lying, hairless, two-left footed freaks.... Den Hartog reveals a massive imagination in these stories-within-stories."

In reviewing the book for *MostlyFiction.com,* Cindy Lynn Speer wrote that *The Perpetual Heartbreak* "might also be a good title for this story. The contrasts between story and confessions, beauty and ugliness, is brilliantly wrought, but there is no joy in this book, only hope that joy may someday come." "Jane's memories accurately reflect the thoughts and fears of a confused and frightened child," commented a *Publishers Weekly* contributor, who added that "the plangent tone of sadness is sustained with grace."

BIOGRAPHICAL AND CRITICAL SOURCES:

PERIODICALS

Booklist, February 1, 2004, Ellen Loughran, review of *Water Wings,* p. 949.

Books in Canada, W. P. Kinsella, review of *Water Wings,* p. 26.

Globe & Mail (Toronto, Ontario, Canada), April 13, 2002, H. J. Kirchhoff, review of *Water Wings;* January 11, 2003, Fiona Foster, review of *The Perpetual Ending.*

Herizons, winter, 2004, Bev Greenberg, review of *The Perpetual Ending,* p. 36.

Kirkus Reviews, January 1, 2003, review of *The Perpetual Ending,* p. 8; December 15, 2003, review of *Water Wings,* p. 1411.

Library Journal, February 1, 2003, Robin Nesbitt, review of *The Perpetual Ending,* p. 114.

Publishers Weekly, February 17, 2003, review of *The Perpetual Ending,* p. 58; February 2, 2004, review of *Water Wings,* p. 59.

Quill & Quire, January, 2001, Padma Viswanathan, review of *Water Wings,* p. 30; December, 2002, Nicholas Dinka, review of *The Perpetual Ending,* p. 25.

Toronto Star, March 25, 2001, review of *Water Wings.*

ONLINE

Curled Up with a Good Book, http://www.curledup. com/ (October 27, 2003), Luan Gaines, review of *The Perpetual Ending.*

MostlyFiction.com, http://mostlyfiction.com/ (July 8, 2003), Cindy Lynn Speer, review of *The Perpetual Ending.*

Rain Taxi Online, http://www.raintaxi.com/ (summer, 2003), Kris Lawson, review of *The Perpetual Ending.**

*   *   *

DERIG, Betty (B.) 1924-

PERSONAL: Born October 17, 1924, in Cambridge, ID; daughter of William M. (a farmer) and Hattie (a teacher and homemaker; maiden name, Lindgren) Carson; married Vincent Francis Derig (in business), September 12, 1948; children: Anna Derig Stark, Paul C., Vincent Francis, Jr. *Ethnicity:* "Anglo." *Education:* Attended Albertson College of Idaho; Washington State University, B.A.; University of Montana, M.A., 1955; further graduate study at Boise State University and Utah State University. *Hobbies and other interests:* Reading, hiking, photography, gardening.

ADDRESSES: Home—P.O. Box 184, Weiser, ID 83672.

CAREER: Treasure Valley Community College, Ontario, OR, instructor in history, 1966-76; photographer, affiliated with Photo Researchers (stock photograph agency). Member of local Friends of the Library.

MEMBER: Garden Writers Association of America, Idaho State Historical Society (member of board of trustees, 1988-94), Pahove-Idaho Native Plant Society, Delta Kappa Gamma.

AWARDS, HONORS: International fellowship, Delta Kappa Gamma; writer of the year award, Idaho Writers League, 1987.

WRITINGS:

(With Florence Sharp) *The Idaho Rambler,* Rambler Press (Weiser, ID), 1982.
Weiser, the Way It Was, Rambler Press (Weiser, ID), 1987.
Roadside History of Idaho, Mountain Press Publishing (Missoula, MT), 1996.
(With Margaret C. Fuller) *Wild Berries of the West,* Mountain Press Publishing (Missoula, MT), 2001.

Contributor of columns and articles to periodicals, including *Idaho Yesterdays, Idaho Heritage, Incredible Idaho,* and *Northwest Travel.*

WORK IN PROGRESS: Researching and photographing "noxious weeds."

SIDELIGHTS: Betty Derig told *CA:* "I get very excited about colorful places and events, whether contemporary or historical, and I want to share the moment. So I am motivated to write. I have been particularly influenced, inspired, and encouraged by the late Bess Foster Smith, an Idaho writer and artist."

BIOGRAPHICAL AND CRITICAL SOURCES:

PERIODICALS

Mother Earth News, October, 2001, review of *Wild Berries of the West,* p. 16.
Wild West, August, 1997, review of *Roadside History of Idaho,* p. 93.

DIJON, Jon
See GRANT, Pete

*   *   *

DONNER, Rebecca

PERSONAL: Born in Vancouver, British Columbia, Canada; immigrated to United States; married; husband's name, Erich. *Education:* University of California—Berkeley, received degree, 1989; Columbia University, M.F.A., 2001.

ADDRESSES: Agent—c/o Author Mail, MacAdam/Cage Publishing, 1900 Wazee St., Ste. 210, Denver, CO 80202. *E-mail*—rjdonner@yahoo.com.

CAREER: Writer. *New Yorker,* New York, NY, intern; KGB Sunday Fiction Series, New York, literary director, 1998-2002.

WRITINGS:

(Editor and author of introduction) *On the Rocks: The KGB Bar Fiction Anthology,* foreword by Denis Woychuk, St. Martin's Griffin (New York, NY), 2002.
Sunset Terrace (novel), MacAdam/Cage (San Francisco, CA), 2003.

SIDELIGHTS: Rebecca Donner is a Canadian-born writer who has lived in Virginia, California, and New York, where she attended Columbia University. For approximately four years, Donner was the literary director of the KGB Fiction Series, held in an East Village room that once was the meeting place for Ukrainian Socialists. Donner's *On the Rocks: The KGB Bar Fiction Anthology* is a collection of writings by authors who had read at the KGB Bar during her tenure. They include Aimee Bender, Mary Gaitskill, Ben Marcus, Joyce Carol Oates, Francine Prose, Judy Budnitz, Elizabeth Tippens, Peter Ho Davies, Dani Shapiro, Philip Gourevitch, and Victoria Redel. Ken Foster, who originated the series in 1994, had previously published *The KGB Bar Reader,* but its success did not guarantee a publisher for Donner, whose new anthology was rejected for nearly a year before it was accepted by St. Martin's Press. *A Publishers Weekly* contributor noted the "originality and artistry" of the stories, which "make for a top-flight anthology, a treat for anyone who wants to sample the best in contemporary fiction."

In an interview for *Smallspiralnotebook.com,* Donner told Felicia C. Sullivan that "in booking authors for the series, I tried to strike a balance between both up-and-coming and established authors, so I thought that the anthology should reflect that balance. I also wanted to feature stories that I felt in some way embodied the spirit of KGB as a place that celebrates risk and invention. Which is not to say that all of the stories in *On the Rocks* are 'experimental'—they are, in fact, very diverse in tone and content and narrative strategy." Donner included "realist" fiction provided by such authors as Gourevitch, Jonathan Lethem, Dale Peck, and Jason Brown, and stories by Marcus and Sylvia Foley "that toy with language and narrative expectation in radical and virtuosic ways." A *Kirkus Reviews* writer called the collection "white lightning in printed form. . . . Enjoyable, terrifying, addictive: the kind of anthology readers deserve."

Donner's debut novel, *Sunset Terrace,* grew out of a short story that was inspired by her childhood. From the age of eight through high school, Donner lived in Los Angeles in subsidized housing occupied primarily by single mothers with children. As she told Ron Hogan in an interview for *Beatrice.com,* "It was a very sad place, but though there was a sense of hopelessness to it, there was a sense of vitality as well."

The story is set in 1983. Elaine Kierson, a college-educated widow whose musician husband took his own life, ekes out an existence as a cook and has moved with her two children eleven times in three years. They are currently living at Sunset Terrace in Los Angeles, where the younger Daisy fits in relatively easily, while nine-year-old Hannah prefers to play with her pet turtle. When Hannah does find friendship, it is with Bridget, a blonde girl her age who shoplifts, sings lewd songs, and whose chain-smoking foster mother, Joan, leaves her with Elaine while she visits her boyfriend. Elaine finds a new relationship with Sam, a divorced man she meets at a singles function, and as she becomes more focused on her new romance, Elaine fails to observe the negative influence Bridget is having on Hannah.

Oregonian reviewer J. David Santen wrote that with *Sunset Terrace* Donner "aptly captures the trauma and confusion of age nine and sets it against an L.A. backdrop fenced with chain-link and crowded highways, covered in broken concrete and sweltering heat and cramped by poverty. There are no postcards from Sunset Terrace." A *Kirkus Reviews* contributor said that "we see through the smoke of Virginia Slims many heartfelt characters, hear through the buzz of their gossip many familiar longings."

BIOGRAPHICAL AND CRITICAL SOURCES:

PERIODICALS

Kirkus Reviews, September 1, 2002, review of *On the Rocks: The KGB Bar Fiction Anthology,* p. 1250; May 1, 2003, review of *Sunset Terrace,* p. 625.
Library Journal, November 1, 2002, Mary Paumier Jones, review of *On the Rocks,* p. 131.
Oregonian, August 3, 2003, J. David Santen, review of *Sunset Terrace,* p. F7.
Publishers Weekly, October 28, 2002, review of *On the Rocks,* p. 49; May 26, 2003, review of *Sunset Terrace,* p. 50.
Times-Picayune, June 8, 2003, Julia Kamysz, review of *Sunset Terrace,* p. 6.

ONLINE

Beatrice.com, http://www.beatrice.com/ (February 27, 2004), Ron Hogan, interview with Rebecca Donner.
Smallspiralnotebook.com, http://www.smallspiralnotebook.com/ (February 27, 2004), Felicia C. Sullivan, interview with Rebecca Donner.

*   *   *

DORKIN, Evan

PERSONAL: Born in Brooklyn, NY. Companion of Sarah Dyer (an artist and writer).

ADDRESSES: Home—New York, NY. *Agent*—c/o Author Mail, SLG Publishing, 577 S. Market St., San Jose, CA 95113. *E-mail*—evandorkin@aol.com.

CAREER: Comic book artist and writer.

AWARDS, HONORS: Eisner Award for Talent Deserving of Wider Recognition, 1995, Best Humor Publication, 1996, for *Milk and Cheese #666,* Best Short Story, 1996, for "The Eltingville Comic-Book, Science-Fiction, Fantasy, and Role-Playing Club in Bring Me the Head of Boba Fett," in *Instant Piano,* issue 3, 1998, for "The Eltingville Comic-Book, Science-Fiction, Fantasy, and Role-Playing Club in The Marathon Men," in *Dork!,* issue 4, 2002, for "The Eltingville Comic-Book, Science-Fiction, Fantasy, and Role-Playing Club in The Intervention," in *Dork!,* issue 9, and Best Writer/Artist, Humor, 2002, for *Dork!;* Harvey Awards, Special Award for Humor, 1996, 2002, and 2003, all for *Dork!* and Best Single Issue or Story, 2001, for *Superman & Batman: World's Funnest.*

WRITINGS:

(Illustrator) Jason Cohen and Michael Krugman, *Generation Ecch!,* Simon & Schuster (New York, NY), 1994.

Superman & Batman: World's Funnest, DC Comics (New York, NY), 2000.

SELF-ILLUSTRATED

Fun with Milk and Cheese (collection of *Milk and Cheese* issues), Slave Labor (San Jose, CA), 1997.

Hectic Planet, Book One: Dim Future (collection of *Hectic Planet* issues), Slave Labor (San Jose, CA), 1998.

Hectic Planet, Book Two: Checkered Past (collection of *Hectic Planet* issues), Slave Labor (San Jose, CA), 1998.

Hectic Planet, Book Three: The Young and the Reckless (collection of *Hectic Planet* issues), Slave Labor (San Jose, CA), 2001.

Dork!: Who's Laughing Now? (collection of *Dork!* issues), Slave Labor (San Jose, CA), 2001.

Circling the Drain (includes stories from *Dork!* issues 7-10 plus new material), Slave Labor (San Jose, CA), 2003.

Adapted Eltingville Club stories for proposed animated television series. Author of scripts, with Sarah Dyer, for animated television series, including *Batman Beyond, Superman,* and *Space Ghost Coast to Coast.* Contributor to various comics titles.

SIDELIGHTS: Evan Dorkin is the creator of iconoclastic comics such as *Milk and Cheese,* about a pair of anthropomorphic dairy products who have gone bad—really bad: they're hostile, destructive, law-breaking drunks—and *Dork!,* an anthology series that features stories of the Eltingville Comic-Book, Science-Fiction, Fantasy, and Role-Playing Club, a group of young people obsessed with these hobbies, allowing Dorkin to satirize comics' fan base.

Dorkin first drew the characters Milk and Cheese as doodles on cocktail napkins and for autograph-seekers at comics conventions, and "had absolutely no idea at the time that the two characters would become somewhat popular and pretty much establish my career," he told an interviewer for the online magazine *X-Entertainment.* He added that he expects to "never stop drawing them in some form or another. . . . I like them too much to abandon them completely." Craig Elliot, in a profile of Dorkin for the Web-based publication *More Goat than Goose,* observed that Dorkin's work "reflects his own thoughts, feelings, and violent fantasies." This is evident, Elliot remarked, in the stories of the Eltingville Club, "four wretched, foul-mouthed geeks . . . driven together more by virtue of their misfit status and common interests than by any obvious affinity for one another." Dorkin, commented *Publishers Weekly* contributor Heidi MacDonald, "is a savage humorist who knows comics geek knowledge inside out."

Dorkin's comics knowledge is also on display in *Superman & Batman: World's Funnest,* a take-off on DC Comics' *World's Finest* title, in which Superman and Batman fought evildoers together. In Dorkin's version, the heroes are killed by two of their longtime nemeses—Mr. Mxyzptlk and Bat-Mite—who then try to outdo each other on a crime spree. They "end up wreaking havoc on both the past and the future, along with all of DC's various alternate universes," reported Bill Radford in the Colorado Springs, Colorado, *Gazette,* adding, "The better you know the DC Universe and all its incarnations, the more you'll be in on the joke."

BIOGRAPHICAL AND CRITICAL SOURCES:

PERIODICALS

Commercial Appeal (Memphis, TN), October 15, 2000, Andrew Smith, "Inimitable Imps Brawl for It All in DC One-Shot," p. H2.

Gazette (Colorado Springs, CO), November 10, 2000, Bill Radford, "'World's Funnest' a Comic Book that Focuses on Mayhem," p. K5611.

Publishers Weekly, December 23, 2002, Heidi Mac-Donald, "Slave Labor Graphics Blows Up," p. 28.

ONLINE

Evan Dorkin/Sarah Dyer Home Page, http://www.houseoffun.com (December 31, 2003).

More Goat than Goose, http://www.moregoatthan goose.com/ (spring, 2000), Craig Elliot, interview with Evan Dorkin.

Punkrocksex.com, http://www.punkrocksex.com/ (August 6, 2003), interview with Evan Dorkin.

Sequential Tart, http://www.sequentialtart.com/ (December 30, 2003), Lee Atchison, interview with Evan Dorkin.

Snard.com, http://www.snard.com/ (August 6, 2003), Paul Freitag, interview with Evan Dorkin.

X-Entertainment, http://www.x-entertainment.com/ (August 12, 2000), interview with Evan Dorkin.*

* * *

DOYLE, Dennis M(ichael) 1952-

PERSONAL: Born April 2, 1952, in Philadelphia, PA; son of Joseph C. and Mary (McVeigh) Doyle; married Patricia M. Dempsey, June 13, 1981; children: Thomas, Michael, Patrick, Christopher. *Education:* LaSalle University, B.A. (English); Ohio University, M.A. (English); Catholic University of America, Ph.D. (religious studies). *Politics:* Democrat. *Religion:* Roman Catholic.

ADDRESSES: Home—362 Marathon Ave., Dayton, OH 45406. *Office*—University of Dayton, Department of Religious Studies, Dayton, OH 45469-1530; fax: 937-229-4330. *E-mail*—Dennis.Doyle@notes.udayton.edu.

CAREER: Educator. University of Dayton, Dayton, OH, professor of religious studies, 1984—.

MEMBER: College Theology Society (chair of research and publications).

WRITINGS:

The Church Emerging from Vatican II: A Popular Approach to Contemporary Catholicism, Twenty-third Publications (Mystic, CT), 1992, revised edition, 2002.

Communion Ecclesiology, Orbis Books (Maryknoll, NY), 2000.

(With son, Patrick Doyle) *Rumors at School,* Paulist Press (Mahwah, NJ), 2000.

Contributor to periodicals, including *Commonweal, National Catholic Reporter,* and *Theological Studies.*

SIDELIGHTS: In *Communion Ecclesiology* educator Dennis M. Doyle examines the modern vision of the Catholic Church. Communion ecclesiology emphasizes "the sacramental and creedal bonds between all Catholic believers," explained Lawrence S. Cunningham in *Commonweal.* In his work, the author "addresses the fact that there are ostensibly competing and/or conflicting understandings of the Church as communion," wrote Mary A. Ehle in a review of Doyle's work for *Theological Studies.* "Doyle seeks a way forward from these conflicts by arguing for the contribution of a communion ecclesiology 'defined more inclusively to embrace a reasonable range of theological approaches.'" Cunningham praised *Communion Ecclesiology,* noting that Doyle "is fair in his exposition of different theological opinions while being open about what he sees as deficiencies."

Doyle told *CA:* "I always wanted to be a writer. I had a major religious conversion in my early twenties. I am intellectually driven. Writing is a large part of what I consider to be my life's work."

BIOGRAPHICAL AND CRITICAL SOURCES:

PERIODICALS

Christian Parenting Today, March, 2001, review of *Rumors at School,* p. 62.

Commonweal, November 9, 2001, Lawrence S. Cunningham, review of *Communion Ecclesiology,* p. 31.

National Catholic Reporter, May 28, 1993, William C. Graham, review of *The Church Emerging from Vatican II: A Popular Approach to Contemporary Catholicism,* p. 40.

Theological Studies, September, 2001, Mary A. Ehle, review of *Communion Ecclesiology,* p. 624.

Du BRUL, Jack B. 1968-

PERSONAL: Born October 15, 1968, in Burlington, VT; married, 2001; wife's name, Debbie. *Education:* George Washington University, B.A. (international relations), 1990.

ADDRESSES: Agent—c/o Author Mail, Onyx Books, Penguin Group, 375 Hudson St., New York, NY 10014. *E-mail*—jack@jackdubrul.com.

CAREER: Writer. Worked variously as a bartender and carpenter.

WRITINGS:

"PHILIP MERCER" SERIES

Vulcan's Forge, Forge (New York, NY), 1998.
Charon's Landing, Forge (New York, NY), 1999.
The Medusa Stone, Onyx (New York, NY), 2000.
Pandora's Curse, Onyx (New York, NY), 2001.
River of Ruin, Onyx (New York, NY), 2002.

SIDELIGHTS: Vermont native Jack B. Du Brul attended boarding school in Connecticut before earning a degree at George Washington University. He moved to Florida after graduation, where he began to write *Vulcan's Forge,* the novel that introduced his ongoing character, geologist Philip Mercer. Du Brul's novels are often set in locations he himself has visited. The plot of this debut novel revolves around the creation of a small volcano below the South Pacific, formed after a Soviet nuclear blast that also forged a new and very valuable type of metal. Decades later, as the submerged island rises to the surface, a plan is formed by a Soviet agent to convince Hawaiians to secede from the union, in the event it breaks through among the islands.

Additional works in the series feature Mercer's exploits around the globe. Figuring in the plot of *Charon's Landing* are a Middle Eastern oil minister, a former KGB scientist, and ecoterrorists involved in international espionage connected with the opening of the oil fields in the Arctic National Refuge. When they are both kidnapped, Mercer, a mining engineer, becomes involved with oil heiress Aggie Johnston. In

The Medusa Stone, Mercer is on a quest to save an old friend who has been kidnapped by Israeli terrorists. His search leads him to the poor African island of Eritrea where the legendary diamond mine of King Solomon may be located. Mercer is charged with saving the world in *Pandora's Curse,* when he uncovers an abandoned U.S. Army base buried under the ice of Greenland and discovers a body still hot with radiation. Clues lead Mercer to the Pandora Project, a Nazi scheme to sell a lethal substance to the highest bidder and which is contained in solid gold boxes made from looted treasure.

The Panama Canal is threatened in *River of Ruin,* and Mercer must subvert a plan by the Chinese to bomb it and pressure the United States into allowing a Chinese takeover of Taiwan. As in all of the Mercer novels, there is a love interest, this time U.S. Army officer Lauren Vanik. And as in his other stories, this one is packed with action, as well as advanced technology. A *Publishers Weekly* contributor wrote that "It's evident at the outset that Mercer and his team will come out on top, but the fun is watching Du Brul untangle his own skillfully woven knots."

BIOGRAPHICAL AND CRITICAL SOURCES:

PERIODICALS

Publishers Weekly, December 8, 1997, review of *Vulcan's Forge,* p. 53; April 12, 1999, review of *Charon's Landing,* p. 53; April 17, 2000, review of *The Medusa Stone,* p. 58; August 27, 2001, review of *Pandora's Curse,* p. 62; October 28, 2002, review of *River of Ruin,* p. 56.

ONLINE

Jack Du Brul Fan Site, http://www.geocities.com/mynamejean/ (March, 2000), interview with Du Brul; (July, 2001), interview with Du Brul.
Jack Du Brul Home Page, http://www.jackdubrul.com (May 14, 2003).*

*   *   *

DUFFY, Peter 1969-

PERSONAL: Born 1969, in Syracuse, NY; *Education:* University of Pittsburgh, received degree.

ADDRESSES: Agent—c/o Author Mail, HarperCollins, 10 East 53rd St., 7th Fl., New York, NY 10022.

CAREER: Journalist.

WRITINGS:

The Bielski Brothers: The True Story of Three Men Who Defied the Nazis, Saved 1,200 Jews, and Built a Village in the Forest, HarperCollins (New York, NY), 2003, published in England as *Brothers in Arms,* Century, 2003.

Contributor to periodicals, including the *New York Times, New York Post, Newsday,* the London *Telegraph,* and *Village Voice.*

SIDELIGHTS: Freelance journalist Peter Duffy spent three years researching and writing *The Bielski Brothers: The True Story of Three Men Who Defied the Nazis, Saved 1,200 Jews, and Built a Village in the Forest* after seeing a reference to "Forest Jews" while surfing the net. He first wrote of the brothers in an article for the *New York Times.* The Bielski brothers, Tuvia, Zus, and Asael, were Jewish millers living in Stankevich, a village near the provincial capital of Novogrudek, a Polish town of approximately six thousand Jews in an area that is part of Belarus. They were not readily accepted by the more urban Jewish families, nor did they fit in with the surrounding peasant population. The family survived by milling grain into flour and meal.

When World War II erupted, Novogrudek came under Soviet rule, and in 1941 the Nazis invaded. Beginning in December of that year, they carried out four campaigns against the Jews, during which five thousand people were killed, including the Bielskis' parents. The brothers fled to the thick forest with their relatives, determined to kill as many Nazis as possible. But under Tuvia's leadership they also reached out to rescue the survivors of the mobile units dispersed to kill Jews. Eventually, the Nazis killed hundreds of thousands, with the cooperation of Poles, Ukrainians, and Lithuanians.

In 1943, the Nazis launched Operation Hermann, the purpose of which was to find and eradicate the forest Jews. As trees were flattened by heavy machinery, the brothers led the people deeper into the woods and into the waters of a swamp, rendering them undetectable to the planes flying overhead. The Bielskis then created a town in eastern Poland that contained a school, synagogue, theater, infirmary, shops for tradesmen, and even a cemetery and jail, which harbored more than one thousand people. Duffy notes that the brothers were not saints. They drank, caroused, and sometimes abused their power. Toward the end, Tuvia killed another Jew in anger.

Michael Skakun reviewed the book for *Jewishpress. com,* noting that "although Duffy conveys the thrill and travail of their extraordinary act of defiance, he is not loath to discuss the compromises and peccadilloes, even the acts of moral outrage, the Bielskis occasionally committed. He gives us the full chiaroscuro effect, painting both the hues of light and shadow that constitute a picture of heroism in extremis." A *Publishers Weekly* contributor wrote that *The Bielski Brothers* "is a story about heroes, and Duffy does a masterful job telling it." And *Tribune Books* writer Rebecca Skloot called this "a haunting book. Along with the brothers' story, Duffy traces the torture and extermination of Jews—a familiar tale that never loses its power—in vivid detail.... Duffy never judges whether the Nazis and their supporters deserved the brutality they experienced at the hands of the Bielski clan, which is a good thing. Readers can decide for themselves."

Unlike other heroes of the Holocaust, the names of the Bielski brothers were lost in history. Asael died in combat, but the remaining two emigrated to Brooklyn. Tuvia died in 1987 and Zus in 1995. Their younger brother, Aron, who had been a scout as a child in the forest, moved to Florida. Survivors of the brothers have accompanied Duffy on tours to promote the book, which has been translated into multiple languages.

BIOGRAPHICAL AND CRITICAL SOURCES:

PERIODICALS

Economist, July 5, 2003, review of *The Bielski Brothers: The True Story of Three Men Who Defied the Nazis, Saved 1,200 Jews, and Built a Village in the Forest,* p. 74.
Kirkus Reviews, May 1, 2003, review of *The Bielski Brothers,* p. 654.

Library Journal, June 1, 2003, Frederic Krome, review of *The Bielski Brothers,* p. 138.

New York Times Book Review, October 5, 2003, Raye Snover, review of *The Bielski Brothers,* p. 24.

Publishers Weekly, May 26, 2003, review of *The Bielski Brothers,* p. 60.

Spectator, August 2, 2003, Carole Angier, review of *Brothers in Arms,* p. 34.

Tribune Books (Chicago, IL), August 24, 2003, Rebecca Skloot, review of *The Bielski Brothers,* p. 3.

ONLINE

Jewishpress.com, http://www.jewishpress.com/ (August 13, 2003), Michael Skakun, review of *The Bielski Brothers.*

*   *   *

DUNCAN, Christine H.

PERSONAL: Born in Salem, NJ; daughter of Joseph and Mildred Hassler; married Gerald Duncan (a steel detailer); children: Melissa, Devin, Gerald, Jr., Russell (stepson). *Education:* Attended University of Florida, 1973-75, San Jose State University, 1976, and Humboldt State University, c. 1978. *Religion:* Christian.

ADDRESSES: Agent—c/o Author Mail, Treble Heart Books, 1284 Overlook Dr., Sierra Vista, AZ 85635-5512. *E-mail*—CHDuncan100@cs.com.

CAREER: Writer.

MEMBER: Sisters in Crime, Electronically Published Internet Connection, Rocky Mountain Fiction Writers.

WRITINGS:

Safe Beginnings (mystery novel), Treble Heart Books (Sierra Vista, AZ), 2002.

WORK IN PROGRESS: Safe House and *Safe Reunion,* additional novels in a mystery series featuring the character Kaye Berreano.

SIDELIGHTS: Christine H. Duncan told *CA:* "I write the Kaye Berreano mystery series because I want to make a statement about domestic violence. I believe that it affects so very many lives, yet as a society we don't really want to talk about it. A lot of people prefer to think it doesn't happen to people like them, and many of us seem to think that the whole problem of domestic violence is covered by having laws against it and battered women's shelters.

"In these books I make an effort to show how stretched the resources of the shelters are. I also make an attempt to show how far short the law can fall from protecting these women.

"Yet I purposely made this a cozy mystery series because I didn't want people to say they couldn't read it because it was too dark, or too graphic. Kaye is a counselor who goes home to her own life and problems, providing a contrast to the shelter. Domestic violence is, unfortunately, a part of life, and I wanted the setting to reflect that."

*   *   *

DYCHTWALD, Maddy Kent 1952-

PERSONAL: Born February 13, 1952, in Newark, NJ; daughter of Stanley and Sally Susan (Gordet) Fusco; married Kenneth Mark Dychtwald (a consultant), November 24, 1983; children: Casey, Zakary. *Education:* New York University, B.A. (magna cum laude), 1974.

ADDRESSES: Office—Age Wave, Inc., 2000 Powell St., Ste. 1680, Emeryville, CA 94608-1861; fax: 925-254-1513. *E-mail*—mdychtwald@maddydychtwald.com.

CAREER: Consultant and speaker. Actress, 1974-83; Dychtwald & Associates (marketing consultants), Emeryville, CA, director of special projects, 1983-86; Age Wave, Inc. (generational marketing consultants), Emeryville, cofounder (with husband), 1986—, director of communications, 1986, vice president of communications, 1987-90, senior vice president of communications, 1990-95, business development.

MEMBER: International Association of Business Communicators, National Association of Female Executives, Screen Actors Guild, American Federation of Television and Radio Actors, American Film Institute.

WRITINGS:

Cycles: How We Will Live, Work, and Buy, Free Press (New York, NY), 2003.

Contributor to journals, including *Journal of Consumer Marketing.*

WORK IN PROGRESS: *Power Trends: Boomer Impact on the New Millennium Generation.*

SIDELIGHTS: Maddy Kent Dychtwald, an authority on generational marketing, cofounded Age Wave with her husband Ken, whose book of the same title was published in 1989. Dychtwald is a frequent speaker before corporations and charts the trends that help businesses plan their marketing campaigns.

Dychtwald noted in a *Journal of Consumer Marketing* article that "we see a tremendous growth in the over-fifty-five population." She also pointed out a shrinking younger population. This is due to the fact that baby boomers had fewer children; more than one fourth had no children, and another fourth had only one. "In a real reversal of the status quo, there are now more Americans over the age of sixty-five than teenagers," Dychtwald stated. From a marketing standpoint, this means that the age group typically targeted by advertising, those from eighteen to thirty-four, is shrinking, while the group of affluent adults over fifty is expanding. Businesses need to be able to see this change of market.

Dychtwald emphasizes the importance of recognizing the needs of older adults and suggests that more products and services must be created to meet them. At the same time, she projects that the boomer generation won't even consider themselves to be seniors until they are about eighty, much older than the previous generations. They will be more active and healthy, often working well beyond traditional retirement age, and will have the largest disposable income of any group, which they will enjoy spending on themselves and their grandchildren.

She felt gerontophobia is most destructive "in the media, which is so youth-obsessed, in marketing, which often portrays old people negatively, and in the workplace, where many young and usually well-meaning managers hold a variety of misconceptions about productivity and aging." Dychtwald said that age prejudice is not fact-based, and named a number of high achievers of later years, including Johann Wolfgang von Goethe, who finished *Faust* after the age of eighty, and Michelangelo Buonarrati, who was appointed chief architect of St. Peter's Cathedral in Rome when he was seventy-one.

In Dychtwald's *Cycles: How We Will Live, Work, and Buy,* she says that people are now living their lives according to cycles, rather than age. These cycles include people remarrying, having children, changing careers, and returning to work at much later ages than have previous generations. A *Publishers Weekly* reviewer believed that many of her observations have been well-known for many years, rendering the book "already behind the times itself."

Cecil Johnson reviewed *Cycles* for *SiliconValley.com,* saying that "the influence of baby boomers in pioneering lifestyle changes is one of the dominant themes of Dychtwald's treatise. She traces their effect upon society from youth through adulthood and to approaching senior citizenship. . . . It is that cyclic, as opposed to linear, approach to living that Dychtwald perceives to be the new wave."

BIOGRAPHICAL AND CRITICAL SOURCES:

PERIODICALS

Discount Store News, June 5, 1995, "A Generation Comes of Age," p. 22.
Journal of Consumer Marketing, fall-winter, 1997, Maddy Kent Dychtwald, "Marketplace 2000: Riding the Wave of Population Change," pp. 271-275.
Publishers Weekly, October 2, 2002, review of *Cycles: How We Will Live, Work, and Buy.*

ONLINE

Maddy Dychtwald Home Page, http://www.maddy dychtwald.com (July 1, 2003).
SiliconValley.com, http://www.siliconvalley.com/ (May 4, 2003), Cecil Johnson, review of *Cycles.**

E

EAKINS, Patricia 1942-

PERSONAL: Born November 16, 1942, in Philadelphia, PA; daughter of Jesse Walter (an electrical engineer and business owner) and Stena Marie (a teacher; maiden name, Osbeck) Eakins; married Peter T. Rodgers (an advertising copywriter and poet), 1966 (divorced, 1969); married Peter Martin (a business owner), April 17, 1982. *Education:* Wellesley College, B.A., 1964; Goddard College, M.F.A., 1977. *Politics:* "New Abolitionist."

ADDRESSES: Home and office—1200 Broadway, Apt. 4C, New York, NY 10001; fax: 973-593-9235. *Agent*—Martha Millard, 293 Greenwood Ave., Florham Park, NJ 07932. *E-mail*—marmillink@aol.com.

CAREER: Freelance writer, editor, and book coach, 1974—; New York Institute of Technology, instructor, 1979-86, adjunct assistant professor, 1986—; Trinity College, Hartford, CT, visiting assistant professor, 1990-94; New School, New York, NY, instructor, 1992-97. Catskill Reading Society, guest readings coordinator, 1985—.

MEMBER: Authors' Guild, National Writers Union, PEN.

AWARDS, HONORS: Fiction fellowship, Creative Artists Program Service (CAPS), New York, 1979; National Endowment for the Arts fellow, 1982, 1987; Charles Angoff Award, *Literary Review,* Fairleigh-Dickinson University, 1986-87; New York Foundation for the Arts fellowship, 1991; Woodstock Guild writer-in-residence, 1992; Agha Khan Prize for fiction, *Paris Review,* 1996, for excerpt from *The Marvelous Adventures of Pierre Baptiste;* Capricorn fiction award, *Writer's Voice,* West Side YMCA, New York, NY, 1997, for *The Marvelous Adventures of Pierre Baptiste;* New York University Press Prize for fiction, 1998, for *The Marvelous Adventures of Pierre Baptiste;* John Gardner fellow in fiction, Bread Loaf writers' conference, 1999.

WRITINGS:

Oono (chapbook), 1982.
The Hungry Girls and Other Stories, illustrated by Judy Sohigian, Cadmus Editions (San Francisco, CA), 1988.
The Marvelous Adventures of Pierre Baptiste: Father and Mother, First and Last (novel), New York University Press (New York, NY), 1999.
Writing for Interior Design, Fairchild Publications (New York, NY), 2004.

American Letters and Commentary, contributing editor, 1999—; *Frigate: A Transverse Review of Books,* editor-in-chief, 2000—. Contributor to periodicals, including *New American Fiction, Race Traitor, Iowa Review, Storia, Paris Review, Parnassus, Conjunctions,* and *Fiction International,* and to collections and anthologies, including *Vital Lines: Contemporary Fiction about Medicine,* edited by Jon Mukand, Ballantine (New York, NY), 1991, and *Transgressions: The Iowa Anthology of Innovative Fiction,* edited by Lee Montgomery and others, University of Iowa Press, 1994.

ADAPTATIONS: The Hungry Girls and Other Stories was adapted for theater by Collision Theory, New York, 1997.

WORK IN PROGRESS: Blood Sisters, a novel; *Black Food: Stories about Bears; Trace Memory: Texts by Patricia Eakins for the Performance Piece by Elizabeth Austin; Fertility Zone and Other Stories; Small Worlds: Prose Poems; Manifesto of a Dead Daughter: Essays and Polemics.*

SIDELIGHTS: Patricia Eakins is a New York City-based award-winning writer whose first book, *The Hungry Girls and Other Stories* recalls the medieval literary form, the bestiary, in that it is a collection of fables that feature unusual, often fantastical, creatures. Eakins's Neones eat radiation but die easily of fright; the Djitsis are serpents that can race in and out of every orifice of a human body in mere seconds, leaving their skins behind. Jonathan Baumbach wrote in the *New York Times Book Review* that Eakins's territory "is in that tangled thicket of the imagination somewhere between Borges and Burroughs, between the fairy tales of Grimm and the magic realism of the South Americans." Baumbach concluded by calling *The Hungry Girls* "a work of imaginative brilliance, a considerable achievement in modest disguise."

The tales are set in diverse time periods and settings, including the Japanese courts and nineteenth-century France. In one story, a mythological forest creature called a banda is charged with the task of warning children to stay off the path to the witch's house. But the banda's tongue is made of velvet, and it has no vocal chords. The children hear only soft whispers that sound like the rustling of leaves.

American Book Review contributor Peter Bricklebank wrote that Eakins's "fanatastic creatures are propelled by the primeval facts of life: finding food, negotiating sex, giving birth, avoiding death, and, if possible, in the case of many of the human characters, turning a small and not insubstantial profit." Bricklebank compared Eakins's work to that of Harold Jaffe, Kathy Acker, and William Burroughs, but added that it is "very much Eakins's own, imbued with an ecological 'fitness' that is one of the many strengths of this collection. The obsession to ingest stretches beyond mere food-chain hierarchies; Nature's checks and balances here extend right into the fairy tale, keeping even good and evil in harmony."

The "girls" of the title are dirt eaters, successive generations of which have grown larger, so that the current girls are as big as houses, and each has at least one young man residing inside her body, with one accompanied by horses and a coach. On the other end of the scale, in the story "Forrago," are very small, rat-like creatures with razor-sharp teeth that inhabit "alleys too dark and narrow even for stand-up whores and small-time thieves." Sex for them and other of Eakins's creatures, means danger. In mating, the Forrago males become stuck, providing food for their partners, who eat their bodies until their male organ finally falls out, only to also be eaten. Ooni males, afraid to enter the bodies of females, which are protected by teeth, instead send a child into the womb with their seed. The females die as soon as they give birth.

"But these are not merely fables of faraway lands and times, of beasts with confounding bodies, of grotesqueries that would perhaps have intrigued the medieval mind but hardly a modern consciousness," continued Bricklebank. "The beasts here are farcical, improbable, ridiculous, yet perfectly adapted and self-sufficient creatures. . . . I give testament to Eakins's ability to bring such impossible beings to life. There's a totality to these creatures and their habits that makes them arresting beyond their inherent freakishness."

Eakins's first novel, *The Marvelous Adventures of Pierre Baptiste: Father and Mother, First and Last,* set in the eighteenth century, is a slave narrative. *Booklist*'s Michele Leber wrote that "the story is told in the style and language of the time and is studded with tales seemingly grounded in legend and myth." Pierre Baptiste is a black slave, who at the age of ten, is sent to work for the master of a Caribbean sugar plantation. He becomes the personal servant of Dufay, assisting him in his work as an amateur naturalist. Dufay has the boy help him with his classification of flora and fauna and allows him to learn to read and write so that he may be even more helpful. Pierre has access to Dufay's vast library and studies on his own and can soon converse at an intellectual level equal to that of Dufay and his acquaintances.

Pierre marries the cook, a disfigured but loving woman with magical powers who is unable to bear children and will, therefore, produce no more slaves. He is friendly to the master's wife, but when she asks for more than he is willing to give, she accuses him of rape. He hops aboard a rum barrel, upon which he writes the address of his hero, naturalist Buffon, and sets out to sea, intent on reaching France. Instead, he washes up on an island where he nurses an injured sea creature back to health, and she repays him by catching fish that she vomits into his mouth. In time, Pierre discovers that he is pregnant and carries to term four "philosofish," that he then begins to educate. At peace, he spends his days with his children and continues writing a history of his life until Dufay's son is shipwrecked on the island, carrying surprising news from the plantation. A *Publishers Weekly* critic called the novel "startlingly creative, memorable work."

Michael Perkins wrote in the *Woodstock Times* that Eakins "is a breathtakingly audacious writer dedicated to unveiling the marvelous, one whose formidable gifts of invention and lyric phrasing are more than commensurate with her boldness. In her first book . . . she dared to create new worlds and new species in language calm, precise, and genuinely poetic: the voice of the inspired fabulist." Of *The Marvelous Adventures of Pierre Baptiste*, Perkins said that "it is difficult to describe a work of such originality. Its strangeness is haunting. Its beauty is undeniable. It is a triumph."

BIOGRAPHICAL AND CRITICAL SOURCES:

PERIODICALS

American Book Review, November, 1989, Peter Bricklebank, review of *The Hungry Girls and Other Stories,* p. 20.
Booklist, May 15, 1999, Michele Leber, review of *The Marvelous Adventures of Pierre Baptiste: Father and Mother, First and Last,* p. 1667.
Kirkus Reviews, March 15, 1999, review of *The Marvelous Adventures of Pierre Baptiste.*
Library Journal, December 15, 1982, review of *Oono,* p. 2306.
New York Times Book Review, February 5, 1989, Jonathan Baumbach, review of *The Hungry Girls and Other Stories,* p. 36; June 27, 1999, Elizabeth Judd, review of *The Marvelous Adventures of Pierre Baptiste,* p. 24.
Publishers Weekly, March 22, 1999, review of *The Marvelous Adventures of Pierre Baptiste,* p. 70.

Woodstock Times, June 17, 1999, Michael Perkins, review of *The Marvelous Adventures of Pierre Baptiste,* p. 2.

ONLINE

Patricia Eakins Home Page, http://www.fabulara.com (December 23, 2003).*

                    *   *   *

EDLOW, Jonathan A. 1952-

PERSONAL: Born December 26, 1952, in MA. *Education:* University of Maryland School of Medicine, graduated 1978.

ADDRESSES: Agent—c/o Author Mail, Yale University Press, P.O. Box 209040, New Haven, CT 06520-9040.

CAREER: Physician. Practicing emergency medicine, 1981—; Beth Israel Deaconess Hospital, Boston, MA, vice chair of the department of emergency medicine; Harvard Medical School, Boston, assistant professor of medicine.

MEMBER: American College of Emergency Physicians.

WRITINGS:

Bull's-Eye: Unraveling the Medical Mystery of Lyme Disease, Yale University Press (New Haven, CT), 2003.

Contributor of medical detective stories to periodicals, including *Ladies' Home Journal* and *Boston.*

SIDELIGHTS: Jonathan A. Edlow, who specializes in emergency medicine, has a particular interest in Lyme disease and other tick-borne illnesses. His *Bull's-Eye: Unraveling the Medical Mystery of Lyme Disease* is a study of the disease first named in Lyme, Connecticut, in the mid 1970s. Two housewives, Judith Mensch and Polly Murray, who observed similar symptoms among members of their families and others in the community, began to document the arthritis, rashes, swelling, and fatigue that are consistent with Lyme. They mapped cases and symptoms without realizing that they were using epidemiological methods, and Murray wrote about their findings in her 1996 book, *The Widening Circle.* As the newly named disease was studied, it became apparent that this was the same disease that had surfaced in other parts of the country and the world over many years.

A Milwaukee dermatologist who had read in a 1958 medical journal of the meningitis and rash caused by a 1930 tick bite in Sweden wrote a paper years later on an American case. The connection was made when U.S. Navy doctors discovered cases at the Groton, Connecticut, submarine base. They, in turn, published their findings in 1976.

Lyme disease is the result of a cycle between deer, ticks, and people. The tick passes a bacterium to humans through its bite. The causative agent of Lyme disease, a spirochete identified in 1982, was later named *Borrelia burgdorferi.* In his book, Edlow studies the history of Lyme disease, the tests used in an attempt to determine its presence, and various treatments. Kenneth R. Dardick wrote in the *Journal of the American Medical Association* that Edlow "has done a masterful job of deconstructing Lyme disease from its caricatured 'bull's-eye' rash to an understanding of the ecology of the complex human-vector-agent relationship."

The author also includes portraits of scientists who have been instrumental in the identification and study of tick-borne diseases, including German doctor Robert Koch, who in the late 1800s became one of the earliest microbiologists after his wife gave him a microscope as a gift. In addition to studying tick-borne diseases, he developed methods of culturing anthrax and tuberculosis. The diagnosis and treatment of Lyme disease remain inexact. Symptoms such as depression and fatigue are often hard to assign to the disease, and some but not all medical practitioners feel that treatment should include long-term antibiotic use. *New York Times Book Review* contributor Andrew C. Revkin felt that "the best thing of all about *Bull's-Eye* is that it lays out the unknowns along with the knowns, the mainstream view along with alternative readings, and thus reveals science for what it is: a perpetual, and admirable, work in progress."

Booklist critic Donna Chavez felt that Edlow's study, in addition to being a source for information on Lyme disease, is also "important for the light it sheds on the nature of scientific inquiry." *New England Journal of Medicine* reviewer Raymond Dattwyler, who called the book "beautifully written," noted that Edlow gives full credit to all who contributed to the understanding and treatment of Lyme disease, including nineteenth-century physicians, the Connecticut mothers, the U.S. Navy physicians, Centers for Disease control staff, the Connecticut Department of Public Health, and Yale University scientists who conducted extensive testing and experimentation. Dattwyler concluded that the book "is written in a clear, readable style that should appeal to both medical professionals and members of the general public."

BIOGRAPHICAL AND CRITICAL SOURCES:

PERIODICALS

Booklist, April 15, 2003, Donna Chavez, review of *Bull's-Eye: Unraveling the Medical Mystery of Lyme Disease,* p. 1437.

Journal of the American Medical Association, December 10, 2003, Kenneth R. Dardick, review of *Bull's-Eye.*

Library Journal, May 1, 2003, Kathy Arsenault, review of *Bull's-Eye.*

New England Journal of Medicine, September 4, 2003, Raymond Dattwyler, review of *Bull's-Eye,* p. 1008.

New York Times Book Review, July 27, 2003, Andrew C. Revkin, review of *Bull's-Eye,* p. 18.*

* * *

EISENBERG, John S. 1956-

PERSONAL: Born September 24, 1956, in Dallas, TX; married Mary Wynne; children: Anna, Wick. *Education:* University of Pennsylvania, B.A. (English), 1979.

ADDRESSES: Agent—c/o Author Mail, Warner Books, 1271 Avenue of the Americas, New York, NY 10020. *E-mail*—John.Eisenberg@baltsun.com; johneberg@home.com.

CAREER: Sportswriter, author. *Baltimore Sun,* Baltimore, MD, sportswriter.

AWARDS, HONORS: Recipient of more than twenty awards, including Sportswriter of the Year, National Society of Sportswriters and Broadcasters.

WRITINGS:

The Longest Shot: Lil E. Tee and the Kentucky Derby, University of Kentucky Press (Lexington, KY), 1996.

Cotton Bowl Days: Growing Up with Dallas and the Cowboys in the 1960s, Simon & Schuster (New York, NY), 1997.

From 33rd Street to Camden Yards: An Oral History of the Baltimore Orioles, Contemporary Books (Lincolnwood, IL), 2001.

Native Dancer: The Grey Ghost: Hero of a Golden Age, Warner Books (New York, NY), 2003.

SIDELIGHTS: John S. Eisenberg has had a long career as a sportswriter with the *Baltimore Sun,* during which time he has written columns and features and covered a range of sporting events. These include the Super Bowl, World Series, Wimbledon, Final Four, Masters, Kentucky Derby, Preakness, Belmont, World Cup, and the Olympics in several countries.

Eisenberg's first book, *The Longest Shot: Lil E. Tee and the Kentucky Derby,* is a study of one of the most extraordinary events in horse racing history: the winning of the 1992 Kentucky Derby run for the roses by an unknown horse named Lil E. Tee, named Lil for his original owner, Lyle Letterman, and E. Tee because as a colt he had an unusual gait and often bellowed for his mother. The horse with the unimpressive pedigree was born on a Pennsylvania farm that raised trotting horses, and he came into the world weak and unable to nurse. Without the benefit of his mother's colostrum, he developed an immune deficiency and was barely saved with injections of antibody-rich blood. He later developed colic and survived stomach surgery that should have meant the end of his career. He was sold several times for sums as low as three thousand dollars and lived in seven states before he turned two.

The plucky horse's future changed under the supervision of owner Cal Partee, trainer Lynn Whiting, and jockey Pat Day. They sensed the potential in the proud animal and found that he possessed lungs and a heart about one third larger than normal. He won the Jim Beam Stakes and finished second in the Arkansas Derby. On the momentous day at Churchill Downs, he faced seventeen other horses, including favorite Arazi, who was compared to the legendary Secretariat, and so he became the seventeen-to-one long shot. But on that Saturday in May, Lil E. Tee showed his stuff and became the one horse out of the 48,000 foals born in 1989 to go on to become one of the approximately one hundred horses to have won the Derby. In all, he ran thirteen races, seven of which he won. In the first year after his win, the horse impregnated fifty mares at $7,500 each, the beginning of his profitable future on a stud farm in Kentucky. Frank Kooistra reviewed *The Longest Shot* in *Aethlon,* calling it "an amazing story." And *Library Journal* contributor David Van de Streek called Eisenberg's account "well-written, enjoyable to read, and guaranteed to move many readers."

Eisenberg's memoir, *Cotton Bowl Days: Growing Up with Dallas and the Cowboys in the 1960s,* is a history that goes back to the National Football League (NFL) franchise's first decade. The author recalls watching games with his father and the Cowboys' first winning year, in 1966, when Eisenberg was ten. For the book, he interviewed many of the stars of the 1960s and 1970s, including Herb Adderley, Bob Lilly, and Don Perkins, and comments on realities he did not come to understand until he was an adult, such as early racism, low salaries, and the character of coach Tom Landry. He notes, too, how the assassination of President John F. Kennedy changed the city in which he was killed. *Booklist* reviewer Wes Lukowsky called the book "a compelling, thoughtful effort that will intrigue even those fans with a marginal interest in the NFL."

Eisenberg turned from football to baseball with *From 33rd Street to Camden Yards: An Oral History of the Baltimore Orioles,* called a "highly readable and anecdotal volume" by *Library Journal* writers Paul Kaplan and Morey Berger. The seven sections of the book are organized chronologically from November 1953, when the St. Louis Browns were moved to Baltimore, to 2000. The book contains interviews with nearly one hundred players, club owners, executives, and broadcasters. Eisenberg moved to Baltimore in

1984, at the end of the Orioles' glory days, but he captures them by including nearly every living figure connected with the club's history.

Native Dancer: The Grey Ghost: Hero of a Golden Age is not only the story of a great horse but also an explanation of how the sport of horse racing drew viewers to their television sets during the early days of the medium. Native Dancer was born in 1950 in the stables of millionaire Alfred Gwynne Vanderbilt. His sire and mare had strong bloodlines, and the young colt was immediately impressive. His color made him stand out from the pack of darker horses, particularly on the black-and-white television screen where he was the star. Native Dancer landed on the cover of *Time* and was twice named Horse of the Year. He won twenty-one of his twenty-two races, but the race he lost was a heartbreaker. It was the 1953 Kentucky Derby, and "Eisenberg gives this loss—by mere inches—all the drama it must have had in its day," wrote *MostlyFiction.com* reviewer Mary Whipple. "Having thoroughly researched every conceivable aspect of his story, Eisenberg writes with the journalistic brio of a true lover of horse racing, and makes the horse, his races, and the people surrounding him live again."

Eisenberg also introduces the reader to jockey Eric Guerin, a blacksmith's son who was raised in rural Louisiana, trainer Bill Winfrey, a Texas native who learned his skills during the Depression, black groom Lester Murray, and Vanderbilt, the millionaire who chose horse racing over business and politics. Vanderbilt's son, Alfred G. Vanderbilt, who was born the same year as Native Dancer, reviewed the book in the *New York Times*. He noted the accomplishments of the descendants of the horse and the fact that, as of his writing, they had "won that last six Kentucky Derbies in a row and eight of the last nine." For example, Funny Cide, winner of the 2003 Kentucky Derby, is a descendant of Native Dancer, but so were the other fifteen entries that year. Vanderbilt noted that like other horses of his time, Native Dancer averaged more than one race a week; horses are now typically rested for three weeks between races.

Vanderbilt listed the events that led to Native Dancer's loss by a head, reflecting that "if all we gauged of the greatness of horses was a performance in one race—or even in the three great races of the Triple Crown—we would miss the most valuable lesson. They are what we would like to be: beautiful and fast and free."

BIOGRAPHICAL AND CRITICAL SOURCES:

BOOKS

Eisenberg, John S., *Cotton Bowl Days: Growing Up with Dallas and the Cowboys in the 1960s,* Simon & Schuster (New York, NY), 1997.

PERIODICALS

AB Bookman's Weekly, June 17, 1996, review of *The Longest Shot: Lil E. Tee and the Kentucky Derby,* pp. 2408-2410.
Aethlon, fall, 1998, Frank Kooistra, review of *The Longest Shot,* pp. 217-218.
Booklist, March 15, 1996, Dennis Dodge, review of *The Longest Shot,* p. 1234; September 15, 1997, Wes Lukowsky, review of *Cotton Bowl Days: Growing Up with Dallas and the Cowboys in the 1960s,* p. 196; March 1, 2001, Wes Lukowsky, review of *From 33rd Street to Camden Yards: An Oral History of the Baltimore Orioles,* p. 1217; May 15, 2003, Dennis Dodge, review of *Native Dancer: The Grey Ghost: Hero of a Golden Age,* p. 1631.
Boston Globe, July 6, 2003, Bill Littlefield, review of *Native Dancer,* p. H6.
Dallas Morning News, September 24, 2003, review of *Native Dancer.*
Fort Worth Star-Telegram, June 11, 2003, review of *Native Dancer.*
Library Journal, March 15, 1996, David Van de Streek, review of *The Longest Shot,* p. 75; February 1, 2001, Paul Kaplan, Morey Berger, review of *From 33rd Street to Camden Yards,* p. 92.
New York Times, June 1, 2003, Alfred G. Vanderbilt, review of *Native Dancer,* Section 8, p. 11.
Publishers Weekly, July 21, 1997, review of *Cotton Bowl Days,* p. 195; March 5, 2001, review of *From 33rd Street to Camden Yards,* p. 71; April 28, 2003, review of *Native Dancer,* p. 61.

ONLINE

Cumberland Times-News Online, http://www.times-news.com/ (August 22, 2001), Mike Burke, review of *From 33rd Street to Camden Yards.*

Horse-Races.net, http://www.horse-races.net/ (March 10, 2004), review of *Native Dancer.*

MostlyFiction.com, http://mostlyfiction.com/ (March 10, 2004), Mary Whipple, review of *Native Dancer.**

*   *   *

EISLER, Barry 1964-

PERSONAL: Born 1964. *Education:* Cornell University, B.A., 1986, J.D., 1989.

ADDRESSES: Agent—c/o Author Mail, G. P. Putnam's Sons, 375 Hudson St., New York, NY 10014. *E-mail*—barry@barryeisler.com.

CAREER: Attorney, author. Hamada and Matsumoto, Tokyo, Japan, attorney; Matsushita Electric and Industrial Co. Ltd., Osaka, Japan, counsel; three years with the U.S. State Department.

WRITINGS:

"JOHN RAIN" SERIES

Rain Fall, Putnam (New York, NY), 2002.
Hard Rain, Putnam (New York, NY), 2003.
Rain Storm, Putnam (New York, NY), 2004.

WORK IN PROGRESS: A fourth "John Rain" novel.

SIDELIGHTS: Attorney Barry Eisler, who has lived and worked in Japan for several years, created the character of Japanese-American Vietnam veteran John Rain for his thriller series that begins in Japan. Rain benefits from Eisler's proficiency in the martial arts—he has a black belt in judo—and is also a lover of jazz, like Eisler.

In the opener, *Rain Fall,* called "rich and atmospheric" by a *Publishers Weekly* critic, the protagonist has become an assassin for hire. Eisler takes Rain through Tokyo's jazz clubs, bars, "love hotels," and the upscale Western shops that flourish there. Rain has no qualms working for anonymous buyers of his creative elimina-

tion service, in part because of his Special Forces training and service during the Vietnam conflict. He has also been alienated from both the cultures of his Japanese father and American mother. Rain plants a microchip on the back of a bureaucrat that interferes with his pacemaker as they ride in a subway, making it appear as if he died of a heart attack. With his techie friend Harry, he meets Midori Kawamura, the dead man's daughter, who is a jazz pianist trained at Julliard. Rain saves her life, although she has no idea that he killed her father, and discovers that a computer disk that Midori's father had planned to give to the press contains revelations of political corruption.

Booklist reviewer Connie Fletcher felt that the book "is weak in characterization. . . . But plot and procedure are real standouts." Wilda Williams added in *Library Journal* that "with plenty of sex, exotic locations, martial arts action, and high-tech wizardry . . . this is the perfect summer brain candy for the testosterone set."

The second book in the series, *Hard Rain,* finds Rain embroiled in a CIA scheme named Crepuscular, the target of which is the Japanese business and political system. Still alone, in spite of occasional relationships, Rain exercises skill in his chosen field. "Hard-boiled down to the ice-cold core of his survival-oriented soul, he's not much more than a machine," commented a *Kirkus Reviews* writer, "but expertly engineered at that, and fascinating to watch in action." A *Publishers Weekly* reviewer, however, said that it is Eisler's "impressive literary skills that make his John Rain such a fascinating, touching, and wholly believable character."

In *Rain Storm,* Rain has accumulated enough enemies and has grown sufficiently weary of the killing business to escape to Brazil. But the CIA convinces him to take on an assignment involving an arms dealer who is supplying South Asian criminal groups, and Rain finds himself back in business and drawn into an international game that may prove to be more than he had counted on.

BIOGRAPHICAL AND CRITICAL SOURCES:

PERIODICALS

Booklist, May 15, 2002, Connie Fletcher, review of *Rain Fall,* p. 1555.

Kirkus Reviews, May 15, 2002, review of *Rain Fall,* p. 683; May 15, 2003, review of *Hard Rain,* p. 698.

Library Journal, July, 2002, Wilda Williams, review of *Rain Fall,* p. 116.

Publishers Weekly, May 27, 2002, review of *Rain Fall,* p. 32; May 26, 2003, review of *Hard Rain,* p. 45.

ONLINE

Barry Eisler Home Page, http://www.barryeisler.com (March 7, 2004).

BookReporter.com, http://www.bookreporter.com/ (March 7, 2004), Joe Hartlaub, review of *Rain Fall.*

BooksNBytes, http://www.booksnbytes.com/ (March 7, 2004), Harriet Klausner, review of *Rain Fall* and *Hard Rain.*

January Online, http://www.januarymagazine.com/ (March 7, 2004), Kevin Burton Smith, review of *Rain Fall.*

Japan.box.sk, http://www.japan.box.sk/ (February 24, 2004), "Barry Eisler: *Hard Rain* Falls on Tokyo.".

Japan Today, http://www.japantoday.com/ (August 21, 2001), Chris Betros, "Eisler Takes to Mean Streets of Tokyo with Japanese-American Hit Man John Rain."

MostlyFiction.com, http://mostlyfiction.com/ (November 12, 2002), Judi Clark, review of *Rain Fall.*

Mystery One Bookstore, http://www.mysteryone.com/ (September, 2002), interview with Barry Eisler.*

*   *   *

ELIE, Paul 1965-

PERSONAL: Born 1965, in NY; married Lenora Todaro. *Education:* Fordham University, B.A. (English); Columbia University, M.F.A.

ADDRESSES: Home—New York, NY. *Agent*—c/o Author Mail, Farrar, Straus and Giroux, 19 Union Square West, New York, NY 10003.

CAREER: Writer and editor. Farrar, Straus, and Giroux, New York, NY, 1993—, became a senior editor.

AWARDS, HONORS: National Book Critics Circle Award nomination, 2004, for *The Life You Save May Be Your Own: An American Pilgrimage.*

WRITINGS:

(Editor) *A Tremor of Bliss: Contemporary Writing on the Saints,* introduction by Robert Coles, Harcourt (New York, NY), 1994.

The Life You Save May Be Your Own: An American Pilgrimage, Farrar, Straus and Giroux (New York, NY), 2003.

Contributor to periodicals, including *New Republic, New York Times Magazine, Commonweal,* and *Spy.*

SIDELIGHTS: Paul Elie was born into a Roman Catholic family and received a Jesuit education at Fordham University. An English major, he took courses in theology, philosophy, and religious art and read books by the four people who became the subjects of his second book, *The Life You Save May Be Your Own: An American Pilgrimage.* They are Flannery O'Conner, the only one of the four born Catholic, and converts Thomas Merton, Dorothy Day, and Walker Percy. Elie has for many years been an editor at Farrar, Straus, and Giroux, a publishing house that released the works of O'Connor, Merton, and Percy. As an editor, Elie has also assembled the writings of twenty contemporary authors for *A Tremor of Bliss: Contemporary Writers on the Saints.*

The four subjects of *The Life You Save May Be Your Own* produced their most influential writings from the 1930s through the 1960s, a period when Catholicism was in favor and evident in films like *The Bells of St. Mary's* and *Going My Way.* There were many people who were converting to Catholicism at the time, as well as activist priests influencing society by becoming involved in the industrial union movement. However, the popularity of the Church waned with the changes that resulted from the Second Vatican Council.

Flannery O'Connor, a Georgia farm girl, died of lupus at thirty-nine in 1964. Her illness caused her to withdrew from a world steeped in fundamentalism to write her fiction, which details the lives of the rural poor in the Protestant South. Much of her work reflects her obsession with the grotesque. Thomas Merton, who lived from 1915 to 1968, could have remained in New York and enjoyed success as a doctor or a writer, but instead he chose to become a cloistered Trappist monk who read medieval philosophy. His autobiography of converting to Catholicism became the 1948 best seller *The Seven Story Mountain.* Merton's writings often blend Christian and Eastern spirituality, ensuring their continued popularity with a variety of readers. Another writer in Elie's book is Walker Percy (1916-1990). He came from an aristocratic Southern family, read Kierkegaard, Dostoevsky, Sartre, and Camus, and wrote existentialist essays before completing his award-winning novel, *The Moviegoer,* and half a dozen others.

All three of these subjects in this volume were defined by their writing, but Dorothy Day was different. Day, who lived from 1897 to 1980, founded the Catholic Worker Movement in 1933 with Peter Maurin to serve the Depression-era poor of New York's Lower East Side. She had a significant influence on unionism, the welfare of the poor, and pacifism. She published eight books of fiction and memoirs, but her most influential writings were to be found in her weekly column in the *Catholic Worker.* Because of her devotion to, and agitation on behalf of, civil rights, economic justice, and peace, many have proposed that Day be named a saint. That may never happen, however, unless the Vatican can overlook her politics, many love affairs, an abortion, and the fact that she had a child out of wedlock. Her influence is felt to this day, as her movement continues through housing, communal farms, and nutrition programs that give people in need a leg up and often a new start on life.

In an interview for *Publishers Weekly,* Elie told Michael Coffey that "there is more 'Catholic' writing coming. . . . Today, if you've been raised in the Catholic tradition, you have to figure it out for yourself. It doesn't come with mother's milk the way it did in the parochial school era, so you have to put the pieces together." The author also said, "It has struck me often that here is a big book, essentially sympathetic to religion, at a time when it seems that nothing but bad things are being done in religion's name. At present, religion is being presented as a mass phenomenon, wholly public, closely overlapping with notions of state and nation. I like to think that my book gives an account of the aspects of religion that might be overlooked—inwardness, the sense of individual personal calling, the constant putting of faith to the test through the encounter with the unbeliever within."

Of *The Life You Save May Be Your Own,* Charles R. Morris wrote in the *New York Times Book Review* that

"Elie's fine study is a freeze frame from another era of the perennial search for truth in a world that lacks self-evident truths, and of four idiosyncratic searchers who sought their own ways to pass it on." Patrick Giles commented in the *Los Angeles Times* that the book "renders these life studies as religious narratives—pilgrimage narratives. . . . Elie weaves their journeys into a tapestry of American Catholicism's incursion into secular life and art. His is a labor of devotion as well as examination, part apologia, part apotheosis. It succeeds because of Elie's skills as a writer and because he is addressing the right subject at the right time."

BIOGRAPHICAL AND CRITICAL SOURCES:

PERIODICALS

Boston Globe, May 18, 2003, Laura Claridge, review of *The Life You Save May Be Your Own: An American Pilgrimage,* p. H8; August 10, 2003, Katherine Powers, review of *The Life You Save May Be Your Own,* p. H9.
Christian Century, May 31, 2003, Joseph Cunneen, review of *The Life You Save May Be Your Own,* p. 23.
Commonweal, March 10, 1995, Anna Harrison, review of *A Tremor of Bliss: Contemporary Writing on the Saints,* p. 24; May 4, 2001, Valerie Sayers, "Being a Writer, Being Catholic: Sometimes the Twain Can Meet," p. 12.
Kirkus Reviews, September 15, 1994, review of *A Tremor of Bliss,* p. 1239; February 1, 2003, review of *The Life You Save May Be Your Own,* p. 203.
Library Journal, November 1, 1994, L. Kriz, review of *A Tremor of Bliss,* p. 81.
Los Angeles Times, August 24, 2003, Patrick Giles, review of *The Life You Save May Be Your Own,* p. R10.
Nation, June 16, 2003, Vince Passaro, review of *The Life You Save May Be Your Own,* p. 26.
New Criterion, June, 2003, Mary Ellen Bork, review of *The Life You Save May Be Your Own,* p. 82.
Newsweek, May 19, 2003, Kenneth L. Woodward, review of *The Life You Save May Be Your Own,* p. 20.
New York Times Book Review, May 18, 2003, Charles R. Morris, review of *The Life You Save May Be Your Own,* p. 34.
Publishers Weekly, October 10, 1994, review of *A Tremor of Bliss,* p. 59; March 10, 2003, review of

The Life You Save May Be Your Own, pp. 63-64; April 7, 2003, Michael Coffey, "Paul Elie: Reading Books With Our Lives," pp. 38-39.

Time, April 14, 2003, Lance Morrow, review of *The Life You Save May Be Your Own,* p. 84.

Wall Street Journal, March 26, 2003, Christopher Willcox, review of *The Life You Save May Be Your Own,* p. D8.

Washington Post, June 1, 2003, Charlotte Allen, review of *The Life You Save May Be Your Own.*

ONLINE

Beliefnet.com, http://www.beliefnet.com/ (March 7, 2004), interview with Paul Elie.

Christianity Today Online, http://www.christianity today.com/ (June 3, 2003), Dick Staub, "The Dick Staub Interview: Paul Elie on 'The Holy Ghost School.'"*

F

FEINBERG, Joel 1926-2004

OBITUARY NOTICE—See index for CA sketch: Born October 19, 1926, in Detroit, MI; died of complications from Parkinson's disease, March 29, 2004, in Tucson, AZ. Philosopher, educator, and author. Feinberg was a highly regarded philosopher who was acclaimed for his writings concerning the limitations of the law and government on public morality. After attending the University of Illinois for a year, he served in the U.S. Army from 1944 to 1946, returning to his studies at the University of Michigan, where he completed his Ph.D. in 1957. His academic career began at Brown University in 1955, followed by teaching positions at Princeton University and the University of California in the mid-1960s. From 1967 to 1977, he was professor of philosophy at Rockefeller University, where he also served as chair of the department from 1971 to 1977. Feinberg then moved on to Tucson in 1977, where he joined the University of Arizona faculty, was head of the philosophy department from 1978 to 1981, and became Regents Professor of Philosophy and Law in 1988. He retired as a professor emeritus in 1994. Feinberg was lauded by his colleagues for his ability to convey complex ideas simply in books such as *Rights, Justice and the Bounds of Liberty: Essays in Social Philosophy* (1980), the four-volume *The Moral Limits of the Criminal Law* (1984-88), and *Freedom and Fulfillment* (1992). In these books he established what he felt should be the limits of government and the law on individuals' personal freedoms. Feinberg, who was also a former president of the American Philosophical Association, continued to lecture widely after his retirement.

OBITUARIES AND OTHER SOURCES:

PERIODICALS

Chicago Tribune, April 6, 2004, Section 3, p. 13.
Los Angeles Times, April 7, 2004, p. B11.
New York Times, April 5, 2004, p. A23.

*   *   *

FEINBERG, Rosa Castro 1939-

PERSONAL: Born January 1, 1939, in New York, NY; daughter of Antonio Castro y Garcia (a cook) and Diana de Llano Castro (a homemaker); married Stephen H. Jones (in insurance business), February, 1959 (divorced, 1966); married Alfred Feinberg (a lawyer), June, 1968 (died August 19, 1975); children: (first marriage) Lincoln H. *Ethnicity:* "Hispanic." *Education:* Florida State University, B.A., M.S.; University of Florida, certificate in foreign language education; University of Miami, Coral Gables, FL, Ph.D.

ADDRESSES: *Office*—c/o Department of Educational Foundations, University Park Campus, Florida International University, Miami, FL 33199. *E-mail*—rcastro@fiu.edu.

CAREER: Teacher of reading, Spanish, science, adult classes in English as a second language, and other subjects at public high schools, Quincy, FL, 1960,

Miami, FL, 1960-61, and Tallahassee, FL, 1961-63; Dade County Public Schools, Miami, FL, high school English teacher and debate coach, 1963-64, junior high school teacher of Spanish, social studies, English as a second language, and bilingual classes, 1964-72; University of Miami, Coral Gables, FL, staff member at Florida School Race Desegregation Consulting Center, 1973-75, assistant director of National Origin Desegregation Assistance Center, 1975-76, associate director, 1977-80, director, 1980-90, director of Bilingual Education Training Program for Administrators, 1983-87, director of Institute for Cultural Innovation, 1986-90, research professor of educational and psychological studies, 1988-90; Florida International University, University Park Campus, Miami, visiting associate professor, 1990-92, associate professor, 1992-2002, adjunct professor, 2003. St. Thomas University, guest lecturer, 1987; University of Chicago, Joyce Lecturer, 1991; guest speaker at other educational institutions, including Arizona State University; workshop coordinator and presenter; public speaker. National Network of Hispanic Educators, chair, 1981-82; Center for Applied Linguistics, member of board of trustees, 1991-96; National Educational Equity Working Group, member, 1993-95; National Coalition of Advocates for Students, member of board of trustees, 1995-98; Coalition for Quality Education, member of board of directors, 1998—. Florida State Task Force on Bilingual Education, member, 1977-79; Florida Post-Secondary Education Planning Commission, member, 1982-87; Florida State Advisory Council on Bilingual Education, chair, 1983-89; Florida State Task Force on Migrant Education, member, 1984-85; Florida State Task Force on Multicultural Education, member, 1991-95. Testified before U.S. Commission on Civil Rights, National Conference on the Education of Hispanics, and White House Initiative on Excellence in Education for Hispanics; consultant to U.S. Department of Health, Education, and Welfare, U.S. Agency for International Development, and Government of Spain. National Conference of Puerto Rican Women, member, 1976—; Spanish American League against Discrimination, member of board of directors, 1976-94, member of executive committee, 1983-86, member of advisory board, 1994—; Coalition of Hispanic American Women, member, 1980-2000. Dade County Housing Finance Authority, commissioner, 1984-86; Miami Capital Development Corp., member of executive committee and board of directors, 1984-86; Dade County Value Adjustment Board, member, 1986-96; Dade County League of Cities, member of board of directors and executive com-

mittee, 1988-95, liaison to Florida League of Cities, 1993-94; Coalition for Quality Education in Dade County, honorary cochair, 1989-95, member of board of directors, 1996—; Dade County Hispanic Heritage Council, member of board of directors, 1992-93. Holmes Braddock Adult Education Center, volunteer, 1998. Member of board of directors, ASPIRA of Florida, 1980-88, ARISE Foundation, 1987-96, and Public Broadcasting System, 1989-96.

MEMBER: National Association of Asian and Pacific American Educators, National Association for Bilingual Education (chair of Committee on Reauthorization of the Bilingual Education Act, 1991-93), Teachers of English to Speakers of Other Languages, National Association for the Advancement of Colored People (life member), Bilingual Association of Florida (president, 1980-82), Sunshine State Teachers of English to Speakers of Other Languages, Florida School Board Association (member of board of directors, 1986-90), New Jersey Teachers of English to Speakers of Other Languages/Bilingual Education Association (honorary life member).

AWARDS, HONORS: Fellow of Southern Scholarship Fund, 1974-76; award from Sunshine State Teachers of English to Speakers of Other Languages, 1979; certificate of appreciation, Miccosukee Tribe of Florida, 1980; named honorary citizen of Tucson, AZ, 1985; Institute fellow, City University of New York, 1986; awards from Maryland Association for Bilingual Education, 1986, and from Hispanic National Bar Association, 1987; Danforth Foundation fellow, 1987-88; National Association for Bilingual Education, Honor Roll Award, 1988, Citizen of the Year Award, 1996; certificate of appreciation, city of Miami, FL, 1988; awards from Association of Foreign Language Teachers of Dade County and Florida Women Lawyers Association, 1989; named woman of the year, Coalition of Hispanic American Women, 1989; named South Florida woman of impact, Community Coalition for Women's History, 1992; award from Colegio de Pedagogos en el Exilio, 1992; ASPIRA of Florida, Madrina Award, 1992, El Pitirre Award, 1996; Gwen Cherry Award, American Association of University Women, 1992; awards from Phi Delta Kappa, 1992-93, and Bilingual Association of Florida, 1993; Nova Education Alumni Association Award, 1993; named alumna of the year, University of Miami Alumni Association, 1993; outstanding service award, Dade Association of Vocational, Adult, Career, and Community Education,

1994; award from Dade Association for Theater Education, 1994-95; Leader in Education Award, Gender Equity Network, 1995; Educator's Award, City of Miami Police Department, 1995; Rosa Castro Feinberg Multicultural Leadership Award established by Dade County Public Schools, 1996; Advocacy in Public Affairs Award, Planned Parenthood of Greater Miami, 1996; awards from Democratic Women's Club of South Florida, 1996, and Legal Services of Greater Miami, 1997; award for legendary leadership in support of immigrant children, Haitian Women of Miami, 2001; Cervantes Outstanding Educator award, Nova Southeastern University and Fischler Graduate School of Education and Human Services Hispanic Advisory Board, 2001.

WRITINGS:

(Editor, with L. Valverde and E. Marquez) *Educating Spanish Speaking Hispanics,* Association for Supervision and Curriculum Development (Alexandria, VA), 1980.
Bilingual Education: A Reference Handbook, American Bibliographical Center-Clio Press (Santa Barbara, CA), 2002.

Contributor to books, including *Bilingual Education for Latino Students,* edited by L. Valverde, Association for Supervision and Curriculum Development (Washington, DC), 1979; and *Beyond Rhetoric: Urban Multicultural Education,* edited by C. A. Ryan and S. L. Woods, Simon & Schuster (New York, NY), 1996. Contributor of articles and reviews to periodicals, including *Theory into Practice, Social Education, Teachers College Record, American School Board Journal, Journal of Language, Culture, and Curriculum, Educational Leadership,* and *Modern Language Journal.* Associate editor, *International Journal: Continuous Improvement Monitor,* 1995—; regional editor, *Hispanic Education Newsletter,* 1981-82; member of editorial board, *NABE Journal,* 1978-81, and *Bilingual Research Journal,* 2001—.

*　　*　　*

FEINSTEIN, Edward 1954-

PERSONAL: Born 1954; married Nina Bieber (a rabbi); children: three. *Education:* University of California at Santa Cruz, B.A.; Jewish Theological Seminary of America, B.Lit.; University of Judaism, M.A.; Columbia University, M.A.

ADDRESSES: Office—Valley Beth Shalom, 15739 Ventura Blvd., Encino, CA 91436. *E-mail*—efeinstein@vbs.org.

CAREER: Rabbi. Ordained, Jewish Theological Seminary of America, New York, NY, 1981; Solomon Schechter Academy, Dallas, TX, founding director; Congregation Shearith Israel, Dallas, associate rabbi; Camp Ramah, CA, executive director, 1990-93; Valley Beth Shalom, Encino, CA, rabbi; Ziegler Rabbinical School, University of Judaism, Los Angeles, CA, lecturer; on the faculties of the Wexner Heritage Foundation and the Whizen Institute on the Family. Former board member of various religious organizations.

AWARDS, HONORS: Rabbi of the Year, Jewish Federation of Greater Los Angeles, 1995-96; Rabbinical Service Award, United Jewish Appeal; Mickey Weiss Award for outstanding alumni, University of Judaism, 2002; Honor Book for Older Readers, Sydney Taylor book awards, Association of Jewish Libraries, 2003, and Top Ten Religious Books for Young Readers citation, American Library Association, both for *Tough Questions Jews Ask: A Young Adult's Guide to Building a Jewish Life.*

WRITINGS:

Tough Questions Jews Ask: A Young Adult's Guide to Building a Jewish Life, Jewish Lights (Woodstock, VT), 2003.

Columnist and contributing editor, *Jewish Journal of Los Angeles;* audio recordings include *The Time of Your Life* and *Out of the Rabbi's Hat* (stories for children).

SIDELIGHTS: Edward Feinstein is a rabbi, as is his wife, Nina, the second woman to be ordained by the Conservative movement. He has written for adults and children, and with his *Tough Questions Jews Ask: A Young Adult's Guide to Building a Jewish Life,* he imagines himself the teacher of a class of Jewish adolescents and answers the questions he feels they would ask and which young people often feel go unanswered because they are not being listened to or taken seriously. Liz Harris wrote in an article for the

Jewish News Weekly of Northern California Online that Feinstein "opens the floodgates for conversation and thoughtful contemplation."

The students, Feinstein imagines, would ask why they should believe in God and if the stories in the Bible are true. They question the value of prayer, why there must be so many rules, and the Jewish traditions themselves. They ask how they can be expected to believe in God when such events as the Holocaust have occurred. These are questions Feinstein has been asked over time by young people, and being the father of children of that age as he wrote the book, Feinstein was in the ideal position to consider the concerns of Jewish teens. "Theology comes alive through Feinstein's cogent analogies and non-dogmatic, down-to-earth style," commented a *Publishers Weekly* contributor. And *Booklist* reviewer Ellen Mandel declared that the volume is "charged with energy and insight."

BIOGRAPHICAL AND CRITICAL SOURCES:

PERIODICALS

Booklist, April 1, 2003, Ellen Mandel, review of *Tough Questions Jews Ask: A Young Adult's Guide to Building a Jewish Life*, p. 139.
Publishers Weekly, April 28, 2003, review of *Tough Questions Jews Ask*, p. 65.

ONLINE

Jewish News Weekly of Northern California Online, http://www.jewishsf.com/ (March 9, 2004), Liz Harris, review of *Tough Questions Jews Ask*.

*   *   *

FEUERMAN, Ruchama King
    See KING, Ruchama

*   *   *

FIELD, Ophelia

PERSONAL: Born in Australia; immigrated to England. *Education:* Attended Christ Church, Oxford, and the London School of Economics.

ADDRESSES: Agent—c/o Author Mail, St. Martin's Press, 175 Fifth Ave., New York, NY 10010.

CAREER: Policy analyst, writer. Human Rights Watch, London, England, policy analyst; *Sunday Telegraph*, London, books consultant.

WRITINGS:

The Favourite: Sarah, Duchess of Marlborough, Hodder & Stoughton (London, England), 2002, published as *Sarah Churchill, Duchess of Marlborough: The Queen's Favourite,* St. Martin's Press (New York, NY), 2003.

Also author of policy reports for Human Rights Watch and contributor to periodicals, including the *Sunday Telegraph.*

SIDELIGHTS: Ophelia Field's first book is an extensive biography published in the United States as *Sarah Churchill, Duchess of Marlborough: The Queen's Favourite.* Sarah Churchill, who lived from 1660 to 1744 and is an ancestor of the late Princess Diana, was vilified in the popular press and by such literary figures as Alexander Pope and Jonathan Swift as being a "cranky old lady." She was born in humble beginnings as Sarah Jennings, but while a servant in the court of Charles II she became very close to Princess Anne and was possibly even her lover, according to Field. She later married John Churchill, who would become the Duke of Marlborough and one of the greatest generals of the eighteenth century. The couple were the seed of the Churchill-Spencer dynasties. Sarah Churchill had considerable influence over both her husband and Queen Anne, and she became the richest and most powerful Englishwomen since Queen Elizabeth I. Sarah, a Whig, attempted to influence the queen's Tory leanings, and she employed what some felt were devious means to advance her goals and increase her fortune.

When Anne replaced Sarah with a new companion, Abigail Masham, Sarah threatened to expose the queen's lesbianism with letters they had exchanged. *Times Literary Supplement* reviewer Carola Hicks noted that Field "points out that the allegations of Queen Anne's lesbianism were meant to taint her with the associated but even worse crime of Roman Catholicism, and therefore unfitness to rule." Eventually, both Sarah and her husband were banished from court, and Sarah turned to writing her memoirs as self-vindication.

Reviewing *The Favourite* in the London *Independent,* Stephen Coote pointed out that Churchill, for all her ambition, manipulations, rages, and vulnerability, "was always a celebrity and often a scapegoat, because she was determined to show what influence a woman could wield over public affairs. She is a marvelous subject for a biography, and Ophelia Field's book, capacious and beautifully detailed, does her full justice, discarding cliched judgements and bringing to light new evidence. It is the first work by a writer who is a master of her craft."

BIOGRAPHICAL AND CRITICAL SOURCES:

PERIODICALS

Booklist, June 1, 2003, Margaret Flanagan, review of *Sarah Churchill, Duchess of Marlborough: The Queen's Favourite,* p. 1734.
English Historical Review, September, 2003, Edward Gregg, review of *The Favourite: Sarah, Duchess of Marlborough,* p. 1059.
Guardian (Manchester, England), June 22, 2002, Kathryn Hughes, review of *The Favourite.*
Independent (London, England), June 27, 2002, Stephen Coote, review of *The Favourite.*
Kirkus Reviews, May 15, 2003, review of *Sarah Churchill, Duchess of Marlborough,* p. 727.
Publishers Weekly, May 12, 2003, review of *Sarah Churchill, Duchess of Marlborough,* p. 56.
Times Literary Supplement, July 19, 2002, Carola Hicks, review of *The Favourite,* p. 11.*

*   *   *

FISCHETTI, Mark

PERSONAL: Male.

ADDRESSES: Office—Scientific American, Inc., 415 Madison Ave., New York, NY 10017.

CAREER: Writer. *Scientific American,* New York, NY, science writer and contributing editor.

WRITINGS:

(Editor) *The Family Business Management Handbook,* Family Business (Philadelphia, PA), 1996.
(With Tim Berners-Lee) *Weaving the Web: The Original Design and Ultimate Destiny of the World Wide Web by Its Inventor,* HarperSanFrancisco (San Francisco, CA), 1999.
(With Elinor Levy) *The New Killer Diseases: How the Alarming Evolution of Mutant Germs Threatens Us All,* Crown (New York, NY), 2003.

Contributor to periodicals, including the *New York Times* and *Smithsonian.* Coeditor of quarterly magazine *Scientific American Presents.*

SIDELIGHTS: Mark Fischetti is a science writer who has collaborated on several books, including *Weaving the Web: The Original Design and Ultimate Destiny of the World Wide Web by Its Inventor.* His coauthor is the inventor and British-born physicist Tim Berners-Lee, who in the 1950s constructed his first computer from a television and other parts. In constructing the Web, he developed the protocols necessary to its success, including the HTML language, and built in the capability that would allow it to work with various operating systems, including Unix, Windows, and Macintosh. A *Publishers Weekly* reviewer noted that Berners-Lee "was very, very right a decade ago, and he's well worth reading now."

The authors write that because Berners-Lee did not develop the Web as a commercial venture it drew in the open society collaborators that helped build it; otherwise, competing startups might have hindered its development as we know it today. Their history goes back to the 1960s, with the foundations of hypertext as developed by Ted Nelson, and Doug Engelbart's invention of the mouse. The authors then move forward to Berners-Lee's earliest work on what would be the Web in his CERN lab in Geneva, Switzerland, and the launching of the Web in 1989. They also provide a history of the earlier development of the Internet, the communications infrastructure that links computers together, which was funded by the U.S. government.

Fischetti and Berners-Lee, furthermore, note the obstacles that had to be overcome to get the Web into the global public domain and the fortunes that were made as a result. Mosaic, the first browser, which was created at the University of Illinois in 1993, was commercialized as Netscape by one of its creators. When the company went public in 1995, its worth skyrocketed to more than four billion dollars after only one day of trading. *Weaving the Web* goes on to address the most current concerns regarding the Web, including the sale of domain names, which can be snapped up by those with the most resources. "Overall," wrote Michael Johnsen in *Video Age International,* "*Weaving the Web* offers a farsighted view of technology's latest development, with both a comprehensive gaze into the past and a realistic window of the future."

Berners-Lee became director of the Massachusetts Institute of Technology-based World Wide Web Consortium, which oversees Web standards. Even though it is often assumed that the "inventor of the World Wide Web" is incredibly wealthy, he is not. It is clear, however, that the Web is universal, and that it is conducive to commercial enterprise.

Fischetti next wrote *The New Killer Diseases: How the Alarming Evolution of Mutant Germs Threatens Us All* with immunologist Elinor Levy. Here they document the symptoms, outcomes, changes, and rates of occurrence for viral and bacterial diseases that include strep, *E. coli,* bovine spongiform encephalopathy (BSE or Mad Cow disease), tuberculosis, HIV, anthrax, West Nile virus, and SARS. Specific cases, such as that of a three-year-old who died of *E. coli* after eating watermelon from a salad bar, put a human face on the deaths that have resulted.

A *Publishers Weekly* contributor felt that *The New Killer Diseases*'s "militaristic language and alarmist tone . . . resemble the scare tactics of political and military propaganda." And Claire Panosian Dunavan, a professor of medicine at the UCLA School of Medicine and a practicing infectious disease and tropical medicine specialist, said in a *Los Angeles Times* article that the book misses "the bigger picture. Since the late 1990s, for example, BSE and West Nile encephalitis have claimed no more than 600 European and American lives in total. In contrast, cerebral malaria (a condition that can be reversed with drugs that cost a dollar or two per patient) has silently killed several million African children, many of whom never

got close to medical help. Now there's a killer disease." However, a *Kirkus Reviews* critic asserted that "given the emergency and headline-making spread from Asia of the mysterious new killer SARS (severe acute respiratory syndrome), the warnings sounded here seem especially timely."

BIOGRAPHICAL AND CRITICAL SOURCES:

PERIODICALS

Booklist, September 15, 1999, Benjamin Segedin, review of *Weaving the Web: The Original Design and Ultimate Destiny of the World Wide Web by Its Inventor,* p. 207.

Inc., October, 1999, review of *Weaving the Web,* p. 93.

Kirkus Reviews, May 1, 2003, review of *The New Killer Diseases: How the Alarming Evolution of Mutant Germs Threatens Us All,* p. 660.

Los Angeles Times, August 24, 2003, Claire Panosian Dunavan, review of *The New Killer Diseases.*

New York Times, October 24, 1999, Katie Hafner, review of *Weaving the Web,* p. 20.

Publishers Weekly, September 13, 1999, review of *Weaving the Web,* p. 72; April 28, 2003, review of *The New Killer Diseases,* p. 56.

Video Age International, January, 2000, Michael Johnsen, review of *Weaving the Web,* p. 14.*

*   *   *

FISHBACK, Mary 1954-

PERSONAL: Born December 18, 1954, in Skinkertown, VA; married John Fishback (a file clerk), September 15, 1974. *Hobbies and other interests:* Growing roses, genealogy, cooking.

ADDRESSES: Home—408 Madison Ct. S.E., Leesburg, VA 20176-3604. *Office*—Thomas Balch History and Genealogy Library, 208 West Market St., Leesburg, VA 20176. *E-mail*—mfishback@leesburgva.org.

CAREER: Loudoun Hospital Center, Leesburg, VA, nurse and phlebotomist, 1973-89; Graydon Manor, Leesburg, VA, nurse and phlebotomist, 1989-99; Town of Leesburg, Leesburg, VA, librarian, 2000—. Loudoun Library Foundation, member, 1990-2003, and coordinator of Book Center; Thomas Balch Library Commission, chair, 1994-99; Thomas Balch History and Genealogy Library, volunteer for nearly thirty years. Northern Virginia Hospice, nurse, 1980-87.

MEMBER: Civil War Roundtable, Loudoun Historical Society (member of board of directors), Loudoun Genealogy Society (president, 1974-96).

AWARDS, HONORS: Service Awards, Loudoun Library Foundation, 2000, 2001; Balch History Award, Thomas Balch History and Genealogy Library, 2000; Balch Honor Award, Thomas Balch Library Commission, 2001.

WRITINGS:

250 Years of Towns and Villages, Arcadia Publishing (Charleston, SC), 1999.
People and Places, Arcadia Publishing (Charleston, SC), 2000.
(With others) *Middleburg Cemeteries, Loudoun County, Virginia,* Willowbend Books (South Deerfield, MA), 2000.
A Family Album, Arcadia Publishing (Charleston, SC), 2001.
Northern Virginia's Equestrian Heritage, Arcadia Publishing (Charleston, SC), 2002.
Leesburg, Arcadia Publishing (Charleston, SC), 2003.

Author of "Loudoun's Legacy," a column in *Loudoun-Times Mirror,* 1987-95. Contributor to periodicals, including *Antique Week.*

WORK IN PROGRESS: A book on the cemeteries of Loudoun County, VA, with others; research on World War II and the Civil War era.

SIDELIGHTS: Mary Fishback told *CA:* "Genealogy is a passion with me! I have volunteered for the Thomas Balch History and Genealogy Library for nearly thirty years. Some of that time was dedicated to save the 1922 library building from being destroyed. Today, since the Town of Leesburg took over the library, Balch Library is one of the premier history and genealogy libraries in the state of Virginia. After a twenty-six-year nursing career, I have found the perfect venue for my second career in teaching genealogy and history writing."

FISHER, Philip A(rthur) 1907-2004

OBITUARY NOTICE—See index for *CA* sketch: Born September 8, 1907, in San Francisco, CA; died March 11, 2004, in San Mateo, CA. Economist, businessman, and author. Fisher was best known as an investment counselor and author of influential, bestselling books on how to invest wisely in the stock market. He studied economics at Stanford University, where he earned his A.B. in 1927 and continued on to graduate study for another year. Not long after this, in 1931, he founded his own investment counseling firm, Fisher & Co., in San Francisco, a company he continued to run until his retirement in 1999. His work was interrupted only by World War II, during which he served as a captain in the U.S. Army Air Corps. Fisher's first book, *Common Stocks and Uncommon Profits* (1958; revised edition, 1960), was a bestseller and is still in print. His advice to research companies thoroughly and hold on to quality stocks as long as possible to get the best return was influential to many investors, including billionaire Warren E. Buffett, who credited Fisher as one of his inspirations. Fisher was also the author of *Paths to Wealth through Common Stocks* (1960), *Conservative Investors Sleep Well* (1975), *Developing an Investment Philosophy* (1980), and *Common Stocks and Uncommon Profits, and Other Writings* (1996).

OBITUARIES AND OTHER SOURCES:

PERIODICALS

Chicago Tribune, April 22, 2004, Section 3, p. 13.
Forbes, April 26, 2004, p. 142.
Los Angeles Times, April 21, 2004, p. B13.
New York Times, April 19, 2004, p. A23.

ONLINE

Mercury News, http://www.mercurynews.com/ (April 20, 2004).

*   *   *

FLEMING, Justin 1953-

PERSONAL: Born March 1, 1953, in Sydney, New South Wales, Australia; son of Justin (a surgeon) and Gwen (a physician; maiden name, Lusby) Fleming; married Fay Brauer (an academic and writer), April 7, 1998; children: Marcus, Lara. *Ethnicity:* "Australian."

Education: University of Sydney, diploma in law, 1978; University College, London, LL.M., 1991. *Hobbies and other interests:* Music, walking, reading.

ADDRESSES: Home and office—110 High St., North Sydney, New South Wales 2060, Australia. *Agent*— Barbara Hogenson, Barbara Hogenson Agency, 165 West End Ave., Suite 19C, New York, NY 10023.

CAREER: Office of the Attorney General, Sydney, New South Wales, Australia, judge's associate, 1974-79; Office of the Commonwealth Crown Solicitor, Sydney, New South Wales, Australia, legal officer, 1979-80; barrister at law in Sydney, New South Wales, Australia, 1980-92, and in Dublin Ireland, 1992. Called to the Bar at King's Inns, Ireland, 1992. Australian National Playwrights' Conference, board member.

MEMBER: Australian Writers' Guild (New South Wales vice president), Irish Bar Association, University College London Alumni Association.

AWARDS, HONORS: New York Play Award, *New Dramatists,* and New South Wales Premier's Literary Award, both 2000, for *Burnt Piano;* resident, Banff Playwrights Colony, Banff, Alberta, Canada, 2000.

WRITINGS:

Hammer (play), produced in Sydney, New South Wales, Australia, at Phillip Street Theater, 1981.
Indian Summer (play), produced in Sydney, New South Wales, Australia, at Phillip Street Theater, 1982.
(Lyricist, with Stephen Edwards and Jonathan Alver) *Crystal Balls* (opera), performed in England, at Sadler's Wells, 1995.
Burnt Piano (play; produced in New York, NY, at Belvoir/Manhattan Theater Club/HB Playwrights Foundation Theater, in Hobart, Australia, at Mainstage Theater, and in Paris, France) Esson Press, 1998.
Harold in Italy (play; produced by Sydney Theater Company), Esson Press, 1998.
The Cobra (play; produced by Sydney Theater Company), Esson Press, 1998.
(Lyricist) *Tess of the d'Urbervilles* (musical play), composed by Stephen Edwards, produced in London, England, at Savoy Theater, 1999-2000.

Coup d'Etat (play), produced in Banff, Alberta, Canada, at Banff Arts Centre, 2002.
Barbarism to Verdict (documentary television series; produced by Southern Star Productions, beginning 1994), HarperCollins, 2002.

Also author of *The Nonsense Boy,* published by Esson Press; a history of the Old Ignatians' Union; a history of the law firm of Carroll & O'Dea; a history of Waverley College; and a television history of cinema.

WORK IN PROGRESS: The Devil's Tango, with Stewart D'Arrietta; *Babel,* with Martin Charnin and Thomas Hodgson; *Shooting the Moon,* a television series; adapting Emile Zola's *Au bonnheur des dames* for the stage.

SIDELIGHTS: Justin Fleming told *CA:* "I write, therefore I am. My work is influenced by my parents, Joe Castley, Hayes Gordon, Richard Wherrett, Tom Stoppard, John Mortimer, Iris Murdoch, David Malouf, Peter Shaffer, Robert Hughes, Samuel Beckett, and Dorothy Hewitt. My inspiration is usually an event, real or imaginary, that triggers an idea. Originally my work was driven by character and idea; now it's that but also more story-driven."

BIOGRAPHICAL AND CRITICAL SOURCES:

PERIODICALS

Back Stage, October 27, 2000, Michael Lazan, "Getting Personal at New Dramatists," p. 49.
Independent (London, England), November 16, 1999, review of *Tess of the d'Urbervilles,* p. 16.
News of the World (London, England), November 14, 1999, Bill Hagerty, review of *Tess of the d'Urbervilles,* p. 60.

*   *   *

FLYNN, Joseph

PERSONAL: Born in Chicago, IL. *Education:* Attended Loyola University of Chicago and Northeastern Illinois University.

ADDRESSES: Agent—c/o Author Mail, Bantam Books, 1745 Broadway, New York, NY 10019. *E-mail*—josephyflynn@josephflynn.com.

CAREER: Writer. Worked variously as a copywriter at advertising agencies, including Foote, Cone, & Belding; J. Walter Thompson; Doyle, Dane, Bernbach; Ogilvy & Mather; and McCann-Erickson.

WRITINGS:

The Concrete Inquisition, Signet (New York, NY), 1993.
Digger, Bantam Books (New York, NY), 1997.
The Next President, Bantam Books (New York, NY), 2000.

Screenplay *Comrades* was optioned by Twentieth-Century Fox.

SIDELIGHTS: Joseph Flynn grew up in a middle-class home in Chicago filled with siblings, aunts, uncles, parents, and grandparents. On his Web site Flynn states: "I grew up on the North Side, in the shadow of Wrigley Field, where I was a White Sox fan in the kingdom of the Cubs. This taught me from the start that I'd have to fight for my place in the world. It was great training for someone who wanted to make his living as a writer." Flynn began his career copywriting for ad agencies. He sold a screenplay that he was working on and began to work on writing novels. His first novel, *The Concrete Inquisition,* was published in 1993.

Flynn's second novel, *Digger,* is about John Fortunato, a Vietnam vetern who has secretly recreated the tunnels of Cu Chi underneath his hometown of Elk River, Illinois. Fortunato, now a photographer, witnesses and captures on film, a brutal killing in his neighborhood. The town is torn apart and erupts into a battlefield. Howard M. Kaplan, writing in the *Denver Post,* called *Digger* "a mystery cloaked as cleverly as (and perhaps better than) any John Grisham work, moves smoothly and swiftly." David Pitt, for *Booklist,* stated, "*Digger* is sure-footed, suspensful, and, in its breathless final moments, unexpectedly heartbreaking."

The Next President, is a thriller that takes place during the 2004 presidential election. There is an assassination plot against Franklin Delano Rawley, America's first black, major-party candidate. J. D. Cade is the assassin blackmailed into the task, but he does not know who is blackmailing him or why this person wants Rawley killed. Cade cannot bring himself to do it and instead tries to discover the identity of his blackmailer whom he plans to kill instead. A reviewer for *Booklist* stated, "Flynn is an excellent storyteller with a well-tuned ear for dialogue and a gift for creating memorable characters placed in believable settings."

BIOGRAPHICAL AND CRITICAL SOURCES:

PERIODICALS

Booklist, August 19, 1997, David Pitt, review of *Digger;* May 15, 2000, review of *The Next President,* p. 1733.
Denver Post, July, 1997, Howard M. Kaplan, review of *Digger.*
Kirkus Reviews, June 15, 1997, review of *Digger.*
Library Journal, July, 1997, Edwin B. Burgess, review of *Digger,* p. 124; April 15, 2000, Robert Conroy, review of *The Next President,* p. 122.
People, October 27, 1997, J.D. Reed, review of *Digger,* p. 1733.
Publishers Weekly, May 8, 2000, review of *The Next President,* p. 205.

ONLINE

Joseph Flynn Home Page, http://www.josephflynn.com (September 24, 2003).
Mystery Guide, http://www.mysteryguide.com/bkflynndigger.html (September 24, 2003), review of *Digger.**

*　　*　　*

FOLEY, Mick 1965-

PERSONAL: Original name, Michael Francis Foley; born June 7, 1965, in NY; son of Jack (a high school athletic director) and Beverly (a physical education teacher) Foley; married, 1992; wife's name, Colette; children: Dewey, Noelle, Michael, Hugh. *Education:* Graduated from State University of New York, Cortland.

ADDRESSES: *Home*—Saint James, NY. *Agent*—Luke Janklow, Janklow and Nesbit Associates, 445 Park Avenue, New York, NY 10022.

CAREER: Professional wrestler, writer. Appeared on the World Wrestling Federation (WWF; now World Wrestling Entertainment [WWE]) Pay-Per-View, 1985-2000, as "Dude Love," "Cactus Jack," and "Mankind"; appeared on Extreme Championship Wrestling (ECW) Hardcore TV, 1994, as "Cactus Jack." Other appearances on televised wrestling events and on *Saturday Night Live* and *The Tonight Show*. Appeared in *Beyond the Mat* (documentary). WWF Commissioner, 2000-01.

AWARDS, HONORS: Three-time WWF Champion; eight-time WWF World Tag Team Champion.

WRITINGS:

Mankind, Have a Nice Day! A Tale of Blood and Sweatsocks, Regan Books (New York, NY), 1999.
Mick Foley's Christmas Chaos, illustrated by Jerry "The King" Lawler, Regan Books (New York, NY), 2000.
Foley Is Good: . . . and the Real World Is Faker than Wrestling, Regan Books (New York, NY), 2001.
Mick Foley's Halloween Hijinx, illustrated by Jill Thompson, HarperCollins (New York, NY), 2001.
Tietam Brown: A Novel, Alfred A. Knopf (New York, NY), 2003.

WORK IN PROGRESS: *Scooter Riley,* a coming-of-age novel.

SIDELIGHTS: Professional wrestler-turned author Mick Foley scored instant successes with his first two books, memoirs that relive his career as the World Wrestling Federation (WWF) star "Mankind," a stage persona who "was a deranged but surprisingly likable fellow in a shirt, tie and Hannibal Lecter mask," according to Alex Tresniowski and Fannie Weinstein in *People* magazine. Foley, born on Long Island, grew up in East Setauket, the son of an athletic director and a gym teacher. He wrestled in high school and, while attending the State University of New York at Cortland, entered professional wrestling in 1983, competing as "Cactus Jack." Foley started out in the minor

leagues of wrestling, as he relates in his best-selling 1999 memoir, *Mankind, Have a Nice Day! A Tale of Blood and Sweatsocks,* fighting for as little as ten dollars a night and sleeping in his car. Initially, as he describes in the memoir, he was the "fall" wrestler, the one who would lose the match to a more popular wrestling star. He went on to develop several more fictional personas for the high-powered entertainment industry of professional wrestling, but his most popular was the good guy, "Mankind." Over the years, however, injuries took their toll on Foley: he lost part of an ear in Munich, a couple of his front teeth were knocked out, and he suffered numerous concussions, broken bones, and other major and minor complaints that finally forced him to leave professional wrestling in 2000, after more than sixteen years in the ring. At that time, Foley was, according to *Newsday*'s Alfonso A. Castillo, "something of a wrestling deity."

In his memoir, *Mankind, Have a Nice Day!,* Foley tells of his personal life in the ring and also how the WWF matches are staged and the endings decided ahead of time. He takes the reader behind the scenes in the wrestling world, an approach that would, according to Patrick Jones in *Voice of Youth Advocates,* "greatly appeal to teens with an avid interest" in the sport. In the end, the book attracted not only teens but also enough adults to send it to the top of *New York Times*'s best-seller list and to sell 754,000 copies. *Time* magazine's Michele Orecklin quipped that the "swift sales" of *Mankind, Have a Nice Day!* "offer incontrovertible proof that wrestling fans can read a work longer than a tattoo." Foley took the success in stride. As he told Tresniowski and Weinstein, "There are better writers, and there are better wrestlers, but there's no better combination of the two. . . . I'm the most successful wrestler-writer of all time."

Until the publication of his 1999 autobiography, Foley may well have been the only wrestler-writer of all time; not long afterward, however, Foley's book inspired an entire new genre of wrestling memoirs. Foley himself got into the trend he had begun, publishing the second installment of his autobiography in 2001, *Foley Is Good: . . . and the Real World Is Faker than Wrestling.* Here the ex-wrestler provides more behind-the-scenes tales of life inside the ropes, and as with the first title, this book too became a best seller. Speaking with Adam Platt in the *New Yorker,* Foley was low-key about his authorial achievements: "This No. 1 seller thing, it's not too different from winning a championship belt. Once a best-seller, always a best-seller. There aren't too many of us out there." Reviewing the work in *Voice of Youth Advocates,* Patrick Jones commented that although the book is "laced with humor, much of it quite raunchy," *Foley Is Good* "tells an often-sad story as Foley realizes that his body is breaking down." According to *Newsday*'s Castillo, the second installment is "loaded with the same candid insights and humor about the pro wrestling industry that made the first book such a success."

Foley went on to pen two best-selling children's books, *Mick Foley's Christmas Chaos* and *Mick Foley's Halloween Hijinx,* before deciding to tackle a novel. Reading J. D. Salinger's *Catcher in the Rye* one day, Foley decided, as he related to Gregory Kirschling in *Entertainment Weekly,* that he could do better: "Hey, if I could write a narrator who was that clear, but also have a story where things happen, then I might have an effective work." Things decidedly happen in the resulting coming-of-age title, *Tietam Brown: A Novel,* including murder, sexual adventures, evil teachers, attempted rape, and first love. Andy Brown, protagonist of the tale, is seventeen and has just been taken out of the detention home where he has been incarcerated for killing a teenager who was trying to rape him. His rescuer is an unlikely one, his long-lost father, Tietam Brown. (Both are named after the Civil War Battle of Antietam.) Andy goes to his father's upstate New York home to start a new life, but is stymied by a coach/ teacher who makes fun of him and by a flock of athletes who also pick on him for his missing ear and deformed left hand. Meanwhile, his weight-lifting father drinks beer, has sex with as many women as he can, and serves as a poor role model for Andy; father and son have an awkward, confused relationship that Andy hopes to understand. The only bright spot in Andy's life is the sudden and unexpected attention paid him by the prettiest girl in school, a born-again Christian named Terri Lynn Johnson. Andy is afraid, however, that he or his father will spoil this chance at love.

Foley's fictional debut had its share of detractors. Writing in the *New York Times Book Review,* Dan Kaufman noted that "what the book lacks isn't action . . . but a character, a scene, or even a scrap of dialogue that feels fresh or unexpected." A critic for *Kirkus Reviews* felt that "Foley gets good seriocomic mileage out of Andy's addled relationship with his volatile, interfering father," and that "one admires . . . charm-

ingly weird images." But for this reviewer, Foley "doesn't know when to tone it down" in this "over-the-top first novel." Similarly, *Booklist*'s Keir Graff found the novel "frustrating," especially because of "supporting characters who are two-dimensional or lack understandable motivation." A contributor for *Publishers Weekly* also commented on Foley's "cartoonish characters," and concluded that "readers in the mood for vigorous pulp may enjoy this steroid-fueled brawl."

Other reviewers found more positive aspects to the novel. *Library Journal*'s Jim Coan found it a "compulsively readable first novel," and went on to observe that Foley "knows how to spin an intriguing if somewhat offbeat tale." Joe Hartlaub, writing on *Bookreporter.com,* while noting that *Tietam Brown* is "hardly an uplifting story," also commented that the book is a "surprisingly confident work for a first novel," and that "some of the passages certainly have the ring of truth about them." Similarly, *Book Page*'s Paul Goat Allen called the novel "highly energetic, breakneck-paced, witty, laugh-out-loud funny and— surprisingly—addictively entertaining." And writing in *Book,* Kevin Greenberg concluded, "Agonizingly tragic, yet ultimately hopeful in its outlook, Foley's novel has us rooting for Andy from the start."

BIOGRAPHICAL AND CRITICAL SOURCES:

BOOKS

Foley, Mick, *Mankind, Have a Nice Day! A Tale of Blood and Sweatsocks,* Regan Books (New York, NY), 1999.
Foley, Mick, *Foley Is Good: . . . and the Real World Is Faker than Wrestling,* Regan Books (New York, NY), 2001.

PERIODICALS

Book, July-August, 2003, Kevin Greenberg, review of *Tietam Brown,* p. 77.
Booklist, May 1, 2003, Keir Graff, review of *Tietam Brown,* pp. 1507-08.
Chicago Sun-Times February 24, 2000, review of *Mankind, Have a Nice Day! A Tale of Blood and Sweatsocks,* p. 40.

Daily Variety, December 1, 2003, Michael Schneider, "Mick Foley's Grappling with CBS Actioner Deal," pp. 5-6.

Entertainment Weekly, July 25, 2003, Gregory Kirschling, "One Giant Leap for Mankind," p. 44; August 1, 2003, Joshua Rich, review of *Tietam Brown,* p. 82.

Houston Chronicle, May 26, 2001, Dinitia Smith, review of *Foley Is Good: . . . and the Real World Is Faker than Wrestling,* p. 9.

Kirkus Reviews, May 1, 2003, review of *Tietam Brown,* p. 626.

Library Journal, June 1, 2003, Jim Coan, review of *Tietam Brown,* p. 164.

Newsday, July 28, 2003, Alfonso A. Castillo, "Ex-Lord of the Ring: After 15 Years of Pounding As a Professional Wrestler, Mick Foley Finds His New Passion—As a Fiction Writer," p. B6.

New York, March 27, 2000, Peter Rainer, "Beyond the Mat," p. 102.

New Yorker, December 20, 1999, Adam Platt, "A Champion in the Ring Takes on the Literary World," pp. 34-35.

New York Times Book Review, August 3, 2003, Dan Kaufman, review of *Tietam Brown,* p. 16.

People, June 11, 2001, Alex Tresniowski and Fannie Weinstein, "Man of Letters," p. 122.

Publishers Weekly, December 11, 2000, "December Publications," p. 79; May 19, 2003, review of *Tietam Brown,* p. 49.

Time, November 15, 1999, Michele Orecklin, "People," p. 124; March 20, 2000, Joel Stein, "Mick Foley Q&A," p. 90.

Times Union, December 5, 1999, Jennifer Weiner, review of *Mankind,* p. J4.

Variety, December 6, 1999, Oliver Jones, "Champ Wrestles Out a Bestseller," p. 6.

Voice of Youth Advocates, February, 2000, Patrick Jones, review of *Mankind, Have a Nice Day!,* p. 420; October, 2001, Patrick Jones, review of *Foley Is Good,* p. 300; June, 2002, Kat Kan, review of *Mick Foley's Christmas Chaos,* p. 110.

Wrestling Digest, August, 2000, Steve Anderson, "Mick Foley Wrestles with Retirement," p. 34; October, 2000, "ECW Avoids Getting Burned," p. 15; December, 2001, Jim Varsallone, "From the Squared Circle to the Best-Seller List," pp. 16-20; October, 2003, Jim Varsallone, "A Novel Approach," pp. 42-48.

ONLINE

BookPage.com, http://www.bookpage.com/ (March 23, 2004), Paul Goat Allen, review of *Tietam Brown.*

Bookreporter.com, http://www.bookreporter.com/ (March 23, 2004), Joe Hartlaub, review of *Tietam Brown.*

MU Online, http://members.aol.com/wumweaverjr/ reviewfigbook.html/ (October 28, 2003), Michael Weaver, Jr., review of *Foley Is Good.*

Official Mick Foley Web site, http://www.mickfoley. com (March 23, 2004).

Pro Wrestling Torch, http://www.pwtorch.com/ (July 25, 2003), Tony Batalla, review of *Tietam Brown.*

Random House Web site, http://www.randomhouse. com/ (March 23, 2004).

Shotgun Reviews, http://www.shotgunreviews.com/ (March 23, 2004), Russ Ray, review of *Foley Is Good.*

Star Tribune Online, http://www.startribune.com/ (July 27, 2003), Graydon Royce, review of *Tietam Brown.*

TV Tome Online, http://www.tvtome.com/ (March 32, 2004).

World Wrestling Entertainment, Inc., http://www.wwe. com/ (June 15, 2003), interview with Mick Foley.

Wrasslin.com, http://www.wrasslin.com/ (October 28, 2003), Philip Nourse, interview with Mick Foley and review of *Tietam Brown.**

*   *   *

FOLLY, Martin H(arold) 1957-

PERSONAL: Born February 6, 1957, in Hackney, London, England; son of Alan (a publisher) and Marjorie (a secretary and homemaker; maiden name, Wood) Folly. *Ethnicity:* "English." *Education:* Sidney Sussex College, Cambridge, B.A. (with honors), 1978; London School of Economics and Political Science, London, Ph.D., 1997. *Politics:* Labour. *Religion:* Church of England. *Hobbies and other interests:* Amateur drama (acting and directing), cricket.

ADDRESSES: Home—1 Tash Pl., New Southgate, London N11 1PA, England. *Office*—Brunel University, Uxbridge, Middlesex UB8 1EH, England. *E-mail*—martin.folly@lineone.net.

CAREER: Brunel University, Uxbridge, Middlesex, England, senior tutor for American studies, 1989—.

MEMBER: British Association for American Studies, British International Studies Association, Society for Historians of American Foreign Relations.

WRITINGS:

People in History (juvenile), Mitchell Beazley (London, England), 1988.
Churchill, Whitehall, and the Soviet Union, 1940-45, Macmillan Publishers (London, England), 2000.

Contributor to periodicals, including *Review of International Studies, Diplomatic History, Journal of American Studies,* and *Diplomacy and Statecraft.* Coeditor of the Internet journal *Entertext.*

WORK IN PROGRESS: The United States in World War II, for Edinburgh University Press (Edinburgh, Scotland); research on Anglo-American Soviet relations in World War II.

SIDELIGHTS: Martin H. Folly told *CA:* "I always loved history. As a ten-year-old I spent a lot of time reading up on the history of the London underground, so it was perhaps natural that I wound up as a historian. But I was also lucky to have schoolteachers who made history interesting and who were very encouraging about my juvenile writing.

"I was always drawn to World War II as a subject. Prime influences on that would be the classic *World at War* television series and all those Airfix models of my youth. Combine that with a longstanding interest in the Soviet Union and you get the inspiration for my studies. As I researched on Anglo-Soviet relations during the war, I became dissatisfied with the way our knowledge of what happened next causes us to view wartime events. How did they look at the time? Participants did not know what was going to happen, but they saw what *had* happened, and their anxiety to prevent a repetition of the desperate war they found themselves in needs to be restored to the center of our understanding of what they did. As I worked on the archives, so I became more interested in the titanic struggle of the Soviet peoples. One day I will write some more on that subject."

*   *   *

FOX, Barry

PERSONAL: Married Nadine Taylor (a registered nurse). *Education:* University of California at Santa Cruz, B.A. (theater), 1979; University of Southern California, M.F.A., 1981; Greenwich University, Ph.D. (professional writing), 1993.

ADDRESSES: Home—23679 Calabasas Rd., #223, Calabasas, CA 91302. *E-mail*—TayFox@aol.com.

CAREER: Speaker and author; *Business Report,* former executive editor; "Housecalls" radio program, Los Angeles, CA, substitute host, 1995-2002; guest on radio and television programs. University of Integrative Studies, Sonora, CA, professor. Chair of the Consumer Advisory Council, American Nutraceutical Association.

WRITINGS:

Foods to Heal By: An A-to-Z Guide to Medicinal Foods and Their Curative Properties, St. Martin's (New York, NY), 1996.
To Your Health: The Healing Power of Alcohol, St. Martin's (New York, NY), 1997.
(With Jason Theodosakis and Brenda Adderly) *The Arthritis Cure: The Medical Miracle that Can Halt, Reverse, and May Even Cure Osteoarthritis,* St. Martin's (New York, NY), 1997.
(With Jason Theodosakis and Brenda Adderly) *Maximizing the Arthritis Cure: A Step-by-Step Program to Faster, Stronger Healing during Any Stage of the Cure,* St. Martin's (New York, NY), 1998.
(With Gabe Mirkin) *The 20/30 Fat and Fiber Diet Plan,* HarperCollins (New York, NY), 1998.
(With Selma Schimmel) *Cancer Talk: Voices of Hope and Endurance from "The Group Room," the World's Largest Cancer Support Group,* Broadway Books (New York, NY), 1999.
(With Gerald Reaven and Terry Kristen) *Syndrome X: Overcoming the Silent Killer that Can Give You a Heart Attack,* Simon & Schuster (New York, NY), 2000.
(With Alexander Mauskop) *What Your Doctor May Not Tell You about Migraines: The Breakthrough Program that Can Help End Your Pain,* Warner Books (New York, NY), 2001.
(With Frederic Vagnini) *The Side Effects Bible: The Dietary Solution to Unwanted Side Effects of Common Medications,* Broadway Books (New York, NY), 2005.

WITH ARNOLD FOX

DLPA to End Chronic Pain and Depression, Pocket Books (New York, NY), 1985.
Wake Up! You're Alive: MD's Prescription for Healthier Living through Positive Thinking, Health Communications (Deerfield Beach, FL), 1988.

Immune for Life: Live Longer and Better by Strengthening Your "Doctor Within," Prima Publications and Communications (Rocklin, CA), 1989.

Making Miracles: Inspiring Mind-Methods to Supercharge Your Emotions and Rejuvenate Your Health, Rodale Press (Emmaus, PA), 1989.

Beyond Positive Thinking: Putting Your Thoughts into Action, Hay House (Carson, CA), 1991.

14-Day Miracle Plan: Inspiring Mind Methods to Supercharge Your Emotions and Rejuvenate Your Health, HarperCollins (New York, NY), 1991.

The Healthy Prostate: A Doctor's Comprehensive Program for Preventing and Treating Common Problems, Wiley (New York, NY), 1996.

Alternative Healing, Career Press (Franklin Lakes, NJ), 1996.

Boost Your Immune System Now!: Live Longer and Better by Strengthening Your "Doctor Within," Prima Publications and Communications (Rocklin, CA), 1997.

WITH WIFE, NADINE TAYLOR

(And with Rene Delorm) *Diana and Dodi: A Love Story,* Tallfellow Press (Los Angeles, CA), 1998.

Arthritis for Dummies, IDG Books Worldwide (Foster City, CA), 2000.

(And with Mark Houston) *What Your Doctor May Not Tell You about Hypertension: The Revolutionary Nutrition and Lifestyle Program to Help Fight High Blood Pressure,* Warner Books (New York, NY), 2003.

Contributor of nearly 200 articles to periodicals. Contributing editor to *Let's Live Magazine.*

SIDELIGHTS: As both a "name" author and a ghost writer, Barry Fox has written a celebrity biography on the tragically shortened romance between Princess Diana and Dodi Al Fayed, numerous self-help and inspirational treatises, and books on a wide variety of health topics, including diet, the immune system, and afflictions such as cancer, arthritis, and hypertension. He is a popular speaker on the lecture circuit. He is also a professor at the University of Integrative Studies, based in Sonora, California and chair of the Consumer Advisory Council for the American Nutraceutical Association, a clearinghouse for information on healthy eating and the health effects of supplements.

With his wife, Nadine Taylor, a trained dietitian, he specializes in bringing current health information to the public in books, articles, and lectures.

One of his popular books has been *The Arthritis Cure: The Medical Miracle that Can Halt, Reverse, and May Even Cure Osteoarthritis,* written with Brenda Adderly and Dr. Jason Theodosakis, an assistant clinical professor at the University of Arizona. Together, the authors recommend an eight-step program including a healthy "joint-building" diet, exercise, maintaining ideal weight, and the careful use of glucosamine and chondroitin sulfates. Some reviewers were skeptical of the advice provided, however. Writing in *Nutrition Forum,* Manfred Kroger predicted, "Like dozens of other books promising simple cures of complicated and perplexing diseases, this book will most likely end up as a remaindered publisher's venture. . . . And years from now, arthritis will still be with us." But other reviewers were more impressed. "The authors, in a clearly illustrated and well-written text, command attention with their research and that of others," wrote *USA Today* contributor Gerald F. Kreyche. Fox, along with Taylor, more recently produced *Arthritis for Dummies,* a "clearly written and simply illustrated guide" to various arthritis treatments and strategies, according to a *Library Journal* reviewer.

In addition to arthritis, Fox has coauthored a number of books on a the considerably more devastating disease of cancer. One of these is *Cancer Talk: Voices of Hope and Endurance from "The Group Room," the World's Largest Cancer Support Group,* written with Selma Schimmel. Herself a longtime cancer survivor, Schimmel founded Vital Options, a support group for young people with cancer, which eventually turned into the Group Room, a radio program on NPR and the world's largest Internet support group to empower cancer patients to take an active role in their treatments rather than see themselves as victims. Issues such as caring for a young child with cancer and dealing with survivor guilt are covered, and there is a great deal of information on the side effects of various treatments, from both experts and forum participants. According to a *Publishers Weekly* reviewer, the book provides a "well-needed, sensitive approach" to treatments and policies, but the real value lies in "the voices of the people affected by cancer who provide hope instead of hopelessness." "Each chapter ends by helpfully summarizing major points, and the book concludes with a long list of support and advocacy organizations," noted *Booklist* contributor William Beatty.

Along with Arnold Fox, the author also completed *The Healthy Prostate: A Doctor's Comprehensive Program for Preventing and Treating Common Problems*. In addition to providing medical information, the Foxes also give advice on effective communication strategies for both doctors and patients and provide alternative treatment options. *Booklist* reviewer Mike Tribby found it, "Easy to use and comprehend." The Foxes also teamed up to write *Immune for Life: Live Longer and Better by Strengthening Your "Doctor Within."* In addition to handy advice about diet and exercise, the book provides an "Outlook on Life Test" and a comprehensive "Nutrition Quiz." *Library Journal* reviewer Allayne Heyduk stated that although there was "nothing new here . . . [the authors] present it in a nice package."

BIOGRAPHICAL AND CRITICAL SOURCES:

PERIODICALS

Booklist, May 15, 1996, Mike Tribby, review of *The Healthy Prostate: A Doctor's Comprehensive Program for Preventing and Treating Common Problems,* p. 1556; May 15, 1999, William Beatty, review of *Cancer Talk: Voices of Hope and Endurance from "The Group Room," the World's Largest Cancer Support Group,* p. 1655.

Library Journal, April 1, 1989, Allayne Heyduk, review of *Immune for Life: Live Longer and Better by Strengthening Your "Doctor Within,"* p. 105; January, 2002, review of *Arthritis for Dummies,* p. 60; September 1, 2003, Janet M. Schneider, review of *What Your Doctor May Not Tell You about Hypertension: The Revolutionary Nutrition and Lifestyle Program to Help Fight High Blood Pressure,* p. 197.

Nutrition Forum, July-August, 1997, Manfred Kroger, review of *The Arthritis Cure: The Medical Miracle that Can Halt, Reverse, and May Even Cure Osteoarthritis,* p. 32.

Publishers Weekly, April 19, 1999, review of *Cancer Talk,* p. 68.

USA Today, January, 1998, Gerald F. Kreyche, review of *The Arthritis Cure,* Magazine section, p. 80.

ONLINE

Barry Fox and Nadine Taylor Home Page, http://www.taylor-fox.com (July 22, 2004).

Barry Fox Home Page, http://www.barryfox.us (July 22, 2004).

FRADY, Marshall (Bolton) 1940-2004

OBITUARY NOTICE—See index for *CA* sketch: Born January 11, 1940, in Augusta, GA; died of cancer March 9, 2004, in Greenville, SC. Journalist and author. Frady was a print and television journalist who was known for his political biographies and his commentaries on the social and political evolution of the American South. An alumnus of Furman University, where he earned a B.A. in 1963, he also graduated from the University of Iowa in 1966. Frady began his journalism career at the Atlanta and Los Angeles bureaus of *Newsweek* magazine. This was followed by a year with the *Saturday Evening Post* in Atlanta and two years with *Harper's*. After writing for *Life* in the early 1970s, Frady moved on to television, working as a writer, correspondent, and host of the program *Closeup* for the American Broadcasting Corporation. His work on the documentary "Soldiers of the Twilight" for *Closeup* earned him an Emmy Award in 1982. He would later also earn awards for the documentaries "To Save Our Schools" (1984) and "The Supreme Court of the United States" (1985). Moving on to ABC's *Nightline*, Frady was a correspondent for that program beginning in 1986, and during the 1990s also worked on television documentaries for public television. Although he would write other biographies, such as *Billy Graham: A Parable of American Righteousness* (1979) and *Jesse: The Life and Pilgrimage of Jesse Jackson* (1996), Frady was often best remembered for his first biography, *Wallace* (1968; revised edition, 1976), the story of Alabama governor and conservative 1968 presidential candidate George Wallace. Originally, Frady had planned to write a southern novel featuring politics, but his time with the governor and those working for him led him to write a nonfiction work that was condemned by Wallace and his supporters as inaccurate and praised by critics as quality journalism; the book was later adapted in 1997 as the miniseries *George Wallace*. Critics also highly lauded Frady's *Southerners: A Journalist's Odyssey* (1980), which was nominated for a Pulitzer in 1981. At the time of his death, Frady was working on a biography of Cuban leader Fidel Castro, and he had just accepted a position as a lecturer in political science and nonfiction writing and as writer in residence at Furman University.

OBITUARIES AND OTHER SOURCES:

PERIODICALS

Chicago Tribune, March 10, 2004, Section 3, p. 12.

New York Times, March 11, 2004, p. A27.
Washington Post, March 11, 2004, p. B6.

*   *   *

FRANCO, Betsy

PERSONAL: Married; husband's name, Douglas; children: James, Thomas, David. *Education:* Stanford University, B.A.; Lesley College, M.Ed.

ADDRESSES: Office—P.O. Box 60487, Palo Alto, CA 94306. *E-mail*—francobe@aol.com.

CAREER: Writer and editor for children and adults; creator of educational materials.

WRITINGS:

Japan, illustrated by Jo Supancich, Evan-Moor, 1993.
Mexico, illustrated by Jo Supancich, Evan-Moor, 1993.
Russia, illustrated by Jo Supancich, Evan-Moor, 1993.
India, illustrated by Jo Supancich, Evan-Moor, 1994.
Nigeria, illustrated by Jo Supancich, Evan-Moor, 1994.
China, illustrated by Jo Supancich, Evan-Moor, 1994.
Brazil, illustrated by Cheryl Kirk Noll, Evan-Moor, 1995.
South Korea, illustrated by Cheryl Kirk Noll, Evan-Moor, 1995.
Italy, illustrated by Susan O'Neill, Evan-Moor, 1995.
Quiet Elegance: Japan through the Eyes of Nine American Artists, Charles E. Tuttle (Boston, MA), 1997.
Sorting All Sorts of Socks, illustrated by Sheila Lucas, Creative Publications (Mountain View, CA), 1997.
Fourscore and Seven, Good Year Books (Glenview, IL), 1999.
Grandpa's Quilt, illustrated by Linda A. Bild, Children's Press (New York, NY), 1999.
Write and Read Math Story Books, Scholastic (New York, NY), 1999.
Unfolding Mathematics with Unit Origami, Key Curriculum, 1999.
Shells, illustrated by Kristin Sorra, Children's Press (New York, NY), 2000.
Why the Frog Has Big Eyes, illustrated by Joung Un Kim, Harcourt, Brace (San Diego, CA), 2000.

Caring, Sharing, and Getting Along, Scholastic (New York, NY), 2000.
Thematic Poetry: On the Farm, Scholastic (New York, NY), 2000.
Twenty Marvelous Math Tales, Scholastic (New York, NY), 2000.
Thematic Poetry: Neighborhoods and Communities, Scholastic (New York, NY), 2000.
Thematic Poetry: Creepy Crawlies, Scholastic (New York, NY), 2000.
201 Thematic Riddle Poems to Build Literacy, Scholastic (New York, NY), 2000.
Thematic Poetry: All About Me!, Scholastic (New York, NY), 2000.
The Tortoise Who Bragged: A Chinese Tale with Trigrams, illustrated by Ann-Marie Perks, Stokes Publishing (Sunnyvale, CA), 2000.
My Pinkie Finger, illustrated by Margeaux Lucas, Children's Press (New York, NY), 2001.
Instant Poetry Frames for Primary Poets, Scholastic (New York, NY), 2001.
Fifteen Wonderful Writing Prompt Mini-Books, Scholastic (New York, NY), 2001.
Clever Calculator Cat, illustrated by Ann-Marie Perks, Stokes Publishing (Sunnyvale, CA), 2001.
Funny Fairy Tale Math, Scholastic (New York, NY), 2001.
Thematic Poetry: Transportation, Scholastic (New York, NY), 2001.
Clever Calculations about Cats and Other Cool Creatures (teacher resource book), Stokes Publishing (Sunnyvale, CA), 2001.
Adding Alligators and Other Easy-to-Read Math Stories, Scholastic (New York, NY), 2001.
Five-Minute Math Problem of the Day for Young Learners, Scholastic (New York, NY), 2001.
Twelve Genre Mini-Books, Scholastic (New York, NY), 2002.
Instant Math Practice Pages for Homework—or Anytime!, Scholastic (New York, NY), 2002.
Six Silly Seals and Other Read-Aloud Story Skits, Teaching Resources, 2002.
Amazing Animals, illustrated by Jesse Reisch, Children's Press (New York, NY), 2002.
Pocket Poetry Mini-Books, Scholastic (New York, NY), 2002.
Silly Sally, illustrated by Stacey Lamb, Children's Press (New York, NY), 2002.
Jake's Cake Mistake, illustrated by Paul Harvey, Scholastic (New York, NY), 2002.
(With Claudine Jellison and Johanna Kaufman) *Subtraction Fun,* Pebble Books, 2002.

(With Denise Dauler) *Math in Motion: Wiggle, Gallop, and Leap with Numbers,* Creative Teaching Press, 2002.

Many Ways to 100, Yellow Umbrella Books (Mankato, MN), 2002.

A Bat Named Pat, illustrated by Bari Weissman, Scholastic (New York, NY), 2002.

Subtraction Fun, Yellow Umbrella Books (Mankato, MN), 2002.

Time to Estimate, Yellow Umbrella Books (Mankato, MN), 2002.

Marvelous Math Word Problem Mini-Books, Scholastic (New York, NY), 2002.

What's Zero?, Yellow Umbrella Books (Mankato, MN), 2002.

Going to Grandma's Farm, illustrated by Claudia Rueda, Children's Press (New York, NY), 2003.

Word Families: Guess-Me Poems and Puzzles, Scholastic (New York, NY), 2003.

Mathematickles!, illustrated by Steven Salerno, Margaret K. McElderry Books (New York, NY), 2003.

Amoeba Hop, illustrated by Christine Lavin, Puddle Jump Press, 2003.

Alphabet: Guess-Me Poems and Puzzles, Scholastic (New York, NY), 2003.

Counting Our Way to the 100th Day!: 100 Poems and 100 Pictures to Celebrate the 100th Day of School, illustrated by Steven Salerno, Margaret K. McElderry Books (New York, NY), 2004.

EDITOR

You Hear Me?: Poems and Writing by Teenage Boys, Candlewick Press (Cambridge, MA), 2000.

Things I Have to Tell You: Poems and Writing by Teenage Girls, photographs by Nina Nickles, Candlewick Press (Cambridge, MA), 2001.

(With Annette Ochoa and Traci Gourdine) *Night Is Gone, Day Is Still Coming: Stories and Poems by American Indian Teenagers and Young Adults,* Candlewick Press (Cambridge, MA), 2003.

Author of numerous workbooks, easy level readers, easy mathematics resource books, and science resource books.

SIDELIGHTS: Betsy Franco's many projects for children range widely across the educational and entertainment spectrums. Franco has written easy level readers for use in schools, mathematics books that rely on games and projects to teach basic skills, and picture books for reading out loud. She has also become known as the editor of three important anthologies of poetry by teenagers: *You Hear Me?: Poems and Writing by Teenage Boys; Things I have to Tell You: Poems and Writing by Teenage Girls;* and *Night Is Gone, Day Is Still Coming: Stories and Poems by American Indian Teenagers and Young Adults.* In these books, the authentic voices of American teens describe what it feels like to be young today.

Franco studied to be a fine artist, and she still loves to paint. When her children were born, however, she realized that she could not spare the time for her visual art, so she decided to try creative writing. One of her favorite challenges is making math fun for children. In books such as *Clever Calculator Cat* and *Many Ways to 100,* students sharpen math skills through activities and riddles. *Mathematickles!* uses the common math signs such as plus, minus, and parentheses in word poems about the seasons and the outdoor world. A *Publishers Weekly* critic praised *Mathematickles!* as a "nimble brain teaser" that "elevates basic mathematical concepts plus wordplay to the level of inspiration."

Inspired by her own teenage sons, Franco decided to solicit poetry from young men for inclusion in an anthology. Skeptics warned that she would not receive enough submissions from teenage boys to fill a book, but she soon had attracted more manuscripts than she could use. *You Hear Me?: Poems and Writings by Teenage Boys* contains frank and honest poetry on every subject of importance to young men, from homosexuality and dating to self-image, family and neighborhood issues, aspirations, and creativity—all written by teenagers. Sharon Korbeck in *School Library Journal* called the book "a fresh approach to hearing what today's youths have to say." *Booklist* correspondent Hazel Rochman found the poems to have "more urgency than many YA novels." She concluded: "Many teens will recognize their search for themselves."

Things I Have to Tell You and *Night Is Gone, Day Is Still Coming* collect the poetry of teenage girls and teenage Native Americans respectively. Both books have received the same warm reviews that greeted *You Hear Me?* A *Horn Book* reviewer wrote of *Things I Have to Tell You:* "Varying in tone, style, and degree of polish, the entries . . . convey moments of strength and weakness, of anger, fear, and joy, commanding our attention from beginning to end." In her *School Library Journal* review of *Night Is Gone, Day Is Still Coming,* Sharon Korbek observed: "Whether they feel oppressed, cheated, or inspired, these young people write from the depths of their souls."

In an interview with *Teenreads,* Franco had some advice for aspiring authors. "You have things to say that no one else can say," she commented. "Just don't give up. Half of being a writer is being stubborn and believing in yourself, not so much in a self-esteem way, but knowing you have something to say. . . . In my case, I found I had to write all kinds of different types of books to make a living, from poetry to nonfiction, from adults to young children. Work very hard."

BIOGRAPHICAL AND CRITICAL SOURCES:

PERIODICALS

Booklist, October 1, 2000, Hazel Rochman, review of *You Hear Me?: Poems and Writings by Teenage Boys,* p. 330.
Horn Book, May, 2001, review of *Things I Have to Tell You: Poems and Writing by Teenage Girls,* p. 343; July-August, 2003, Susan Dove Lempke, review of *Mathematickles!,* p. 472.
Publishers Weekly, June 16, 2003, review of *Mathematickles!,* p. 70.
School Library Journal, October, 2000, Sharon Korbeck, review of *You Hear Me?,* p. 183; May, 2001, Sharon Korbeck, review of *Things I Have to Tell You: Poems and Writing by Teenage Girls,* p. 164; August, 2003, Sharon Korbeck, review of *Night Is Gone, Day Is Still Coming: Stories and Poems by American Indian Teens and Young Adults,* p. 184.

ONLINE

Betsy Franco Home Page, http://www.betsyfranco. com (December 12, 2003).
Candlewick Press, http://www.candlewick.com/ (December 12, 2003), "Betsy Franco."
Teenreads, http://www.teenreads.com/ (December 12, 2003), interviews with Franco.*

FRIEDMAN, Debra 1955-

PERSONAL: Born July 19, 1955. *Education:* Attended York University, Toronto, 1974-76, Nova Scotia College of Art and Design, 1977, and Visual Studies Workshop, Rochester, NY, 1978; School of the Museum of Fine Arts, Boston, MA, B.F.A., 1981; School of the Art Institute of Chicago, M.F.A., 1985.

ADDRESSES: Home—18 Langford Ave., Toronto, Ontario, Canada M4J 3E3.

CAREER: Art photographer, 1980—. *Exhibitions:* MIT Creative Photography Lab, 1980; Idee Gallery, Toronto, 1983, 1985, and 1988; SE Centre for Photographic Studies, Daytona, FL, 1984; Toronto Photographers Workshop, 1985; Cincinnati Academy of Art, 1985; Illinois Development Finance Authority Building, 1985; UCLA Art Department, 1986; Burlington Cultural Centre, Burlington, Ontario, 1988; Zwiazek Polskich Artystow Fotografikow, Krakow, Poland, 1989; Artichok, Oss Netherlands, 1990; Winnipeg Art Gallery, 1990, Jane Corkin Gallery, 1990; Toronto Image Works, 1992; Betty Rymer Gallery, Chicago, IL, 1994; Stephen Bulger Gallery, Toronto, 1995; Ryerson Gallery, Toronto, 1996; The Photo Passage, Toronto, 1999; Museum of Contemporary Canadian Art, Toronto, 2000; York Quay Centre, Toronto, 2001; Luft Gallery, Toronto, 2002; Pikto Gallery, Toronto, 2003. Work is permanently collected by City of Toronto Archives, Polaroid Corporation, Pende Fine Arts, Canada Council Art Bank, Illinois State Art Museum, and Art Institute of Chicago, as well as private and corporate collections.

AWARDS, HONORS: Grants from Ontario Arts Council, 1984, 1986, 1988, 1996, 1998, and 2000; grants from Polaroid Corp., 1985, 1986, and 1993; State of Illinois Art Gallery purchase award, 1985; Artichok Festival grant, 1989; residency fellowship, Hambidge Centre, 1993.

WRITINGS:

Picture This: Fun Photography and Crafts, Kids Can Press, 2003.

Creator of brochures and posters for corporate and civic clients, including United Steelworkers of America, Jobs Ontario Training Fund, and Ontario Women's Directorate.*

FRISCH, Walter 1951-

PERSONAL: Born February 26, 1951, in New York, NY; son of Raymond J. and Darcy (Miller) Frisch; married Anne-Marie Bouche, August 27, 1981; children: Nicholas. *Education:* Yale, B.A., 1973; University of California, Berkeley, M.A., 1977; Ph.D., 1981.

ADDRESSES: Office—Department of Music, 621 Dodge Hall, Columbia University, 2960 Broadway, New York, NY 10027.

CAREER: Columbia University, professor, 1982—; writer.

MEMBER: American Musical Society; American Brahms Society.

AWARDS, HONORS: National Endowment for the Humanities fellowship, 1985-86, for individual research; Deems Taylor awards, American Society of Composers, Authors, and Publishers, 1985, 1990.

WRITINGS:

(Editor) *Schubert: Critical and Analytical Studies,* University of Nebraska Press (Lincoln, NE), 1986.
(Editor) *Brahms and His World,* Princeton University Press (Princeton, NJ), 1990.
Brahms and the Principle of Developing Variation, University of California Press (Berkeley, CA), 1993.
The Early Works of Arnold Schoenberg, 1893-1908, University of California Press (Berkeley, CA), 1993.
Brahms: The Four Symphonies, Schirmer Books (New York, NY), 1996.
(Editor) *Schoenberg and His World,* Princeton University Press (Princeton, NJ), 1999.

Editor of *19th Century Music.*

SIDELIGHTS: Walter Frisch told *CA:* "I am interested in writing about Western classical music in a way that can appeal both to specialists and the informed listener. Writing about music can be technical and detailed but not impenetrable. I seek to enhance a reader's appreciation of familiar masterworks by composers such as Brahms, Schubert, and Schoenberg."

BIOGRAPHICAL AND CRITICAL SOURCES:

PERIODICALS

American Record Guide, September-October 1997, John P. McKelvey, review of *Brahms: The Four Symphonies,* pp. 296-298.
Music & Letters, May, 1995, Nick Chadwick, review of *The Early Works of Arnold Schoenberg: 1893-1908,* p. 307.
New York Review of Books, October 22, 1998, Charles Rosen, review of *Brahms: The Four Symphonies,* p.64.
Notes, June, 1995, Seve Neff, review of *The Early Works of Arnold Schoenberg: 1893-1908,* p. 1289; September 2000, Walter B. Bailey, review of *Schoenberg and His World,* p. 143.*

*   *   *

FROUD, Brian 1947-

PERSONAL: Born 1947, in Winchester, England; married, wife's name, Wendy (a sculptor, dollmaker, and puppetmaker); children: Toby. *Education:* Maidstone College of Art, B.A. (with honors), 1971.

ADDRESSES: Agent—c/o author correspondence, Harry N. Abrams, Inc., 110 E. 59th St., New York, NY 10022.

CAREER: Artist, illustrator, creative consultant to films, including *The Dark Crystal,* 1983, and *Labyrinth,* 1986. *Exhibitions:* Work has been exhibited in England and America.

AWARDS, HONORS: ASFA Best Interior Illustration Award and Hugo Award for best original artwork, both 1995.

WRITINGS:

The Land of Froud, Peacock Press (New York, NY), 1977.
(With Alan Lee) *Faeries,* Harry N. Abrams (New York, NY), 1978.

The Faeries Pop-Up Book, 1980.

Goblins, Macmillan (New York, NY), 1983.

(With Terry Jones) *The Goblins of Labyrinth: Invented and Illuminated by Brian Froud; Captured and Catalogued by Terry Jones,* Henry Holt (New York, NY), 1986.

(With Charles de Lint) *The Dreaming Place,* Atheneum (New York, NY), 1990.

(With Terry Jones) *Lady Cottington's Pressed Fairy Book,* Turner Publications (Atlanta, GA), 1994, reprinted, Harry N. Abrams (New York, NY), 2002.

(With Charles de Lint) *The Wild Wood,* Bantam Books (New York, NY), 1994.

(With Terry Jones) *The Goblin Companion: Invented and Illustrated by Brian Froud; Captured and Catalogued by Terry Jones,* Turner Publications (Atlanta, GA), 1996.

(With Terry Jones) *Strange Stains and Mysterious Smells: Quentin Cottington's Journal of Faery Research,* Simon & Schuster (New York, NY), 1996.

Good Faeries/Bad Faeries, Simon & Schuster (New York, NY), 1998.

(With Jessica Macbeth) *The Faeries' Oracle,* Fireside Books (New York, NY), 2000.

(With Ari Berk) *Brian Froud's the Runes of Elfland: Visions and Stories from the Faerie Alphabet,* Harry N. Abrams (New York, NY), 2003.

(With J. J. Llewellyn) *The World of the Dark Crystal,* Harry N. Abrams (New York, NY), 2003.

ILLUSTRATOR

Charles Lamb, *A Midsummer Night's Dream,* Franklin Watts (New York, NY), 1972.

Margaret Mahy, *The Man Whose Mother Was a Pirate,* Atheneum (New York, NY), 1972.

Margaret Mahy, *Ultra-Violet Catastrophe! Or, The Unexpected Walk with Great-Uncle Magnus Pringle,* Parents' Magazine Press (New York, NY), 1975.

Mary Norton, *Are All the Giants Dead?,* Harcourt, Brace (New York, NY), 1975, Magic Carpet Books (San Diego, CA), 1997.

Alexander Theroux, *Master Snickup's Cloak,* Paper Tiger (Limpsfield, Surrey, England), 1979.

Charles De Lint, *The Dreaming Place,* Atheneum (New York, NY), 1990.

Charles De Lint, *Brian Froud's Faerielands: The Wild Wood,* Bantam (New York, NY), 1994.

Patricia A. McKillip, *Brian Froud's Faerielands: Something Rich and Strange,* Bantam (New York, NY), 1994.

(Designer) Wendy Froud and Terri Windling, *The Winter Child,* Simon & Schuster (New York, NY), 2001.

ADAPTATIONS: Froud and his artwork are featured in the documentary film *The Fairy Faith.*

SIDELIGHTS: The image of faeries has changed considerably since Brian Froud began his artistic career in the 1970s. Through his influential drawings and books, Froud has introduced the idea that faeries (the Old English spelling) come in many shapes and personalities—that some are indeed the pleasant pixies of animated cartoons, while others can be sinister, sad, or flirtatious. Froud's book *Faeries,* a bestseller in its time, has had enormous influence on film, general illustration, and fantasy, as the artist has channeled old Celtic folklore and earlier generations of faery pictorials into new and vibrant work.

An essay by Terri Windling on Froud's Web site had this to say about *Faeries:* "Here, in all their beautiful, horrible glory were the faeries of old British legends, undiluted by greeting card sentiment: gorgeous and grotesque (often at the same time), creatures of ivy, oak and stone—born out of the British landscape, as potent, wild and unpredictable as a force of nature."

Most illustrators wait for a story manuscript and then create the pictures to go with it. Froud has sometimes worked this way, but on other occasions he turns the process on its head and creates the pictures first. In those cases he then works closely with a writer to fashion a text that fits the pictures. Some of Froud's projects, including *Lady Cottington's Pressed Fairy Book* and *The Goblin Companion: Invented and Illustrated by Brian Froud; Captured and Catalogued by Terry Jones,* urge readers to pay close attention to how the illustrations sometimes subtly contradict the accompanying text. On Froud's Web site, Windling observed: "If there can be said to be a painterly equivalent to the literary school of Magical Realism, then the work of Brian Froud exemplifies it. . . . To open the heavy wood door of [his] house is to open a gate that leads back through time and into the faerielands."

Froud has also worked as a consultant to films, including the Jim Henson puppet movie *The Dark Crystal.* Additionally, his work lends itself to the playing card format, and he has created numerous faery cards and card sets that can be used to play games or to commune with the otherworldly folk. In an online interview, Froud encouraged others to see faeries the way he sees them and draws them—from a wellspring of creativity. "Faeries are seen through the heart, not through the eyes," he said. "Remember that faeries inhabit the interior of the earth and the interior of all things, so look, in the first place, in the interior of yourself. Allow them to materialize in your mind's eye. If you let Faery live within you, you can likewise live within Faery."

BIOGRAPHICAL AND CRITICAL SOURCES:

PERIODICALS

Library Journal, May 1, 2003, Michael Rogers, review of *The World of the Dark Crystal,* p. 160.

Los Angeles Magazine, December, 1982, Tom Link, review of *The World of the Dark Crystal,* p. 318.

Magazine of Fantasy and Science Fiction, April, 1995, Charles de Lint, review of *Lady Cottington's Pressed Fairy Book,* p. 36; June, 2001, Charles de Lint, review of *The Faeries' Oracle,* p. 26; May, 2004, Charles de Lint, review of *Brian Froud's the Runes of Elfland: Visions and Stories from the Faerie Alphabet,* p. 30.

New York Times Book Review, November 7, 1982, review of *The World of the Dark Crystal,* p. 51.

Publishers Weekly, June 13, 1980, review of *The Faeries' Pop-Up Book,* p. 74; September 9, 1983, Jean F. Mercier, review of *Goblins,* p. 65; December 20, 1993, review of *Brian Froud's Faerielands: The Wild Wood,* p. 54; October 3, 1994, review of *Brian Froud's Faerielands: Something Rich and Strange,* p. 54; August 14, 2000, "Faeries, Spells, and Magic," p. 343; September 10, 2001, review of *The Winter Child,* p. 66.

School Library Journal, February, 1991, Susan L. Rogers, review of *The Dreaming Place,* p. 93; April, 1999, Frances Reiher, review of *Good Faeries/ Bad Faeries,* p. 164.

Time, January 3, 1983, Richard Corliss, review of *The Dark Crystal,* p. 82.

ONLINE

World of Froud, http://www.worldoffroud.com (June 7, 2004), author's home page.*

FUMAROLI, Marc 1932-

PERSONAL: Born June 10, 1932 in Marseilles, France.

ADDRESSES: Home—11 rue de l'Université 75007 Paris, France. *Office*—Collège de France, 52 Rue due H.E. Cardinal Lemoine, 75231 Paris cedex 05, France.

CAREER: Writer, educator, and professor of rhetoric. Sorbonne, Paris, France, 1976; Collège de France, Titular professor, chair of rhetoric and European society of 16th and 17th centuries, 1986—; University of Chicago, professor, 1996—. *Commentaire,* editor-in-chief, 1978—. *XVIIe Siècle* (journal), director, 1981-1986; member of advisory council, Bibliohèque Nationale, 1988-92; Society of Friends of the Louvre, president, 1996; Academy Française, member, 1995; High Committee of National Celebrations, member, 1998—.

AWARDS, HONORS: Chevalier Légion d'honneur, des Palmes académiques; Officer ordre national du Mérit; Commander, des Artes et des Lettres.

WRITINGS:

(Editor) *Mémoires de Henri De Campion, Suivis de Trois Entretiens Sur Divers Subjects d'Histoire, de Politique, et de Morale,* Mercure de France (Paris, France), 1967.

(Editor) *L'Illusion comique, comédie,* Larousse (Paris, France), 1970.

A Rebours/J.-K Huysmans, Gallimard (Paris, France), 1977.

L'Age de l'éloquence: rhé et "res literaria," de la Renaissance au seuil de l'époque classique, Champion (Paris, France), 1980.

(Editor) *Le Statut de la littérature: Mélanges offerts á Paul Bénichou,* Droz (Geneva, Switzerland), 1982.

(With Marianne Grivel) *Devises pour les Tapisseries du Roi,* Herscher (Paris, France), 1988.

L'inspiration du poéte de Poussin: Essai sur Lallégorie du Parnasse, Ministére de la culture, de la communication, des grands travaux et du Bicentenaire (Paris, France), 1989.

Eroi e Oratori: Retorica e Drammaturgia Secentesche, Il Mulino (Bologna, Italy), 1990.

(With Noemi Hep, Bernard Tocanne, and Roger Zuber) *Précis de Littérature Française du XVII siécle,* PUF (Paris, France), 1990.

Héroes et Orateurs: Rhétorique et Dramatureis Cornéliennes, Droz (Geneva, Switzerland), 1990.

L'Etat Culturel: Une Religion Moderne, Editions de Fallois (Paris, France), 1991.

Le Genre des Genres Littéraires Français: La Conversation, Oxford University Press (New York, NY), 1992.

Res Libraria, Edizioni dell'elefante (Rome, Italy), 1994.

La diplomatie de l'esprit: de Montaigne á La Fontaine, Hermann (Paris, France), 1994.

L'école du Silence: le Sentiment des Images au XVIIe Siécle, Flammarion (Paris, France), 1994.

(With Tzvetan todorov) *Mélanges sur l'oeuvre de Paul Bénichou* Gallimard (Paris, France), 1995.

Le Poéte et le Roi: Jean de la Fontaine en son Siécle, Editions de Fallois (Paris, France), 1997, published as *The Poet and the King: Jean de La Fontaine and His Century,* translated by Jane Marie Todd, University of Notre Dame Press (Notre Dame, IN), 2002.

Rome dans la Méoire et l'Imagination de l'Europe: Celebrazione sul Campidoglio del Cinquantesimo Anniversario Della Fondazione dell'Unione, Unione Internazionale degli istituti di archeologia, storia et storia dell'arte in Roma (Rome, Italy), 1997.

Vie de Napoléon, Editions de Fallois (Paris, France), 1999.

Rorme et Paris: Capitales de la République Européenne des Lettres, preface by Volker Kapp, afterword by Giovanni Pozzi, LIT (Hamburg, Germany), 1999.

Nicolas Poussin: Sainte Françoise Romaine Annonçant á Rome la fin de la Peste, Réunion des musée nationaux: Louvre, Service culturel (Paris, France), 2001.

Quand l'Europe Parlait Français, Fallois (Paris, France), 2001.

Chateaubriand: Poésie et Terreur, Fallois (Paris, France), 2003.

La Mythologie Gré-Latine à Travers 100 Chefs-d'oeuvre de la Peinture, Presses de la Renaissance (Paris, France), 2004.

Contributor of numerous articles to scholarly publications and journals, including *New Republic* and *Diogenes.*

SIDELIGHTS: Writer and professor Marc Fumaroli is a prolific author of widely praised works on French political, intellectual, and cultural history. A career academic, Fumaroli is professor of rhetoric and society in Europe at the Collége de France.

In *L'Age de l'éloquence: rhé et "res literaria," de la Renaissance au seuil de l'époque classique,* Fumaroli presents a richly detailed study of the history of rhetoric in Europe. The 1980 book "is modestly described in the preamble as a contribution to the history of rhetoric in modern Europe," wrote Peter France in *Modern Language Review.* "It is in fact easily the most significant contribution to date to the history of French rhetoric, but it is far more than this." In addition to in-depth discussion of rhetorical theory, Fumaroli also provides scholarly insight into "the practice of eloquence," France wrote, and the history of French prose in the sixteenth and seventeenth centuries. Because of its focus on rhetoric, the book can also be considered "a major contribution to the history of mentalities and indeed to the history of society," France remarked. "By means of a *tour de force* of organization, the author has ensured that the vast store of erudition on which he has drawn is properly subordinated to a powerful central thesis," wrote Terence Cave in *Times Literary Supplement.*

Beginning with a study of Cicero as an exemplary figure, the book examines early forms of rhetoric and their interplay. "Cicero represented different things at different times and to different people," France observed. Fumaroli explores Cicero's changing context. Cicero, France commented, "appears here above all as the figure of the urbane, yet serious middle way which will eventually be that of French classicism." The first part of the book "is a history of the ciceronian *ideal* of eloquence," Cave observed. "Fumaroli is not concerned with the technical detail of rhetorical pedagogy," Cave remarked, but is instead concerned with "the history of an idea, of the institutions which promoted it, and of the individuals who gave it expression." The remaining portions of the book provide detailed and subtle analysis of the "the opposing rhetorical traditions of the Society of Jesus and the Gallican *parlementaires,*" France wrote. "The three strands of Fumaroli's book thus converge at a key moment in the history of French culture," Cave noted, specifically in the time of Richelieu and his strict central control, during the flourishing of the French court, during the conflict between the rhetorical styles of France and Rome, and "above all between neo-Latin humanism and vernacular *belles-lettres,*" Cave observed.

Although the book "is a heavy one and takes time to read," France remarked, "no specialist should grudge the time taken to read a work of this importance." Fumaroli's book "stands alone in its range and synthetic power," commented Cave in another *Times Literary Supplement* review. Fumaroli "shows enormous still in attaching the endless permutations of broad conceptual categories," such as ciceronianism, "the sublime," and related intellectual abstractions "to verifiable historical evidence and thus in giving them a local precision." Cave also called the book an "outstanding successor" to other works in the field, and named it "compulsory reading" for persons interested in French culture, literature, and rhetoric.

Fumaroli's *Héroes et Orateurs: Rhétorique et Dramatureis Cornéliennes* contains "a rich and often fascinating gathering of pieces" and essays that "express a distinctive vision of seventeenth-century French culture," Peter France wrote in *French Studies*. In *Précis de Littérature Française du XVII siécle*, Fumaroli "provides a dazzling panorama of the century's early years, frequently quoting from inaccessible but consistently apt and illuminating texts," wrote Peter Bayley in *French Studies*. With *Quand l'Europe Parlait Français*, Fumaroli offers a collection of essays on the use of French as the language of the elite; the history, cultural meaning, and linguistic virtues of French; and the erosion of the French language in the face of increased use of English. "Fumaroli's stimulating and elegant preface to this book is an extended essay on the circumstances that led to the supremacy of the French language throughout Europe and beyond in the eighteenth century," wrote John Rogister in *Times Literary Supplement*. It also examines the use of French by foreigners who adopted French as their main language during the eighteenth century. In terms of the current battle for the purity of the language, "Fumaroli does not give way to pessimism," Rogister observed. "In his view, anyone who wants to escape from conformity or from the age of mass communication need only to resort to French of the old school."

Fumaroli argues in favor of humanistic culture for its own sake in *L'Etat Culturel: Une Religion Moderne*. "The argument of Marc Fumaroli's elegant book, *L'Etat Culturel*, is plain and deeply felt," wrote Patrice Higonnet in *Times Literary Supplement*. "Humanistic culture is the highest kind of self-expression," Higonnet wrote, and "it is an end in itself," available to all through the virtue of liberal education "which empowers all men and women regardless of their social rank. Different human beings will seek transcendence in different ways," Higonnet observed, "but their answers—provided they are reflective and sincere—will all have

universal resonance." France, according to Fumaroli, exemplified the pinnacle of this type of culture of self-expression.

"In the past few decades, however, a cancer, as Fumaroli sees it, has steadily been eating away at French and Parisian culture," Higonnet remarked. "In the place of dialogue and confrontation, instead of enlightened discourse, the French have been substituting the false values of l'Etat culturel." Empty concepts, pretentious attitudes, facile behaviors, and remnants of American counterculture have been wrongly offered to the French "as the essence of modern [French] culture," Higonnet wrote. Fumaroli criticizes the new French National Library, the work of French universities, national politics, and the actions of the state in his quest to reinvigorate culture in France and Paris. *L'Etat Culturel* is an "important book," Higonnet wrote. To some, Fumaroli will appear as "a learned curmudgeon, disillusioned by modern life," while others will see him more sympathetically as "a wise but confirmed pessimist," Higonnet observed. To Fumaroli, systematic dismantling of the "l'Etat culturel" will allow "new and vital cultural forms" to be born out of the wreckage, reinvigorating French culture and allowing a new generation of cultivated residents to emerge.

Fumaroli turns his attention to art in *Nicolas Poussin: Sainte Françoise Romaine Annonçant á Rome la fin de la Peste*. Fumaroli provides an in-depth analysis of the Poussin's painting, *Sainte Françoise Romaine*, upon its acquisition and exhibition by the Louvre. "No more appropriate an author could have been found," Charles Dempsey wrote in *Burlington Magazine*, "and Fumaroli has responded with an invaluable analysis of the painting and its full artistic, cultural, religious, and historical context." Of particular note and "Especially satisfying," Dempsey commented, "is Fumaroli's sure-footed treatment of the sequence of visual metaphors deployed by Poussin in the background of the painting."

With *The Poet and the King: Jean de La Fontaine and His Century*, Fumaroli "has written the finest and most perceptive of all the innumerable accounts of La Fontaine," wrote Charles Rosen in *New York Review of Books*. Jean de La Fontaine is regarded by Fumaroli and others to be the greatest French lyric poet of the seventeenth century, Rosen observed, and the book presents an in-depth study of the poet and the political and cultural environment he lived in, placing La Fontaine within "the intellectual context of his time," wrote Maya Slater in *French Studies.*

La Fontaine had hoped for a prosperous period of royal patronage under the auspices of superintendent of finances, Nicolas Fouquet. A "popular and impressive figure," Fouquet had successfully negotiated peace among factions that had risen up against the brutal and absolutist policies of the infamous Cardinal Richelieu, Rosen wrote. Fouquet was a patron of the arts on a grand scale, and La Fontaine had every reason to believe that such patronage would continue. However, shortly after a luxurious party given by Fouquet for the entire French court, Fouquet was ordered arrested by King Louis XIV and charged with treason and embezzlement. "There is no question that Fouquet's wealth had been acquired by methods that were strictly criminal; these methods were also widespread, commonplace, and expected," Rosen observed. "The arrest of Fouquet was a disaster" for La Fontaine, Rosen remarked. "He had been protected and generously supported by the superintendent, and he remained loyal to him for decades, helping in his defense, and writing with considerable eloquence a plea for a pardon or more generous treatment."

La Fontaine's support for Fouquet put him at odds with Louis XIV, and he continually risked ruination at the whim of the king. Other poets, writers, artists, and creative sorts of the time suffered as well. "Marc Fumaroli shows how the fall of Fouquet destroyed the hopes of a generation of creative artists who had anticipated a golden age of patronage under the enlightened minister," wrote Maya Slater in *Times Literary Supplement.* Jay Freeman, writing in *Booklist,* called *The Poet and the King* an "engrossing account of the struggles of a creative man against a smothering tyranny." The book "is almost as much about Louis XIV as about La Fontaine: the absolutist politics and the consequent attempt to enforce an official style by the King and his ministers are continuously present throughout the book," Rosen remarked. "Fumaroli's distaste for the King is as evident as his remarkable admiration of the poet, and he treats Louis XIV with unmitigated Ferocity." Slater observed that "Fumaroli's approach to La Fontaine is always perceptive and convincing," and Rosen concluded that "Fumaroli's study is a meditation on the plight of the artist under such a ruler [as Louis XIV] during the imposition of an absolutist, centralized political regime."

BIOGRAPHICAL AND CRITICAL SOURCES:

PERIODICALS

American Historical Review, October, 2003, Michael Moriarty, review of *The Poet and the King: Jean de La Fontaine and His Century,* pp. 1224-1225.
Booklist, May 1, 2002, Jay Freeman, review of *The Poet and the King,* p. 1499.
Burlington Magazine, January, 2002, Charles Dempsey, review of *Nicolas Poussin: Sainte Françoise Romaine Annonçant á Rome la fin de la Peste,* pp. 31-33.
Choice, January, 2003, C. E. Campbell, review of *The Poet and the King,* p. 831.
English Historical Review, February, 2004, Roger Mettam, review of *The Poet and the King,* p. 213.
French Review, October, 1980, Jacques Barchilon, review of *Précis de Littérature Française du XVII siécle,* p. 160; May, 1983, Henri Peyre, review of *Le Statut de la littérature: Mélanges offerts á Paul Bénichou,* pp. 935-936.
French Studies, July, 1991, Peter France, review of *Héroes et Orateurs: Rhétorique et Dramatureis Cornéliennes,* pp. 318-319; July, 1992, Peter Bayley, review of *Précis de Littérature Française du XVII siécle,* pp. 327-330; April, 1998, Maya Slater, review of *Le Poéte et le Roi; Jean de La Fontaine en son siécle,* p. 202.
Historical Journal, March, 1995, Peter N. Miller, review of *Héroes et Orateurs: Rhétorique et Dramatureis Cornéliennes,* pp. 161-173.
Library Journal, June 1, 2002, Scott Hightower, review of *The Poet and the King,* p. 147.
London Review of Books, March 23, 1995, Malcolm Bull, review of *L'école du Silence: le Sentiment des Images au XVIIe Siécle,* pp. 31-32.
Modern Language Review, January, 1982, Peter France, review of *L'Age de l'éloquence: rhé et "res literaria," de la Renaissance au seuil de l'époque classique,* pp. 203-205.
New York Review of Books, December 18, 1997, Charles Rosen, "The Fabulous La Fontaine," review of *Le Poéte et le Roi; Jean de La Fontaine en son siécle,* pp. 38-39.
Times Literary Supplement, February 27, 1981, Terence Cave, "The Ciceronian Ideal," review of *L'Age de l'éloquence: rhé et "res literaria," de la Renaissance au seuil de l'époque classique,* p. 236; February 14, 1992, Patrice Higonnet, review of *L'Etat Culturel: Une Religion Moderne,*

pp. 3-4; October 28, 1994, Terence Cave, review of *La diplomatie de l'esprit: de Montaigne á La Fontaine,* p. 26; October 28, 1994, Terence Cave, review of *L'Age de l'éloquence: rhé et "res literaria," de la Renaissance au seuil de l'époque classique,* p. 26; May 3, 1996, Malcolm Bowie, review of *Le Statut de la littérature: Mélanges offerts á Paul Bénichou,* p. 6; April 25, 1997, Peter France, review of *Le Poéte et le Roi; Jean de La Fontaine en son siécle,* p. 12; October 25, 2002, Maya Slater, review of *The Poet and the King: Jean de La Fontaine and His Century,* p. 30; May 3, 2002, John Rogister, review of *Quand l'Europe Parlait Français,* p. 8.

ONLINE

University of Notre Dame Press Web site, http://www.undpress.nd.edu/ (July 2, 2003), description of *The Poet and the King.**

G

GAGLIANO, Eugene M. 1946-

PERSONAL: Surname is pronounced *Gall*-iano; born May 14, 1946, in Niagara Falls, NY; son of Michael V. and Caroline H. Gagliano; married Carol Gagliano (a teacher), October 10, 1970; children: Gina, Jared, Darin, Nathan. *Education:* State University of New York at Cobleski, B.S. *Religion:* Catholic. *Hobbies and other interests:* Gardening, camping, canoeing, hiking, painting, and singing.

ADDRESSES: Home—20 Hillside Dr., Buffalo, WY 82834. *E-mail*—egagliano@wyoming.com.

CAREER: Elementary school teacher in Honeoye, NY, 1969-73; teacher in a K-5 country school, Buffalo, WY, 1973-77; elementary school teacher in Buffalo, WY, 1977-2003; full-time writer and lecturer, 2003—.

MEMBER: Society of Children's Book Writers and Illustrators, Wyoming Writers, Wind Writers.

AWARDS, HONORS: Arch Coal Teacher Achievement Award, 2001; Western Horizon Award from Wyoming Writers, 2002, for *Secret of the Black Widow.*

WRITINGS:

Secret of the Black Widow, White Mane Kids (Shippensburg, PA), 2002.
Inside the Clown, Publish America, 2003.
C Is for Cowboy: A Wyoming Alphabet, illustrated by Susan Guy, Sleeping Bear Press (Chelsea, MI), 2003.

WORK IN PROGRESS: Falling Stars, a novel about Alzheimer's Disease; *My Veggie Friends* (children's poetry); research on the Loretto Chapel.

SIDELIGHTS: Eugene M. Gagliano once commented: "My seventh grade English teacher, Mrs. Erwin, recognized and encouraged my writing. Thanks to her, I had my first poem published in the school newspaper. I continued to write poetry and have it published in numerous national anthologies throughout high school and college.

"As an elementary teacher, and father of four children, I've read a lot of children's literature and met many authors, like Wilson Rawls, Marguerite Henry, Ken Thomasma, Bruce Coville, Will Hobbs, and Roland Smith who all inspired me to want to write for children. My wife, Carol, encouraged me to take a writing correspondence course through the Institute of Children's Literature, even though we couldn't afford it. This helped further develop my writing skills.

"I received a full scholarship to attend the Highlights Writers Conference, which was a turning point in my life. I was inspired by award-winning author Pam Conrad, to write my first published book, *Secret of the Black Widow,* after attending her workshop.

"Katherine Patterson, Patricia MacLachlan, Eve Bunting, Will Hobbs, Roland Smith, and Ben Michelsen are some of the authors I respect and admire.

"I was thrilled to write *C Is for Cowboy: A Wyoming Alphabet,* because it gave me the opportunity to tell about the beauty and wonders of my adopted state. I wanted Wyoming children to learn to appreciate and take pride in their state.

"In *Secret of the Black Widow*, children come to realize that it's best to face their fears, and that all children have the same feelings despite their differences.

"*Inside the Clown* addresses the issues of teenage suicide and depression. I wanted teenagers to understand that there is always hope and a way out.

"Hopefully my work will touch the hearts of those who read it. It's important to me that my readers make connections to their own lives. Making readers aware of the beauty and joy in life, as well as the tragedy is another goal. I want to make children see the humor in life and make them laugh.

"My best writing time is in the morning, so after taking my golden retriever, Rosie, for a long walk, I write. In summer, I divide my day between my two passions, writing and gardening. When I was teaching I would write mainly on the weekends or during breaks at school. I use a computer, but sometimes a pencil and paper is all that I need.

"Four words define my success as a writer: practice, persistence, patience, and prayer. I love children and relate well to them, and so I wanted to write books they would enjoy while learning about life."

*　　*　　*

GARCÍA, C(elso-) R(amön) 1921-2004

OBITUARY NOTICE—See index for *CA* sketch: Born October 31, 1921, in New York, NY; died of cardiovascular disease February 1, 2004, in Boston, MA. Physician, educator, and author. García is best remembered for his research that helped lead to the creation of an effective birth control pill. He completed undergraduate studies at Queens College in 1942 and received his medical degree three years later at Long Island College of Medicine. After serving in the U.S. Army Medical Corps from 1943 to 1948, he finished his residency in Brooklyn and moved to Puerto Rico, where he was assistant professor of obstetrics and gynecology for two years at the University of Puerto Rico. It was here that he began to build on the research initiated by doctors John Rock and Gregory Pincus and others, work that he would later continue when he

returned to Massachusetts in 1955 and would lead to the effective birth-control treatment now called "the pill." He worked in Brookline for ten years as a surgeon and as a senior scientist and director of the training program in the physiology of reproduction at the Worcester Foundation for Experimental Biology in Shrewsbury for two years. In 1962, García joined the Harvard Medical School faculty as an instructor in obstetrics and gynecology. Most of his academic career, however, was spent at the University of Pennsylvania, where he was on the faculty from 1965 until 1992, the year he became William Shippen Jr. professor emeritus. García published several books concerning reproduction, including *Human Fertility: The Regulation of Reproduction* (1977), *Current Therapy of Infertility, 1984-1985* (1984), and *Current Therapy in Surgical Gynecology* (1986). Much honored for his contributions to reproductive science, García received many awards, including, most recently, an M.D. Master Teaching award from the SUNY Alumni Association in 1989, a Recognition award from APGO Wyeth-Ayerst in 1993, a Frank L. Babbott award from SUNY in 1995, and a Science Leadership award from the Global Alliance for Women's Health in 2000.

OBITUARIES AND OTHER SOURCES:

PERIODICALS

Chicago Tribune, February 23, 2004, Section 4, p. 9.
Los Angeles Times, February 17, 2004, p. B9.
New York Times, February 16, 2004, p. A19.
Washington Post, February 20, 2004, p. B7.

*　　*　　*

GARDELL, Mattias

PERSONAL: Male. *Education:* Earned Ph.D.

ADDRESSES: Office—CEIFO, Stockholm University, 106 91 Stockholm, Sweden. *E-mail*—mattias.gardell@ceifo.su.se.

CAREER: University of Stockholm, Stockholm, Sweden, associate professor of religious history.

WRITINGS:

In the Name of Elijah Muhammad: Louis Farrakhan and the Nation of Islam, Duke University Press (Durham, NC), 1996.

Gods of the Blood: The Pagan Revival and White Separatism, Duke University Press (Durham, NC), 2003.

Vad ar Rasism?, Natur och Kultur (Stockholm, Sweden), 2005.

Globalisering och Politisk Islam, Leopard Forlag (Stockholm, Sweden), 2005.

SIDELIGHTS: Mattias Gardell is a University of Stockholm professor who specializes in the history of religions. While working on his doctorate, he wrote his dissertation on the Nation of Islam (NOI) and its leader Louis Farrakhan. This later developed into Gardell's first book, *In the Name of Elijah Muhammad: Louis Farrakhan and the Nation of Islam.* The book is an in-depth discussion of the origins of the NOI in America, the rise to leadership by Farrakhan, and the unique belief system and contradictory elements of the NOI that led *Political Studies* contributor Richard H. King to comment that the NOI "stands to orthodox Islam in somewhat the same manner as the Mormon Church stands to orthodox Christianity." In fact, Bill Maxwell noted in the *St. Petersburg Times* that "one of the book's best features is its examination of the Nation in relationship to mainstream Islam."

Gardell traces this unique form of Islam to its origins in 1930s America, speculating that, as Dennis Walker reported in the *Journal of Muslim Minority Affairs,* "some kind of Druze from Syria-Lebanon-Palestine—perhaps the second-generation scion of an immigrant family?—was the founder." The original leaders of the NOI, Elijah Muhammad and his son, then combined this belief system with others in a way that made it more relevant to the difficult urban poverty that many African Americans were experiencing during the Great Depression, which began with the collapse of the U.S. stock market in 1929. Walker related, "Gardell balances analysis of sources as heterogeneous as the Qur'an, esoteric Sufism, Shi'ite sects and, in regard to North American sources, Christian, theosophical and Freemasonic writings that had been articulating a sense that humans are fallen gods before Wali Fard Muhammad and Elijah in their turn reinvented such American anthropomorphism in the early 1930s." The author

then discusses Farrakhan's rise to leadership. Farrakhan, whose name was originally Louis Eugene Walker and whose original career was as a musician under the stage name Calypso Gene, was a favorite of Elijah Muhammad, and he became a leader in the NOI after Muhammad's death in 1975. The NOI then split, as Farrakhan took his followers in one direction and Elijah's son took other believers in a direction that was closer to Sunni Muslim orthodoxy. Farrakhan's teachings, in comparison, were very unorthodox. He preached a vision of Armageddon, in which all the trappings of white society, which he associated with the devil, would be destroyed to give rise to a new civilization dominated by blacks.

Even more odd, according to Gardell, is Farrakhan's assertion that God is watching Earth from an artificial "Mother Ship" and that he sends observers to the planet which are perceived as UFOs. "In one such encounter," related Malise Ruthven in the *Times Literary Supplement,* "Farrakhan meets the Honourable Elijah Muhammad, the occulted Messiah, who confirms his authority as Leader. A scroll containing the sacred scriptures has been placed in the back of Farrakhan's brain to be revealed in its entirety in the fullness of time. While awaiting deliverance, the faithful must purify themselves, eschewing meat, junk food, alcohol, drugs, sexual promiscuity—all devil's weapons aimed specifically at enslaving African Americans." The result of this belief system is a unique vision that blends both constructive and destructive ideals. On the one hand, the NOI feels that white society must eventually be destroyed, and one disturbing trait of this belief system is its anti-Semitism; on the other, Farrakhan's followers have worked fervently to eliminate crime, poverty, and ignorance within their communities, thus offering a ray of hope to many inner-city neighborhoods.

Gardell relied on interviews with Farrakhan and members of the NOI for much of the research in his book, but some reviewers of *In the Name of Elijah Muhammad* found that this and the author's strict objectivity is, in some ways, detrimental to the book. "So closely does Gardell stick to elucidating rather than judging the NOI perspective that at times he seems to identify with it," observed King in *Political Studies.* However, King praised Gardell's book for revealing the NOI as an anti-democratic religion advocating black supremacy and anti-Semitism. Also praising Gardell for his research and thoroughness, other critics found the author's first book to be very valuable. Walker, for one, called it "the best-researched and most comprehensive survey published thus far of the evolution of protest Islam among Black Americans, albeit as viewed from that post-1977 period of the movement shaped under the leadership of Louis Farrakhan Muhammad." And Ruthven in *Times Literary Supplement* declared it a "masterful study" that is the "first comprehensive scholarly treatment of Farrakhan and the NOI."

Beginning in 1996, Gardell became fascinated by the infusion of Nordic pagan beliefs into the radical white separatist movement in North America and Europe. Again conducting extensive research and interviews on the subject, he completed *Gods of the Blood: The Pagan Revival and White Separatism* in 2003. Followers of this movement, who believe in white supremacy and racial purity, have been increasingly attracted to beliefs in the Old Norse gods, and they are therefore sometimes called "Odinists" after the god Odin. "Gardell mainly focuses on neo-Vikingism, but other pagan traditions have proved attractive," commented *Books & Culture* reviewer Philip Jenkins, who added that Gardell is not criticizing the neo-pagan movement, most of whose adherents are in no way racist extremists. The author's thesis is actually aimed at explaining the rise of this neo-Nazi pagan movement. Gardell "argues cogently that the rise of racist paganism is a reaction to globalism," stated Daniel Levitas in *History: Review of New Books*, "which white supremacists fear will destroy their presumed racial integrity through genetic and cultural homogenization." Although a *Publishers Weekly* reviewer found that the academic tone of *Gods of the Blood* sometimes makes for dry reading, the critic asserted that this "well-researched book offers never-before-seen glimpses of the visions and goals of racist pagans."

BIOGRAPHICAL AND CRITICAL SOURCES:

PERIODICALS

American Studies, fall, 1997, Julius E. Thompson, review of *In the Name of Elijah Muhammad: Louis Farrakhan and the Nation of Islam,* p. 160.
Books & Culture, November-December, 2003, Philip Jenkins, "The Other Terrorists," p. 8.

Canadian Journal of Political Science, September, 1997, Martha Lee, review of *In the Name of Elijah Muhammad,* p. 581.
History: Review of New Books, fall, 2003, Daniel Levitas, review of *Gods of the Blood: The Pagan Revival and White Separatism,* p. 4.
Journal of American History, June, 1997, review of *In the Name of Elijah Muhammad,* p. 299.
Journal of Muslim Minority Affairs, October, 1998, Dennis Walker, review of *In the Name of Elijah Muhammad.*
Journal of the American Academy of Religion, winter, 1997, C. S'thembile West, review of *In the Name of Elijah Muhammad,* p. 889; fall, 1997, review of *In the Name of Elijah Muhammad,* pp. 889-892.
New York Review of Books, September 19, 1996, Gary Wills, "A Tale of Three Leaders," pp. 61-74.
Political Studies, June, 1995, Richard H. King, review of *In the Name of Elijah Muhammad,* pp. 369-370; June, 1998, King, "Book Reviews," p. 369.
Publishers Weekly, September 16, 1996, review of *In the Name of Elijah Muhammad,* p. 66; May 12, 2003, review of *Gods of the Blood.*
St. Petersburg Times (St. Petersburg, FL), November 17, 1996, Bill Maxwell, review of *In the Name of Elijah Muhammad,* p. D5.
Times Higher Education Supplement, March 21, 1997, Paul Gilroy, "Nothing but Good Faith," p. 25.
Times Literary Supplement, May 30, 1997, Malise Ruthven, review of *In the Name of Elijah Muhammad.*
Virginia Quarterly Review, spring, 1997, "Notes on Current Books: National and International Affairs."

ONLINE

Duke University Press, http://www.dukeupress.edu/ (October 28, 2003).

*   *   *

GART, Murray Joseph 1924-2004

OBITUARY NOTICE—See index for *CA* sketch: Born November 9, 1924, in Boston, MA; died of complications from heart surgery, March 31, 2004, in Michellville, MD. Journalist, editor, and author. A longtime correspondent for *Time* magazine and editor with

Time-Life, Gart was remembered as the last editor to head the now-defunct *Washington Star.* After serving with the U.S. Army during World War II, he completed his undergraduate work at Northeastern University in 1949. Though his major had been economics, he started a career in journalism as a reporter for the Honolulu *Star-Bulletin* in 1949. The early 1950s saw Gart working as a reporter and editor for small papers in Kansas and New Jersey, but these posts led to a job as the Toronto bureau chief for the Time-Life News Service in 1955. Gart would remain with Time-Life for the rest of his career, working in various positions in Boston, Chicago, and London during the early 1960s and reporting on events in Asia and the Middle East; in the late-1960s, he was assistant managing editor for *Forbes* magazine, becoming chief of the Time-Life office in New York City in 1969 and assistant managing editor of *Time* magazine in 1972. When Time-Life purchased the *Washington Star* newspaper, Gart was named its editor in 1978. The paper, which had once been one of the prominent newspapers in the country, had fallen into financial problems, however, because of competition from the *Washington Post* and from television news programs. While his reporters praised Gart, some of his staff complained about the editor's management style. While many felt that Gart helped improve the quality of the writing in the *Washington Star,* he was unable to turn the newspaper's finances around, and it folded in 1981. After this, Gart worked as an associate for the Foreign Policy Institute at Johns Hopkins from 1982 to 1984 and remained a consultant to Time-Life until 1989. Even upon retiring, however, Gart was active in several organizations, including working as director of the Middle East Institute in 1988, and of American Near East Refugee Aid in 1993, and serving on the board of directors for Geopolitics of Energy from 1985 to 1994 and for the Washington Institute on Foreign Affairs. A former editor of *Cosmos Journal,* he was a member of the Cosmos Club, where he helped to promote international forums. For this work, the club awarded him a distinguished service award in 2003.

OBITUARIES AND OTHER SOURCES:

PERIODICALS

Chicago Tribune, April 2, 2004, Section 3, p. 11.
New York Times, April 3, 2004, p. A25.
Washington Post, April 3, 2004, p. B7.

GEARY, Joseph
(Patrick Lynch, a joint pseudonym)

PERSONAL: Born in England. *Education:* Attended Oxford University.

ADDRESSES: Home—Los Angeles, CA, and France. *Agent*—c/o Author Mail, Pantheon Publicity, 1745 Broadway, New York, NY 10019.

CAREER: Author.

WRITINGS:

Spiral (novel), Pantheon Books (New York, NY), 2003.
Mirror, Simon & Schuster (New York, NY), 2004.

WITH PHILIP SINGTON; UNDER JOINT PSEUDONYM PATRICK LYNCH

The Annunciation, Heinemann (London, England), 1993.
The Immaculate Conception, Heinemann (London, England), 1994.
Carriers, Random House (New York, NY), 1995.
Omega, Dutton (New York, NY), 1997.
The Policy, Dutton (New York, NY), 1998.
Figure of Eight, Dutton (New York, NY), 2000.

SIDELIGHTS: After writing several novels with Philip Sington under the joint pseudonym Patrick Lynch, Joseph Geary's debut solo novel, *Spiral,* gained wide acclaim among critics. A thriller that combines a murder mystery with the underground world of unscrupulous art collectors, *Spiral* is the tale of a struggling English biographer named Nick Greer, who becomes obsessed with the life of a long-dead artist named Frank Spira. After five years of work, his biography on Spira is almost complete when Greer learns that Spira's former lover, Jacob Grossman, is still alive and living in New York City. Flying to New York, Greer finds Grossman, who is now a homeless bum in his eighties. During his interview, Grossman tells Greer about Spira's great painting *The Incarnation,* which the artist supposedly destroyed in Tangier back in 1957. However, Grossman thinks it still exists and that Greer is trying to find it. After the interview, Grossman is brutally murdered, and Greer, the last to see him, becomes a suspect in the murder investigation. But Greer also becomes a subject of interest to Tony Reardon, a mobster who once financed Spira and who is now looking for *The Incarnation,* which, if it exists, is estimated to be worth millions. Realizing he has opened up a deadly can of worms, Greer sets off to find the truth in Tangier, where he is nearly murdered himself as he tries to put together the pieces of the Spira puzzle and publish his biography before another writer beats him to the scoop.

"In this accomplished work," asserted *Booklist* contributor Keir Graff, "[Geary] has breathed life into an increasingly familiar mystery milieu—the art world." Calling the novel "smart, complex and insightful," a *Publishers Weekly* reviewer complimented the author's "tight, multilayered plot." And Maureen Corrigan, writing in *Newsday,* added, "Part of the fun of *Spiral* derives from the assurance with which Geary conjures up Spira's life and beat movement contacts. The rest of the nervous excitement derives from the breakneck plot, which twists, turns and zig-zags like an abstract rendering of the Brooklyn-Queens Expressway at rush hour."

BIOGRAPHICAL AND CRITICAL SOURCES:

PERIODICALS

Booklist, May 1, 2003, Keir Graff, review of *Spiral,* p. 1542.

Forbes, August 13, 2003, Michael Maiello, review of *Spiral.*

Kirkus Reviews, May 1, 2003, review of *Spiral.*

Library Journal, June 1, 2003, Ronnie H. Terpening, review of *Spiral,* p. 164.

Newsday, August 24, 2003, Maureen Corrigan, "Beach Books: Mysteries of Money and Art," p. D36.

Publishers Weekly, April 14, 2003, review of *Spiral,* p. 45.*

*   *   *

GIENOW-HECHT, Jessica C. E. 1964-

PERSONAL: Born December 25, 1964, in Essen, West Germany (now Germany); daughter of Herbert (an attorney) and Imina (an attorney) Gienow; married Heiko Hecht (a psychologist), August 12, 1995; children: Imina Juliane. *Ethnicity:* "Caucasian." *Education:* Earned B.A. degree in Aachen, Germany; University of Virginia, M.A., 1990, Ph.D., 1995. *Religion:* Protestant.

ADDRESSES: Office—Charles Warren Center for Studies in American History, Emerson Hall, Harvard University, Cambridge, MA 02138. *E-mail*—gienow@ fas.harvard.edu.

CAREER: University of Bielefeld, Bielefeld, Germany, postdoctoral fellow in history, 1995-96; Martin-Luther-University, Halle-Wittenberg, Germany, deputy director of Center for U.S. Studies, 1996-99; Harvard University, Cambridge, MA, John F. Kennedy fellow at Center for European Studies, 1999-2000, fellow at Charles Warren Center for Studies in American History, 2000-02, lecturer in History and Literature Program, 2002—. Worked as a trainee in journalism and advertising and as a clerk at a winery in Bordeaux, France.

MEMBER: American Historical Association, Society for Historians of American Foreign Relations, DGFA.

AWARDS, HONORS: Stuart Bernath Prize for best first book in diplomatic history, 1999, and Myrna Bernath Prize for best book in diplomatic history written by a woman, 2000, both for *Transmission Impossible: American Journalism as Cultural Diplomacy in Postwar Germany, 1945-1955;* fellow of German Marshall Fund.

WRITINGS:

Transmission Impossible: American Journalism as Cultural Diplomacy in Postwar Germany, 1945-1955, Louisiana State University Press (Baton Rouge, LA), 1999.

(Editor, with Frank Schumacher) *Culture and International History,* Berghahn Books (New York, NY), 2003.

Contributor to periodicals. Member of editorial board, *Diplomatic History.*

WORK IN PROGRESS: Sound Diplomacy: Music, Emotions, and Politics in Trans-Atlantic Relations since 1850 (tentative title), publication by University of Chicago Press (Chicago, IL) expected in 2004.

SIDELIGHTS: Jessica C. E. Gienow-Hecht told *CA:* "For at least five generations, the women in my family (notably on my German mother's side) have aspired to become writers, novelists, and historians. Most of them wrote in private; some published individual works; none, however, became a full-time writer. I consider myself the first one to realize this ambition. I have been wanting to write ever since I was a child. I could barely read and write when I began borrowing my mother's portable typewriter to compose letters, stories, and poems. When I was ten, I 'published' my first newspaper and sold it to my godmother, Tante Annelie. The paper was titled *Die Welt* and carried news from our home town, interviews, along with fictional news from around the world. When I was twelve, I produced a mock copy of *Emma,* at the time the leading feminist journal in Germany, in which I reprinted a fictional interview by *Emma* with my mother (whose opinion about women's emancipation remained ambivalent). I had barely graduated from high school when I began writing for several German newspapers in the Rhineland, Hamburg, Munich, and Berlin, while also working as a text trainee for an advertising firm in Düsseldorf. Yet it was during my stint as an exchange student in the history department of the University of Virginia that I—inspired by a host of English-language scholarship ranging from Richard Hofstetter to Lawrence Levine—decided to become a historian and a writer. Today, I write most of my prose in English along with an occasional article in German.

"Likewise, I became interested in the things I write bout when I was still a child. I grew up in the Federal Republic in the 1960s and 1970s where the presence of American troops and American culture had a profound impact on German life. This was also the time when young Germans in particular began to come to terms with *Vergangenheitsbewältigung* (mastering the past). My youth was inhabited by the heroes of George Lucas's *Star Wars* along with the demons of the first holocaust documentaries aired on public television in the mid-1970s. More than any other age bracket, my generation grappled with the paradox of living in a postwar consumer society, inspired by the American economic model and protected by American soldiers, while at the same time accepting responsibility for a German past in which it had not participated. Because of my background, I have focused my writing over the past twelve years on cross-cultural relations, 'trans-atlanticism,' emotions, and, most recently, the power of music in the international arena.

"My current book manuscript, *Sound Diplomacy: Music, Emotions, and Politics in Trans-Atlantic Rela-*tions *since 1850,* retraces the efforts of European governments to export culture as an instrument of diplomacy in order to befriend America, a nation that promised to be a rising star in the international arena. While the French capitalized on art and the British on social ties and literature, the German Reich exported the symphony as its most precious cultural good. As a result, in the United States the image of the German musician as a gifted and attractive man who knew how to express his feelings became a symbol for Germany's cosmopolitan culture, while the art of Brahms and Beethoven evoked precisely the respect for German greatness, *Heimat,* and emotionalism that Reich officials wanted to convey. The emergence of cultural hierarchy in America, then, constituted an international affair orchestrated by tough European artists, policy makers, and cultural administrators.

"My personal goal as a writer and as a historian is to make a difference in the world of international relations. I have lived in four different countries, and I have learned that to be cosmopolitan means to feel estranged wherever one is. But it also means to comprehend and tolerate diversity much better. Many scholars in the profession have recently begun projects designed to internationalize the study and teaching of American history, an effort I have become deeply involved with. Students of U.S. history should be acquainted with the view of American history from the perspective of scholars outside the United States; they should be stimulated in new ways by what they hear and learn—just as any cosmopolitan feels when confronted with a different culture. I do not only write from an international perspective—I am an international human being."

BIOGRAPHICAL AND CRITICAL SOURCES:

PERIODICALS

Choice, May, 2000, R. Halverson, review of *Transmission Impossible: American Journalism as Cultural Diplomacy in Postwar Germany, 1945-1955.*

*   *   *

GIMPEL, Erich 1910-1996

PERSONAL: Born 1910, in Germany; died, 1996, in Germany. *Education:* Studied high-frequency transformers and radio engineering.

CAREER: Spy. Telefunken, radio engineer, 1935-1939; German spy, 1939-45.

WRITINGS:

Agent 146: The True Story of a Nazi Spy in America, Thomas Dunne Books (New York, NY), 2003, originally published in Germany as Spion fur Deutschland, 1957.

SIDELIGHTS: Erich Gimpel grew up in Merseburg, Germany, and was interested in radio from a young age. After graduating from high school, he studied high-frequency transformers and then became a radio engineer.

In 1935, Gimpel was hired by Telefunken, the largest radio company in Germany. He was sent to Peru, where he worked for the firm. The job paid well and was not very demanding, and Gimpel lived luxuriously. When the German embassy there asked him to do some minor spy work, Gimpel agreed. He observed ships in the port at Lima and socialized with American army officers stationed there, gleaning bits of information about their operations. He was not subtle enough, though, and the officers eventually became suspicious of him. He was arrested and sent to the United States, which had just entered World War II,to Germany, and was ultimately returned to Germany.

Gimpel continued his spy training in Hamburg, Germany, and became a very good agent. The Nazi government asked him to devise a way to blow up the Panama Canal. Although Gimpel thought this was a ridiculous idea, he did come up with a plan to transport disassembled planes across the Atlantic on German submarines, put them back together on a Caribbean island, and then use them to bomb the canal. The German authorities were so impressed with this idea that they approved it. In 1944, shortly before the mission was scheduled to begin, the German authorities canceled it in order to send Gimpel to the United States.

Gimpel's partner in this new mission was William Colepaugh, an American traitor. Although Colepaugh had been born in Niantic, Connecticut, the son of an American father and a German mother, he had decided to work for Nazi Germany as a spy.

In December of 1944, Gimpel and Colepaugh were rowed to shore in Frenchman Bay, Maine, from a German submarine. Their mission was to learn everything they could about the American atomic bomb and then send the information back to Germany. They were also supposed to join with other agents, who would sneak into the United States from South America, to sabotage American defense plants.

The two men took the train from Maine to Boston and then to New York City, where they were arrested. Gimpel was sentenced to be hanged, but through a series of events, he escaped this fate. After President Franklin Delano Roosevelt's death, there were no executions during a period of national mourning, and when the Americans defeated the Germans, his execution was commuted to life imprisonment by President Harry S. Truman. Gimpel served eleven years in American prisons, including Alcatraz. In 1956, he earned parole and was sent back to Germany, where he lived until his death in 1996.

Gimpel tells the story of the mission and its aftermath in Agent 146: The True Story of a Nazi Spy in America. The book was originally published in Britain and Germany in 1957, and was published in the United States in 2003.

In Boston.com, Bob MacDonald noted that although many readers would initially be offended by the subject matter of the book "How can one feel empathy for a Nazi or want to hear his side of the story?" However, McDonald wrote, "Gimpel was not a [Nazi] party member; rather, he was a man who thought of himself as a patriot fighting for his country and later becoming disillusioned." Sherryl Connelly wrote in the New York Daily News that the book is "a log of terse episodes" and commented that in places it "reads like a boiled-down spy thriller."

BIOGRAPHICAL AND CRITICAL SOURCES:

PERIODICALS

Booklist, December 1, 2002, Gilbert Taylor, review of Agent 146: The True Story of a Nazi Spy in America, p. 643.
Kirkus Reviews, November 1, 2002, review of Agent 146, p. 1587.

Library Journal, December, 2002, Elizabeth Morris, review of *Agent 146,* p. 148.

Newsweek, February 10, 2003, Andrew Nagorski, "An Eerily Timely Tale of Fanaticism," p. 68.

Publishers Weekly, November 25, 2002, review of *Agent 146,* p. 53.

ONLINE

Boston.com, http://www.boston.com/ (April 23, 2003), Bob MacDonald, review of *Agent 146.*

New York Daily News Online, http://www.nydailynews. com/ (January 17, 2003), Sherryl Connelly, review of *Agent 146.**

*　　*　　*

GLANCY, Diane 1941-

PERSONAL: Born Helen Diane Hall, March 18, 1941, in Kansas City, MO; daughter of Lewis and Edith (Wood) Hall; married Dwane Glancy, May 2, 1964 (divorced, March 31, 1983); children: David, Jennifer. *Education:* University of Missouri, B.A., 1964; Central State University (Edmond, OK), M.A. (creative writing), 1983; University of Iowa, M.F.A., 1988. *Religion:* Christian.

ADDRESSES: Home—3508 W. 73rd Terr., Prairie Village, KS 66208. *Office*—Department of English, Macalester College, 1600 Grand, St. Paul, MN 55105.

CAREER: Macalester College, St. Paul, MN, assistant professor of English, beginning 1988, became professor. Artist-in-residence of the Oklahoma State Arts Council, 1982-92; has traveled for the U.S. Information Agency to Syria and Jordan.

AWARDS, HONORS: Fellowship, University of Iowa Writers' Workshop; Pegasus Award, Oklahoma Federation of Writers, 1984, for *Brown Wolf Leaves the Res and Other Poems;* named laureate for the Five Civilized Tribes, 1984-86; Lakes and Prairies Award, *Milkweed Chronicle,* 1986, for *One Age in a Dream;* Oklahoma Theater Festival Award, 1987, for *Segwohi;* Five Civilized Tribes Playwriting Prize, 1987, for *Weebjob;* Aspen Summer Theater Award, 1988, for *Stick-horse; Iron Woman* was selected by Nicholas Christopher as the 1988 Capricorn Poetry Prize winner; Charles Nilon Minority Fiction Award, 1990, for *Trigger Dance;* fellowship from the National Education Association and Minnesota State Arts Board, and National Endowment for the Arts poetry fellowship, both 1990; North American Indian Prose Award, University of Nebraska Press, and American Book Award, Before Columbus Foundation, both 1992, both for *Claiming Breath;* National Endowment for the Humanities, 1992; Sundance Institute Native American Screenwriter's fellowship, UCLA, 1998; McKnight Fellowship/Loft Award of Distinction in Creative Prose, 1999; Many Voices Fellowship, Playwrights Center, Minneapolis, 2001; Thomas Jefferson Teaching/Scholarship Award, Macalester College, 2001; Cherokee Medal of Honor, Cherokee Honor Society, 2001; National Federation of State Poetry Societies, Stevens Poetry Award, 2001; Arts & Science Dsitinguished Alumni Award, University of Missouri, 2003; National Endowment for the Arts grant, 2003; Juniper Prize, 2004, for *Primer of the Obsolete.*

WRITINGS:

Drystalks of the Moon, Hadassah Press (Tulsa, OK), 1981.

Traveling On, Myrtlewood Press (Tulsa, OK), 1982.

Brown Wolf Leaves the Res and Other Poems, Blue Cloud Quarterly Press (Marvin, SD), 1984.

(Editor with C. W. Truesdale) *Two Worlds Walking: Short Stories, Essays, and Poetry by Writers with Mixed Heritages,* New Rivers Press (New York, NY), 1994.

(Editor, with Mark Nowak) *Visit Teepee Town: Native Writings after the Detours,* Coffee House Press (Minneapolis, MN), 1999.

The Shadow's Horse, University of Arizona Press (Tuscon, AZ), 2003.

SHORT STORIES

Trigger Dance, Fiction Collective Two (Boulder, CO), 1990.

Firesticks: A Collection of Stories, University of Oklahoma Press (Norman, OK), 1993.

Monkey Secret (short stories), TriQuarterly Books (Evanston, IL), 1995.

The Voice That Was in Travel: Stories, University of Oklahoma Press (Norman, OK), 1999.

NOVELS

The Only Piece of Furniture in the House: A Novel, Moyer Bell (Wakefield, RI), 1996.

Pushing the Bear: A Novel of the Trail of Tears, Harcourt Brace (New York, NY), 1996.

Flutie, Moyer Bell (Wakefield, RI), 1998.

The Closets of Heaven: A Novel of Dorcas, the New Testament Seamstress, Chax Press (Tuscon, AZ), 1999.

Fuller Man, Moyer Bell (Wakefield, RI), 1999.

The Man Who Heard the Land, Minnesota Historical Society Press (Saint Paul, MN), 2001.

The Mask Maker, University of Oklahoma Press (Norman, OK), 2002.

Designs of the Night Sky, University of Nebraska Press (Lincoln, NE), 2002.

Stone Heart: A Novel of Sacajawea, Overlook Press (Woodstock, NY), 2003.

POETRY

One Age in a Dream, illustrated by Jay Moon, Milkweed Editions (Minneapolis, MN), 1986.

Offering: Aliscolidodi, Holy Cow! Press (Duluth, MN), 1988.

Iron Woman, New Rivers Press, 1990.

Lone Dog's Winter Count, West End Press (Albuquerque, NM), 1991.

Boom Town, Black Hat (Goodhue, MN), 1995.

Primer of the Obsolete, Chax Press (Tuscon, AZ), 1998, reprinted, University of Massachusetts Press (Amherst, MA), 2004.

(Ado)ration, Chax Press (Tuscon, AZ), 1999.

The Relief of America, Northwestern University Press (Chicago, IL), 2000.

The Stones for a Pillow, 2001.

ESSAYS

Claiming Breath, University of Nebraska Press (Lincoln, NE), 1992.

The West Pole, University of Minnesota Press (Minneapolis, MN), 1997.

The Cold-and-Hunger Dance, University of Nebraska Press, 1998.

In-between Places, University of Arizona Press (Tuscon, AZ), 2004.

PLAYS

Segwohi, produced in Tulsa, OK, 1987.

Testimony, produced in Tulsa, OK, 1987.

Webjob, produced in Tulsa, OK, 1987.

Stick Horse, produced in Aspen, CO, 1988.

The Lesser Wars, produced in Minneapolis, MN, 1989.

Halfact, produced in San Diego, CA, at Modern Language Association Conference, 1994.

War Cries: A Collection of Plays, introduction by Kimberly Blaeser (includes *Weebjob, Stick Horse, Bull Star, Halfact, Segwohi, The Truth Teller, Mother of Mosquitos, The Best Fancy Daner the Pushmataha Pow Wow's Ever Seen,* and *One Horse*), Holy Cow! Press, 1997.

American Gypsy: Six Native American Plays, University of Oklahoma (Norman, OK), 2002.

Also author of plays *Jump Kiss* and *The Woman Who Was a Red Deer Dressed for a Deer Dance.* Contributor to *I Tell You Now: Autobiographical Essays by Native American Writers,* edited by Brian Swann and Arnold Krupat, University of Nebraska Press, 1987; and *Talking Leaves,* edited by Craig Lesley, Bantam (New York), 1991; *Braided Lives: An Anthology of Multicultural American Writing,* Minneapolis Humanities Commission, 1991; *Stiller's Pond: New Fiction from the Midwest,* edited by Jonis Agee, Roger Blakely, and Susan Welch, New Rivers, 1991; *The Heartlands Today,* edited by Larry Smith and Nancy Dunham, Bottom Dog (Huron, OH), 1991; *EarthSong, Sky Spirit: Short Stories of Contemporary Native American Experience,* edited by Clifford Trafzer, Doubleday, 1993; *Inheriting the Land: Contemporary Voices from the Midwest,* edited by Mark Vinz and Thom Tammaro, University of Minnesota Press, 1993; *The Pushcart Prize XVIII: Best of the Small Presses, 1993-1994,* edited by Bill Henderson, Pushcart, 1994; and *Freeing the ! First Amendment: Critical Perspectives on Freedom of Expression,* edited by Robert Jensen and David Allen, New York University Press, 1995.

SIDELIGHTS: Diane Glancy is a poet, playwright, short story writer, essayist, and novelist who often explores the quest for spirituality among mixed-race characters. One-eighth Cherokee, Glancy identifies herself with the Native American and mixed-blood characters she writes about, and like some other contemporary Native American writers, she experiments with genres and styles in an attempt to give expression to the reality of mixed-blood peoples. "The difference in Glancy's writing has to do with her attempts to construct Native American texts by combining oral and written traditions, fusing the visual and verbal, mixing poetry and prose, and experimenting with the arrangement of the text on the page," noted Julie LaMay Abner in *Dictionary of Literary Biography.* Though not all of her experiments are successful, Glancy has won numerous awards for her writings and critical applause for her deeply felt, poetic depictions of marginalized characters. Wendy Murray Zoba, writing in *Books and Culture,* commented on Glancy's quiet childhood, noting that eventually, Glancy "found the one voice that held the others together. Or the voice found her. It came through her writing. The result has been a body of work that defies literary convention." Zoba continued, "If she is hard to categorize, she has nevertheless found readers."

Known first as a poet, Glancy began to garner significant critical attention with the publication of collections of short stories and autobiographical poem-essays. *Firesticks,* a collection of nineteen stories and novellas, centers on Native American characters in contemporary, urban settings who, critics noted, are hard to distinguish from non-Native Americans in their troubled and dreary lives. "Glancy invests her prose with tremendous emotional resonance . . . in tales that often seem more like poems than conventional short stories," remarked a reviewer for *Publishers Weekly* of this work. *The Cold-and-Hunger Dance,* a collection of essays and poems, shares with the earlier volume an emphasis on "the importance of the written word and the act of writing," observed Mary B. Davis in *Library Journal.* In the pieces gathered here, Glancy explores the tangle of emotions evoked by witnessing ceremonies held by tribes other than her own, and universalizes her personal experience as the child of parents with differing cultural backgrounds. In pursuit of melding her Christian beliefs with her Nativist spirituality, Glancy reworks several Native legends to "bizarre" effect, according to a reviewer for *Publishers Weekly,* who classified *The Cold-and-Hunger Dance* as "a strange and insipid tome from a writer who has done much better."

Like *The Cold-and-Hunger Dance, Claiming Breath* is a collection of short, related, autobiographical pieces that often meld genres. Often inspired by long stretches traveling across Oklahoma toward schools where Glancy taught poetry to Native American students in her role as artist-in-residence for the Oklahoma State Arts Council, the author muses on marriage and divorce, the uncanny influence of her Cherokee grandmother on her identity, and attempts to reconcile Native American spiritualism with her own Christian-based beliefs. The result is a "wildly uneven grab-bag in the form of a journal," according to a critic for *Kirkus Reviews,* who found "fresh language and banality, fine prose-poetry and self-indulgence," side by side in *Claiming Breath.* Nevertheless, the volume may serve as a model for those who advocate journal writing as "a road to self-actualization," this critic concluded.

The West Pole is another unusual collection of autobiographical prose and poetry musings on Glancy's attempts to define her identity as a Native American writer. But, like *Claiming Breath,* critics found the pieces of mixed value. "Glancy has a gift for language," proclaimed *Library Journal* critic Vicki Leslie Toy Smith, "but . . . she seems to stop writing before she has exhausted a subject." Similarly, a reviewer for *Publishers Weekly* found the collection "at best only sporadically rewarding," though Glancy's efforts at "deftly blending Indian beliefs and mythology with European Christianity" are "refreshing" compared to the angrier and more divisive sentiments found in much other Native American writing.

With her first novel, *Pushing the Bear: A Novel of the Trail of Tears,* Glancy retells the grueling tale of the thousands of Cherokee Indians who were forced to leave their home lands in North Carolina, Alabama, Georgia, and Tennessee and walk to reservations in Oklahoma. The journey has gone down in history as the Trail of Tears, because so many people died along the way from exposure and disease. Glancy's historical novel centers on a young woman and her family, with numerous secondary characters including soldiers who enforced the march, white clergy, and Indians of all ages whose sufferings are recounted in the first-person. Critics focused much of their attention on Glancy's successful incorporation of a wealth of historical material relating to the forced march, and the evocative voice of her myriad characters to tell "an exquisitely sad tale," in the words of *Booklist* reviewer Kathleen Hughes. "The voices that comprise the narrative are vigorous, and the period details convincing but not obtrusive," claimed a critic for *Kirkus Reviews.* Moreover, *Pushing the Bear* exemplifies, according to a reviewer for *Publishers Weekly,* "the Cherokee conception of story as the indestructible chain linking people, earth and ancestry-a link that becomes, if not unmitigated salvation, then certainly a salve to the spirit."

Almost simultaneously with the publication of *Pushing the Bear,* Glancy published another novel, *The Only Piece of Furniture in the House,* a coming-of-age story that, in its focus on the spiritual life of its protagonist, set the pattern for future novels by the author. In *The Only Piece of Furniture in the House,* Rachel Hume grows up the second oldest of nine children born to a deeply religious mother and her itinerant railway worker husband in the American South and Southwest. When Rachel meets and marries Jim, a soldier, her new life in military housing tests her religious faith as she is surrounded by people who daily break the rules she has learned to live by. In the midst of a postpartum depression, Rachel returns to her childhood home only to realize she must learn to face the world or give up her marriage. A reviewer for *Publishers Weekly* praised Glancy's "expressive prose [which] evocatively captures the intriguing complexity of life in the Bible Belt South."

Like *The Only Piece of Furniture in the House,* the protagonist of *Flutie* is an adolescent girl struggling to reconcile her powerful spiritual life with the realities of her emotionally and materially deprived surroundings. A contributor for *Kirkus Reviews* observed that "Glancy demonstrates a strong and very particular gift for catching the way in which spiritual yearnings work on an untutored mind." In this novel, Flutie Moses sees stories in everything and everyone around her, but can hardly speak to anyone with whom she is not intimate, and thus much of the narrative is given over to accounts of Flutie trying to speak. "This quite beautiful novel proves unexpectedly moving in the ways Glancy finds to write the sounds of silence," remarked Grecian A. Decanted in *Booklist.* Flutie's visions lead her toward a Cherokee spiritualism that is unavailable to the rest of her family, and in a book she gains inspiration from the legend of Philohela, whose brother-in-law cut out her tongue to prevent her from accusing him of raping her. With her newfound powers of speech, Flutie graduates from high school and prepares to attend college to follow her dream of studying geology. The result is "a story of great emotional honesty and power," averred Carolyn Ellis Gonzalez in *Library Journal.*

As in her earlier novels, the protagonist of *Fuller Man* is a young woman predominantly struggling with the role of religious faith in her life. Halley Willie, her sister Nearly, and her brother Farley each must find his or her own way among the battles between their devout mother and skeptical father. "In single images, remarks and disjunct scenes, as if from a journalist's notebook, Halley lays out each important moment of her maturation, from grade school to middle age," as she teeters between faith and doubt, according to a reviewer for *Publishers Weekly.* Like *The Only Piece of Furniture in the House,* the journey toward spiritual healing in the form of fundamentalist Christianity documented by Glancy's narrative in *Fuller Man* was noted by critics for its sympathetic treatment, a rare find in contemporary American literature. While the contributor for *Kirkus Reviews* found Glancy's efforts marred by her unusual, sometimes "cryptic," storytelling methods, "Glancy's determination to plumb an unfashionable question in fiction—how faith or the lack of it shapes and sustains our lives—is admirable."

The Man Who Heard the Land and *The Mask Maker* come at fiction from a more poetic angle than Glancy's previous novels. In the first, a teacher of environmental literature turns to his Native American roots to begin to get through his depression. The results, according to Mary Margaret Benson in her *Library Journal* review "are mixed: his life is still troubled . . . but he has a fuller understanding of himself." *The Mask Maker,* which Debbie Bogenschutz of *Library Journal* called a "truly dynamic" experiment, tells the story of a mixed-blood Native American mother, who deals with her feelings and emotions through the traditional artwork of the mask. Glancy accompanies her text with Bible passages and the thoughts of the main character in her own voice, each featured on the side of the page.

Designs of the Night Sky falls somewhere between a collection of stories and a novel; main character Ada works in a library and reads accounts of the Trail of Tears. Confronting problems in her own life and delving into historical accounts of tragedy, Ada seeks comfort in Christianity and at the Dust Bowl roller rink. The novel changes back and forth between the historical forced migration of the Cherokee and Ada's life and the stories of her family members. Debbie Bogenschutz in her *Library Journal* review called the book "an engaging novel," while a critic for *Kirkus Reviews* considered the book, perhaps in spite of its non-traditional format, "at its core a probing, honest tale." Howard Meredith, writing for *World Literature*

Today, noted, "In every sense, this is Glancy's most ambitious endeavor."

In 2003, Glancy took on the challenge of presenting historical heroine Sacajawea in a novel format. Though it had been done before, Glancy's approach gave the story a new twist; while using a second-person voice to give Sacajawea's perspective on the Lewis and Clark expedition, Glancy featured excerpts from the Louis and Clark journals on a second column on the page. The narrative is two-fold; one gives the historical perspective of the white explorers, the other the thoughts of a young Native American woman. Sacajawea, a Shoshone woman who had been kidnapped by the Hidatasa tribe and then sold to a Canadian trapper as his second wife, was pregnant with the trapper's child when she served as a translator for the expedition. Glancy's depiction of Sacajawea neglects none of her strength of character; Margaret Flanagan of *Booklist* wrote that "Sacajawea is blessed with an inner vision that puts and earthy and vibrant spin on each individual experience and encounter." A reviewer for *Publishers Weekly* thought that many of Sacajawea's responses were "predictable," however, the critic concluded, "Glancy's sharply observed details and lyrical stylings make for a lively, thought-provoking read"; a critic for *Kirkus Reviews* considered the book "a brilliantly artistically ambitious retelling." In *Library Journal,* Debbie Bogenschutz claimed "the interest in this retelling lies in the contrast between the two parties' journals"; Anne G. Myles in *North American Review* similarly commented, "This doubling is the narrative's most distinctive and difficult feature, as Glancy executes it literally, graphically on the page." Myles continued, "Such readerly dislocation is surely part of the point: we find ourselves, like the protagonist, out of our element; we have to work out for ourselves what kind of authority two incommensurable perspectives have within the novel and within our understanding of the truth."

Glancy defines herself as a Native American writer, and her fiction and nonfiction writings alike treat the consequences of that self-definition, especially for her spiritual life. Admiring critics point to the evocative language she uses to create characters besieged by inner lives whose expression is not welcome in the worlds they inhabit, which are marked by poverty in the material, emotional, and spiritual senses. "Her work is a refreshingly honest depiction of contemporary American Indian life with common themes that are easily accessible to Indian and non-Indian readers alike: mixed-bloodedness, heritage, colonialism, middle age, feminism, divorce, death, power, and survival," wrote Abner in *Dictionary of Literary Biography.* While some critics find her autobiographical collections of short prose and poetry less satisfying than her novels, accusing the author of failing to take on the important questions she raises in-depth or with logical precision, the journal-like musings found in *Claiming Breath* and *The West Pole* are valued by other critics as a model for readers seeking identity and self-worth in times of trouble.

AUTOBIOGRAPHICAL ESSAY:

Diane Glancy contributed the following autobiographical essay to *CA:*

THE COLD-AND-HUNGER DANCE

> *. . . therefore I set my face like a flint*
>
> (Isaiah 50:7)

I had a hunger for words. The house I lived in as a child was quiet. I was quiet. I was three before I had a sibling. My mother handled the words. I wanted someone to listen. I wanted someone to talk to.

I wanted my own voice forming my will.

I wanted books. The fortified cities of them.

I wanted to be a maker of those fortifications. A fortifier. Because my parents are gone and they were once young and sturdy. Though they also tore down. And were torn down.

I was born between two cultures. My father was Cherokee. My mother, English and German. But we weren't enough Cherokee to be accepted as Indian, nor was I white enough to be accepted as white. I could walk in both worlds. I could walk in neither. I lived in a no-man's-land. A no-man's-land that moved.

In a poem called "Oklahoma Land Run," in *The Relief of America,* I have a line, "jiggling like a pea in a, Prince Albert tobacco tin." I always have felt I rolled around.

Diane Hall with her father—"Sitting on the fortified wall; 'my rock and fortress' (Psalms 31:3)," 1941

My father worked for the stockyards in Kansas City. He was transferred several times. I went to several schools in the Midwest. Francis Willard in Kansas City. Flackville in Indianapolis. Normandy in St. Louis. I graduated from the University of Missouri in 1964, from the University of Central Oklahoma in 1983, and from the University of Iowa Writer's Workshop in 1988. I have been at Macalester College in St. Paul, Minnesota, since then. I write and teach Native American literature and creative writing in its many forms—poetry, fiction, creative nonfiction, scriptwriting.

I've always wanted to tell stories. To tell them in my own way. According to oral tradition, I could speak with the trail of voices. I could talk with my own voice, and the process of my words could change the structure of the story. I could speak indirectly if I wanted. Talking about one thing while meaning another.

The Judeo-Christian heritage, which is full of stories of expanding boundaries, and church, where I heard those stories, have been a part of my middle-class life also.

I think I am a Christian because of the words in the Bible. The sturdiness of them. The oratures of them.

> *He stretcheth out the north over the empty place, and hangeth the earth upon nothing.*
>
> *(Job 26:7)*

> *He bindeth up the waters in his thick clouds; and the cloud is not torn under them.*
>
> *(Job 26:8)*

> *He hast set a bound that the waves may not pass over, that they turn not again to cover the earth.*
>
> *(Psalms 104:9)*

> *Will ye not tremble at my presence, who have placed the sand for the bound of the sea; and though its waves toss themselves, yet can they not prevail; though they roar, they cannot pass over.*
>
> *(Jeremiah 5:22)*

I felt an *unformedness* I wanted form for. Or maybe I wanted boundaries for. It was through words. The stories of them. Their *storyness.* It was the Word God held out as a pole for me to take a hold of.

There is something in the Bible. A relativity of *change-ableness,* yet an absolute dry-ground in the flood. The waves could come so far, but no farther. Jesus was a construct of voice and a centering in the turmoil I felt.

Sometimes, even in the Native American experience, I hear about Jesus.

In the Newberry Library, during a research fellowship, I found a story.

Now here is a Ute Sundance story told by Mollie Cloud.

this is about the Sundance, it was long time ago; there were two of them, an old man and an old woman, she was his mother, the one who acted as his mother; and he was lonely, the (young) man was, without relatives, they had all perished (in an epidemic); so he would just hunt around, he went hunting, wandering around, through the cedar-grown country, it was around Mancos Creek long time ago;

so as he hunted around, he didn't kill (anything), he didn't kill any deer; so the next day he went out again, having killed no deer (the day before), he again went hunting; and once again he returned (empty-handed);

so then . . . he became very lonely; he . . . having no relatives; so then later on he brooded, and he became lonely; so he decided to kill himself, to shoot himself in the head, right there on the rocky slope; he was sitting on a rocky hillside, he was going to kill himself;

so then, having not yet loaded his gun, all of a sudden an owl hooted right behind him; he had hobbled his horse . . . where he had hobbled it . . . right behind it there (the owl) cried;

so he quit trying to kill himself, sitting there on the slope, sitting on the rocky hillside; then all of a sudden, for whatever reason, he got angry; "Why is it" he said, "that the owl is calling me? So that I shouldn't kill myself!" he said, he thought;

then his horse . . . (the owl) kept hooting toward where his horse was, the owl did; when he was sitting, when he was sitting, right behind him, it hooted; and it kept leading him toward the horse, it kept hooting; he had hobbled his horse quite a distance back;

so then, while he was sitting . . . I mean . . . he stepped (up on) his horse; then all of a sudden his . . . he mounted it and turned back, going home; it was very far; then when he arrived, he told his Grandmother: "being so

"I remember the empty bookcases beside the fireplace in our living room. I don't remember having many books. Yet, I'm on the front steps of my house, age two and a half, reading," 1943

lonely, I almost killed myself" he said, "because I was so lonely" he said; "Why are you so lonely?" asked his Grandmother, "I'm still around, you shouldn't do it!" she said;

well, the next day he went out again; he had a dream in his sleep (that night), of a deer going that way, across the rocky mesa . . . it was a flat rocky mesa . . .

so (going across that country), there were indeed tracks, of a deer going across the rocky mesa; then, the young man thought, someone was whistling right there; there was a small arroyo there, and suddenly from across it, there was a whistling; so he looked that way, he kept tracking the deer, its spoor; and right there (in front of him) there was a White-Man standing, on a white horse, all dressed in white; it was a White-Man; "What manner of dress is that?" the Young Man thought. "It must be the White-Man's way" he thought; so he stood and looked at him, and the White-Man called him: "Come here!" he told him; so the Young Man approached slowly; and the White-Man spoke to him then;

he spoke in all languages . . . then . . . eee . . . he spoke English (first), next he spoke Spanish, but the Young Man didn't understand . . . he then spoke (in the languages of) all the people who live on earth, he spoke all of them;

finally he spoke to him in his own Ute language, finally, but before that he spoke to him in Navajo . . . and that the Young Man understood; what the White-Man spoke last was Ute, and the Young Man understood it;

now the White-Man showed him . . . he showed him . . . he showed him his hand where he had been nailed . . . and his ribs where he had been stabbed; "How come you are like that?" the Young Man asked; he was indeed a whole person there was nothing . . . there was nothing missing about him;

the Young Man himself was sort of an orphan he understood (only) when the White-Man spoke Navajo, or in Ute; he didn't understand any English; and he didn't know anything about it, that this was the White-Man who had been nailed (to the cross) on the hillside; of what the White-Man told him he knew nothing; "Who is this one?" he wondered; and indeed, it was Jesus, it was him, he was bearded, he had long hair.

well then . . . the story goes . . . "I will talk to you now" Jesus said, "about this business yesterday of you wanting to shoot yourself in the head" he said; "You shouldn't do it, even though you may be an orphan" he said then, "I will talk to you now" he said; "It is because of his influence that you did it" he said; and lo, just next to Jesus there was a Dark Man standing, with a hook nose, like a cowboy, just like that type, wearing a big hat, with spurs, decked up in his finery, riding a well-made saddle; and his horse had fierce eyes, it

was pitch black; and lo, it was the Devil himself it was him; so the Young Man stood and watched (him); it was because of his power that he was going to shoot himself in the head (the day before); that's what Jesus told him;

the Young Man was scared, watching the Devil, Jesus showed him to him; then (he said): "I am the one who stopped you (from killing yourself), disguised as an owl, I'm the one who hooted at you, I'm the one who led you away" he told him then; so the Young Man said: "Yes" he said, "I was feeling very dejected when I did it" he said, "That's why I (tried to) do it" he told him, the Young Ute told Jesus;

so Jesus told him: "I will now tell you" he said, "you . . . you . . . 'I'm lonely' that's what you said" he said; "Now I'll show you your relatives; your relatives are indeed alive, your older brother" he said, "is standing right there" he said, "indeed I've brought him here" he said;

and lo, right alongside Jesus there was a person standing, his older brother; so the Young Man stood there looking at him; "alright" asked Jesus, "do you recognize him?" he asked; "yes, he's my older brother" said the Young Man, "and he's been dead for a long time"; "No" Jesus told him, "he's not dead, he's alive, up in heaven, up there above the earth": he said, "he's alive there, (together with) many others"; that's what he told him, he told him;

then Jesus continued: "Yes" he said, "he just came to see you, because you were lonely, you said so yourself; now he knows where you live" he said; so the Young Man said: "Alright" he said, "it's alright by me" he said;

then Jesus said: "Now I am going to tell you the story" he said, "of this land, the way it is going to be in the future" he said; "right now I . . . right now all this land is full of Indians; but just like that (it will fill with) Whites" he said; "They'll speak all (kinds of) language, it will all be mixed" he said, telling him the story; "And these church goers, there'll be all kinds, there'll be all kinds, a jumble of congregations with all kinds of names . . . church goers . . ." he said; "They'll have (different) names, those congregations" he said; "And as to these Indians, the ones here now, the Indians, they'll become this way too; now, here standing (next to you) is the one you were longing for" he said; "So what will become of you now? These Indians (around you), they don't . . . understand (about all this)" Jesus continued; "So . . . you . . . we-two will now tell you about the way the Indians will practice (religion); they will eat Peyote, or they will Sundance; of the two, which one do you choose?" "The Sundance . . . that's the kind I choose" said the Young Man, "the Sundance. But my relatives don't practice any of it" he continued, "they don't Sundance. Of what you describe, they practice nothing. But I will practice that kind" he said;

"Now I . . . Alright" said Jesus; "You yourself will be the (Sundance) Chief, and I will then give you the things with which you'll do it, what you'll Sundance with, what will be done" he said . . . that's what he told him . . . so the Young Man agreed, and he did exactly that way, when he practiced the next summer; when they did it then, they just did it for practice, with only a few people;

the following summer, it was supposed to be very big, with many people doing it; and then the Sundancers were to be all dressed up exactly the same way; the Young Man also had the same outfit, with an Eagle-Whistle and all, and drums . . . the way they were going to do it . . . that's what Jesus told him, so that's why the Young Man did it (that way); and when they practiced, they did it with the singing;

now then, after having finished the practice, he . . . he, one Indian, an envious one, came over across, with his hat . . . the center pole was very, it was very tall; so he hung his hat up there (on the center pole) after they had practiced; that person went mad afterwards, and he ran away; and lo, his house . . . inside his hat there was a yellow (cloth) bundle (of bad medicine); he was bad-mouthing (the Sundance), he was a bad one, he did it . . . so he went mad;

Diane, with her mother and brother, David, 1950

then the Young Man . . . Jesus had also told him: "that . . . don't . . ." (some people) were bad-mouthing the Young Man when he practiced the Sundance; so then he . . . when they kept doing that to him, that crowd spoke ill of him; so later: "When they speak ill of you, I myself will (come and) take you away (to me)" that's what Jesus had told him . . . "When you had practiced it (the Sundance), I will take you away (to me), if they speak ill of you, that crowd . . ."

so then when the Young Man practiced that way, those people indeed bad-mouthed him; Jesus had told him (about it) long before that; at that time he had also told him many (other) things . . .

so then the next summer . . . the next day . . . the next summer when (the Sundance) was supposed to take place, he died then . . . just . . . the Young Man died, after they bad-mouthed him; there were quite a few there when he practiced, and they all were dressed exactly the same fine style; well, there was that woman inside there where the crowd (of Dancers) was supposed to be, two women; they were supposed to sit across (from the Sundancers); they weren't supposed to Sun-dance, only to sit; that's how it was to be, supposedly;

and he had also said . . . the Son of God . . . "You must also do like this, I tell you" he said; he told him about everything, about what will become of everything on this earth, the way it will happen, about that, he told him; The Indian will disappear, he said, with only a few surviving, alive; they will have to marry their own kin, he said then, because they would have become so few, he said;

that's how it is nowadays, just as he said, with the White-Men having become so numerous; they all go to churches, and (Jesus said that) they'd all be arguing with each other, all those religions, he told him; they . . . all over their churches they would be shooting each other; that's what has happened now, Jesus told him (about it), that's what Jesus said . . .

I myself often sit and think about it, knowing all this; I keep thinking, about that; knowing all this . . .

so Jesus told him about everything, about all that is on this earth; that's how it is, the way it has become; they even called-up the Indians (to serve) overseas; it has become that way . . .

long time ago . . . that way he . . . it was long ago, there remain other things, that he also said; this earth would break open, he said, and the water would begin to rise, he said; un-less they do the Sundance, unless they run it real good and proper, unless he run it well;

that Sundance is powerful Medicine, (that's) where the Sundancing Indian would get his Medicine-power; it's that way that they've come (to have Medicine-Power); and with it

in their hands, like this (gesture), they would always ward off (bad medicine); that is, if one does the Sundance well, that's what (Jesus) said, if one does it real well; that wandering young Ute was to become a Medicine man;

nowadays I often sit and think about all this; (about how) they do it the wrong way, those who do it, those who do the Sundance; it is the wrong way, it is;

it is Jesus who said it; when I think about it now . . . there's much more to it, what I will say, there's much more to it that (Jesus) had said; there's no end to it, the way this (the Sundance) has become; he's the one who said that . . . it's him, the Son of God; there's much more to it, I myself know only some of it, I don't know all of it, I don't remember (all of) what he said, what he said; whatever it be, it has become like that, the way (Jesus) said it, to him, to the Ute man, it's what he said, to the Medicine-Man; I've said it now, this is just about as far as I know, not very much . . .

Jesus told him this, to him, to the Ute man: "when you return when you go back home . . . when you go back, I'll give you one horse" he told him then; so then later the Young Man went back, back home . . . "That horse will catch up with you" he had told him; "It'll be a black spotted one, a small one, not very big"; and indeed that happened;

but then he couldn't, when he was going back home he couldn't catch it; he came along it four, three (times); but it kept disappearing that-a-way; and then afterwards it would come back, but the Young Man didn't carry anything (to catch it with), he didn't have anything, he wasn't carrying a rope with him, so he didn't catch it then; heee . . . circling around four times with the horse, he kept coming up to it as he was returning home; but he didn't have . . . anything with which to catch it; that one . . . that horse . . . that's the one that the Young Man was supposed to ride go-ing all over this land; he had said that, he had told him, God . . . the Son of God; the Young Man saw him; then when he returned home he . . . then . . . it was like that . . . he

"My brother and me at the Pacific," 1950

didn't catch it, the horse ran way, that-a-way; it was supposed to be gentle, the horse, it was supposed to be a good one;

I sit and think about it, this is the story they used to tell me, my long-gone relatives; that's how come I know it, about how the Sundance used to be . . .

(Here the speaker digressed into how the Sundance is currently done.)

so the young man . . . he returned home then, and he lived on; but later he died; he is the one who told (his people) about the Sundance; but he did not do it himself; he died (before that);

after he died, when he was lying in state, a rainbow appeared, right above; and everything was there (on the funeral pyre), everything, what the Ute man would have worn dancing, Sundancing, it was all there, the bundle he would have (carried), his eagle whistle, what he was supposed to wear, and whatever else he had; he had done it all properly, it was like that . . . he was a real Indian;

that's what she said . . . she used to tell me this, my late mother, when she told me stories . . . I have told it now, where it all comes from; this is as far as it goes, what I know.

(The Ute name for the Sundance, "tagau-wunuvaci," means "standing hungry." In this story it is referred to most often as "tagu-nhka-pi" ["hunger-dance"]. Sometimes it is also referred to simply as "wunu-vaci" ["standing"]. Some speakers say that the name of the Young Ute man who received the Sundance from Jesus was "tuu-naci-too-pu" ["Black Cane"]. He is said to have been the older brother of Peter Spencer, and thus, the son of a Ute man named "nuu-saaquaci" ["Ghost Person"].)

*

Those Sundances would go on in secret. The Indian couldn't practice his religion openly until the Religious Freedom Act of 1978. For nearly a hundred years the Sundance was illegal. It wasn't the tradition my father was from anyway. He'd come from northern Arkansas, where his father had been a country doctor and his mother a Cherokee woman. His religion came in the form of church.

My father also liked to travel. From Kansas City, we made trips to my grandparents' farm in Kansas and my father's mother in Viola, Arkansas We went to California to visit my Aunt Helen, and to Itasca State Park in Minnesota.

When we lived in Indiana, we went to Lake Michigan and the sand dunes, Turkey Run State Park, and Washington D.C., Jamestown and Williamsburg. When we lived in St. Louis, we made trips to Florida and to the Lake of the Ozarks in Missouri, where Aunt Mu and Uncle Carl had a cabin.

I remember feeling limits, but when I look at the photo album, there was also migration.

When I was eight or nine, I had to take swimming lessons at Paseo High School in Kansas City. I still have an image of that pool. The shape of it, shallow on one end, deep on the other, something like the state of Oklahoma where I lived much of my adult life. The weight of it filled with water. I was under water, swimming for the surface. I could see light. I swam toward it. When I think back on those early years, it was my father who was the light. My Aunt Mil in her saddle shoes was the one who held out the pole. Because she was never angry with me.

Diane with her brother, David, at Itasca State Park, Minnesota, 1951

I never did learn to swim.

It was an overwhelming experience that stands as a dominant image of my childhood.

That swimming pool is still in my head. I drain it with my writing. My mother's unhappiness as a mother. Her disapproval of me. Whether it was my darkness intruding upon her, or something disagreeable in me, we had conflict.

But that point of fear and drowning is the undercurrent of my writing.

Words are a netting, a surface of waves, which disrupt the joint of process. Wind patterns on the lake. Interrelated and touching one another. Though it seems they don't. I feel the frustration of words in their bondage of having to explain.

A swimming pool full of waves. That was my adolescence.

> *He had seven sons and three daughters . . .*
> *and their father gave them inheritance among*
> *their brethren.*
>
> *(Job 42:13-15)*

Though I felt I was nothing, I knew I had an inheritance. I struggled through self-devaluation and fear and inferiority and isolation. There was a steel wire that ran though my life. Wherever it came from. A combination of several sources, probably. Self-will and determination. An aunt without children, who approved of me. A house with two parents that remained whole though broken. The words from the Bible.

> *He hath compassed the water with a boundary.*
>
> *(Job 26:10)*

When I write a story, I feel those variables moving in different patterns. I think it's why I write in several genres. The imagination moves across the landscape and enters the text, and takes part in the forming of the creative act, which unites my fragments in a loose bonding, which moves to other bondings of other fragments, and makes sources of energy spots.

Writing is the creating of a *source structure.*

In wording and naming the act of living, the experience of shaping out of shapelessness, a determination, a determinacy, speaks a continuum of will and fortitude and not giving up.

When I was rejected and rejected and rejected, the words were still there, the writing, that is. I kept writing. And the manuscripts piled up. I sent them out, received them back, sent them out again. The title of my second collection of drama, *Cargo,* probably came from carrying all those words around.

Now that I'm older, I think, looking back, what it was to live my life. It was long ago and I wanted to write and I wrote when my two children napped, and I had a file cabinet, and then I bought another to hold what I had written. I moved it with me, from Oklahoma to Iowa to Minnesota, and twice since I've lived in Minnesota.

Words are a dynamic of self seeking connection.

> Waves cropping a lake.
> A lake cropping its waves.

Words are the reflection of water in the pool of the eye.

> A place I was looking for
> made of images of meaning.
> A more-than-one on which to focus.

> A flag in the wind.
> Someone speaking from far way.
> I can see the mouth move.
> I see it like a flag in the wind.

There is a crosspool of floodings in the complexities of current. There is a voice saying, "hold on, it will connect and *go somewhere,*" in a broken surface on which words spread into many genres.

From 1964 to 1983, I was married to Dwane Glancy. The image I have from those years was a dream I had once, early in the marriage. I was trying to drive a loaded eighteen-wheeler up a sandy incline.

Those were the years I began writing.

I also wanted to return to school. After I got my BA. at the University of Missouri, it was twenty years before I continued my education. My years as an undergraduate had been unsettled. Insecure. I couldn't study. I didn't think I could. My grades suffered.

The turmoil of my life still circled. Everything fell back on me. I worked with poetry and then story. I worked with creative nonfiction, drama, and the novel. It wasn't until 1984 that I had anything published.

Two early novels, *The Only Piece of Furniture in the House* and *Fuller Man,* written during my marriage, weren't published for fifteen years. I began *Monkey Secret,* my third collection of short stories, as an undergraduate at the University of Missouri. I remember writing one of the sections, "The Wooden Tub," in my first creative writing class. It was nearly thirty years before the other parts of the story were finished and published.

My historical novel, *Pushing the Bear,* about the 1838 Trail of Tears, the removal of 13,000 Cherokee from the southeast to Indian Territory, took nearly eighteen years to write. In the afterward, I tell how I first saw the outdoor drama in Tahlequah, Oklahoma. My daughter and I had driven from Tulsa to see it. Over the years, the many voices in the novel came to my imagination during research or travel. Or sometimes when I was doing something else, there would be Maritole or Knobowtee. It's where I heard them anyway, in the imagination. A series of voices, a story of many voices walking the trail, telling their side of it.

When I was in New York to talk to my publisher about the novel, I visited the Smithsonian Museum of the American Indian in the Custom House. I saw a Seminole robe which was a patchwork of color and geometric design. I thought of my novel as a patterning of voices with dialogue and conflicts unfolding in relationship to one another. When I saw a northwestern tribe "button blanket," I thought of my novel as a "voice blanket." My grandmother on my mother's side made quilts. Maybe in sewing the scattered voices together in the novel, I'm doing what she did, only in a different way.

I also thought of *Pushing the Bear* as the noise of voices after their sound has stopped.

The title came to me when I was at the Gilcrease Museum in Tulsa, down among the shelves in the storage rooms. I saw a small ivory statue of an Eskimo man pushing the rump of a bear. "Pushing the Bear" came immediately to mind.

*

Sometimes my writing comes quickly. My next novel, *Flutie,* was written in 1995-96. It's the story of a young woman who is shy and cannot speak, but through circumstance and ceremony and an act of the will, she finds her voice and speaks.

I'm glad each piece comes in its own way. Writing is a continual process, changing as it goes.

I have the title for a new novel, *An American Language,* and something else called, *The Man Who Heard the Land,* is there. And something called, *America's First Parade,* is there after that. I feel my words coming and coming. I don't think I'll ever get them all down.

I have a piece of dialogue from *An American Language.* "Imagine a place without its own language. Well, it has a language. It's just not its own."

I was thinking about our American language when I was traveling in Germany recently. I said that I felt limited when I traveled because I only had one language. But someone said, "It's the right one."

At the conference in Munich, I was talking about the experimentation I liked to do with the American language. I talked about the possibilities of changing syntax. The possibilities for opening the language to accommodate minority and women's voices. How in not having ownership over language, it expands to do what you want to do as a writer. The Germans said that the German language didn't have that capacity. If you changed a word in German, or tried to stretch it, you'd feel that something was wrong.

Maybe our language is more fluid. Elastic. It's what I want language to be, anyway.

It's also what I want genres to be. I think it's why I began experimenting with the short-story collections I wrote. My first two short fiction books, *Trigger Dance* and *Firesticks,* were written in Oklahoma, where I lived with my husband and children. They contain first-person narratives and short short fiction pieces as well as traditional short stories. *Firesticks* begins with a story about Louis, who is colorblind and tries to imagine color. The book then continues with a personal essay, then a poetic piece about a truck driver, and then the first section of the title piece, "Firesticks." Then there's another personal-voice piece and another chapter of "Firesticks." Then more stories and personal-voice pieces with more parts of "Firesticks" woven between them. I think I wrote the book that way because I felt the fragmentation of my own life, and of my father's heritage, in the breaking up of a solid place.

I've already mentioned *Monkey Secret,* my third collection. It is also a broken-voice piece. The book is three short stories followed by the novella, "Monkey Secret." That monkeys were once men was an idea I got from the *Popol Vuk,* the Mayan council book.

On the cover flap, the editor, Reginald Gibbons, writes:

> Glancy's tales of Native American life explore the essential American territory, the border-between: between past and present, between native and immigrant cultures, between self and society.
>
> The short novel, "Monkey Secret," combines traditional Native American storytelling and contemporary narrative techniques to explore the coming of age of a young girl of mixed race and heritage in rural northern Arkansas. Jean Pierce narrates her passage from childhood to maturity with typically Native American circularity and digression. Each chapter of "Monkey Secret" is like a single perfect bead on a string; Jean's impressionistic vignettes—growing up with her extended family at their farm in Haran, Arkansas, spending summers at the cabin on Bull Shoals Lake, depparting for college and returning to find her mother dying—are threaded with the twin strands of her complex culture and her desperate love for her cousin Cedric.
>
> In its gaps and hesitations, the qualifications of thought and feeling, the meditative self-reflexiveness, Glancy's work interrogates narrative form while revealing the individuality and authenticity of her characters.

I had wanted to call the novella, "Portrait of an Artist as a Young Woman," but I knew I couldn't get into those waters. It's about a young woman who lives in the crevice between the Christian world of her father and the mythic Cherokee world of her mother, and uses words to bridge the two irreconcilable worlds that are always moving apart from one another. One of the sections in the novella, however, is called "Sketches of an Artist as a Young Woman." I remember visiting Bull Shoals Lake in Arkansas when we went to see my father's mother. I remember being in a rowboat on *big water.* I also used the experiences I had at my Uncle Carl's cabin on the Lake of the Ozarks.

During my 1995-96 sabbatical year at Macalester College, I finished my fourth collection of short stories, *The Voice That Was in Travel*. It also moves between the personal and distant voice, but there is more of a "settledness" of pieces.

In 1995, *Trigger Dance* was translated into German and published by S. Fischer in Frankfurt. It's the reason I've traveled to Germany several times for readings and conferences. I also went to Italy, Syria, and Jordan for U.S. Information Service tours.

Creative nonfiction is a genre with a moving definition. Memoir, autobiography, diary writing, journal keeping, travel pieces, essays on various subjects, assemblages of experiences and reflections, and experimentation with the variables of composition. *Claiming Breath* and *The West Pole* are collections of creative nonfiction, combining lectures and book reviews with personal essays and fragmented prose pieces, all the while moving between traditional and disconnected writing styles, shifting the text, breaking into the sentence structure. Expanding the boundaries. Somehow communicating the ideas.

I'm now working on my third book of creative nonfiction called, *In the Spirit of the Mind*.

I have nine manuscripts of unpublished poetry I work on at various times. *The Relief of America, The Deer Rider, Asylum in the Grasslands, (Ado)ration, Generally He Gave Us Plenty of Room, Necessary Departures*. Well, two of them, *Still Life with Mazie in the Cornfields* and *Warrior Woman* are chapbooks, and *Passionate Visions* is a selected work.

Drama is a fifth genre field. *War Cries* is a book of nine of my plays. *Cargo* is my second. "Lesser Wars," "American Gypsy," "Cargo," "Jump Kiss," and "The Woman Who Was a Red Deer Dressed for the Deer Dance" are the plays I've worked on recently.

Now I'm working on a piece called, "The Women Who Loved House Trailers." The main characters are three women: Oscar, a welder, Jelly, a weaver of strips of birchbark into small canoes, and Berta, a collector of stories.

Like "The Woman Who Was a Red Deer Dressed for the Deer Dance," which was written after I saw a red papier-mâché dress made by visual artist Carolyn Erler, this piece will also be interdisciplinary.

The house trailers will be the three women who come to terms with themselves. The house trailers will be their roaming hearts. The house trailers will be the groups of their extended families they learn to accept. The house trailers will be the moving stories of their different lives. The house trailers also will be the cultures of several continents, which is another addition to the multidimensional aspect of the new wave of oral tradition I'm trying to create, which is interlocking cultures. Well, I'm just beginning to write this fictional/poetic/ dramatic piece, and already I can see the long trail. Jelly will make wheels for her canoes. Oscar will weld wheels. Berta's stories will be mobile. In the three women's relationships, their problems and limitations will be made portable and rolled away. With love and blow kisses from the welder's torch.

Native American storytelling is an act of *gathering* many voices to tell a story. One voice alone is not enough because we are what we are in relationship to others, and we each have our different way of seeing. NA writing is also an alignment of voices so the story comes through. A *relational stance* is the construct of the writing. In my short stories, poems, and creative nonfiction I can follow the rules of conflict/resolution, one point-of-view, plot, and the usual, but there is something essential in Native storying that is not included, which is a migratory and interactive process of the moveable parts within the story. It's also the element of Native American oral tradition told with what it is not—the written word—then returned to what it is by the act of the voice. There's not a name for it in the genre field, but I'mm trying to give solid nomenclature to something that is a moving process, and resists naming, other than a new oral tradition.

I think writing exists, in part, for healing, not only in the writer, but also for the reader/hearer. For instance, in Navajo sand paintings, the painter aligns the design in the sand to the hurt in the one needing healing, and the alignment draws the hurt into the painting, and the painting is destroyed, and the ailment along with it. Storying should do the same. It is much needed in a culture with a high alcoholism rate, poverty, and a struggle for racial esteem.

America is taking out of the melting pot what didn't melt: our voices and styles of storytelling. We are a fractured, pluralistic society, which our art should reflect. I think understanding cultures is the byword for our society. It seems to me that art is the medium for understanding not only the differences between cultures, but within cultures as well. There is a vast difference between the Plains Indian and the Woodland cultures.

*

Sometimes, in the long cold of a Minnesota winter, I think about my writing. Especially when I'm chopping ice that's several inches thick on my sidewalk. Especially when I'm shoveling snow. The last storm, my snow shovel froze in a mound of old snow where I'd jabbed it. I had to shovel with a shovel with a broken handle.

At night, when the ice on the roof shifts, the house moans and knocks with stories.

Over the years, I have written because I was hungry for words.

I have written because I was cold.

I think I've waited my whole life to teach, travel, read my poetry and fiction in bookstores and at conferences.

Like my father, I want to be on the road. The autumn of my sabbatical after receiving tenure, I had a fellowship at the Provincetown Art Center in Massachusetts, I drove from St. Paul to the other side of Cleveland the first day. And from the other side of Cleveland to Provincetown. 1465 miles in two days.

There was something I had to get through. Maybe like a piece of writing.

There were names I found, like Ashtabula County in Ohio, I had to get down.

And there were the *trucks—Yellow Transit. National Carriers. Transcontinental Registered Lines. Roadway. Consolidated Freight. Wells Fargo. j B. Hunt.. North American. Burlington. Falcon. Tuscarora. Mayflower.*

Some without names.

The turnpikes east of Wisconsin are walled cities. I felt locked on the highway with the truckers. But I was away from classes and department and committee meetings and grading papers.

There were seven tollgates through Chicago alone where I waited in the exhaust of their dust.

Alter two days by myself on the road, weary and spaced, my sense of identity, which is tied to place, was gone. I was one of those nameless trucks floating over the road. Disconnected. But in the movement of my car was place, I remembered. Migration was a state.

And I was in the walled city of my car.

If I could be from anywhere, it would be Ashtabula. If I could be with anyone, it would be one of those truckers. Those wedding-cake grooms up there decorated with lights. I would follow his truck across the Atlantic, if there was a highway there.

*

My children are grown and my relatives are gone, and I am with my words now.

Water I can't swim.

Water you are blank as I am.

Water you can swim.

Water you can hold me up.

Sometimes I think of my father, who left his rural Cherokee heritage to be a real American—a Boy Scout leader—a provider for his family. I remember the hollowness and anger in him because he had a blank place wheree heritage should have been.

But I had a doll cart with two wheels my father made, and I'd pull my two dolls to a weeded lot by my house and play there all day mashing berries for food, playing out what was in my imagination. There was a life

"My cousin, Susan, who is Aunt Helen's daughter, and me on our grandparents' farm; my father made my wooden doll cart," 1951

of the mind in which there was the making of metaphor, a development and insight into the relationship of parts—the likeness of differences—the difference of likenesses—the connectives and disconnectives—the making of something. I thhink I continue pushing my doll cart to the woods with my writing.

Because I didn't have music or mathematics or science—I made analogies. I made stories. But the principles of discovery and relationships may be the same.

The language of the imagination has the function of talking through the connections which underlie things. I am in a relationship to something outside myself. I have a connection to words, and as I work, they connect with something larger.

I feel the variability. The layering of expanding thought processes, the opportunities, the options, the embellishment and elaborations. I generate my own life in the development of thought through words.

I have a reliable construction of change and the unexpected. I have a gist of certainty. My writing is a generator. A source of Something—of words—of reasoning—

They brought me to the place where I am now. It's a full life full of ordinariness, really. I had twenty years as a wife and mother. I've been divorced thirteen. My children are on their own in different cities. This was a time dreaded by my mother's generation in the fifties. What do you do after the children are gone? Who are you outside your husband and family?

Those years with my children were meaningful—and I miss them sometimes. But now I get up in the morning and have coffee and read the newspaper and go to my word processoor and go through my thoughts, and go back through them, and find that road into what I am saying. I guess it's always been Main Street under the Elms.

I remember the decency of my parents despite their problems and economic straits—the unfairness they knew. My mother as a woman. My father as a man who had to live without part of himself. I remember the ddisillusionment, the boredom, I guess, of their marriage. The tediousness of life we all know. My anger at them—

But the carcasses of cattle hung upside down in the stockyards where my father worked, and Christ hung right side up on his cross in church. There was faith in the bloodshed of Christ for the atonement of our shortcomings and sins. Christianity as a strained metaphor, so to speak. A thought process that links. Something like sand, which can be a boundary of the sea and a conduit of healing in a painting.

I have my own life now. I have a small house in St. Paul. When it's twenty degrees below or when there are twenty inches of snow in one afternoon, my brother calls from Missouri and asks what I'm doing there. But I can shovel my walk and mow the lawn and reach the windows when I wash them. I have a sense of self in my thinking, which is an internal landscape. There are elements in the world that could wipe me out, but I have a heritage of survival. I just have to hold on to it.

"My first dance," 1956

Somewhere as a child, the cold-and-hunger dance passed into me. Awkward. Intrusive. A routine of writing and rewriting and rewriting and waiting.

But there was a Ute Sundance story circling. A mix of cultures. A change in the way of saying. A text you can't quite get ahold of. An accomplishment despite failure.

> If someone is deer hunting and can't kill a deer. If someone is alone. A white man on a white horse appears. Before which he'd been an owl. Speaking languages until after he finds the Ute to speak. The Devil on a black horse causing the Ute to deconstruct. The white man showing the Ute his dead relatives while deer hunting and not killing deer. A forecast of the mix of American culture. Religions of varied interpretations. A Sundance to dance a certain way. It was the Ute's choice. Jesus would take him away if anyone laughed. It seems they did. Though the Ute only practiced the Sundance and couldn't really do that. Nor a small black spotted horse the Ute couldn't catch. Robust and he didn't quite have the rope with which to catch. Couldn't seem anything in the haplessness of his story. But the horse was there anyway. And the rainbow appeared over.

The eagle-whistle and drums after overseas service. Through bondage to the fact of slipping. Yet the Ute dying significantly. In the long cold winter of the Sundance where I live.

I am always thinking about the importance of story. I've heard many Native American writers say that our words are our most important possession. They define what we are.

Stories give us our sense of meaning. But what exactly is a story? How does it work?

Dan Taylor, in *The Healing Power of Stories* (Doubleday, 1996), says that "a story is the telling of the significant actions of characters over time." But where should the definition go from there?

When I was in Germany, I visited the *Forum der Technik,* the science museum, in Munich. On the second floor, I saw a huge DNA double helix. Somehow I thought, that's how a story works.

Our lives are made of the joining of words into stories into meaning into integral parts of our being. In the same way, maybe, that we're made of DNA, which carries the chemical traditions from generation to generation.

There also was an explanation of genetic coding on the second floor of the museum, and though it was in German, I could see two things linking. I felt, likewise, our minds hold up their hands to hook on to a story. A possibility of meaning. The mind and the story connect and coil with other stories to form the structure of thought. There is a combining of elements.

Later, I was reminded of Reginald Gibbons's comment about the chapters of the novella "Monkey Secret" "threaded with the twin strands" of Jean Pierce's culture and her love for her cousin. There are always undercurrents working in the subconscious to make connections.

When I returned from Germany, Jim Straka, biochemist and visiting professor at Macalester College, talked to me about the DNA I had seen in Germany, since the language explaining it, as I said, had been in German. As he told me about A, T, G, C, the four bases on the strands of DNA, we agreed the DNA structure could be a metaphor for story.

There was the possibility of a correspondence. The meaning and sound of the spoken words, the hearing and interpretation of them, the telling of them again in one's own way.

The four bases holding hands. Their carefulness in which hands they hold.

The DNA making protein, which, in combination with the DNA, makes cells to make organs to make organisms. There is a circularity in the fact that DNA makes protein which is necessary to make more DNA.

As story must be heard and processed to make more story.

The drift and change.

Somehow I could make the transference.

*

It's always been those small connections. I lived in Oklahoma when I met Gerald Stern at a writers' conference in Tucson. He encouraged me to apply to the Iowa Writer's Workshop. I was in the farmhouse I rented in Iowa when Alvin Greenberg called from Macalester College. Could I come up and look the school over? He'd heard my name at an Associated Writing Program's conference where he had asked for names when he was thinking of changing and expanding the English Department faculty.

And I was there with determination like flint that was going to spark. I came from no intellectual tradition or background. I was supposed to be quiet, invisible, to survive. But I could feel the fortifier moving. I could feel the spark of the human mind.

I could move to Minnesota and teach. I could step to one place after another in the landscape of the classroom: writing and Native American literature. I

could take one trip after another in a continual migration of readings: from the Hungry Mind Bookstore in St. Paul, to the Loft in Minneapolis, to the University of Alabama in Tuscaloosa, to the Phillips public Library in Eau Claire, Wisconsin, to the Summer Writer's Conference at the University of Iowa in Iowa City, to the Just Buffalo Literary Center in Buffalo, New York, to the Olean Public Library in Olean, New York, to the Conference on Christianity and Literature at Baylor University in Waco, Texas, to Southwestern Oklahoma State University in Weatherford, Oklahoma, to the Quartz Mountain Writer's Conference for the Oklahoma Arts Institute in Lone Wolf, Oklahoma, to Hope College, Holland, Michigan, to a roundtable discussion, "Myth and Ritual, Desire and Cognitive Science," at the University of Alabama in Huntsville, to a Writer's Conference at Concordia College in Moorhead, Minnesota, to the University of Rochester in Rochester, New York, to the University of Arizona in Tucson, to the International Conference for the Short Story in Ames, Iowa, to the Arts Guild Complex in Chicago, to the Matthews Opera House in Spearfish, South Dakota, to Northland College in Ashland, Wisconsin, to the Left Bank Bookstore for the Writer and Religion Conference at Washington University in St. Louis, Missouri, to the Modern Language Association presentation of my play *Halfact,* in San Diego, California.

I could take research trips, driving back along the Trail of Tears from Georgia, Tennessee, Kentucky, Illinois, Missouri, Arkansas, Oklahoma, stopping at state parks and museums along the way. In the same two-year period, I could travel to Rosebud Reservation and drive across Montana. I could fly to the Squaw Valley Writers' Conference in California for a screen-writing workshop. I could drive to Provincetown, Massachusetts, for a month's fellowship. Another time, I could drive through New England.

I could spend two months in Australia. I could go to Japan in addition to the U.S. Information Service trips. All of which I've done and written about in my poems and stories and novels and creative nonfictions.

I could read for Fiction Collective II, the University of Oklahoma Press, and the Native American Prose Award for the University of Nebraska Press. I could be on the 1995 National Endowment for the Arts panel, the Jerome Travel Grant panel, and serve as judge for several poetry competitions, such as the National Federation for State Poetry Societies.

I could follow the turns of narrative truth in their pivotal and moving processes. Their several directions and points of departures and returns. I could see truth as a collaborative work, a country of imagination, a series of integral histories integrated into how one reads the narrative.

In other words, my words could be about the impossibility of arriving at one place of wholeness, but getting somewhere in the neighborhood.

I could feel the parts of myself, unthreaded by my name also. Helen Diane Hall Glancy. With an Indian name someone gave me that means "Happy Butterfly Woman." A name I would need in the moving and changing places I've lived my life. I was named after my Aunt Helen, my mother's sister. But I've never been called by that name, though it appears as my name on official documents. And my married name, Glancy, speaks of an Irish heritage I don't have.

But when I married, a long time ago, I don't remember the option of keeping my own name, Diane Hall, or returning to it once I had children.

I've turned one blank space after another forming my identity, but all those spaces, threaded one after one, coiling together like rope, is who I am.

GEOGRAPHIES OF LANGUAGE

Diane Glancy contributed the following update in 2004:

> I am a sojourner as my fathers were.
>
> *(Psalm 39:12)*

I can't put my finger on it as yet. But I feel the borders of it. A book of roads.

I find notes I've made of the land. *The late October trees were red; the sky, mauve; the underclouds, a brownish, rust red.* On that particular trip on I-94 across North Dakota, I listened to the Psalms as I traveled—they rolled by as a moving landscape—the Psalms were taken out of their numbered order, though I knew that each verse had iits place within the Psalm,

and that each Psalm had its place within the Psalms, and that the book of Psalms had its place among the other books in the Old Testament. But listening while driving, instead of reading in a chair in my room, the Psalms traveled the road.

> A stunting of Psalm 136:
> to him who paved the earth above the waters
> to him who made the sun to rule the day
> the moon the stars to rule the night
> who struck Egypt in their firstborn
> and brought Israel out from among them
> who divided the Red Sea
> and made Israel pass through
> but overthrew Pharaoh and his army
> to him who led his people through the wilder-
> ness
> who slew kings and gave their land for a
> heritage.

Who is this God? I still ask. It is the same God the people believed in who came to this country and displaced the native tribes. But it is this God who gave meaning to my life. I hear his voice in the migration across the land, maybe the same way my ancestors knew the Maker by their movement across the land, only now I know his name is Christ. Migration was not only to get from one place to another, summer to winter camp, or following buffalo herds during the hunt, but migration was a process for the development of oneself as a human being—for knowing one's relationship to the larger, spiritual realm.

I made note of the outgoing of the evening across the North Dakota furrows: the land was a roadshow. Words from the land filled the hollow of driving across it. I liked the migratory aspect, the spatial positioning. I saw the earth by the geography of its language.

On another trip, this time down I-35 to visit my family in Kansas City, a duck flapped its wings to get over the interstate, not graceful, not soaring hawk-like over the road. Often I feel I flap like the duck to possible marshlands or wetlands that may be nearby. There are long streaks across the sky where planes crossed. I make this trip once a month, sometimes more, while teaching full time and traveling to conferences and readings. 439 miles. Six and a half hours. A stop in Des Moines for gas and two short rest stops. On the road, because I have done it so often, there is a

"My brother, my parents, and me in front of our house in St. Louis," 1959

sense of purpose, of destination, of task, of achievement. I am cut off from small duties. I am connected to larger ones: thought, endurance, survival. There is a heightened *sense of being* when I am on the road.

My road trips began as a child. My mother's parents lived on a Kansas farm seventy miles south of Kansas City, Missouri. I don't remember exactly how many times we traveled there, but according to the photos in my mother's old album, it was often. I got used to *going*. My father's mother was in Arkansas, though we didn't travel there often.

While I was growing up, my father worked for Armour's and was transferred several times: from Kansas City, Missouri, to Indianapolis, to St. Louis, to Reading, Pennsylvania, back to Kansas City, to St. Joseph, Missouri, to Denver, to Chicago, to Iowa. The old packing houses with wooden floors were deteriorating. It was my father's job to make recommendations: leave them for a few more years or take them down.

I have moved many times on my own. I also drove for a living. During the 1980s, I was Artist-in-Residence of the State Arts Council of Oklahoma, getting out my Oklahoma map every Sunday, finding the small western Oklahoma town where I would spend a week, teaching writing, helping students read their work in front of a class, and whatever else the teacher required.

Travel has been a part of my writing process also. For *Pushing the Bear,* my novel of the 1838-39 Cherokee

Trail of Tears, I drove the nine hundred miles from New Echota, Georgia, to Fort Gibson, Oklahoma. It was in driving the land, that I found the voices of the characters. For *Flutie,* my novel of a native girl so shy she couldn't speak, I made trips from Minnesota back to Oklahoma to pick up images of the land and to remember the voices. For *Stone Heart: A Novel of Sacajawea,* about the young Shoshoni woman who traveled with Lewis and Clark, I spent the summers of 2000 and 2001 following the Missouri and Columbia rivers from Fort Mandan, North Dakota, to Fort Clatsop, Oregon, while listening to *The Journals of Lewis & Clark* on tape. The second summer, I continued onto Texas, for the wedding of my son, a journey of nearly six thousand miles from St. Paul back to St. Paul.

For the Native American, stories often were embedded in journey, and the journey or migration usually was followed by teepee-drawings depicting experiences during the journey. Now a journal replaces the drawings:

The sun will not smite you (Isaiah 49:10) was the verse I started with on the second, longer trip—comforting since I was going to make a long, circular journey that included a drive through the Nevada desert on my way to Texas. Amusing also, because June 24th when I left, I passed through a downpour west of Minneapolis around 7:00 a.m. I wrote: lightning, thunder, downpour, miles of incoming traffic, water across the road in low places, thunder, lightning, a lighter sky, windshield wipers down a notch. Open sky. Open road.

I had several purposes for the trip: a poetry conference in Oregon, continued research on *Stone Heart: A Novel of Sacajawea* for the two hundredth anniversary of the Lewis and Clark expedition, and the wedding. The previous summer I had driven along the Missouri and Columbia rivers, but had not been through the Bitterroot Mountains in Idaho, especially the two mountain passes, Lemhi and Lolo, where Lewis and Clark nearly starved and froze to death in the late autumn of 1805.

Lemhi Pass in Idaho is on a single-lane dirt road that climbs through the pines to just over seven thousand feet, and then descends. I had several boxes of books to take to the conference, my wedding clothes for my son's wedding in Texas, a large suitcase for the twenty

days I would be gone, a small bag to carry into the motel at night. I even had my grandson's car seat in the backseat my daughter had given me the last time I was in Kansas City so they wouldn't have to carry it to the wedding in Texas on the plane. I also travel with a file box where I keep projects on which I'm working, another box of maps and tablets of paper and books on tape such as the Bible and *The Journals of Lewis & Clark.* I had a case of Chippewa Spring Water. I also had my old cat carrier because my son found a litter of four motherless kittens, and I was going to bring back one or two. Of course, I had my lap top and portable printer. A large purse. Hanging clothes. Loose shoes and assorted other articles. A few rocks and pine cones I picked up along the way. All this I took up the hairpin curves and dust of the dirt road to Lemhi pass, my ears popping in the altitude, my car continuing to climb.

My car had 65,161 miles on the odometer when I left June 24th. It had 71,110 miles when I returned July 13th. The car was a few boxes of books lighter. But basically everything returned with me in good order. I even forgot to leave the car seat at my daughter's when I passed through Kansas City on I-35 on my way back from Texas to Minnesota. But I would be returning the next weekend for my second grandson's Dedication. I also returned with my cat carrier, though I left the cats in Texas.

After the poetry conference, I drove to Texas: south through Oregon, northern California into Nevada because I wanted to see Walker Lake and Grant Mountain where the Ghost Dance began, an interesting phenomena among Native Americans in the late nineteenth century. When I write about something, I have to be on the land where the story happened. I pick up the setting, and a sense of the story. Land informs the piece. How can we sing the Lord's song in a strange land? (Psalm 137:4) How can I write words that don't connect to the land? I think the land somehow carries the voices that have passed there, or some vestige of them. It's where I get the words I write. As I am finishing one project, such as Sacajawea, I like to start another. Or several others. This new project is called, *The Dance Partner,* and is about the Ghost Dance, or the Messianic dances that took place among the Native Americans when they realized their way of life was coming to an end. No one knows what happened, but after reading an account by Kicking Bear, it seems like there was divine intervention, or some sort of revival, to prepare the Indians for what was ahead. Did Christ appear in America to the Indians in visions and dreams during the Ghost Dances from 1888-1890? Does anything like that happen any longer? Did nothing happen and it only seemed like something? It was an issue I wanted to pursue.

I picked up a rock from Walker Lake, made some notes, and continued the trip. From Nevada, I crossed into Arizona at Hoover Dam. Ahead, there was a checkpoint before the drive across the dam. There was a line of cars and a long wait. Maybe it was slow because it was tourist season. Maybe it was the aftermath of 9/11, cars pulled off to the side, trunks open. Then I drove across Arizona, New Mexico, and into Texas. My son now lives in Rhome which is about twenty miles northwest of Fort Worth. Those three days I drove from Oregon to Texas, all that way through the Nevada desert and the southwest, there was cloud cover. So there was the promise. It was still hot. And there was sun from time to time. But there was cloud cover and the sun did not *smite* me.

I like to be on the road by myself, for a while anyway. I want to do it because I can. My family is raised. I am alone. I want to do it while I still can. Besides, I couldn't figure out any other way to get everywhere I had to go with everything I needed to take. There wasn't time to go one place, fly back home, fly to another place. Research was part of the trip also.

I had worried about the long trip before I left. I worried about my responsibility for the wedding. The rehearsal dinner for thirty-seven people. The flowers. I also helped with other expenses because my son teaches high-school and his funds are limited. My daughter's-in-law parents are gone, so she had no one to help her. My former husband is gone also. I was the only parent able to help. Last winter, I received one invitation after another to give a talk or reading, for which I get paid. The money for the wedding began to collect and everything is paid for.

I also worried about my ability to drive day after day without anyone to talk to, with the loneliness of traveling alone (though I like it, as I said), of having the responsibility of deciding where to eat, where to sleep, where to stop for gas. I remember buying gas and passing the next station where it was ten cents a gallon cheaper. I remember driving in Montana and look-

ing at my gas tank and seeing it nearly on empty and how did I let that happen where gas stations are far apart? Fortunately I made it to Billings, though I couldn't have gone much farther. I remember the motels by the traintracks I didn't notice when I checked in. The motels with thin walls and creaking doors when I was trying to sleep.

I was not around the rivers that were flooding in Texas that summer, but on the high, northern plains. My minety year-old former mother-in-law, hearing on television of the water, thinking all of Texas had flooded, and forgetting my son was on his honeymoon, called and told him to drive to the nearest hotel on high land and stay there. When she understood it was me who was in the house, she told me to do the same. As always with her, I said I would without trying to explain the situation.

I killed my first scorpion in Texas. I knew they were in the house. My son had told me. It was small, I didn't have to fight it with a broom, just lift my shoe and stomp it several times. A hawk made off with one of the four kittens. I saw him circling the next few days as I stood outside guarding the kittens when I let them out of the hot garage. My son wants them to be outside cats, and I honor what he wants, though I don't always agree.

My son is thirty-seven. I have been with him during low points in his life. He had surgery to repair holes in his lungs when he was in high school. Later, he had surgery to repair the passage that goes from the kidney to the bladder. He was in the Persian Gulf during Desert Storm. Then he lived with me in St. Paul while he went to Bethel College. This was seven or eight years ago. Then he went off to Texas by himself to teach high school. At the wedding I saw him dancing with his new wife, surrounded by friends.

We have been made low. We have been brought high.

A passage I found in the Bible as I read during my travels: I appoint unto you a kingdom, as my father has appointed unto me; That you might eat and drink at my table in my kingdom (Luke 22:29-30.) *I have given you a kingdom.* I felt that kingdom in Texas. The kingdom of my family who had come for the wedding: my son and daughter, my son-in-law and new daughter-in-law, Joseph and Charlie, my two grandsons with a third child on the way, my brother and his family, my two cousins.

The importance of family is another aspect of native life (even though alcohol, drugs, neglect, child and wife abuse are epidemic in the poverty of reservation life).

On the return trip, I listened to a tape, *The Gift of the Jews: How a Tribe of Desert Nomads Changed the Way Everyone Thinks and Feels,* by Thomas Cahill. Our values, ethics, ideas, our western civilization, itself, came from the Jews. The Jews broke cyclic thinking. All things became possible: history, the individual, even the concept of time itself. The history of the Jews is the story of God breaking into the human consciousness. We see the change from gods made with human attributes to humanity made in God's image.

It is in the private time on the road that I return to myself. Often, it is a time to think. A time of seeing in the light of the road. A time in which I pick up the rhythms of writing. The long stretches of development. Driving always is a release.

As a Christian, I have a foundation of strength, yet I'm often broken, weeping, groaning. I am made of dust, yet I am clothed with a house which is from heaven (II Corinthians 5:2). At my death, my mortality will be swallowed up into life. Sometimes I can almost feel real life start. In prayer. And those times of long travel when I feel that connection to the beyond—it is just a step into travel across the universe that must be waiting, something like the journey into the beyond during thhe Ghost Dance.

This is about a journey. It also is about contradictions:

To receive, I must give.

On the road, I often have watched the hawks with their wings outspread, gliding on the air currents that rise from passing traffic.

Christianity began with a Diaspora, an outward movement from its center. By the time John wrote the book of Revelation, he was writing to seven churches all with different understandings and practices of Christianity. By the third century A.D. Constantine ruled Rome and made Christianity the official religion and bound it to the state or Empire. This was the rise of the Catholic Church which remained until Martin Luther nailed his thesis to the Wittenberg door in 1517 proclaiming, "The Just Shall Live by Faith." Luther broke Christianity into Catholic and Protestant. The Protestant tried to return to the New Testament roots—a sense of personal commitment to Christ without a priest, but it resulted in a range of believers united mainly by their diisagreements on the interpretation of the scripture. Since the reformation, there has been further splintering of the splintered. Further denominations within denominations. (Christianity also has its brutal history of Crusades, Holy Wars, Inquisitions, and the burning of heretics that it should acknowledge, as America should hear the voices from its history.)

But somewhere in all the brokenness and contradiction, Christ reigns.

These are the words I receive. Encouragement mostly. Sometimes correction.

In Texas, there is the flat land, a few clumps of trees in the distance, the sky with clouds so bright and heavy you think Jesus will step through any minute.

Because I asked to know things. To see things I had not seen. To travel further than I had traveled. Because I asked to be more than I am. I asked to drive that migration of faith across new land. I asked for another kingdom: of travel, of *road.*

I have a colleague from the east coast who says the driving I do must be different from the driving she is used to. She dreads driving on the crowded roads. But my driving usually is by choice and it is on the open road. Driving in traffic at rush hour is not the road travel I'm talking about.

Returning to Minnesota, I drove north through Texas and Oklahoma. It was good to see again the red soil, the red ponds. There was a terrible rain storm as I passed through Oklahoma City. At times, I could hardly see the road, but I knew where I-35 turned right and where it veered left. Then I continued north

Diane Glancy

through the flint hills of Kansas, into Missouri, staying a night with my daughter and her family in Kansas City, before continuing through Iowa back to Minnesota.

The only problem on the whole trip was inside the Minnesota border when I filled the car with gas one last time, but couldn't find my wallet. I take care of my wallet when I travel. Money, credit card and a photo i.d. are a life-line when you are miles from anyone you know. You are nothing without them. It's what people want from you. It makes the travel happen. I took everything out of my large purse, my file box of maps, and books on tape I carry in the front seat on the rider's side. I looked under both front seats. I had paid for gas in Bethany, Missouri; I was sure I put the wallet back in my purse. I had stopped at a rest stop in Iowa. Had I forgotten to lock the door? Did someone reach inside and take it? No, I was sure I had locked the doors. I couldn't figure out what had happened. I went through everything again. No wallet. I went inside with my check book. The clerk wouldn't take my check. Someone would have to come and pay. I didn't know anyone who would

drive one hundred miles from St. Paul to pay for my gas. I asked to see the manager. He would only take a check if I had a photo ID. I said, it's in the wallet I can't find. We talked a long time. They had gotten too many bad checks. My check was not bad, I said. I had nowhere to turn. He finally made a call to my bank, and said he would take my check. As I got in the front seat of the car, the seat pulled away a little from the console, and I saw where my wallet had fallen. I don't know how it got there. As I said, I always take care to put it back into my large purse, which is always on the floor board in the front seat. I went back inside and told the clerk I could pay cash since I'd found my wallet, but she only wanted to write my driver's license number on the check I had given her.

It is awful to be on the road without money. It must be what it feels like to live without faith, or worse, to be near death without Christ as Savior.

Another contradiction:

It is finished, yet gird yourself. There is a long way to go.

Then said I, Lo, I come: in the volume of the book it is written. Psalm 40:7

Are my wanderings not in a book? Psalm 56:8

Are there not many books within the book?

A book of the records of the fathers? Ezra 4:15

A book of records of the chronicles? Esther 6:1

A book of remembrance? Malachi 3:16

A book of the road?

BIOGRAPHICAL AND CRITICAL SOURCES:

BOOKS

Dictionary of Literary Biography, Volume 175: *Native American Writers of the United States,* Gale (Detroit, MI), 1997.

Native North American Almanac, Gale (Detroit, MI), 1994.

Notable Native Americans, Gale (Detroit, MI), 1995.

PERIODICALS

Booklist, August, 1996, p. 1881; March 15, 1998, p. 1201; December 15, 2000, Donna Seaman, review of *Flutie,* p. 787; January 1, 2003, Margaret Flanagan, review of *Stone Heart: A Novel of Sacajawea,* p. 847.

Books and Culture, May, 2001, Wendy Murray Zoba, "The Voice that Found Her," p. 32.

Kirkus Reviews, January 15, 1992; June 15, 1996; February 15, 1998; September 1, 1999, p. 1331; September 15, 2002, review of *Designs of the Night Sky,* p. 1348; November 15, 2002, review of *Stone Heart,* p. 1642.

Library Journal, February 1, 1989, p. 66; December, 1990, p. 162; March 1, 1992, p. 91; April 1, 1993, p. 134; July, 1996, p. 158; November 1, 1996, p. 106; March 15, 1997, p. 70; March 1, 1998, p. 127; November 15, 1998, p. 67; September 1, 2001, Mary Margaret Benson, review of *The Man Who Heard the Land,* p. 233; March 1, 2002, Debbie Bogenschutz, review of *The Mask Maker,* p. 138; September 1, 2002, Nancy Pearl and Jennifer Young, "Native Voices, Old and New," p. 244; September 15, 2002, Howard Miller, review of *American Gypsy: Six Native American Plays,* p. 62; November 1, 2002, Debbie Bogenschutz, review of *Designs of the Night Sky,* p. 128; January, 2003, Debbie Bogenschutz, review of *Stone Heart,* p. 154.

Mpls.St.Paul Magazine, August, 1994, p. 28.

New York Times Book Review, April 11, 1993, p. 29; October 1, 1995, p. 32; January 5, 1997, p. 18; May 17, 1998, p. 40.

North American Review, November-December, 2003, Anne G. Myles, "Writing the Go-Between," pp. 53-58.

Publishers Weekly, February 1, 1993, p. 76; June 17, 1996, p. 47; October 7, 1996, p. 59; February 10, 1997, p. 76; March 16, 1998, p. 55; August 31, 1998, p. 57; May 31, 1999, p. 89; August 23, 1999, p. 45; December 23, 2002, review of *Stone Heart,* p. 43; October 6, 2003, review of *The Shadow's Horse,* p. 81.

World Literature Today, July-September, 2003, Howard Meredith, review of *Designs of the Night Sky,* p. 151.

GLEN, Paul (Michael) 1965-

PERSONAL: Born March 10, 1965, in Chicago, IL; son of Marren Jay and Ann (Elcrat) Glen. *Education:* Cornell University, B.A., 1988; Northwestern University, M.B.A. (marketing, organizational behavior, and strategy), 1991.

ADDRESSES: Office—3253 Malcolm Ave., Los Angeles, CA 90034; fax: 310-694-0451. *E-mail*—info@leadinggeeks.com.

CAREER: Management consultant and educator. SEI Information Technology, Chicago, IL, consultant, 1988-95, Los Angeles, CA, regional manager, 1995-99; C2 Consulting, Marina Del Rey, CA, founder, 1999—. Taught at the University of Southern California and Loyola Marymount University.

MEMBER: Institute of Management Consultants, American Society for Training and Development, Academy of Management, and National Speakers Association.

AWARDS, HONORS: getAbstract Business and Finance Book Prize, Financial Times (Germany), 2003, for *Leading Geeks: How to Manage and Lead People Who Deliver Technology.*

WRITINGS:

Leading Geeks: How to Manage and Lead People Who Deliver Technology ("Warren Bennis Signature" series), Jossey-Bass (San Francisco, CA), 2003.

Author of monthly column for *Computerworld.*

SIDELIGHTS: Paul Glen drew on his own experience in the world of management, marketing, and software and hardware development when writing *Leading Geeks: How to Manage and Lead People Who Deliver Technology.* Glen, who on his Web site is described as "a self-proclaimed geek," dismisses the stereotypes typically associated with geeks and instead notes the qualities found in developers that are essential to performing the kinds of tasks expected of them. He advises on the management of people who despise meetings and who don't particularly like to be managed by managers who usually know less than they do. Glen includes a twelve-part model that demonstrates how "knowledge workers" contribute to an organization.

In an interview posted at *ZDnet* online, Glen said that he would define a geek as anyone who works on the technical side of IT (information technology). He added, "When geeks perceive that someone in their work environment is ineffective due to incompetence or aberrant behavior, they have a tendency to dismiss that person completely. They also take great pride in their work and take criticism personally. If a manager says a particular interface makes no sense, he has to understand that's like telling a geek his child is ugly. They put extraordinary effort into the creative solution of a technical or business problem, and they take it personally if that solution is criticized."

A reviewer for London-based *Information Age* noted that the use of the word geek is more acceptable in the United States, where there is a kind of pride in being categorized as such, whereas in England, the term has negative connotations. The reviewer said of the book that "at times, it is an almost anthropological text, detailing the many apparent differences between the rules and mindset of 'normal' society and the geek sub-tribe; it also explains how the apparently egalitarian geek society has its own hierarchy and politics that can be understood and molded."

Glen makes the point that because geeks are the people who deliver innovation and support it, a manager would be wise to adapt his style to theirs. Geeks tend to be unimpressed by power, are task-oriented, and work best in an environment that is orderly and efficient.

Paul B. Brown reviewed *Leading Geeks* in *CIOInsight,* commenting that "it should come as no surprise that they [geeks] hate ambiguity in any guise. But it's no use saying, 'Too bad. By definition, business is riddled with ambiguity, paradoxes, and contradictions, and the geeks just have to learn to adjust.' Instead, Glen argues, managers must take a different approach, constantly showing techies how their work fits into the bigger picture."

A *Publishers Weekly* contributor wrote that Glen provides "ample material on what works with geeks and what doesn't," and deemed his advice "easily readable" and "exceptionally useful."

BIOGRAPHICAL AND CRITICAL SOURCES:

PERIODICALS

CIOInsight, November 2, 2002, Paul B. Brown, review of *Leading Geeks: How to Manage and Lead People Who Deliver Technology.*
Information Age (London, England), September 10, 2003, review of *Leading Geeks.*
Publishers Weekly, October 21, 2002, review of *Leading Geeks,* p. 63.

ONLINE

C2 Consulting, http://www.c2-consulting.com/ (April 8, 2004).
Paul Glen Home Page, http://www.leadinggeeks.com (October 24, 2003).
ZDnet, http://www.zdnet.com.au/ (June 26, 2003), interview with Paul Glen.

*   *   *

GOBODO-MADIKIZELA, Pumla

PERSONAL: Born in Cape Town, South Africa; children: one son. *Education:* Fort Hare University (social work, psychology); Rhodes University, M.A.; University of Cape Town, Ph.D. (clinical psychology).

ADDRESSES: Office—Dept. of Psychology, University of Cape Town, Rondebosch 7701, Cape Town, South Africa. *Agent*—c/o Author Mail, Houghton Mifflin, 222 Berkeley St., Boston, MA 02116. *E-mail*—pgobodo@humanities.uct.ac.za.

CAREER: Human rights activist and educator. University of Transkei, South Africa, instructor; served with the Truth and Reconciliation Commission, 1996—; University of Cape Town, Cape Town, South Africa, associate professor of psychology; Unilever Ethics Centre, University of Natal, Pietermaritzburg, South Africa, adjunct professor. Brandeis Ethics Center, Coexistence Program, faculty affiliate; taught in the United States at Harvard University, Brandeis University, Wellesley College, and Tufts University.

AWARDS, HONORS: Awards from Harvard University, University of Southern California, Tufts University, and the University of Michigan; peace fellowship, Radcliffe Institute for Advanced Studies; Harvard Divinity School fellow, 2000-01; honorary doctor of laws degree from Holy Cross College, 2002.

WRITINGS:

A Human Being Died That Night: A South African Story of Forgiveness, Houghton Mifflin (Boston, MA), 2003, published as *A Human Being Died That Night: A South African Woman Confronts the Legacy of Apartheid,* Mariner Books (Boston, MA), 2004.

Contributor to periodicals, including *Journal of Humanistic Psychology, Washington Post,* and *Los Angeles Times,* and to works by others, including *Truth and Lies: Stories from the Truth and Reconciliation Commission in South Africa,* edited by J. Edelstein, New Press (New York, NY), 2001.

SIDELIGHTS: South African professor and clinical psychologist Pumla Gobodo-Madikizela has long been involved with human rights issues and frequently lectures on the topics of vengeance and forgiveness. During the 1980s, she served as an expert witness for attorneys representing black anti-apartheid activists, and because of her work on behalf of children in the Eastern Cape region in the early 1990s, she was appointed chair of a UNICEF project that studied the state of children in South Africa. Beginning in 1996, Gobodo-Madikizela served as one of the ten members, along with Nelson Mandela, of South Africa's Truth and Reconciliation Commission (TRC).

The history leading up to the establishment of the commission goes back several decades to the period when the African National Congress (ANC), led by Mandela, carried out peaceful protests against the cruelty of apartheid. On March 21, 1960, a demonstration of several thousand protested the pass laws that increased control over blacks by requiring that they carry internal passports. The police fired into the crowd, killing sixty-seven and wounding 186, including women and children. With this act of aggression the ANC became more radical, and Mandela was ultimately arrested and imprisoned.

Over the next three decades, black South African political activists and others suffered record numbers of tortures, killings, and detainments, and police who were afforded nearly unlimited power were able to cover up their activities. But in the early 1990s, President B. W. Botha and his administration faced up to the fact that the country was being torn apart by violence. He released Mandela and established the Convention for a Democratic Election in South Africa (CODESA). In 1994, the majority put Mandela in office.

But there was still the issue of how the crimes of apartheid could be reconciled, and thus the TRC was formed, a commission that not only dealt with the human rights violations of the government, but also those committed by the resistance. In all, some 22,000 victims testified before the commission, which included Gobodo-Madikizela. During the period in which she was teaching in the United States, she began her account of the history behind the TRC and her work on the commission, titled *A Human Being Died That Night: A South African Story of Forgiveness.*

A writer for the Web site *Women Waging Peace* wrote that "the most profound experience of Pumla's career with the TRC was witnessing the incredible phenomenon of forgiveness between victims and perpetrators. The desire by the many victims to meet their perpetrators was something she had never imagined would happen," and that experience gave her a feeling of hope.

One of the major witnesses before the commission was death squad leader Eugene de Kock, a former police colonel dubbed "Prime Evil" for his role in the mass killings. He was sentenced to 212 years in a Pretoria prison for his crimes. De Kock used bombs and other devices to kill anti-apartheid leaders, and he reached across borders, as well as within South Africa itself, to capture guerrillas and infiltrators. He then used whatever means necessary to extract information, including brainwashing, poisoning, and torture. Amazingly, women whose husbands and sons became the victims of his crimes eventually forgave him when he expressed his remorse.

Beginning in 1997, Gobodo-Madikizela interviewed de Kock for nearly fifty hours, as he sat in prison chained to a stool that was bolted to the floor for her protection. Early in the book she makes references to the *Silence of the Lambs* character Hannibal Lector.

Richard Byrne commented in *Washington Post Book World* that "much of the book's narrative comes from Gobodo-Madikizela's tentative movement toward understanding and, ultimately, forgiving de Kock—without at the same time diminishing his many crimes. One signature moment comes during an interview with de Kock, who is convulsed with remorse at relating his own actions; Gobodo-Madikizela reaches out to touch the man's 'trigger hand,' only to be caught up short by immediate, personal revulsion and the larger implications of her gesture of kindness."

Time's Lance Morrow noted that "the gesture startled them both. Around such moments, Gobodo-Madikizela has composed a beautiful moral document that is without a whisper of easy grace."

Robert I. Rotberg reviewed the book in *Christian Science Monitor*, saying that Gobodo-Madikizela "believes that reciprocal acts of apology and forgiveness heal by breaking the bonds of hatred that tie victims and kin inextricably to those who did them harm. Forgiveness rises above the terrible act, refusing to be captured forever by evil. De Kock needed, pleaded for, his interlocutor's understanding. He became human again through her empathy."

Gobodo-Madikizela compares the work of the TRC with present-day ideas of revenge as a mode of justice. A *Kirkus Reviews* contributor felt that "there's much forgiving to be done in this world, and this primer in compassion makes a fine start."

Byrne concluded by saying, "*A Human Being Died That Night* is a personal journey, yet it also offers a blueprint of hope for the Balkans, the Middle East—and anywhere else that systemic violence has ruptured human relations."

BIOGRAPHICAL AND CRITICAL SOURCES:

PERIODICALS

Booklist, December 15, 2002, Hazel Rochman, review of *A Human Being Died That Night: A South African Story of Forgiveness,* p. 712.
Christian Science Monitor, February 27, 2003, Robert I. Rotberg, review of *A Human Being Died That Night.*

Kirkus Reviews, November 15, 2002, review of *A Human Being Died That Night,* p. 1673.
Library Journal, February 1, 2003, James Thorsen, review of *A Human Being Died That Night,* p. 101.
Publishers Weekly, January 20, 2003, review of *A Human Being Died That Night,* p. 74.
Time, January 27, 2003, Lance Morrow, review of *A Human Being Died That Night,* p. 60.
Washington Post Book World, February 16, 2003, Richard Byrne, review of *A Human Being Died That Night,* p. 4.

ONLINE

Women Waging Peace, http://www.womenwagingpeace.net/ (July 2, 2003), Pumla Gobodo-Madikizela, "Reconciling the Past."*

*   *   *

GOLD, Bernice

PERSONAL: Born in Montreal, Quebec, Canada; daughter of a psychiatrist; married Alan Gold (a doctor); children: five. *Education:* McGill University, B.S.; Concordia University, music degree. *Hobbies and other interests:* Swimming, caring for dogs.

ADDRESSES: Home—Montreal, Quebec, Canada. *Office*—P.O. Box 23, Victoria Station, Montreal, QC, Canada H3Z 2V4. *E-mail*—agold@videotron.ca.

CAREER: CBC Radio, Montreal, Quebec, Canada, freelance broadcaster; writer. Teacher of remedial subjects to children with learning disabilities, McGill-Montreal Children's Hospital Learning Centre, Montreal.

MEMBER: Canadian Children's Book Centre, Society of Children's Book Writers and Illustrators, Writers' Union of Canada, CanCopy, Quebec Writers' Federation, Canadian Society of Children's Authors, Illustrators and Performers, Children's Literature Round Table of Montreal.

AWARDS, HONORS: Best Bet citation, Ontario Library Association, 1999, for *My Four Lions.*

WRITINGS:

My Four Lions, illustrated by Joanne Stanbridge, Annick Press (Vancouver, British Columbia, Canada), 1999.
Strange School, Secret Wish, Beach Holme Publishing (Vancouver, British Columbia, Canada), 2001.

WORK IN PROGRESS: This Horse of a Different Color, a novel for horse-lovers; *Take Me With You,* a picture book on Canadian geese; *Millie's War,* a juvenile fantasy; and *Amy's Fortune,* an adventure tale.

SIDELIGHTS: Bernice Gold is a musician, a teacher, and a mother of five grown children. She moved into writing as a way to revisit her own happy childhood. Although Gold's books are not strictly biographical, they do capture the warmth of growing up with an active imagination and with dreams that take time and effort to realize. Gold once commented that she writes stories because she spent so many pleasant hours reading as a child in a home filled with books. "When I was growing up," she recalled, "my brother, sister, and I had our own bookshelves and right beside them, a shabby old red leather chair. You could lose yourself in its arms and find yourself in the story. I loved being a part of the story. I think that writing helps to keep me there, on the inside, which is just where I want to be."

My Four Lions is a book for juvenile readers that shows one plucky youngster's solution to a common problem. Ben walks home from school on a snowy afternoon and lets himself into his apartment. While waiting for his mother to return from work, Ben conjures a jungle with a campfire, surrounded by his four lion friends who sometimes need to be reassured about the growing darkness. In return for Ben's reassurance, the lions guard him when his mother tucks him in to sleep for the night. A reviewer for *Resource Links* found *My Four Lions* appealing for "Gold's ability to combine a heartwarming, simple story with the realities of everyday urban life."

In *Strange School, Secret Wish,* Jenny Merrill dreams of owning the beautiful violin she sees in Eaton's catalogue. But she lives in a train car, and her family cannot afford any luxury items. Secretly Jenny hatches a plan to raise the money she will need for the violin—and eventually she enlists the help of family and friends to realize her dream. In *Resource Links,* Gillian Richardson described Jenny as a "likeable character" whose challenges will appeal to other children who must balance ambitions against family obligations. Richardson concluded: "This is a pleasant story, with a unique setting that will introduce students to a chapter of Canadian history in a rural community."

BIOGRAPHICAL AND CRITICAL SOURCES:

PERIODICALS

Resource Links, December, 1999, review of *My Four Lions,* p. 5; February, 2002, Gillian Richardson, review of *Strange School, Secret Wish,* p. 10.
School Library Journal, March, 2000, Maryann H. Owen, review of *My Four Lions,* p. 197.

ONLINE

Bernice Gold Home Page, http://www.bernicegold.ca (December 11, 2003).

*   *   *

GOLDBERG, Danny

PERSONAL: Son of Victor Goldberg; married Rosemary Carroll (an attorney); children: Katie, Max. *Education:* Attended University of California at Berkeley. *Religion:* Jewish.

ADDRESSES: Home—New York, NY. *Office*—Artemis Records, 130 5th Ave., 7th Floor, New York, NY 10011. *E-mail*—info@dannygoldberg.com.

CAREER: Involved in politics, New York, NY, and worked for *Billboard* magazine; vice president of Swan Song Records and founder and co-owner of Modern Records; owner and president of Gold Mountain Entertainment (personal management firm), 1983-92; Atlantic Records, Los Angeles, CA, senior vice president, 1992, president, 1993-94; Warner Bros. Records, chair and chief executive officer, 1995;

Mercury Records, president, 1996-97, chair and chief executive officer, 1998; *Tikkun* magazine, co-publisher, 1997-2001; Artemis Records, chair and chief executive officer, 1998—; president and chief executive officer of Sheridan Square Entertainment. Also worked as a television commercial and film producer in the 1980s, co-producing and directing *No Nukes* (documentary), 1980, co-producing voter registration commercials for MTV, 1984, and producing "Rock against Drugs" commercials, 1986. President, American Civil Liberties Union Foundation of Southern California; member of board of directors, New York Civil Liberties Union executive committee, Rock the Vote, Creative Coalition, Nation Institute, Jewish Television Network, and the Abraham Fund; served on the board for the Hollywood Policy Center and the Show Coalition.

WRITINGS:

(Editor, with father, Victor Goldberg, and Robert Greenwald) *It's a Free Country: Personal Freedom in America after September 11,* RDV Books (New York, NY), 2002.
Dispatches from the Culture Wars: How the Left Lost Teen Spirit, Miramax (New York, NY), 2003.

SIDELIGHTS: Music company executive and political activist Danny Goldberg has long-held, strong beliefs about the importance of free speech and a free American culture, and his books reflect these beliefs. His first publication, *It's a Free Country: Personal Freedom in America after September 11,* was edited with Robert Greenwald and Goldberg's father, Victor, with whom he at one time published the Jewish political magazine *Tikkun.* A collection of essays by political pundits, mostly from the political Left, the book warns of the dangerous consequences to America's political freedoms brought about by the passage of the Patriot Act after terrorist attacks of September 11, 2001. Although *Library Journal* writer Thomas J. Baldino complained that the essay collection does not offer a balanced perspective on this issue, the critic still felt "this lively book should be added to the collections of larger public libraries."

Goldberg authored his first book, *Dispatches from the Culture Wars: How the Left Lost Teen Spirit,* in 2003. Drawing on his vast experience in the music industry, the author combines his political and cultural views to examine his notion that the Democrats have damaged their political prospects because they have distanced themselves from America's youth culture. Meanwhile, the Republicans have become savvier in appealing to young voters; Goldberg feels the consequences will be that liberal views will lose ground in American politics. This evolution, says Goldberg, began in the 1980s with President Ronald Reagan's charismatic Hollywood appeal, and the situation became worse when Democrats such as Al Gore's wife, Tipper, began actively attacking America's popular culture by organizing the Parents Music Resource Center. "Tipper," writes Goldberg, "legitimized to many liberal baby boomers the snobbish, indeed arrogant, notion that their children were being exposed to music far less moral than the songs they'd grown up with." When Gore ran for president in 2000, Goldberg continues, he further alienated young voters by selecting the "stuffy" Joe Lieberman as a running mate. With the Gore-Lieberman ticket as their only other choice, young voters found the George W. Bush-Dick Cheney campaign much more appealing than they might otherwise have.

Dispatches from the Culture Wars "leaves the reader feeling like they've just finished a class taught by an exhipp[i]e college professor with cool music tastes and a fiery passion for liberal politics," said Wes Orshoski in his *Billboard* assessment. Some critics found this unique perspective on American politics particularly refreshing. As one *Publishers Weekly* contributor asserted, "Here is that rare breed of book that can deconstruct gangsta rap as effectively as it analyzes the 1988 presidential election." However, David Weigel, writing in *Reason,* felt that Goldberg was off the mark in using the musical tastes of politicians as a barometer for how well Washington is connected to the country's voters. "Goldberg's thesis is more fun than a prescription drug plan," commented Weigel. "And it definitely comes from the gut. But in the end, *Dispatches from the Culture Wars* fundamentally misunderstands politics, pop culture, and the connections between them. By equating aesthetics with ideology, Goldberg makes a common but serious mistake: He thinks you can tell a person's politics from the music she listens to." *Library Journal* reviewer Thomas A. Karel similarly felt that Goldberg's views are "unrealistic," but he asserted that "the great value of [Goldberg's] book is as an insider's tour of American cultural life from the Sixties to the present."

BIOGRAPHICAL AND CRITICAL SOURCES:

PERIODICALS

Billboard, July 26, 2003, Wes Orshoski, "Goldberg: Checking the Left," p. 59.

Economist, September 7, 2002, "Easy to Lose; Civil Liberties."

Kirkus Reviews, May 1, 2003, review of *Dispatches from the Culture Wars: How the Left Lost Teen Spirit,* p. 655.

Library Journal, October 1, 2002, Thomas J. Baldino, review of *It's a Free Country: Personal Freedom in America after September 11,* p. 116; May 15, 2003, Thomas A. Karel, review of *Dispatches from the Culture Wars,* p. 105.

Publishers Weekly, August 26, 2002, "September 11: Before and After," p. 53; April 7, 2003, review of *Dispatches from the Culture Wars,* p. 54.

Reason, March, 2004, David Weigel, "Talkin' 'Bout Regeneration."

Rolling Stone, July 10, 2003, Lewis Macadams, review of *Dispatches from the Culture Wars.*

Washington Post, August 26, 2003, Ann Hornaday, review of *Dispatches from the Culture Wars,* p. C01.

ONLINE

Danny Goldberg Home Page, http://www.danny goldberg.com (April 8, 2004).

*   *   *

GOLDING, Theresa Martin 1960-

PERSONAL: Born February 27, 1960, in Philadelphia, PA; daughter of James J. (an attorney) and Kathryn Martin; married Gilbert J. Golding (an attorney); children: Jennifer, Michael, Mary Kathryn. *Education:* LaSalle University, B.A., 1982; Georgetown University Law Center, J.D., 1985.

ADDRESSES: Home—New Hope, PA. *Agent*—c/o author correspondence, Boyds Mills Press, 815 Church St., Honesdale, PA 18431. *E-mail*—gjg874@aol.com.

CAREER: Writer.

WRITINGS:

Kat's Surrender, Boyds Mill Press (Honesdale, PA), 1999.

The Secret Within, Boyds Mills Press (Honesdale, PA), 2002.

Memorial Day Surprise, illustrated by Alexandra Artigas, Boyds Mills Press (Honesdale, PA), 2004.

The Truth about Twelve, Boyds Mills Press (Honesdale, PA), 2004.

SIDELIGHTS: Theresa Martin Golding is a native of Philadelphia, where she grew up in a row house. As a child she dreamed of being a writer, but the adults in her life encouraged her to pursue a more financially reliable career. Golding attended law school at Georgetown University, but even there she was observing people and situations that she would later adapt for novels. Now an adult, she told *Boyds Mills Press,* she hopes to make writing books her "real job."

Kat, the heroine in Golding's *Kat's Surrender,* is trying to understand life in the wake of her mother's death. A lonely thirteen-year-old who takes no pleasure in the activities she once enjoyed, Kat finds solace in the company of an old man she calls "the General." When Kat's friend Maggie is injured in a hit-and-run accident, circumstances point to the General as the perpetrator of the crime. It is up to Kat to investigate and learn the truth about the accident, and about her own deep feelings as well. *Booklist* critic Chris Sherman found Kat "an appealing character" and noted that Golding "has an ear for kids' dialogue."

In *The Secret Within,* young Carly finds herself in a difficult situation with nowhere to turn for help. The victim of an abusive father, Carly must deliver mysterious packages for him. She deliberately avoids finding out what the packages contain, and she lies to friends and well-meaning adults who want to help her. As her circumstances become more desperate, however, Carly realizes that she is protecting a criminal and putting herself in great danger. GraceAnne A. De-Candido in *Booklist* described *The Secret Within* as "a tale that will holds readers until the end." In *School Library Journal,* Miriam Lang Budin called the novel "suspenseful, . . . solid [and] well-paced."

BIOGRAPHICAL AND CRITICAL SOURCES:

PERIODICALS

Booklist, October 15, 1999, Chris Sherman, review of *Kat's Surrender,* p. 444; September 15, 2002, GraceAnne A. DeCandido, review of *The Secret Within,* p. 231.
School Library Journal, August, 2002, Miriam Lang Budin, review of *The Secret Within,* p. 184.

ONLINE

Boyds Mills Press, http://www.boydsmillspress.com/ (June 7, 2004) "Theresa Martin Golding."

*   *   *

GOODAVAGE, Maria 1962-

PERSONAL: Born 1962; married Craig Hanson; children: Laura Hanson. *Education:* Studied at Northwestern University. *Hobbies and other interests:* Travel.

ADDRESSES: Home—San Francisco, CA. *Agent*—c/o Author Mail, St. Martin's Griffin, 175 Fifth Ave., New York, NY 10010.

CAREER: Journalist and author. *USA Today,* former staff writer.

MEMBER: Outdoor Writers Association of California.

WRITINGS:

The California Dog Lover's Companion, Foghorn Press (San Francisco, CA), 1994, revised triannually, fourth edition published as *The Dog Lover's Companion to California: The Inside Scoop on Where to Take Your Dog in the Golden State,* Avalon Travel Publications (Emeryville, CA), 2002.
The Dog Lover's Companion in the Bay Area, Avalon Travel Publications (Emeryville, CA), 2002.

(With Jay Gordon) *Good Nights: The Happy Parents' Guide to the Family Bed (and a Peaceful Night's Sleep!),* St. Martin's Griffin (New York, NY), 2002.

SIDELIGHTS: Maria Goodavage began her writing career as a correspondent for *USA Today,* a job that required her to travel throughout the state of California. After 1989 she chose to travel with her dog, an Airedale named Joe the Dog, and the process of learning the ins and outs of finding dog-friendly hotels resulted in both a list of places in California that accepted canines and the idea for two books. Goodavage's *The Dog Lover's Companion to California: The Inside Scoop on Where to Take Your Dog in the Golden State* and the spin-off volume, *The Dog Lover's Companion in the Bay Area,* have spawned a series of books dedicated to dog travel. Joe the Dog eventually graduated to a starring role in a popular children's film called *Here's Looking at You, Kid!* in 2001, with the voice of actor Ed Asner; Goodavage subsequently did her traveling with a yellow Labrador named Jake the Dog.

"Dogs have attained family status in many circles," Goodavage explained to John Flinn in the *San Francisco Chronicle.* "With more couples, families and individuals refusing to leave their dogs at home when vacationing, the California [tourist lodging] market has responded." Cheri Sicard, reviewing *The Dog Lover's Companion to California* for *Fabuloustravel.com,* exclaimed: "If you're planning to travel to California . . . you owe it to yourself and your furry friends to get this guide!"

Goodavage's interests include sleep research, a subject she studied at Northwestern University. She also had first-hand experience with sleep-related issues while parenting her daughter, Laura, and consequently undertook several studies on correlations on a child's sleep habits and social skills. Together with Jay Gordon, Goodavage coauthored *Good Nights: The Happy Parents' Guide to the Family Bed (and a Peaceful Night's Sleep!).* Annette V. Janes, reviewing *Good Nights* for *Library Journal,* wrote that "the authors conducted impressive research and present it convincingly. Though not for everyone, this book provides a good alternative to dealing with those difficult 'night nights.'"

BIOGRAPHICAL AND CRITICAL SOURCES:

PERIODICALS

Library Journal, August, 2002, review of Good Nights: The Happy Parents' Guide to the Family Bed (and a Peaceful Night's Sleep!), p. 132.
San Francisco Chronicle, February 16, 1996, Reynolds Holding, "Author Curbs Alleged Copycat," p. D1; May 19, 2002, review of The Dog Lover's Companion to California: The Inside Scoop on Where to Take Your Dog in the Golden State, p. C1.
Time, January 27, 2003, review of Good Nights.

ONLINE

Dog Lover's Companion Web site, http://www.dogloverscompanion.com/ (July 15, 2003).
Fabuloustravel.com, http://www.fabuloustravel.com/ (March 24, 2001), review of The Dog Lover's Companion to California.*

*   *   *

GORMAN, Carol
(Jane Ballard, a pseudonym)

PERSONAL: Born in Iowa City, IA; daughter of a pediatrician and a homemaker; married Ed Gorman (a writer); children: Ben. Education: University of Iowa, B.A.

ADDRESSES: Agent—c/o author correspondence HarperCollins, Inc., 10 E. 53rd St., 7th Floor, New York, NY 10022.

CAREER: Middle school teacher in Cedar Rapids, IA, prior to 1984; writer, 1984—. Conducts writing workshops and makes presentations in elementary and middle schools; part-time instructor, Coe College.

AWARDS, HONORS: Best books for the teen age citation, New York Public Library, 1987, for America's Farm Crisis; outstanding book citation, American Library Association and Ethical Culture Book Award,
both 1987, both for Chelsey and the Green-Haired Kid; children's choice list, International Reading Association, 1994, for Die for Me, and 1995, for Graveyard Moon; Missouri Mark Twain Award, Sequoyah Children's and Young Adult Book Award, South Carolina Children's, Junior, and Young Adult Book Award, Washington Children's Choice Picture Book and Sasquatch Reading Award, and West Virginia Children's Book Award, all 2002, all for Dork in Disguise.

WRITINGS:

America's Farm Crisis, Franklin Watts (New York, NY), 1987.
Chelsey and the Green-Haired Kid, Houghton Mifflin (Boston, MA), 1987.
Pornography, Franklin Watts (New York, NY), 1988.
T. J. and the Pirate Who Wouldn't Go Home, Scholastic (New York, NY), 1990.
The Biggest Bully in Brookdale, Concordia Publishing House (St. Louis, MO), 1992.
It's Not Fair, illustrated by Rudy Nappi, Concordia Publishing House (St. Louis, MO), 1992.
Die for Me, Avon Books (New York, NY), 1992.
Graveyard Moon, Avon Books (New York, NY), 1993.
The Great Director, illustrated by Rudy Nappi, Concordia Publishing House (St. Louis, MO), 1993.
Skin Deep, illustrated by Rudy Nappi, Concordia Publishing House (St. Louis, MO), 1993.
Nobody's Friend, illustrated by Rudy Nappi, Concordia Publishing House (St. Louis, MO), 1993.
The Richest Kid in the World, illustrated by Rudy Nappi, Concordia Publishing House (St. Louis, MO), 1993.
Brian's Footsteps, illustrated by Ed Koehler, Concordia Publishing House (St. Louis, MO), 1994.
The Taming of Roberta Parsley, illustrated by Ed Koehler, Concordia Publishing House (St. Louis, MO), 1994.
Million Dollar Winner, illustrated by Ed Koehler, Concordia Publishing House (St. Louis, MO), 1994.
The Rumor, illustrated by Ed Koehler, Concordia Publishing House (St. Louis, MO), 1994.
The Miraculous Makeover of Lizard Flanagan, HarperCollins (New York, NY), 1994.
Jennifer-the-Jerk Is Missing, Simon & Schuster (New York, NY), 1994.
Back from the Dead, Avon Books (New York, NY), 1995.

Lizard Flanagan, Supermodel?, HarperCollins (New York, NY), 1998.

Dork in Disguise, HarperCollins (New York, NY), 1999.

(Editor with husband, Ed Gorman) *Felonious Felines,* Five Star Press (Unity, ME), 2000.

Dork on the Run, HarperCollins (New York, NY), 2002.

A Midsummer Night's Dork, HarperCollins (New York, NY), 2004.

Also author of adult books under pseudonym Jane Ballard; ghostwriter for mystery series books.

SIDELIGHTS: Carol Gorman did not plan to become a professional writer. Trained as an actress and a teacher, Gorman took up writing for children because her husband, novelist Ed Gorman, encouraged her to try. Gorman's willingness to experiment has paid off in a selection of novels for middle school and upper elementary grade readers, including straight mysteries, comic adventures, and humorous tales of budding adolescence. Gorman is best known for her recurring characters, including Jerry Flack the "dork" and Lizard Flanagan the tomboy, who learn to celebrate their uniqueness in a middle-school culture that encourages conformity.

The daughter of a pediatrician and a homemaker, Gorman grew up in Iowa. As a student she gravitated to the stage and won leading roles in college dramas, including *West Side Story* and *Peter Pan.* After graduating from college, she settled in Iowa and taught seventh grade. In the meantime, her husband was having success as an author of adult mysteries, and he suggested she try writing for children. "I probably would never have started writing if I hadn't married a writer," Gorman said in an interview with *Book Report.*

After writing two nonfiction books for middle-school readers, Gorman moved into fiction. One of her early successes was *Chelsey and the Green-Haired Kid.* Wheelchair-bound Chelsey and her green-haired friend become detectives after Chelsey witnesses a suspicious accident. Part of the plot revolves around Chelsey's disability and how she lives with it, a theme that brought Gorman awards and national attention for the title. Other Gorman mysteries such as *Die for Me* and *Graveyard Moon* also received citations as best books for younger or struggling readers.

Jerry Flack is the hero of several Gorman novels, including *Dork in Disguise, Dork on the Run,* and *A Midsummer Night's Dork.* Jerry wears glasses and loves science. Can he survive in middle school, or should he try to change his image? In *Dork in Disguise,* Jerry tries looking and acting "cool" in hopes of winning the interest of the popular crowd in general and a girl named Cinnamon in particular. Instead he discovers the friendship of Brenda, a female dork who recognizes one of her own. In *Dork on the Run,* Jerry decides to run for class president even though his opponent is a popular kid who will stop at nothing to scare, embarrass, and humiliate Jerry. Success comes when Jerry uses his own dorkiness as a selling strategy for the campaign. "If there was ever a quintessential book on dealing with bullies, this is it," wrote Tina Zubak in her *School Library Journal* review of *Dork on the Run.* Zubak also called the book "a thoughtful read and a discussion starter." *Horn Book* reviewer Peter D. Sieruta praised *Dork on the Run* as a "fast-paced story that will appeal to the dork in us all."

Lizard Flanagan got her nickname when her brother couldn't pronounce "Elizabeth." As the heroine of two books, *The Miraculous Makeover of Lizard Flanagan* and *Lizard Flanagan, Supermodel?* she struggles with the transition from a rough-and-tumble tomboy to an adolescent sportswoman who is also interested in makeup and boys. Helping Lizard make this transition is Zach, an old friend who becomes a boyfriend over the course of the two novels, and Lizard's twin brother, Sam, who helps to keep her grounded. In her *Booklist* review of *The Miraculous Makeover of Lizard Flanagan,* Kay Weisman concluded that Gorman covers adolescent issues "with a refreshing sense and good humor that will appeal to middle-grade readers everywhere." Reviewing *Lizard Flanagan, Supermodel?* in the *School Library Journal,* Connie Tyrrell Burns wrote: "In the face of those stereotypical dual preoccupations of sixth-grade girls—boys and bodies—Lizard is a refreshing character."

Sometimes during her school visits, Gorman will be asked if she ever knew a dork like Jerry Flack. Then she admits it: She was once a dork herself. More to the point, she thinks most preteens suffer moments when they feel like dorks or are convinced that they look like a dork. "I think everyone can identify with how Jerry Flack feels," she said in an interview with the *Des Moines Register.* Gorman has endowed Jerry and his sidekick Brenda with believable personalities and moments of quiet triumph and self-satisfaction.

BIOGRAPHICAL AND CRITICAL SOURCES:

PERIODICALS

Booklist, June 1, 1994, Mary Harris Veeder, review of *Jennifer-the-Jerk Is Missing,* p. 1816; October 15, 1994, Kay Weisman, review of *The Miraculous Makeover of Lizard Flanagan,* p. 426; November 15, 1998, GraceAnne A. DeCandido, review of *Lizard Flanagan, Supermodel?,* p. 590; September 1, 1999, Shelley Townsend-Hudson, review of *Dork in Disguise,* p. 133; July, 2000, Jenny McLarin, review of *Felonious Felines,* p. 2012; June 1, 2002, Francisca Goldsmith, review of *Dork on the Run,* p. 1722.

Book Report, March/April, 1996, Sharron McElmeel, "Carol Gorman," p. 22.

Center for Children's Books Bulletin, May, 1994, Deborah Stevenson, review of *Jennifer-the-Jerk Is Missing,* p. 287; September, 1999, Fern Kory, review of *Dork in Disguise,* p. 12.

Des Moines Register (Des Moines, IA), May 7, 2002, Joanne Boeckman, "Kids, Adults Identify with 'Dork,'" p. 3.

Horn Book, spring, 1995, Christine Hepperman, review of *The Miraculous Makeover of Lizard Flanagan,* p. 76; spring, 1999, Erica L. Stahler, review of *Lizard Flanagan, Supermodel?* p. 66; January, 2000, Peter D. Sieruta, review of *Dork in Disguise,* p. 75; September-October, 2002, Peter D. Sieruta, review of *Dork on the Run,* p. 572.

Kirkus Reviews, June 15, 1994, review of *Jennifer-the-Jerk Is Missing,* p. 845.

Publishers Weekly, March 13, 1987, Diane Roback, review of *Chelsey and the Green-Haired Kid,* p. 86; June 6, 1994, review of *Jennifer-the-Jerk Is Missing,* p. 66; September 27, 1999, review of *Dork in Disguise,* p. 106.

Reading Teacher, October, 1995, review of *The Miraculous Makeover of Lizard Flanagan,* p. 155.

School Library Journal, June-July, 1987, Judy Greenfield, review of *Chelsey and the Green-Haired Kid,* p. 95; November, 1987, Eldon Younce, review of *America's Farm Crisis,* p. 118; November, 1988, Judie Porter, review of *Pornography,* p. 136; June, 1994, Jana R. Fine, review of *Jennifer-the-Jerk Is Missing,* p. 128; October, 1994, Connie Tyrell Burns, review of *The Miraculous Makeover of Lizard Flanagan,* p. 426; October, 1998, Connie Tyrell Burns, review of *Lizard Flanagan, Su-*

permodel?, p. 135; September, 1999, Susan L. Rogers, review of *Dork in Disguise,* p. 225; June, 2002, Tina Zubak, review of *Dork on the Run,* p. 138.

ONLINE

Carol Gorman Home Page http://www.carolgorman. com (September 17, 2003).

Institute for Children's Literature, http://www.institute childrenslit.com/ (September 17, 2003), "Rx for Writers: 'Humor in Fiction' with Carol Gorman."*

*   *   *

GRALLA, Cynthia

PERSONAL: Female. *Education:* Doctoral student at the University of California, Berkeley.

ADDRESSES: Agent—c/o Author Mail, Ballantine Books, Random House, 1745 Broadway, New York, NY 10019.

CAREER: Writer and graduate student. Worked as a hostess in Tokyo, Japan.

WRITINGS:

The Floating World, Ballantine Books (New York, NY), 2003.

Contributor to *Salon.com.*

WORK IN PROGRESS: A novel about a supermodel who is a saint.

SIDELIGHTS: Cynthia Gralla's debut novel *The Floating World* is set in Japan and builds on her own experiences there. *Asian Reporter* critic Joseph Eaton described it as "a female-narrated *Heart of Darkness* set partly in the underbelly of Tokyo's pleasure districts."

Liza, the story's protagonist, is a Princeton graduate student who travels to Tokyo to study butoh, an avant-garde dance that evolved from the horrors of World War II and is referred to as the dance of utter darkness. When she arrives, she finds work as a hostess in a Ginza bar, where she acts as companion to men who come to drink and sing karaoke. Up to this point, the story somewhat parallels Gralla's own experiences, but then the story takes its fictional turn.

Liza has several lovers, including Carlo, who wears the garb of a monk and calls her Princess Amida, political radical Mark, and the student she left behind at Princeton. She stops eating and becomes involved with Maboroshi, the leader of the maiko, a group of subversive apprentice geisha who wander the streets at night dressed in traditional costumes. She changes jobs to work with Maboroshi at an exclusive nyoutaisushi restaurant, where sushi and other delicacies are arranged on the naked bodies of beautiful women, who are essentially tables from which the wealthy patrons can pick and choose their food. *Book*'s Kelli Daley noted that Gralla learned about these restaurants from an American friend, but when she asked some of her customers at the bar to take her, they didn't comply.

The "floating world" of the title refers to the world of pleasures of classical Japan several centuries ago, according to *Asian Review of Books* contributor Peter Gordon. "This is a bizarre, dark world," he added. "Whether due to her lack of daily sustenance or the sinister powers around her, Liza begins to lose touch with reality, or at least everyday reality, and *her* world begins to float."

Gordon wrote that Liza is somewhat nihilistic, a characteristic increased by the macabre slice of Japanese culture that she inhabits. Furthermore, "her intelligence, her understanding of avant-garde dance, seem—rather than protecting her—to draw her into the extremes of 'the body as art,' 'sex as art,' and ultimately 'death as art.'"

A *Publishers Weekly* contributor wrote that "Gralla succeeds in creating an intelligent contemporary heroine whose perceptive insights illuminate past and future, East and West."

BIOGRAPHICAL AND CRITICAL SOURCES:

PERIODICALS

Asian Reporter, April 22, 2003, Joseph Eaton, review of *The Floating World,* p. 12.

Book, January-February, 2003, Kelli Daley, review of *The Floating World.*

Booklist, March 15, 2003, Kristine Huntley, review of *The Floating World,* p. 1274.

Kirkus Reviews, December 1, 2002, review of *The Floating World,* p. 1718.

Publishers Weekly, January 20, 2003, review of *The Floating World,* pp. 54-55.

ONLINE

Asian Review of Books, http://www.asianreviewof books.com/ (June 20, 2003), Peter Gordon, review of *The Floating World.**

* * *

GRAMMATICO, Maria 1941-

PERSONAL: Born December, 1941, in Erice, Sicily, Italy.

ADDRESSES: Home—Erice, Sicily, Italy. *Office*—Pasticceria Grammatico, Via Vittorio Emanuele 14, 91016 Erice, Italy. *Agent*—c/o Author Mail, William Morrow and Co., 10 East 53rd Street, New York, NY 10022.

CAREER: Confectioner and author. Founder and proprietor of Pasticceria Grammatico, Erice, Sicily, Italy.

WRITINGS:

(With Mary Taylor Simeti) *Bitter Almonds: Recollections and Recipes from a Sicilian Girlhood,* photographs by Mark Ferri, illustrations by Maria Vica Costarelli, W. Morrow (New York, NY), 1994.

SIDELIGHTS: Maria Grammatico is a Sicilian confectioner who has gained fame for her almond pastries. Her life story, as related in *Bitter Almonds: Recollections and Recipes from a Sicilian Girlhood,* "reads like the rough draft of a novella by someone like Alice Munro," according to *Los Angeles Times* contributor Michelle Huneven. Born on the rugged and isolated west coast of Sicily in 1940, Grammatico grew up in a poor farming family. When her father died of a heart attack in 1952, and with three other mouths to feed and a fourth on the way, Maria's mother sent her and her younger sister to San Carlo, the local orphanage run by Franciscan nuns. There, they fell into a harsh regime. Their pregnant mother was not allowed to see them for a year, until she had given birth, for the nuns did not want the young girls to see a pregnant woman. The children of the orphanage helped in the single enterprise of this cloistered orphanage: the production of almond pastries.

For ten years, Grammatico shelled and ground almonds and helped with the mixing and baking of the cookies, biscuits, and cream tarts that the nuns sold through the iron gate of San Carlo. Then, believing she was called to a religious life, Grammatico entered a Carmelite convent, but the life was not for her. She suffered a nervous breakdown and, at the age of twenty-two, was sent home. Recovering, she had to do something to earn a living. There had been scant education in the orphanage; the one thing she did know was how to make marzipan and other delicacies. Though the nuns forbade taking any of their recipes to the outside world, Grammatico remembered how to make a rich variety of such delicacies. Starting out with a crude wood-burning oven, a rolling pin, and a manual nut grinder, Grammatico opened up a confectionery shop in Erice, Sicily, that grew over the years to two successful shops that attracted tourists from around the world.

In the early 1990s, Grammatico shared her life story as well as numerous recipes with American writer Mary Taylor Simeti, who taped the woman's tale. Published in 1994, *Bitter Almonds* provides "vivid recollections of a vanished culture and way of life," according to a *Kirkus Reviews* critic. A reviewer for *Publishers Weekly* likewise praised these "bittersweet recollections . . . [that] lend depth to this slender volume of Italian recipes." Writing in the *Boston Globe*, Sheryl Julian felt that the book "will keep you . . . enthralled." Julian further noted that *Bitter Almonds* is "an important book, not only because Grammatico's story is fascinating, but also for the thoughtfulness and care that Simeti took in bringing her subject to the page." Nancy McKeon of the *Washington Post* noted that Grammatico's tale is related "with a savvy story-teller's instinct for the details that will seem most exotic." The recipes in the book range

from traditional cannoli to anise biscuits, Genoa cakes, and marzipan. The *Kirkus Reviews* critic concluded that Grammatico's book is an "eloquent celebration of food and a woman who learned the hard way how to prepare it."

BIOGRAPHICAL AND CRITICAL SOURCES:

PERIODICALS

Boston Globe, December 7, 1994, Sheryl Julian, review of *Bitter Almonds: Recollections and Recipes from a Sicilian Girlhood,* p. 77.
Kirkus Reviews, May 1, 2003, review of *Bitter Almonds,* p. 666.
Los Angeles Times, December 15, 1994, Michelle Huneven, review of *Bitter Almonds,* p. 14.
Publishers Weekly, September 26, 1994, review of *Bitter Almonds,* p. 65.
Washington Post, November 2, 1994, Nancy McKeon, review of *Bitter Almonds,* p. E1.

ONLINE

BuySicilian Home Page, http://www.buysicilian.it/ (March 25, 2004).
ChefShop.com., http://chefshop.com/ (March 25, 2004).
Frommer's Online, http://www.frommers.com/ (March 25, 2004).*

*   *   *

GRANT, Pete
(A pseudonym; Jon Dijon, Paul Kuehn, additional pseudonyms)

PERSONAL: Male. *Education:* Attended University of Connecticut, 1941; completed M.D.

ADDRESSES: Agent—c/o Author Mail, Newmark Publishing, P.O. Box 603, South Windsor, CT 06074.

CAREER: Surgeon and author. Chair of cancer commission for American College of Surgeons. *Military service:* U.S. Navy; served as a pilot in Night Torpedo Squadron, 1941-45.

MEMBER: American Cancer Society (president of Hartford Unit and Connecticut Division), New England Cancer Society (president).

WRITINGS:

(Under pseudonym Paul Kuehn) *Breast Care Options: A Cancer Specialist Discusses Breast Care Options, Risk Factors, and How to Cope with Breast Cancer,* Newmark Publishing (South Windsor, CT), 1986.

(Under pseudonym Paul Kuehn) *Breast Care Options for the 1990s,* Newmark Publishing (South Windsor, CT), 1991.

(Under pseudonym Jon Dijon) *Who Is Robin?* (novel), Newmark Publishing (South Windsor, CT), 1993.

UNDER PSEUDONYM PETE GRANT

Night Flying Avenger, Newmark Publishing (South Windsor, CT), 1990.

The Surgical Arena, Newmark Publishing (South Windsor, CT), 1993.

Destination 2020 White House (novel), Newmark Publishing (South Windsor, CT), 1999.

The Medical Supreme Court (novel), Newmark Publishing (South Windsor, CT), 2001.

SIDELIGHTS: Pete Grant, Jon Dijon, and Paul Kuehn are all pen names used by a prominent surgeon and World War II naval pilot who chooses to remain anonymous as an author. He has drawn on both his wartime experience and his medical career to provide the foundation for the thrillers and nonfiction titles that he writes. As Paul Kuehn, he has written two nonfiction titles on the treatment options available to those diagnosed with breast cancer, as well as the risk factors to watch out for; as Jon Dijon and Pete Grant, he is the author of several novels.

His first Pete Grant novel, *Night Flying Avenger,* was described by his publisher as "autobiographical historical fiction." Pretending to be the subject of his own novel, the author has written the story of a young man named Pete Grant, who joins the navy right after Pearl Harbor and sees action as a pilot in both the Atlantic and Pacific theaters. Blessed with unusually good eyesight, Grant proves extremely valuable in a navy plagued by primitive radar and landing instruments. Soon he is put to work flying dangerous nighttime operations against German subs and later in the bloody battles as U.S. forces island-hopped toward the Japanese mainland. "Although the book is clearly heartfelt, it is poorly organized, confusing, and awkwardly written," wrote *Library Journal* reviewer Edwin Burgess. In a more favorable assessment, a *Kirkus Reviews* contributor found that "the flying is as hair-raising as anything in Tom Cruise's *Top Gun.*"

Grant turned next to the genre of medical thriller. As Jon Dijon, he published *Who is Robin?,* the story of a frantic, nationwide search for an androgynous, possibly HIV-positive transsexual who may be involved in a double murder. At least one reviewer was disappointed in "Jon Dijon." "Bad grammar . . . unnecessary explanations . . . even egregious bathos, this book has it all," maintained *Library Journal* reviewer Rex Klett. The same year, the author published *The Surgical Arena,* again as Pete Grant writing about Pete Grant. This time, Grant is a surgeon who takes the reader through a series of fictionalized operations and consultations, while elaborating on issues such as malpractice and socialized medicine. The author "is at his best when describing his work and . . . at his worst when trying to develop a plot," maintained a *Publishers Weekly* contributor. "As a novel writer, he fails to include the element of suspense. . . . It's a shame, because Grant can write," concluded *Library Journal* reviewer Ralph DeLucia.

In his more recent novels, Grant has incorporated overtly political interests while being less autobiographical. In *Destination 2020 White House* he tells the story of Kelli Fitzgerald, the granddaughter of a naval flier who decides to become a navy pilot herself. Overcoming sexual harassment, the hostility of some superiors, and violent threats, Fitzgerald becomes a Top Gun fighter pilot and a Gulf War veteran, ultimately landing a choice assignment as an aide to the secretary of the navy. She gives this up to settle down with an old flame and raise a family. But boredom drives her to reenter politics, first in Congress and then as a presidential candidate. Although finding Kelli "robotic and cold," a *Publishers Weekly* reviewer noted that her "bid for the presidency . . . is neatly executed and adds some texture to the narrative."

The author next published another political thriller, *The Medical Supreme Court.* Starting with the kidnapping of three Supreme Court justices by an odd alliance of Islamic terrorists and Montana militia members, the book progresses through a series of curious events, including the resignation of five justices, a number of controversial constitutional amendments, and ultimately the calling of another constitutional convention by President Palmer. What comes out of this is a series of rules covering term limits, as well as the establishment of a Medical Supreme Court to evaluate the health of political officeholders and judges and oversee controversial medical lawsuits. Throughout all this, President Palmer must deal with foreign policy threats and save her own teenage daughter from danger. "Grant's enjoyable, optimistic yarn also comes as quite a relief—a good story without sex and violence," commented *Booklist* reviewer William Beatty.

BIOGRAPHICAL AND CRITICAL SOURCES:

PERIODICALS

Booklist, September 15, 2001, William Beatty, review of *The Medical Supreme Court,* p. 191.
Kirkus Reviews, April 15, 1990, review of *Night Flying Avenger,* p. 518.
Library Journal, April 1, 1990, Edwin Burgess, review of *Night Flying Avenger,* p. 136; August 1, 1993, Rex Klett, review of *Who Is Robin?,* p. 159; September 1, 1993, Ralph DeLucia, review of *The Surgical Arena,* p. 221.
Publishers Weekly, March 11, 1990, Sybil Steinberg, review of *Night Flying Avenger,* p. 248; August 30, 1993, review of *The Surgical Arena,* p. 74; August 16, 1999, review of *Destination 2020 White House,* p. 62.*

*   *   *

GRANT DUFF, Sheila 1913-2004

OBITUARY NOTICE—See index for *CA* sketch: Born May 11, 1913, in London, England; died March 19, 2004. Journalist and author. Duff was best known for her pre-World War II reporting and her staunch stand against Germany's annexation of Czechoslovakia. Developing a great distaste for war after her father was killed during World War I, she was raised in a liberal household that encouraged her education at St.

Margaret Hall, Oxford, where she earned a B.A. in 1934. After working for the *Chicago Daily News* for a year, her concern for Czechoslovakia began in 1936, when she was assigned as the Prague correspondent for the London *Observer.* Opposed to both Adolph Hitler and the Communists' interests in Czechoslovakia, she was committed to a belief that nonviolence and a free country were in the best interests of that nation. Her first book, *German and Czech: A Threat to European Peace* (1937) dealt with the subject, as did *Europe and the Czechs,* the bestseller that was released in 1938, the same year the international community conceded Czechoslovakia to Germany. Back in England in 1937, Duff served as an advisor to Winston Churchill and worked for the British Foreign Office in the Press Section as an expert on foreign research, where she remained from 1939 to 1961; during the war, she also worked for the British Broadcasting Corporation. It was during World War II, as well, that she formed a romantic relationship with Adam von Trott zu Stolz, the famous conspirator who planned Hitler's assassination and who later was killed for it; their correspondence were later published in her *A Noble Combat: The Letters of Shiela Grant Duff and Adam von Trott zu Stolz, 1931-1939* (1988). After an unsuccessful first marriage, Duff married a Russian named Micheal Sokolov Grant, and the two of them led a peaceful existence living and working on farms in England and Ireland. In 1982, Duff published her memoirs about her pre-war life in *The Parting of Ways: A Personal Account of the Thirties.*

OBITUARIES AND OTHER SOURCES:

PERIODICALS

Daily Telegraph (London, England), March 27, 2004, p. 34.
Guardian (London, England), April 3, 2004, p. 19.
Independent (London, England), April 12, 2004, p. 31.

*   *   *

GRAVES, Russell A. 1969-

PERSONAL: Born October 17, 1969, in Mesquite, TX; son of Harold (a welder) and Ona (a homemaker; maiden name, Thorton) Graves; married Kristy Baker (an educational aide), September 11, 1993; children: Bazlee Lee Ann. *Ethnicity:* "White." *Education:* East

Texas State University, B.S. *Politics:* Republican. *Religion:* Baptist. *Hobbies and other interests:* Photography, hunting, fishing.

ADDRESSES: Home and office—706 Avenue I S.E., Childress, TX 79201; fax: 940-937-3649. *E-mail*—russell@russellgraves.com.

CAREER: Childress Independent School District, Childress, TX, teacher, 1993—. Childress County Historical Museum, member of board of directors.

MEMBER: Vocational Agriculture Teachers Association of Texas, Texas Outdoor Writer's Association.

AWARDS, HONORS: Named Agriscience Teacher of the Year, 2001.

WRITINGS:

Managing Wildlife as an Enterprise, John Deere Publishing, 1997.
The Prairie Dog: Sentinel of the Plains, Texas Tech University Press (Lubbock, TX), 2001.
The Hunting Dogs, Krause Publications (Iola, WI), 2002.

WORK IN PROGRESS: Communicating in the Agriculture Industry, publication by Delmar Learning (Clifton Park, NY) expected in 2005; research on prairie dogs.

SIDELIGHTS: Russell A. Graves told *CA:* "My primary reason for writing is to capture the experiences of my life and what I have witnessed and offer them to a broader audience. My work is influenced by nature and by writers and photographers such as Wyman Meinzer, David Sams, Jan Reid, and Bill O'Reilley. My writing is inspired by the beauty of nature and my longing to capture its essence."

BIOGRAPHICAL AND CRITICAL SOURCES:

PERIODICALS

Booklist, January 1, 2002, Nancy Bent, review of *The Prairie Dog: Sentinel of the Plains,* p. 785.

GRAY, Christopher 1950-

PERSONAL: Born 1950.

ADDRESSES: Home—New York, NY. *Office*—Office for Metropolitan History, 246 West 80th St., No. 8, New York, NY 10024. *E-mail*—MetHistory@aol.com.

CAREER: Architectural historian, columnist, writer. Office for Metropolitan History, New York, NY, founder and director, 1975—. *New York Times,* "Streetscapes" columnist, 1987—.

WRITINGS:

Blueprints: Twenty-Six Extraordinary Structures, Simon & Schuster (New York, NY), 1981.
Changing New York: The Architectural Scene, Dover Publications (New York, NY), 1992.
(Editor) *Fifth Avenue, 1911, from Start to Finish in Historic Block-by-Block Photographs,* Dover Publications (New York, NY), 1994.
(With David Stravitz) The Chrysler Building: Creating a New York Icon Day by Day, Princeton Architectural Press (New York, NY), 2002.
New York Streetscapes: Tales of Manhattan's Significant Buildings and Landmarks, research by Suzanne Braley, Harry N. Abrams (New York, NY), 2003.

Contributor to *Avenue* and *House and Garden.* Contributor to *New York,* Vendome Press, 1980.

SIDELIGHTS: The author and editor of four books, Christopher Gray is a specialist on New York City architecture. Founder of the Office for Metropolitan History, Gray has also penned a weekly column, *Streetscapes,* for the *New York Times* since 1987, in which he details the history and architecture of the city, with a focus on Manhattan. Gray's columns also emphasize preservation policies and practices.

Gray's first book, *Blueprints: Twenty-Six Extraordinary Structures,* is not centered on New York, though some of the buildings, such as the Chrysler and Empire State Building, as well as the Statue of Liberty, are landmarks of the city. Gray includes blueprints for well-known landmarks—buildings and non-buildings—with brief descriptions and photographs of the actual structures. His eclectic list includes the White House, the Golden Gate Bridge, the Volkswagen Beetle, a few cathedrals, a dirigible, the Concorde, the Hoover Dam, the Pentagon, and even a lunar rover. Some of the fold-out blueprints are four feet in length in this "delightful compilation," as Philip Morrison described the offbeat book in *Scientific American.* For Paul Goldberger, reviewing the title in the *New York Times Book Review,* it was a "silly idea that yields an altogether enticing book." Goldberger went on to call Gray's work a "celebration of the blueprint" and to praise the "brief but clear description" accompanying each entry. A reviewer for the *Village Voice* found the collection "only half campy." The same contributor further noted that the "blueprints are of uneven beauty but great interest."

In 1992 Gray collected more than one hundred of his *New York Times* columns for the book *Changing New York: The Architectural Scene,* introducing and describing edifices such as the Metropolitan Museum of Art and the Russian Tea Room, and sites from Park Avenue to Washington Mews in Greenwich Village. Helen Felice Pryor, writing in *New Technical Books,* praised the book as "lavishly illustrated with historical photographs." Gray narrows his focus to one street in New York with his 1994 *Fifth Avenue, 1911, from Start to Finish in Historic Block-by-Block Photographs,* which makes good use again of historical photographs of the creation of the heart of Manhattan.

Gray once more gathered a sampling of his *New York Times* columns for the 2003 *New York Streetscapes: Tales of Manhattan's Significant Buildings and Landmarks.* This time Gray culled 190 of the best-loved columns that appeared in the newspaper's real estate section weekly for fifteen years. Collected here are tales of famous and obscure sites and structures and of the people who inhabited them. Gray's choices range from the oldest bar in Manhattan to skyscrapers. Paula Frosch observed in a *Library Journal* review that Gray "writes with the loving eye of the city dweller and the profound curiosity of the newly arrived settler." A contributor for *Publishers Weekly* commented that Gray is surely "something more than an architectural historian," and praised the book's text as a combination of "elegant architectural writing" and "gossipy and historical anecdotes."

BIOGRAPHICAL AND CRITICAL SOURCES:

PERIODICALS

Library Journal, June 15, 2003, Paula Frosch, review of *New York Streetscapes: Tales of Manhattan's Significant Buildings and Landmarks,* p. 67.
New Technical Books, November, 1992, Helen Felice Pryor, review of *Changing New York: The Architectural Scene,* p. 1469.
New Yorker, November 18, 2002, Claudia Roth Pierpoint, "The Silver Spire."
New York Times Book Review, December 12, 1982, Paul Goldberger, review of *Blueprints: Twenty-Six Extraordinary Structures,* p. 12.
Publishers Weekly, May 12, 2003, review of *New York Streetscapes,* p. 61.
Real Estate Weekly, April 4, 2001, "Christopher Gray to Lecture on Beekman Place," p. 23.
Scientific American, April, 1983, Philip Morrison, review of *Blueprints,* pp. 32-33.
Village Voice, December 21, 1982, review of *Blueprints,* p. 66.

ONLINE

City Journal Online, http://www.city-journal.org/ (March 25, 2004).
City Review Online, http://www.thecityreview.com/ (March 25, 2004).
Society of Architectural Historians Web site, http://www.sah.org/index.html/ (1998).*

*   *   *

GRAY, Deborah D. 1951-

PERSONAL: Born November 28, 1951, in PA; daughter of Gerald (a farmer) and Patricia (a registered nurse) Gray; married, 1982; children: three. *Ethnicity:* "Caucasian." *Education:* Syracuse University, M.A. (social work), 1981, M.P.A., 1981. *Politics:* Independent. *Religion:* Christian. *Hobbies and other interests:* Hiking, reading in all areas of human development, playing with dog.

ADDRESSES: *Office*—8011 118th Ave. NE, Kirkland, WA 98033; fax: 425-483-2957. *E-mail*—DeborahD Gray@aol.com.

CAREER: Social Worker. North Slope Borough School District, Alaska, counselor, 1975-76; Regional Perinatal Center, Upstate Medical Center, Syracuse, NY, social worker, 1979-81; Catholic Community Services, Mt. Vernon, WA, therapist, 1982-84; New Hope Child and Family Services, Seattle, WA, casework supervisor, 1988-93; private practice as a clinical social worker, Kirkland, WA, 1993—. Antioch University's foster care and adoption therapy post-graduate certificate program, core faculty; Portland State University's foster care and adoption therapy post-graduate certificate program, faculty.

MEMBER: National Association of Social Workers, Association for Treatment and Training in the Attachment of Children, Families for Russian and Ukrainian Adoption (advisory board member).

WRITINGS:

Attaching in Adoption: Practical Tools for Today's Parents, Perspectives Press (Indianapolis, IN), 2002.

Contributor to periodicals, including *Adoptive Families of America* and various professional and parent newsletters.

WORK IN PROGRESS: A book on trauma, neglect, and attachment.

SIDELIGHTS: Deborah D. Gray had nearly twenty years of experience as a clinical social worker in the fields of children's therapy, child placement, and foster and adoption counseling when she wrote *Attaching in Adoption: Practical Tools for Today's Parents.*

Gray specializes in the areas of attachment, grief, and trauma and works primarily with children who have been adopted through the foster care system or international orphanages. She teaches information and techniques that can help when abuse, deprivation, or long periods spent in foster care make attachment formation with adoptive parents difficult. In her private practice, parents are often involved in the therapy sessions, providing comfort and safety and working to meet the needs of the children while dealing with attachment-related problems.

In her book, Gray documents the healthy attachment stages by age and notes how grief, cultural change, and trauma can interfere with the normal attachment process. She advises parents to learn more about their child's background and to provide a structured, nurturing environment. Gray addresses the issue of delayed emotional development and how to spot such conditions as fetal alcohol syndrome, posttraumatic stress disorder, autism, learning disabilities, and attention deficit disorder. She also discusses interracial and cross-cultural adoptions and provides a list of resources, including books, journal articles, organizations, and Web sites, where parents can find help. A *Publishers Weekly* contributor felt that "while the book is densely written, it will nevertheless be invaluable for adoptive parents." *Library Journal's* Alice Hershiser wrote that "this book appears to be the only one that so thoroughly summarizes attachment." She felt *Attaching in Adoption* to be "of considerable value."

BIOGRAPHICAL AND CRITICAL SOURCES:

PERIODICALS

Library Journal, May 15, 2002, Alice Hershiser, review of *Attaching in Adoption: Practical Tools for Today's Parents,* p. 120.
Publishers Weekly, April 15, 2002, review of *Attaching in Adoption,* p. 58.

*   *   *

GRAY, Spalding 1941-2004

OBITUARY NOTICE—See index for *CA* sketch: Born June 5, 1941, in Providence, RI; died of an apparent suicide c. January 10, 2004, in NY. Actor and author. Though he appeared in a number of character roles in such Hollywood films as 1984's *The Killing Fields,* Gray was most acclaimed for his onstage monologues, which combined wit, angst, and comedy in such popular productions as *Swimming to Cambodia.* Troubled throughout his life by his mother's suicide when he was a child, Gray was an unremarkable student at Emerson College, where he earned a B.A. in 1965. He moved to New York City, where he found work as a dish washer and joined the experimental Performance Group actors. It was also in New York that he met Elizabeth LeCompte, with whom he would found the Wooster Group acting troupe in 1977. His first jobs in film, though, were roles in pornographic films, though he would later deny this. With LeCompte, he began writing experimental plays, including *Sakonnet Point* (1975) and *Rumstick Road* (1977), which explored his mother's mental illness. Along with *Nyatt School,* the three plays formed the trilogy he called *Three Places in Rhode Island,* which were first performed together in 1979. His first monologue, *Sex and Death to the Age 14* (1979), also delved into Gray's troubled childhood. This was followed, in quick succession, by the monologues *Booze, Cars, and College Girls, India (and After),* and *A Personal History of the American Theatre.* Finding more success as an actor by the 1980s, Gray began appearing in films as a character actor in such movies as *Straight Talk* (1992), *The Paper* (1994), and *Diabolique* (1996). Living in Cambodia for eight weeks while shooting the 1984 movie *The Killing Fields,* he turned this experience into his most successful monologue, *Swimming to Cambodia,* which enjoyed a two-year run. Gray continued to draw on his personal struggles in life in further monologues through the 1980s and 1990s, including *Travels through New England* (1986), *Monster in a Box* (1992), *Gray's Anatomy* (1993), and *It's a Slippery Slope* (1996). In the 1990s, he also penned a collection of short stories, *Seven Scenes from a Family Album* (1981), and a novel, *Impossible Vacation* (1992). His last published work was 1999's *Morning, Noon, and Night.* Divorced from his first wife in 1991, Gray remarried but continued to struggle with depression, especially after a debilitating car accident in 2001. After being reported missing by his family, his body in the East River near Brooklyn in March 2004; investigators suspected suicide, though the cause of Gray's death remains unknown.

OBITUARIES AND OTHER SOURCES:

BOOKS

Contemporary Theatre, Film, and Television, Volume 24, Gale (Detroit, MI), 2000.

PERIODICALS

Chicago Tribune, March 9, 2004, Section 1, p. 5.
Independent (London, England), March 10, 2004, p. 34.

New York Times, March 9, 2004, p. A1; April 14, 2004, p. C15.
Times (London, England), March 10, 2004, p. 38.
Washington Post, March 9, 2004, p. B4.

*   *   *

GREENWOOD, Leigh 1942-

PERSONAL: Born September 16, 1942, in NC; father (an educator) and mother (an educator); married, 1972; wife's name, Anne (a nurse); children: Heather, Chris, Cameron. *Education:* University of North Carolina, B.A., M.A. *Hobbies and other interests:* Gardening.

ADDRESSES: Office—P.O. Box 470761, Charlotte, NC 28226. *E-mail*—leighgwood@aol.com.

CAREER: Writer. Worked for more than thirty years as a music teacher; also worked as a church organist and choir director. Guest on television programs, including *Entertainment Tonight.*

MEMBER: Romance Writers of America (past member of board of directors; past president), Novelists Inc., PASIC.

AWARDS, HONORS: Two Maggie Awards; twice named author of the year by Carolina Romance Writers; Bookstores that Care Network Award for best sequel; *Romantic Times,* six K.I.S.S. Awards and career achievement award.

WRITINGS:

ROMANCE NOVELS

Wyoming Wildfire, Zebra Books (New York, NY), 1987.
Wicked Wyoming Nights, Zebra Books (New York, NY), 1989.
Colorado Bride, Zebra Books (New York, NY), 1990.
Seductive Wager, Zebra Books (New York, NY), 1990.
Sweet Temptation, Zebra Books (New York, NY), 1991.
Rebel Enchantress (also known as *Bold Enchantress*), Zebra Books (New York, NY), 1992.

Scarlet Sunset, Silver Nights, Zebra Books (New York, NY), 1992.

Arizona Embrace, Kensington Publishing (New York, NY), 1993.

(With Peg Sutherland) *Only You,* Harlequin Enterprises (Buffalo, NY), 1997.

Just What the Doctor Ordered, Silhouette Books (Buffalo, NY), 1998.

Married by High Noon, Silhouette Books (Buffalo, NY), 1999.

Winner's Circle, Volume 1, Zebra Books (New York, NY), 1999.

Love on the Run, Leisure Books (New York, NY), 2000.

Texas Bride, Leisure Books (New York, NY), 2002.

Texas Homecoming, Leisure Books (New York, NY), 2002.

Undercover Honeymoon, Silhouette Books (Buffalo, NY), 2002.

Born to Love, Leisure Books (New York, NY), 2003.

Family Merger, Silhouette Books (Buffalo, NY), 2003.

Independent Bride, Leisure Books (New York, NY), 2004.

ROMANCE NOVELS; "THE COWBOYS" SERIES

Jake, Leisure Books (New York, NY), 1997.
Ward, Leisure Books (New York, NY), 1997.
Chet, Leisure Books (New York, NY), 1998.
Buck, Leisure Books (New York, NY), 1998.
Jake, Leisure Books (New York, NY), 1999.
Pete, Leisure Books (New York, NY), 1999.
Sean, Leisure Books (New York, NY), 1999.
Drew, Leisure Books (New York, NY), 2000.
Luke, Leisure Books (New York, NY), 2000.
Matt, Leisure Books (New York, NY), 2001.

ROMANCE NOVELS; "SEVEN BRIDES" SERIES

Fern, Leisure Books (New York, NY), 1994.
Iris, Leisure Books (New York, NY), 1994.
Daisy, Leisure Books (New York, NY), 1995.
Laurel, Leisure Books (New York, NY), 1995.
Rose, Leisure Books (New York, NY), 1996.
Lily, Leisure Books (New York, NY), 1996.
Violet, Leisure Books (New York, NY), 1996.

Also author of *The Captain's Caress,* Harlequin Enterprises (Buffalo, NY). Work represented in anthologies, including *Old-Fashioned Southern Christmas,* Leisure Books (New York, NY), 1994; *Their First Noel,* Leisure Books (New York, NY), 1995; *Christmas Spirit,* Loveswept (New York, NY), 1997; and *Winter Wonderland,* Loveswept (New York, NY), 1999.

WORK IN PROGRESS: The Reluctant Bride, a historical western romance novel.

SIDELIGHTS: Leigh Greenwood told *CA:* "Okay, let's get the hard stuff out of the way right up front. I am a man. I know men aren't supposed to write romance, but I do, and I don't intend to quit. It's fun.

"If you're still mad, you can blame it on my wife. I wouldn't have known what romance was if, after I got married in 1972, romances hadn't started collecting all over the house. They were everywhere I looked, in the den, on the kitchen table, in the living room, stacked along one whole wall in the bedroom, even in the bathroom. When my wife wasn't cooking or taking care of the children, she was reading a romance. I admit I was a little supercilious about her choice of reading material. After all, I was reading Dickens, Hemingway, Austen, the classics! I started calling them her 'sin, lust, and passion' books. I said it so often that my daughter started calling them Mommy's 'celeste' passion books. I thought it was riotously funny. My wife didn't. One day, after what I'm certain was a typically rude remark (you have to understand I'd never read a romance, just looked at the covers and made a snap judgment), she threw a book at me and told me to read it or shut up.

"Being an obedient husband (my wife's expletive deleted!), I read the book. It was Georgette Heyer's *These Old Shades.* I loved it. To this day it's one of my favorite books. Being thoroughly hooked, I searched new and used bookstores until I'd collected every book Georgette Heyer ever wrote. After reading them all several times, I asked my wife to suggest some other books. Since I have a minor in history, she started me on a diet of the icons of early historical romance: Kathleen Woodiwiss, Rosemary Rogers, Jennifer Blake, Bertrice Small, and Johanna Lindsey. By now, I was completely addicted.

"Somewhere along the line, I read that women could make decent money (more than I could as a music teacher) writing historicals, so I tried to get my wife to write one. She told me she couldn't write, that I ought to write one. I said I couldn't think of a plot. This went back and forth for some time until I said if she'd give me a plot, I'd write a book. She said, 'I've lost everything.' It wasn't a plot, but it must have been enough. I sat down and started writing; 889 pages later, I had finished my first romance.

"I didn't know much about writing, and nothing at all about the romance market, so I had to write two more books and join the Romance Writers of America before I knew enough to sell my first book. *Wyoming Wildfire* was published in 1987. Since then I've written more than thirty other books and some novellas.

"I'm older than sixty now, so I call writing my mid-life crisis career. I taught music and worked as an organist and choir director for more than thirty years before retiring to write full-time. I've been married for more than thirty years. My wife is a nurse, but after years of working in a hospital on weekends to help make ends meet, she took a full-time job with a health maintenance organization. She said she was too old to be a hospital nurse any longer. I think having three children and being married to me just wore the poor lady down! We have three grown children, who are momentarily occupying distant parts of these United States. I enjoy gardening when I can find time off from writing and my duties as husband, father-at-a-distance, and slave to the family cat."

*   *   *

GRIFFITH, Jim

PERSONAL: Male.

ADDRESSES: Office—eBay Inc., 2145 Hamilton Avenue, San Jose, CA 95125.

CAREER: eBay, customer relations, 1996—, Customer Support Training program, manager, 1999—; eBay University, traveling training program for using the Internet auction services, trainer, "dean," 2000—.

WRITINGS:

The Official eBay Bible: The Most Up-to-Date, Comprehensive How-to Manual for Everyone from First-Time Users to People Who Want to Run Their Own Business, Gotham Books/Penguin (New York, NY), 2003.

SIDELIGHTS: Jim Griffith became an ambassador for the online auction service eBay in 1999, after organizing the company's first customer support service. Thereafter, he began traveling the country providing seminars on how to use eBay not only to sell the occasional item, but also to set up a home business. In these seminars, part of what is called eBay University, Griffith covers the basics of posting an item, from taking a picture to deciding on price to choosing the right descriptive words in order to get the most responses or "hits."

Griffith put his expertise between the covers of a book with the 2003 *The Official eBay Bible: The Most Up-to-Date, Comprehensive How-to-Manual for Everyone from First-Time Users to People Who Want to Run Their Own Business.* Noting that "an object sells on eBay every 1.7 seconds," a contributor for *Publishers Weekly* pointed out that Griffith "dexterously walks readers through the site, with impressive practical know-how about buying and selling." The same reviewer praised the "depth of Griffith's commonsense knowledge and the clarity of his writing." Mike Maza, reviewing the title in the *Knight Ridder/Tribune News Service,* commented that Griffith's guide would "get newbies up to speed quickly," while Ann Lloyd Merriman noted in the *Richmond Times* that Griffith's "detailed instructions on use of the site" make his book "more comprehensive" than earlier guides to eBay. "'If you're going to sell on eBay, you're going to have competition, so you need to know what you're doing,'" Griffith told Sue Kidd of the *King County Journal Online.*

BIOGRAPHICAL AND CRITICAL SOURCES:

PERIODICALS

Knight Ridder/Tribune News Service, June 4, 2003, Mike Maza, review of *The Official eBay Bible: The Most Up-to-Date, Comprehensive How-to Manual for Everyone from First-Time Users to People Who Want to Run Their Own Business;* February 20, 2004, Terry Jackson, "eBay University to Help People Become Active Sellers."
Publishers Weekly, April 28, 2003, review of *The Official eBay Bible,* p. 58.
Richmond Times (Richmond, VA), June 22, 2003, Ann Lloyd Merriman, review of *The Official eBay Bible,* p. E5.

ONLINE

King County Journal Online, http://www.kingcounty journal.com/ (February 6, 2004), Sue Kidd, "eBay University a Primer on How to Sell Your Stuff."
The Official eBay Bible, http://pages.ebay.com/griff/ (March 25, 2004).*

* * *

GUBERNICK, Lisa Rebecca 1955-2004

OBITUARY NOTICE—See index for *CA* sketch: Born June 28, 1955, in Los Angeles, CA; died of colon cancer March 16, 2004, in New York, NY. Journalist and author. Gubernick was an entertainment correspondent for *Forbes* and the *Wall Street Journal.* Graduating from Bryn Mawr College in 1978, she began her journalism career as a finance writer for the *American Lawyer* and the spin-off publication *Takeover Control Alert.* During the early 1980s, she also wrote for *Securities Week* and *East Side Express.* In 1984, she joined the *Forbes* staff, later becoming its Hollywood correspondent from 1987 to 1990, when she was promoted to senior editor. In 1998, she left the magazine to work for the *Wall Street Journal,* where she again wrote for the entertainment section. Gubernick was also the author of two books, *Squandered Fortune: The Life and Times of Huntington Hartford* (1991) and *Get Hot or Go Home: Trisha Yearwood, the Making of a Nashville Star* (1993).

OBITUARIES AND OTHER SOURCES:

PERIODICALS

New York Times, March 17, 2004, p. A21.

H

HAMPTON-JONES, Hollis

PERSONAL: Married Stone Jack Jones (a musician, artist, and writer).

ADDRESSES: Home—Nashville, TN. *Agent*—c/o Author Mail, Riverhead Books Publicity, 375 Hudson St., New York, NY 10014.

CAREER: Writer, model.

WRITINGS:

Vicious Spring (novel), Riverhead Books (New York, NY), 2003.

SIDELIGHTS: Hollis Hampton-Jones presents an eighteen-year-old lap-dancing, drug-hazed, born-again Christian as the protagonist of her first novel, 2003's *Vicious Spring.* Christy is a troubled youth who flees her staunchly religious Nashville family. But the life she discovers in the outside world is not what she was expecting, as she falls into drug addiction and the arms of a thirty-three-year-old boyfriend, Del, and takes up the easiest work she can find: lap dancing in a strip club. Christy is apathetic about her choices, noted a critic for *Kirkus Reviews* who commented that she "displays no interest in life and little ability to get one."

Christy's departure from her home is precipitated by the death of her younger sister, Lizzy, in a car accident. Thereafter, she can no longer tolerate her "Jesus-freak mother and leering pothead father," as the *Kirkus Reviews* contributor described her parents. She moves in with Del, a bouncer at a strip club, and is dubbed Sugar, working as a stripper and lap dancer and developing a cocaine addiction. As Christy's life spirals downward out of control, Hampton-Jones keeps her narration cool and distant. Several reviewers noted the author's narrative style, including Paul Griffith who wrote in *Nashville Scene Online* that "to her credit, the author attempts to maintain a moral and emotional distance from Christy." Yet according to the same critic, this approach leads to problems, for "Hampton-Jones makes no attempt to account for Christy's aloofness from the seediness around her." Thus, according to Griffith, what is missing from the book is "substance," and what the reader gets is mere "titillation."

Other reviewers voiced similar reservations. For Julia LoFaso, writing in *Library Journal,* "the novel feels overwritten" and is "ultimately disappointing." For Emily Simon, reviewing the novel in the *Buffalo News,* the story "feels totally faked, like an unusually bad episode of [the television drama] 'Crossing Jordan.'" Not all reviewers were so negative, however. A contributor to London's *Observer Online* called the book a "little bit *American Beauty,* a little bit *Catcher in the Rye* for crueler times." The same reviewer also felt that "Christy has enough innocence to make her tragic and make us care." And writing on *PopMatters Online,* Bunmi Adeoye dubbed Hampton-Jones' debut novel a "svelte, trendy book."

BIOGRAPHICAL AND CRITICAL SOURCES:

PERIODICALS

Buffalo News (Buffalo, NY), May 4, 2003, Emily Simon, review of *Vicious Spring,* p. F4.

Kirkus Reviews, February 15, 2003, review of *Vicious Spring,* p. 256.

Library Journal, May 15, 2003, Julia LoFaso, review of *Vicious Spring,* p. 124.

ONLINE

Austin Chronicle Online, http://www.austinchronicle. com/ (June 20, 2003), Jessica Garratt, review of *Vicious Spring.*

Fictitious Records, http://www.fictitiousrecords.com/ (March 27, 2004).

Nashville Scene Online, http://www.nashvillescene. com/ (May 1, 2003), Paul Griffith, "Sex and the City, Nashville Author's Debut Has Lots of Titillation, But Little Else."

Observer Online, http://books.guardian.co.uk/ (June 29, 2003), review of *Vicious Spring.*

PopMatters Online, http://www.popmatters.com/ (August 27, 2003), Bunmi Adeoye, review of *Vicious Spring.**

*   *   *

HARDWICK, Phil 1948-

PERSONAL: Born June 20, 1948, in Mendenhall, MS; married; children: two. *Education:* Belhaven College, B.S., 1982; Millsaps College, M.B.A., 1984. *Religion:* Episcopalian.

ADDRESSES: Home—P.O. Box 55804, Jackson, MS 39296-5804. *E-mail*—phil@philhardwick.com.

CAREER: Mississippi Valley Gas Co., Jackson, MS, vice president for ten years; also worked as a police officer and state investigator. Mississippi Economic Development Council, past president; member of Mississippi Sports Hall of Fame and Museum and Leadership Jackson. *Military service:* U.S. Army, 1968.

MEMBER: Mystery Writers of America, Mississippi Main Street Association (member of board of directors).

AWARDS, HONORS: Two editorial awards, International Association of Business Communicators.

WRITINGS:

MISSISSIPPI MYSTERIES SERIES

Found in Flora, Flora Chamber of Commerce (Flora, MS), 1997.

Captured in Canton, Canton Chamber of Commerce (Canton, MS), 1997.

Justice in Jackson, Quail Ridge Press (Brandon, MS), 1997.

Newcomer in New Albany, Quail Ridge Press (Brandon, MS), 1997.

Vengeance in Vicksburg, Quail Ridge Press (Brandon, MS), 1998.

Collision in Columbia, Quail Ridge Press (Brandon, MS), 1998.

Conspiracy in Corinth, Quail Ridge Press (Brandon, MS), 1999.

Cover-up in Columbus, Quail Ridge Press (Brandon, MS), 2001.

Sixth Inning in Southaven, Quail Ridge Press (Brandon, MS), 2002.

Mishap in Macon, Quail Ridge Press (Brandon, MS), 2003.

Author of "From the Ground Up," a biweekly column in *Mississippi Business Journal.*

WORK IN PROGRESS: Another mystery novel set in a Mississippi town.

SIDELIGHTS: Phil Hardwick told *CA:* "I love a good mystery. Early in my career I solved real ones. These days I'm a professional economic developer who spends his spare time writing mysteries. My 'Mississippi Mysteries' series, featuring private eye Jack Boulder, grows every year with the addition of another novella or two set in a Mississippi town. I plan to expand to other states in 2004."

BIOGRAPHICAL AND CRITICAL SOURCES:

PERIODICALS

Clarion-Ledger (Jackson, MS), July 7, 2002, interview by Sid Salter, p. G2.

ONLINE

Phil Hardwick Home Page, http://www.philhardwick. com (August 22, 2003).

HARTE, Amanda

PERSONAL: Born in Davenport, IA. *Education:* Syracuse University, B.A.

ADDRESSES: Home—P.O. Box 597, New Providence, NJ 07974-0597. *E-mail*—amanda.harte@sff.net.

CAREER: Writer.

WRITINGS:

ROMANCE FICTION

Strings Attached, Avalon Books (New York, NY), 2000.
North Star, Leisure Books (New York, NY), 2000.
Moonlight Masquerade, Avalon Books (New York, NY), 2001.
Imperfect Together, Avalon Books (New York, NY), 2001.
Rainbows at Midnight, Leisure Books (New York, NY), 2002.
Carousel of Dreams, Leisure Books (New York, NY), 2002.

"THE WAR BRIDES" TRILOGY

Dancing in the Rain, Avalon Books (New York, NY), 2003.
Whistling in the Dark, Avalon Books (New York, NY), 2004.
Laughing at the Thunder, Avalon Books (New York, NY), in press.

SIDELIGHTS: Amanda Harte told *CA:* "Although my books have been inspired by a myriad of things—everything from a snippet of a song overheard in a restaurant to a chance encounter with a carousel horse in (of all places) a highway rest area—and although the time frames and settings have ranged from medieval France to modern-day New Jersey, all of my books have one thing in common: the healing power of love and the ability of people to surmount seemingly impossible obstacles. Yes, I believe in happy endings!"

HARTLEY, Aidan 1965-

PERSONAL: Born 1965, in Kenya; married; wife's name Claire; children: two. *Education:* Studied English at Balliol College, Oxford, and politics at London University.

ADDRESSES: Home—Laikipia, Kenya. *Agent*—c/o Author Mail, Grove/Atlantic, 841 Broadway, 4th Floor, New York, NY 10003. *E-mail*—info@thezanzibarchest.com.

CAREER: Journalist. Foreign correspondent for the Reuters news agency, *Financial Times,* and the London *Times.* Cofounder, African Environment News Services (AENS; online African-wide environmental news and information service).

WRITINGS:

The Zanzibar Chest: A Story of Life, Love, and Death in Foreign Lands, Atlantic Monthly Press (New York, NY), 2003.

Author of column for the *Spectator.*

SIDELIGHTS: Aidan Hartley is an African-born, British-educated journalist whose first book, *The Zanzibar Chest: A Story of Life, Love, and Death in Foreign Lands,* chronicles not only a family history, but also Hartley's fifteen years of experience as a correspondent in flash points from Rwanda to Bosnia. Hartley's family history figures strongly in his tale, and he details some four generations of it, from his great-great grandfather, who defended British settlements in New Zealand and won a Victoria Cross for his efforts to his own father, who was a colonial officer in Africa in the 1920s and went on to help build dams in Arabia.

Hartley's book takes its title from a hand-carved chest that the author discovered upon his father's death. Inside were the diaries of his father's best friend, Peter Davey, whose death half a century earlier was something of a mystery. Hartley, by this time himself burnt out by covering tragedy and mayhem throughout Africa and Europe in the 1990s, followed the trail of this diary to southern Arabia, in a search not only to reveal the enigma of Davey's death but also to come to terms with his own life. The resulting book contains, as Rob Nixon noted in the *New York Times Book Review,* "three trapped, potential others, each banging on the lid and hollering for air." The three tales are the saga of Hartley's family, the search for Peter Davey, and a memoir of a journalist who has seen too much famine and genocide. For Nixon, the various themes of Hartley's book did not mesh well, or were too large to be contained by the others. "An unresolved imperial nostalgia suffuses *The Zanzibar Chest*—a yearning not for empire but for the purposeful lives of action that empire allowed men like Hartley's father and Peter Davey to sustain," Nixon commented. However, the same reviewer noted that "no such sentimentality mars the Rwanda and Somalia sections of the book. Skillfully and with deceptive simplicity, they deliver the deepest hauntings." Similarly, Joshua Hammer, writing in *Newsweek International,* felt that "one of the few shortcomings in Hartley's book is the diversion he makes into the life of Peter Davey. . . . Hartley would like us to see parallels between his own life and that of the unfortunate Davey, another expatriate." For Hammer the "most vivid part of Hartley's memoir is the meltdown of Somalia in the early 1990s." Hammer went on to observe that "Hartley's narrative is far more than a travelogue from hell, however. It is a cry of moral outrage. . . . Hartley has fashioned a mesmerizing story of pain and loss." Writing in *National Geographic Adventure,* Anthony Brandt also commended Hartley's book as "affecting," and observed that the author is "excellent with facts."

More praise for *The Zanzibar Chest* came from a contributor to the *Economist,* who called it a "lyrical, passionate memoir," and from *Booklist* critic Vernon Ford, for whom the work was a "fascinating odyssey." Writing in London's *Daily Telegraph,* Janine di Giovanni observed that "there is no conventional narrative here; it's more a succession of tense, sad vignettes knitted together as the author remembers them." The result is "moving," the critic concluded. Other critics on both sides of the Atlantic applauded Hartley's work. For a contributor to *Publishers Weekly, The Zanzibar Chest* is a "mesmerizing chronicle," and a "sweeping, poetic homage to Africa." Anthony Stattin, writing in the London *Sunday Times,* called it a "muscular, heartbreaking book." And Bart McDowell, reviewing the book in the *Washington Times,* noted that Hartley's work "must rank with other great journalistic memoirs."

BIOGRAPHICAL AND CRITICAL SOURCES:

PERIODICALS

Booklist, July, 2003, Vernon Ford, review of *The Zanzibar Chest: A Story of Life, Love, and Death in Foreign Lands,* p. 1859.

Daily Telegraph (London, England), January 17, 2004, Janine di Giovanni, review of *The Zanzibar Chest,* p. 6.

Economist, July 26, 2003, review of *The Zanzibar Chest,* p. 77.

Kirkus Reviews, May 1, 2003, review of *The Zanzibar Chest,* pp. 657-658.

National Geographic Adventure, August, 2003, Anthony Brandt, review of *The Zanzibar Chest,* p.31.

Newsweek International, September 8, 2003, Joshua Hammer, review of *The Zanzibar Chest,* p. 59.

New York Times Book Review, August 24, 2003, Rob Nixon, review of *The Zanzibar Chest,* p. 22.

Publishers Weekly, April 7, 2003, review of *The Zanzibar Chest,* p. 53.

Spectator, July 19, 2003, Matthew Leeming, review of *The Zanzibar Chest,* pp. 35-36.

Sunday Times (London, England), December 7, 2003, Anthony Stattin, review of *The Zanzibar Chest,* p. 48.

Washington Times, August 31, 2003, Bart McDowell, review of *The Zanzibar Chest,* p. B8.

ONLINE

African Environmental News Services, http://www.aens.org/ (March 27, 2004).

BookPlace, http://www.thebookplace.com/ (March 27, 2004), Chris Martin, interview with Aidan Hartley.

Connection, http://www.theconnection.org/ (September 18, 2003).

Official Aidan Hartley Web Site, http://www.thezanzibarchest.com (March 27, 2004).*

*　　*　　*

HATHAWAY, Robin 1934-

PERSONAL: Born February 12, 1934, in Philadelphia, PA; daughter of John W. Hathaway (an artist and teacher) and Elizabeth McCloy (an artist); married Robert Alan Keisman (a cardiologist); children: two daughters. *Ethnicity:*"English/Irish/French." *Educa-*

tion: Smith College, B.A. (English), 1956. *Politics:* Independent. *Religion:* Presbyterian. *Hobbies and other interests:* Photography.

ADDRESSES: *Home*—247 E. 33rd St., #3D, New York, NY 10016. *E-mail*—robdoneit@aol.com.

CAREER: Author, photographer. Former owner of Barnhouse Press, Philadelphia, PA; teacher of mystery writing at the Gotham Writers Workshop, New York, NY.

MEMBER: International Crime Writers Association, Mystery Writers of America, Sisters in Crime.

AWARDS, HONORS: Winner of St. Martin's Press/Malice Domestic Prize, 1997 (prize was publication of first novel, *The Doctor Digs a Grave*); Agatha Award, 1998, for *The Doctor Digs a Grave*.

WRITINGS:

"ANDREW FENIMORE MYSTERY" SERIES

The Doctor Digs a Grave, St. Martin's Press (New York, NY), 1998.
The Doctor Makes a Dollhouse Call, Thomas Dunne Books (New York, NY), 2000.
The Doctor and the Dead Man's Chest, Thomas Dunne Books (New York, NY), 2001.
The Doctor Dines in Prague, Thomas Dunne Books (New York, NY), 2003.

OTHER

Scarecrow ("Jo Banks Mystery" series), Thomas Dunne Books (New York, NY), 2003.

Contributor of short stories to periodicals, including *Ellery Queen's Mystery Magazine* and *Alfred Hitchcock Mystery Magazine.*

WORK IN PROGRESS: Two mystery novels, *The Doctor Rocks the Boat* and *Satan's Pony.*

SIDELIGHTS: Robin Hathaway is a New York City-based writer who has created two mystery series, both with doctors as the central characters. In writing her mysteries, Hathaway is assisted with the medical details by her cardiologist husband.

Hathaway's longer running series features cardiologist Andrew Fenimore, an old-fashioned doctor who has a solo practice out of his townhouse in Philadelphia. Andrew, who has become disillusioned with HMOs and the impersonal healthcare system, still makes house calls, and his only staff is Mrs. Doyle, an elderly nurse and secretary. He has a cat named Sal, and his girlfriend, Jennifer Nicholson, runs an antiquarian bookstore with her father.

In the first book in the series, *The Doctor Digs a Grave,* Andrew befriends Horatio, a hispanic youth who is attempting to bury his dead cat in a public park in an affluent downtown Philadelphia neighborhood. As they lay the pet to rest, they uncover the body of a Lenni Lenape (or Delaware) girl, buried in an upright position facing east, as is the Lenape custom. Andrew has two puzzles to solve—whether the girl's death was natural or the result of a crime, and why she was buried in this location, which they discover is actually an ancient burial ground.

A *Publishers Weekly* contributor wrote that Hathaway "deserves a wide readership for this smooth and entertaining blend of jargon-free medical lore, little-known historical facts, and credible mystery plotting." *School Library Journal*'s Pat Bangs commented that the book turns the history of this tribe, "the doctor's unconventional avocation as a P.I., and a cast of lovable but eccentric characters into a well-crafted tale of suspense."

In *The Doctor Makes a Dollhouse Call,* Andrew is summoned by elderly patients Judith and Emily Pancoast to their Jersey shore mansion when their niece, Pamela, is poisoned on Thanksgiving. Hers and subsequent deaths all occur on holidays and are somehow connected to the sisters' dollhouse, which is an exact replica of their Victorian home and in which each member of the family is represented by their own doll. Horatio is now helping in Andrew's office, assisting Mrs. Doyle, who leads a geriatric karate class in the basement. "An unexpected conclusion, mixed with charm and tragedy, tops off this expert tale," wrote a

Publishers Weekly reviewer. *Booklist* critic John Rowen called the doctor and Mrs. Doyle "realistic yet appealingly quirky characters."

The third book of the series, *The Doctor and the Dead Man's Chest,* finds Andrew with fifty acres and a treasure map, left to him by a patient, but when he inspects the land, he finds it to be a muddy and mosquito-ridden swampland. Close by is another elderly patient, Lydia Ashley, who lives with her granddaughter, Susan, and Andrew takes advantage of the opportunity to stop and see her. He becomes concerned about her heart when he learns that someone has been leaving rotting dead carcasses in her barn, and tossing smoke bombs and messages to sell through her windows.

Andrew dispatches Mrs. Doyle to stay with them, and she looks for clues among their acquaintances, help, and others in the community. When Horatio is stabbed during a gang initiation, Andrew sends him to Lydia's as well, so that he might recuperate and keep on eye on things. The troubles continue as Mrs. Doyle is shot at and abducted and Lydia's heart medications are tampered with. Andrew discovers the identity of the culprits and rescues Mrs. Doyle with the help of Jennifer. "Charming, with interesting tidbits about colonial brickwork and coins," commented a *Kirkus Reviews* contributor. "If Fenimore is a bit dull, Mrs. Doyle, Horatio, and Jennifer more than take up the slack."

Andrew travels to Europe in *The Doctor Dines in Prague,* to visit the Czech Republic, the birthplace of his mother. Upon reaching Prague, he attempts to phone his cousin, Anna Borovy, and her husband, without success. When he finally visits their apartment, he finds their young daughter, Marie, surviving on crackers. Not knowing what misdeeds have occurred, Andrew chooses to send Marie to the United States before beginning an investigation, aided by his cousin's friend, Ilsa Tanacek. Jennifer arrives, and soon they are immersed in a conspiracy with political implications. A *Publishers Weekly* contributor wrote that Andrew "is a mild-mannered hero neither handsome nor particularly dashing, yet his kindness and generosity will endear him to many readers." Jenny McLarin wrote in *Booklist* that although the emphasis of this series has been "atmosphere over adventure, the fourth Dr. Fenimore story stands out as suspenseful as well as charming."

Jo Banks, the protagonist of Hathaway's second series, bears no resemblance to Andrew, except for her resistance to "the establishment." She is a twenty-something family-practice doctor who flees New York City, deeply affected by the death of a young patient. In the first story, *Scarecrow,* Jo is staying at a motel in Bayside, New Jersey, and is asked to treat the ill woman in the adjoining room. The woman recovers and, with her husband, leaves without paying. Motel owners Maggie and Paul Nelson ask Jo to stay on as the motel's on-call doctor, which she agrees to do, and the next time she sees the errant couple they are guests of Becca, a runaway to whom Jo had offered a lift. Becca and her aunt disappear, and Jo is presented with the possibility that the two are responsible for this and the disappearance of the Nelsons' son, as well as for the dead man who is found inside the garb of a scarecrow. Jo relies on Tom Canby, an expert in house restoration, to help her with the mystery that leads to her own brush with death. Jo is also the on-call provider for other motels in the area, and travels by motorcycle. Her motel doctoring leads to interesting situations and provides her with plenty of opportunities for sleuthing. A *Kirkus Reviews* critic noted the story's "offbeat heroine, crusty local characters, and a fine sense of menace." McLarin called *Scarecrow* "an affectionate portrayal of small-town life."

Hathaway told *CA:* "When I was ten, I had rheumatic fever and was confined to bed for six months. To entertain me my mother gave me Agatha Christies to read. I also was an avid radio listener (TV hadn't been invented yet). I discovered if I turned the dial all the way to the right I could pick up police calls-robberies, fires, accidents, and on a good day, even a homicide! One day in an effort to keep me occupied, my mother gave me a pad of paper and a pencil and told me to write her a story. It was a terrible mystery-but that was the beginning.

"I hope my books will entertain. Give readers a few hours in which they can escape into another world, meet some new people. My greatest ambition is to be reread-to have people come back to my books, even though they know the answer to the puzzle—and reread them because they enjoy returning to the setting and being with the characters."

BIOGRAPHICAL AND CRITICAL SOURCES:

PERIODICALS

Booklist, December 15, 1999, John Rowen, review of *The Doctor Makes a Dollhouse Call,* p. 759;

November 15, 2001, Jenny McLarin, review of *The Doctor and the Dead Man's Chest,* p. 557; February 15, 2003, Jenny McLarin, review of *Scarecrow,* p. 1053; September 15, 2003, Jenny McLarin, review of *The Doctor Dines in Prague,* p. 215.

Kirkus Reviews, September 15, 2001, review of *The Doctor and the Dead Man's Chest,* p. 1326; February 1, 2003, review of *Scarecrow,* p. 188; September 1, 2003, review of *The Doctor Dines in Prague,* p. 1102.

Library Journal, April 1, 2003, Rex Klett, review of *Scarecrow,* p. 133; October 1, 2003, Rex Klett, review of *The Doctor Dines in Prague,* p. 120.

Publishers Weekly, March 16, 1998, review of *The Doctor Digs a Grave,* p. 57; December 20, 1999, review of *The Doctor Makes a Dollhouse Call,* p. 60; October 15, 2001, review of *The Doctor and the Dead Man's Chest,* p. 50; October 13, 2003, review of *The Doctor Dines in Prague,* p. 61.

School Library Journal, October, 1998, Pat Bangs, review of *The Doctor Digs a Grave,* p. 161.

ONLINE

Robin Hathaway Home Page, http://www.robin hathaway.com (June 1, 2004).

*   *   *

HAZELWOOD, Robert R.
(Roy Hazelwood)

PERSONAL: Male; married; wife's name Peggy.

ADDRESSES: Home—Southern VA. *Agent*—c/o Author Mail, St. Martin's Press, 175 Fifth Ave., New York, NY 10010.

CAREER: Federal Bureau of Investigation, agent beginning 1971, supervisory agent with Behavioral Science Unit, FBI Academy, beginning 1978; retired; Academy Group, Inc., Manassas, VA, forensics consultant. Writer and speaker. *Military service:* U.S. Military Police Corps; served as major.

WRITINGS:

(With Park Elliott Dietz and Ann Wolbert Burgess) *Autoerotic Fatalities,* Lexington Books (Lexington, MA), 1983.

(With Ann Wolbert Burgess) *Practical Aspects of Rape Investigation: A Multidisciplinary Approach,* CRC Press (Boca Raton, FL), 1987, third edition, 2001.

(As Roy Hazelwood; with Stephen G. Michaud) *The Evil That Men Do: FBI Profiler Roy Hazelwood's Journey into the Minds of Sexual Predators,* St. Martin's Press (New York, NY), 1998.

(As Roy Hazelwood; with Stephen G. Michaud) *Dark Dreams: Sexual Violence, Homicide, and the Criminal Mind,* St. Martin's Press (New York, NY), 2001.

Contributor to over forty professional journals.

SIDELIGHTS: Robert R. "Roy" Hazelwood has worked for the Federal Bureau of Investigation for over twenty-two years, sixteen of which he spent in the Bureau's Behavioral Science Unit. He has become one of the country's leading experts in the complex, and often perplexing, world of sexual criminals, serial killers, and other such offenders. Now retired from the bureau and currently living in southern Virginia with his wife, Hazelwood has allied with the Academy Group, Inc., a forensic consulting firm whose clients range from government and industry to criminal justice. In addition to his FBI service, Hazelwood also served as a major for the U.S. Military Police Corps. Exposed to excessive violence throughout his long career, Hazelwood decided to share his knowledge and has published over forty journal articles as well as several books on the topic. He has also teamed up writer Stephen G. Michaud to share his vast first-hand knowledge in the books *The Evil That Men Do: FBI Profiler Roy Hazelwood's Journey into the Minds of Sexual Predators* and *Dark Dreams: Sexual Violence, Homicide, and the Criminal Mind.*

The Evil That Men Do documents Hazelwood's FBI career as an expert assigned to explore and uncover the motivations and psychology of sexual predators. At first his role was not highly respected within the bureau, but after he developed a successful method for entering the minds of serial killers and rapists, Hazelwood helped transform sexual crime investigation into a well-respected area of study.

Upon beginning his FBI career, Hazelwood quickly realized that no serious study had ever been made of serial rapists. As he notes in *The Evil That Men Do:* "There'd been hundreds of rape studies done, but no one had ever looked at serial rapists." Deciding to conduct some research of his own, Hazelwood gathered forty-one men from twelve different states, all of whom had been imprisoned for rape. Combined, these individuals were responsible for 837 rapes and had attempted approximately 400 more. While at the conclusion of his research Hazelwood found no comprehensive reason why some individuals act out and others do not, he did acquire the necessary skills and knowledge to co-found the Violent Criminal Apprehension Program (VICAP) with Robert Ressler and John Douglas. This FBI program serves the purpose of profiling serial killers.

The Evil That Men Do follows Hazelwood's career through several well-known criminal cases, among them the notorious Tawana Brawley case of 1987, the Lonely Heart Killer case, the "Ken and Barbie" killings, the Atlanta child murders, and the 1989 explosion on the USS *Iowa* that killed forty-seven people. Also included are case studies, biographical information, and statistics. A reviewer for *Publishers Weekly* stated that "Michaud is most interesting when he ably summarizes Hazelwood's groundbreaking work and least interesting when he slips into simple hagiography of the dedicated lawman." Christopher Lehmann-Haupt commented in the *New York Times,* "In fact, you learn so much from cases like these that by the end, in a chapter called 'You Be the Analyst,' you find you are able to put together many of the clues in the 1986 rape-murder of a young typist in the FBI's San Antonio office."

Michaud and Hazelwood have also teamed up to write *Dark Dreams: Sexual Violence, Homicide, and the Mind.* This time taking the investigations and psychological aspects of each individual case a bit further, techniques and psychological profiles of the offenders are openly discussed by the authors. Hazelwood shares his tactics for successfully tracking down these very same perpetrators and also recounts the dangers he has faced in the course of doing his job.

BIOGRAPHICAL AND CRITICAL SOURCES:

PERIODICALS

New York Times, February 4, 1999, Christopher Lehmann-Haupt, review of *The Evil That Men Do: FBI Profiler Roy Hazelwood's Journey into the Minds of Sexual Predators,* p. E8
Publishers Weekly, December 14, 1998, review of *The Evil That Men Do,* p. 66.

ONLINE

Holtz Brink Publisher Web site, http://www.holtzbrinck publisher.com/ (October 1, 2003).*

* * *

HAZELWOOD, Roy
See HAZELWOOD, Robert R.

* * *

HEARD, Nathan C(liff) 1936-2004

OBITUARY NOTICE—See index for *CA* sketch: Born November 7, 1936, in Newark, NJ; died of complications from Parkinson's disease March 16, 2004, in Newark, NJ. Educator, journalist, and author. Heard was a novelist best known for his stories about life on the tough streets of Newark. Originally having ambitions of being a baseball player, Heard was a high school dropout when he ran into trouble with the law and was imprisoned for eight years for armed robbery and parole violation. While serving his time at the New Jersey State Prison, boredom led him to books. He read the works of such authors as Richard Wright, James Baldwin, and Norman Mailer; he also read pulp novels. Convincing himself that he could do better than the pulps, he penned his first novel, *Howard Street* (1968), while still in prison. The book became a bestseller, earning Heard an income that sustained him for ten years. His writing also led to jobs as a columnist and writing speeches for Newark mayor Kenneth A. Gibson; and he taught creative writing at Fresno State College for a year and was an assistant professor of English at Rutgers University from 1970 to 1972. Other novels followed his debut, including *To Reach a Dream* (1972), *A Cold Fire Burning* (1974), *When Shadows Fall* (1977), and *The House of Slammers* (1983). In addition to these pursuits, Heard explored acting, taking on roles in such films as 1973's *Gordon's War.*

OBITUARIES AND OTHER SOURCES:

PERIODICALS

Chicago Tribune, March 23, 2004, Section 3, p. 11.
Los Angeles Times, March 23, 2004, p. B13.

New York Times, March 23, 2004, p. A20.
Washington Post, March 22, 2004, p. B6.

* * *

HEINRICH, Will 1978(?)-

PERSONAL: Born c. 1978, in New York, NY. *Education:* Graduated from Columbia University.

ADDRESSES: Agent—c/o Author Mail, Charles Scribner's Sons, 1230 Avenue of the Americas, New York, NY 10020.

CAREER: Writer. *Harper's* magazine, intern, 2001.

WRITINGS:

The King's Evil (novel), Scribner's (New York, NY), 2003.

SIDELIGHTS: Will Heinrich's first novel, *The King's Evil,* appeared in 2003 and was dubbed a "brooding and suspenseful . . . debut" by a *Publishers Weekly* critic. Heinrich, a recent graduate from Columbia University and an intern at *Harper's* magazine when he sold the book to Scribner, has fashioned a tale that "asks provocative questions about the nature of good and evil," according to the reviewer.

Joseph Malderoyce, the protagonist and narrator of Heinrich's "creepy Gothic tale," as Mark Rozzo described it in the *Los Angeles Times,* is a former lawyer who has left his practice and moved to remote and rural Bettley to spend his free time studying tuberculosis, the disease that killed both his wealthy parents. Their deaths, in fact, brought Malderoyce into his patrimony, allowing him to quit his loathed work as a lawyer. Malderoyce has other passions, too: as a youth he was inspired to become a painter after seeing a Piet Mondrian exhibition. Practicality, however, forced him to set such dreams aside, and he has long regretted that youthful decision. As Rozzo put it, "Joseph [Malderoyce] is the perfect embodiment of how the rash notions of adolescence reverberate into middle age."

Into this quiet, remote life comes a stranger, a teenager named Abel who camps out at Malderoyce's doorstep one stormy night. The older man takes the youth in, an act of kindness and charity with alarming consequences. The mysterious Abel, who is something of an alter ego for Malderoyce, is less than a perfect guest, ruining slides Malderoyce has prepared, manipulating visitors or being downright rude to them, and eventually turning violent. Malderoyce sees the evil in the youth and feels he must "cure" him of it in the same manner that early kings were supposed to be able to cure a patient of tuberculosis by their touch. He is at once repelled by and attracted to the youth, who is by turns simply a surly outsider and a vision of Malderoyce's younger self. The denouement is, as the critic for *Publishers Weekly* noted, "a disturbing moral lesson about the power of violence to expunge evil." The reviewer also felt that though Heinrich's "narrative initially has a gripping immediacy, its schematic nature soon becomes irksome."

Other reviewers focused more on the chilling aspects of this tale. For example, a writer for *Kirkus Reviews* called young Abel a "tyrant adolescent and a troll out of Grimm." For *Library Journal* contributor Jim Coan, Heinrich's tale about dealing with the "darker forces of one's personality has psychological, philosophical, and even biblical overtones."

BIOGRAPHICAL AND CRITICAL SOURCES:

PERIODICALS

Kirkus Reviews, May 1, 2003, review of *The King's Evil,* p. 629.
Library Journal, May 1, 2003, Jim Coan, review of *The King's Evil,* pp. 155-156.
Los Angeles Times, September 7, 2003, Mark Rozzo, review of *The King's Evil,* p. R14.
Publishers Weekly, May 26, 2003, review of *The King's Evil,* p. 45.

ONLINE

eReader.com, http://www.palmdigitalmedia.com/ (March 28, 2004).*

HEMINGWAY, Hilary 1961(?)-

PERSONAL: Born c. 1961, in FL; daughter of Leicester Hemingway; married Jeffry P. Lindsay; children: one daughter. *Education:* University of Miami, graduated 1984 (with honors). *Hobbies and other interests:* Volunteering for the American Diabetes Research Foundation.

ADDRESSES: Home—Cape Coral, FL. *Agent*—c/o Author Mail, Rugged Land, LLC, 276, Canal St., Fifth Floor, New York, NY 10013.

CAREER: Writer, television producer, and documentary filmmaker.

MEMBER: American Diabetes Association (member of south coastal region board of directors).

AWARDS, HONORS: Has won state and national awards for her unproduced screenplay "A Light within the Shadow."

WRITINGS:

(With Jeffry P. Lindsay) *Dreamland: A Novel of the UFO Cover-Up,* Forge (New York, NY), 1995.
(With Jeffry P. Lindsay) *Dreamchild,* Tom Doherty Associates (New York, NY), 1998.
(With Jeffry P. Lindsay) *Hunting with Hemingway: Based on the Stories of Leicester Hemingway,* Riverhead Books (New York, NY), 2000.
(With Carlene Brennen) *Hemingway in Cuba,* Rugged Land (New York, NY), 2003.

Also author of the *Hemingway Florida Guidebook* and an unproduced screenplay titled "A Light within the Shadow."

ADAPTATIONS: Hunting with Hemingway was adapted for audiocassette, Highbridge, 2000, and narrated by the authors.

SIDELIGHTS: Hilary Hemingway, who is the niece of famous author Ernest Hemingway, is the "family's best hope to carry on the literary line," noted a contributor for *People* magazine. Teaming up with her writer-husband, Jeffry P. Lindsay, she has penned two UFO/alien abduction thrillers, as well as a pair of books about aspects of her illustrious uncle's life.

In *Dreamland: A Novel of the UFO Cover-Up* and its 1998 sequel, *Dreamchild,* Hemingway blends detective novel and science fiction concepts. With *Dreamland* the author takes as a given that there was a UFO crash at Roswell, New Mexico, in the 1940s, and that the military is keeping aliens from that craft under close supervision. In the meantime, they are also creating a new super weapon as part of Project Joshua. Stanley Katz is involved in the project, and when his wife, Annie, who is pregnant once again after many miscarriages, mysteriously loses her unborn child, she and her husband begin to suspect alien abduction. The novel was greeted by *Booklist* contributor Emily Melton as "a sort of E.T. meets Darth Vader story," and was recommended for readers who "love a good sci-fi tale full of flying saucers and ripping good action." A contributor to *Publishers Weekly,* however, called the book a "lackluster thriller," whose "narrative suffers from a brittle superficiality." *Booklist* contributor Candace Smith commented that there is "loads of action" in this book, but that it "reads like a TV script" and has characters who "tend to be cookie-cutter."

Hemingway again collaborated with her husband with *Hunting with Hemingway: Based on the Stories of Leicester Hemingway.* This book is purported to be a partial transcript of fireside tales that Hemingway's father, Leicester—himself a writer—recorded on tape about his and his brother Ernest's hunting adventures. Such tall tales involve fighting cobras, tigers, bears, and even Nazis. But the book is also, as Carol Peace Robins noted in the *New York Times Book Review,* a "personal journey as [Hilary Hemingway] ponders her father's suicide." Like his brother and father before him, Leicester Hemingway committed suicide; in his case it was as a result of depression over the diabetes that would have led to the amputation of both his legs. Because of the complicated narrative structure in which the tapes are related to an English professor in search of Hemingway material and then in turn transcribed by the author and her husband, as well as their young daughter, Robins also commented that the book "lacks focus" because of the "excess of remarkers remarking [that] is cloyingly artificial." A contributor to *Publishers Weekly* was less encouraging, calling the book a *disappointing narrative* that seems "apocryphal"; and *Library Journal* contributor Michael Rogers felt that many of the anecdotes related are "so over the top that they should be regarded as fiction." However, reviewing the audiobook version, *Booklist* critic Karen Harris found it an "engaging blend of truth and family legend."

Teaming up with photographer Carlene Brennen, Hemingway mines more of her uncle's life and adventures in *Hemingway in Cuba,* a book that combines passages from Hemingway's eight novels written while he lived in Cuba with text providing insights into his daily life there, including his wives, lovers, passion for fishing, and anti-Nazi activities, until he was forced to leave with the advent of Castro's regime. Many reviewers praised the author's chapters dealing with more recent attempts by the Cuban authorities to establish a Hemingway research center at the author's former house, Finca Vigia. Janice Byrne, for example, wrote in the *Hemingway Review* that "perhaps the most important chapters in *Hemingway in Cuba* come at the end of the book where Hilary Hemingway reveals the status of Hemingway research in Cuba today." A *Publishers Weekly* critic, while noting that the text is "uneven," went on to praise the "gorgeous layout" with its generous use of sepia-tone photos, and concluded that "this volume earns its place on any Hemingway fan's shelf." Similarly, *Newsday* critic Spencer Rumsey said the book is "lavishly produced," and further noted that it "bring[s] to life an important period in the life of this man of letters, long overlooked because of the tensions between Castro's Cuba and the United States." Curtis Morgan, reviewing the title in the *Miami Herald Online* thought that "the book has an intimate feel," and that Hemingway "sprinkles similar passages from [Ernest Hemingway's] novels, and it's interesting to see how experience replayed in fiction—sometimes closely, sometimes cruelly or tenderly tweaked."

BIOGRAPHICAL AND CRITICAL SOURCES:

PERIODICALS

Booklist, February 15, 1995, Emily Melton, review of *Dreamland: A Novel of the UFO Cover-Up,* p. 1064; May 15, 1998, Candace Smith, review of *Dreamchild,* p. 1601; March 1, 2003, Karen Harris, review of *Hemingway in Cuba* (audiobook), p. 1295; May 15, 2003, Steve Paul, review of *Hemingway in Cuba,* p. 1632.

Diabetes Forecast, April, 1999, "Hilary Hemingway: Supporting Diabetes through the International Hemingway Festival," p. 89.

Hemingway Review, fall, 2003, Janice Byrne, review of *Hemingway in Cuba,* pp. 123-126.

Library Journal, July, 2000, Michael Rogers, review of *Hunting with Hemingway: Based on the Stories of Leicester Hemingway,* p. 91; May 15, 2003, Michael Rogers, review of *Hemingway in Cuba,* pp. 89-90.

Newsday, July 27, 2003, Spencer Rumsey, review of *Hemingway in Cuba,* p. E5.

New York Times Book Review, August 6, 2000, Carol Peace Robins, review of *Hunting with Hemingway,* p. 16.

People, July 22, 1985, "Hilary Hemingway May Be a Mariel Look-alike, but She's Out to Stake Her Claim on Papa's Turf," p. 79.

Publishers Weekly, January 23, 1995, review of *Dreamland,* p. 61; June 26, 2000, review of *Hunting with Hemingway,* p. 63; April 28, 2003, review of *Hemingway in Cuba,* p. 57.

ONLINE

Miami Herald Online, http://www.miami.com/mld/miamiherald/ (October 26, 2003), Curtis Morgan, "Deconstructing a Famous Uncle and His Life in Cuba."*

* * *

HENSLEY, Christopher 1972-

PERSONAL: Born October 7, 1972, in Greenville, TN; son of Virginia S. Norton Payne. *Ethnicity:* "White." *Education:* East Tennessee State University, B.S. (summa cum laude), 1993; Mississippi State University, M.S., 1995, Ph.D., 1997. *Politics:* Democrat.

ADDRESSES: Home—292 Woodland Lane, Mount Sterling, KY 40353. *Office*—Institute for Correctional Research and Training, 114 Rader Hall, Morehead State University, Morehead, KY 40351; fax: 606-783-5006. *E-mail*—ch.hensley@moreheadstate.edu.

CAREER: Northeastern State University, Tahlequah, OK, assistant professor of sociology, 1997-99; Morehead State University, Morehead, KY, assistant professor of sociology and director of Institute for Correctional Research and Training, 1999—. Guest on media programs.

MEMBER: Academy of Criminal Justice Sciences, American Correctional Association, American Society of Criminology, Southern Criminal Justice Association.

AWARDS, HONORS: Grants from Kentucky Department for Mental Health/Mental Retardation Services, Kentucky Department of Juvenile Justice, Administrative Office of the Courts of Kentucky, and Prevent Child Abuse Kentucky.

WRITINGS:

(Editor and contributor) *Prison Sex: Practice and Policy,* Lynne Rienner Publishers (Boulder, CO), 2002.

(Editor, with Richard Tewksbury) *Sexual Deviance: A Reader,* Lynne Rienner Publishers (Boulder, CO), 2002.

Contributor to professional journals and other periodicals, including *USA Today, Justice Professional, American Journal of Criminal Justice, International Journal of Offender Therapy and Comparative Criminology, Journal of Interpersonal Violence, Journal of Offender Rehabilitation, Journal of Criminal Justice Education, Journal of Men's Studies, Urban Researcher,* and *Journal of Correctional Health Care.* Member of editorial board, *Journal of African American Men,* 1999-2001, and *Prison Journal,* 2000—.

* * *

HERMAN, Stephen L. 1946-

PERSONAL: Born April 11, 1946, in Hickory, NC; son of Johnson Oliver and Mary Francis (Akin) Herman; married June 2, 1992; wife's name, Debbie Virginia; stepchildren: Richard, Ryan. *Ethnicity:* "Caucasian." *Education:* Lee College, A.A.S.; Catawba Valley Technical College, graduate. *Politics:* Conservative. *Religion:* Christian. *Hobbies and other interests:* Woodworking, stained glass.

ADDRESSES: Home—135 PR 52336, Pittsburg, TX 75686.

CAREER: Teacher of electrical technology for thirty years, including positions at Lee College, Baytown, TX, and Randolph Technical College, Asheboro, NC. *Military service:* U.S. Army; served in Vietnam.

AWARDS, HONORS: Excellence in Teaching Award, Haliburton Education Foundation.

WRITINGS:

(With Walter N. Alerich) *Industrial Motor Control,* Delmar Publishers (Albany, NY), 1985, 4th edition, 1999.

Electronics for Industrial Electricians, Delmar Publishers (Albany, NY), 1985, 3rd edition, 1995.

(With Bennie L. Sparkman) *Electricity and Controls for Heating, Ventilating, and Air Conditioning,* Delmar Publishers (Albany, NY), 1986, 4th edition published as *Electricity and Controls for HVAC/R,* 2000.

(With John R. Duff) *Alternating Current Fundamentals,* Delmar Publishers (Albany, NY), 3rd edition, 1986, 6th edition, 2000.

(With Robert L. Smith) *Electrical Wiring: Industrial,* Delmar Publishers (Albany, NY), 6th edition, 1987, 11th edition, 2002.

(With Crawford G. Garrard) *Practical Problems in Mathematics for Electricians,* Delmar Publishers (Albany, NY), 4th edition, 1987, 6th edition, 2002.

Delmar's Standard Textbook of Electricity, Delmar Publishers (Albany, NY), 1993, 3rd edition, Delmar Learning (Clifton Park, NY), 2004.

Electrical Studies for Trades, Delmar Publishers (Albany, NY), 1997, 2nd edition, 2002.

(With Donald E. Singleton) *Delmar's Standard Guide to Transformers,* Delmar Publishers (Albany, NY), 1997.

Electrician's Technical Reference: Theory and Calculations, Delmar Publishers (Albany, NY), 1998.

(With Walter N. Alerich) *Electric Motor Control,* Delmar Publishers (Albany, NY), 6th edition, 1998, 7th edition, 2003.

Electrician's Technical Reference: Transformers, Delmar Publishers (Albany, NY), 1999.

Electrician's Technical Reference: Industrial Electronics, Delmar Publishers (Albany, NY), 1999.

Electrical Transformers and Rotating Machines, Delmar Publishers (Albany, NY), 1999.

The Complete Lab Manual for Industrial Electricity, Delmar Publishers (Albany, NY), 2001.

Electronics for Electricians, 4th edition, Delmar Publishers (Albany, NY), 2002.

Practical Problems in Mathematics for Electronic Technicians, 6th edition, Delmar Learning (Clifton Park, NY), 2003.

Residential Construction Academy: Electrical Principles, Delmar Learning (Clifton Park, NY), 2003.

*   *   *

HERRICK, James A. 1954-

PERSONAL: Born 1954; married; children: four. *Education:* University of California, Fresno, B.A. (speech communication, magna cum laude), 1976; University of California, Davis, M.A. (rhetoric), 1978; University of Wisconsin, Madison, Ph.D. (communication arts), 1986.

ADDRESSES: Home—35 East 28th St., Holland, MI 49423. *Office*—Department of Communication, Hope College, 126 E. 10th St., Holland, MI 49422-9000. *E-mail*—herrick@hope.edu.

CAREER: Hope College, Holland, MI, instructor, 1984-90, associate professor, 1990-93, professor, 1997—, Guy Vander Jagt Professor of Communication, 2001—, department chair, 1993-2002.

AWARDS, HONORS: Wisconsin Alumni Research Foundation fellowship, 1982; Lilly Foundation grant, 1988; Knight Foundation fellowships, 1990, 1991; various teaching and research grants and awards.

WRITINGS:

Critical Thinking: The Analysis of Arguments, Gorsuch Scarisbrick (Scottsdale, AZ), 1991.

Argumentation: Understanding and Shaping Arguments, Gorsuch Scarisbrick (Scottsdale, AZ), 1995, revised edition, Strata (State College, PA), 2004.

The History and Theory of Rhetoric: An Introduction, Gorsuch Scarisbrick (Scottsdale, AZ), 1997, third edition, Pearson Education (Boston, MA), 2004.

The Radical Rhetoric of the English Deists: The Discourse of Skepticism, 1680-1750 ("Studies in Rhetoric/Communication" series), University of South Carolina Press (Columbia, SC), 1997.

The Making of the New Spirituality: The Eclipse of the Western Religious Tradition, InterVarsity Press (Downers Grove, IL), 2003.

Contributor of entries to the *New Dictionary of National Biography,* 1999-2000; contributor to academic journals and periodicals, including *Quarterly Journal of Speech, Michigan Association of Speech Communication Journal, Washington Times, Chicago Tribune, Detroit Free Press,* and *San Francisco Examiner.* Manuscript reviewer, referee, and editorial board member for various academic publications and journals.

SIDELIGHTS: James A. Herrick has written a number of volumes about his specialty, rhetoric and communications. Among these texts is *The Radical Rhetoric of the English Deists: The Discourse of Skepticism, 1680-1750.* Central to Herrick's study are the doctrines of the principal Deists and his emphasis on their rhetoric. *Criticism* critic Justin Champion called the volume "a bold work that sets out to underscore the importance of radical anti-Christian discourses to the history of freedom in eighteenth-century English debate. . . . Herrick argues for a heroic, radical, and populist account of deism, located in clubs, coffee houses, secret guild and clandestine meetings. One of the key premises of his account is the claim that exploring the 'rhetoric' of deistical writings and controversies is critical to refurbishing their reputation and importance." Champion concluded by saying that the book has value "as an overview of the types of debate which convulsed English literary and political discourse in the eighteenth century. It is a very accomplished starting point which should encourage scholars to take seriously the survival and power of radical discourse in the eighteenth century."

John C. Adams wrote in a review for *Argumentation* that "Herrick's book does what it sets out to do and along the way leaves bibliographic traces that are a catalogue of nearly all of the period's primary sources." Adams further stated that the book "provides a scholarly context for understanding rhetoric's play in the depths and surfaces of Christianity's problematic encounter with life's meaning and purpose."

BIOGRAPHICAL AND CRITICAL SOURCES:

PERIODICALS

Argumentation, February, 1999, John C. Adams, review of *The Radical Rhetoric of the English Deists: The Discourse of Skepticism, 1680-1750,* pp. 119-121.
Criticism, fall, 1999, Justin Champion, review of *The Radical Rhetoric of the English Deists,* p. 554.
Heythrop Journal, April, 2001, E. M. Knottenbelt, review of *The Radical Rhetoric of the English Deists,* pp. 208-210.
Library Journal, May 1, 2003, William P. Collins, review of *The Making of the New Spirituality: The Eclipse of the Western Religious Tradition,* p. 120.
Studies in English Literature, 1500-1900, summer, 1998, Donna Landry, Gerald MacLean, review of *The Radical Rhetoric of the English Deists,* p. 553.
Theological Studies, March, 1999, Melvyn New, review of *The Radical Rhetoric of the English Deists,* p. 192.

*　　*　　*

HERRICK, William 1915-2004

OBITUARY NOTICE—See index for *CA* sketch: Born January 10, 1915, in Trenton, NJ; died January 31, 2004, in Old Chatham, NY. Author. Herrick was best known for his espionage and war novels. A veteran of the Spanish Civil War, during which he fought against Francisco Franco's army as part of the Abraham Lincoln Brigade, Herrick fictionalized this experience in his novel *Hermanos!* (1969). Before becoming a novelist, however, he worked as a court reporter from 1943 to 1969. By late 1960s, his fiction was seeing print, beginning with *The Itinerant* (1967), which was followed by nine more novels and the memoir, *Jumping the Line: The Adventures and Misadventures of an American Radical* (1998). Among his other novels, his most ambitious were the three comprising an espionage trilogy: *Shadows and Wolves* (1980), *Love and Terror* (1981), and *Kill Memory* (1984). His last novel was *Bradovich* (1990).

OBITUARIES AND OTHER SOURCES:

BOOKS

Dictionary of Literary Biography 2001 Yearbook, Gale (Detroit, MI), 2002.

PERIODICALS

New York Times, February 9, 2004, p. A25.
Washington Post, February 10, 2004, p. B7.

*　　*　　*

HICKMAN, John (Kyrle) 1927-2001

PERSONAL: Born July 3, 1927; died in 2001; son of J. B. and Joan Hickman; married Jennifer, 1986; children: two sons, one daughter. *Education:* Trinity Hall, Cambridge, (history). *Hobbies and other interests:* History and golf.

CAREER: Diplomat. U.K. High Commission, Wellington, 1959-62; H.M. Diplomatic Service, joined 1965, posted to British Embassy, Madrid, Spain, 1966, Consul-General, Bilbao, Spain, 1967, Deputy High Commissioner, Singapore, 1969-71; ambassador to Ecuador, 1977-81, and Chile, 1982-87, alternate chairman, Belize Independence Conference, 1981; head of Southwest Pacific Department, 1971-74; counsellor in Dublin, Ireland, 1974-77; director, Anaconda (South America) Inc., 1988-2001. *Military service:* Royal Army, 45th Field Regiment, Commonwealth Brigade,1948-50.

MEMBER: Anglo-Ecuadorian Society (chairman, 1988-91), Anglo-Chilean Society.

AWARDS, HONORS: Gran Oficial, Order of Merit (Chile), 1992.

WRITINGS:

The Enchanted Islands: The Galapagos Discovered, Anthony Nelson (Oswestry), 1985.
News from the End of the Earth: A Portrait of Chile, St. Martin's Press (New York City), 1998.

Contributor of historical articles to periodicals.

SIDELIGHTS: A retired British diplomat who spent a great deal of his career in South America, John Hickman wrote two informative works about that part of the world. His *The Enchanted Islands: The Galapagos Discovered,* published in 1995, provides an overview of the mysterious Galapagos off the coast of Ecuador, where Hickman spent several years as British ambassador. Reviews of *The Enchanted Islands,* were generally positive. Douglas C. Spanner in *British Book News* called the book "fascinating and tastefully produced," and J. A. Steers in the *Geographical Journal* subbed it "readable, interesting and informative."

The nine islands of the Galapagos chain are all volcanic and had no aboriginal residents. Passing sailors first discovered the island's Chimu culture, which pre-dated the Inca era in Peru, and while Spanish and British sailors explored the islands, few stayed for any length of time, finding the land inhospitable. The Galapagos were made famous when Charles Darwin arrived there in the *Beagle* in 1835 to study the flora and fauna of the area.

The Enchanted Islands provides details about the flora and fauna that so fascinated Darwin, and at the same time outlines interesting historical facts about the islands. For example, Scotsman Alexander Selkirk, after spending four years marooned on Juan Fernandez Island in the Galapagos, became the model for Daniel Defoe's novel *Robinson Crusoe.* Large areas of the islands, which have a permanent population of around 6,000, are now nature preserves.

As Chilean ambassador from Great Britain from 1982 to 1987, Hickman was in a good position to evaluate the recent history of Chile when he wrote *News from the End of the Earth: A Portrait of Chile,* published in 1998. Mark L. Grover in *Library Journal* called the book a "readable and well-written" introduction for those not familiar with the history of Chile. Although calling the book somewhat "Anglocentric," Grover valued the way Hickman brought his personal experience to bear on the story he tells. Kenneth Maxwell in *Foreign Affairs* deemed the book "succinct and balanced."

After many decades of stability, Chile was the scene of much upheaval beginning in the late 1960s. Marxist President Salvador Allende was overthrown by the forces of General Augusto Pinochet in 1973, after Allende's attempts at reform put the country into dire economic conditions. The Pinochet era was marked by civil rights abuses against many citizens, but also by a growing and healthy economy in Chile. When that economy began to decline in 1982, Pinochet was forced out. In *News from the End of the Earth: A Portrait of Chile,* Hickman's focus is largely on the Pinochet regime, noting that a number of American-trained economists helped the country to open its markets. He also discusses the role of Chile during the Falklands war and brings up the possibility that the Pinochet regime may have supplied intelligence information to Great Britain during that conflict. Hickman is no apologist for Pinochet, however; he also compliments the work of the Commission on Truth and Reconciliation, established in 1990 to look into human rights abuses during Pinochet's reign.

News from the End of the Earth gained an unexpectedly large readership when its publication coincided with Pinochet's arrest in London for alleged crimes against Chilean citizens.

BIOGRAPHICAL AND CRITICAL SOURCES:

PERIODICALS

British Book News, July, 1985, p. 443.
Foreign Affairs, March, 1999, p. 150.
Geographical Journal, March, 1986, pp. 101-102.
Library Journal, November 15, 1998, p. 80.*

* * *

HOFFMAN, Mat 1972-

PERSONAL: Born January 9, 1972, in Oklahoma City, OK; son of Matthew (a medical supplies salesman) and Geovanna Hoffman; married Jaci Keel (a ballet dancer), 1993; children: two. *Hobbies and other interests:* Sky diving and other extreme sports.

ADDRESSES: Office—Hoffman Enterprises, P.O. Box 18931, Oklahoma City, OK 73154. *Agent*—Brian Dubin, William Morris Agency, 1325 Avenue of the Americas, New York, NY 10019.

CAREER: Amateur freestyle BMX stunt bicyclist, 1984-88; professional freestyle BMX vert-ramp bicyclist, 1988—. Ten-time vert world champion; high air world record holder. Founder and president, Hoffman Promotions and Hoffman Bikes; producer, director, and host of bicycle competitions and television shows for ESPN2, including *Kids in the Way, HBtv,* and *Mat's World;* organizer of show tours, including Sprocket Jockey Bicycle Stunt Team, Crazy Freakin' Bikers Series, and Mat Hoffman's Crazy Freakin' Stunt Show. Consultant to movies, including *Keep Your Eyes Open, Ultimate X, Triple X, Jackass: The Movie,* and *Tomb Raider 2.* Participant, Tony Hawk's Boom Boom Huck Jam. Co-producer of video games, including *Mat Hoffman's Pro BMX* and *Mat Hoffman's Pro BMX 2.*

AWARDS, HONORS: Numerous gold, silver, and bronze medals for BMX bicycle events and X Games events; Action Sports Lifetime Achievement Award from ESPN, 2002.

WRITINGS:

(With Mark Lewman) *The Ride of My Life* (autobiography), HarperCollins (New York, NY), 2003.

SIDELIGHTS: Pioneering athlete Mat Hoffman is one of the greatest vert-ramp bicycle riders in the world. With his daring extreme stunts and imaginative original moves, Hoffman has helped to establish freestyle BMX bike racing as an international sport with an ever-growing audience. Nicknamed "The Condor," Hoffman has seemed to defy gravity by becoming airborne on his custom-made bicycles and executing flips, turns, and other moves so radical that he had to name them himself. He is one of very few Americans who—as himself—is the star of two video games.

Hoffman began doing stunts on his bike when he was still a boy, and by the time he was thirteen he qualified to race as an amateur at national freestyle BMX events. At sixteen he turned pro and began a long domination of freestyle bicycle competitions that includes ten world championships, the high air world record, and the creation of more than 100 new tricks for vert—ramp biking. The championships have exacted a toll—he has suffered more than forty-five broken bones, has endured multiple concussions, and has undergone numerous surgical procedures, some of them for life-threatening injuries. Hoffman told the London *Observer* that the thrill of aerial stunt biking

is worth the pain of the inevitable wipe-outs. "In the end, I think it defines how much I love what I do," he said. "To taste all the pleasure and success you have to be prepared to take all the pain and failures too. And I am."

As one of the early international stars of vert-ramp biking, Hoffman wisely noted that the sport was gaining in popularity. He formed his own production company to produce television and traveling shows that have brought in new viewers and participants. He also designed his own bicycles out of necessity and turned that into an international industry, Hoffman Bikes. Now in the twilight of his years as a competitor, he is well poised to continue making important contributions to his sport.

Most people are just embarking on their life careers at age thirty, but Hoffman had accomplished so much that he was ready to look back and write an autobiography. *The Ride of My Life,* co-authored with Mark Lewman, explores his life from the time he left school to compete in amateur events through his many years of top-level competition, to his success as the head of two companies. Written in a manner that can be enjoyed by both adults and children, *The Ride of My Life* includes numerous pictures of Hoffman executing his signature stunts and enjoying the accolades that came with his championships. In a *Library Journal* review of the book, Jamie Watson noted that while Hoffman's story might be enjoyed most by fans of extreme sports, "anyone could find inspiration from the success and pleasure he has gotten from hard work, passion, and desire."

In his London *Observer* profile, Hoffman said he has no plans to quit riding, despite the mounting physical damage he sustains from the effort. "I just want to see what I can do with my body and my bike," he said. "And challenge it daily. My motivation is not competition. I ride under the current terms, that I'm dealt with my body. And I enjoy riding as it is now as opposed to comparing it to anything else."

BIOGRAPHICAL AND CRITICAL SOURCES:

PERIODICALS

Daily News (Los Angeles, CA), August 16, 2003, Ramona Shelburne, "Bike Stunt Vert," p. S8.
Library Journal, May, 2003, Jamie Watson, review of *The Ride of My Life,* p. 181.

News Journal (Wilmington, DE), November 10, 2002, Holly Norton, "Extreme Sports Stars Mix It up on Tour," p. D1.

Observer (London, England), June 9, 2002, Matthew O'Donnell, "Up Where He Belongs: Mat Hoffman Is the King of BMX," p. 25.

People Weekly, September 16, 2002, Jason Lynch, "Leapin' Wizard: What's Biker Mat Hoffman's Most Awesome Stunt? Turning Himself into a Successful CEO," p. 101.

ONLINE

Hoffman Bikes, http://www.hoffmanbikes.com/ (June 8, 2004).*

*   *   *

HOLZ, Cynthia 1950-

PERSONAL: Born 1950, in New York, NY; married; children: one son. *Education:* City University of New York, Queens College, B.A. (English), 1971.

ADDRESSES: Home—Toronto, Ontario, Canada. *Agent*—c/o Author Mail, Thomas Allen Publishers, 145 Front St. East, Suite 209, Toronto, Ontario M5A 1E3, Canada.

CAREER: Writer and educator. *Business Week,* Toronto, Ontario, Canada, correspondent, beginning in 1976; Ryerson Polytechnic University, Toronto, Ontario, Canada, teacher of creative writing, 1990—; Toronto Public Library, Toronto, Ontario, Canada, writer-in-residence, 1999.

WRITINGS:

Home Again (short stories), Random House Canada (Toronto, Ontario, Canada), 1989.

Onlyville (novel), illustrated by Gerard Brender à Brandis, Porcupine's Quill (Erin, Ontario, Canada), 1994.

The Other Side, Second Story Press (Toronto, Ontario, Canada), 1994.

Semi-Detached, Key Porter Books (Toronto, Ontario, Canada), 1999.

A Good Man, Thomas Allen Publishers (Toronto, Ontario, Canada), 2003.

Contributor to periodicals, including *Quill & Quire, Ottawa Citizen,* and Toronto *Globe & Mail.*

SIDELIGHTS: Cynthia Holz is a novelist and author of short stories. *Home Again,* her debut work, is a collection of stories that "concentrate on gloomy, repressed lives; people are dangerous containers that threaten to explode," according to Beverley Daurio in *Books in Canada.* The stories often feature female protagonists, "everyday heroines beating against the current, sometimes allowing themselves to be carried along by it," wrote Zsuzsi Gartner in *Quill & Quire.* Daurio added that the "most memorable characters" in *Home Again* are the women, and she complimented Holz's narrative voice, "a cold, precise voice, fascinating while it is telling a story, patronizing when it editorializes."

Onlyville concerns the spiritual and emotional crisis facing Anna Berman, a twenty-nine year old who tries to escape her troubled life by fleeing to her abandoned family cottage in Onlyville, a seacoast town. There, in the words of *Quill & Quire* reviewer Sandra Martin, Anna "dives in to the past, hoping to emerge refreshed and unfettered by the ghost of her mother," who drowned fifteen years earlier. Anna is soon joined, however, by her boyfriend and several members of her family. By the end of the novel, observed Chris Knight in the *Canadian Book Review Annual,* "Anna is leaving Onlyville again to find peace—but she leaves with a peace she has found there as well."

After her housemate commits suicide, an unemployed actress learns that his ghost still inhabits her kitchen in *The Other Side.* Though her own life is in chaos, Holly tries to help her dead friend, Marc, find the courage to "cross over." "Holz has set up a profound situation in a whimsical context," according to *Canadian Book Review Annual* contributor Martha Wilson, who stated that the author's "use of humor . . . can feel clumsy and heavy-handed." *Quill & Quire* reviewer Janet McNaughton called the work "a seriously comedic novel," but also remarked that Holz raised an important question: "Is a life like Holly's, a life without clear direction or purpose, worth living?"

A couple reexamines their relationship after more than three decades of marriage in *Semi-Detached,* "a sparely and buoyantly written" work according to Toronto *Globe & Mail* contributor Daurio. Barbara and Elliot Rifkin agree to live independently while still sharing a house, and to the consternation of friends and family, they divide their home into two separate living areas and begin dating other people. "Holz has a powerfully good time teasing her readers, and dangles her characters in their dilemmas mercilessly," Daurio stated.

Holz published her fourth novel, *A Good Man,* in 2003. The work follows Izzy Schneider, a man torn by grief and loss after his friend is murdered.

BIOGRAPHICAL AND CRITICAL SOURCES:

PERIODICALS

Books in Canada, June-July, 1989, review of *Home Again,* p. 26; summer, 1994, Maureen McCallum Garvie, review of *Onlyville,* p. 56.

Canadian Book Review Annual, 1994, Chris Knight, review of *Onlyville,* pp. 162-163; 1998, Martha Wilson, review of *The Other Side,* pp. 186-187; 1999, Sarah Robertson, review of *Semi-Detached,* p. 171.

Canadian Literature, summer, 2003, Sara Crangle, "Inside the House," pp. 188-191.

Globe & Mail (Toronto, Ontario, Canada), August 28, 1999, Beverly Daurio, "Welcome to Our Tiny, Delicate World," p. D17.

Quill & Quire, May, 1989, Zsuzsi Gartner, review of *Home Again,* p. 19; March, 1994, Sandra Martin, "Mother & Child Reunion," p. 71; December, 1997, Janet McNaughton, review of *The Other Side,* pp. 24, 26; August, 1999, Mary Soderstrom, review of *Semi-Detached,* p. 32.

ONLINE

Thomas Allen Publishers Web site, http://www.thomas-allen.com/ (April 16, 2004), "Cynthia Holz."
Writers' Union of Canada Web site, http://www.writers union.ca/ (April 16, 2004), "Cynthia Holz."*

HOSSEINI, Khaled 1965-

PERSONAL: Born 1965, in Kabul, Afghanistan; immigrated to the United States, 1980. *Education:* Santa Clara University, B.A. (biology), 1988; University of San Diego, M.D., 1993. *Hobbies and other interests:* Soccer, racquetball, writing, involved in charities Paralyzed Vets of America and Aid the Afghan Children.

ADDRESSES: Office—The Permanente Medical Group, 555 Castro St., 3rd Fl., Mountain View, CA 94041. *E-mail*—khaled@khaledhosseini.com.

CAREER: Practicing physician specializing in internal medicine, 1996—; The Permanente Medical Group, Mountain View, CA, physician, 1999—.

AWARDS, HONORS: Original Voices Award, Borders Group, 2004, for *The Kite Runner.*

WRITINGS:

The Kite Runner, Riverhead Books (New York, NY), 2003.

ADAPTATIONS: The Kite Runner was adapted for audio (unabridged; eight cassettes), read by the author, Simon & Schuster, 2003.

SIDELIGHTS: Khaled Hosseini was born in Kabul, Afghanistan, the son of a diplomat father and teacher mother. In 1976 the family was relocated to Paris, France, where they remained until 1980 following the Soviet takeover of Afghanistan. They were then granted political asylum in the United States and moved to San Jose, California. Hosseini's parents left everything behind and relied on welfare until they were able to get back on their feet. Hosseini became a physician, but he had always loved to write. His debut novel, *The Kite Runner,* was called "painful, moving, remarkable" by *Library Journal* reviewer Michael Adams, who reviewed the audio version. In the book, Hosseini returns to the pre-Soviet Afghanistan of his childhood and relates his feelings for a servant who had lived in the household, a man who taught him to read and write. "Rather than settle for a coming-of-age or travails-of-immigrants story, Hosseini has folded them both into this searing spectacle of hard-won personal salvation," wrote a *Kirkus Reviews* critic. "All this, and a rich slice of Afghan culture too: irresistible."

The story spans four decades and is told by the protagonist, Amir, who as an adult is a writer living in California. His story goes back to his childhood in Kabul, when the quiet, motherless boy yearns for attention from his successful father, Bapa, but finds a friend in Hassan, the son of his father's servant. Amir resents sharing his father's affection with the loyal and talented Hassan, but when Amir wins a kite-flying contest, his father finally gives him the praise he craves. But in that single incident, he loses Hassan, who goes after a downed kite and is attacked and raped by Assef, the town bully. Because of his feelings of guilt for not helping his friend, Amir pushes Hassan away, even accusing of him of theft, and eventually, the family leaves the community.

The story then fast forwards to the adult Amir, who has fled Afghanistan during the Russian occupation, moved to the bay area of California, married a beautiful Afghan woman, and became a successful writer. His father has died of cancer, but in 2001 his father's partner, who knows the history of Amir and Hassan, calls from Pakistan. He tells Amir that Hassan and his wife have been executed by the Taliban, leaving their son, Sohrab. He suggests that Amir owes a debt to Hassan, and Amir agrees. He returns to find Sohrab in the custody of Assef, and it is then that he finally stands up to the man who had raped his friend.

Edward Hower wrote in the *New York Times Book Review* that "Hosseini's depiction of prerevolutionary Afghanistan is rich in warmth and humor but also tense with the friction between the nation's different ethnic groups." The critic added, "The novel's canvas turns dark when Hosseini describes the suffering of his country under the tyranny of the Taliban.... The final third of the book is full of haunting images." *School Library Journal* reviewer Penny Stevens called *The Kite Runner* a "beautifully written first novel." And a *Publishers Weekly* contributor called the novel "stunning," adding that "it is rare that a book is at once so timely and of such high literary quality."

BIOGRAPHICAL AND CRITICAL SOURCES:

PERIODICALS

Booklist, July, 2003, Kristine Huntley, review of *The Kite Runner,* p. 1864.

Kirkus Reviews, May 1, 2003, review of *The Kite Runner,* p. 630.
Kliatt, November, 2003, Nancy C. Chaplin, review of *The Kite Runner* (audiobook), p. 50.
Library Journal, April 15, 2003, Rebecca Stuhr, review of *The Kite Runner,* p. 122; November 15, 2003, Michael Adams, review of *The Kite Runner* (audio), p. 114.
New York Times Book Review, August 3, 2003, Edward Hower, review of *The Kite Runner,* p. 4.
Publishers Weekly, May 12, 2003, review of *The Kite Runner,* p. 43.
School Library Journal, November, 2003, Penny Stevens, review of *The Kite Runner,* p. 171.
Times (London, England), August 30, 2003, review of *The Kite Runner,* p. 17.

ONLINE

Khaled Hosseini Home Page, http://www.khaledhosseini.com (March 12, 2003).
Weekend Edition Sunday, http://www.npr.org/ (July 27, 2003), Liane Hansen, interview with Khaled Hosseini.*

*   *   *

HOUSE, Tom 1962-

PERSONAL: Born 1962, in Long Island, NY. *Education:* State University of New York at Stony Brook, M.A. (English), Ph.D. coursework.

ADDRESSES: Home—East Hampton, NY. *Home and office*—P.O. Box 856, Wainscott, NY 11975-0856. *Agent*—Mitchell Waters, Curtis Brown, Ltd., 10 Astor Place, New York, NY 10003. *E-mail*—tomhouse1@aol.com.

CAREER: Writer. Formerly worked as a bartender on Long Island, NY; State University of New York at Stony Brook, professor of English.

WRITINGS:

The Beginning of Calamities: A Novel, Bridge Works (Bridgehampton, NY), 2003.

Contributor to anthologies, including *Best American Gay Fiction,* Little, Brown, 1997, 1998; and *Men on Men,* Plume, 2000. Contributor to *Christopher Street, Harper's, Puerto del Sol, Western Humanities Review, New England Review, Chicago Review, Antioch Review, Other Voices,* and other periodicals.

SIDELIGHTS: Tom House was raised in East Islip, Long Island where he attended Catholic school as a child, and he uses this familiar setting as the backdrop for in his well-received debut novel, *The Beginning of Calamities.* The novel takes place in the 1970s, as fifth-grader Danny Burke completes his Easter play titled *The Passion and Resurrection of Christ.* When Danny's young teacher, Liz Kaigh learns about the accomplishment, she is quick to scoop it up as an opportunity for her class to perform. However, the more popular students in Danny's class reject the idea of performing the play, leaving Danny and a leftover collection of oddballs to compose the cast. While their teacher refers to herself as "Queen of the Lepers", comical problems soon begin to arise. The chosen narrator has a terrible lisp, and the young girl playing Mary Magdalene is cut from the play at the last minute due to her mother's mortification that her daughter will be playing a prostitute. Meanwhile Danny has increasingly begun to identify with the lead character of Christ through his vilification and nudity, and he discovers a newfound freedom in the possibility in he himself might be gay. In an effort to obtain the lead role for himself, Danny concocts a plan to sabotage the other Jesus candidates, however he must first overcome his incredible shyness and tendency to stutter before he can take the stage. In addition to his own personal differences, Danny must deal with the negative effects of his Valium addicted mother Carol, whose vocal lack of faith in her son leads her to push him to take a minor role in the play.

While acknowledging the limitations of House's first novel, several critics were enthusiastic about his sensitive coming-of-age story. A reviewer for *Publishers Weekly* noted of *The Beginning of Calamities* that while "House writes with a sure hand about Danny's loneliness and longing, he never quite gets the novel's comic pacing right." Other critics found more to like in the novel, a contributor to *Kirkus Reviews* stated that the author's penchant for "underlying sarcasm leaves an aftertaste of wistful cynicism." Maureen Neville, writing in *Library Journal,* also complimented House's fiction debut and praised him as an "accomplished" author of short fiction. "Mixing pathos,

irreverence, and a sense of befuddled impending doom," Neville maintained, *The Beginning of Calamities* acts as an "emotional roller coaster ride—one that makes the curious reader hold on until the final pages." While noting that the "unexplained, unrealistic absence of Danny's father from all semblance of family life" is problematic, C. Kevin Smith nonetheless praised House's debut as "enjoyable, well-written, and original," adding in his *Lambda Book Report* review that the play's the thing: "in the laborious, often hilarious, process of the play's advance from conception to performance" House creates "a metaphor for the continuous drama of childhood." In *The Beginning of Calamities,* the critic concluded, the reader discovers "true passion in the imagination of childhood—the inseparable rapture of faith and desire."

Discussing the craft of fiction writing in an interview with Jeffery Obser for the *East Hampton Star,* House commented: "Usually I write about embarrassment. Whenever someone feels humiliated, it indicates strong things are going on that make good fiction."

BIOGRAPHICAL AND CRITICAL SOURCES:

PERIODICALS

Booklist, June 1, 1987.
Kirkus Reviews, April 15, 2003, review of *The Beginning of Calamities,* p. 559.
Lambda Book Report, December, 2003, C. Kevin Smith, "Passion Play," p. 18.
Library Journal, April 15, 2003, Maureen Neville, review of *The Beginning of Calamities,* p. 122.
Publishers Weekly, April 28, 2003, review of *The Beginning of Calamities,* p. 46.

ONLINE

Tom House Web site, http://www.HouseStories.net (April 5, 2004).*

*   *   *

HUCHTHAUSEN, Peter 1939-

PERSONAL: Born 1939.

ADDRESSES: Agent—c/o Author Mail, Viking Press, 375 Hudson Street, New York, NY 10014.

CAREER: U.S. Navy, retired 1990; commanded River Patrol Section in Vietnam War; served as U.S. Naval Attaché in Yugoslavia, Romania, and Soviet Union.

WRITINGS:

(With Nguyen Thi Lung) *Echoes of the Mekong,* Nautical and Aviation Publishing Co. of America (Baltimore, MD), 1996.

(With Igor Kurdin and R. Alan White) *Hostile Waters,* St. Martin's Press (New York, NY), 1997.

Frye Island: Maine's Newest Town, a History, 1748-1998, Heritage Books (Bowie, MD), 1998.

K-19: The Widowmaker: The Secret Story of the Soviet Nuclear Submarine, National Geographic Books (Washington, DC), 2002.

October Fury, John Wiley & Sons (Hoboken, NJ), 2002.

America's "Splendid" Little Wars: A Short History of U.S. Military Engagements, 1975-2000, Viking (New York, NY), 2003.

ADAPTATIONS: Hostile Waters and *K-19: The Widowmaker: The Secret Story of the Soviet Nuclear Submarine,* were both made into motion pictures.

SIDELIGHTS: A retired naval officer and Vietnam veteran, Peter Huchthausen also served as an attaché in various East European capitals, where he met a number of his Russian counterparts in one of the most dramatic Soviet-American confrontations, the Cuban Missile Crisis. Since retirement from the navy, he has drawn on his military and diplomatic experiences to write about some dramatic incidents in Cold War history, including the sinking of the Soviet submarine, K-19.

Five years after graduating from the Naval Academy, Huchthausen found himself commanding a riverboat on the Mekong in Vietnam. On one patrol he and his crew rescued a wounded ten-year-old girl, Nguyen Thi Lung. The crew adopted her, paying for her health care and then her schooling, but eventually they lost touch with her. Many years later, Nguyen was able to get in touch with Huchthausen and, under his sponsorship, arrange to immigrate to the U.S. The two collaborated on *Echoes of the Mekong,* "a small gem of a dual memoir in which [Huchthausen and Lung] tell amazing, intersecting tales of war and peace," in the

words of a *Kirkus Reviews* contributor. Huchthausen took part in some of the most fearsome fighting, including the American response to the catastrophic Tet Offensive. Lung survived the war, only to face constant threats from vengeful North Vietnamese eager to hunt down an American "collaborator." "The key to this book's freshness is the respective naiveté of its main characters. In the end, the two seem to have retained something of their innocence despite all their fearful experiences—a characteristic somewhat unusual in personal narratives about this tragic war," noted *Naval War College Review* contributor Robert Shenk.

Huchthausen followed up with another interesting collaboration, this time with Soviet naval officer Igor Kurdin and thriller writer R. Alan White. They tell the story of K-219 in *Hostile Waters,* "a riveting account . . . of a hell-and-high-water incident toward the Cold War's end, in which a missile-bearing Soviet submarine sank within a few hundred miles of North Carolina," in the words of a *Kirkus Reviews* contributor. Suffering the usual bad maintenance of late-Soviet-era, the nuclear submarine K-219 still patrolled the Atlantic coast of the U.S. After one of the missile silos springs a leak, Soviet Captain Igor Britanov faces lethal gas, the loss of both of his reactors, and a fire belowdecks. Moscow wants him to salvage the sub, risking an explosion that would have flooded the East Coast with deadly radiation. Instead, he scuttles his sub, under the watchful eyes of the U.S. Navy. Drawing on interviews, declassified documents, and their own naval experiences, the authors tell the story of this dramatic incident, and the subsequent court martial of the officers. "Captain Britanov and the men of K-219 emerge from these exciting, occasionally melodramatic, pages as legitimate heroes in a real-life struggle with the sea, their superiors, and their system," wrote a *Publishers Weekly* reviewer. The book became the basis for an HBO movie in the summer of 1997.

A few years later, Peter Huchthausen served as technical advisor on *K-19: The Widowmaker,* a major motion picture depicting the tale of another doomed Soviet submarine, this one at the height of the Cold War in 1961. Huchthausen's companion book, *K-19: The Widowmaker: The Secret Story of the Soviet Nuclear Submarine,* again tells the dramatic tale of submarine crew struggling to fend off a meltdown that could set off a world war, in the face of dangerous interference from Moscow. "This well-researched-and-written book tells a captivating story that could not have been told a few years ago," wrote *Library Journal* reviewer Mark Ellis.

Huchthausen has established a reputation as a careful researcher and interviewer in bringing to life two Soviet submarine accidents that might have set off a world war. But he himself was a participant in one of the Cold War's most dramatic, and dangerous, incidents—the Cuban Missile Crisis. While a great deal has been written about the Kennedy-Kruschev standoff, most of these accounts focus on the politicians and the diplomats. *October Fury* tells the story of the actual participants in Kennedy's blockade of Cuba—the sailors. Based on an antisubmarine destroyer, Huchthausen experienced and recounts all the tension of a force trying to prevent the Russians from getting through, while avoiding any incident that would set off open war. And once again, he draws on the recollections of Soviet submariners to provide a view from below the waves, including Soviet officers who were authorized to launch nuclear-tipped missiles if necessary. "Huchthausen succeeds admirably in portraying sympathetically the sailors who would have been the first to die if war had been declared," concluded *Library Journal* reviewer Karl Helicher.

BIOGRAPHICAL AND CRITICAL SOURCES:

PERIODICALS

Booklist, July, 2003, Roland Green, review of *America's "Splendid" Little Wars: A Short History of U.S. Military Engagements, 1975-2000*, p. 1859.

Kirkus Reviews, December 1, 1995, review of *Echoes of the Mekong*, p. 1683, June 15, 1997, review of *Hostile Waters*, p. 928; May 15, 2003, review of *America's "Splendid" Little Wars*, p. 729.

Library Journal, September 15, 2002, Mark Ellis, review of *K-19: The Widowmaker*, p. 76, September 15, 2002, Karl Helicher, review of *October Fury*, p. 76; July, 2003, Mark E. Ellis, review of *America's "Splendid" Little Wars*, p. 103.

Naval War College Review, autumn, 1998, Robert Shenk, review of *Echoes of the Mekong*, pp. 138-139.

Publishers Weekly, July 14, 1997, review of *Hostile Waters*, p. 76; May 26, 2003, review of *America's "Splendid" Little Wars*, p. 63.*

HUNTLEY, Paula (Bowlin) 1944-

PERSONAL: Born December 31, 1944, in Little Rock, AR; daughter of Paul Richard (a business owner) and Rosemary (a librarian and homemaker; maiden name, Rhodes) Bowlin; married Edwin S. Villmoare, III (a law professor); children: (first marriage) Paul Robert Wrapp; (stepsons) Brian, Paul. *Education:* Lindenwood University, B.A. (history), 1966; Southern Methodist University, M.A. (history), 1971.

ADDRESSES: Home—P.O. Box 318, Bolinas, CA 94924. *Agent*—Lorraine Kisly, Shickshinny, PA. *E-mail*—paula@bookclubofkosovo.com.

CAREER: English teacher and marketing consultant.

WRITINGS:

The Hemingway Book Club of Kosovo (memoir), Jeremy P. Tarcher (New York, NY), 2003.

SIDELIGHTS: Paula Huntley's memoir *The Hemingway Book Club of Kosovo* is based on the journal she kept during the nearly one year, from 2000 to 2001, that she lived in Prishtina, Kosovo. Her intention was not to write a book; rather, she wanted to document every minute spent there. She carried notebooks during the day, jotting down conversations and facts, and transferred them to her computer at night. She was convinced to publish her writings when she returned to the United States.

She accompanied her husband, who had volunteered for an American Bar Association project to help create a new legal system, and Huntley, who had been an English teacher decades earlier, prepared herself beforehand to teach English as a second language, so that she would also have something to offer the people of that war-torn country where North Atlantic Treaty Organization (NATO) peacekeeping forces continued to patrol.

Teaching materials were nearly nonexistent, so when Huntley found a copy of *The Old Man and the Sea*, she photocopied it and began a book club for her Albanian students, who ranged in age from fifteen years to middle age. She found that they were quick to identify with the protagonist in Ernest Hemingway's tale, and when they finished it, Huntley introduced them to other American writers. Jesse Oxfeld quoted Huntley in a *Book* review as noting, "The book club began to come into the class, and the class became the club." Huntley became close to many of her students as a result of this extra effort and the trust and caring that grew between them.

A *Publishers Weekly* reviewer wrote that "Huntley's journal not only shares their stories, but reminds readers that by volunteering, people get back more than they give." Melissa Brown reviewed the book for *Bookreporter.com,* finding that "Huntley is the epitome of a great teacher—one who goes above and beyond the call of duty to help her students succeed."

Huntley heard the stories of her students, of torture, rape, and killings committed by the Serbians, and of the refugee camps. She observes the poverty that continues to engulf the population of the Yugoslavian province, and she relates what she was told about the apartheid of the 1990s and Slobodan Milosevic's ethnic cleansing of Albania Muslims from 1998-99, which left 10,000 civilians dead and 860,000 homeless.

In an interview with Huntley published on the *Penguin Putnam* Web site, she was asked why Hemingway's book worked so well. She replied, "It's a fable of the triumph of hope and courage over adversity. For the students, the book was the story of their personal lives, of their country. . . . My students also loved the old man's relationship with the young boy." That mentoring relationship, she felt, made them think about the ones they share with "the older people in their families, whom they revere. They spoke to me of their grandparents, their older aunts and uncles, who had come through the years of apartheid and ethnic cleansing with 'eyes that were cheerful and undefeated.'" Huntley returned home in April 2001, but remains in touch with Kosovar friends through email.

In a review for *Hope* magazine, Sara Terry wrote that "while her sympathies are clearly with her students, Huntley still challenges their blanket hatred of Serbs and their desire to have a mono-ethnic country, ruled by and for Albanians." Terry said that "she also displays a humble self-knowledge often lacking among internationals at work in post-conflict situations," and added, "Huntley offers no solutions, no analysis. But what does light this book is her persistent faith in the power of connectedness, of nurturing the human spirit, of the obligations that we, as human beings, have to one another."

Star-Telegram Online contributor Lev Raphael stated that *The Hemingway Book Club of Kosovo* "makes for gripping, heartbreaking reading," and described it as "a book that is stirring and nearly impossible to put down."

BIOGRAPHICAL AND CRITICAL SOURCES:

BOOKS

Huntley, Paula, *The Hemingway Book Club of Kosovo,* Jeremy P. Tarcher (New York, NY), 2003.

PERIODICALS

Book, January-February, 2003, Jesse Oxfeld, review of *The Hemingway Book Club of Kosovo,* p. 31.
Booklist, February 1, 2003, Elsa Gaztambide, review of *The Hemingway Book Club of Kosovo,* p. 965.
Hope, March-April, 2003, Sara Terry, review of *The Hemingway Book Club of Kosovo.*
Kirkus Reviews, January 1, 2003, review of *The Hemingway Book Club of Kosovo,* p. 40.
Library Journal, February 1, 2003, Mary V. Welk, review of *The Hemingway Book Club of Kosovo,* p. 104.
Publishers Weekly, December 16, 2002, review of *The Hemingway Book Club of Kosovo,* pp. 52-53.

ONLINE

Bookreporter.com, http://www.bookreporter.com/ (July 7, 2003), Melissa Brown, review of *The Hemingway Book Club of Kosovo.*
Paula Huntley Home Page, http://www.hemingway bookclubofkosovo.com (October 28, 2003).
Penguin Putnam, http://www.penguinputnam.com/ (July 7, 2003), interview with Paula Huntley.
Star-Telegram Online (Dallas-Fort Worth), http://www. dfw.com/ (March 2, 2003), Lev Raphael, review of *The Hemingway Book Club of Kosovo.**

J

JACOBS, George 1927-

PERSONAL: Born 1927, in New Orleans, LA.

ADDRESSES: Home—Palm Springs, FL. *Agent*—c/o Author Mail, HarperCollins, 10 East 53rd St., 7th Fl., New York, NY 10012.

CAREER: Valet for Frank Sinatra, 1953-68; master chef and carpenter.

WRITINGS:

(With William Stadiem) *Mr. S: My Life with Frank Sinatra,* HarperEntertainment (New York, NY), 2003.

SIDELIGHTS: George Jacobs waited a long time to finally publish his biography *Mr. S: My Life with Frank Sinatra.* While employed by noted American singer and actor Frank Sinatra as his valet and self-proclaimed right-hand man between 1953 and 1968, Jacobs saw everything: the good, the bad, and the ugly. "George was like one of the Rat Pack. Frank took him everywhere," stated William Stadiem, who co-wrote the book with Jacobs. Rumor has it that Jacobs waited as long as he did to publish his book because of threats from Sinatra's lawyer, who died in 1999. In his book he provides Sinatra fans and critics alike with a "fuller understanding of the object of their fascination," according to Mike Tribby in *Booklist.*

Jacobs came into Sinatra's employ as the singer's career was rebounding following his Oscar-winning role in the 1952 film *From Here to Eternity,* and he continued to work for Sinatra for more than thirteen years. During this period he bore witness to Sinatra's rise to power and fame, as the entertainer associated with beautiful Hollywood starlets like Ava Gardner, Marlene Dietrich, and Greta Garbo as well as future president John F. Kennedy and several Mafia members. Among the many stories he tells, Jacobs recounts romantic affairs between Sinatra and starlets like Marilyn Monroe and Lauren Bacall, and maintains that he witnessed Kennedy take cocaine with British actor Peter Lawford, a member of the famed Rat Pack. Jacobs did more than act as Sinatra's chauffeur; he also often found himself entertaining these very same high-profile guests himself. Aside from giving Kennedy a back massage, he danced with Monroe, drank with Ava Gardner, and even played jazz with the prince of Monaco—while Sinatra supposedly pursued Princess Grace.

In the end, it was because of his informal relationship with Sinatra that Jacobs lost his job. In 1968 public interest was once again shifting away from Sinatra; as his music grew less popular, he found himself in a troubled marriage to actress Mia Farrow while many of his mob friends were in jail or in exile. When a paparazzi photographed Jacobs dancing with Sinatra's wife at a popular Beverly Hills nightspot, Sinatra fired his chauffeur in a fit of anger.

Jacobs' overall tone in *Mr. S* is informative; as Mike Tribby noted in *Booklist,* his "main man comes off much better than in many other biographies," and a *Kirkus Reviews* contributor referred to the book as "Deliciously gossipy, yet Sinatra is recalled with affection rather than spite." "As close as I was, I couldn't miss these things," Jacobs notes in his book, which a *Publishers Weekly* contributor praised as a "mostly respectful portrait" but added: "One only wishes the book included more of Jacobs."

BIOGRAPHICAL AND CRITICAL SOURCES:

PERIODICALS

Book, May-June 2003, Patrick Beach, review of *Mr. S: My Life with Frank Sinatra,* p. 24.
Booklist, May 1, 2003, Mike Tribby, review of *Mr. S: My Life with Frank Sinatra,* p. 1563.
Kirkus Reviews, April 15, 2003, review of *Mr. S: My Life with Frank Sinatra,* p. 586.
Publishers Weekly, April 12, 2003, review of *Mr. S: My Life with Frank Sinatra.*

ONLINE

HarperCollins Web site, http://www.harpercollins.com/ (April 5, 2004).*

*   *   *

JACOBSON, Judy 1947-

PERSONAL: Born January 2, 1947, in Detroit, MI; daughter of James (an educational administrator) and Edith Arlene (Reynold) Mathieson; married Harry Jacobson, April 2, 1970; children: Todd, Jodi. *Education:* Eastern Michigan University, B.A., 1968.

ADDRESSES: Agent—c/o Author Mail, Clearfield Co., 200 East Eager St., Baltimore, MD 21202.

CAREER: Worked for public schools in Livonia, MI, and at Starkville Public Library, Starkville, MS; Mississippi State University, Mississippi State, worked at library; Oktibbeha County Heritage, Starkville, worked as museum curator.

MEMBER: American Association of Professional Genealogists, Starkville League of Women Voters (president), Daughters of the American Revolution.

WRITINGS:

Southold Connections, Clearfield (Baltimore, MD), 1991.
Massachusetts Bay Connections, Clearfield (Baltimore, MD), 1992.
Detroit River Connections, Clearfield (Baltimore, MD), 1994.
A Genealogist's Refresher Course, Clearfield (Baltimore, MD), 1995, 2nd edition, 1996.
Alabama and Mississippi Connections, Clearfield (Baltimore, MD), 1999.
A Field Guide for Genealogists, Clearfield (Baltimore, MD), 2001.

*   *   *

JARRETT, (John) Derek 1928-2004

OBITUARY NOTICE—See index for *CA* sketch: Born March 18, 1928, in Whyteleafe, Surrey, England; died March 28, 2004, in Truro, England. Historian, educator, and author. Jarrett was an authority on eighteenth-century England and France and was most recently acclaimed for editing Horace Walpole's *Memoirs of the Reign of King George III.* After serving in the Royal Air Force during World War II, he earned a B.A. at Keble College, Oxford, in 1951, followed by a B.Litt. and M.A. in 1955. The next year, Jarrett took a post as senior history master at Sherborne School, where he remained until 1964. He then joined the University of London's Goldsmith's College. Beginning work there as a lecturer in eighteenth-century British history, Jarrett rose to the position of principal lecturer in history in 1971. Fascinated by the inextricable relationship between Britain and France over the centuries, Jarrett's first book, *Britain: 1688-1815* (1965), became a standard textbook on the subject. He followed this with more history works, such as *Begetters of Revolution: England's Involvement with France, 1759-1789* (1973), *The Ingenious Mr. Hogarth* (1976), and *Three Faces of Revolution: Paris, London, and New York in 1789* (1989). His last work was the ambitious edition of Walpole's *Memoirs of the Reign of King George III* (1999), which many critics have considered a masterful work of scholarship.

OBITUARIES AND OTHER SOURCES:

PERIODICALS

Independent (London, England), April 1, 2004, p. 34.
Times (London, England), May 10, 2004, p. 29.

JOHNSON, Donald S. 1932-

PERSONAL: Born 1932.

ADDRESSES: Home—Boydens Lake Rd., Perry, ME 04667.

CAREER: Sailor, writer. University of Southern Maine, Portland, ME, guest curator of Smith Center for Cartographic Education Osher Map Library nautical exhibition *Charting Neptune's Realm: From Classical Mythology to Satellite Imagery,* 2000-01.

WRITINGS:

Charting the Sea of Darkness: The Four Voyages of Henry Hudson, International Marine (Camden, ME), 1993.
Phantom Islands of the Atlantic, Goose Lane (Fredericton, New Brunswick, Canada), 1994, revised edition published as *Phantom Islands of the Atlantic: The Legends of Seven Lands that Never Were,* Walker and Co. (New York, NY), 1996.
La Salle: A Perilous Odyssey from Canada to the Gulf of Mexico, Cooper Square Press (New York, NY), 2002.

Contributor to maritime magazines and journals, including *Ocean Navigator, Practical Boat Owner,* and *Sea History.*

SIDELIGHTS: Sailor Donald S. Johnson has crossed the Atlantic Ocean five times in a twenty-seven foot sailboat and has written several books of maritime history. Among them are *Charting the Sea of Darkness: The Four Voyages of Henry Hudson,* called "an excellent account" by Clarence J. Murphy in *Science Books & Films.* Johnson notes that only four years of Hudson's life can be accounted for. In addition, no likeness of Hudson has survived to give us a clue as to his appearance. Johnson introduces the book by explaining the search by the English and the Dutch for a northwest or northeast passage to the Orient. He also notes the earlier voyages of explorers that include the Cabots, Cartier, Frobisher, and Davis.

Johnson devotes one chapter each to the four voyages taken by Hudson beginning in 1607. Each chapter has a prologue and a journal that contains excerpts from the third book of Samuel Purchas's *Purchas His Pilgrims,* published in London in 1625. This book includes portions of Hudson's original logs and those of his mate, Robert Juet, and a passenger, Abacuck Prickett. Next comes an epilogue that discusses the voyage and the journal, and finally, a concluding piece contains maps and illustrations. Hudson's ship, the *Half Moon,* is described in the appendices, as are North Atlantic currents and statistics regarding boat speed and distances. On the *Half Moon,* which was amazingly small, just sixty-five feet long and fourteen feet wide, Hudson and his crew endured bad weather, unsanitary conditions, and inadequate and spoiled food.

Johnson draws from the journals and logs in studying the explorations of the waterway now known as the Hudson River. These documents reflect Hudson's admiration for the Native Americans he met, but also show that he was liberal in supplying them with alcohol and in kidnapping them. Douglas A. Sylva noted in the *New York Times Book Review* that Johnson "also recounts Hudson's growing obsession with locating a northwest passage, an obsession that ultimately led to mutiny in 1610." Hudson died when he, his son, and a handful of sick sailors were set adrift in a small boat.

Phantom Islands of the Atlantic was revised and reprinted as *Phantom Islands of the Atlantic: The Legends of Seven Lands that Never Were.* The seven islands were figments of the imaginations of voyagers and navigators disoriented by storm or fog, mistaking their position when they made landfall without benefit of navigational instrumentation. These fictional islands, along with sightings of monsters of the deep, were added to early maps. Johnson provides a history of these seven islands, which include the Isle of Demons, supposedly located off Newfoundland and populated by mythical creatures, St. Brendan, named for a sixth-century Irish monk, and an island named for fifth-century St. Ursula, whose traveling companions were 11,000 virgins. Other missing islands are Frisland, Buss Island, the Isle of Seven Cities, and Hy-Brazil, supposedly off the coast of Ireland.

A *Publishers Weekly* contributor wrote that "this admirably researched and well-written account, with numerous maps and illustrations, vividly illustrates how interesting the often-overlooked science of geography can be." "There are plenty of good stories here," remarked John Kenny in *Library Journal.* Amelie Southwood wrote in the *New York Times Book Review* that "the legends behind the phantom islands . . . are fascinating."

Rene-Robert Cavalier, Sieur de la Salle was the seventeenth-century explorer who is the subject of Johnson's *La Salle: A Perilous Odyssey from Canada to the Gulf of Mexico.* La Salle was the first to navigate the Mississippi River from the Great Lakes to the Gulf of Mexico, thereby taking claim to a huge section of North America that he named Louisiana. Johnson documents the European effort to control this continent and provides new information about La Salle's other expeditions on the Ohio River and in Texas and his last, during which he was killed by his men after failing to reach the mouth of the Mississippi from the Caribbean. Information recovered with the discovery of La Salle's ship *Belle* in 1995 now brings that history into view.

Johnson was guest curator of the nautical exhibit *Charting Neptune's Realm: From Classical Mythology to Satellite Imagery,* offered by the University of Southern Maine's Smith Center for Cartographic Education. The exhibit ran until 2001 but remains available at the Osher Map Library Web site.

BIOGRAPHICAL AND CRITICAL SOURCES:

PERIODICALS

Booklist, December 15, 1996, Brad Hooper, review of *Phantom Islands of the Atlantic: The Legends of Seven Lands that Never Were,* p. 697.

Library Journal, December, 1996, John Kenny, review of *Phantom Islands of the Atlantic,* p. 130; October 1, 2002, Margaret Atwater-Singer, review of *La Salle: A Perilous Odyssey from Canada to the Gulf of Mexico,* p. 113.

New York Times Book Review, January 3, 1993, Douglas A. Sylva, review of *Charting the Sea of Darkness: The Four Voyages of Henry Hudson,* p. 14; February 16, 1997, Amelie Southwood, review of *Phantom Islands of the Atlantic,* p. 19.

Publishers Weekly, October 14, 1996, review of *Phantom Islands of the Atlantic,* p. 69.

Science Books & Films, May, 1993, Clarence J. Murphy, review of *Charting the Sea of Darkness,* p. 105.

ONLINE

University of Southern Maine, Smith Center for Cartographic Education, Osher Map Library Web site, http://usm.maine.edu/maps (August 15, 2003).*

*   *   *

JOHNSON, Doug(las A.) 1952-

PERSONAL: Born July 29, 1952, in Sac City, IA; son of Darrell (a crop duster and farmer) and Joan (a carpenter and homemaker; maiden name, Gotsch) Johnson; married Anne M. Hanson (a library media specialist), February 14, 2002; children: Carrie Ann Johnson Roberts, Brady Allan. *Ethnicity:* "Caucasian." *Education:* University of Northern Colorado, B.A., 1976; University of Iowa, M.A., 1979.

ADDRESSES: Home—46813 Cape Horn Rd., Cleveland, MN 56017. *Office*—Mankato Area Public Schools, 1351 South Riverfront Dr., Mankato, MN 56002-8713. *E-mail*—dougj@doug-johnsoncom.

CAREER: Stuart-Menlo Schools, Stuart, IA, English teacher, 1976-78; West Branch Schools, West Branch, IA, English teacher and librarian, 1979-84; Aramco Schools, Dhahran, Saudi Arabia, library media specialist, 1984-89; St. Peter Schools, St. Peter, MN, library media specialist, 1989-91; Mankato Area Public Schools, Mankato, MN, director of media and technology, 1991—. Minnesota State University—Mankato, adjunct faculty member. Mankato Downtown Kiwanis, member.

MEMBER: International Society for Technology in Education, American Association of School Librarians, Minnesota Educational Media Organization.

WRITINGS:

The Indispensable Librarian: Surviving (and Thriving) in School Media Centers in the Information Age, Linworth Publishing (Worthington, OH), 1997.

The Indispensable Teacher's Guide to Computer Skills, Linworth Publishing (Worthington, OH), 2002.

Teaching Right from Wrong in the Digital Age, Linworth Publishing (Worthington, OH), 2003.

Author of "Head for the Edge," a column in *Library Media Connection.*

WORK IN PROGRESS: Revising *The Indispensable Librarian: Surviving (and Thriving) in School Media Centers in the Information Age.*

SIDELIGHTS: Doug Johnson told *CA:* "Why do I write for publication? Well, of course I write for the big bucks, huge prestige, and pure adulation of millions of fans. While the limousines, champagne on first-class flights, and attractive strangers constantly opening their bank accounts and boudoirs to me gets tiresome, having my own line of fashion apparel saves me from having to shop for clothes. Oh, sorry, I got lost in fantasy for a moment.

"I write for publication because I have to write anyway. Much of what I write about comes from dealing with challenges at my day job as media and technology director for Mankato Public Schools. As a part of making an effective media program work, tools need to be developed, policies written, programs planned, and philosophies clarified. Things seem to run better in my district when they are written down in black and white. Problems, new projects, and good questions from students, staff, and the public all require that I write about them, even if it is only to help me clarify my own thinking. I also figure that, if I am struggling with an issue, others may be as well.

"Writing keeps me current. There is no incentive like knowing others will be reading what one has written to force one to stay current on technologies and trends in education. I like reading futurists, and it's a real challenge to try to figure out the implications of their predictions for my school and profession. While I was never much for doing 'research' in high school or college, using information to find solutions to problems is actually interesting. I still detest having to write footnotes, however.

"Writing helps me keep my day job (I think). I mess up on my job a lot. Anyone who really tries out new methods of teaching and working should be expected to fail on a regular basis. (If you don't, you are probably not reaching far enough.) So every now and then, it is nice to be able to slip an article or column to the superintendent, board member, or even my own staff. I hope they think, 'Gee, others think this guy has some credibility. Maybe he isn't as crazy as I think he is.'

"Publishing returns the favor to others from whom I have borrowed. I have learned so much from the people I consider to be the real experts in media and technology. A partial list includes Loertscher, Eisenberg, Simpson, Berger, Batton, Haycock, Donham, Jukes, McKenzie, and a whole raft more. And it isn't just the big dogs who help me. I steal my best ideas from practicing media specialists and technologists who speak at conferences, write for journals, and contribute to *LM_Net.* I am a great believer in the 'stone soup' mentality. When everyone contributes to the pot, the soup is richer for it.

"I write knowing that I've helped someone. It's the rare conference or week of e-mails when I don't get a thank-you from a media specialist or technologist to tell me they have been able to somehow use what I've written. Whether it is a tool that someone has found effective, the description of a plan that someone has gotten to work in his or her district, or a column that persuaded a local decision-maker, wonderful people come forward to say thank you. It makes all the sunny mornings I spend writing instead of playing worth it. Thanks back to you.

"I write because I'm on a mission from God. Heaven knows that nobody goes into education (or writes for it) to make money. As educators, our satisfaction comes from actually believing we are doing something that will make the world a more humane place in which to live. The ultimate goal of professional writing is to improve professional practice that in turn improves the lives of kids. I not only encourage, but I expect all members of our profession to write for publication. While it may never improve your bank account, you'll get jewels in your crown for lighting those lamps against darkness and hell. And please, toss in a little humor and poetry when you do."

* * *

JONES, Solomon 1969(?)-

PERSONAL: Born c. 1969 in Philadelphia, PA; married; children: one daughter. *Education:* Temple University, B.A. (cum laude), 1998.

ADDRESSES: Agent—c/o Author Mail, St. Martin's Press, 175 Fifth Ave., New York, NY 10010. *E-mail*—info@solomonjones.com.

CAREER: Philadelphia Weekly, Philadelphia, PA, senior contributing editor; Salvation Army of Eastern Pennsylvania and Delaware, former regional director of public relations; Philadelphia Committee to End Homelessness, former director of development and outreach; Calvary Baptist Church of Philadelphia, volunteer public relations director.

WRITINGS:

Pipe Dream, Random House (New York, NY), 2001.
The Bridge, St. Martin's Press (New York, NY), 2003.

Contributor to *Philadelphia Inquirer, Philadelphia Magazine,* and *Philadelphia Tribune.*

SIDELIGHTS: Solomon Jones has written two novels set in the urban decay of big city America. His first novel, *Pipe Dream,* draws on his own past as a drug addict to present a story of a police frame-up, while in *The Bridge* a young girl goes missing from a Philadelphia housing project. "Jones, who grew up in the Philadelphia projects and knows his subject well, is a talent to watch," a critic for *Publishers Weekly* contended. In the early 1990s, Jones was a crack addict who was living in the streets. A chance opportunity to write a story for a newspaper aimed at the homeless led to his being hired at the *Philadelphia Inquirer.* He is currently a recovered addict and a staff member of the *Philadelphia Weekly.*

Pipe Dream begins with the murder of a crusading Puerto Rican city councilman in a Philadelphia crack house. Accused are four crack addicts who happened to be on the scene when the shooting occurred. They quickly find themselves hunted by the police even though they are innocent of the crime. Their efforts to avoid capture and wrongful conviction are recounted by Samuel Everett "Black" Jackson, one of the accused addicts, in a statement made to his lawyer before trial. "The chase is compelling," a critic for *Publishers Weekly* noted, "but even more involving is the way Jones slowly reveals each character's story, presenting in convincing and heartbreaking detail how each was sucked into dead-end addiction." "There are in-your-face scenes of scams, set-ups, burglaries, shootings and blackmail," according to Anthony C. Davis in the *Black Issues Book Review.* "This book is like a train wreck: It's a ghoulish scene, but hard to look away

from." Reviewing *Pipe Dream* for *Booklist,* Wes Lukowsky called the novel "a shocking, visceral portrayal of the crackhead's world—a nightmare of desperate need, constant despair, and hovering death."

The world of crack addiction is familiar to Jones. He explained in an "Author Q and A" posted on the *Random House Web site* that "the idea for *Pipe Dream* came from my own experience with crack addiction. For a number of years I struggled on and off with an addiction that I never thought would suck me in the way that it did. There were times when my addiction left me homeless for weeks or months at a time. There were times when nothing was more important than getting that next hit. So the idea for the novel was there, imbedded in my own experiences." Speaking to Steve Baltin in *Venice* online, Jones admitted: "*Pipe Dream* helped me look at my addiction, what it did to the people around me, and the community in general."

In *The Bridge* Jones tells the story of nine-year-old Kenya Brown, the daughter of a recovering addict mother, who goes missing from Philadelphia's East Bridge Housing Project. Detective Kevin Lynch, who grew up in the housing project, and Roxanne Wilson, a black single mother, are the officers assigned to the case. The prime suspect seems to be a suspected child abuser, Sonny Williams, who is the boyfriend of Kenya's drug-dealing aunt Judy. But when Sonny cannot be found, the ensuing search for him leads to larger political implications. "Like a rock dropped in a pond," Keir Graff stated in *Booklist,* "the crime has effects that ripple outward to encompass other building residents, then other Philly projects, then the whole city." "This tale," Harriet Klausner remarked in an online review for *BooksnBytes,* "has a deeper message about an abundant society ignoring abject poverty and its consequences." Rex Klett in the *Library Journal* praised "Jones's authentic dialog, gritty sketches of crack dens and project buildings, and amazing character interactions."

BIOGRAPHICAL AND CRITICAL SOURCES:

PERIODICALS

Black Issues Book Review, July, 2001, Anthony C. Davis, review of *Pipe Dream,* p. 32.
Booklist, May 1, 2001, Wes Lukowsky, review of *Pipe Dream,* p. 1636; March 15, 2003, Keir Graff, review of *The Bridge,* p. 1279.

Kirkus Reviews, March 1, 2003, review of *The Bridge,* p. 335.

Library Journal, October 1, 2001, Robert A. Berger, review of *Pipe Dream,* p. 140; April 1, 2003, Rex Klett, review of *The Bridge,* p. 134.

Publishers Weekly, July 9, 2001, review of *Pipe Dream,* p. 44; March 31, 2003, review of *The Bridge,* p. 45.

ONLINE

BooksnBytes.com, http://www.booksnbytes.com/ (October 1, 2003), Harriet Klausner, review of *The Bridge.*

Random House Web site, http://www.randomhouse. com/ (October 1, 2003), "Author Q and A."

Solomon Jones's Home Page, http://www.solomon jones.com (April 14, 2004).

Venice Online, http://www.venicemag.com/ (October 1, 2003), Steve Baltin, "Solomon Jones Confronts His Pipe Dream."*

*   *   *

JUSKA, Jane 1933(?)-

PERSONAL: Born c. 1933; married (divorced, 1972); children: Andy. *Hobbies and other interests:* Singing, hiking.

ADDRESSES: Home—Berkeley, CA. *Agent*—c/o Author Mail, Villard, Random House, 201 East 50th St., New York, NY 10022.

CAREER: Former high-school English teacher; volunteer teacher at San Quentin prison.

WRITINGS:

(Editor with Mary Ann Smith) *The Whole Story: Teachers Talk about Portfolios,* National Writing Project (Berkeley, CA), 2001.

A Round-heeled Woman: My Late-Life Adventures in Sex and Romance, Villard (New York, NY), 2003.

WORK IN PROGRESS: A book about her teaching career and the challenges of finding intellectually equal partners.

SIDELIGHTS: Jane Juska grew up in a small town in Ohio. Throughout her childhood she was raised to obey men, taking no thrill in her sexuality for fear of developing a bad reputation. However, at the age of sixty-seven, finding herself living in Berkeley, California, divorced from her first and only husband, and finally retiring from her long career as an English teacher, Juska decided to take control of her own sexual destiny. After realizing that all the volunteer commitments and art museums in the world could not fill the void of actual human touch, she decided to place a personal ad in the *New York Review of Books* in the fall of 1999. "Before I turn 67—next March—I would like to have a lot of sex with a man I like. If you want to talk first, Trollope works for me." Within a month's time she received sixty-three responses, and took a year to follow them up. She recorded her experiences of these encounters and published them as *A Round-heeled Woman: My Late-Life Adventures in Sex and Romance.*

Juska decided to weave her story in the form of a novel, believing that readers would find her story too fantastical to be true. In addition to recounting her numerous sexual encounters with men of varying characters, she also tells the story of her life: her small-town upbringing, her unhappy marriage and divorce, her alcoholism and weight gain. As a result of her ad, Juska finds herself entangled with men from age thirty-two to eighty four, from all walks of life, some charming and caring and others less amiable. In the end it was one of these male companions who convinced Juska to break free from a stifling writing group and write her book as an autobiography and true testament of her life.

Throughout her memoir Juska tells her tale with riveting honesty and a comedic air that engages readers. "Expressive and touching: readers will be rooting for Juska to get all that she wants," stated a reviewer for *Kirkus Reviews,* while Ilene Cooper in *Booklist* praised the novel as a "refreshingly honest, remarkably candid story" that illustrates "the courage shown by a round-heeled woman who decided it was time to pursue passion with a vengeance." Calling *A Round-heeled Woman* "wryly comic and bittersweet," *Library Journal* contributor Martha Cornog added that Juska comes across as an intellectual "Everywoman confronting the legendary meat market of romance."

BIOGRAPHICAL AND CRITICAL SOURCES:

PERIODICALS

Booklist, April 15, 2003, Ilene Cooper review of *A Round-heeled Woman: My Late-Life Adventures in Sex and Romance,* p. 1431.

Kirkus Reviews, February 15, 2003, review of *A Round-heeled Woman,* p. 285.

Library Journal, March 15, 2003, Martha Cornog review of *A Round-heeled Woman,* p. 91.

New York Times, April 27, 2003, Alex Witchel review of *A Round-heeled Woman.*

Publishers Weekly, March 3, 2003, review of *A Round-heeled Woman,* p. 62.

ONLINE

Salon.com, http://www.salon.com/ (June 6, 2003), Stephanie Zacharek, review of *A Round-heeled Woman.**

K

KACHTICK, Keith

PERSONAL: Born in TX. *Education:* Iowa Writer's Workshop. *Religion:* Buddhist.

ADDRESSES: Home—New York, NY. *Agent*—c/o Author Mail, HarperCollins, 10 East 53rd St., New York, NY 10022.

CAREER: Writer. Lineage Project, New York, NY, senior instructor.

WRITINGS:

Hungry Ghost: A Novel, HarperCollins (New York, NY), 2003.

Contributor to periodicals including *Esquire, Texas Monthly, New York Times Magazine,* and the *Missouri Review.*

SIDELIGHTS: Keith Kachtick is a practicing Buddhist. He is a senior intructor at the Lineage Project, a non-profit Dharma-based organization that runs meditation classes in youth prisons. Kachtick's writings have appeared in numerous periodicals and his first novel, *Hungry Ghost,* was published in 2003.

Hungry Ghost focuses on freelance photographer Carter Cox. Carter is thirty-nine-years old, a fledgling Buddhist, and full of bad habits, but longs to better his ways. He meets Mia Malone at a Buddhist retreat.

Mia is a twenty-six-year-old Catholic and determined to remain a virgin until she is married. Carter falls hard for Mia and convinces her to come on a photo shoot to Morocco with him. Although some reviewers felt that the second-person narrative of *Hungry Ghost* was hard to read, Joanne Wilkinson, a reviewer for *Booklist,* noted, "First-novelist Kachtick proves himself an inventive storyteller when he presents two versions of the trip to Morocco." In a review for the *New York Times,* Pico Iyer stated that Kachtick "writes with an assurance and verve that fling us without trepidation into the confusions of an earnest philanderer."

BIOGRAPHICAL AND CRITICAL SOURCES:

PERIODICALS

Booklist, April 1, 2003, Joanne Wilkinson, review of *Hungry Ghost,* p. 1378.
Kirkus Reviews, March 15, 2003, review of *Hungry Ghost,* p. 419.
Library Journal, May 1, 2003, Christine Perkins, review of *Hungry Ghost,* p. 156.
New York Times, July 27, 2003, Pico Iyer, review of *Hungry Ghost.*
Publishers Weekly, April 28, 2003, review of *Hungry Ghost,* p. 48.*

* * *

KAPLAN, Carter 1960-

PERSONAL: Born April 15, 1960, in KY; son of Sidney Joseph (a professor of sociology) and Patricia Ann (a book store manager; maiden name, Carter; later surname, Weiss) Kaplan. *Ethnicity:* "American." *Edu-*

cation: University of Toledo, B.A., M.A.; also earned Ph.D. *Politics:* "Jeffersonian." *Religion:* "Independent Presbyterian." *Hobbies and other interests:* Musical composition, mountain climbing, museums, looking at buildings, conversation.

ADDRESSES: Office—Mountain State University, Beckley, WV 25802. *E-mail*—kplnf@aol.com.

CAREER: Yeshiva University, New York, NY, adjunct assistant professor, 1997; College of St. Elizabeth, Morristown, NJ, assistant professor, 1998-99; Shippensburg University, Shippensburg, PA, assistant professor, 1999-2000; Mountain State University, Beckley, WV, associate professor of English and philosophy, 2001—. Architectural writer.

MEMBER: New Jersey College English Association (member of board of trustees, 1998-2002).

WRITINGS:

Critical Synoptics: Menippean Satire and the Analysis of Intellectual Mythology, Fairleigh Dickinson University Press (Madison, NJ), 2000.

WORK IN PROGRESS: A Greek play reminiscent of the comedy of Aristophanes; research on abstract thinking, approached from the perspective of Milton and Wittgenstein.

SIDELIGHTS: Carter Kaplan told *CA:* "Although I have written stories from childhood, I was first motivated to write seriously in my late teens after immersing myself in the fantastic tales of pulp writers from the thirties, particularly Robert E. Howard, Clarke Ashton Smith, and H. P. Lovecraft. Such examples led me to entertain notions of becoming a famous and reclusive fantasy writer, and I indulged visions of myself living in a Scottish castle with a mailbox overflowing with royalty checks. As I embarked upon these early projects, however, I discovered two things that prevented me from fulfilling my ambition: I disliked writing the sort of fantasy that is commercially viable; and I possessed a keen interest in philosophy that I was reluctant to control when it surfaced in my writing. Rather than the writers of generic fantasy, I found myself identifying strongly with people like Rabelais, Petronius, Mary Shelley, Wittgenstein, Swift, and Melville. What this meant for me was a year of frustrated attempts to write fantasy, followed by twenty years of producing material characterized by interweaving threads of multi-level thematic sophistication, misleading allusions, ultra-violent forays into psychological disaffection and detachment, and terse philosophical analysis. I suppose I style my work 'satire,' though I am earnest in striving for that modernist insinuation that whispers to the reader, 'Something new has been pioneered in this work of art you're now clutching, and you ought to bow down to it.'

"Such writing did not stuff my mailbox with royalty checks, nor did I find myself set to purchase that castle in Scotland, so instead I turned, ironically, to the university, which had been the very same target of some of my most vitriolic declamations. Not unlike that lesser species of rebel who 'bites the hand who feeds him,' I plugged along, taking my doctorate from one of the most undistinguished English programs in the country, and writing a dissertation (later to be revised and published as *Critical Synoptics: Menippean Satire and the Analysis of Intellectual Mythology*) that was an attack on the 'postmodern' university, thinly veiled as a study of satire. One of the chapters of this multi-genre work is taken from one of my novels, featuring a description of a 'well connected world class poet' who thrashes a gang of literary theorists with a prosthetic arm torn from the shoulder of a deconstructionist. What makes my graduate school period (which I describe as Ph.D. boot camp) particularly odd was the members of the English department itself, who stand in my memory as epitomizing a sort of conservative news-magazine columnist's nightmare of contemporary university clichés: tenured radicals, New Left nihilists, amoral Marxists in Volvos, and lower-middle-class bureaucratic thugs—the wilted flower of the Woodstock nation maintaining a sort of permanent adolescent siege from behind the ramparts of their pinched brows, fat jaws, maroon scarves, and baggy denim dungarees. Actually, their nihilism was a front, as were their orthodox left-wing pretensions. They were no more than simple, run-of-the-mill mad persons.

"Writing comes very easily to me, which is probably a reflection or a 'function' of the efforts of my parents, who read to me from the time I was a small child. I don't use notebooks or outlines, relying instead on my memory and the odd sentence or image that often returns to pester me, as if to say, 'Don't forget to write me down.' Most of my work consists in stringing such images together with a narrative of some kind, usually fast-paced. Verisimilitude and the suspension of disbelief are very important to me, and I've shied away from fantastic worlds and comic book heroes, instead creating wonderful effects through writing about eccentric and loquacious individuals who have credible—though improbable—adventures. Events that appear either fantastic or surreal early in a work are later explained away by providing rational explanations, after the technique of Mrs. Radcliffe in her gothic mysteries, or Jane Austen in *Northanger Abbey.* My latest work is a play, a Greek comedy after the style of Aristophanes."

* * *

KAUFMAN, Lynne

PERSONAL: Born in the Bronx, NY; married; husband's name, Steve (a physician), 1957; children: Dan, Jen. *Education:* Hunter College, B.A.; Columbia University, graduate degree.

ADDRESSES: Agent—Susan Gurman Agency, 865 West End Ave., #15A, New York, NY 10025.

CAREER: Playwright and author. University of California, Berkeley Extension, staff member for thirty years, became director of travel study programs.

AWARDS, HONORS: Will Glickman Playwriting Award and Best New Play Award, Bay Area Critics' Circle/*San Francisco Chronicle,* both for *The Couch;* New American Plays Award, Kennedy Center/National Endowment for the Arts, for *Speaking in Tongues;* Best New Play in California Award, Theaterworks, for *Our Lady of the Desert.*

WRITINGS:

PLAYS

The Couch (first produced in San Francisco, CA, at the Magic Theatre, 1985), Dramatist's Play Service, 1998.

Roshi, first produced in San Francisco, CA, 1987.
Speaking in Tongues, first produced in San Francisco, CA, at the Magic Theatre, 1989.
Our Lady of the Desert, first produced at Theatreworks (California), 1991.
Shooting Simone (first produced in Louisville, KY, at the Actors Theatre of Louisville, 1993), Dramatic Publishing, 1994.
Fifty/Fifty, first produced by the Theatre Artists of Marin (California), 1994.
Fakes, first produced at the Florida Studio Theatre, 1997.
The Last Game Show, first produced in Washington, DC, at Horizons Theatre, 2000.
The Next Marilyn, first produced at the Florida Studio Theatre, 2003.
Daisy in the Dreamtime, first produced in New York, NY, at the Abingdon Theatre, 2003.
Picasso, first produced in San Francisco, CA, 2003.

OTHER

Slow Hands (novel), Mira Books (New York, NY), 2003.
Wild Women's Weekend (novel), Mira Books (New York, NY), 2004.

Contributor to periodicals, including *Redbook, Cosmopolitan,* and *McCall's.*

SIDELIGHTS: Lynne Kaufman wrote short stories for more than ten years before concentrating on plays for nearly two decades. While at a 1980s conference on Jungian psychology, she was intrigued with the relationship between Jung, his wife, Emma, and his mistress, a young patient named Toni Laufer. The three traveled together, and the two women ran the Jung Society. Based upon this history, Kaufman wrote "Phallic Symbols," which drama critic Martin Esslin recommended for production at the Magic Theater, but with a title change: it became *The Couch.*

Bernard Weiner reviewed the play in the *San Francisco Chronicle,* noting that Kaufman "takes a whack at no less than Sigmund Freud and Carl Jung. The two genius psychoanalysts—the elderly Freud with his childhood-sex reductionism, the philandering forty-year-old Jung with his search for the godhead—are shown behaving like two eccentric and silly boys squabbling over possession of a prize marble." The critic added, "But what makes the play sing is the comedy to be mined in romantic and psychoanalytic disputes, not the important philosophical distinctions between Freud and Jung."

Kaufman followed *The Couch* with *Roshi,* a play about the changing lives of a group of graduating law students, including Sam, who chooses a Zen life over his girlfriend and a law career but who ultimately fails as leader of the religious community. *San Francisco Chronicle* critic Steven Winn wrote that "at one obvious level, *Roshi* can be read as a kind of parable about the dangers and corruptions of religious power—of any power once placed in the hands of a hubristic leader." Winn noted, however, that "it's not clear why Sam feels so drawn to the Zen life in the first place and whether it's mistaken ideology or mere opportunism that leads him to his misdeeds."

Speaking in Tongues, Kaufman's next play, finds Lucia, the daughter of James Joyce, attempting to seduce her father's assistant, Patrick Gregory. *Los Angeles Times* critic John Godfrey wrote that on one level the play "begs comparison to Tennessee Williams's *A Streetcar Named Desire.* Both plays deal with a protagonist woman struggling with her untapped sexuality, and in both plays, the protagonist's trauma leads to a complete mental breakdown."

The love affair of Simone de Beauvoir and Jean-Paul Sartre is the subject of the playwright's *Shooting Simone.* The couple were together for nearly their entire lives, but never married, in part because of his involvement with other women. In Kaufman's play, she focuses on the dynamic that develops when Beauvoir's country cousin, Olga, shows up in Paris. Sartre is smitten, but it is Beauvoir whom Olga seeks out. The play then fast forwards to 1980 and a journalist named Kate, who confronts de Beauvoir about her life as Kate prepares to shoot a documentary about her heroine.

More recent plays by Kaufman include *Fakes* and *The Last Game Show.* The former is set in Holland, during the years between 1937 and 1947, and is based on a true story. Hans Van Meegeren is a painter whose work has been dismissed by the critic Bredius. In order to exact his revenge, Van Meegeren, aided by his lover, the art dealer Caroline Haller, concocts a scheme to

embarrass Bredius. Van Meegeren paints a fake Vermeer that Bredius declares a masterpiece. But Van Meegeren's ego comes into play, and he continues painting forgeries, which end up in the collection of Hermann Goering, Hitler's minister of culture. *The Last Game Show* is set in purgatory. The premise is that the winner of a game show will gain entry to heaven, while the loser goes to hell. The contestants are Martin Heidegger, father of existential phenomenology, and Hannah Arendt, author of *Origins of Totalitarianism. Washington Post* contributor Nelson Pressley noted that "Alex and Luna, the show's hosts ... ironically grill the philosophers with the same holier-than-thou attitude that Heidegger and Arendt sometimes used in their careers.... And the game's ruthless either/or format—winner/loser, truth/lie—is terrific at weeding out equivocations and moral inconsistencies."

In Kaufman's debut novel, *Slow Hands,* two sisters inherit one million dollars from their mother, who has attached the condition that they open a business together. After pondering where to put the money, Sara and Coralee open a bordello for women in a beautiful Victorian house in Berkeley, a spa-like retreat where four young male Zen students satisfy the needs of the female clients. A *Kirkus Reviews* contributor wrote that the establishment "caters to the unloved, unhappy, and merely horny as a lot of high-minded rationalization of this implausible enterprise is bandied about and politically correct motivation is duly provided." Dave Ford, who interviewed Kaufman for the *San Francisco Chronicle,* wrote that the author "rails against a youth-obsessed American culture that leaves women in middle age, and beyond, feeling invisible. 'I see so many women of a certain age who don't have a partner, or who do, but that sense of womanliness, of sensuality, of being admired and being touched goes away,' she says. 'And there's such a loss.' *Slow Hands* addresses that loss."

BIOGRAPHICAL AND CRITICAL SOURCES:

PERIODICALS

Kirkus Reviews, May 15, 2003, review of *Slow Hands,* p. 704.
Los Angeles Times, April 22, 1991, John Godfrey, review of *Speaking in Tongues,* p. 1; June 11, 1993, Jan Breslauer, review of *Speaking in Tongues,* p. 23.

St. Petersburg Times, March 18, 1994, Susan Eastman, review of *Shooting Simone,* p. 23; May 13, 1997, John Fleming, review of *Fakes,* p. 2B.

San Francisco Chronicle, February 3, 1985, Ruthe Stein, "*The Couch:* Playwright Analyzes Jung's Menage a Trois," p. 22; February 8, 1985, Bernard Weiner, review of *The Couch,* p. 72; January 29, 1987, Steven Winn, review of *Roshi,* p. 58; June 17, 2003, Dave Ford, "She Takes Sensuality Seriously: *Picasso* Playwright Advocates for Senses," p. D2.

Sarasota Herald Tribune, April 18, 1997, Jay Handelman, review of *Fakes,* p. 3B.

Washington Post, March 8, 2000, Nelson Pressley, review of *The Last Game Show,* p. C9.

Washington Times, May 21, 1996, Nelson Pressley, review of *Shooting Simone,* p. C11.

ONLINE

Lynne Kaufman Home Page, http://www.lynnekaufman.com (March 14, 2004).

*   *   *

KELLER, Edward B. 1955-

PERSONAL: Born December 28, 1955, in New York, NY; son of Harold and June G. Keller. *Education:* University of Pennsylvania, B.A., 1977, M.A., 1979.

ADDRESSES: Home—300 W. 23rd St., Apt. 2N, New York, NY 10011. *Office*—Roper ASW, 205 E. 42nd St., 14th Floor, New York, NY 10017. *E-mail*—ekeller@roper.com.

CAREER: Yankelovich, Skelly & White, Inc., New York, NY, research associate, 1979-80, senior associate, 1980-82, vice president, 1982-86; Roper ASW, New York, NY, chief executive officer, 1986—. Member of advisory board, Annenberg School.

MEMBER: International Communications Association, Issues Management Association, American Association of Public Opinion Research.

AWARDS, HONORS: Ayer scholar, 1977.

WRITINGS:

(With Jon Berry) *The Influentials,* Free Press (New York, NY), 2003.

Contributor of articles to professional journals, magazines, and newspapers.

SIDELIGHTS: Edward B. Keller is chief executive officer of Roper ASW, a worldwide firm that researches market trends and advises companies how to expand brand loyalty and product recognition. Together with another Roper executive, Jon Berry, Keller has written *The Influentials,* a book about the ten percent of people who, by personal preference and word of mouth, influence the popularity of emerging products and services. Keller and Berry identify "influentials" as socially active, generally middle income individuals whose buying habits are two to three years ahead of the general public. The authors demonstrate that "influentials" spurred the move to fuel efficient cars in the 1970s, bought home computers in the 1980s, and moved to the Internet and cell phones soon after these options became available. It is the word of mouth advice of the "influentials" that has popularized such technical innovations as the Internet, while bypassing other products such as e-books. Keller and Berry also suggest that these "influentials" can sway national elections and international public policy.

The Influentials includes profiles of specific influential individuals from the mayor of Richmond, Indiana, to a participant in the Iditarod. The authors suggest that businesspeople who understand the thinking of "influentials" will be able to tailor products that will appeal to a much more vast portion of the populace. *Booklist* correspondent Barbara Jacobs praised the book for being based on "the solid research of six decades of even more solid research" and called *The Influentials* "a fact-filled yet intriguing read." A writer for the Web site *Children Come First* observed: "Both an intellectual adventure and a hands-on marketing manual, *The Influentials* is an extraordinary gold mine of information and analysis that no business can afford to ignore." A *Publishers Weekly* reviewer likewise concluded that Keller and Berry's theories "are compelling and exceedingly well researched, and should be a boon to anyone looking to promote the next big thing."

BIOGRAPHICAL AND CRITICAL SOURCES:

PERIODICALS

Booklist, December 15, 2002, Barbara Jacobs, review of *The Influentials,* p. 712.

Library Journal, December, 2002, Stephen Turner, review of *The Influentials,* p. 143.

Publishers Weekly, November 18, 2002, review of *The Influentials,* p. 52.

USA Today, February 17, 2003, Diane Scharper, "The Influentials Set USA's Pace from the Middle of the Pack."

ONLINE

Children Come First, http://www.childrencomefirst. com/ (June 23, 2003), review of *The Influentials.*

Innsbrook Today Online, http://www.innsbrooktoday. com/ (June 23, 2003), Hilary Burns, "Off the Shelf," review of *The Influentials.*

Wirelessweek, http://www.wirelessweek.com/ (June 23, 2003), Sue Marek, "Researcher Studies Influentials in Technology."*

*   *   *

KERSEY, (Patrick) Colin 1947-

PERSONAL: Born October 8, 1947, in Yukon, FL; son of Stanley P. (former mayor of Auburn, WA) and Lorrayne G. (president of a realty company) Kersey; married Joyce A. Tonucci (a trainer), July 19, 1984; children: Jesse (daughter). *Education:* Western Washington University, B.A. (English), 1969; Western Washington University, B.A. (Education), 1970; University of Washington, B.A. (Advertising), 1976. *Politics:* Independent. *Religion:* Protestant. *Hobbies and other interests:* Travel, motorcycling.

ADDRESSES: Home—1205 Pine Street, Huntington Beach, CA 92648. *Agent*—Victoria Sanders, Victoria Sanders & Associates LLC, 241 Avenue of the Americas Suite 11H, New York, NY, 10014. *E-mail*—kersey@earthlink.net.

CAREER: Self-employed for over twenty years in advertising and marketing with agencies in Washington and California; and author. Board member, Huntington Youth Shelter, 1989-90.

AWARDS, HONORS: Bruce L. Williams Award for Volunteerism, 1991, for writing, producing, and directing a video about homeless children.

WRITINGS:

Soul Catcher, St. Martin's Press (New York, NY), 1995.

SIDELIGHTS: After working for many years in advertising, in 1995 Colin Kersey published his first novel, *Soul Catcher,* which a contributor to *Kirkus Reviews* described as "a rousing supernatural thriller." Kersey told *CA:* "Two forces propel my writing: a love of language and a growing fascination with advertising.

"Currently a resident of Huntington Beach, California, Colin Kersey grew up in Auburn, Washington. He studied fiction and poetry writing at Western Washington University and the University of Washington, earning degrees in English, Education, and Advertising. For the past twenty years, he has created advertising for some of the better known American and Japanese companies.

"Following his move to southern California in 1983, he studied novel writing for three years with bestselling mystery writer Elizabeth George. In 1991, he started Camp Pines Writers, a weekly critique group. Kersey's first novel, *Soul Catcher,* was sold at auction to St. Martin's Press in 1994 and published in November, 1995."

Soul Catcher begins with a shaman's final quest, the search for a "boy with no ears," whom he saw in a vision. When a gang of street punks murders him in a Seattle alley, the shaman calls on a wind spirit to finish his quest and avenge his death. As the wind spreads destruction and panic through the city, a few characters band together to resist it: twelve-year-old Evan Baker, who is deaf; his mother, a public relations hack; public defender Paul Judge, who is Native American; a retired school teacher; and a down-and-out journalist. A reviewer for *Publishers Weekly* compared Kersey's multiple-perspective style to that of Stephen King and Dean Koontz. A contributor to *Library Journal* likened him to Koontz and Clive Barker and called the Seattle setting "lovingly and accurately portrayed."

Kersey told *CA*, "I write in snatches: before work, in client's offices, in restaurants, whenever and wherever I can, given the fact that advertising still pays the bills. A first time author may sound pretentious when talking about his or her 'work.' Nevertheless, perhaps because I've come at writing by the long road, I've thought about it a good deal. The search for love, grace, and beauty in a world wrestling with intolerance, injustice, and violence is my beat. I consider myself a Western writer: I have a particular need to explore and write about the landscape and the people who inhabit it, especially the people of the Northwest where I was raised. I am inspired by and enjoy writing about the handicapped, whom I find heroic. My mission is to touch people. Being a writer is the most difficult and rewarding pursuit I know of."

BIOGRAPHICAL AND CRITICAL SOURCES:

PERIODICALS

Kirkus Reviews, September 1, 1995, review of *Soul Catcher.*
Library Journal, October 15, 1995, review of *Soul Catcher.*
Publishers Weekly, September 18, 1995, review of *Soul Catcher.**

*   *   *

KIDD, Diana 1933-2000

PERSONAL: Born 1933, in Melbourne, Australia; died 2000, in London, England; married, husband's name, Simon; children: two sons and a daughter. *Education:* Trained as a primary school teacher in Australia.

CAREER: Taught English to migrant workers' children in Australia; writer.

AWARDS, HONORS: Victorian Premier's Literary Award for Children's Literature and shortlist citation for Australian Children's Book of the Year award, both 1990, both for *Onion Tears;* shortlist citation, Victoria Premiers Literary Award, 1992, shortlist citation, Australian Children's Book Council Book Award (junior readers section), 1992, and Australian Multi-cultural Award for Children's Literature (junior fiction section), 1993, for *The Fat and Juicy Place;* shortlist citation, Australian Children's Book Council Book of the Year Award, 1997, for *I Love You, Jason Delaney;* Australian Children's Book Council Book of the Year Award (young readers division), Diversity in Health Children's Book Award, FAW Award, and Family Award for Children's Books, all 2001, all for *Two Hands Together.*

WRITINGS:

Onion Tears, illustrated by Lucy Montgomery, Viking (Australia), 1990, Puffin (London, England), 1994.
The Fat and Juicy Place, Angus & Robertson (Australia), 1992.
Spider and the King (Young Bluegum), HarperCollins (Australia), 1995.
Two Hands Together, Penguin Books Australia (Australia), 2000.

Also author of *The Day Grandma Came to Stay,* 1988; picture book, *Paddymelon,* illustrated by Maxim Svetlanov, 1994; and *I Love You, Jason Delaney,* 1996.

SIDELIGHTS: Diana Kidd drew the inspiration for her novels from her years teaching English to the children of migrant workers in Australia. She wanted to convey to an Australian reading public that children of different ethnic and cultural backgrounds had similar feelings and goals and should be treated with respect and consideration. The late author's several novels, including *The Day Grandma Came to Stay, Onion Tears,* and *The Fat and Juicy Place* all concern themselves with people stuck between cultures, comfortable nowhere, and yearning for whole acceptance, usually by the mainstream Australian society in which they have come to live.

Kidd was born and raised in Australia, but after working for awhile as a primary school teacher in her hometown of Melbourne, she embarked on a bohemian tour of Europe that included lengthy stays in Greece, England, and Spain. Only after marrying an Englishman did she return to Australia to raise her family and resume the teaching profession. She became a published author relatively late in life, releasing *The Day Grandma Came to Stay* in 1988, when she was fifty-five. Her most productive decade as a writer was the

1990s, when she garnered nominations and awards in Australia for *Onion Tears, The Fat and Juicy Place,* and *I Love You, Jason Delaney.* She died the day her most highly awarded book, *Two Hands Together,* was sent to the printer. The citations for that title included the coveted Australian Children's Book Council Book of the Year Award.

Kidd's novel *Onion Tears* explores the life of Nam-Huong, a fictitious young refugee who has left her entire family behind in war-ravaged Vietnam to live with a restaurateur in Australia. Emotionally drained by her experiences in Vietnam, Nam-Huong must learn to feel again, and she does so with the help of a sensitive teacher and with her adoptive "Auntie." To quote Nancy Vasilakis in *Horn Book,* "Nam's longing for her family permeates the novel, whose lean and unaffected prose is tinged with ineffable sadness." Phyllis G. Sidorsky in *School Library Journal* maintained that the story "is sympathetic and well told, giving children an idea of how noncombatants . . . suffered during the Vietnam War."

The Fat and Juicy Place and *Two Hands Together* examine the difficulties faced by Aboriginal children who try to live within their ancient culture while simultaneously attempting to assimilate into mainstream Australian society. In preparation for these books Kidd actually spent time camping with Aboriginal Australians on the coast of New South Wales and elsewhere. Unfortunately, Kidd died before *Two Hands Together* earned its critical and commercial success in Australia.

While relatively unknown in America, Kidd was highly respected in her home country and in Great Britain. She was on an extended book tour in England and Spain when she died in London in 2000. On the *HarperCollins* Web site, a commentator wrote that she was "not only a talented and gifted writer, but a giving and wise soul who always gave much more than she expected back. Her humanity was so clearly visible, and she remained open to discovery, delight and surprise in people all around her."

BIOGRAPHICAL AND CRITICAL SOURCES:

PERIODICALS

Horn Book, May-June, 1991, Nancy Vasilakis, review of *Onion Tears,* p. 330.

Publishers Weekly, February 22, 1991, Diane Roback and Richard Donahue, review of *Onion Tears,* p. 218.
School Library Journal, June, 1991, Phyllis G. Sidorsky, review of *Onion Tears,* p. 108.

ONLINE

HarperCollins Publishers, http://www.harpercollins.com.au/authors/ (December 15, 2003), biography of Kidd.*

*   *   *

KING, Gary C.

PERSONAL: Born in Farmington, MO; married; wife's name Teresita; children: Kirsten, Sarah. *Ethnicity:* "Caucasian." *Hobbies and other interests:* Travel, reading.

ADDRESSES: Agent—Peter Miller, PMA Literary and Film Management, 45 West 21st St., 6th Floor Rear, New York, NY 10010. *E-mail*—garycking@earthlink.net.

CAREER: Writer.

WRITINGS:

TRUE CRIME ACCOUNTS

Blood Lust: Portrait of a Serial Sex Killer, Onyx Books (New York, NY), 1992.
Driven to Kill, Pinnacle Books (New York, NY), 1993.
Web of Deceit, Pinnacle Books (New York, NY), 1994.
Blind Rage, Onyx Books (New York, NY), 1995.
(With Don Lasseter) *Savage Vengeance,* Pinnacle Books (New York, NY), 1996.
The Texas 7, St. Martin's Press (New York, NY), 2001.
Murder in Hollywood, St. Martin's Press (New York, NY), 2001.
An Early Grave, St. Martin's Press (New York, NY), 2001.

Angels of Death, St. Martin's Press (New York, NY), 2003.

The Good Neighbor, St. Martin's Press (New York, NY), 2004.

Contributor to magazines in England and the United States, including *True Detective.*

*   *   *

KING, Michael 1945-2004

OBITUARY NOTICE—See index for *CA* sketch: Born December 15, 1945, in Wellington, New Zealand; died in a car accident March 30, 2004, near Auckland, New Zealand. Historian, journalist, and author. King was considered a leading expert on the indigenous Maori people of New Zealand and was often credited with helping to ease tensions between the native peoples and European settlers. Originally, his goal was to become a journalist. Completing a bachelor's degree at Victorian University in 1967, he began his career at the *Waikato Times* in 1968. It was while writing stories about the native Maoris that his focus began to shift. He continued to write, as well as teaching journalism at the University of Papua New Guinea and Victoria University Extension Department, during the 1970s, while completing his doctorate at the University of Waikato in 1978. The 1970s also saw the publication of his first titles about the Maori, including *Moko-Maori Tattooing in the Twentieth Century* (1972) and *Te Puea* (1977). Having become a historian, King felt that, as a descendant of European settlers, in order to understand the Maori he would need to learn their language, which he did thoroughly. He became a sympathetic ear to the concerns of New Zealand's native people, who were often discriminated against by the white government, and he received wide praise of his balanced biographies and histories of the Maori. Among his many important works are *New Zealand: Its Land and Its People* (1980), *Whina: A Biography of Whina Cooper* (1983), *New Zealand* (1987), the autobiographical *Pakeha: The Quest for Identity in New Zealand* (1991) and *Being Pakeha Now: Reflections and Recollections of a White Native* (1999), and *Wrestling with the Angel: A Biography of Janet Frame* (2000). In 2003, he completed *The Penguin History of New Zealand,* which became a phenomenal bestseller in his native country, selling over seventy thousand copies. Named to the Order of the British Empire in 1988 for his services, King was considered a consensus builder, a living bridge between the Maori and European New Zealanders. In addition to his writing, he was a researcher at the University of Auckland in the 1980s and 1990s, conducting workshops there in the early 1980s, and worked for a number of nonprofit groups, such as the Auckland Institute and Museum Council, the Chatham Islands Conservation Board, the Waikato Conservation Board, and the Hahei Marine Reserve management committee. He also was a member of the Janet Frame Literary Trust and was a judge for literary awards.

OBITUARIES AND OTHER SOURCES:

PERIODICALS

Guardian (London, England), April 1, 2004.
Los Angeles Times, April 1, 2004, p. B11.
Washington Post, April 2, 2004, p. B9.

*   *   *

KING, Ruchama,
(Ruchama King Feuerman)

PERSONAL: Married Yisrael Feuerman (a writer, psychotherapist, and fund-raiser); children: four. *Education:* Brooklyn College, MFA (creative writing). *Religion:* Jewish.

ADDRESSES: Home—Passaic, NJ. *Office*—c/o Author Mail, St. Martin's Press, 175 Fifth Avenue, New York, NY 10010. *Agent*—Ann Rittenberg, Ann Rittenberg Literary Agency, 1201 Broadway, Suite 708, New York, NY 10001.

CAREER: Writer.

WRITINGS:

(Under name Ruchama King Feuerman) *The Secret of the Hotel Dela Rosa,* Aura Press (Brooklyn, NY), 1996.

(Under name Ruchama King Feuerman) *The Marvelous Mix-Up: And Other Tales of Reb Shalom,* illustrated by Vitality Romanenko, Hachai Publishing (Brooklyn, NY), 1997.

Seven Blessings, St. Martin's (New York, NY), 2003.

Contributor of stories to journals and magazines.

SIDELIGHTS: Ruchama King is the author of a well-received 2003 novel, *Seven Blessings,* set in a contemporary Orthodox Jewish community in Jerusalem. King, a native of Silver Spring, Maryland, moved to Israel when she was seventeen, and spent the next ten years living and working in Jerusalem, where she studied and taught Torah, and did volunteer work with the disabled. "'I was there in the Eighties,'" King told Lisa Haddock in the Bergen County, New Jersey *Record.* "'Everyone thinks of Jerusalem as a place to die for now. . . . But Jerusalem is a place to live for and to live in and love.'" During her years in Jerusalem, King, the daughter of an Ashkenazi father and a Moroccan-born Sephardi mother, lived with a matchmaker.

King returned to the United States in the early 1990s, married, and earned a master of fine arts degree in creative writing from Brooklyn College. She began publishing stories in small magazines, and also published two books under her married name, Ruchama King Feuerman. Her 1996 *The Secret of the Hotel Dela Rosa* is a detective story featuring Bina Gold, while her 1997 book, *The Marvelous Mix-Up: And Other Tales of Reb Shalom,* is a collection of three long tales for middle-grade readers featuring the wise Reb Shalom who lives in the Jewish town of Keppel.

With *Seven Blessings,* published under her maiden name, King utilizes the material from her Jerusalem years. "King's skillful prose reveals the heartbreak and the joy involved in trying to find the right partner," according to a contributor for *Aish.com,* "and her beautiful descriptions of the city make Jerusalem a place that readers will not wish to depart." In an interview with the same contributor, King noted, "I wanted to write an honest book, and yet I feared going overboard in my honesty." For King, other writings about Orthodox Jews have often missed the mark. She wanted to depict real people in real-life situations. "'Matchmaking and romance are the perfect camou-

flage for thornier issues,'" the author told Lisa Haddock in the *New Jersey Jewish News Online.* "'Along the way, you can slip in a little Torah, a little God, a little coming to grips with the dark side of your own soul and self.'" Thus King decided to set her story against the backdrop of matchmakers at work.

King features expatriate men and women in Jerusalem in the pre-Intifada 1980s: Beth, an independent thirty-nine-year-old American woman is at the center of action; the rather arrogant American artist, Binyamin who is a headache for the matchmakers; and the matchmakers themselves, Tsippi, a Holocaust survivor, and the alluring Judith, both of whom need a little help with their own marriages. Each character struggles towards love and self-fulfillment in this novel which puts a "fresh spin" on the subject of matchmaking, according to Andrea Kempf in *Library Journal.* Kempf also found that King's depiction of the Orthodox and ultra-orthodox Jewish community is "as warm and engaging as any in contemporary literature," and that her characters "jump off the page and into the hearts of her audience."

For a *Publishers Weekly* critic, *Seven Blessings* was a "bustling" title, with "richly detailed descriptions of Jerusalem" and "sympathetic characters [that] make this a fully realized novel." Similarly, a critic for *Kirkus Reviews* thought the same novel was a "tender, enlightening debut that, urban setting aside, reads like a comedy of provincial manners." And for Haddock, writing in the *New Jersey Jewish News,* the book "is a love letter to the faith that King cherishes," a "passion," according to Haddock, that "fuels a compelling story about the search for love—of God, of Torah, of life, of soul mates—in the land of Israel."

BIOGRAPHICAL AND CRITICAL SOURCES:

PERIODICALS

Kirkus Reviews, June 1, 2003, review of *Seven Blessings,* p. 772.

Library Journal, May 15, 2003, Andrea Kempf, review of *Seven Blessings,* p. 125.

Publishers Weekly, May 12, 2003, review of *Seven Blessings,* pp. 39-40.

Record (Bergen County, NJ), November 13, 2003, Lisa Haddock, "Seeking God and Soul Mates in Jerusalem," p. L4.

ONLINE

Aish.com, http://www.aish.com/ (February 22, 2004), "Seven Blessings: Q and A with the Author."

New Jersey Jewish News Online, http://www.njjewishnews.com/ (February 12, 2004), Lisa Haddock, "NJ Author Tells 'Passionate' Story of Israeli Singles Seeking Soul Mates."

St. Martin's Press Web site, http://www.stmartins.com/ (October, 30, 2003). *

* * *

KIYAMA, Henry Yoshitaka 1885-1951

PERSONAL: Born January 9, 1885, in Neu, Tottori Prefecture, Japan; immigrated to United States, 1904; returned to Japan, 1937; died, April 24, 1951. *Education:* Attended San Francisco Art Institute.

CAREER: Artist, teacher.

AWARDS, HONORS: New York Art Students League scholarship.

WRITINGS:

The Four Immigrants Manga: A Japanese Experience in San Francisco, 1904-1924 (original Japanese-language edition *Manga Yonin Shosei* was self-published in San Francisco, 1931), translation, introduction, and notes by Frederik L. Schodt, Stone Bridge Press (Berkeley, CA), 1999.

SIDELIGHTS: When Yoshitaka Kiyama arrived in San Francisco from Japan in 1904 at the age of nineteen, he took the name of Henry. Kiyama stayed in the United States for thirty years, studying art and mastering Western techniques and became a well-respected artist whose works, many of which have survived, were widely exhibited. He had a studio at 1902 Sutter Street in San Francisco's Japantown. Kiyama returned to Japan for the last time in 1937, and while he was there, war broke out, forcing him to remain. He taught school in his hometown of Neu and continued creating his own works until his death in 1951.

Kiyama also created what may have been the first graphic novel approximately seven years before an American comic book was published. In 1927, he had his work on exhibition at the Golden Gate Institute, and in addition to his drawings and paintings, he displayed fifty-two episodes of a cartoon created in the style of American comic strips titled *Manga Hokubei Iminshi,* or *A Manga North American Immigrant History.* It represented the lives of Kiyama and friends who had taken the names of Charlie, Fred, and Frank and covered the period from 1904, when the young students first arrived, to 1924. Kiyama, who deliberately used a style that was crude and cartoony, similar to that seen in American strips, hoped that it would be carried by a newspaper, but it was perhaps too long, or too documentary, and it was never picked up. Kiyama had the work printed while visiting in Japan in 1931, and returned to self-publish it in the United States as *Manga Yonin Shosei* or *The Four Students Manga.* The work was praised by people prominent in the Japanese community, as well as by the consul general of Japan.

Frederik L. Schodt came across a copy of the work in a Berkeley library in 1980 and began to translate it. He later published it as *The Four Immigrants Manga: A Japanese Experience in San Francisco, 1904-1924.* Kiyama's edition was handwritten in Meiji-period Japanese, but where other ethnic groups, including Chinese and English speakers appear in the story, they speak their own languages. This hand lettering remains, supplemented with English text, and some panels are reversed to accommodate the left-to-right flow of English. *Historian* reviewer Benson Tong called the volume "charming, yet poignant."

Joe Lockard, who reviewed the new version for *Bad Subjects* online wrote that Schodt's "combination of scholarship, advocacy, and conscientious translation has achieved exemplary results here. The translation notes and historical comments are valuable and necessary complements to the manga; the cultural history becomes far more accessible to the uninitiated."

The four immigrants represent a life of both personal and legislative racism in California as they work in a series of low-level jobs from houseboy to field and orchard worker, grateful for their wages, still higher than those they would receive in Japan. Fred hopes to succeed in farming, Frank in the import and export business, Charlie in the study of American politics, and Henry, like his creator, in art. Most of the episodes are set in the city, however, and there are many that provide histories of the 1906 earthquake and fire, the Spanish flu, World War I, immigrant marriage customs, and property rights, or the lack thereof. The four never assimilate, but rather adapt in a society that still mistakes the Japanese consul for a Chinese servant. They lose money in risky ventures and reach various levels of success.

"Kiyama's drawing style adds frequent touches of humor to these episodes and the manga storyline," wrote Lockard. "The noses of babies drip, men slouch down the street, and storekeepers assume a protective posture. A wry verbal wit joins this visual wit, as the immigrant characters observe their situation with occasional anger but no malice. Where it arises, Kiyama's anger animates his humor. It is an attitude like this that would make this manga so attractive as a teaching text."

Richard von Busack noted in a review for *Metroactive* online that "as Schodt writes, there's something in *The Four Immigrants Manga* to offend everyone. Schodt hastens to apologize for the racism, adding that Kiyama learned to draw African American and Chinese stereotypes from the newspapers of the day. But the ugly side of the immigrant experience rounds out *The Four Immigrants Manga* and makes it more than just an interesting antiquity."

A writer for *Rational Magic* online noted that one of the things that comes through is the sense of humor of the friends and other Japanese immigrants. The reviewer wrote that "some of the things that happened to them were really quite terrible, such as when Charlie and Frank were bundled onto a truck at gunpoint and driven out of Turlock with a warning never to return, or when Charlie's request to gain his precious citizenship was denied, even after he'd fought on behalf of the United States. Yet the characters can still dismiss their bad fortune with a wry sentence or even a joke."

"From subjects as mundane as cooking and selling shoes to sensitive topics like the death of a parent and the great San Francisco earthquake, Kiyama exhibits a gentle humor that appeals to readers of all cultures," wrote Robert L. Humphrey in *American Studies International*. "This must have been very difficult to do at the time, for much of Kiyama's art deals with the strong anti-Asian feelings that were building up on the West Coast and which eventually prevented his return."

BIOGRAPHICAL AND CRITICAL SOURCES:

PERIODICALS

American Studies International, June, 1999, Robert L. Humphrey, review of *The Four Immigrants Manga: A Japanese Experience in San Francisco, 1904-1924*, pp. 107-108.

Booklist, September 15, 1998, Gordon Flagg, review of *The Four Immigrants Manga*, p. 184.

Historian, summer, 2000, Benson Tong, review of *The Four Immigrants Manga*, p. 877.

Library Journal, November 1, 1998, Stephen Weiner, review of *The Four Immigrants Manga*, pp. 76, 78.

Pacific Historical Review, May, 2000, Brian M. Hayashi, review of *The Four Immigrants Manga*, p. 271.

ONLINE

Bad Subjects, http://eserver.org/bs/reviews/ (February 14, 2000), Joe Lockard, review of *The Four Immigrants Manga*.

Metroactive, http://www.metroactive.com/ (June 3, 1999), Richard von Busack, review of *The Four Immigrants Manga*.

Rational Magic, http://www.rationalmagic.com/ (August 12, 2003), review of *The Four Immigrants Manga*.*

*   *   *

KLEIMAN, Robert 1918-2004

OBITUARY NOTICE—See index for *CA* sketch: Born October 1, 1918, in New York, NY; died of cardiovascular disease March 22, 2004, in Washington, DC. Journalist, educator, and author. Kleiman, who was associated with the *New York Times* for two decades, was well known as an authority on European-American political relations. Graduating from the University of

Michigan in 1939, his first job was with the *Washington Post,* where he was a reporter for two years. Next, he worked as the White House correspondent for the *New York Journal of Commerce.* With the onset of World War II, he served in the Office of War Information, where in 1942 he continued his work as White House correspondent, only this time for the Voice of America. During the war, Kleiman became involved in psychological warfare, helping to organize an operation in Burma that became a model for this new method of undermining the enemy. With the war over, he returned to journalism, first as an associate editor in Washington, D.C., for *U.S. News & World Report,* and then as a correspondent in Germany and France. In 1962, Kleiman was briefly the bureau chief in Paris for the Columbia Broadcasting System. The next year, he joined the staff at the *New York Times,* where he would remain, with the exception of a stint with the International Institute for Strategic Studies in London from 1972 to 1973, until 1983. Beginning in the 1980s, Kleiman turned his expertise in foreign affairs to the classroom, teaching at such institutions as Stanford University, the University of Maryland, Columbia University, and Union College; in the late 1980s, he was also a visiting research fellow at the Royal Institute of International Affairs in London, England. A member of the Council on Foreign Relations, the Overseas Press Club, the American Academy of Arts and Sciences, the Authors Guild, and the Century Club, Kleiman, who was a Phi Beta Kappa and member of Sigma Delta Chi, published *Atlantic Crisis: American Diplomacy Confronts a Resurgent Europe* in 1964.

OBITUARIES AND OTHER SOURCES:

PERIODICALS

Los Angeles Times, March 26, 2004, p. B13.
New York Times, March 25, 2004, p. C16.
Washington Post, March 25, 2004, p. B6.

* * *

KLEIN, Adam

PERSONAL: Male. *Education:* Attended the University of Iowa; San Francisco State University, M.A. (fiction writing).

ADDRESSES: Agent—c/o Author Mail, Serpent's Tail, 4 Black Stock Mews, London N4 2BT, England.

CAREER: Writer, musician, composer. Worked as a caseworker, San Francisco, CA; Roman Evening, band member, 1999—; Peace Corps, Bangladesh, 2003—.

WRITINGS:

The Medicine Burns, Serpent's Tail (London, England), 1995.
(With Thomas Avena) *Jerome: After the Pageant,* Bastard Books (San Francisco, CA), 1996.
Tiny Ladies, Serpent's Tail (London, England), 2003.

Klein's stories have been published in various journals and magazines, including *BOMB* magazine, and in the anthology, *Men on Men 5.* As a composer, with Michael Mullen, Klein has released CDs, including *Together Now* (recorded with the band Roman Evening), 2001, *Tiny Ladies,* 2003, and *Heaven Will Not Delay a Traveler,* 2004.

WORK IN PROGRESS: A novel, *The Forks.*

SIDELIGHTS: Adam Klein is a writer and musician whose published books include a collection of short stories, *The Medicine Burns,* a monograph on artist Jerome Caya, *Jerome: After the Pageant,* and a novel, *Tiny Ladies.* A graduate of San Francisco State University's fiction program, Klein signed his first book contract above San Francisco's legendary City Lights bookshop.

Klein's short story collection, *The Medicine Burns,* is interconnected by a central narrative voice. Stories include "Club Feet," about the inexorable bond between mother and child as a result of an inherited deformity, "India," the story of a man with AIDS who escapes everyday reality, and the title tale, which deals with a gay adolescent's battle with acne and first love. *Lambda Book Report* reviewer, Raphael Kadushin thought that the stories in this collection "have a classical feel to them." Kadushin went on to note that the tales are "almost uniformly bleak," and that if there were "weak spots" among them, the book "more than compensates for these with some powerful, bittersweet stories," such as "Club Feet" and the "long seamless story titled 'India.'"

For *Booklist* contributor Whitney Scott, Klein's "strong stories limn the lives of people living on the fringes," and is a "strong addition to gay and lesbian literature." A reviewer for *Publishers Weekly* found the tales "brief slices of bitterness," and that Klein's "direct, economical language hammers these stories home with a single stroke." And a critic for *Kirkus Reviews* added more praise to this debut book, calling it "harrowing, and yet exquisite, unflinching, and compelling."

Klein next turned his hand to biography and art in his collaborative effort with Thomas Avena in documenting the work of San Francisco artist, Jerome Caya. "That book . . . was an enormous undertaking and a very emotional process," Klein told a contributor for *Delusions of Adequacy.* "Jerome was deteriorating from AIDS and went blind during the process." The book, *Jerome: After the Pageant,* was published a year after Caya's death from AIDS, and is, according to Eric Bryant, writing in *Library Journal,* a "surprisingly uplifting record of a talent brought down in his prime."

Klein is also a long-time musician, and in 1999 joined forces with the band Roman Evening, releasing a CD, *Together Now,* not long after. In 2003, he published his first novel, a story that utilizes some of his own experiences as a social worker in San Francisco. *Tiny Ladies* tells the story of Carrie, who has had a disastrous affair with one of the clients, Victor, whom she was serving as a caseworker in San Francisco. Now working in the Midwest, she is assigned Hannah as a client and finds new strength and optimism as a result. Carrie could use some strength, as she has made some bad choices in her life. Victor was one of these; he treated her badly and murdered a friend of hers. Sexually abused as a teenager and a former junkie, Carrie could use a social worker in her own life. As Hannah and Carrie grow closer, they realize how similar they are, both "burdened with a history of bad choices and lethal violence," according to a *Kirkus Reviews* contributor. This same reviewer found the book a "bold and worthwhile attempt," but also observed that there is "just simply too much of everything: sex, drugs, guilt, alienation, regret, anomie." For this critic, Klein's talents were better served in the short story. However, Daniel Mitchell, reviewing the novel in *Ink 19,* thought that the "suspense and latent desire in *Tiny Ladies* is masterful." Mitchell commended the "sexual tension" between Hannah and Carrie and also praised Klein's descriptive powers as "worthy of note." Mitchell

concluded that the novel was a "well-written, interesting, and fascinating look at a side of life few of us ever experience." Klein also composed a set of songs to go with the book, released as the 2003 CD, *Tiny Ladies,* "an immediate, accessible pop record," according to Tim Whalley writing for *Fakejazz.com.*

BIOGRAPHICAL AND CRITICAL SOURCES:

PERIODICALS

Booklist, June 1, 1995, Whitney Scott, review of *The Medicine Burns,* p. 1729.
Kirkus Reviews, May 15, 1995, review of *The Medicine Burns,* p. 661; February 15, 2003, review of *Tiny Ladies,* p. 259.
Lambda Book Report, July-August, 1995, Raphael Kadushin, review of *The Medicine Burns,* pp. 23-24.
Library Journal, December, 1996, Eric Bryant, review of *Tiny Ladies,* p. 87.
Publishers Weekly, May 22, 1995, review of *The Medicine Burns,* p. 54.

ONLINE

Delusions of Adequacy, http://www.adequacy.net/ (October 30, 2003), interview with Adam Klein.
Fakejazz.com, http://www.fakejazz.com/ (August 15, 2003), Tim Whalley, review of *Tiny Ladies.*
Guardian Online, http://books.guardian.co.uk/ (April 26, 2003), Rachel Hore, review of *Tiny Ladies.*
Ink 19, http://www.ink19.com/ (August, 2003), Daniel Mitchell, review of *Tiny Ladies.**

*   *   *

KÖNIG, Franz 1905-2004

OBITUARY NOTICE—See index for *CA* sketch: Born August 3, 1905, in Rabenstein, Pielach, Austria-Hungary; died March 13, 2004, in Vienna, Austria. Priest, educator, and author. König was an influential cardinal in the Catholic Church and was considered an important bridge builder between the Church and the Communist countries of eastern Europe. Educated at the Pontifical Gregorian University's Bible Institute, he earned a theology degree in 1930 and was ordained a priest in 1933. In his early career, he served the

Church in Lille, France, as a parish priest and then was a cathedral curate in St. Poelten, as well as a secondary school teacher. During World War II, he was a chaplain and teacher, and after the war König was a university professor in Vienna and Salzburg. His work began to draw the attention of his superiors as early as 1947, and in 1956 he was made the archbishop of Vienna, a post he held until 1985; he was elevated to cardinal in 1958. The turning point of his service came in 1960 while visiting Yugoslavia. He became more aware of Marshal Tito's oppressive rule there and vowed to do something about it, not only for Yugoslavia but for all eastern European countries. Arguing for more Church involvement in the East, he helped shape the Roman Catholic Church's policies there. He was the first Catholic prelate to manage to visit the sequestered Cardinal Jozsef Mindszenty, who was hiding from the Communists at the U.S. embassy in Budapest; he made regular visits to Poland, Romania, and Serbia to establish better relations with those countries; and he has been credited with strongly influencing the election of Cardinal Karol Wojtya of Poland to Pope in 1978, rather than having another Italian cardinal become head of the Church. A president of the Secretariat for Non-Believers from 1965 to 1980 and of Pax Christi International from 1985 to 1990, König remained actively involved in the international community all his life; he was also a prolific author, publishing such works as *Kirche im Aufbruch* (1966), *Das zeichen Gottes: Die Kirche in unserer Zeit* (1973), and *Kardinal Franz König: Ansichten eines engagierten Kirchenmannes* (1991).

OBITUARIES AND OTHER SOURCES:

PERIODICALS

Independent (London, England), March 15, 2004, p. 34.
Los Angeles Times, March 15, 2004, p. B9.
New York Times, March 15, 2004, p. A23.
Times (London, England), March 15, 2004, p. 27.
Washington Post, March 14, 2004, p. C10.

*   *   *

KOPLOW, David A. 1951-

PERSONAL: Born May 21, 1951, in Sioux Falls, SD; son of Bernard (a real estate agent) and Minette (a homemaker; maiden name, Friedman) Koplow; married Karen Jones (a bookkeeper), October 7, 1974;

children: Justin, Brian, Alexander. *Education:* Harvard University, B.A., 1973; attended Queen's College, Oxford, 1973-75; Yale Law School, J.D., 1978. *Politics:* Democrat.

ADDRESSES: Home—1032 Carper St., McLean, VA 22101. *Office*—Georgetown University Law Center, 600 New Jersey Ave., NW, Washington, DC 20001. *E-mail*—koplow@law.georgetown.edu.

CAREER: U.S. Arms Control and Disarmament Agency, Washington, DC, attorney and advisor, 1978-81; Georgetown University Law Center, Washington, DC, professor of law, 1981—, director of Center for Applied Legal Studies. U.S. Department of Defense, Washington, DC, Deputy General Counsel for International Affairs, 1997-99.

AWARDS, HONORS: Rhodes Scholar, 1968.

WRITINGS:

Testing a Nuclear Test Ban: What Should Be Prohibited by a "Comprehensive" Treaty?, Dartmouth Publishing (Aldershot, England), 1996.
By Fire and Ice: Dismantling Chemical Weapons while Preserving the Environment, Gordon and Breach (Amsterdam, Netherlands), 1997.
Smallpox: The Fight to Eradicate a Global Scourge, University of California Press (Berkeley, CA), 2003.

Contributor to books, including *Shadows and Substance: The Chemical Convention,* 1993, *Encyclopedia of the United States Congress,* 1995, and *Arms Control and the Environment,* 2001. Contributor to scholarly journals, including *Arms Control Today, New York University Law Review,* and *Maryland Law Review.*

SIDELIGHTS: Georgetown University professor David A. Koplow, an expert on biological warfare issues, is the author of *Smallpox: The Fight to Eradicate a Global Scourge,* a work that "insightfully and reasonably examines the complex issue of whether the two remaining official stocks of smallpox virus should be destroyed," according to Pascal James Imperato in the *Journal of Community Health.* Smallpox, a deadly virus that has killed millions of people over the centuries, was deemed eradicated from the earth in

1977. The two remaining stocks are stored at the Centers for Disease Control and Prevention in Atlanta, Georgia, and the Russian State Research Center of Virology and Biotechnology in Novosibirsk, Russia. A reviewer in *Publishers Weekly* called Koplow's work an "accessibly written analysis of smallpox policy," and Imperato remarked that Koplow "meticulously and even-handedly analyzes the cases for and against extermination within the broader contexts of bioterrorism, environmental law and policy, the morality of purposeful extinction, and the role of the World Health Organization."

BIOGRAPHICAL AND CRITICAL SOURCES:

PERIODICALS

Booklist, December 15, 2002, William Beatty, review of *Smallpox: The Fight to Eradicate a Global Scourge,* p. 715.
Journal of Community Health, October, 2003, Pascal James Imperato, review of *Smallpox,* p. 390.
Journal of the American Medical Association, November 19, 2003, Douglas J. Wear, review of *Smallpox,* p. 2610.
Library Journal, January, 2003, Tina Neville, review of *Smallpox,* p. 144.
New Statesman, March 31, 2003, Michael Barrett, "Germ Rights," p. 54.
Publishers Weekly, November 18, 2002, review of *Smallpox,* p. 54.
Quarterly Review of Biology, March, 2004, Frank Fenner, review of *Smallpox,* pp. 114-115.
Times Educational Supplement, February 21, 2003, Christopher Wills, "A Deadly Dance with Diseases on Death Row," p. 28.
Wall Street Journal, December 4, 2002, Nancy de Wolf Smith, review of *Smallpox,* p. D10.

ONLINE

Georgetown Law Web site, http://www.law.georgetown.edu/ (April 17, 2004), "David A. Koplow."*

*   *   *

KRUEGER, Lesley

PERSONAL: Born in Vancouver, British Columbia, Canada; married Paul Knox (a foreign correspondent). *Education:* University of British Columbia, graduate.

ADDRESSES: Agent—c/o Author Mail, Penguin Books Canada Ltd., 10 Alcorn Ave., Suite 300, Toronto, Ontario M4V 3B2, Canada.

CAREER: Educator and fiction writer. Ryerson University, Toronto, Ontario, Canada, faculty member. Writer-in-residence, Tasmanian Writers' Centre and Varuna Writers' Centre.

WRITINGS:

(With Dayv-James French and Rohinton Mistry) *Coming Attractions,* Oberon Press (Ottawa, Quebec, Canada), 1986.
Hard Travel, Oberon Press (Ottawa, Quebec, Canada), 1989.
Poor Player, Oberon Press (Ottawa, Quebec, Canada), 1993.
Drink the Sky, Key Porter Books (Toronto, Ontario, Canada), 1999.
Foreign Correspondences: A Traveler's Tales, Key Porter Books (Toronto, Ontario, Canada), 2000.
The Corner Garden, Penguin (Toronto, Ontario, Canada), 2004.

SIDELIGHTS: Lesley Krueger is a Canadian writer who has published short stories, novels, and a travel memoir. Much of her writing, both fiction and nonfiction, concerns South America and is based on her many travels in the region with her husband, a foreign correspondent with the Toronto *Globe & Mail.*

Krueger's *Poor Player* is a novel in which Canadian actor Jack Hall travels to Central America to involve himself in the struggle for human rights. On the way, he stops off in Mexico to visit a journalist friend, Hugh Bruce, and to learn Spanish. Narrated by Bruce, who sees the world only through his literary and historical blinders, and focusing on Hall, a shallow and colorless character, the novel depicts the inability of North Americans to truly understand the societal problems in Mexico, even when they find themselves surrounded by those problems. "Krueger's narrative makes the gap between cultures extremely clear," Guy Beauregard noted in *Canadian Literature.* "Mexico represents the meeting point of northern idealism with southern realism," Elizabeth Mitchell added in *Quill and Quire.* "Class distinctions, superstitions, and the clashing of traditional beliefs with modern society are aspects of Mexican daily life that [North American governments] cannot begin to understand."

Drink the Sky, Krueger's second novel, is set in Brazil where environmentalist Todd Austen is doing work in the Amazon while his wife Holly stays behind with their children in Rio de Janeiro. Holly uses her time alone to pursue her interest in art, creating paintings inspired by stories of Charles Darwin's stay in the region. She also has an affair with a musician and must deal with another man who may be a child abuser. The couple's problems are echoed in the larger problems Todd encounters in the Amazon, where a mining company is exploiting the local Indians and despoiling the environment. As in Krueger's previous novel, "the Austens' Canadian experience is of little use in understanding the machinations at play around them," Maureen Garvie explained in *Quill & Quire.* "*Drink the Sky* is a powerful, timely, harrowing, and immensely readable book," John Walker concluded in the *Canadian Book Review Annual.* "Krueger adds another richly textured canvas to her gallery with her new novel," Loranne Brown wrote in the Toronto *Globe & Mail.*

Foreign Correspondences: A Traveler's Tales is partly a travel memoir and partly an effort by Krueger to understand the lives of her immigrant grandparents, who came to Canada from Sweden and Scotland. While she speaks of her own travels throughout the world, Krueger also tries to recapture the bravery and feelings of dislocation of her own family members. The book, Susan Highes wrote in *Quill & Quire,* "is full of richly detailed descriptions." "Ultimately, *Foreign Correspondences* is about the human need to find a sense of place in the world," Jo-Anne Mary Benson concluded in the *Canadian Book Review Annual.*

Krueger's *The Corner Garden* is a young-adult novel about fifteen-year-old Jessie Barfoot, who has recently moved to Toronto with her mother and her mother's new husband. Feeling alone in the world, Jessie unexpectedly befriends the elderly neighbor Martha von Tellingen, whose own experiences as a young girl in Nazi-occupied Holland are interwoven into the book's diary-like structure. "This demanding book challenges its readers," Margaret Mackey stated in *Resource Links,* adding that *The Corner Garden* "provides considerable food for thought as a reward."

In an interview posted on the *Penguin Books Canada Web site,* Krueger revealed that *The Corner Garden* was based on her own childhood in Vancouver, British Columbia. When she was eight years old her father, recently released from the Canadian Army, built a house for the family on Vancouver's north side. The German family next door had a beautiful garden which Krueger enjoyed secretly visiting to "make what I thought were improvements," something that did not earn the appreciation of her neighbors. The German woman who owned the garden, unable to have children of her own, nonetheless enjoyed the young girl's company and treated her well. "And so I began to think about the war, a garden, a neighbour, and *The Corner Garden* grew," Krueger recounted.

BIOGRAPHICAL AND CRITICAL SOURCES:

PERIODICALS

Books in Canada, February, 1994, Gary Draper, review of *Poor Player,* p. 48.
Canadian Book Review Annual, 1999, John Walker, review of *Drink the Sky,* pp. 175-176; 2000, Jo-Anne Mary Benson, review of *Foreign Correspondences: A Traveler's Tales,* p. 52.
Canadian Literature, spring, 1991, Lesley D. Clement, review of *Hard Travel,* pp. 151-153; winter, 1995, Guy Beauregard, review of *Poor Player,* pp. 139-141.
Globe & Mail (Toronto, Ontario, Canada), April 17, 1999, Loranne Brown, review of *Drink the Sky,* p. D15.
Maclean's, December 4, 2000, review of *Foreign Correspondences,* p. 87.
Quill & Quire, January, 1994, Elizabeth Mitchell, review of *Poor Player,* p. 33; May, 1999, Maureen Garue, review of *Drink the Sky,* p. 34; July, 2000, Susan Hughes, review of *Foreign Correspondences,* pp. 36-37.
Resource Links, February, 2003, Margaret Mackey, review of *The Corner Garden,* p. 41.

ONLINE

Penguin Books Canada Web site, http://www.penguin.ca/ (October 2, 2003), interview with Krueger.*

KUBERT, Joe 1926-

PERSONAL: Born October 12, 1926, in Yzerin, Poland; immigrated to United States; son of Jacob (a kosher butcher) and Etta (Reisenberg) Kubert; married Muriel Fogelson, July 8, 1951; children: David, Daniel, Lisa, Adam, Andrew.

ADDRESSES: Office—Joe Kubert's World of Cartooning, 37B Myrtle Ave., Dover, NJ 07801; fax: 973-537-7699. *E-mail*—kubert@earthlink.net.

CAREER: Comic book artist, illustrator. DC Comics, New York, NY, director of publications, 1967-76; founder and president of Joe Kubert School of Cartoon and Graphic Art, 1976—. International Museum of Cartoon Art, advisory board. *Military service:* Served in the U.S. Army.

MEMBER: New York Press Club, Society of Illustrators, National Cartoonist Society (past president).

AWARDS, HONORS: Burroughs Award, 1972; National Cartoonist Society awards, 1974, 1980; Inkpot Award, 1977; Big Five Collectors Society Award (hall of fame), 1997; Bob Clampett Humanitarian Award, 1997; Comic Con award for teaching, 1997; United Kingdom art award, special achievement, 1997; Will Eisner Award, 1997, for best graphic novel; Harvey Award, 1997; Jack Kirby Award, 1997; Will Eisner Hall of Fame Award, 1998; Ignatz Award.

WRITINGS:

Abraham Stone: Country Mouse City Rat, Malibu Graphics, 1992.
(With others) *Rise of the Midnight Sons: Ghost Rider/ Morbius/Darkhold/Nightstalkers/Spirits of Vengeance,* Marvel (New York, NY), 1993.
(Illustrator) Bill Black and Ralph Mayo, *Golden-Age Greats: Fighting Females,* AC Comics/Paragon Press, 1995.
(Illustrator, with Joe Madureira) Scott Lobdell, *X-Men: Legionquest,* Marvel (New York, NY), 1996.
(Illustrator, with others) *The Origin of Generation X,* Marvel (New York, NY), 1996.
(Illustrator, with son, Adam Kubert) *X-Men Visionaries,* Marvel (New York, NY), 1996.

Fax from Sarajevo: A Story of Survival, Dark Horse Comics (Milwaukie, OR), 1996.
(Illustrator, with son, Andy Kubert) Scott Lobdell, *Onslaught: "The Awakening,"* Marvel (New York, NY), 1997.
Superheroes: Joe Kubert's Wonderful World of Comics, Watson-Guptill Publications (New York, NY), 1999.
(With others) *Batman Black and White,* DC Comics (New York, NY), 1999.
(With Gardner Fox and Murphy Anderson) *The Hawkman Archives,* DC Comics (New York, NY), 2000.
(With Nicky Wright) *The Classic Era of American Comics,* McGraw-Hill/Contemporary Books (New York, NY), 2000.
(With others) *Enemy Ace: War in Heaven,* DC Comics (New York, NY), 2001.
Tor (two volumes), DC Comics (New York, NY), 2001-2002.
(Illustrator) Stan Lee, *Just Imagine Stan Lee Creating the DC Universe,* DC Comics (New York, NY), 2002.
(With Carmine Infantino) *Jesse James: Classic Western Collection,* Vanguard Productions (Somerset, NJ), 2003.
(Illustrator) Claudio Nizzi, *Four Killers,* Volume 1: *The Lonesome Rider,* Dark Horse Comics (Milwaukie, OR), 2003.
Yossel: April 19, 1943, ibooks, 2003.

Illustrator of and contributor to comic book series, including *Hawkman, Dr. Fate, Sgt. Rock, Enemy Ace, Flash, Firehair, Newsboy Legion,* and *Tarzan;* creator of strip "Tales of the Green Beret."

SIDELIGHTS: Joe Kubert entered the world of comics at the age of twelve as an inker while he was attending the High School of Music and Art in New York City. His first published work appeared during the 1940s, and he illustrated and inked for various publishers. Kubert served in the U.S. Army during the 1950s, became a freelancer upon his return, and with his friend, Norman Maurer, he developed the process that led to the 3-D comic book. Among the titles that used this process were *Tor* and *Mighty Mouse.* Kubert then began working primarily for National (now DC Comics), creating two outstanding war features with writer Robert Kanigher. *Sgt. Rock* and *Enemy Ace: War in Heaven* are still praised to this day for the realism of Kubert's artwork. The central character of the former first appeared in *Our Army at War,* while the German aviator of the latter was first seen in *Star-Spangled War Stories.*

Michael Uslan wrote in *America at War* that Kubert's "highly stylized, gritty, piercing illustrations embody all the horrors of war and the intricacy of detailed war machines. When Kubert's soldiers crawl across Italy on their bellies, you see the pain, the weariness, the insanity of war in the faces of the soldiers. . . . It is Kubert's hard-hitting interpretation of war that the readers have been viewing since the early days of *Our Army at War,* and it is his style that acts as the model for nearly every artist who has followed him."

Kubert drew superheroes like *Hawkman* and then took a respite from comic books to draw the strip "Tales of the Green Beret," based on the book by Robin Moore. The strip ended after two years, in part because of antiwar sentiment.

After returning to DC, Kubert was assigned to a number of new titles, including *Tarzan.* His work on the series was deemed outstanding, and he was chosen to write, edit, and draw *Tarzan of the Apes,* and also to adapt other Edgar Rice Burroughs' texts.

Fax from Sarajevo: A Story of Survival is Kubert's graphic novel about the 1992-1994 experiences of Ervin Rustemagic, a comics agent Kubert had met years earlier at an Italian comics convention, and with whom he stayed in touch and developed a friendship. Rustemagic was working from his office in Holland in March 1992 when he faxed Kubert a message, telling him that he and his family were returning to Dobrinja, a suburb of Sarajevo. His wife and children were homesick, and the situation seemed to have calmed. When they returned, however, the conflict escalated, and Serb bombing destroyed their home and possessions. They took refuge in another building, and over two years, Rustemagic faxed Kubert, sometimes more than once a day, communicating conditions in the war zone. Because he had media credentials, Rustemagic was able to escape first, then get his family out. They were granted citizenship in Slovenia and relocated there.

Kubert used the information from these faxes in writing and drawing his black-and-white documentary of the experiences of the family. "The graphic novel format is ideally suited to bring the events to life in a compelling way," wrote Betsy Levine in *School Library Journal. Booklist*'s Gordon Flagg wrote that Kubert's work "renders political conflict understandable and with plenty of personal impact."

Yossel: April 19, 1943 is a graphic novel in which Kubert has inserted himself as the young boy who is the central character. Kubert's family left Poland for the United States in 1926, the year of his birth, and the boy Yossel lives in the Warsaw ghetto at an age that approximates Kubert's own if his family had remained. His rough, penciled drawings dramatically emphasize the horrors of the concentration camps and the ghetto uprising. Flagg wrote that "the visual looseness . . . conjures a potent intimacy that adds to the story's impact."

Peter Siegel reviewed *Yossel* for *Artbomb.net* online, writing that Kubert's uninked and unfinished drawings give the story the appearance of a sketchbook, "but it's a truly perfect companion to the raw and often graphic story he's telling here. *Yossel* is the accomplished artist in the twilight of his career mustering his powers one more time to give us his most sincere achievement."

A *Publishers Weekly* contributor wrote that Kubert's "signature graphic style . . . marks him as one of mainstream comics' most talented and celebrated interpreters of the horrors of war."

BIOGRAPHICAL AND CRITICAL SOURCES:

BOOKS

Contemporary Graphic Artists, Gale (Detroit, MI), Volume 1, pp. 164-166.
Uslan, Michael, editor, *America at War,* Simon & Schuster (New York, NY), 1979.

PERIODICALS

Booklist, October 1, 1996, Gordon Flagg, review of *Fax from Sarajevo: A Story of Survival,* p. 315; October 15, 2003, Gordon Flagg, review of *Yossel: April 19, 1943,* p. 400.

Publishers Weekly, September 23, 1996, review of *Fax from Sarajevo,* p. 72.

School Library Journal, June, 1997, Betsy Levine, review of *Fax from Sarajevo,* pp. 151-152.

ONLINE

Artbomb.net, http://www.artbomb.net/ (January 3, 2004), Peter Siegel, review of *Yossel: April 19, 1943.*

Dark Horse Comics Online, http://www.darkhorse.com/ (January 3, 2004), interview with Kubert.

Kubert's World, http://www.kubertsworld.com (January 3, 2004), author's home page.*

*　　*　　*

KUDLINSKI, Kathleen V. 1950-

PERSONAL: Born October 5, 1950, in Philadelphia, PA; daughter of William J. and Grace Veenis; married Hank Kudlinski, July 3, 1972; children: Elizabeth, Henry. *Education:* University of Maine, B.S., 1972. *Politics:* "Compassionate liberal and environmentalist."

ADDRESSES: Home—95 Alden Dr., Guilford, CT 06437. *Agent*—Susan Cohen, Writer's House, 21 W. 26th St., New York, NY 10010. *E-mail*—kathkud@aol.com.

CAREER: Writer. Weekly columnist, "The Naturalist," *New Haven Register,* New Haven, CT, 1988—. Has also worked as an elementary school classroom teacher; makes frequent visits to classrooms to talk about writing and book production. Chairperson, Guilford, CT Community Fund, 2003.

MEMBER: Society of Children's Book Writers and Illustrators.

AWARDS, HONORS: "Master Teaching Artist" citation, Connecticut Commission for the Arts, 1998; NSTA-CBC "notable children's book in the field of science" citation, 1999, for *Dandelions; Learning Magazine* Teacher's Choice Awards, 2003, for *It's Not Easy Being Green* and *Food for Life!*

WRITINGS:

Rachel Carson: Pioneer of Ecology, McGraw Hill (New York, NY), 1988.

Juliette Gordon Low, America's First Girl Scout, Viking (New York, NY), 1989.

Hero over Here: A Story of World War I ("Once upon America" series), Viking (New York, NY), 1990.

Pearl Harbor Is Burning: A Story of World War II ("Once upon America" series), Viking (New York, NY), 1990.

Animal Tracks and Traces, Franklin Watts (New York, NY), 1991.

Night Bird: A Story of the Seminole Indians, Viking (New York, NY), 1993.

Earthquake!: A Story of Old San Francisco ("Once upon America" series), Viking (New York, NY), 1993.

Lone Star: A Story of the Texas Rangers ("Once upon America" series), Viking (New York, NY), 1994.

Facing West: A Story of the Oregon Trail ("Once upon America" series), Viking (New York, NY), 1994.

Marie: An Invitation to Dance, Simon & Schuster (New York, NY), 1996.

Shannon: A Chinatown Adventure ("Girlhood Journeys" series), Simon & Schuster (New York, NY), 1996.

Shannon: Lost and Found ("Girlhood Journeys" series), Simon & Schuster (New York, NY), 1997.

Shannon: The Schoolmarm Mysteries, San Francisco, 1880 ("Girlhood Journeys" series), Simon & Schuster (New York, NY), 1997.

Popcorn Plants, Lerner (New York, NY), 1998.

Venus Flytraps, photographed by Jerome Wexler, Lerner (New York, NY), 1998.

Dandelions, Lerner (New York, NY), 1999.

My Tree, McGraw Hill (New York, NY), 2000.

My Body Is Changing: Now What Do I Do?, McGraw Hill (New York, NY), 2000.

Rosa Parks, Young Rebel, Simon & Schuster (New York, NY), 2001.

Harriet Tubman, Freedom's Trailblazer, Simon & Schuster (New York, NY), 2002.

It's Not Easy Being Green, Newbridge Educational Publishing, 2003.

Food for Life!, Newbridge Educational Publishing, 2003.

Sojourner Truth, Voice of Freedom, Simon & Schuster (New York, NY), 2003.

The Spirit Catchers, Watson-Guptill (New York, NY), 2004.

What Do Roots Do?, NorthWord Press, 2004.
Boy, Were We Wrong about Dinosaurs!, Dutton (New York, NY), 2005.
The Sunset Switch, NorthWord Press, 2005.
Boy, Were We Wrong about the Solar System!, Dutton, in press.

Contributor to *Camelot: A Collection of Original Arthurian Stories,* edited by Jane Yolen, Philomel (New York, NY), 1995. Columnist for *The Agawam Advertiser,* 1980-84, and *The Springfield Sunday Republican,* 1984-87. Some of Kudlinski's books have been translated into Japanese.

WORK IN PROGRESS: A historical novel based in Harper's Ferry, West Virginia.

SIDELIGHTS: Kathleen V. Kudlinski is a prolific author of historical fiction, biographies, and science books that reflect her passionate interest in the natural world and preserving its treasures. She once commented: "My family was always on the move when I was growing up. In each new town I searched anew for people to talk to. Books—and their authors—were the only friends who traveled across the country with me. Unlike anyone else in my family, I loved nature and art and I had a secret longing to be great someday.

"I spent my days climbing trees to look into nests or digging in streambeds to find salamanders. Books by Robert McClung and, later, Sally Carrigher and Rachel Carson, honored my interest. I could ask any nature question, however odd or embarrassing, and find the answers for myself—in books. When I wasn't nature watching, I was drawing birds, horses, castles, or monsters. 'How-to' books showed me ways to sketch and paint. I read dozens of biographies looking to see how people became great.

"I never thought about becoming a great author. I thought writers were tidy people with good grades and perfect spelling. My bedroom was always full of shed snake skins and feathers, piles of books, art projects, and camping gear. My report card was a mess and my spelling was worse.

"During high school in Westport, Connecticut, I volunteered at a local museum, sketching, caring for wild animals, and teaching about nature. It seemed a perfect match for my talents and hobbies. I studied science in college at the University of Maine where I met my future husband, Hank. After we graduated in 1972, I decided to teach in schools instead of museums. For three years I taught science at an elementary school in North Carolina in a classroom crowded with cages of gerbils and snakes, parakeets and tarantulas. For three years after that, my animals and I taught fifth grade in New Hampshire. I had found a way to be important in the lives of many kids, doing what I love.

"Then my husband took a new job in Massachusetts where there was no need for school teachers—even those with dozens of classroom animals. I spent months trying to find something to do with my life. When I saw an ad for a conference of the Society of Children's Book Writers and Illustrators in nearby Northampton, Massachusetts, I decided to drop in.

"One of the speakers, Jane Yolen, was as excited and happy with writing as I had been with teaching. I bought her book, *Writing for Children,* and stood in a long line waiting for her to sign it. As we inched along I thought about perhaps trying to write, someday. But Jane didn't write 'good luck' in the book. In black ink, she wrote 'from one writer to another.'

"I stumbled away from the table, my life changed. The great Jane Yolen had given me permission to think of myself as an actual writer. I went home and began work on my first book. Over the next four years, Jane and I became friends, I had two children and dozens of rejections. I wrote for magazines and newspapers, doing stories about nature.

"Every month I met with a writer's group, led by Jane and including Robert McClung and Patty MacLachlan. We talked about getting books published and then critiqued each other's books in progress. The encouragement and support of these famous people kept me from being discouraged by rejections. I finally signed a book contract for *Rachel Carson, Pioneer of Ecology* six years after Jane told me I was a writer.

"In 1985 our family moved to Connecticut where we still live. I've written more than two dozen books here, sitting at my desk overlooking a deep, wild pond. Sometimes now I take my computer up to our log cabin in the woods of Vermont. I write about the things that fascinate me: nature and art and greatness. Every week I write and illustrate a newspaper article about nature, too. In writer's groups, I pass on the same encouragement I got when I was just beginning. I often visit classrooms, where I talk about writing well and the joy of finding a life full of the things you love."

Kudlinski's writing career demonstrates how a professional can earn respect, and a good living, as a children's writer. She is equally at home with historical fiction and science writing and has contributed to two popular series, "Once upon America" and "Girlhood Journeys." Both of those series introduce middle-grade readers to real events in American history through the first-person adventures of fictitious heroes and heroines. In *Lone Star: A Story of the Texas Rangers,* for instance, eleven-year-old Clay Andrews dreams of becoming a Ranger so that he can hunt down and kill the Indians who murdered his father. As the action unfolds, Clay actually meets some Texas Rangers and eventually learns, to his dismay, that their brand of "justice" is more senseless and brutal than that of the Comanches who made Clay an orphan. In *Booklist,* Chris Sherman found *Lone Star* to be "a slice of history, thoughtfully presented."

Hero over Here was one of the first "Once upon America" titles. Theodore is too young to go away to Europe to fight in the First World War. Chafing at his lost chances for adventure, he is frightened—and then galvanized—when his mother and sister become deathly ill during the worldwide influenza epidemic of 1918. Diane Roback in *Publishers Weekly* liked the way Kudlinski's descriptions "breathe color and life" into a topic that most students find only in dull history texts. Other Kudlinski titles dealing with American history include *Earthquake!: A Story of Old San Francisco, Night Bird: A Story of the Seminole Indians,* and *Pearl Harbor Is Burning!: A Story of World War II.*

The "Girlhood Journeys" series bears certain similarities to the "American Girl" books made so popular by Pleasant Company. In the case of the "Girlhood Journeys" series, however, the heroines range widely through historical eras and are not necessarily stereotypical American girls. Kudlinski has written three novels about one such adventuress, *Shannon: A Chinatown Adventure, Shannon, Lost and Found,* and

Shannon: The Schoolmarm Mysteries, San Francisco, 1880. Shannon is a nineteenth-century Irish immigrant who is old enough to miss her former home and to make astute observations about her new home, San Francisco. In *Shannon: A Chinatown Adventure,* Shannon comes to terms with her homesickness by orchestrating the liberation of a young Chinese girl who is enslaved to a local merchant. Julie Shatterly in *School Library Journal* commended the book for its "suspense" and "likable characters." *Shannon: The Schoolmarm Mysteries* concerns itself more directly with prejudice. Even though Shannon is Caucasian, she finds that, because she is Irish, other whites shun her. This brings her closer to her Chinese friends, who are themselves victims of racism. Joan Zaleski in *School Library Journal* appreciated the "strong female characters" that Kudlinski has presented in "historically accurate" circumstances.

One of Kudlinski's most popular science titles is *Venus Flytraps.* Written for the youngest audience interested in the natural world, *Venus Flytraps* introduces the fascinating carnivorous plant, describes its life in the wild, and offers advice on growing it in a home environment. With a nod to ecology, Kudlinski urges children to be careful not to buy Venus Flytraps that have been taken from the wild, only those that have been bred domestically. According to Ruth S. Vose in *School Library Journal,* the author presents her topic in "clear, simple sentences," yet conveys a great deal of information for children and adults. In *Booklist,* Carolyn Phelan called *Venus Flytraps* "a good look at an ever popular plant." Kudlinski's titles *Boy, Were We Wrong about Dinosaurs!* and *Boy, Were We Wrong about the Solar System!* update and rectify older theories on the sciences of paleontology and astronomy. These titles are also for young readers or middle grade students ready to explore scientific topics on their own.

BIOGRAPHICAL AND CRITICAL SOURCES:

PERIODICALS

Booklist, May 1, 1994, Chris Sherman, review of *Lone Star: A Story of the Texas Rangers,* p. 1602; May 1, 1997, Chris Sherman, review of *Shannon, Lost and Found: San Francisco, 1880,* p. 1494; December 1, 1998, Carolyn Phelan, review of *Venus Flytraps,* p. 678.

Publishers Weekly, April 13, 1990, Diane Roback, review of *Hero over Here,* p. 64; November 11, 1996, review of *Shannon: A Chinatown Adventure,* p. 76.

School Library Journal, February, 1992, Phyllis K. Kennemer, review of *Pearl Harbor Is Burning!: A Story of World War II,* p. 87; May, 1993, Yvonne Frey, review of *Night Bird: A Story of the Seminole Indians,* p. 106; August, 1993, Ruth S. Vose, review of *Earthquake! A Story of Old San Francisco,* p. 164; June, 1994, George Gleason, review of *Lone Star,* p. 132; August, 1994, Sally Bates Goodroe, review of *Facing West: A Story of the Oregon Trail,* p. 154; September, 1996, Julie Shatterly, review of *Shannon: A Chinatown Adventure,* p. 204; April, 1998, Joan Zaleski, review of *Shan-*non: *The Schoolmarm Mysteries,* p. 102; January, 1999, Lisa Wu Stowe, review of *Popcorn Plants,* p. 116; March, 1999, Ruth S. Vose, review of *Venus Flytraps,* p. 196.

ONLINE

Kathleen V. Kudlinski Home Page, http://www. kathleen-v-kudlinski.com (December 15, 2003).

*   *   *

KUEHN, Paul
    See GRANT, Pete

L

LADY BARKER
See STEWART, Mary Anne

*   *   *

LADY BROOME
See STEWART, Mary Anne

*   *   *

LAKE, Jo-Anne 1941-

PERSONAL: Born February 23, 1941, in London, Ontario, Canada; daughter of John and Mina Rankin; married Maurice Lake (a management consultant), July 6, 1961; children: Michelle Lake Goslin, Sherri, Jonathan. *Education:* York University, B.A., 1984, B.Ed., 1985; Niagara University, M.S., 1987. *Hobbies and other interests:* Skiing, golfing, walking, rollerblading, dancing, collecting shoes, reading, writing, collecting spinning tops.

ADDRESSES: Agent—c/o Author Mail, Stenhouse Publishers, 477 Congress St., Suite 4B, Portland, ME 04101-3451. *E-mail*—joannelake@rogers.com.

CAREER: Elementary schoolteacher in London, Ontario, Canada, 1961-63, and Oshawa, Ontario, Canada, 1963-65; University of Western Ontario, London, instructor in mathematics, 1965; elementary schoolteacher, 1968-80; middle-school teacher, 1981-83; teacher in a program for gifted students, 1983-85;

Durham District Board of Education, Whitby, Ontario, Canada, consultant, 1986-90, administrator, 1991-2000; writer, public speaker, and educational consultant, 2000—. University of Toronto, instructor in elementary science. Sciencents, cofounder. Community volunteer.

MEMBER: International Reading Association, National Science Teachers Association, Ontario Principals Association.

WRITINGS:

Imagine, Pembroke (Markham, Ontario, Canada), 1993.
Life Long Learning, Pembroke (Markham, Ontario, Canada), 1997.
Literature and Science Breakthroughs: Connecting Language and Science Skills in the Elementary Classroom, Stenhouse Publishers (Portland, ME), 2000.

Contributor to education and library journals.

WORK IN PROGRESS: You Can't Stop Time, Round and Round I Go, Hidden Treasures, The Wonderful World of Spinning Tops, and *Where Is Cedar?,* all for children; "The Cinderella Complex," "a research project on the retirement phase and its impact on a cross-section of diverse individuals."

SIDELIGHTS: Jo-Anne Lake told *CA:* "My greatest source of inspiration for my writing in the area of science came from my mother's love of nature. Throughout my childhood years I learned to appreciate the simplest things in life. The song of a blue jay, the wonder in observing a Baltimore oriole's nest, the architecture of a spider web, the sound of a babbling brook: these memories and more are part of my soul and continue to speak to me when I write about yet another wonder! And now, my grandchildren continue my mother's legacy. They are the major source of my ideas for new writing. For example, when my grandchildren received a pet hedgehog called Cedar, we experienced a pet's life together. When Cedar ran away, I prepared a manuscript for publication titled *Where Is Cedar?*

"Another source of motivation for my writing is travel. I have been fortunate to have traveled the world. Along the way I became a collector; I have collected more than sixty spinning tops and observed spinning-top contests in Kalatan, Malaysia. My love of spinning tops was the source of three manuscripts: *Round and Round I Go, Hidden Treasures,* and *The Wonderful World of Spinning Tops.*"

*   *   *

LARSGAARD, Chris 1967-

PERSONAL: Born 1967, in San Francisco, CA. . *Education:* Attended university in California.

ADDRESSES: *Agent*—c/o Author Mail, Delacorte, 1745 Broadway, New York, NY 10019.

CAREER: Writer. Private investigator, c. 1990—.

AWARDS, HONORS: Shamus Award shortlist for best P.I. first novel, Private Eye Writers of America, 2001, for *The Heir Hunter.*

WRITINGS:

The Heir Hunter (crime novel), Delacorte (New York, NY), 2000.

WORK IN PROGRESS: Two more novels, including a possible prequel to *The Heir Hunter.*

SIDELIGHTS: Chris Larsgaard is a private investigator who used his knowledge in finding heirs to unclaimed fortunes for the basis of his debut novel, *The Heir Hunter.* An heir hunter is a special type of investigator who locates family members who are entitled to money left by their relatives that has gone unclaimed for one reason or another. Usually, this type of work involves relatively routine work looking through public record files and other documents, but in the case of Larsgaard's main character, Nick Merchant, the work digs up government secrets and life-threatening adventure.

When Nick teams up with his ex-girlfriend, Alex Moreno, to find out who should get the twenty-two million dollars left behind by Gerald Jacobs, a deceased resident of Hudson, New York, they discover that Jacobs was part of the FBI witness protection program. Further investigation leads the team on a chase that takes them from Washington, D.C., to Switzerland, as they discover links involving everything from secret Swiss bank accounts and Nazis to a federal government cover up. All the while, they are pursued by agents linked to powerful people who will do anything to keep Merchant and Moreno from learning the truth.

Although reviewers of *The Heir Hunter* found minor flaws in the book that they attributed to Larsgaard's inexperience as a novelist, many critics had high praise for this debut effort. A *Publishers Weekly* contributor noted that the author "gives a bit too much plot away" and that Larsgaard has an occasional tendency to "overwrite," but the critic concluded that "this fine debut oozes authenticity and provides a fascinating glimpse into the quixotic and dangerous realm of high-stakes 'assets recovery.'" Similarly, *Booklist* writer Gary Niebuhr noted that although Larsgaard occasionally stretches credibility, the reviewer appreciated how the author "keeps things moving and does a good job with character development." Finally, *Denver Post* contributor Ron Franscell, commenting that the author's hero has less authority than a character who is a policeman or government investigator but more experience than an amateur sleuth, enjoyed how Larsgaard introduces readers to "a whole new sleuthing subspecies, thankfully more closely related to medical examiners and investigative reporters than precocious cats and nosy nuns."

Larsgaard explained, in a *Wag* interview with Woody Arbunkle, that he was inspired to write *The Heir*

Hunter when he noticed that no one had yet written a crime novel featuring a hero involved in his line of work. "I had a good feeling that the concept would be well-received because it presented a niche of private investigation which few people know about," he told Arbunkle. After the success of his debut novel, Larsgaard plans to write more, starting with "something a bit more daring, although it will involve a few of the same elements of *The Heir Hunter,* such as changed identities and such. I plan on writing another heir-finding book soon, however; I'm seriously thinking of making it a prequel to the original."

BIOGRAPHICAL AND CRITICAL SOURCES:

PERIODICALS

Booklist, January 1, 2000, Gary Niebuhr, review of *The Heir Hunter,* p. 884.
Denver Post, February 13, 2000, Ron Franscell, review of *The Heir Hunter.*
Library Journal, February 15, 2000, Jane Jorgenson, review of *The Heir Hunter,* p. 197.
Publishers Weekly, December 6, 1999, review of *The Heir Hunter,* p. 51.

ONLINE

Wag, http://www.thewag.net/ (August 1, 2000), Woody Arbunkle, "The Wag Chats with Chris Larsgaard."*

* * *

LEE, Jae 1972-

PERSONAL: Born June 22, 1972.

ADDRESSES: Agent—c/o Author Mail, Marvel Enterprises, Inc., 10 East 40th St., New York, NY 10016. *E-mail*—jaelee@aol.com.

CAREER: Graphic artist. Illustrator for publishers, including Image and Marvel Comics.

AWARDS, HONORS: Eisner Award for Best New Series, 1999, for *The Inhumans.*

WRITINGS:

ILLUSTRATOR

The Sentry, written by Paul Jenkins, Marvel Comics (New York, NY), 2001.
The Inhumans, written by Paul Jenkins, Marvel Comics (New York, NY), 2001.
Fantastic Four: 1, 2, 3, 4 (Marvel Knights), written by Grant Morrison, Marvel Comics (New York, NY), 2004.

Writer and illustrator of *Hellshock.* Illustrator of comic book series, including *Beast, X-Men, Namor, Youngblood Strikefile, Wildcats* trilogy, *X-Factor,* and *Spider-Man.*

SIDELIGHTS: Jae Lee broke into the comics industry just out of high school by illustrating one of Scott Lobdell's *Beast* stories for Marvel Comics Presents in 1991. He had met an *X-Men* writer at a New York convention and sent samples for over a year before being asked to contribute to the series. He then drew for the *Namor* series by John Byrne and moved to Image to work on *Youngblood Strikefile* and the *Wildcats* trilogy. He also drew some issues of *X-Factor* and one issue for the *Spider-Man* series before launching his own *Hellshock,* which grew out of a four-issue miniseries.

Hellshock is about a female psychiatrist who encounters the spiritual being Daniel in a New York City hospital. Lee's work is also represented in a number of Marvel collections.

In an *Orcafresh.net* interview with Lee, Mary Stronach wrote that Lee "is most at home drawing natural scenes." "I love nature," said Lee. "I hate crowd scenes and drawing man-made items. I'd hate to do *Star Trek;* it would be my worst project."

BIOGRAPHICAL AND CRITICAL SOURCES:

ONLINE

Orcafresh.net, http://www.orcafresh.net/ (August 13, 2003), Mary Stronach, interview with Jae Lee.*

LEE, Jennifer 1968-

PERSONAL: Born January 9, 1968, in Seoul, Korea; naturalized U.S. citizen; daughter of Sangrin (a professor) and Wonja (a nurse) Lee. *Ethnicity:* "Korean." *Education:* Columbia University, B.A., 1986, M.A., 1995, Ph.D., 1998.

ADDRESSES: Office—Department of Sociology, University of California—Irvine, Irvine, CA 92697-5100.

CAREER: University of California—Irvine, Irvine, assistant professor, 2000-02, associate professor of sociology, 2003—. Center for Advanced Study in the Behavioral Sciences, Palo Alto, CA, fellow, 2002-03.

MEMBER: American Sociological Association.

WRITINGS:

Civility in the City, Harvard University Press (Cambridge, MA), 2002.

WORK IN PROGRESS: Asian American Youth, for Routledge (New York, NY), completion expected in 2004.

*   *   *

LENTZ, Harold H(erbert) 1910-2004

OBITUARY NOTICE—See index for *CA* sketch: Born June 11, 1910, in Nevada, IA; died March 11, 2004, in Lima, OH. Minister, administrator, and author. Lentz is remembered for leading Carthage College through an important transitional period as the campus moved from Carthage, Illinois, to Kenosha, Wisconsin. He was educated at several institutions, earning his A.B. at Wittenberg University in 1932, his B.D. from Hamma School of Theology in 1935, his master's from Oberlin College in 1939, and his doctorate from Yale in 1943. Ordained a Lutheran clergyman in 1935, he served as a pastor in Ashland, Ohio, during the 1930s and 1940s before being named president of Carthage College in 1951. By the next year, the Kenosha campus was opened, and under Lentz's administration the college saw its enrollment grow six hundred percent. He continued to serve as president until his retirement in 1976, and in gratitude Carthage awarded him an honorary doctorate in 1987. Lentz was the author of *A History of Wittenberg College: 1845-1945* (1945), *Reformation Crossroads* (1953), and *The Miracle of Carthage* (1974).

OBITUARIES AND OTHER SOURCES:

PERIODICALS

Chicago Tribune, March 15, 2004, Section 1, p. 13.

ONLINE

Carthage College, http://www.carthage.edu/ (March 12, 2004).
ELCA News, http://stlconline.org/elcanews/ (March 16, 2004).

*   *   *

LEVENDOSKY, Charles (Leonard) 1936-2004

OBITUARY NOTICE—See index for *CA* sketch: Born July 4, 1936, in Bronx, NY; died of colon cancer March 14, 2004, in Casper, WY. Editor, educator, and author. Levendosky was the editor of the *Casper Star-Tribune*'s editorial page, as well as the author of books of poetry. Despite his later work in journalism, his original area of study was mathematics and physics, and he earned a B.S. in 1958 and a B.A. in 1960 from the University of Oklahoma; he then received a master's in education from New York University in 1963 and taught high school math and science on the U.S. Virgin Islands for two years. Moving to New York in 1967, he taught at New York University for several years, eventually becoming an assistant professor of English in 1970. Publishing his first poetry book in 1970, *Perimeters,* Levendosky became poet-in-residence at Georgia Southern College that year. He also was associate director of Project Radius for the Georgia Commission on the Arts in 1971 and 1972. Levendosky next moved to Wyoming to become poet-in-residence for the Wyoming Council on the Arts and director of the Poetry Programs of Wyoming. During this time, he continued to publish poetry collections, such as *Words & Fonts* (1975), *Aspects of the Vertical* (1978), and *Distances* (1980). In 1982, Levendosky accepted a job as arts editor, columnist, and editorial page editor for the *Casper Star-Tribune,* for which he became known for his editorials on free speech, conservation, and civil liberties; he also created the newspaper's First Amendment Web site—FACT— which earned him an American Library Association (ALA) award in 1995 and an *Editor and Publisher* award for best original feature for an online newspaper service in 1996. More poetry books were published in the early 1980s, including *Wyoming Fragments* (1981) and *Nocturnes* (1982), and in 1988 Levendosky was named poet laureate of Wyoming. His last poetry collections were *Hands and Other Poems* (1986) and *Circle of Light* (1995). In addition to the above honors, Levendosky was given the ALA's Intellectual Freedom Round Table's John Phillip Immroth Memorial Award and, in 1999, the Freedom to Read Foundation named him to its Roll of Honor.

OBITUARIES AND OTHER SOURCES:

PERIODICALS

Library Journal, March 24, 2004.
Rocky Mountain News (Denver, CO), March 19, 2004, p. B15.

*   *   *

LEWIS, Wendy A. 1966-

PERSONAL: Born February 10, 1966, in Ottawa, Ontario, Canada; married; husband's name Rob; children: Amelia, Maddie. *Education:* University of Toronto, B.A., 1988; also attended Seneca College.

ADDRESSES: Home—Uxbridge, Ontario, Canada. *Agent*—c/o Author Mail, Red Deer Press, MLT 813 2500 University Dr. N.W., Calgary, AB, Canada T2N 1N4.

CAREER: Retail store owner, 1989-93; public relations, marketing, and sales manager for a retirement community, 1994-96; writer, 1996—.

AWARDS, HONORS: Writing for Children contest winner, Writer's Union of Canada, and Canada Council grant, both 2000; Vicky Metcalf Short Story Award, Canadian Authors Association, 2001, for "Revelations."

WRITINGS:

Graveyard Girl (stories), Red Deer Press (Calgary, Alberta, Canada), 2000.
(With Marilyn Metts) *In Abby's Hands,* illustrated by Peter Ledwon, Red Deer Press (Calgary, Alberta, Canada), 2004.

Contributor of short stories to anthologies, including *All Join In,* Prentice Hall Ginn (Canada), 1999; *In My World,* Prentice Hall Ginn (Canada), 1999; and *Just Watch Me,* Prentice Hall Ginn (Canada), 1999.

WORK IN PROGRESS: Picture books and chapter books; a novel for young adults.

SIDELIGHTS: In an online interview with the University of Manitoba, Wendy A. Lewis said: "I like writing about characters in their teen years, when relationships, whether with other young people or family members, are so important. I'm also interested in how the fairytales we grow up with are buried in our subconscious and come back to haunt our relationships later in life." Lewis has brought those preoccupations to bear on her debut collection of short stories, *Graveyard Girl,* a linked series of tales about a group of children and teens who have participated in a re-enactment of the wedding of Prince Charles and Lady Diana Spencer. Some of the tales are set in 1983, around the time of the celebrated royal wedding, and others take place ten years later, as the younger children who participated in the mock event come of age themselves. The stories are anchored by the recollections of Ginger, the "Graveyard Girl" of the title.

"What I tried to do in *Graveyard Girl* was create a snapshot of young people in a small town," Lewis explained in her online interview. "I've always been fascinated by projects, like a play, that kids are working on. You look around, and see the range of personalities: there's always a shy person, the bubbly, outgoing one, the athletic jock, and so on. I don't mean stereotypes; I hope the characters in *Graveyard Girl* have more depth than that."

Graveyard Girl grew out of writing workshops Lewis attended from 1994 through 1996, in which she shared and honed her work. In her interview she said: "Now, if young people ask me, 'How do you become a writer?' I say, 'Write, write and write more! Writing is a craft that you learn, over time, by practising . . . A LOT.'"

A *Publishers Weekly* critic of *Graveyard Girl* admired the way the various characters struggle with challenges that are at once unique and universal. A teenage couple have a child and begin to raise it despite their parents' disapproval. Another character grieves as his sister battles cancer. "Graveyard Girl" herself is haunted by her past and by her lasting love for a young man who has left town for a career as a professional hockey player. The *Publishers Weekly* reviewer noted that the "characters are sympathetic" and the collection contains "tender moments." In her *Booklist* review, Anne O'Malley concluded of *Graveyard Girl:* "The characters are compelling and the stories deeply felt."

BIOGRAPHICAL AND CRITICAL SOURCES:

PERIODICALS

Booklist, January 1, 2001, Anne O'Malley, review of *Graveyard Girl,* p. 940.
Publishers Weekly, February 19, 2001, review of *Graveyard Girl,* p. 92.
School Library Journal, May, 2001, Sandra L. Doggett, review of *Graveyard Girl,* p. 156.

ONLINE

University of Manitoba Outreach, http://www.umanitoba.ca/outreach/ (November 25, 2000), interview with Lewis.*

*   *   *

LIGON, Samuel

PERSONAL: Married; children: two. *Education:* New School, M.F.A.

ADDRESSES: *Home*—Madison, WI. *Agent*—c/o Author Mail, HarperCollins, 10 East 53rd St., New York, NY 10022.

CAREER: Writer and teacher.

WRITINGS:

Safe in Heaven Dead, HarperCollins (New York, NY), 2003.

Contributor of stories to periodicals, including *Story Quarterly, Manoa, Other Voices,* and *Cimarron Review.*

SIDELIGHTS: A *Publishers Weekly* reviewer claimed that Samuel Ligon's debut novel, *Safe in Heaven Dead,* "instantly seizes and holds the imagination . . . few readers will remain unmoved by the agonizing questions that drive this story." *Safe in Heaven Dead* revolves around Robert Elgin, a man running away from his problems. Elgin, married with two children, is a labor negotiator in Michigan. Things become unbearable as he is swept up in political scandals at work and his five-year-old daugther is sexually abused. Elgin goes on the run with a call-girl, Carla, whom he falls in love with. Ligon writes the novel from different perspectives and in a nonlinear style. It is told from Robert Elgin's point of view and from Carla's first-person viewpoint. In a review for *January Magazine,* David Abrams concluded, "As *Safe in Heaven Dead* gradually unspools, we become more and more engrossed in the characters and the circumstances that put them in their private hells."

BIOGRAPHICAL AND CRITICAL SOURCES:

PERIODICALS

Kirkus Reviews, February 1, 2003, review of *Safe in Heaven Dead,* pp. 167-68.
Library Journal, March 1, 2003, Marriane Fitzgerald, review of *Safe in Heaven Dead,* p. 120.
New York Times Book Review, June 8, 2003, Charles Salzberg, review of *Safe in Heaven Dead,* p. 24.
Publishers Weekly, March 15, 2003, review of *Safe in Heaven Dead.*

ONLINE

Art Savant, http://www.artsavant.com/ (April 8, 2003), Lydia Arnold, interview with the author.

January Magazine, http://www.januarymagazine.com/ (October 30, 2003), David Abrams, review of *Safe in Heaven Dead.**

*   *   *

LINDGREN, David T(readwell) 1939-

PERSONAL: Born March 1, 1939, in Ipswich, MA; married first wife; wife's name, Nancy (divorced); married Dora Currea (an economist), August 22, 1977; children: Jeffrey Treadwell, Christopher Gage, Alexander Holt. *Ethnicity:* "Anglo-Saxon." *Education:* Boston University, A.B., 1960, M.A., 1962, Ph.D., 1970. *Politics:* Republican. *Religion:* Protestant. *Hobbies and other interests:* Reading, sports, saxophone.

ADDRESSES: Home—3229 Klingle Rd. N.W., Washington, DC 20008. *Agent*—American Literary Agents of Washington, Inc., 1429 G St. N.W., Suite 317, Washington, DC 20005. *E-mail*—lindgren@uio.satnet. net.

CAREER: Central Intelligence Agency, Washington, DC, imagery analyst, 1964-66; Dartmouth College, Hanover, NH, professor of geography and department head, 1966-2001. Consultant to Central Intelligence Agency, National Aeronautics and Space Administration, and U.S. Department of the Interior.

AWARDS, HONORS: Honorary M.A., Dartmouth College, 1981; grant from John D. and Catherine T. MacArthur Foundation, 1987; Distinguished Graduate Award, Boston University, 1992.

WRITINGS:

Land Use Planning and Remote Sensing, Martinus Nijhoff Publishing (Boston, MA), 1985.
Trust but Verify: Imagery Analysis in the Cold War, Naval Institute Press (Annapolis, MD), 2000.

WORK IN PROGRESS: No Ordinary Summer, a novel set in the year 1942; *In All Good Conscience,* a fictional work about a college president who attempts to cover up a sex scandal.

BIOGRAPHICAL AND CRITICAL SOURCES:

PERIODICALS

Aerospace Power Journal, winter, 2000, review of *Trust but Verify: Imagery Analysis in the Cold War,* p. 112.
Bulletin of the Atomic Scientists, January, 2001, review of *Trust but Verify,* p. 70.
Survival, summer, 2001, Frank Asbeck, review of *Trust but Verify,* p. 162.
Technology and Culture, October, 2001, Dwayne A. Day, review of *Trust but Verify,* p. 822.

*   *   *

LOBINGER, Fritz 1929-

PERSONAL: Born January 22, 1929, in Passau, Germany; son of Herman and Martha (Schreiner) Lobinger. *Ethnicity:* "German." *Education:* Earned D.Th. *Religion:* Roman Catholic. *Hobbies and other interests:* Hiking, boating.

ADDRESSES: Home and office—53 Cathcart St., Aliwal North 9750, South Africa; fax: 051-633-3078. *E-mail*—bishaliw@intekom.co.za.

CAREER: Roman Catholic priest; served in Regensburg diocese in Germany for one year; missionary in South Africa, fourteen years; Missiological Institute, Lumko, South Africa, staff member, seventeen years; bishop of Aliwal North, South Africa, c. 1986—.

WRITINGS:

Katechisten als Gemeindeleiter, Schwarzach (Munich, Germany), 1971.
How Much Can Lay People Do?, (Lumko, South Africa), 1973.
Towards Non-dominating Leadership, (Lumko, South Africa), 1978.
Like His Brothers and Sisters: Ordaining Community Leaders, Claretians (Manila, Philippines), 1998, Crossroad Publishing (New York, NY), 1999.

SIDELIGHTS: Fritz Lobinger told *CA:* "My primary motivation for writing is to influence the way the Church is moving, both on the level of the communities and on the level of the universal Church. Being a leader of the Church as priest and now as bishop, I see the need for developments in the Church, and I want to assist these developments according to the way I see ahead of us.

"What influences my work is first of all my involvement in the communities of the Church in the Third World. I live with communities, I see the way people react, the way they long for new horizons. They long for new ways of participation in the Church and in the world. I see also what hinders them. This motivates and influences me. Something else that influences me is the observation of other parts of the Church, especially parts of the young churches in the Third World.

"My writing process usually begins by trying something out: processes to be tried out, pilot programs to be tried out in communities, small writings to be discussed so that I can see the reactions. Then I try out the ideas among coworkers, and finally I write a publication.

"The subjects I have chosen are always about participation of all members of the Church and about community-building in the Church. What makes us a community of equals? What makes us a community where all can participate? When I see that this participation and this community-building is hindered or how it can be increased, then I look for ways of getting this going, either by practical steps or by writing or by both."

BIOGRAPHICAL AND CRITICAL SOURCES:

PERIODICALS

Theological Studies, September, 2001, Ray R. Noll, review of *Like His Brothers and Sisters: Ordaining Community Leaders,* p. 659.

*   *   *

LOEB, Jeph 1958-

PERSONAL: Born January 29, 1958, in Stamford, CT; married; wife's name, Christine; children: Sam, Audrey. *Education:* Columbia University, B.A., M.A. (film).

ADDRESSES: Agent—c/o Author Mail, DC Comics, 1700 Broadway, New York, NY 10019.

CAREER: Writer, screenwriter, comics creator, producer, and publisher. Screenplays include *Teen Wolf, Commando, Burglar,* and *Firestorm;* Awesome Entertainment, cofounder and publisher; *Buffy the Vampire Slayer* (animated television series), executive producer; *Maurice Sendak's Seven Little Monsters* (television series), Public Broadcasting Service (PBS), writer and producer; *Smallville* (television series), Warner Brothers, consulting producer.

AWARDS, HONORS: Eisner Award, 1999, for *Batman: The Long Halloween.*

WRITINGS:

PLOTS AND SCRIPTS; SELECTED TITLES

Batman: Haunted Knight: The Legends of the Dark Knight Halloween Specials: Three Tales of Halloween in Gotham City (contains *Batman: Legends of the Dark Knight Halloween Special, Batman: Madness: Legends of the Dark Knight: A Tale of Halloween in Gotham City,* and *Batman: Ghosts: A Tale of Halloween in Gotham City, Inspired by Charles Dickens' A Christmas Carol*), DC Comics (New York, NY), 1995.
X-Men: The Age of Apocalypse, Marvel (New York, NY), 1995.
X-Men: Dawn of the Age of Apocalypse, Marvel (New York, NY), 1996.
Onslaught: To the Victor, Marvel (New York, NY), 1997.
Wolverine Gambit Victims, Marvel (New York, NY), 1997.
Batman: The Long Halloween (contains thirteen issues of the miniseries), DC Comics (New York, NY), 1998.
Superman for All Seasons, DC Comics (New York, NY), 1999.
Superman: No Limits, DC Comics (New York, NY), 2000.
The Witching Hour, DC Comics (New York, NY), 2000.
Batman: Dark Victory, DC Comics (New York, NY), 2001.

Superman: Endgame, DC Comics (New York, NY), 2001.

Superman: 'Til Death Do Us Part, DC Comics (New York, NY), 2002.

Superman: Our Worlds at War, DC Comics (New York, NY), 2002.

Superman: The Ultimate Guide, DK Publishing (New York, NY), 2002.

Superman: President Lex, DC Comics (New York, NY), 2003.

Daredevil: Yellow, Marvel (New York, NY), 2003.

Spider-Man: Blue, Marvel (New York, NY), 2003.

Batman: Hush, DC Comics (New York, NY), Volume 1, 2003, Volume 2, 2004.

Hulk: Gray, Marvel (New York, NY), 2004.

Writer for additional graphic novels and comic books for series and miniseries, including *Batman, Superman, The Avengers, Captain America, Coven, Daredevil, Fighting American, Generation X, The Savage Hulk, Kaboom, Spiderman, Wolverine, X-Force, X-Men,* and *Challengers of the Unknown.*

SIDELIGHTS: Jeph Loeb is well-known for his association with both *Batman* and *Superman* comics, as well as many others, including Marvel's comics, but the writer's first stories were screenplays for films, including *Teen Wolf,* starring Michael J. Fox, and *Commando,* starring Arnold Schwarzenegger, both of which could be considered live-action comics.

In an interview with a *BBC Online* contributor, Loeb said that his first writing job was as a freelancer for DC Comics. *Challengers of the Unknown,* his miniseries for DC, paired him up in 1992 with his frequent collaborator, illustrator Tim Sale.

"We're probably best known for *Batman: The Long Halloween,* a year-long detective serial we did for DC featuring Batman," said Loeb. "It won numerous awards, including the Eisner, which in the world of comic books is equivalent to an Emmy. We also did *Superman for All Seasons,* which was a graphic retelling of the Superman origin in a pulp-spun Norman Rockwellian kind of way. Between those two things, while I was still writing and producing movies and television, I suddenly had a new career in the comic book industry."

Anna Jellinek reviewed *Batman: The Long Halloween* for *Dark Star* online, calling it "a successful return to the Year One underworld created by Frank (*Sin City*)

Miller. Loeb brings back gangsters such as Carmine 'The Roman' Falcone, and underused villains like Solomon Grundy." Batman's relationships with Falcone and District Attorney Harvey Dent are important to the story, and in the case of the latter, shows how Dent became Two-Face. Batman is caught up in the murders of mafia crime family members who are killed on holidays during every month of the year by a killer dubbed "Holiday."

Reviewing *Batman: The Long Halloween* for *11th Hour* online, Yannick Belzil wrote that it is "the prime example of how a storyline should treat Batman, by putting him in his natural element: a mystery. . . . Writer Jeph Loeb has crafted a story that is unique to the characters. It's a complex murder mystery, but it's also a Batman story. It couldn't have been done with another character or setting—it belongs solely to the Caped Crusader." Belzil felt that "we're not often treated to the emotional side of Batman, other than the personal tragedy that took his parents away, but this story reveals his feelings about his city and the people that surround him."

In *Superman for All Seasons,* Clark has recently arrived in Metropolis from Smallville and is at the beginning of his career. His story is told through several narrators, including his father, Lois Lane, Lex Luthor, and Lana Lang. Tom Knapp reviewed the book for *Rambles* online, commenting that this "is a pleasant, low-key book which, in the end, will likely stick with you far longer than the usual book about supervillains and massive brawls."

Patrick M. Gerard interviewed Loeb for the *Unofficial Golden-Age Superman Site,* asking him about his beginnings with Superman. Loeb mentioned that in the 1970s, when he was twelve or thirteen years old, he sent a script to Superman writer Elliot S! Maggin, who has inspired Loeb over the years. Of the character, Loeb said that Superman "is so simple to identify with—you put on a cape and you fly around the house. Great stuff. All comics lead from that single point of creation. He's important!" Loeb said that "the one thing that makes him Superman is really Clark. That's an interesting character. He has two wonderful parents who instill in him a spark of goodness, but even after he leaves, he uses his powers to help others."

With *Batman: Dark Victory,* Batman is the Dark Knight in a story that begins where *Batman: The Long Halloween* ends and is set in Gotham City during the period in which such Batman opponents as the Joker are gaining a foothold. The character of Robin/Dick Grayson is not introduced until the end, a move that *Counterculture*'s Sion Smith said "gives the pacing a much-needed depth and a slant on the story that makes it so much fresher than its predecessors." Smith praised the characterizations of the Riddler, Two Face, and Albert the butler, adding that "this has all the look and feel of a real labor of love."

Batman: Hush, Volume 1, collects the first five installments of a twelve-part series that brings together Loeb, illustrator Jim Lee, and inker Scott Williams. Batman's opposition includes Poison Ivy and Killer Croc, and at the same time, he pursues the luscious Catwoman. Other DC characters, including Superman, make appearances, but all are being subtly controlled by a mysterious manipulator. A *Publishers Weekly* contributor wrote that "Loeb is especially talented at underwriting, not crowding the page full of long explanations and snappy patter; after all, readers have known these characters for years."

Loeb also wrote and produced *Maurice Sendak's Seven Little Monsters* for public television, a children's show by the creator of *Where the Wild Things Are.* Loeb's television credits also include the animated version of *Buffy the Vampire Slayer,* which he left before it went into production to become consulting producer for *Smallville.* Loeb told an interviewer for *Comics Continuum* online that *Smallville* is "Superman for this generation. I like the way the characters interact; the cast is wonderful and the whole 'making of a hero' is very appealing to me. . . . It very much reminds me of the graphic novel *Superman for all Seasons* . . . in terms of tone, and that makes me very comfortable on what is unquestionably the hottest show on television."

BIOGRAPHICAL AND CRITICAL SOURCES:

PERIODICALS

Booklist, July, 2003, Gordon Flagg, review of *Batman: Hush,* Volume 1, p. 1856.

Library Journal, September 1, 2003, Steve Raiteri, review of *Batman: Hush,* Volume 1, p. 142.

Publishers Weekly, July 21, 2003, review of *Batman: Hush,* Volume 1, pp. 176-177; September 29, 2003, review of *Superman: President Lex,* pp. 45-46.

ONLINE

11th Hour, http://www.the11thhour.com/ (June, 2000), Yannick Belzil, review of *Batman: The Long Halloween.*

AllNerdReview.com, http://www.allnerdreview.com/ (August 13, 2003), review of *Batman: Haunted Knight: The Legends of the Dark Knight Halloween Specials: Three Tales of Halloween in Gotham City.*

BBC Online, http://www.bbc.co.uk/ (September 23, 2003), interview with Jeph Loeb.

Comic Book Resources, http://www.comicbook resources.com/ (July 10, 2003), Arune Singh, "Don't Mess with the 'S': Jeph Loeb Talks Superman/Batman" (interview).

Comics Continuum, http://www.comicscontinuum. com/ (June 6, 2002), interview with Jeph Loeb.

Counterculture, http://www.counterculture.co.uk/ (August 13, 2003), Sion Smith, review of *Batman: Dark Victory.*

Dark Star, http://www.darkstarorg.demon.co.uk/ (August 13, 2003), Anna Jellinek, review of *Batman: The Long Halloween.*

KryptonSite, http://www.kryptonsite.com/ (December, 2002), Craig Byrne, interview with Jeph Loeb.

Ninth Art, http://www.ninthart.com/ (October 26, 2001), John Connors, review of *Batman: The Long Halloween.*

Rambles, http://www.rambles.net/ (November 17, 2001), Tom Knapp, review of *Superman for All Seasons.*

Superman-Comics.com, http://superman.ws/superman-comics/ (August 13, 2003), Jeph Loeb, "About Superman for All Seasons."

Unofficial Golden-Age Superman Site, http://www. superman.ws/kal-l/superman/ (October 22, 1999), Patrick M. Gerard, interview with Jeph Loeb.*

*   *   *

LOHREY, David T. 1955-

PERSONAL: Born August 25, 1955, in Coldspring, NY; son of Sherwood (a theater director) and Joan (a painter) Lohrey; married Yuka Miyawaki (an accountant), July 22, 1985. *Ethnicity:* "White." *Education:* University of California—Berkeley, B.A., 1981; California State University—Los Angeles, M.A., 1994. *Politics:* Independent.

ADDRESSES: Office—c/o New Jersey City University, 2039 Kennedy Blvd., Jersey City, NJ 07305. *E-mail*—davlohrey@msn.com.

CAREER: Playwright. New Jersey City University, Jersey City, NJ, adjunct professor.

MEMBER: Dramatists Guild of America, Drama Desk: New York Association of Theater Critics, Editors, and Reporters, Theater Alliance of Greater Philadelphia.

WRITINGS:

PLAYS

Betterland (drama; e-book), Singlelane.com, 2000.
Jigsaw Confession (drama; e-book), Singlelane.com, 2000.
One, Two, Three (comedy; e-book), Singlelane.com, 2001.
In a Newark Minute (comedy; e-book), Singlelane. com, 2001.
Sperm Counts (comedy; e-book), Singlelane.com, 2002.
Peace of Mind (drama; e-book), Singlelane.com, 2002.

Contributor to the Internet theater magazine *Curtainup. com.*

WORK IN PROGRESS: Bluff City, a screenplay, completion expected in 2004; research on Japanese feudalism and on Caribbean revolutionaries.

SIDELIGHTS: David T. Lohrey told *CA:* "I'm inspired by the example of other writers—not necessarily by their writings, but by their lives and struggles. The example of solitary hard work often unrewarded keeps me going, but I am always moved by examples of these well done."

*   *   *

LOPEZ, Jack 1950-

PERSONAL: Born February 2, 1950, in Lynwood, CA; son of Robert and Agripina (Estavillo) Lopez; married Patricia Geary (a novelist), 1988; children: Denis. *Ethnicity:* "Latino." *Education:* Portland State University, B.A., 1983; University of California—Irvine, M.F.A., 1987.

ADDRESSES: Home—Redlands, CA. *Agent*—c/o Author Mail, University of Arizona Press, 355 South Euclid Ave., Suite 103, Tucson, AZ 85719. *E-mail*—jack.lopez@csun.edu.

CAREER: Writer. Orange Coast College, Costa Mesa, CA, instructor, 1987; University of Redlands, Redlands, CA, instructor, 1988; California State University, Northridge, professor of English, 1989—.

AWARDS, HONORS: First Place Short Story, Ninth Chicano Literary Prize, 1983, for "The Boy Who Swam with Dolphins;" University fellow, University of California, 1986, 1987; National Hispanic Scholar Award, 1987; Pushcart Prize, XVIII, Special Mention, 1994, for "In the South;" First Place Best Literary Stories, Latino Literary Hall of Fame, 2002, for *Snapping Lines.*

WRITINGS:

Cholos and Surfers: A Latino Family Album, Capra Press (Santa Barbara, CA), 1998.
Snapping Lines: Stories ("Camino del sol" series), University of Arizona Press (Tucson, AZ), 2001.

Work represented in anthologies, including *Mirrors beneath the Earth, Iguana Dreams, Pieces of the Heart,* and *Muy Macho;* contributor to periodicals, including *Massachusetts Review, Quarterly West,* and *Blue Mesa Review.*

WORK IN PROGRESS: Young adult novel for Little, Brown.

SIDELIGHTS: In his first book, a collection of essays titled *Cholos and Surfers: A Latino Family Album,* Lopez writes about the Latino condition, but moreover about the human condition. The stories about his family offer up the love and pain that exist in every family. Some of his pain is extreme. The brother he admired died of AIDS in 1987.

In the first chapter, titled "Ordinary Wisdom," Lopez writes, "My family, of course, never recovered from this. Though we all knew my brother was at risk, we all knew he was gay, we all knew he'd taken heroin, we all knew he'd lived in New York City at the height of the post 1960s hedonism, and had lived there into the early 1980s, when many artists were dying, still we thought we were blessed. Things that raw and 'life-and-death' wouldn't happen to us."

In the stories of *Snapping Lines,* Lopez writes primarily of lone young men looking for love and trying to find themselves in a world without borders. One finds himself preparing to do prison time, while another discovers that his beautiful wife as been adulterous. The collection is published as part of the University of Arizona's Latino literary series. A *Kirkus Reviews* contributor described the tales in *Snapping Lines* as "rich, moody Chicano adagios."

BIOGRAPHICAL AND CRITICAL SOURCES:

PERIODICALS

American Book Review, January-February, 2002, T. R. Hull, review of *Snapping Lines: Stories,* p. 10.
Kirkus Reviews, February 1, 2001, review of *Snapping Lines,* p. 143.

*   *   *

LORD, Tony 1949-

PERSONAL: Born 1949.

ADDRESSES: Office—c/o Author Mail, Frances Lincoln, Ltd., 4 Torriano Mews, London NW5 2RZ England.

CAREER: Research chemist; National Trust, England, gardens adviser, 1979-89; *Royal Horticultural Society's Plant Finder,* principal editor; author, photographer, horticultural consultant, lecturer.

MEMBER: Royal Horticultural Society (member, Floral A Committee, Trials Committee, Reginald Cory Memorial Cup Committee, Advisory Panel of Nomenclature and Taxonomy; chairman of Floral Trials Subcommittee; chairman of United Kingdom Plant Breeders' Rights Controller's Advisory Panel for Herbaceous Plants), National Trust (Gardens Panel), Horticultural Taxonomy Group.

AWARDS, HONORS: Garden Writers' Guild "Best General Gardening Book" Award, 1994, for *Best Borders;* Garden Club Book Selection, 2002, for *Encyclopedia of Planting Combinations: The Ultimate Visual Guide to Successful Plant Harmony.*

WRITINGS:

(Compiler of Historical Plant Lists) Roy C. Strong, *Small Period Gardens: A Practical Guide to Design and Planting,* Rizzoli (New York, NY), 1992.
Best Borders, Frances Lincoln Ltd. (London, England), 1994, Penguin Books (New York, NY), 1996.
(Photographer) Rosemary Verey, *Rosemary Verey's Making of a Garden,* with watercolors by Hilary Wills, Henry Holt (New York, NY), 1995.
Gardening at Sissinghurst, Macmillan (New York, NY), 1996, paperback edition published as *Planting Schemes from Sissinghurst,* Frances Lincoln Ltd. (London, England), 2003.
(Photographer) George Plumptre, *Classic Planting: Featuring the Gardens of Beth Chatto, Christopher Lloyd, Rosemary Verey, Penelope Hobhouse, and Many Others,* Ward Lock (London, England), 1998.
Designing with Roses, Trafalgar Square Publishing (North Pomfret, VT), 1999.
Encyclopedia of Planting Combinations: The Ultimate Visual Guide to Successful Plant Harmony, photography by Andrew Lawson, Firefly Books (Toronto, Ontario, Canada), 2002.

SIDELIGHTS: Respected English horticulturalist, photographer, and author Tony Lord began his career as a chemist before becoming a gardens adviser to Britain's National Trust. He studied at the Royal Botanic Gardens at Kew and has served as editor of the Royal Horticultural Society's annual publication the *Plant Finder* for several years, where he applies codes of nomenclature to more than 70,000 plants.

Lord compiled the plant lists for Roy C. Strong's book *Small Period Gardens: A Practical Guide to Design and Planting.* He was photographer for Rosemary Verey's *Making of a Garden* and George Plumptre's *Classic Planting.* Lord has also written four books of his own: *Best Borders,* which won a Garden Writers'

Guild award in 1994; *Gardening at Sissinghurst; Designing with Roses;* and *Encyclopedia of Planting Combinations: The Ultimate Visual Guide to Successful Plant Harmony.*

Lord's *Best Borders* examines the border plants in twelve famous gardens—eleven English and one French—revealing the history of each over generations, showing design plans and color schemes, and explaining at length how to plant and maintain the borders. He has supplied his own brilliantly colored photographs, using a full-page photo to show the whole border and smaller close-ups for detail, with Latin names for flowers and plants. Divided into chapters according to formality, season, and color, the book also includes a list of the best gardens to tour in Britain, Canada, and the United States. Mary Keen, in the *Spectator,* called it "the definitive 'Border Book'" and "required reading for any serious artist gardener." April Austin, of the *Christian Science Monitor,* found the book to be "an English garden lover's dream." Carol McCabe, of *Early American Life,* commented, "There's great stuff here for any gardener who's interested in experimenting with color and design, even in the smallest flower bed." Ann Lovejoy, in *Horticulture,* praised *Best Borders* as "one of the most stimulating garden books to appear in recent years." She concluded, "Lord's photographs are worth the price of the book in themselves."

Lovejoy also commended Lord for his photographs in *Rosemary Verey's Making of a Garden,* calling them "delectable." Beth Clewis Crim, in *Library Journal,* wrote that the book is "brimming with glorious color photographs."

In *Gardening at Sissinghurst,* Lord goes into rich detail about the history, design, planting, maintenance, and evolution of the famous garden begun by Vita Sackville-West and Harold Nicolson in 1930. One of the world's most-visited public gardens today, it is divided into "rooms" that burst with color throughout the growing season. Lord also tells how Pam Schwerdt and Sibylle Kreutzberger, joint head gardeners at Sissinghurst from 1959 to 1991, continued Miss Sackville-West's tradition even after the gardens passed to the National Trust. Christopher Reed, in *Horticulture,* wrote, "This is a fine book and worth owning whether or not you have been to Sissinghurst or intend to go there. It's a pleasure to read, lovely to look at, and packed with useful information." Carol Cubberly, in

Library Journal, thought it "would be a fine addition to any collection of landscape architecture, horticulture, or gardening." Dora Galitzki, in the *New York Times Book Review,* commented that Lord looks at the gardens "with as much attention to the 'how' and the 'why' as the 'what.'" Mary Keen, in the *Spectator,* found the book to be "an analytical and detailed appraisal of the way the place is run," with "something new to learn" on each page.

Designing with Roses is a thorough treatment of the history and art of growing roses, whether in separate beds, in borders, or in mixed gardens. As in his other books, Lord supplies the photographs. Phillip Oliver, in *Library Journal,* called them "sumptuous" and the book a "worthy treatment" on roses. Carol Bishop Miller, in *Horticulture,* praised the book's "Pick of the Bunch" list of suggestions for types of roses to grow for any purpose. Miller thought Lord's chapters "deal with using roses intelligently and imaginatively" and offer "delicious combinations of color and texture." Mary Keen, in the *Spectator,* wrote, "Show me a gardener who shuns roses and they might manage without Dr. Lord. Everyone else will wonder how they coped before this indispensable work appeared."

Lord's *Encyclopedia of Planting Combinations,* with photos by Andrew Lawson, a Garden Writers' Guild Garden Photographer of the Year, features more than 1,000 plants in some 4,000 beautiful combinations. Lord lists bulbs, annuals, climbers, shrubs and small trees, roses, and perennials. Every aspect of design, planting, and care is covered. Carol Haggas, of *Booklist,* wrote, "If there is a better organized gardening book available, its existence is unknown." Thoroughly cross-referenced, with hardiness zone maps for Europe, North America, Australia, and New Zealand, the book gives common and botanical names for all plants and uses symbols to show light, moisture, and soil conditions most favorable to each. S. C. Awe, in *Choice,* called the book "essential for . . . aspiring gardeners everywhere." Nancy Myers, in *Library Journal* described it as "a stunning book that is destined to become an essential reference on combining plants."

BIOGRAPHICAL AND CRITICAL SOURCES:

PERIODICALS

Booklist, November 1, 2002, Carol Haggas, review of *The Encyclopedia of Planting Combinations: The Ultimate Visual Guide to Successful Plant Harmony,* p. 465.

Choice, January, 2003, S. C. Awe, review of *The Encyclopedia of Planting Combinations,* p. 804.

Christian Science Monitor, February 23, 1995, April Austin, review of *Best Borders,* p. B1.

Early American Life, December, 1995, Carol McCabe, review of *Best Borders,* p. 57.

Horticulture, Gardening at Its Best, February, 1995, Ann Lovejoy, review of *Best Borders,* p. 66; March, 1996, Ann Lovejoy, review of *Rosemary Verey's Making of a Garden,* p. 66; October, 1996, Christopher Reed, review of *Gardening at Sissinghurst,* p. 72; January, 2000, Carol Bishop Miller, review of *Designing with Roses,* p. 84.

Library Journal, December, 1995, Beth Clewis Crim, review of *Rosemary Verey's Making of a Garden,* pp. 141-142; May 15, 1996, Carol Cubberly, review of *Gardening at Sissinghurst,* p. 78; August, 1999, Phillip Oliver, review of *Designing with Roses,* p. 126; October 15, 2002, Nancy Myers, review of *The Encyclopedia of Planting Combinations,* p. 62.

New York Times Book Review, June 16, 1996, Dora Galitzki, review of *Gardening at Sissinghurst,* Section 7, p. 19.

Spectator, November 26, 1994, Mary Keen, review of *Best Borders,* p. 52; December 2, 1995, Mary Keen, review of *Gardening at Sissinghurst,* pp. 41-42; November 27, 1999, Mary Keen, review of *Designing with Roses,* p. 57.

ONLINE

Horticultural Taxonomy Group, http://www.hortax.org.uk/ (June 4, 2001), "Tony Lord".

iCanGarden.com, http://www.icangarden.com/ (April 3, 2003), review of *The Encyclopedia of Planting Combinations.**

* * *

LOVATO, Charles F(rederick) 1937-1987

PERSONAL: Born May 23, 1937, in Santo Domingo Pueblo, NM; died, 1987. *Education:* Attended Native American school in Santa Fe, NM; studied art with Jose Rey Toledo.

CAREER: Painter, potter, bead maker, and textile artist. *Exhibitions:* Work represented in group exhibitions, including shows at Heard Museum, Hastings College Art Center, and Wheelwright Museum of the American Indian; work collected at Center for Great Plains Studies at University of Nebraska, Heritage Center Collection at Pine Ridge, SD, Indian Pueblo Cultural Center, National Museum of the American Indian, and Museum of Northern Arizona. *Military service:* U.S. Navy.

AWARDS, HONORS: Numerous awards, 1967-87, including award from Heard Museum Guild Indian Fair and Market, 1968; Bialac Purchase Award, 1969, 1971; Inter-Tribal Indian Ceremonial Award, 1969; annual awards, Philbrook Museum, 1970-71, 1979; awards from Scottsdale National Indian Art Exhibition, 1970, and Red Cloud Indian Art Show, 1971; Keney Award, 1971-72; Avery Award, 1977; and Elkus Award.

WRITINGS:

(And illustrator) *Life under the Sun* (poetry), Sunstone Press (Santa Fe, NM), 1982.

BIOGRAPHICAL AND CRITICAL SOURCES:

BOOKS

St. James Guide to Native North American Artists, St. James Press (Detroit, MI), 1998, pp. 336-338.*

* * *

LOWRY, Bates 1923-2004

OBITUARY NOTICE—See index for *CA* sketch: Born June 23, 1923, in Cincinnati, OH; died of pneumonia March 12, 2004, in Brooklyn, NY. Historian, educator, and author. Lowry was a specialist in art and architecture history and former director of the Museum of Modern Art and National Building Museum. He served in the U.S. Army during World War II, and it was while in France and Germany that he became interested in art and architecture. He studied art history at the University of Chicago after the war, earning his doctorate in 1955. Lowry's academic career began at the University of California at Riverside, where he was an assistant professor in the mid-1950s. Next, he was an assistant professor at the Institute of Fine Arts at New York University from 1957 to 1959, followed by four years as professor and chair of the art department at Pomona College. He performed similar duties at Brown University from 1963 to 1968, the year that Museum of Modern Art director Rene D'Harnoncourt selected him to be his successor. Unfortunately, D'Harnoncourt died shortly thereafter in an auto accident, and Lowry had difficulties gaining support from the museum's trustees after the abrupt transition. Resigning from the museum in 1969, he joined the faculty at the University of Massachusetts, where he was a professor of art and department chair for the remainder of the 1970s. In 1980, Lowry's knowledge of architecture led to his being selected as director of the new National Building Museum in Washington, D.C., which opened in 1985. But although Lowry's knowledge of architecture was never in question, he did not enjoy fundraising and working to stay in the good graces of politicians. He left in 1987 to focus on writing and research. Among his publications are *Renaissance Architecture* (1962), *Building a National Image: Architectural Drawings for the American Democracy, 1789-1912* (1985), and *The Silver Canvas: Daguerreotype Masterpieces from the J. Paul Getty Museum* (1998), which he wrote with his wife, Isabel. He and his wife were also the founders of the Dunlap Society, which was created to develop educational materials about art. A member of the Smithsonian Institute's editorial board, Lowry edited the College Art Association's Monograph series during the 1950s and 1960s, the *Art Bulletin* from 1965 to 1968, and the *Architecture of Washington, D.C.* from 1977 to 1979.

OBITUARIES AND OTHER SOURCES:

PERIODICALS

Los Angeles Times, March 22, 2004, p. B9.
New York Times, March 18, 2004, p. C17.
Washington Post, March 17, 2004, p. B6.

*   *   *

LYNCH, Patrick
    See GEARY, Joseph

M

MacDOUGALL, (George) Donald (Alastair) 1912-2004

OBITUARY NOTICE—See index for CA sketch: Born October 26, 1912, in Glasgow, Scotland; died March 22, 2004, in London, England. Economist, educator, and author. MacDougall played an important role as an advisor to his government from World War II through the 1970s. Educated at Balliol College, where he earned a master's degree in 1936, he was an assistant lecturer at the University of Leeds when he was selected to advise Winston Churchill on economic matters involving the war with Germany. Although still very young at the time, MacDougall was considered brilliant by many who credited him as an important factor in winning the war. For example, his calculations concerning supply shipping helped prevent Germany's efforts to starve England into a surrender. After the war, he was also instrumental in planning for the post-war reconstruction of Europe. MacDougall returned to academia as a fellow at Wadham College, Oxford, in the late-1940s and 1950s, also serving as first bursar from 1958 to 1964. He was back in government work in 1964, however, when he accepted a post as director-general of England's Department of Economic Affairs. During this time, his efforts focused on encouraging planned economic growth, including improving communication between government, businesses, and labor. From 1969 to 1973, MacDougall was an advisor to the Treasury, leaving government work to be chief economic advisor to the Confederation of British Industry until his retirement in 1984. A former officer in the Royal Economic Society, who was president from 1972 to 1974, the economist's service to his country did not go unrecognized, and he was knighted in 1953. He was the author of several books, including *The Dollar Problem* (1957), *Studies in Political Economy* (1975), and *Don and Mandarin: Memoirs of an Economist* (1987).

OBITUARIES AND OTHER SOURCES:

PERIODICALS

Financial Times, March 24, 2004, p. 4.
Independent (London, England), March 23, 2004, p. 34.
Times (London, England), March 29, 2004, p. 26.

* * *

MacLEAN, Glynne 1964-

PERSONAL: Born April 17, 1964, in Christchurch, New Zealand. *Education:* Waikato Unversity, B.A., 1984.

ADDRESSES: *Agent*—Michael Gifkins, Michael Gifkins & Associates, P.O. Box 6496, Auckland, New Zealand; michael.gifkins@xtra.co.nz. *E-mail*—glynne@paradise.net.nz.

CAREER: Writer. Has also worked in travel industry; designer of commercial Web sites.

AWARDS, HONORS: Children's Literature Foundation of New Zealand Notable Book, 2004, for *The A'nzarian Chronicle, Book One: Roivan.*

WRITINGS:

(Self-illustrated) *The A'nzarian Chronicle, Book One: Roivan,* Penguin Books New Zealand (Auckland, New Zealand), 2003.
Love in Shades of Grey (adult novel), Penguin Books New Zealand (Auckland, New Zealand), 2004.

Author of regular computer column for *Chatterbox* magazine, New Zealand, 1999—. Contributor of poetry, essays, and short fiction in ezines and in *Niederngasse: The Journal of Winning Poetry.*

WORK IN PROGRESS: Book Two of *The A'nzarian Chronicle.*

SIDELIGHTS: Glynne MacLean once commented: "I write both literary fiction and sci fi. I see the universe, past, present, and imagined, as providing an unlimited canvas. Writing sci fi allows me to examine issues and scenarios beyond the constraints of the prevailing definition of political correctness."

BIOGRAPHICAL AND CRITICAL SOURCES:

ONLINE

A'nzarian Chronicle, http://www.roivan.co.nz/ (December 14, 2003), information about MacLean's science fiction.
Glynne MacLean Home Page, http://www.glynne.co. nz/ (December 14, 2003).

*   *   *

MACMILLAN, Malcolm (Bruce) 1929-

PERSONAL: Born January 1, 1929, in Perth, Western Australia; son of Ian Stewart and Mabel Evelyn (Sinclair) Macmillan; children: Luisa Ann Macmillan Tanter, Ian Scott, Gregor James. *Ethnicity:* "Australian." *Education:* University of Western Australia, B.Sc., 1950; University of Melbourne, M.Sc., 1964; Monash University, D.Sc., 1992. *Politics:* "Communist in search of a party." *Hobbies and other interests:* Traditional jazz, chamber music, wine.

ADDRESSES: Office—School of Psychology, Deakin University, Burwood, Victoria 3125, Australia. *E-mail*—m.macmillan@deakin.edu.au.

CAREER: Australian Council for Educational Research, research assistant, 1955; Department of Health, Melbourne, Victoria, Australia, began as psychologist at Mental Hygiene Branch, became senior psychologist, 1955-64; Monash University, Melbourne, Victoria, Australia, senior lecturer in psychology, 1965-94; Deakin University, Burwood, Victoria, Australia, adjunct professor of psychology, 1994—. University of Wisconsin—Madison, visiting professor, 1972-73; Cambridge University, visiting scholar, 1979; Stanford University, visiting professor, 1979; University of Arizona, visiting professor, 1989; University of Pittsburgh, visiting fellow at Center for Philosophy of Science, 1993; Northern Michigan University, visiting professor, 1999; Oxford University, visiting fellow at McDonnell Centre for Cognitive Neurosciences, 2002; guest lecturer at other institutions, including New York University, New School for Social Research, and University of Beijing; public speaker in Australia and abroad.

MEMBER: International Society for the History of the Neurosciences (founding member), Cheiron: International Society for the History of the Behavioral Sciences, Australian Psychological Society (founding member; fellow; president, 1984-85), American Psychological Society (fellow), History of Science Society (United States).

AWARDS, HONORS: Association of American Publishers Award, professional and scholarly publishing division, 2001, for *An Odd Kind of Fame: Stories of Phineas Gage;* inaugural prize for "book making the most outstanding and original contribution to the history of the neurosciences in the period between 1999 and 2001," 2002.

WRITINGS:

The Historical and Scientific Evaluation of Psychoanalytic Personality Theory, Department of Psychology, Monash University (Melbourne, Victoria, Australia), 1974.
Freud Evaluated: The Completed Arc, North-Holland (Amsterdam, Netherlands), 1991.

Evaluating Freud: The Poor Students' Guide, Department of Psychology, Monash University (Melbourne, Victoria, Australia), 1992.

Critical Introductory Lectures on Psychoanalysis, Monash University (Melbourne, Victoria, Australia), 1993.

An Odd Kind of Fame: Stories of Phineas Gage, MIT Press (Cambridge, MA), 2000.

Contributor to books, including *Sigmund Freud: Critical Assessments,* Volume 1, edited by L. Spurling, Routledge (London, England), 1989; *Freud and the History of Psychoanalysis,* edited by T. Gelfand and J. Kerr, Analytic Press (Hillsdale, NJ), 1992; *Classic Cases in Neuropsychology,* edited by C. Code and others, Erlbaum (East Sussex, England), 1996; and *Psychoanalytic Knowledge and the Nature of Mind,* edited by M. C. Chung and C. Feltham, Palgrave (London, England), 2003. Contributor of articles and reviews to academic journals, including *Psychological Inquiry, Journal of Nervous and Mental Disease, British Journal of Medical Psychology, Developmental Medicine and Child Neurology, Journal of Autism and Childhood Schizophrenia, Brain and Cognition, Australian Psychologist,* and *American Imago.* Book review editor, *Australian Journal of Psychology,* 1966-72; member of editorial board, *Journal of the History of the Neurosciences,* 1996—, and *History of Psychology,* 1997—.

WORK IN PROGRESS: A study of pioneer brain surgeon William Macewen.

SIDELIGHTS: Malcolm Macmillan told *CA:* "My primary motivation for writing is to report scientific research and to evaluate scientific theories, especially by considering their historical development. My work is particularly influenced by Marx and Engels. My inspiration is curiosity. I get an idea; I think and read about it; I get confused and swamped; a framework develops (by itself); and I set about writing."

BIOGRAPHICAL AND CRITICAL SOURCES:

PERIODICALS

Isis, March, 2002, Kieran O'Driscoll, review of *An Odd Kind of Fame: Stories of Phineas Gage,* p. 138.

Journal of Neurology, Neurosurgery, and Psychiatry, July, 2001, John Hodges, review of *An Odd Kind of Fame,* p. 136.

Journal of the American Medical Association, January 10, 2001, Randolph W. Evans, review of *An Odd Kind of Fame,* p. 215.

Lancet, February 17, 2001, Paul Crichton, review of *An Odd Kind of Fame,* p. 566.

Quarterly Review of Biology, December, 2001, Jonathon Erlen, review of *An Odd Kind of Fame,* p. 521.

Science, October 27, 2000, John C. Marshall, review of *An Odd Kind of Fame,* p. 718.

Student BMJ, June, 2001, Sally-Ann S. Price, review of *An Odd Kind of Fame,* p. 213.

*   *   *

MANDEL, Miriam B. 1942-

PERSONAL: Born June 23, 1942, in San Juan, Puerto Rico; immigrated to Israel, 1979; daughter of Paul (an architect) and Gertrude S. (an office manager) Bauer. *Education:* Attended Harpur College of the State University of New York and Ohio State University. *Hobbies and other interests:* Music (particularly opera), twentieth-century art, bullfighting.

ADDRESSES: Office—Department of English, Tel Aviv University, Ramat Aviv, Israel; fax: 972-3-640-7312. *E-mail*—mbmandel@post.tau.ac.il.

CAREER: Rutgers University, New Brunswick, NJ, editorial assistant in Graduate School of Education, 1968-71; Tel Aviv University, Ramat Aviv, Israel, member of faculty, 1979—, currently senior lecturer in English. Translator from Spanish into English.

MEMBER: Modern Language Association of America, American Literature Association, Hemingway Society, Fitzgerald Society.

AWARDS, HONORS: Grants from United States-Israel Educational Fund, 1990, John F. Kennedy Library, 1991, 1995, and National Endowment for the Humanities, 1995-98.

WRITINGS:

Reading Hemingway: The Facts in the Fictions, Scarecrow Press (Lanham, MD), 1995.

Hemingway's Death in the Afternoon: The Complete Annotations, Scarecrow Press (Lanham, MD), 2002.

Hemingway's The Dangerous Summer: The Complete Annotations, Scarecrow Press (Lanham, MD), 2003.

Contributor to books, including *Literature and Life: Making Connections in the Classroom,* edited by Patricia Phelan, National Council of Teachers of English (Urbana, IL), 1990; *Hemingway Repossessed,* edited by Kenneth Rosen, Praeger (Westport, CT), 1994; and *Notable Women: Female Critics and the Female Voice in Hemingway,* edited by Lawrence Broer and Gloria Holland, University of Alabama Press (Tuscaloosa, AL), in press. Contributor to periodicals, including *Studies in Short Fiction, Persuasions, International Fiction Review, Housman Society Journal, Hemingway Review, Journal of Modern Literature,* and *Resources for American Literary Study.*

WORK IN PROGRESS: *Hemingway's Nonfiction: Annotating Africa and France* (tentative title), for Scarecrow Press (Lanham, MD); editing *A Companion to Hemingway's "Death in the Afternoon,"* Camden House/Boydell & Brewer (Rochester, NY).

SIDELIGHTS: Miriam B. Mandel told *CA:* "Even before I was born, my life took many unexpected turns. Because of Hitler's persecution of the Jews, my parents moved from Vienna, Austria, where the family had lived for generations, to San Juan, Puerto Rico, where I was born. As a result, my brother and I grew up trilingual (German, Spanish, English), and this 'multiculturality' has shaped my life in a variety of ways. Another unexpected turn was my immigration to Israel in 1979, which added Hebrew to my life, and my life at Tel Aviv University, where I was required to publish. This demand led to an active writing career that I had never envisioned for myself. Writing my books has been extremely pleasurable, and I recommend historical research and literary annotation to all aspiring scholars. It helps one read, think, observe, and enjoy places and activities which one might never have otherwise encountered.

"I find that research makes any subject more interesting. My research on Hemingway, facilitated by my ability to read all the languages he knew, has led me to—among the many subjects which interested

him—bullfighting. The bullfight established the moral and cultural background of several of Hemingway's best short stories and two of his major novels (*The Sun Also Rises* and *For Whom the Bell Tolls*). The subject so fascinated Hemingway that he wrote two entire nonfiction volumes about it: *Death in the Afternoon* (his longest book) and *The Dangerous Summer* (the last book he wrote). Studying it, I too became fascinated by the history of bullfighting, its contemporary manifestations, and its significance to Spanish culture and art, as well as to Hemingway's aesthetics.

"From Austrian backgrounds to Puerto Rican beginnings to Israeli maturity to the pleasures of the Spanish plaza, it has been an interesting life. I wonder where it will take me next."

BIOGRAPHICAL AND CRITICAL SOURCES:

PERIODICALS

College Literature, June, 1997, Stephen P. Clifford, review of *Reading Hemingway: The Facts in the Fictions,* p. 172.

Hemingway Review, fall, 1995, Earl Rovit, review of *Reading Hemingway,* p. 105; fall, 2002, Keneth Kinnamon, review of *Hemingway's Death in the Afternoon: The Complete Annotations,* p. 118.

*   *   *

MANICKA, Rani

PERSONAL: Born in Malaysia; immigrated to England; divorced. *Education:* Earned degree in economics; studied management training in Germany.

ADDRESSES: *Home*—England; Malaysia. *Office*—c/o Author Mail, Viking, 375 Hudson St., New York, NY 10014.

CAREER: Businessperson and author. Ran a restaurant in London, England.

AWARDS, HONORS: Commonwealth Writers Prize, 2003, for *The Rice Mother.*

WRITINGS:

The Rice Mother, Sceptre (London, England), 2002, Viking (New York City), 2003.

SIDELIGHTS: Malaysian native Rani Manicka published her first novel *The Rice Mother,* after the book was the subject of a bidding war between publishers. Manicka, who had previously worked in the restaurant business in her adopted country of England before turning to writing, was inspired to write the book by her grandmother in Malaysia. Manicka was influenced by how hard she fought in her life, and *The Rice Mother*'s main character, Lakshmi, also overcomes many difficult circumstances. In addition to winning the Commonwealth Writers Prize, *The Rice Mother* was also nominated for the International IMPAC Dublin Literary Award in 2004.

The Rice Mother revolves around Lakshmi, a native of Ceylon who moves to Malaysia as a teenager in about 1930 to marry Ayah, who has lied about his circumstances. By the time Lakshmi is nineteen years old, she has six children, and Japan has invaded the country. Ayah is tortured by the Japanese. Lakshmi's beloved daughter Mohini also disappears, and is raped and presumed murdered by the invaders, adding to the legacy of tragedy in the family. Despite such horrors, Lakshmi pushes her family forward. They have success in business and in their personal lives because of her, but also experience much loss. Told from various first-person narratives, the chronicle of *The Rice Mother* includes the point of view of Lakshmi's children, their partners, her grandchildren, and her great-grandchildren. Hwee Hwee Tan of *Time International* felt that Manicka's "characters were original, its canvas broad, and Manicka's radiant prose brings out all the dark lushness of her ultimately tragic tale." Though a reviewer for *Publishers Weekly* commented that Manicka was "syrupy" in her depiction of such areas as youth, the reviewer also acknowledged that the characters' "voices were distinct, and prismatic sketches form a cohesive and vibrant saga."

BIOGRAPHICAL AND CRITICAL SOURCES:

PERIODICALS

Booklist, June 9, 2003, Kristine Huntley, review of *The Rice Mother,* p. 1956.

Books Magazine, autumn, 2002, review of *The Rice Mother,* p. 21.
Kirkus Reviews, May 15, 2003, review of *The Rice Mother,* p. 707.
Library Journal, April 15, 2003, Andrea Kempf, review of *The Rice Mother,* p. 123.
Observer (London, England), September 22, 2002, Hephizibah Anderson, "If you're not sure how to make a sari, read on," p. 17.
Publishers Weekly, June 9, 2003, review of *The Rice Mother,* p. 34.
Time International, March 10, 2003, Hwee Hwee Tan, "Matriarch of Malaysia: Rani Manicka's debut novel, *The Rice Mother,* sets a family saga in unexplored literary territory," p. 59.

ONLINE

Bookreporter.com, http://www.bookreporter.com/ (November 3, 2003), Sarah Rachel Egelman, review of *The Rice Mother.*
Guardian Unlimited, http://books.guardian.co.uk/ (September 22, 2002), Hephizibah Anderson, "Local colour."
Penguin Putnam, http://www.penguinputnam.com/ (November 3, 2003), "A Conversation with Rani Manicka" (November 3, 2003), summary of *The Rice Mother.*
Red Hot Curry, http://www.redhotcurry.com/ (November 3, 2003), review of *The Rice Mother.*
Sawnet Review, http://www.umiacs.umd.edu/users/sawweb/sawnet/ (November 3, 2003), review of *The Rice Mother.**

*   *   *

MATSUI, Yayori 1934-2002

PERSONAL: Born April 12, 1934 in Kyoto, Japan; died of liver cancer, December 27, 2002, in Tokyo, Japan. *Education:* Attended college in MN and Paris. *Hobbies and other interests:* Swimming, yoga, painting, music, clothing.

CAREER: Author, journalist, educator, and women's rights activist. *Asahi Shimbun* newspaper, Tokyo, Japan, reporter, staff writer, and correspondent, stationed in Japan, the United States, and Singapore,

1961-1994. Founded Asian Women in Solidarity, 1976, the Asia-Japan Women's Resource Center in Tokyo, 1995, and the organization, Violence against Women in War; taught at various universities.

WRITINGS:

Tamashii ni fureru Ajia, Asahi Shinbunsha (Tokyo, Japan), 1985.

Onnatachi no Ajia, Iwanami Shoten (Tokyo, Japan), 1987, translation published as *Women's Asia,* Zed Books (Atlantic Highlands, NJ), 1989.

Ajia, onna, minshu, Shinkansha (Tokyo, Japan), 1987.

Ajia kara kita dekasegi rodoshatachi, Akashi Shoten (Tokyo, Japan), 1988.

Shimin to enjo: Ima nani ga dekiru ka, Iwanami Shoten (Tokyo, Japan), 1990.

Ajia ni ikiru kodomotachi, Rodo Junposha (Tokyo, Japan), 1991.

NGO, ODA enjo wa dare no tame ka: Hihon to Doitsu daisan sekai, Akashi Shoten (Tokyo, Japan), 1992.

Ajia no kanko kaihatsy to Nihon, Shinkansha (Tokyo, Japan), 1993.

Nihon o tou Ajia: Kaihatsu, josei, jinken, Buraku Kaiho Kenkyujo (Osaka, Japan), 1994.

Onnatachi ga tsukuru Ajia, Iwanami Shoten (Tokyo, Japan), 1996, translation by Noriko Toyokawa and Carolyn Francis published as *Women in the New Asia: From Pain to Power,* Zed Books (New York, NY), 1998.

SIDELIGHTS: One of first female journalists in Japan, Yayori Matsui was also an author of note whose works focused on the rights of women in Asia. Born in 1924, Matsui was the daughter of Christian missionaries and received an international education, studying in both the United States and France. Returning to Japan after her studies abroad, Matsui stopped off in various Asian countries and was confronted, for the first time, with the face of poverty, an experience that informed much of her later work. In 1961 she began as a reporter for the Tokyo newspaper, *Asahi Shimbun,* and it was clear from the outset that she would not be shunted off into the women's section, writing only about food and fashion. Concentrating on social issues, she was one of the first to break stories about birth defects caused by the use of the sedative thalidomide, as well as to investigate Minamata disease, which is caused by mercury poisoning.

Introduced to the feminist movement while on a trip to the United States, she also began campaigning against the growing sex tourism industry in Asia. Posted in Singapore in 1981, Matsui uncovered the excesses of the Japanese occupation forces during World War II; in particular, she focused on the Japanese Army's use of so-called "comfort women," some 200,000 Asian females that the military forced into sexual slavery. The fact that those responsible for this crime had never been brought to justice outraged Matsui, and she campaigned vigorously for the rest of her life to that end.

Among Matsui's books on women in Asia, two have been translated into English. *Women's Asia,* originally published in 1987, is a book that looks at "the relationship between Japan and other countries from the perspective of women," according to Pam Keesey writing in *Women's Studies International Forum.* Included in the study are examinations of child prostitution and the sex tourism industry, the use of women as cheap labor, and violence to women, including rape and child abuse. For Matsui, the role of Japanese women in a wider Asian context was one of ambivalence. "We Japanese women play a double role," she wrote in her book. "We are discriminated against in Japanese society and, at the same time, we benefit from the exploitation of other Asian women. . . . We are both victims and oppressors." Matsui used personal testimony and examples in her book, describing "women's resistance with the same eloquence and attention to detail that she uses in describing the horrifying details of their exploitation," according to Keesey. "Matsui more than does justice to her subject," Keesey concluded. Jane Hutchinson, writing in the *Journal of Contemporary Asia,* found the book to be "comprehensive in its coverage and in its subject matter," documenting the condition of women in seventeen Asian countries. For Sylvia Hale in *Pacific Affairs,* Matsui's book "provides interesting and often moving journalistic descriptions," and Sue Ellen Charlton, reviewing the work in *Women and Politics,* noted that "Matsui's tone is personal, with the result that the reader feels an intimate connection with the plight of the village women, migrants and dowry victims she describes."

In her 1996 title, *Women in the New Asia: From Pain to Power,* Matsui presents an updated view of females in Asian countries in a "lucidly written book [that] offers a broad view of the lives of women in Thailand, the Philippines, Thailand, Korea, Nepal, Hong Kong and China," according to R. Sooryamoorthy, writing in *Journal of Third World Studies.* Again, as in her earlier work, Matsui employs largely personal observation to demonstrate how women in Asia suffer from social conditions including domestic violence, sexual slavery, and prostitution. When writing of conditions in Japan, for example, Matsui shows that that country's sex industry generates as much income as the defense budget of Japan. Matsui also explores the ravages of HIV among females, and the speed with which it is spreading in Asian countries. Sooryamoorthy concluded, "The author, on the whole, has succeeded in giving [an] overall view of the position of women in Asian countries, with clear insights and interesting narratives." Writing in *Asian Affairs,* Delia Davin also had praise for *Women in the New Asia,* noting that "this book contains an immense amount of information that will no doubt contribute to the growing awareness of the price paid for economic growth by the most vulnerable members of society." Davin also thought that, despite some "shortcomings," such as the conversion of names from Chinese to English and what Davin considered a somewhat "superficial" approach in places, Matsui's book "should be read by all who are interested in Asian women in the modern world." Similarly, Maila Stivens, reviewing the same work in *Journal of Southeast Asian Studies,* felt that *Women in the New Asia* "is a highly readable introduction to some aspects of gender relations in contemporary Asia."

Matsui retired from her newspaper position in 1994, but remained active in women's rights to the very end of her life. In 2000, her organization, Violence against Women in War brought together a people's tribunal in the Hague over the issue of Japan's use of "comfort women," collecting testimony from survivors who spoke before lawyers and judges from the United Nations. In October of 2002, she went to Afghanistan, examining the condition of women there. Returning to Japan, she was diagnosed with liver cancer, but continued working on a project to open the Women's Museum in Tokyo in 2006. She died on December 27, 2002. "As a charismatic, energetic, and utterly stubborn woman in a male-dominated society, Matsui left her mark on everyone she met," wrote Joachim Bergstroem in a *World Press Review* appreciation of the journalist and activist.

BIOGRAPHICAL AND CRITICAL SOURCES:

BOOKS

Matsui, Yayori, *Women's Asia,* Zed Books (Atlantic Highlands, NJ), 1989.

PERIODICALS

Asian Affairs, June, 2000, Delia Davin, review of *Women in the New Asia: From Pain to Power,* pp. 208-209.
Journal of Contemporary Asia, January, 1991, Jane Hutchinson, review of *Women's Asia,* pp. 129-131; March, 2001, Indira Arumugam, review of *Women in the New Asia,* p. 133.
Journal of Southeast Asian Studies, June, 2002, Maila Stivens, review of *Women in the New Asia,* pp. 345-346.
Journal of Third World Studies, spring, 2002, R. Sooryamoorthy, review of *Women in the New Asia,* pp. 210-212.
Pacific Affairs, winter, 1990, Sylvia Hale, review of *Women's Asia,* pp. 546-547.
Women and Politics, fall, 1992, Sue Ellen Charlton, review of *Women's Asia,* pp. 109-112.
Women's Studies International Forum, May-June, 1992, Pam Keesey, review of *Women's Asia,* pp. 431-432.

ONLINE

Palgrave Macmillan Web site, http://www.palgrave-usa.com/ (July 8, 2003).
Spinifex Press, http://www.spinifexpress.com.au/ (March 20, 1999), Lucy Sussex, review of *Women in the New Asia.*

OBITUARIES:

PERIODICALS

Los Angeles Times, January 8, 2003, Mark Magnier, "Yayori Matsui, 68," p. B10.
New York Times, January 5, 2003, Wolfgang Saxon, "Yayori Matsui, Campaigner," p. A27.

World Press Review, March, 2003, Joachim Bergstroem, "Yayori Matsui: Championing Women of Asia," p. 46.*

* * *

MAYES, Linda C(arol) 1951-

PERSONAL: Born October 14, 1951, in Sewanee, TN. *Education:* University of the South, B.A. (summa cum laude), 1973; Vanderbilt University, M.D., 1977; attended Western New England Institute for Psychoanalysis, 1986-2000.

ADDRESSES: Home—20D Harbour Village, Branford, CT 06405. *Office*—Yale Child Study Center, Yale University, 230 South Frontage Rd., P.O. Box 107900, New Haven, CT 06520-7900. *E-mail*—linda.mayes@ yale.edu.

CAREER: Vanderbilt University, Nashville, TN, intern, 1977-78, resident in pediatrics, 1978-80, fellow in neonatology, 1980-82; Yale University, New Haven, CT, fellow in Robert Wood Johnson General Academic Pediatrics Program, 1982-84, research fellow in pediatrics at Yale Child Study Center, 1984-85, assistant professor, 1986-89, Elizabeth Mears and House Jameson Assistant Professor of Child Development, 1989-90, Elizabeth Mears and House Jameson Associate Professor of Child Development, 1990, Arnold Gesell Associate Professor of Child Psychiatry, Pediatrics, and Psychology, 1991—, fellow at Morse College, 1990—, fellow at Bush Center on Social Policy, 1994—, coordinator of early childhood section, Yale Child Study Center, 1996—, codirector of Early Childhood Education Consortium, 1997—. Western New England Institute for Psychoanalysis, faculty member, 2001—; University of London, visiting professor at University College, 2001. National Center for Clinical Infant Programs, fellow, 1984-85; National Institute of Child Health and Human Development, adjunct scientist, 1990—. Gesell Institute, board member, 1991-2000; Menninger Clinic, visiting scholar, 2001. City of New Haven, member of Special Commission on Infant Health, 1992-96.

MEMBER: World Association for Infant Psychiatry, Ambulatory Pediatric Association, Society for Research in Child Development, American Psychoanalytic Association (chair of Fund for Psychoanalytic Research, 2000—), Association of Child Psychoanalysis, Neurobehavioral Teratology Society, Cognitive Neuroscience Society, Connecticut Council of Child Psychiatrists, Phi Beta Kappa, Sigma Xi, Alpha Omega Alpha.

AWARDS, HONORS: Research and Teaching Award, Ambulatory Pediatrics Association, 1985; Johnson & Johnson Advanced Pediatric Research Award, 1984-85; D.Sc., University of the South, 1994; Heinz Hartmann Award, New York Psychoanalytic Association, 1999; grants from numerous organizations and agencies, including Maternal and Child Health Bureau, Connecticut Department of Children and Families, Harris Foundation, National Institute of Mental Health, March of Dimes Birth Defects Foundation, Smith Richardson Foundation, Robert Wood Johnson Foundation, National Institute on Child Health and Human Development, and National Institute on Drug Abuse.

WRITINGS:

(Editor, with W. S. Gilliam, and contributor) *Comprehensive Psychiatric Assessment of Young Children,* W. B. Saunders Co. (Philadelphia, PA), 1999.
(With D. J. Cohen and others) *The Yale Child Study Center Guide to Understanding Your Child: Healthy Development from Birth to Adolescence,* Little, Brown and Co. (New York, NY), 2002.

Contributor to books, including *Attention, Development, and Psychopathology,* edited by J. A. Burack and J. T. Enns, Guilford Press (New York, NY), 1997; *The Vulnerable Child,* edited by T. Cohen, M. H. Etezady, and B. L. Pacella, International Universities Press (Madison, CT), 1999; *The Scientific Basis of Child Custody Decisions,* edited by R. M. Galatzer-Levy and L. Kraus, John Wiley and Sons (New York, NY), 1999; *Environmental Effects on Cognitive Abilities,* edited by R. J. Sternberg and E. L. Grigorenko, Lawrence Erlbaum Associates (Mahway, NJ), 2001; and *Child and Adolescent Psychiatry: A Comprehensive Textbook,* edited by M. Lewis, Williams & Wilkins (Philadelphia, PA). Contributor of articles and reviews to periodicals, including *Current Psychology of Cognition, Journal of Developmental and Behavioral Pediatrics, Infant Mental Health, Psychoanalytic Study of the Child, Child Psychiatry and Human Development,*

Journal of Clinical Anesthesia, Journal of Applied Developmental Psychology, Pediatrics, Development and Psychopathology, and *Journal of Infant, Child, and Adolescent Psychotherapy.* Editor of special issues, *Seminars in Perinatology,* 1989, 1997; member of editorial board, *Journal of the American Psychoanalytic Association,* 2001—.

BIOGRAPHICAL AND CRITICAL SOURCES:

PERIODICALS

Booklist, February 1, 2002, Vanessa Bush, review of *The Yale Child Study Center Guide to Understanding Your Child: Healthy Development from Birth to Adolescence,* p. 913.
Library Journal, February 15, 2002, Douglas C. Lord, review of *The Yale Child Study Center Guide to Understanding Your Child,* p. 172.
M2 Best Books, March 21, 2002, review of *The Yale Child Study Center to Understanding Your Child.*
Publishers Weekly, January 21, 2002, review of *The Yale Child Study Center Guide to Understanding Your Child,* p. 84.

*   *   *

McCORD, Margaret 1916-2004

OBITUARY NOTICE—See index for *CA* sketch: Born November 7, 1916, in Durban, South Africa; died March 29, 2004, in Carlisle, MA. Author. McCord is best remembered for her award-winning biography *The Calling of Katie Makanya: A Memoir of South Africa* (1995). The subject of her biography was a woman she had known since childhood as the Zulu translator who worked at the hospital that McCord's father founded in South Africa. The road that led to the writing of the book was long, however. McCord left South Africa to study at Oberlin College in Ohio, where she earned a B.A. in 1939. After spending a year as an art teacher in South Africa, she returned to the United States, was married in 1941, and spent her days as a homemaker while also working a variety of jobs, including as an executive secretary at Cornell University Nursery School during World War II, as a screen story analyst for Warner Bros. in the early 1950s, and as a travel agent in the 1970s and 1980s.

The work on her biography, which would later win the 1996 Alan Paton Award, began in 1954, just months before Makanya's death. McCord spent several weeks recording Makanya's personal story, but the writing did not come about until some four decades later. The result, however, was a very personal view into the racially divided nation of South Africa that also won a CNA Literary Award in 1996 and a New York Library Young Adult Award.

OBITUARIES AND OTHER SOURCES:

PERIODICALS

Chicago Tribune, April 12, 2004, Section 4, p. 7.
Los Angeles Times, April 10, 2004, p. B21.

ONLINE

UCLA Faculty Women's Club, http://www.bol.ucla.edu/~uclafwc/ (May 13, 2004).

*   *   *

McCRORY, Donald P(eter) 1943-

PERSONAL: Born June 29, 1943, in Ballynahinch, Northern Ireland; son of Thomas and Eileen (Macallister) McCrory. *Ethnicity:* "White British male." *Education:* Kingston University, London, B.A. (German, Spanish, geography), 1967; Birkbeck College, B.A. (Spanish), 1969; King's College, London, M.A. (Spanish), 1970, B.A. (French), 1972; University of London, Ph.D. (Spanish), 1978; School of African and Oriental Studies, earned certificate in South Asian studies, 1994. *Politics:* Green Party. *Religion:* "New Age." *Hobbies and other interests:* Travel, sport, opera, yoga, ecology, New Age philosophy.

ADDRESSES: *Office*—42 Lea Rd., Preston, Lancashire PR2 1TP, England. *E-mail*—donald_mccrory@yahoo.co.uk.

CAREER: Secondary school teacher, early 1970s; North East Surrey College of Technology, Ewell, Surrey, England, lecturer in modern languages, 1974-84;

American International University in London, London, England, head of Spanish and German departments, 1984-2001; retired; Royal Society of Geographers, fellow, 1997. Teacher of yoga. Member, Oxford University Institute of Educational Technology Network.

MEMBER: British Wheel of Yoga, Royal Society of Geographers.

AWARDS, HONORS: International and British prizes for poetry; winner of six prizes in competitions sponsored by the Royal Society of Geographers.

WRITINGS:

(Author of explanatory text) Miguel de Cervantes, *The Captive's Tale,* Aris & Philips (Warminster, England), 1994.
(Author of introduction and notes) Hermann Hesse, *Siddhartha,* Picador (London, England), 1998.
No Ordinary Man: The Life and Times of Miguel de Cervantes, Peter Owens (London, England), 2002.

Contributor to periodicals, including *Treffpunkt, Vida Hispánica, Journal of the Association of Italian Teachers, Journal of the Modern Languages Association,* and *Linguist.*

POETRY

The Conscious Light, Outposts, 1978.
Another World, Outposts, 1980.
Wind on the Skin, Outposts, 1983.
The Sweet Taste of Goodness, Outposts, 1986.
A Piece of Glass, 1990.
New Beginnings (collected poetry), Bekal, Surbiton, 1993.

WORK IN PROGRESS: Off the List; a novel about relationships; *What If . . . ,* a novel for young adults that "is, in part, a reaction to 'Pottermania;'" *Unconditional Love,* a full-length drama.

SIDELIGHTS: A linguist and poet, Donald P. McCrory has written *No Ordinary Man: The Life and Times of Miguel de Cervantes,* a biography of the sixteenth-century Spanish-born author of *Don Quixote.*

A diplomat, prisoner, soldier, and poet, Cervantes led an exciting and unlikely life before writing the best-selling *Don Quixote* and earning international fame. McCrory's biography draws on recently unearthed family materials concerning Cervantes, as well as on McCrory's own knowledge of Spanish history. McCrory's book, the first new biography of Cervantes to be published in twenty years, is "a thoroughgoing and credible biography that opts for carefully researched conclusions over hearsay," in the opinion of Nedra C. Evers in the *Library Journal.*

McCrory told *CA:* "I have been influenced by major European authors: Shakespeare, Cervantes, Goethe, Voltaire, Dickens, T. S. Eliot, D. H. Lawrence.

"Ever since childhood I have loved literature and foreign languages. Poetry was my favorite medium until I became a serious academic and wrote what many would call erudite articles for important modern language journals in the United Kingdom. This led to the writing of academic texts and to biographical studies and to the recent well-reviewed biography on Cervantes.

"I believe the Cervantes principle of combining entertainment and wisdom is the best recipe for creative works. After a lifetime of study and reading, I feel I have a great deal to contribute to modern thinking and real life issues and I can do this best through writing and the media.

McCrory further noted his "strong and abiding interest in ancient India. I have studied Sanskrit in both London and Poona, India; followed Vedic philosophical teachings ever since 1963; have visited Indian seven times; and have stayed in several ashrams. Hence my interest in yoga and in the Hindi language.

"I took early retirement to focus on writing and on being published and on reaching the widest possible market! On a more personal note, although I no longer teach modern languages I spend several vacations on both language courses in Germany, France, Spain, and Italy and by attending opera festivals abroad; I hope to add Portuguese to my language repertoire soon."

BIOGRAPHICAL AND CRITICAL SOURCES:

PERIODICALS

Choice, September, 1995, review of *The Captive's Tale,* p. 126; December, 2002, E. H. Friedman, review of *No Ordinary Man: The Life and Times of Miguel de Cervantes,* p. 637.

Herald (Glasgow, Scotland), March 9, 2002, review of *No Ordinary Man,* p. 12.

Library Journal, September 15, 2002, Nedra C. Evers, review of *No Ordinary Man,* p. 63.

Publishers Weekly, June 3, 2002, review of *No Ordinary Man,* p. 81.

Sunday Times (London, England), May 26, 2002, Humphrey Carpenter, review of *No Ordinary Man,* p. 41.

Times Literary Supplement, July 12, 2002, A. J. Close, review of *No Ordinary Man,* p. 3.

*　　*　　*

McCULLOUGH, James P., Jr. 1936-

PERSONAL: Born October 13, 1936, in Baton Rouge, LA; son of James P. and Willie (Howell) McCullough; married January 17, 1964; wife's name, Rosemary F. (a librarian); children: Michael J., John P., Kristin R. *Ethnicity:* "Caucasian." *Education:* University of Georgia, Ph.D. *Politics:* Democrat. *Religion:* Republican.

ADDRESSES: Office—Department of Psychology, Virginia Commonwealth University, Richmond, VA 23284-9005. *E-mail*—jmccull@vcu.edu.

CAREER: Virginia Commonwealth University, Richmond, professor of psychology.

MEMBER: American Psychological Association (fellow).

WRITINGS:

Treatment for Chronic Depression: Cognitive Behavioral Analysis System of Psychotherapy, Guilford Press (New York, NY), 1999.

Skills Training Manual for Diagnosing and Treating Chronic Depression: Cognitive Behavioral Analysis System of Psychology, Guilford Press (New York, NY), 2001.

Also author of the booklet, "Patient Manual for CBASP," Guilford Press (New York, NY), 2002.

McDONNELL, Patrick 1956-

PERSONAL: Born March 17, 1956, in NY; married; wife's name Karen (a writer). *Education:* School of Visual Arts, B.A., 1978.

ADDRESSES: Agent—c/o Author Mail, Andrews McMeel Universal, 4520 Main St., Kansas City, MO 64111-7701.

CAREER: Graphic artist, writer, cartoon creator, musician, sculptor, and artist. Steel Tips (band), New York, NY, drummer, c. 1970-1981. Humane Society of the United States, board of directors.

AWARDS, HONORS: Max und Moritz Prize, Germany, 1996, for best international cartoon artist; Genesis Award, Ark Trust, 1997 and 1999, for outstanding contribution to animal rights by a cartoonist; Adamson Statuette, Swedish Academy of Comic Art, 1997; Harvey Award, 1997, 1999, 2001, 2002, and 2003, for best syndicated strip; Best Comic Strip of the Year Award, National Cartoonists Society, 1998; Ruben Award, National Cartoonists Society, 1999.

WRITINGS:

MUTTS COLLECTIONS

Mutts, foreword by Charles M. Schulz, Andrews McMeel (Kansas City, MO), 1996.

Cats and Dogs, Andrews McMeel (Kansas City, MO), 1997.

More Shtuff, Andrews McMeel (Kansas City, MO), 1998.

Yesh!, Andrews McMeel (Kansas City, MO), 1999.

Mutts Sundays, Andrews McMeel (Kansas City, MO), 1999.

Our Mutts, Andrews McMeel (Kansas City, MO), 2000.

Mutts: Sunday Mornings, Andrews McMeel (Kansas City, MO), 2001.

A Little Look-See, Andrews McMeel (Kansas City, MO), 2001.

Mutts: What Now?, Andrews McMeel (Kansas City, MO), 2002.

I Want To Be the Kitty, Andrews McMeel (Kansas City, MO), 2003.

Mutts: The Art of Patrick McDonnell, Harry N. Abrams (New York, NY), 2003.

Sunday Afternoons: A Mutts Treasury, Andrews McMeel (Kansas City, MO), 2004.

Dog-Eared: Mutts Nine, Andrews McMeel (Kansas City, MO), 2004.

OTHER

(With wife, Karen McDonnell, and others) *Krazy Kat: The Comic Art of George Herriman,* Harry N. Abrams (New York, NY), 1986.

Bad Baby (collection), Fawcett Columbine (New York, NY), 1988.

(Illustrator) Daniel Evan Weiss, *100% American,* Poseidon Press (New York, NY), 1988.

(Illustrator) *They Said It!: 200 of the Funniest Sports Quips and Quotes,* Oxmoor House (New York, NY), 1990.

Comic strips include "Mutts" (King Features Syndicate) and "Bad Baby" (for *Parents* magazine); illustrator of Russell Baker's column in *New York Times* magazine, "Scorecard" column for *Sports Illustrated,* "Bright Ideas" for *Parade,* and the "Laughter" page for *Reader's Digest;* illustrator for other periodicals, including *Time* and *Forbes.*

ADAPTATIONS: Gibson Greetings created a line of greeting cards based on "Mutts."

SIDELIGHTS: Cartoonist Patrick McDonnell is the creator of the comic strip "Mutts," which is syndicated in hundreds of newspapers in the United States, as well as in dozens of other countries. It features Earl the dog and Mooch the cat. Earl is in part based on McDonnell's own dog of the same name, and lives with Ozzie, while Mooch lives with neighbors Millie and Frank. Other animal characters include Sid the fish. McDonnell's animals talk to each other but keep their animal characteristics. McDonnell was drawing dogs for years before he and Karen moved to a house with a yard where they could have a dog. They got Earl, and when Karen found a calico kitten in a parking garage, they also adopted Meemow, and the two animals became McDonnell's companions as he began to draw "Mutts."

Editor & Publisher's David Astor felt that McDonnell "knows how to write, too. But here, again, McDonnell is not your typical modern-day cartoonist. While many of his peers produce comics with a hip, cynical edge, McDonnell prefers a kinder, gentler, 'stop-and-smell-the-roses' approach. . . . McDonnell also bucks the trend of more topicality in comics by trying to keep the 'real world' from entering 'Mutts.' His canine and feline costars think about food, sleep, the weather, and other basics of life as they get in and out of all kinds of humorous situations."

McDonnell is a multitalented artist and musician. After graduating from New York's School of Visual Arts, he continued to play with his band Steel Tips as he entered the world of professional graphic art. He illustrated Russell Baker's column in the *New York Times* magazine for ten years and drew a variety of subjects for *Sports Illustrated*'s "Scorecard" section. He freelanced for a number of other publications, including *Parents* magazine, for which he wrote his "Bad Baby" strip, editions of which were collected in one volume in 1988. Although McDonnell and his wife are not parents themselves, he relied on memory and the antics of his nephew Kevin for inspiration.

"Mutts" was born in 1994, shortly before Bill Watterson's "Calvin and Hobbes" was discontinued, and "Mutts" soon filled the empty space left in many newspapers. Strips have been collected into volumes at an average rate of once per year.

McDonnell is a great admirer of the work of "Peanuts" creator, the late Charles M. Schulz, who provided the foreword for McDonnell's first collection, titled simply *Mutts.* Schulz wrote that the best compliment he could give was that McDonnell "keeps coming up with ideas I wish I had thought of myself." Schulz especially enjoyed Earl, that "new and perfect little dog."

McDonnell and Karen also cowrote, with others, *Krazy Kat: The Comic Art of George Herriman,* a collection of thirty-one years of the work of another cartoonist admired by McDonnell. Add to that list Walt Kelly ("Pogo"), Elzie Segar ("Thimble Theatre" and "Popeye"), Richard Outcault ("Buster Brown"), Percy Crosby ("Skippy"), Chester Gould ("Dick Tracy"), and Harold Gray ("Little Orphan Annie").

"Mutts" has won many awards, including several Harvey Awards. This is a peer-chosen acknowledgment by people in the comics industry and is named for Harvey Kurtzman, creator of *Mad* magazine. He has also been honored for his work on behalf of animals.

"Mutts" contains subtle messages, as with the depiction of a dog who is always chained. In 1998, McDonnell began doing a special series approximately twice a year to promote the adoption of shelter animals. The first of these featured a cat named Tom Tom, who finally finds a home with a little girl. Shelters acknowledge that these strips have been responsible for increased adoptions, and McDonnell has been honored by the Ark Trust for his contributions to animal rights. He also serves on the board of directors of the National Humane Society.

BIOGRAPHICAL AND CRITICAL SOURCES:

PERIODICALS

Editor & Publisher, November 16, 1996, David Astor, "It's Reigning a Cat and Dog in Hit Strip," pp. 40-41.
Sports Illustrated, September 28, 1987, Donald J. Barr, "'Scorecard' illustrator Patrick McDonnell," p. 4; March 13, 1989, Donald J. Barr, review of *Bad Baby,* p. 4.

ONLINE

"Mutts" Home Page, http://muttscomics.com/ (August 12, 2003).
Pet Press (Los Angeles), http://www.thepetpress-la.com/ (October, 1999), Lori Golden, "The Cartoonist Who Is King of the 'Mutts.'"*

*   *   *

McGREEVY, John T.

PERSONAL: Male. *Education:* University of Notre Dame, B.A. (history), 1986; Stanford University, A.M. (history), 1987; Stanford University, Ph.D. (history), 1992.

ADDRESSES: Home—South Bend, IN. *Office*—Department of History, 219 O'Shaughnessy Hall, University of Notre Dame, Notre Dame, IN 46556-0368; fax: (219) 631-4268. *E-mail*—John.T.McGreevy.5@nd.edu.

CAREER: Educator and historian. Harvard University, Cambridge, MA, former assistant professor; University of Notre Dame, Notre Dame, IN, currently associate professor of history and chair of department. Distinguished lecturer for Organization of American Historians, 2004-05.

AWARDS, HONORS: Mellon Foundation Interdisciplinary Graduate fellowship, 1990-92; John Gilmary Shea Prize, American Catholic Historical Association, 1996, for *Parish Boundaries: The Catholic Encounter with Race in the Twentieth-Century Urban North;* American Council of Learned Societies fellowship, 1996-97; Erasmus Institute fellowship, 1999; Louisville Institute Major Project grant, 1999-2000.

WRITINGS:

Parish Boundaries: The Catholic Encounter with Race in the Twentieth-Century Urban North, University of Chicago Press (Chicago, IL), 1996.
Catholicism and American Freedom: A History, Norton (New York, NY), 2003.

Contributor to books, including *Major Problems in American Religious History,* edited by Patrick Allitt, Houghton, 1999; *The Challenge of American History,* edited by Louis Masur, Johns Hopkins University Press, 1999; and *Governance, Accountability, and the Future of the Catholic Church,* edited by Francis Oakley and Bruce Russett, Continuum, 2003. Contributor to periodicals, including *Commonweal, American Quarterly, Journal of American History,* and *Religion and American Culture.*

SIDELIGHTS: John T. McGreevy, an associate professor of history at the University of Notre Dame, studies the history of Catholics in America. His first two books, *Parish Boundaries: The Catholic Encounter with Race in the Twentieth-Century Urban North* and *Catholicism and American Freedom: A History,* are both about this subject.

"*Parish Boundaries* is clearly the most comprehensive and thoroughly researched analysis of urban, northern Catholics and race published in America," declared *Journal of Social History* reviewer Timothy Kelly. The book examines the dilemma that formerly all-white

Catholic parishes in northern cities faced when African-Americans began streaming from the South into those cities after World War I. McGreevy argues that Catholics had a stronger bond with their neighborhoods than did Protestants and Jews, because Catholic parishes were defined by geography. Because of this geographic focus, Catholics and Catholic churches invested much in creating a strong, frequently ethnic neighborhood built around their parish church and school. As Protestant and Jewish worshippers fled to the suburbs, their churches often picked up and followed—an option that was not open to the geographically defined Catholic parishes. Thus, Catholics, more frequently than Protestants and Jews, found themselves remaining in urban neighborhoods and, because they were so emotionally and spiritually invested in their neighborhoods, working to protect it from—as they viewed them—the "invading" African-Americans. "After finishing [*Parish Boundaries*], readers are apt to think that they always knew that Catholics played a pivotal role in the way race relations evolved in the great cities of the north since the 1920s," Philip Gleason commented in *Journal of American Ethnic History*. "But that is only because McGreevy makes the case so convincingly."

In his second book, *Catholicism and American Freedom*, McGreevy examines the different views of freedom held by America's Protestant founders and its Catholic citizens. The book, described as "ambitiously conceived, prodigiously researched, and beautifully executed" by Philip Gleason in a *Church History* article, contains an intellectual history both of American Catholic social thought and of anti-Catholic, Protestant reactions to it. The divide is between Catholics who believe that freedom is found in being part of a unified, righteous community that submits to the Church's moral authority on social issues, and Protestants who believe that freedom of conscience to make up one's own mind on those issues, and even the freedom to decide in error, is a necessary component of political freedom. McGreevy examines a number of American political divides where these two competing conceptions came into play, from the nineteenth-century arguments over slavery to twentieth-century debates on contraception, abortion, and other issues of sexuality. "There is nothing in American Catholic historiography that comes close to rivaling [McGreevy's three-chapter discussion of the latter issues] in scope of coverage, nuance of interpretation, or depth of research," wrote Gleason. "It is a remarkable tour de force." "All in all," Richard John

Neuhaus concluded in *First Things, Catholicism and Freedom* "is the most informative, analytically insightful, and even-handed account we have of the troubled relationship between Catholicism and the American experiment."

BIOGRAPHICAL AND CRITICAL SOURCES:

PERIODICALS

America, December 6, 1997, Dominic P. Scibilia, review of *Parish Boundaries: The Catholic Encounter with Race in the Twentieth-Century Urban North,* pp. 26-28; July 21, 2003, Thomas Murphy, review of *Catholicism and American Freedom: A History,* p. 27.

American Historical Review, December, 1996, Robert Orsi, review of *Parish Boundaries,* pp. 1640-1641.

Booklist, May 1, 2003, Margaret Flanagan, review of *Catholicism and American Freedom,* pp. 1556-1557.

Books and Culture, March-April, 2004, Allen Guelzo, review of *Catholicism and American Freedom,* pp. 22-23.

Catholic Historical Review, January, 1998, R. Scott Appleby, review of *Parish Boundaries,* pp. 157-159.

Choice, November, 2003, J. C. Scott, review of *Catholicism and American Freedom,* p. 559.

Church History, September, 1997, Jay P. Dolan, review of *Parish Boundaries,* pp. 668-670; December, 2003, Philip Gleason, review of *Catholicism and American Freedom,* pp. 910-911.

Commonweal, July 12, 1996, Don Wycliff, review of *Parish Boundaries,* pp. 23-24.

Crisis, April 1, 2004, John C. Chalberg, review of *Catholicism and American Freedom.*

Ethnic and Racial Studies, March, 1998, Michael P. Hornsby-Smith, review of *Parish Boundaries,* pp. 367-369.

First Things, August-September, 2003, Richard John Neuhaus, review of *Catholicism and American Freedom,* pp. 66-71.

Historical Journal, June, 1999, Amy S. Greenberg, review of *Parish Boundaries,* p. 519.

Journal of American Ethnic History, winter, 1998, Philip Gleason, review of *Parish Boundaries,* pp. 83-85.

Journal of American History, September, 1997, James T. Fisher, review of *Parish Boundaries,* pp. 614-617.

Journal of Social History, winter, 1998, Timothy Kelly, review of *Parish Boundaries,* pp. 480-482.

Journal of Urban History, May, 2000, Arnold R. Hirsch, review of *Parish Boundaries,* p. 519.

Kirkus Reviews, March 1, 2003, review of *Catholicism and American Freedom,* p. 366.

Library Journal, March 15, 2003, Anna M. Donnelly, review of *Catholicism and American Freedom,* p. 89.

Nation, September 22, 2003, JoAnn Wypijewski, review of *Catholicism and American Freedom,* p. 40.

New York Times, May 3, 1997, Peter Steinfels, "How Anxiety about Catholicism Helped Shape the Outlook of Modern American Intellectuals," pp. 10, 29; August 3, 2003, Michael J. Lacey, review of *Catholicism and American Freedom,* p. 13.

New York Times Book Review, August 25, 1996, Richard Wightman Fox, review of *Parish Boundaries,* p. 24.

Publishers Weekly, March 31, 2003, review of *Catholicism and American Freedom,* p. 59.

Review of Politics, winter, 1998, Cyprian Davis, review of *Parish Boundaries,* pp. 186-189.

Reviews in American History, June, 1997, Jay P. Dolan, review of *Parish Boundaries,* pp. 282-287.

Seattle Post-Intelligencer, July 3, 1996, review of *Parish Boundaries,* p. C2.

Star-Ledger (Newark, NJ), February 7, 1999, Bob Armbruster, review of *Parish Boundaries,* p. 8.

ONLINE

Organization of American Historians, http://www.oah.org/ (June 15, 2004), "2004-2005 OAH Distinguished Lectureship Program."

University of Notre Dame, http://www.nd.edu/ (June 15, 2004), "John T. McGreevy."*

*   *   *

McKENZIE, Nancy Affleck 1948-

PERSONAL: Born February 19, 1948, in Princeton, NJ; daughter of James G. and Callie K. Affleck; married Bruce Gordon McKenzie (an executive entrepreneur), June 10, 1972; children: Elizabeth, Catherine, Caroline. *Education:* Mount Holyoke College, B.A. (magna cum laude), 1970; Tufts University, M.A., 1973. *Hobbies and other interests:* Sailing, horseback riding, baseball, reading.

ADDRESSES: Agent—Jean Naggar, Jean V. Naggar Literary Agency, 216 E. 75th St., New York, NY 10021.

CAREER: Thorobrook Farm, Rye, NY, stable manager, 1986-90; president of her own desktop publishing company, 1989-2000. Writer.

MEMBER: Authors Guild, Phi Beta Kappa.

AWARDS, HONORS: "Discovery of the Year" citation from Del Rey Books, 1993, for *The Child Queen;* Washington Irving Medal from Westchester Library Association, NY, 1994, for *The Child Queen.*

WRITINGS:

The Child Queen (also see below), Del Rey (New York, NY), 1994.

The High Queen (also see below), Del Rey (New York, NY), 1995.

Queen of Camelot (contains *The Child Queen* and *The High Queen*), Del Rey (New York, NY), 2002.

Grail Prince, Del Rey (New York, NY), 2003.

Prince of Dreams, Del Rey (New York, NY), 2004.

Senior editor, *Childbirth Instructor Magazine,* 1994-99.

WORK IN PROGRESS: A young adult series of novels about young Guinevere; researching ancient Egypt and the life of Akhenaten.

SIDELIGHTS: Nancy Affleck McKenzie covers familiar ground in her novels, but she does so in innovative ways. McKenzie is the author of a series of books based on the King Arthur legends. In the case of her work, however, it is the important secondary characters—Queen Guinevere, Lancelot, and Galahad—who assume center stage and tell their versions of life in Camelot. McKenzie's debut novel, *The Child Queen,* explores Guinevere's childhood and young adulthood in the kingdoms of her father and uncle.

Young Guinevere is resourceful, intelligent, and brave, but she fails to see the enmity she has engendered in her cousin Elaine, who wants to be Arthur's queen. *Locus* reviewer Carolyn Cushman praised *The Child Queen* as "heavily researched, with a strong sense of history and legend." *Voice of Youth Advocates* correspondent Sarah Flowers felt that "the writing is lively and the characters likable and/or interesting."

In the sequel, *The High Queen,* Guinevere helps Arthur to rule Camelot and raises Arthur's illegitimate son Mordred as if he were her own. *The High Queen* also examines Guinevere's love affair with Lancelot from Guinevere's perspective. In her *Voice of Youth Advocates* critique of the novel, Rebecca Barnhouse concluded: "It's pleasant to get the old story from a woman's point of view." Both *The Child Queen* and *The High Queen* have been reprinted in one volume, titled *Queen of Camelot.* In a review for the online *Crowsnest SF Magazine,* Jacqueline Kirk commended McKenzie for portraying "a Guinevere that has more to her than just a pretty face."

McKenzie continues the King Arthur saga with *Grail Prince,* a retelling of the life of Sir Galahad, son of Lancelot and Elaine. Raised by his bitter mother and neglected by his father, Galahad grows up with a jaundiced view of women. Vowing celibacy, Galahad joins Arthur's court in time to witness the king's death and to be charged with a quest to unite the sword Excalibur with a grail and a spear that belonged to a prior king of Britain. For Galahad, the quest becomes an entrée into manhood and a means by which he finally prepares to fall in love. On the *What You Need to Know about Sci-Fi/Fantasy* Web site, Clara Null Houston wrote of *Grail Prince:* "This is not the dry as dust retelling of old tales. This is an epic adventure with believable people." Jennifer Baker in *Library Journal* called the book a "tale of abiding love and enduring hope," and a *Publishers Weekly* critic found it to be an "engrossing medieval fantasy." A *Galacticum.com* contributor declared: "Not since *The Mists of Avalon* has an author so brilliantly reimagined and brought to life the enduring Arthurian legends."

McKenzie told *CA:* "My favorite books are historical novels that envelope the reader in a different place and time, such as *Middlemarch* or *The Jewel in the Crown* or *Tai Pan* or *The Game of Kings.* Mary Renault's books are among my favorites—ancient Greece has always fascinated me—and so are Mary Stewart's four books about Merlin the Enchanter in the days of King Arthur. Mary Stewart's vision of fifth-century Britain inspired my Guinevere books (*The Child Queen, The High Queen,* and *Queen of Camelot*). I wanted to make this much-maligned legendary character accessible to modern readers.

"I like getting inside my characters and finding out what makes them tick, and all of my books are character studies at heart. But I also like plots that roll right along at a decent place, so the character studies are wrapped around a good story.

"I've always had an interest in the deeper questions posed by humans since time began: What is holiness? What are the forces that drive us? What makes a leader? What should we value? How should we behave toward one another? You don't need to read my books on this level, but you can.

"Thus far, my published books are all Arthurian adventures/romances, but I am deeply interested in ancient Egyptian culture and hope to write an archaeologically up-to-date life of Akhenaten in the near future."

BIOGRAPHICAL AND CRITICAL SOURCES:

PERIODICALS

Booklist, December 1, 2002, Margaret Flanagan, review of *Grail Prince,* p. 646; December 1, 2003, Margaret Flanagan, review of *Prince of Dreams,* p. 655.

Library Journal, November 15, 2002, Jennifer Baker, review of *Grail Prince,* p. 102.

Locus, July, 1994, Carolyn Cushman, review of *The Child Queen,* p. 35.

Publishers Weekly, July 18, 1994, review of *The Child Queen,* p. 241; December 23, 2002, review of *Grail Prince,* p. 50; November 10, 2003, review of *Prince of Dreams,* p. 46.

Voice of Youth Advocates, December, 1994, Sarah Flowers, review of *Child Queen,* p. 288; October, 1995, Rebecca Barnhouse, review of *The High Queen,* p. 235.

ONLINE

About SF/Fantasy, http://scifi.about.com/ (May 5, 2003), Clara Null Houston, review of *Grail Prince.*

Crowsnest SF Magazine, http://www.computercrows
nest.com/ (May 5, 2003), Jacqueline Kirk, review
of *Queen of Camelot.*

Nancy McKenzie Home Page, http://www.nancy
mckenzie.com (May 5, 2003).

Romance Readers Connection, http://www.theromance
readersconnection.com/ (May 5, 2003), Mellanie
Crowther, review of *Grail Prince.*

Simegen.com, http://www.simegen.com/ (May 5,
2003), Harriet Klausner, review of *Grail Prince.**

*   *   *

McMANUS, Antonia 1952-

PERSONAL: Born November 17, 1952, in Ballycastle,
County Mayo, Ireland; daughter of Anthony (a school
principal) and Mary (a school vice principal) Murphy;
married Kenneth McManus (a school principal),
August 22, 1974; children: Kenneth. *Education:* May-
nooth, B.A. (with first class honors) and Higher
Diploma of Education (with honors), 1986; Trinity
College, Dublin, Ph.D., 2000. *Politics:* "Varies." *Religion:* Roman Catholic.

ADDRESSES: Home—139 Kirwin Ave., Avondale,
Trim, County Meath, Ireland. *E-mail*—ktmcmanus@
lircom.net.

CAREER: Convent of Mercy, Trim, County Meath,
Ireland, teacher, 1985-86; teacher at a Roman Catholic
high school, Trim, 1986-93; Trinity College, Dublin,
Ireland, lecturer in education, 1993-2003; Froebel College of Education, Sion Hill, Blackrock, County Dublin, Ireland, lecturer, 2002—.

WRITINGS:

The Irish Hedge School and Its Books, 1695-1831,
Four Courts Press (Dublin, Ireland), 2002.

WORK IN PROGRESS: Research on the history books
read in hedge schools.

SIDELIGHTS: Antonia McManus told *CA:* "The
subject of my book was the topic I selected to research
for my doctoral thesis. The topic is in an area of the
history of Irish education which hasn't been revisited
on a major scale since P. J. Dowling's pioneering work
The Hedge Schools of Ireland appeared in 1932.

"My interest in hedge schools and their books was
stimulated while I was a research student in the master
of education program at Trinity College. Having read
Dowling's book, I found that my interest in the Irish
poets of the eighteenth century was rekindled once
more. As an undergraduate, their poetry had laid a
profound impression on me, especially the 'aisling' or
vision poetry of Eoghan Rua Ó Súilleabháin (1748-
1784). I was impressed by the tenacity of the poets
who rose above their miserable social conditions to
write such poetic works and by the fact that their
poetry was remarkably free of bitterness, despite the
fact that their patrons, the Gaelic chieftains, had been
dispossessed of their lands following the Elizabethan
wars (1601) and later the Williamite wars (1689-1691).
I was no doubt influenced by Daniel Corkery's lyrical
defense of eighteenth-century Munster poets in his
book *The Hidden Ireland* (1924). However, it was Vi-
vien Mercier's *The Irish Comic Tradition* (1962) which
helped to shape my view that whatever the poets
lacked in poetic ability, they more than adequately
compensated for in their spirited approach to life, when
they resorted to satire and humor in order to poke fun
at the new landowners, and in order to entertain their
own people during very difficult times.

"Having read Dowling's book, I learned that almost
every Irish poet of the eighteenth century was also a
hedge schoolmaster. This came as little surprise to me
because I believed that their creative ability, coupled
with their generosity of spirit and liberal outlook on
life, equipped them well for a life in the teaching
profession. However, I was keen to learn more about
the social conditions of the period, the historical
background which forced the hedge schoolmasters to
operate underground for almost ninety years, and how
they succeeded in becoming the dominant educators in
Ireland for well over a century.

"I was also interested to learn more about the curriculum in the hedge schools, which was more
extensive and liberal than the utilitarian curriculum
which was available to the poor in England or indeed
in the rival educational institutions in Ireland.

"Finally, I was greatly surprised by the quantity and
diversity of the books read in the hedge schools,
considering the poverty of the children who attended

them. Contemporary writers and conservative elements in Irish society, in the early nineteenth century, were deeply critical of a small number of these books, claiming that they had either a subversive sub-text or were immoral in content and were therefore unsuitable matter for children to read. I was keen to explore the possibility that there was some basis for these concerns, and I felt that a detailed study of a selected sample of the most controversial books (as well as a representative sample of the range of other books read) merited an in-depth analysis. I was therefore very pleased to be allowed the privilege and pleasure of undertaking research in this area of Irish educational history."

*   *   *

McPHEE, Sarah (Collyer) 1960-

PERSONAL: Born 1960. *Education:* Harvard University, A.B. (art history), 1982; Columbia University, M.A., 1988, Ph.D. (art history), 1997.

ADDRESSES: Office—Department of Art History, Emory University, 128 Carlos Hall, Atlanta, GA 30322. *E-mail*—smcphee@emory.edu.

CAREER: Educator and author. Metropolitan Museum of Art, New York, NY, assistant editor and writer, 1984-86; Emory University, Atlanta, GA, assistant professor, 1995-2001, associate professor of art history, 2001—.

AWARDS, HONORS: James Bowdoin Writing Prize, Harvard University, 1982; Mellon fellow in the humanities, 1986-88, 1992-93; Mellon Foundation grants, 1986, 1988; Metropolitan Museum of Art Jane and Morgan Whitney fellowship, 1993-94, and Chester Dale fellowship, 1994-95; Emory University Faculty Development Awards, 1996, 1997, 1998, 1999, 2000, Title VI grant, 1997, course development grant, 1999, Faculty Research Award, 1999; Massee-Martin grant, 1998; Millard Meiss Subvention grant, 2000, for *Bernini and the Bell Towers.*

WRITINGS:

(With others) *Filippo Juvarra: Drawings from the Roman Period 1704-1714, Part II,* Elfante (Rome, Italy), 1999.
Bernini and the Bell Towers: Architecture and Politics at the Vatican, Yale University Press (New Haven, CT), 2002.

Contributor to books, including *Filippo Juvarra el'architettura europea,* 1998; contributor to periodicals, including *Journal of the Society of Architectural Historians, Studi Piemontesi,* and *Burlington.* Contributor to exhibition catalogues.

SIDELIGHTS: With expertise in seventeenth-and eighteenth-century Italian art and architecture, writer and educator Sarah McPhee illuminates the work of architect Gian Lorenzo Bernini and his failed efforts to construct the twin bell towers, or campanili, that were to have completed Michelangelo's St. Peter's Basilica in her book *Bernini and the Bell Towers: Architecture and Politics at the Vatican.*

Beginning his undertaking in 1638, the noted architect and artist was commissioned by Pope Urban VIII due to Bernini's success in numerous other projects throughout Rome. The two massive towers slowly took shape, and by 1643 they had begun to take shape. While the southern tower was almost completed, the northern tower was halted as funds were siphoned from the work to pay for the pope's War of Castro against Italy's powerful Farnese family. While many Vatican wags—including those architects who had been overlooked in favor of the younger Bernini—viewed Bernini's designs as too tall and massive to appropriately grace the top of St. Peter's, work on the project stopped altogether when large cracks appeared in the main Basilica. Bernini's critics were quick to attribute them to the architect's ineptitude and overambitious project. With his reputation now in shambles, Bernini watched as his work was demolished under the orders of succeeding Pope Innocent X. Ironically, his inability to court papal favor following the death of Urban had much to do with the discontinuation of the tower project, as McPhee makes clear; in any case, as Andrew Hopkins noted in the *Times Literary Supplement,* "From the moment that Bernini's project was dropped, calumnies that have permanently stained his reputation and have persisted for over three centuries began to circulate." With her book, Hopkins added, McPhee provides Bernini vindication.

In what *America* contributor Franco Mormando dubbed "an awe-inspiring, laudable monument of scholarship," McPhee researched archives and libraries throughout Europe, as well as drawing on her own technical expertise, to sort out the facts of the bell tower fiasco. According to *Bernini and the Bell Tow-*

ers the damage to the main Basilica was the fault of the project's first architect, Carlo Maderno, who preceded Bernini on the project and began construction of inadequate foundations—St. Peter's is in fact constructed on a flood plain. Pope Urban, too, is not without blame; according to McPhee, his insistence that the towers serve as a fitting monument to his ambition resulted in their bulk, and the unnecessary demolition of the towers was the result of inter-Vatican rivalries and petty jealousies. Noting that *Bernini and the Bell Towers* is not for the general reader, Mormando praised the work as "the definitive study on this topic," citing her "extremely detailed, technical investigation and closely reasoned analysis of the facts." Hopkins also praised her detailed work, noting that "Architectural historians will appreciate McPhee's close attention to the drawings and her clarification of the roles played in this intriguing saga."

BIOGRAPHICAL AND CRITICAL SOURCES:

PERIODICALS

America, April 21, 2003, Franco Mormando, S.J., review of *Bernini and the Bell Towers: Architecture and Politics at the Vatican.*.
Building Design, January 31, 2003, Emma Dent Coad, "Troubled Waters," p. 14.
Library Journal, April 1, 2003, Paul Glassman, review of *Bernini and the Bell Towers,* p. 94.
Times Literary Supplement, April 4, 2003, Andrew Hopkins, "Felled by the Bells," p. 11.

ONLINE

Emory University Web site, http://www.emory.edu/ (May 15, 2004), "Sarah McPhee."*

*   *   *

MEE, Bob

PERSONAL: Male.

ADDRESSES: Office—Telegraph Group, Ltd., 1 Canada Sq., Canary Wharf, London E14 5DT, England.

CAREER: Journalist. *Daily Telegraph,* London, England, boxing correspondent; *Boxing News,* assistant editor; *Independent on Sunday,* London, England, writer; ITV, London, England, production; Sky Sports, Isleworth, England, production.

WRITINGS:

(With Steve Bunce) *Boxing Greats: An Illustrated History of the Ring,* Courage Books (Philadephia, PA), 1998.
(With Mickey Duff) *Twenty and Out: A Life in Boxing,* HarperCollins Willow (London, England), 1999.
Bare Fists: The History of Bare-Knuckle Prize-Fighting, HarperCollins Willow (London, England), 2000, Overlook Press (Woodstock, NY), 2001.

Also coauthor of *Lords of the Ring* with Peter Arnold.

SIDELIGHTS: Bob Mee has been covering the British and international boxing scene for over twenty years, as an assistant editor for *Boxing News,* a writer for the *Independent on Sunday,* and most recently the boxing correspondent for the *Daily Telegraph.* Along the way he has written and cowritten several boxing books, including histories and biographies.

Several of Mee's book projects are survey histories, such as *Boxing Greats: An Illustrated History of the Ring* with Steve Bunce and *Lords of the Ring* with Peter Arnold. Mee also helped colorful fight promoter Mickey Duff pen his autobiography, *Twenty and Out: A Life in Boxing.* The *New Statesman*'s Tony van den Bergh praised Mee for pulling off "a minor miracle in somehow corralling Mickey Duff's avalanche of words into a disciplined order" and "captur[ing] the atmosphere of this miscalled noble art, with its tang of cigar smoke, wintergreen and cheap cigarettes."

Mee set out on his own in 2001 with *Bare Fists: The History of Bare-Knuckle Prize-Fighting,* a meticulously researched history of the sport from the early 1700s until the arrival of the Marquis of Queensberry rules in the late 1800s. Mee also briefly examines bare-knuckle fighting in the twentieth century, as the brutal sport went underground in the age of gloves. Wes Lukowsky, writing for *Booklist,* delighted in *Bare Fists*'s tales of the ring's colorful figures and marathon bouts, calling the book "a vivid chronicle of the freewheeling bare-knuckle era." A contributor for *Kirkus Reviews* appreciated the book's "wildly inclusive" historical detail, but found fault with Mee's prose, noting that the "300-year history is too lackluster," and "too often . . . reads like a telephone directory." A *Publishers Weekly* critic also found the "well-researched, blocky accounts" of the fights and fighters compelling, but noted that Mee's "enthusiasm and devotion" to his subject probably will not win over those uninterested in the sweet science.

BIOGRAPHICAL AND CRITICAL SOURCES:

PERIODICALS

Booklist, April 1, 2001, Wes Lukowsky, review of *Bare Fists: The History of Bare-Knuckle Prize-Fighting,* p. 1442.
Kirkus Reviews, March 15, 2001, review of *Bare Fists,* p. 389.
New Statesman, January 24, 2000, Tony van den Bergh, review of *Twenty and Out: A Life in Boxing,* p. 54.
Publishers Weekly, May 14, 2001, review of *Bare Fists,* p. 65.*

* * *

MEHTA, Gita 1943-

PERSONAL: Born 1943, in Delhi, India; daughter of Biju Patnaik (a freedom fighter and political leader); married Ajai Singh Mehta (a publishing executive); children: one son. *Education:* Graduate of University of Bombay and Cambridge University.

ADDRESSES: Agent—c/o Author Mail, Nan A. Talese, Doubleday Broadway Group, Random House, 1745 Broadway, New York, NY 10019.

CAREER: Author and journalist. Director of documentary films for the British Broadcasting Corporation (BBC) and National Broadcasting Company (NBC).

WRITINGS:

Karma Cola: Marketing the Mystic East, Simon and Schuster (New York, NY), 1979, reprinted, Vintage Books (New York, NY), 1994.

Raj: A Novel, Simon and Schuster (New York, NY), 1989.
A River Sutra (stories), Nan A. Talese (New York, NY), 1993.
Snakes and Ladders: Glimpses of India, Nan A. Talese (New York, NY), 1997.

Contributor to periodicals, including *Vogue.*

SIDELIGHTS: Gita Mehta is an Indian-born author who attended Cambridge University, where she met her husband, Ajai Singh "Sonny" Mehta. He later became president of Alfred A. Knopf, an imprint of Random House, in New York, one of the three locations the couple and their son call home, the other two being London, England and Delhi, India.

Mehta was born in Delhi to a father who was a well-known freedom fighter and who later became the leader of the state of Orissa. Because of her family's strong political views, her grandmother wanted her named Joan of Arc, but the name given her can be interpreted to mean song of freedom. When Mehta was two weeks old, her father was imprisoned for his activities on behalf of Indian liberation, and when she turned three, their mother placed her and her brother in boarding school so that she could help her husband.

As Erin Soderberg noted in an article for *Voices from the Gaps,* the idea for Mehta's first book, *Karma Cola: Marketing the Mystic East* evolved from a 1979 publishing industry cocktail party she attended with her husband. Mehta, who was wearing a traditional sari, was accosted by a guest who insisted that she explain karma, and upon hearing her response, another guest urged her to put her ideas to paper. In three weeks' time, Mehta had written the satirical essays that comprise the volume, and which examine the 1960s influx of foreigners to India during the hippie-era obsession with Indian mysticism.

Soderberg wrote that Mehta "blends humor with witty observations, constructing a book that presents her own impressions through the experiences of many."

Raj: A Novel reveals how life was lived under colonialism through the eyes of Jaya Singh, a highly born Indian woman. Soderberg felt that Jaya Singh was a strong female character, and she said of Mehta that "while her intelligence is obvious and her opinions clear, she is ultimately not interested in pressing her political impressions onto her reader, but presents historical facts with gentle persuasion in a beautifully woven tapestry."

A River Sutra is a novel that weaves half a dozen stories together, all of which have the sacred river Narmada as a common connection. The main character is a retired civil servant who wants only to spend his remaining years by the river, running a government-owned inn, but his peace is interrupted by a stream of pilgrims, including a monk, teacher, executive, courtesan, musician, and minstrel.

Indira Karamcheti wrote in *Women's Review of Books* that "all other things being equal, in many ways this is a satisfying book, full of lovely stories. . . . A unifying theme is announced by the title word 'sutra,' which the thoughtfully included glossary defines as 'literally, a thread or string. Also a term for literary forms, usually aphoristic in nature.' So Mehta, using the Narmada river as a narrative structuring device to thread these stories together, at the same time suggests that a philosophical or ethical principle can be pulled, perhaps in aphoristic form, from the river's symbolic presence in the stories." Love is the thread that runs through the tales that Karamcheti noted "are full of oriental philosophy and extravagance, physical passion and spiritual possession, lust and loot, beauty and booty, renunciation and titillation."

A *Publishers Weekly* contributor said that "Mehta does not avoid the controversies of life in her homeland, including the caste system and political/religious rivalries; rather, she willingly exposes its complexities."

Snakes and Ladders: Glimpses of India is a collection of essays about India since its independence in 1947. *Publishers Weekly* writer Wendy Smith, who interviewed Mehta upon the publication of *Snakes and Ladders,* wrote that "among the essays are a moving portrait of a cooperative bank that enables women to buy themselves out of bonded labor and start their own businesses; a tribute to the 'faceless, nameless, all-enduring Indian voter' who has continued to believe in democracy despite notorious government corruption and Indira Gandhi's 1975 State of Emergency declaration (under which Mehta's father was again impris-

oned); and a delicious evocation of India's colorful pavement booksellers and the kind of reading 'uninhibited by literary snobbisms' they promoted."

Mehta told Smith that she wrote many essays that she did not include in the volume "because they required too much pre-information. I wanted to make modern India accessible to Westerners and to a whole generation of Indians who have no idea what happened twenty-five years before they were born."

Mehta also talked with Smith about the troubles inherent in being married to "one of the most powerful people in international publishing," as Smith put it. "Imagine: you're working on a book, and Gabriel Garcia Marquez comes for a drink—you think, 'Does the world really need me?' And these nightmare sales figures for other writers; I hear Sonny say, 'Well, we've sold twelve million copies' of something, and I think, 'Oh my God!' That's why, when I'm really into a book, I go to London [where their son lives]."

In addition to her writing, Mehta has directed documentary films about India, the Bangladesh war, the Indo-Pakistan war that resulted in the creation of Bangladesh, and the elections in the former princely states. Her journalistic background lends itself to her writings, which explore the people, history, and culture of India. Soderberg concluded that Mehta "has the unique opportunity to collect the richness of living on three continents, and it is this rarity of perspective that gives her a uniquely witty and frank ability to define her vision of India through her work."

BIOGRAPHICAL AND CRITICAL SOURCES:

BOOKS

Literature of Developing Nations for Students: Presenting Analysis, Context, and Criticism on Literature of Developing Nations, Volume 2, Gale (Detroit, MI), 2000.

PERIODICALS

Booklist, May 1, 1997, Donna Seaman, review of *Snakes and Ladders: Glimpses of India,* p. 1477.
Economist, June 21, 1997, review of *Snakes and Ladders,* pp. R3-R4.

Forbes, June 16, 1997, Shailaja Neelakantan, review of *Snakes and Ladders* and interview with Gita Mehta, p. 284.

Globe & Mail, August 19, 1989, Valerie Fitzgerald, review of *Raj: A Novel.*

New Statesman & Society, June 18, 1993, Boyd Tonkin, review of *A River Sutra,* p. 41.

New York Times Book Review, June 22, 1989, review of *Raj.*

Publishers Weekly, March 29, 1993, review of *A River Sutra,* pp. 33-34; April 7, 1997, review of *Snakes and Ladders,* p. 82; May 12, 1997, Wendy Smith, "Gita Mehta: Making India Accessible" (interview), pp. 53-54.

Time, December 24, 1979, review of *Karma Cola: Marketing the Mystic East.*

Washington Post Book World, March 21, 1989, Florence King, review of *Raj.*

Women's Review of Books, January, 1994, Indira Karamcheti, review of *A River Sutra,* pp. 20-21.

ONLINE

India Star Review of Books, http://www.indiastar.com/ (September 23, 2003), C. J. S. Wallia, interview with Gita Mehta.

Voices from the Gaps, http://voices.cla.umn.edu/ (April 8, 1999), Erin Soderberg, biography of Gita Mehta and review of *Snakes and Ladders.**

*   *   *

MERRITT, E. B.
See WADDINGTON, Miriam

*   *   *

METZGER, Robert A(lan) 1956-

PERSONAL: Born May 21, 1956, in Los Angeles, CA. *Education:* University of California, Los Angeles, B.S., 1980, M.S., 1980, Ph.D. (electrical engineering), 1983.

ADDRESSES: Agent—c/o Author Mail, Ace, Putnam Berkley Group, 200 Madison Ave., New York, NY 10016. *E-mail*—ram@rametzger.com.

CAREER: Engineer, journalist, and novelist. Hughes Research Laboratories, Malibu, CA, research scientist and electrical engineer, c. 1980s; Georgia Institute of Technology, Atlanta, research scientist and electrical engineer, beginning 1990s. *Compound Semiconductor* magazine, cofounder.

MEMBER: Science Fiction and Fantasy Writers of America, National Association of Science Writers, Institute of Electrical and Electronics Engineers.

AWARDS, HONORS: Nebula Award nominee for best novel, 2002, for *Picoverse.*

WRITINGS:

Quad World, Roc (New York, NY), 1991.
Picoverse, Ace (New York, NY), 2002.

Author of columns, "What If?" for *Aboriginal SF* and "State of the Art" for *Science Fiction Writers of America Bulletin.* Contributor of short stories to periodicals, including *Aboriginal SF, Amazing, Magazine of Fantasy and Science Fiction, Science Fiction Age, Weird Tales,* and *Wired.*

SIDELIGHTS: Robert A. Metzger, a scientist and a columnist for the *Science Fiction Writers of America Bulletin,* is also the author of the 2002 Nebula Award-nominated *Picoverse.* As Metzger stated on his Web site, "I'm an engineer of the electrical variety (not to be confused with a physicist), a writer of science fiction, and a reporter of technology. In reality I wear only one hat—these three areas have so merged that there is no separating them."

Picoverse, according to *SciFi.com* reviewer Bob Koester, is a "rewarding yarn with some new spins on the idea of alternate universes." In the work, a team of physicists headed by Professor Horst Wittkowski develops the Sonomak, a fusion power project with almost limitless potential. After a disastrous experiment, the project is taken over by the mysterious Alexandra Mitchell, who uses the Sonomak to create a picoverse—a new, miniature universe—which she enters. Her actions set off "a chain of events that whirls the characters . . . through multiple picoverses and time periods," wrote *Booklist* critic Bryan Baldus. *SF*

Site Online contributor Lisa DuMond stated that Picoverse "races through a plot far more complex than the simple twist of knot pictured on the cover," adding that "With realities shifting from one universe to the next, the motives and loyalties of the characters shift rapidly, leaving readers unable to completely trust anyone in the book until their intentions are proven." A Publishers Weekly reviewer remarked that "This fast-paced romp through multiple manmade universes from Metzger will appeal to hard SF fans who like their science served straight up."

BIOGRAPHICAL AND CRITICAL SOURCES:

PERIODICALS

Analog, March, 2002, Tom Easton, review of Picoverse, pp. 132-137.
Booklist, March 1, 2002, Bryan Baldus, review of Picoverse, p. 1099.
Library Journal, November 15, 1991, Jackie Cassada, review of Quad World, p. 111; March 15, 2002, Jackie Cassada, review of Picoverse, p. 111.
Locus, December, 1991, Charles N. Brown and Scott Winnett, review of Quad World, p. 54.
Publishers Weekly, February 11, 2002, review of Picoverse, pp. 166-167.

ONLINE

Deep Outside Science Fiction, Fantasy, and Horror, http://www.clocktowerfiction.com/ (April 19, 2004), A. L. Sirois, "Outside in Review."
Robert A. Metzger Home Page, http://www.rametzger.com (April 19, 2004).
SciFi.com, http://www.scifi.com/ (April 19, 2004), Bob Koester, "Off the Shelf."
SF Site Online, http://www.sfsite.com/ (April 19, 2004), Lisa DuMond, review of Picoverse.*

*   *   *

MEYER, Sam 1917(?)-2003

PERSONAL: Born c. 1917, in Decorah, IA; died of a stroke, January 11, 2003, in Chicago, IL; married; wife's name Sarah; children: Robin, Lindy, June. Education: University of Iowa, B.A. (commerce; cum laude), 1940; University of Chicago, M.A., 1948; Loyola University, Chicago, Ph.D. (English), 1960.

CAREER: Educator and author. Civilian Conservation Corps, 1938-39; Tennessee Valley Authority, Wilson Dam, AL, junior clerk, 1940-41; Goldblatt's (department store), Chicago, IL, director of profit sharing and pension plan, 1946-48; St. Charles High School, Chicago, teacher of English and journalism, 1949-51; Bensenville High School, teacher, 1952-55; Morton College, Cicero, IL, professor of English, 1955-68, chairman of language arts department, 1968-75, professor emeritus, 1975-2003. Military service: U.S. Navy, active duty, 1941-46; during World War II served in Cuba and Algeria; postwar served at Glenview Naval Air station, Glenview, IL; U.S. Naval Reserves, 1946-75; attained rank of captain.

AWARDS, HONORS: George Washington Honor Medal, Freedoms Foundation of Valley Forge, 1991, for "Religion, Patriotism, and Poetry in the Life of Francis Scott Key."

WRITINGS:

An Interpretation of Edmund Spenser's Colin Clout, University of Notre Dame Press (Notre Dame, IN), 1969.
Paradoxes of Fame: The Francis Scott Key Story, Eastwind Publishing (Annapolis, MD), 1995.

Contributor to periodicals, including Naval Officer, Retired Officer, Maryland Historical Magazine, Journal of American Composition, Rhetoric Society Quarterly, and Navy Supply Corps Newsletter.

SIDELIGHTS: Educator and author Sam Meyer was widely recognized as the biographer of Francis Scott Key, who wrote the lyrics to the national anthem.

Meyer was born of immigrant parents and grew up during the Great Depression. He served with the Civilian Conservation Corps, and at the same time continued studying toward his bachelor's degree. Meyer was working as a clerk at the Wilson Dam in Alabama, a Tennessee Valley Authority project, when World War II erupted. In 1941, he joined the U.S. Navy, and because he could type and had a college degree, he was given the rank of yeoman first class and a position with naval intelligence at Guantanamo Bay, Cuba.

In 1943, Meyer was commissioned as an ensign in the Naval Reserve Supply Corps and posted first in Algeria, and then stateside following the war until his discharge in 1946. He remained in the Reserves until 1975. While studying for his master's degree, Meyer worked for Goldblatt's department store in Chicago, then became an English teacher in Chicago high schools. Twelve years later, after acquiring a Ph.D., he became a professor at Morton College.

A frequent contributor to military and historical journals, Meyer was also the author of a number of volumes, including *An Interpretation of Edmund Spenser's Colin Clout,* a study of the work of the Irish poet. Brad Webber wrote in a *Chicago Tribune* obituary that "Meyer's natural curiosity led him to a career that included everything from an academic analysis of esoteric Renaissance poetry to an essay distilling the meaning of colors in the titles of John D. MacDonald's hard-boiled crime sagas."

Meyer's research of titles led to his fascination with the title of "The Star-Spangled Banner" and ultimately to his study of the patriotic and humble man who wrote the lyrics, and whose biography he penned as *Paradoxes of Fame: The Francis Scott Key Story.*

OBITUARIES:

PERIODICALS

Chicago Tribune, January 14, 2003, Brad Webber, p. 12.
Navy Supply Corps Newsletter, May-June, 2003, Frank J. Allston, p. 48.*

* * *

MICHELSON, Karin 1953-

PERSONAL: Born February 14, 1953, in Montreal, Quebec, Canada; daughter of Gunther (a journalist) and Eva (Jeske) Michelson; married Russell M. Deer. *Education:* Harvard University, Ph.D., 1983.

ADDRESSES: Office—Department of Linguistics, State University of New York—Buffalo, Buffalo, NY 14260.

CAREER: State University of New York—Buffalo, associate professor of linguistics.

WRITINGS:

(Editor) *Three Stories in Oneida,* translated and told by Georgina Nicholas, National Museums of Canada (Ottawa, Ontario, Canada), 1981.
A Comparative Study of Lake-Iroquoian Accent, Kluwer Academic (Boston, MA), 1988.
(Editor, with Donna B. Gerdts) *Theoretical Perspectives on Native American Languages,* State University of New York Press (Albany, NY), 1989.
(With Mercy Doxtator) *Oneida-English/English-Oneida Dictionary,* University of Toronto Press (Toronto, Ontario, Canada), 2002.

* * *

MILLER, Leslie Adrienne 1956-

PERSONAL: Born October 22, 1956, in Medina, OH; daughter of Ray G. (a lawyer and judge) and Martha Ann (Fergason) Miller; married William Nevin Simonds, August, 1978 (divorced February 19, 1980); married David Williamson (an orchestral musician), September 30, 2000; children: (second marriage) Sebastian Dante. *Ethnicity:* "Caucasian." *Education:* Stephens College, B.A., 1978; University of Missouri, M.A., 1980; University of Iowa, M.F.A., 1982; University of Houston, Ph.D., 1991. *Politics:* Democrat. *Religion:* Methodist.

ADDRESSES: Home—956 Portland Ave., St. Paul, MN 55104. *Office*—Department of English, University of St. Thomas, St. Paul, MN 55105-1096; fax: 651-962-5623. *E-mail*—lamiller@stthomas.edu.

CAREER: Teacher in an adult education program, Columbia, MO, 1977; junior high school English teacher, Columbia, MO, 1978; University of Missouri—Columbia, instructor in English, 1979-80, 1981-82; Catonsville Community College, instructor, 1982; Goucher College, instructor, 1982-83; Stephens College, Columbia, MD, director of Creative Writing Program, 1983-87; University of Houston, Houston, TX, instructor, 1987-90; University of Oregon, Eugene, OR, visiting writer, 1990; University of St. Thomas, St. Paul, MN, began as assistant professor, became associate professor, 1991-2002, professor of English, 2002—. Instructor at University of Maryland—Baltimore County, 1982-83, Johns Hopkins Center for Talented Youth, 1983, and Washington College, Chestertown, MD, 1984-85; University of Minnesota, guest lecturer, 2001. *Open Places,* managing editor, 1985-87; judge of writing and scholarship competitions.

MEMBER: Modern Language Association of America, Associated Writing Programs, Poets and Writers, Loft Writers Center.

AWARDS, HONORS: President's Award, *Ohio Journal,* 1985; Writers at Work poetry fellowships, *Quarterly West,* 1987, 1988; Stanley Hanks Chapbook Award, St. Louis Poetry Center, 1987, for *No River;* Pushcart Prize, 1988, for "Epithalamium;" Ann Stanford Poetry Prize, *Southern California Anthology,* 1988, for "Influenza;" PEN Southwest Discovery Award, 1988; grant from Arts Symposium of Houston, 1989; Stanley Young fellow in poetry, Breadloaf Writers Conference, 1989; Billee Murray Denny Poetry Award, 1989, for "Keeping My Place in the Line;" poetry fellow, National Endowment for the Arts, 1989; Strousse Award, *Prairie Schooner,* 1991, for three poems; cultural exchange fellow in Berlin, Germany, Goethe-Institut, 1992; fellow, Minnesota State Arts Board, 1993, 1997; Loft McKnight Awards, 1993, 1998; Minnesota Book Award nominations in poetry, 1994, for *Ungodliness,* and 1999, for *Yesterday Had a Man in It;* grant for Indonesia, U.S. International Education Program, 1995; Poetry Award, *Nebraska Review,* 1996; resident at NALL Artists Colony, Vence, France, 1997-98; fellow at Hawthornden Castle International Writers Retreat, 1997; Loft Minnesota grant, 1998; resident at Fundación Valparaío, Almería, Spain, 1999; resident at Le Château de Lavigny, Lavigny, Switzerland, 2000.

WRITINGS:

(With Matthew Graham) *Hanging on the Sunburned Arm of Some Homeboy* (poetry chapbook), Domino Impressions Press (Iowa City, IA), 1982.

No River (poetry chapbook), St. Louis Poetry Center (St. Louis, MO), 1987.

Staying up for Love (poetry), Carnegie-Mellon University Press (Pittsburgh, PA), 1990.

Ungodliness (poetry), Carnegie-Mellon University Press (Pittsburgh, PA), 1994.

Yesterday Had a Man in It (poetry), Carnegie-Mellon University Press (Pittsburgh, PA), 1998.

Eat Quite Everything You See (poetry), Graywolf Press (St. Paul, MN), 2002.

Work represented in anthologies, including *Anthology of Magazine Verse and Yearbook of American Poetry,* 1984; *Yellow Silk: An Erotic Anthology,* Crown/Harmony, 1990; *Writing Poems,* Little, Brown (Boston, MA), 1995; *Motives for Writing,* Mayfield Publishing, 1995; and *Are You Experienced? Baby Boom Poets at Midlife,* University of Iowa Press, 2002. Contributor of poetry, essays, and reviews to magazines, including *Luna, Big Muddy: Mississippi Journal, Willow Springs, Colorado Review, Seneca Review, Rattle, North Stone Review, Crab Orchard Review, Gulf Coast,* and *Harvard Review. Open Places,* member of editorial staff, 1977, contributing editor, 1981; editor, *Narcissus,* 1978, and *Midlands,* 1980; member of editorial staff, *Pavement,* 1981-82; contributing editor, *Telescope,* 1985.

WORK IN PROGRESS: Consummate Geographies, a poetry collection.

SIDELIGHTS: Leslie Adrienne Miller told *CA:* "I write poems for many of the same reasons that I travel, to disabuse myself of the notion that I know anything at all about who and what I am. Why I begin a poem or a journey should be different from why and how I end it. If where I begin doesn't shift in a palpable way during the acts of writing, moving, or being, I've failed.

"The obvious and grandiose reasons one writes or moves to and through distant places: to mark the passing of time, to fend off cruelty, silence, nothingness; to reduce the general incomprehensibility of life by some fraction; because speaking anything clearly and compellingly in English seems almost, but not quite, impossible—the idea that there are other languages improves the odds. One writes, or moves, because all the unsaid things that accumulate in a day, a week, a year, a lifetime, a history, many histories, are noisy; because everything fits: the sweetness, the 'ha-ha,' and the 'get lost;' because it is satisfying to stumble on a temporary illusion of order, to mark one's place in a community, a geographical location, a psychological and/or linguistic conflict.

"Also there are the 'inobvious' and inglorious reasons for writing or traveling, those (dare we admit them) personal, petty, and routinely denied reasons: escape, revenge, eat your heart out; because something hurt, someone didn't pay attention; because love was lost, some truth didn't come home, there is gratuitous misery. One writes to get the reader to agree to the 'ouch,' the 'oh,' the 'quoi,' and 'warum' of it all; because prose like this and life itself are dull, abstract. Poetry is the only mode wherein the movement of interior and exterior life can be simultaneous, if not momentarily merged into one possibly eloquent gesture."

Miller added: "I grew up in Zanesville, Ohio, a small town in the southeastern corner of the state, the daughter of a lawyer father who ran for and won posts as county and circuit court judges and a grade school teacher mother who was also the soul of my father's political ambitions. Southeastern Ohio was James Wright country. My parents played bridge with Ted Wright, James's brother. Poetry was that close, but I had to go far away to find out how close I had been to those sons of steelworkers.

"I began writing when I began to discover my own consciousness. I must have been twelve or thirteen. As I came into consciousness, I also came into shyness; the more I regarded my own baffling sense of self, the more I shrank from others, and so poetry became a secret language with which I explored the interior of this emerging sensibility. I suspect that most adolescents write in some kind of secret interior language as they imagine and construct their own personalities, but some of us kept doing it, and so had to name what it was we were writing. Poetry. One of my high school English teachers gave me that name for what I was doing, and once I had the name, I had a world: Sylvia Plath and Edna Millay, Sara Teasedale and Marianne Moore were among my first meaningful encounters with poetry.

"I went to Stephens College for women in Missouri in 1974, and though I regarded myself as a serious writer of poems by then, I had no clue that writing poems was something I might actually do for a living. In my four years at Stephens I was offered extraordinary opportunities as a young writer, but I also had the opportunity to study with a variety of visiting writers. By the time I was twenty-one, I had met and worked with many of the most exciting women writers of the day. I also published my first poem in a nationally recognized literary magazine, *Beloit Poetry Journal.*

"After Stephens College, I enrolled at the University of Missouri and studied there for two years with the poet Larry Levis. His work had an enormous impact on my own work at this time. His work with Spanish surrealism influenced, not only his own poems, but those of his students who were privy to his obsessions during those years. When Levis and his wife, poet Marcia Southwick, moved to the Iowa Writers' Workshop in 1980, I headed for Iowa, too.

"In Iowa the competition was stiff, and though years later I learned just how unhappy many of my peers had been there, I myself view my two Iowa years as some of the most exciting of my life. I studied first with Marvin Bell, who gave me the tools I needed to write the new narrative poetry. Donald Justice also taught in Iowa those two years, and in my second year there, Jane Cooper came to teach. Working with Jane was like coming home for me. An ardent feminist, Cooper gave me faith in my own voice and encouraged my poems about female subjects which, to be honest, did not seem to be entirely welcome in many of the other Iowa workshop classes.

"Not least among the important influences of my Iowa years were my fellow and sister students. So many of them went on to publish fine books, and I've always counted myself lucky to have been in such a stellar class. A small group of created our own 'salon,' the idea of poets Julia Wendell and Jack Stephens. Our little half dozen poets met every Friday night for two years, to share meals and poems. In 1982 I moved to Baltimore, Maryland, with a group from our salon. We continued to work together as poets. In a sense, we took Iowa City with us when we left. I taught creative writing in a state-run program for gifted children and taught part-time at five different colleges and universities.

"Between 1983 and 1987, I directed the creative writing program at Stephens College and served as managing editor of *Open Places.* I also spent several years developing, directing, and teaching in the creative writing program at the Perry Mansfield Summer Arts School and Camp in Steamboat Springs, Colorado, and published my chapbook *No River.* In 1987 I moved to the University of Houston to finish the last leg of my educational journey. There I studied in four concentration areas: British romanticism, British medieval literature, classical rhetoric and criticism, and poetry. In 1990 Carnegie-Mellon University Press published my first full-length volume of poems, *Staying up for Love.* The poems in that collection were written over the ten preceding years and demonstrate my growth the discovery of a 'voice.' In 1990 I held the generous John and Becky Moores fellowship at the university, a full year's fellowship free from teaching to enable me to study for my comprehensive exams and to complete another collection, *Ungodliness,* a volume of pieces very much informed by my studies in British literature. Though it did not appear in print until 1994, the writing of that volume occurred almost exclusively during my years in Houston.

"In 1991 I accepted a tenure track job in creative writing at the University of St. Thomas, where I have taught ever since. The newfound stability of a full-time, tenure line job with benefits enabled me to begin to realize a lifelong dream of extended travels abroad. It was during a residency at the Literarisches Colloquium, a writers' center in Berlin, that I began to write many of the poems in *Yesterday Had a Man in It.* In 1995 I was awarded an arts international travel grant, on which I traveled extensively in Indonesia, and continued to work on the poems for that collection. In 1997 I spent most of my sabbatical year in France at a small artists' colony, and in Scotland at Hawthornden Castle. In both France and Scotland I worked on the volume of poems that would become *Eat Quite Everything You See.*"

BIOGRAPHICAL AND CRITICAL SOURCES:

PERIODICALS

American Book Review, June-July, 1990, review of *Staying up for Love,* p. 2.

Arkansas Democrat Gazette, April 26, 1998, Andrea Hollander Budy, review of *Yesterday Had a Man in It.*

Choice, September, 1994, B. Quinn, review of *Ungodliness,* p. 1.

Columbia Missourian, January 25, 1984, "Poet Uses Childhood to Find Life's Lessons."

Houston Metropolitan, January, 1990, review of *Staying up for Love.*

Kansas City Star, April 26, 1987, "Voices of Missouri Women."

Minneapolis Star Tribune, June 19, 1994, review of *Ungodliness;* July 14, 2002, "Got Roots? Five Poets Expose Their Regional Affinities in New Collections."

Minnesota Literature, February, 1998, review of *Yesterday Had a Man in It.*

Minnesota Monthly, December, 1995, review of *Ungodliness,* p. 110.

North Stone Review, Number 14, 2002, Marjorie Buettner, review of *Eat Quite Everything You See.*

Ohioana Quarterly, fall, 1990, Marianna Hofer, review of *Staying up for Love;* fall, 1995, review of *Ungodliness;* spring, 1999, Gretchen Geralds, review of *Yesterday Had a Man in It.*

Publishers Weekly, June 17, 2002, review of *Eat Quite Everything You See,* p. 61.

St. Louis Post-Dispatch, August 2, 1987, review of *No River.*

Siren, November, 1990, Jeff Troiano, review of *Staying up for Love.*

View from the Loft, September, 1998, interview by Heid Erdrich, pp. 4, 13-14.

Virginia Quarterly Review, summer, 1990, review of *Staying up for Love,* p. 3.

Washington Post Book World, May 6, 1990, review of *Staying up for Love;* November 13, 1994, review of *Ungodliness,* p. 51.

*   *   *

MINDLIN, Michael 1923-2004

OBITUARY NOTICE—See index for *CA* sketch: Born March 11, 1923, in New York, NY; died of lung cancer March 7, 2004, in New York, NY. Entertainment executive and author. Mindlin worked as a publicity and production executive in the theater and for movies. After attending Duke University from 1942 to 1943, he served as a navigator in the U.S. Army Air Forces during World War II. After the war, instead of returning to school he found a job as an office boy working for Warner Bros. This introduced him to the behind-the-scenes world of entertainment, and he quickly became involved in publicity for theater on Broadway and at the Cape Playhouse in Massachusetts during the late 1940s. After a stint as advertising and publicity director for the Ballet Russe in Monte Carlo, and for Lopert Films, he worked on such films as *Summertime* (1955) and *Trapeze* (1956). During the 1950s, he was publicity director for Figaro, Inc., and a production associate for David Merrick, for whom he produced several Broadway productions, including *Gypsy.* In the 1960s, he worked in London and then became vice president of advertising and publicity at Filmways, Inc., from 1965 to 1969; during the early 1970s he was vice president for the East Coast for

Warner Bros. and an independent producer for Paramount Pictures and Frank Yablans, Inc. He was the author, with actor Tony Randall, of the book *Which Reminds Me* (1989), and more recently turned his memoirs into an Off-Broadway monologue, which he later turned into an as-yet-unpublished book. Mindlin was also known for co-producing and directing the documentary *A Journey to Jerusalem.*

OBITUARIES AND OTHER SOURCES:

PERIODICALS

Daily Variety, March 18, 2004, p. 14.
Los Angeles Times, March 11, 2004, p. B13.

*   *   *

MINETOR, Randi (S.) 1958-

PERSONAL: Born December 2, 1958, in Rochester, NY; daughter of Al (in sales) and Annette (a secretary; maiden name, Kershenbaum) Bassow; married Nic Minetor (a lighting designer), September 16, 1990. *Ethnicity:* "Caucasian, Jewish." *Education:* State University of New York—Buffalo, B.A., 1980; University of Rochester, M.A., 1988. *Politics:* Democrat. *Religion:* Jewish. *Hobbies and other interests:* Birding, home renovation.

ADDRESSES: Home and office—Minetor and Co., Inc., 32 Bengal Terr., Rochester, NY 14610-2809; fax: 585-271-2813. *E-mail*—randi@minetor.com.

CAREER: Worked in the late 1970s as a rewriter for the *Dallas Morning News,* Dallas, TX; Geva Theater, Rochester, NY, director of audience development, 1984-87; Saphar and Associates, Inc., Rochester, vice president, 1988-98; Minetor and Co., Inc., Rochester, president, 1998—. Geva Theater, member of board of directors, 1996—; Housing Opportunities, Inc., member of board of directors, 2000—; Rochester Women's Network, member.

MEMBER: National Association of Women Business Owners.

AWARDS, HONORS: Prism Award, 2001, for copywriting for a shaken-baby-syndrome campaign.

WRITINGS:

Breadwinner Wives and the Men They Marry, New Horizon Press (Far Hills, NJ), 2002.

Also works as a journalist, film critic, and public relations writer. Contributor to periodicals, including *Dallas Observer.*

WORK IN PROGRESS: Housework Confidential, a book on what men say about housework; two novels.

SIDELIGHTS: Randi Minetor told *CA:* "Rainer Maria Rilke once said that the key question writers must ask themselves is whether they *must* write. In my case, the answer is yes. I must write, and I do write every day, sometimes in joyous bursts of creativity or, more often, in the slower-paced, methodical way required for intelligent nonfiction.

"I began writing for a living at twenty-one, both as a freelancer for the *Dallas Observer* and as the day rewriter (my 'beat' was death and weather) for the *Dallas Morning News.* Since then, I have made my living as a film critic, journalist, advertising and public relations writer and, most recently, as a writer of feature material for trade magazines in between select client projects. I have known since I was eight years old that I could only live up to my own standards if I became an author. I published my first book recently, and I am now deep into the research for a second nonfiction book, while I work on two novels as well.

"My nonfiction work focuses on the challenges faced by successful working women, in an era that both embraces and shames us. Here in the twenty-first century, millions of women in the United States earn far more money than our husbands do—but our society still expects us to succeed at home, as brilliantly talented mothers and homemakers, without a lick of help from our lower-earning husbands. When we turn out to be mediocre housekeepers or uninspired cooks, we chastise ourselves for our 'failures.' This dichotomy reveals itself in dual-income homes across America and around the world, regardless of which spouse earns the higher income.

"With my books, I try to bring hope to successful women while calling national attention to this bizarre double standard that we perpetuate in our own homes. My next book, *Housework Confidential,* will shed some light on men's attitudes toward housework by asking them directly about their role, their expectations, and the obstacles—real and imagined—that keep them from participating at home.

"My greatest influences were the feminists of the 1960s and 1970s, whose work led me to understand my own potential. Betty Friedan's groundbreaking books, Gloria Steinem's remarkable example and, later, Margaret Atwood's extraordinary fiction—especially *The Edible Woman* and *The Handmaid's Tale*—all have been critically important to my own work.

"I write on a Macintosh laptop computer and do most of the work on my books at a local Starbucks, where the background sounds blend to shut out the distractions of cell phones, pagers, and e-mail. When I am deep into a manuscript, I will write four to six hours daily, beginning in the mid-morning. Writing, for me, is a job—a wonderful, magical job—so I do not turn it into a vehicle for martyrdom or agony. Writing for me is a healthy, exciting activity that increases my productivity, sharpens my senses, and forces my ideas to coalesce."

BIOGRAPHICAL AND CRITICAL SOURCES:

ONLINE

Minetor Companies Web site, http://www.minetor.com/ (March 2, 2004).

* * *

MLODINOW, Leonard 1954-

PERSONAL: Born 1954; children: Alexi, Nicholai. *Ethnicity:* "Caucasian." *Education:* University of California at Berkeley, Ph.D.; completed postdoctoral studies at California Institute of Technology.

ADDRESSES: Home—1970 La France Ave., South Pasadena, CA 91030.

CAREER: Writer. *Night Court,* writer; *Star Trek: The Next Generation,* story editor; Scholastic, Inc., New York, NY, research and development.

WRITINGS:

Euclid's Window: The Story of Geometry from Lines to Hyperspace, Free Press (New York, NY), 2001.
Feynman's Rainbow: A Search for Beauty in Physics and in Life, Warner Books (New York, NY), 2003.

Author of episodes of television series, including "Hell Week," *MacGyver,* American Broadcasting Company, 1987; "Shield of Honor," *Hunter,* National Broadcasting Company, 1989; "The Dauphin," *Star Trek: The Next Generation,* Paramount Television, 1989.

SIDELIGHTS: Leonard Mlodinow took a slightly circular route from holding a post-doctoral fellowship in physics at CalTech to writing popular science books for lay audiences. Along the way he spent some time in Hollywood, writing for television sitcoms and such marginally physics-friendly shows as *MacGyver* and *Star Trek: The Next Generation.* But though it took almost twenty years, Mlodinow did return to the science and scientists he was inspired by as a young scholar.

In 2001 Mlodinow published *Euclid's Window: The Story of Geometry from Lines to Hyperspace,* a study of geometry that set out to explain how Euclid's theories on the three dimensions set the stage for our understanding of the universe, even as they were rendered obsolete by scientists such as Carl Fredrich Gauss and his eighteenth-century ideas about curved space. Descartes, Einstein, and Witten all make appearances as Mlodilnow carries his history into the twenty-first-century and current string-theory speculations about eleven dimensions. Amy Brunvand of *Library Journal* found the effort a "surprisingly exciting history" that "does an excellent job of explaining the importance of the study of geometry." In *Booklist* Gilbert Taylor enjoyed how Mlodinow's humorous and "lively exposition" propelled the book forward. However, a critic for *Publishers Weekly* felt that that the joking tone gives "the false, probably unintentional impression that the subject itself is dull or inaccessible."

Mlodinow followed up *Euclid's Window* with 2003's *Feynman's Rainbow: A Search for Beauty in Physics and in Life*, in which he recounted his early-'80s conversations with famed physicist Richard Feynman. While doing his post-doctoral work at CalTech, Mlodinow underwent a crisis of self-doubt. Eventually he sought out his idol and departmental colleague Feynman iand the two engaged in long discussions of not just science, but life in general. Mlodinow taped some of their conversations, and transcripts of those tapes form the nucleus of *Feynman's Rainbow*. When combined with Mlodinow's anecdotes about his life at CalTech, the result is, according to a contributor to *Kirkus Reviews,* an "inspiring and very readable portrait of a free-spirited genius."

BIOGRAPHICAL AND CRITICAL SOURCES:

PERIODICALS

Booklist, March 1, 2001, Gilbert Taylor, review of *Euclid's Window: The Story of Geometry from Lines to Hyperspace*, p. 1215.
Kirkus Reviews, April 1, 2003, review of *Feynman's Rainbow: A Search for Beauty in Physics and in Life*, p. 522.
Library Journal, March 15, 2001, Amy Brunvand, review of *Euclid's Window*, p. 103.
Publishers Weekly, March 5, 2001, review of *Euclid's Window*, p. 74.
Science News, June 14, 2003, review of *Feynman's Rainbow*, p. 383.

ONLINE

Time Warner Bookmark, http://www.twbookmark.com/ (September 7, 2003).
Wigglefish, http://www.wigglefish.com/ (June 5, 2001), review of *Euclid's Window* and interview.*

*   *   *

MONOSON, S. Sara 1960-

PERSONAL: Born March 23, 1960, in New York, NY; daughter of David B. and Muriel Monoson; married Michael Berns, May 15, 1994; children: Alexander. *Education:* Brandeis University, B.A., 1981; London School of Economics and Political Science, University of London, M.Sc., 1982; Princeton University, Ph.D., 1993.

ADDRESSES: Office—Department of Political Science, Northwestern University, Evanston, IL 60208. *E-mail*—s-monoson@northwestern.edu.

CAREER: Northwestern University, Evanston, IL, assistant professor, 1993-2000, associate professor of political science and classics, 2001—.

AWARDS, HONORS: Best first book award, Foundations of Political Thought Section, American Political Science Association, 2001, for *Plato's Democratic Entanglements: Athenian Politics and the Practice of Philosophy.*

WRITINGS:

Plato's Democratic Entanglements: Athenian Politics and the Practice of Philosophy, Princeton University Press (Princeton, NJ), 2000.

Contributor to periodicals, including *Political Theory.*

BIOGRAPHICAL AND CRITICAL SOURCES:

PERIODICALS

Ethics, April, 2002, Richard Mulgan, review of *Plato's Democratic Entanglements: Athenian Politics and the Practice of Philosophy*, p. 631.

*   *   *

MORRIS, Bill 1952-

PERSONAL: Born 1952.

ADDRESSES: Agent—c/o Author Mail, Simon & Schuster, 1230 Avenue of the Americas, New York, NY 10020.

CAREER: Greensboro News and Record, Greensboro, NC, columnist.

WRITINGS:

Motor City (novel), Washington Square Press (New York, NY), 1992, published as *Biography of a Buick,* Granta (London, England), 1992.
All Souls' Day (novel), Avon (New York, NY), 1997.

Contributor to *Granta 38: We're So Happy!,* edited by Bill Buford, Granta (London, England), 1991.

SIDELIGHTS: A reporter and columnist, Bill Morris has an eye for the details that add up to a bigger story. In his novels, he has trained this eye on the past, bringing distinctive American eras to life through seminal events, cameos of the famous, and the thoughts and actions of characters that typify their times. In his first novel, *Motor City,* his subject is the 1950s, and the seminal event is the design of the 1954 Buick Century by the hard-charging, hard-drinking designers at General Motors. The novel "amply demonstrates that the '50s were the first American decade that could be caricatured by the brand names of its material goods," noted critic Frank Rich in the *New Republic,* "and Morris recaptures the clean, voluptuous pleasure of it all. At times his book suggests, not necessarily pejoratively, that America had been freshly plastered over with that home-decorating miracle known as Con-Tact paper. . . . After applying his figurative contact, however, Morris inevitably must strip it away to reveal what is hidden underneath."

From salesmen who pressure a war vet into buying a car he cannot properly operate to a general manager who uses spies and McCarthyite dirty tricks to keep his designs from falling into the hands of rival companies, Morris describes both the drive and the hucksterism of the era. According to mystery writer Loren Estleman in the *Washington Post Book World,* the book "paints a disturbingly accurate picture of an industrial leviathan rolling fat on the profits from its biggest year, oblivious to the faint rumble from the factories of the Far East and the cancerous cells feeding on its own vitals." Numerous cameos, including Marilyn Monroe, Elvis Presley, Jack Kerouac, and a Ray Kroc about to launch the McDonalds hamburger on an unsuspecting world, further illustrate the contradictions of the era. "Although the '50s collage sometimes wears thin," concluded a *Publishers Weekly* reviewer, "Morris displays the zealous detachment of a sociologist as he exposes fissures in the decade's bland materialism."

Morris' next novel, *All Souls' Day,* is set on the eve of the Vietnam War, which would forever change the world of *Motor City.* Navy veteran Sam Malloy, shattered by his participation in some particularly nasty secret missions in Vietnam, has fled to Bangkok to quietly run a hotel. When U.S. Information Service agent Anne Sinclair shows up and starts sharing her own suspicions about where the American involvement in Vietnam is heading, Malloy finds himself gradually drawn back into the shadowy world he had left behind. Eventually, the two stumble upon a plot to assassinate South Vietnamese president Ngo Dinh Diem, the event that drew the United States into the bloody tangle of Vietnamese politics for the next twelve years. "The problem is that his protagonists . . . are simply too nice to be interesting," complained a *Publishers Weekly* reviewer. But a *Kirkus Reviews* contributor found the book to be "an angry, moving, ingenious blend of fact and fiction about the early stages of the war in Vietnam."

BIOGRAPHICAL AND CRITICAL SOURCES:

PERIODICALS

Entertainment Weekly, June 27, 1997, Vanessa V. Friedman, review of *All Soul's Day,* p. 115.
Independent on Sunday (London, England), July 26, 1992, William Leith, "Dreams of Tail-Fins and Gas-Guzzling."
Kirkus Reviews, April 1, 1997, review of *All Souls' Day.*
Library Journal, May 1, 1992, D. Bogey, review of *Motor City,* p. 119.
Literary Review, spring, 1995, Krzystof Lisowski and Ewa-Hryniewicz Yarbrough, review of *All Soul's Day,* p. 356.
New Republic, September 7, 1992, Frank Rich, review of *Motor City,* pp. 38-43.
New Statesman & Society, July 24, 1992, Roz Kaveney, "First Loves," p. 42.
New York Times, July 7, 1992, Michiko Kakutani, "Promise and Betrayal of the American Dream."
Observer (London, England), August 23, 1992, Valentine Cunningham, "All Revved Up and Nowhere to Go," p. 47.
Publishers Weekly, April 13, 1992, review of *Motor City,* p. 41; April 21, 1997, review of *All Souls' Day,* p. 58.
Washington Post Book World, June 14, 1992, Loren Estleman, review of *Motor City,* p. 38.*

MOSS, Eric Owen 1943-

PERSONAL: Born July 25, 1943, in Los Angeles, CA. *Education:* University of California at Los Angeles, B.A., 1965; University of California at Berkeley, M.Arch., 1968; Harvard University, M.Arch., 1972.

ADDRESSES: Office—Eric Owen Moss Architects, 8557 Higuera St., Culver City, CA 90232-2535; fax: 310-839-7922. *E-mail*—mail@ericowenmoss.com.

CAREER: Southern California Institute of Architecture, Los Angeles, director and professor of design, 1974—; Eric Owen Moss Architects, Culver City, CA, founder, 1975—. Eliot Noyes chair, Harvard University, 1990; Eero Saarinen Chair, Yale University, 1991. Lecturer at University of Michigan, National Building Museum, Pratt Institute, Rice University, Dallas Museum of Art, and other institutions. *Exhibitions:*Work has been exhibited at Queens Museum of Art, Max Protetch Gallery, and Venice Biennale.

AWARDS, HONORS: American Institute of Architects AIA/LA Award, 1977, 1979, 1983, 1988, 1990, 1991, and 1992; Architectural Record Interiors Award, 1984; Los Angeles Chamber of Commerce Design Award, 1984; AIA/CC Award, 1986, 1988, and 1991; National AIA Honor Award, 1988, 1989, and 1992; Award in Architecture, American Academy of Arts and Letters, 1999; AIA/LA Gold Medal Award, 2001.

WRITINGS:

Eric Owen Moss: Buildings and Projects 1, introduction by Wolf D. Prix, Rizzoli (New York, NY), 1991.
Eric Owen Moss, Rizzoli (New York, NY), 1992.
Lawson-Westen House, 1995.
Eric Owen Moss: The Box, 1996.
Eric Owen Moss: Buildings and Projects 2, Rizzoli (New York, NY), 1996.
Eric Owen Moss, Rizzoli (New York, NY), 2000.
Gnostic Architecture, 1999, Monacelli Press (New York, NY), 2003.
Eric Owen Moss: Buildings and Projects 3, Rizzoli (New York, NY), 2003.

SIDELIGHTS: Eric Owen Moss is an architect and director of the Southern California Institute of Architecture. His buildings are, according to David

Bryant in *Library Journal,* "jaggedly of our time: twisted metal, glass in arrangements that look lethal, concrete serving as cheap permanent mass, and wood as a random accent." "Moss," Thomas Fisher explained in *Progressive Architecture,* "is a master of the non sequitur, joining things that seem unrelated to reveal deeper affinities." Writing in the *Los Angeles Times Book Review,* Leon Whiteson described Moss as "one of a group of . . . Los Angeles architects who have won international recognition for the boldness and verve of their designs." Moss has designed buildings around the world, including in southern California, Havana, Vienna, London, and St. Petersburg, Russia.

Moss is especially known for his collaborative efforts alongside real estate developer Frederick Smith to revitalize Culver City, California, an industrial town with old factories and warehouses. Moss often converts these existing structures into new buildings for different uses. The Pittard Sullivan headquarters in Culver City incorporates a brick wall and the bowstring trusses from the factory that once occupied the site. "There is a lively dialogue between old and new," as Michael Webb described the building in *Interiors.* "A tilted cylinder serves as a lofty entrance atrium; a tilted cube as a second-floor conference room." The Culver City headquarters of the Gary Group made use of existing warehouses. Jayne Merkel in *Art in America* described the design: "Moss has cut apart concrete block warehouses . . . to insert offices; he covered them with various odd-shaped skylights and hung chains, wheels, Plexiglas panels, pipes and a sloping extra wall on the outside."

Describing his approach to architecture, Moss writes in his book *Gnostic Architecture* that it "is not about faith in a movement, a methodology, a process, a technique, or technology. It is a strategy for keeping architecture in a perpetual state of motion." Moss's buildings, as Andrew Ballantyne wrote in the *Times Literary Supplement,* "look like acts of insurrection. They celebrate the possibilities of particular circumstances, take advantage of unique opportunities, are concerned with the 'here' and 'now' of their inception and development. . . . They have the appearance of robust practicality and cultivated imperfection."

Moss has presented his designs in a series of books that also offer his reflections on how and why he designed them. The first of a series, his *Eric Owen Moss: Buildings and Projects* was described by D. P.

Doordan in *Choice* as "one of the best new books on contemporary radical architecture." Doordan praised Moss for explaining "complex ideas in a clear and evocative manner." "Throughout the book," Fisher noted, "there echo the existential dilemmas of our times—the loss of certainty, the death of religion, the impossibility of universal truth."

BIOGRAPHICAL AND CRITICAL SOURCES:

BOOKS

de Boissière, Olivier, *Eric Owen Moss Architecte: Lindblade Tower and Paramount Laundry, Reconversion à Culver City, Californie, USA* Demi-Circle (Paris, France), 1991.

Steele, James, *Eric Owen Moss* (interview), Academy Group (London, England), 1992.

Steele, James, *PS: A Building by Eric Owen Moss,* 1998.

PERIODICALS

Architectural Record, February, 1997, Suzanne Stephens, "Eric Moss's Samitaur Building, His Latest Project in the Culver City Section of Los Angeles, Plays against Type," p. 52.

Architecture, January, 2003, Bay Brown, "Eric Owen Moss Architects," p. 34.

Art in America, February, 1994, Jayne Merkel, reviews of *Eric Owen Moss: Buildings and Projects,* pp. 33-38.

Choice, May, 1992, D. P. Doordan, review of *Eric Owen Moss: Buildings and Projects,* p. 1383.

Interiors, September, 1998, Michael Webb, "Pittard Sullivan," p. 84; October, 1999, review of *Gnostic Architecture,* p. 86.

Library Journal, April 1, 2003, David Bryant, review of *Eric Owen Moss: Buildings and Projects 3,* p. 95.

Los Angeles Times Book Review, July 12, 1992, Leon Whiteson, review of *Eric Owen Moss,* p. 6.

Progressive Architecture, August, 1992, Thomas Fisher, review of *Eric Owen Moss: Buildings and Projects,* p. 77; January, 1995, "Ince Theater," p. 104.

Times Literary Supplement, May 29, 1992, Andrew Ballantyne, review of *Eric Owen Moss: Buildings and Projects,* p. 16.

ONLINE

Eric Owen Moss Architects Web site, http://www.eric owenmoss.com (October 7, 2003).*

*   *   *

MUNÉVAR, Gonzalo 1945-

PERSONAL: Born 1945, in Barranquilla, Colombia; son of Gonzalo and Delia Munévar; married second wife, Susan Greenshields (a clinical psychologist); children: Ryan (first marriage). *Education:* California State University, B.A., 1970, M.A., 1971; University of California, Berkeley, Ph.D., 1975. *Politics:* "19th Century liberal, in the tradition of J. S. Mill." *Hobbies and other interests:* Soccer, classical music, movies, travel.

ADDRESSES: Office—Department of Humanities, Social Sciences and Communication, Lawrence Technological University, 21000 West Ten Mile Rd., Southfield, MI 48075-1058. *Agent*—Peter Scolney, 100 WIlshire Blvd., Suite 1300, Santa Monica, CA 90401. *E-mail*—munevar@ltu.edu.

CAREER: Educator, consultant, and writer. San Francisco State University, lecturer, 1975-76; University of Nebraska, Omaha, assistant professor, 1976-85, professor, 1985-86, Nebraska Foundation Professor of Philosophy, 1986-89; Evergreen State College, Olympia, Washington, professor of history and philosophy of science, 1989-97; Lawrence Technological University, Southfield, Michigan, professor and chair, Department of Humanities, Social Sciences and Communication, 1999—. Stanford University, Stanford, California, visiting associate professor of philosophy, faculty fellow at Stanford Humanities Center, 1983-84; University of Newcastle, Australia, visiting research professor in evolutionary epistemology, summer, 1986, summer, 1987; Instituto de Filosofía, Madrid, Spain, visiting research professor, fall, 1987; Universidad de Barcelona, Spain, visiting research professor, winter, 1988; Universidad de Santiago de Compostela, Spain, visiting research professor, spring, 1988; University of Edinburgh, Scotland, fellow, Institute for Advanced Study in the Humanities, summer, 1989; Kobe Shodai University, Kobe,

Japan, visiting professor, spring-summer, 1993; University of Washington, Seattle, visiting professor of philosophy, spring, 1994; University of California, Irvine, visiting professor of philosophy, 1997-99.

MEMBER: American Philosophical Association, Philosophy of Science Association, American Association for the Advancement of Science.

AWARDS, HONORS: Distinguished Research Award, University of Nebraska at Omaha, 1986; Ethel Wattis Kimball fellowship, Stanford Humanities Center; Black Heron Press Award for social fiction, 1999, for *The Master of Fate.*

WRITINGS:

Radical Knowledge: A Philosophical Inquiry into the Nature and Limits of Science, with foreword by Paul K. Feyerabend, Hackett (Indianapolis, IN), 1981.
(Editor) *Beyond Reason: Essays on the Philosophy of Paul Feyerabend,* Kluwer Academic Publishers (Boston, MA), 1991.
(Editor) *Spanish Studies in the Philosophy of Science,* Kluwer Academic Publishers (Boston, MA), 1996.
Evolution and the Naked Truth: A Darwinian Approach to Philosophy, Ashgate (Brookfield, VT), 1998.
The Master of Fate (novel), Black Heron Press, 1999.
(Editor, with John Preston and David Lamb) *The Worst Enemy of Science?: Essays in Memory of Paul Feyerabend,* Oxford University Press (New York, NY), 2000.

Contributor of essays in philosophy, short stories, poetry, and literary criticism to periodicals.

WORK IN PROGRESS: Alex and *The Night of the Red Moon* (novels); *The Dimming of Starlight: The Philosophy of Space Exploration; Loose Ends* (screenplay); *A Theory of Wonder: A Naturalistic Account in the Revolution in the Philosophy of Science;* adapting Gunther Stent's *Nazis, Women and Molecular Biology* as a screenplay.

SIDELIGHTS: Interdisciplinary scholar, professor, and author Gonzalo Munévar has taught philosophy, history, science, literature, mathematics, and writing at the college level. His particular field of interest is the philosophy of science. A native of Colombia, he has been a visiting professor at universities throughout the world. Munévar has written and edited several books on philosophy and is the author of an award-winning novel, *The Master of Fate,* which is set in his native country.

Munévar's first book, *Radical Knowledge: A Philosophical Inquiry into the Nature and Limits of Science,* explores the theories of Paul Feyerabend, Karl Popper, Konrad Lorenz, Ernst Mach, Herbert Spencer, Henri Poincaré, and others in developing a discourse on the limitations of the cumulative body of scientific knowledge as a product of biologically based human intelligence. Steven Walt, in a somewhat negative review for *Ethics,* stated that "Munévar's treatment is superficial and too brief throughout" and that his suggestion of institutional rationality "is handled in four paragraphs despite its importance" to the author's argument. Allen Scult, in a review for the *Quarterly Journal of Speech,* concluded: "Munévar, like most evolutionary epistemologists, is bound to stress the importance of encouraging the multiplication of competing scientific perceptions. Likewise, he is driven to call for means whereby even initially implausible theories can be protected from premature refutation." A contributor to *Choice* described the book as a "lively discussion of the limits of scientific knowledge . . . in the tradition of T. S. Kuhn."

Munévar's first novel, *The Master of Fate,* is the story of a middle-class Colombian teenager, Oscar Moreira, growing up during the 1950s and attending a Catholic boarding school in Bogatá. When Oscar's father's business fails and the family is beset with financial troubles, Oscar reacts to the changes in a more negative way than does his brother, Homero. As his father takes out his frustrations on Oscar and Homero and his mother struggles to maintain peace and sanity, Oscar adopts a stubborn and aloof manner that alienates those around him. Forced to attend a national university rather than the elite school he had hoped for, he falls behind in his studies. Homero, on the other hand, chooses to make the best of the family's losses. When his father dies, Oscar must confront his choices and try to salvage his future. A reviewer for *Black Heron Press* described the novel as "both existential and realistic." A *Publishers Weekly* contributor noted the "often stunningly blunt dialogue of teenagers exchanging boasts and sexual secrets" and concluded that "Oscar's inner life registers as an uncompromising study of the psychological origins of resentment."

Munévar also coedited *The Worst Enemy of Science?: Essays in Memory of Paul Feyerabend,* a book of essays in memory of the philosopher Paul K. Feyerabend, about whom the author has frequently written. Alfred Nordmann, in a review for *Ethics,* commented that "Feyerabend's views become more challenging with the quality of the questions put to him."

BIOGRAPHICAL AND CRITICAL SOURCES:

BOOKS

Directory of American Scholars, ninth edition, Volume 4: *Philosophy, Religion, and Law,* Gale (Detroit, MI), 1999.

PERIODICALS

Choice, November, 1982, review of *Radical Knowledge: A Philosophical Inquiry into the Nature and Limits of Science,* p. 447.
Ethics, January, 1983, Steven Walt, review of *Radical Knowledge,* p. 419; October, 2001, Alfred Nordmann, review of *The Worst Enemy of Science? Essays in Memory of Paul Feyerabend,* p. 197.
Publishers Weekly, November 15, 1999, review of *The Master of Fate,* p. 55.
Quarterly Journal of Speech, August, 1984, Allen Scult, review of *Radical Knowledge,* pp. 307-309.

ONLINE

Black Heron Press Web site, http://mav.net/blackheron/ (February 29, 2000), review of *The Master of Fate.*
Lawrence Technological University Web site, http://www.ltu.edu/ (November 5, 2003), "Faculty and Staff: Gonzalo Munévar."

*   *   *

MURRAY, Yxta Maya

PERSONAL: First name is pronounced "Eeek-sta"; born in Long Beach, CA. *Education:* University of California—Los Angeles, BA; Stanford University, J.D., with distinction.

ADDRESSES: Office—Burns-309, Loyola Law School, 919 South Albany Street, Los Angeles, CA 90015-1211. *E-mail*—yxta.murray@lls.edu.

CAREER: Loyola Law School, Loyola Marymount University, Los Angeles, CA, professor, 1995—; writer. Worked as law clerk for Honorable Harry Hupp, Central District of California, and Honorable Ferdinant Fernandez, Ninth Circuit Court of Appeals, Pasadena, CA.

AWARDS, HONORS: Whiting Award for exceptionally promising emerging writer of fiction, 1999.

WRITINGS:

Locas, Grove Press (New York, NY), 1997.
What It Takes to Get to Vegas, Grove Press (New York, NY), 1999.
The Conquest, Rayo (New York, NY), 2002.

Also author of short stories and articles, including "Becoming Latina," published on *Latina.com.*

SIDELIGHTS: Yxta Maya Murray wrote in an article for the online publication *Latina.com* that she was named for the legendary Aztec princess Ixtaccihuatl. The princess died upon hearing the false rumors of the death of her warrior-lover, Popocatepetl. Upon returning from battle and finding his lovely princess dead, Popo carried Ixta's body to the top of the mountain, and the two of them, to this day, watch over Mexico City. This story did not stop her classmates in Long Beach, California, where Murray grew up, from teasing her about her "tongue-twisting name." She did, however, gain self-confidence from having been named for such a legend. She has gone on to pursue two successful careers, in law and in writing.

In the online publication *Stanford Lawyer,* Murray explained that her work in law and her creative writing inform one another. Her stories, she stated, make her feel as if she were writing "little love letters to the community." Her first work of fiction, *Locas,* was described by Margaret Regan in *Tucson Weekly* as giving "razor-sharp life to *la vida* in a down-and-out Los Angeles barrio." Regan also referred to the novel as being a "horrifying new book." The story deals with the notorious gangs of Los Angeles and, especially, their women, the *locas*. The two main characters are the teenagers Cecilia and Lucia, who seem mainly interested in pleasing the male gang leaders. Cecilia hopes for little more than to get pregnant, but Lucia is more ambitious. She does not like what happens to most women in her community, who spend their days tending small babies and their nights being abused by the men. Lucia, according to Regan's article, is "Tough, smart and mean to the bone." She wants to be a *jefa*, a leader of a gang.

"Murray details these two girls' grim histories," wrote Rachel Stoll for *New York Times*, "with little sentimentality and much skill." Celeste Fremon in *Los Angeles Times* also praised Murray's writing skill, stating that her work is "fierce and persuasive." Yet the critic nonetheless questioned the accuracy of Murray's story. She feared that many people who are not familiar with the real life aspects of gang culture will believe that Murray's book provides a "genuine visit to the hidden and dangerous world of gangs." Concluding her review, Fremon wrote, "As a coming-of-age fable, Murray's story is passionate, poetic and, in so many ways, dazzling, but as a window into real life, it's a saddening misstep." *Chicago Tribune Books* critic Jody Miller was also concerned about how Murray tells her story. Miller wrote, "Murray's artistic license leads to an unrealistic portrait of the nature of girls' involvement in gangs." However, Miller also noted that in the end, "the story is a compelling read."

What It Takes to Get to Vegas tells the story of Rita Zapata, who dreams of rising out of poverty by marrying a boxer. According to Cara Mia Di Massa in *Los Angeles Times Book Review*, Murray's story "offers a swift, compelling portrait of the East L.A. boxing scene and a woman's place in it." The focus in the story is definitely on the women; male characters are present but are seen only through the women who attempt to control them. *LA Weekly*'s Ben Ehrenreich described the male characters in Murray's second novel as providing "sex and status, but are for the most part little more than objects maneuvered in a game played by women." Billy Navarro is the boxer whom Rita clings to. He provides only a few elements of Rita's dream and shatters the rest of it with violence. "Everything that she [Rita] gains," wrote a reviewer for *Publishers Weekly*, "she attains by deceit." Rita finally achieves her dreams, but her slide back down the other side is swift. One of the good qualities of

this book is that Murray does not judge her characters, the *Publishers Weekly* reviewer stated, but rather allows readers to come to their own conclusions.

The Conquest, Murray's third novel, is a story about Sara Gonzales, a rare-book restorer for the Getty Museum. As the story opens, Sara has just begun working on a manuscript written by a sixteenth-century woman called Helen, an Aztec princess. Helen was abducted by Fernando Cortez and taken to Europe for the benefit of the pope. When Sara brings Helen's manuscript to the attention of her boss and colleagues, they tell her that the story is nothing but fiction. Sara is determined to prove them wrong. In order to do so, she must dig into piles of old manuscripts and letters, a task that keeps her at work until late, affecting her relationship with her long-time boyfriend, Karl.

Two stories unfold in this novel. One deals with Sara and her struggles; the other focuses on Helen. Sara's life, however, proves to be the more complicated as she gets lost in indecision. Her boyfriend Karl has announced that he plans to marry another woman; and although Sara does not want to lose him, she cannot give him the time that their relationship demands.

"The great strength of *The Conquest*", wrote Colleen Quinn for the online publication *Bookreporter.com*, "is its sensuality." Whether Murray is describing a love scene or the luxuriant paper of an old manuscript, or a delicious meal with European royalty, "she is contagious in her enjoyment of every gleam, every drop, every stroke." Another critic, this one from *Publishers Weekly*, found that the weaving of the two women's stories provided the most interest. "The subplot about Sara's literary sleuthing ties the two stories neatly together and gives the book a satisfying edge of suspense," the reviewer wrote.

BIOGRAPHICAL AND CRITICAL SOURCES:

PERIODICALS

Chicago Tribune Books, May 11, 1997, Jody Miller, "Twp Authors Look at Girls, Gangs and Violence," review of *Locas,* p. 6.
Kirkus Reviews, September 1, 2002, review of *The Conquest,* pp. 1255-1256.

LA Weekly, September 3-9, 1999, Ben Ehrenreich, "Eastside, Westside," review of *What It Takes to Get to Vegas.*

Library Journal, April 1, 1997, Lawrence Rungren, review of *Locas,* p. 128; June 1, 1999, Dianna Moeller, review of *What It Takes to Get to Vegas,* p. 176.

Los Angeles Magazine, November, 2002, Ariel Swartley, review of *The Conquest,* pp. 134-136.

Los Angeles Times Book Review, June 15, 1997, Celeste Fremon, "Homegirls," review of *Locas,* pp. 10-11; August 29, 1999, Cara Mia Di Massa, review of *What It Takes to Get to Vegas,* p. 4.

New York Times, August 24, 1997, Rachel Stoll, review of *Locas,* p. 19; October 3, 1999, Barbara Sutton, review of *What It Takes to Get to Vegas,* p. 21.

Publishers Weekly, March 3, 1997, review of *Locas,* p. 62; June 28, 1999, review of *What It Takes to Get to Vegas,* p. 53; September 9, 2002, review of *The Conquest.* p. 42.

ONLINE

Bookreporter.com, http://www.bookreporter.com/ (January 7, 2003), Colleen Quinn, review of *The Conquest.*

Stanford Lawyer Online, http://www.law.Stanford.edu/alumni/lawyer/ (spring, 2000), issue 57, "Alumni Profiles."

Tucson Weekly Online, http://www.tucsonweekly.com/ (June 5-June 11, 1997), Margaret Regan, "'Locas' Takes a Hard Look at an Even Harder Life.*"

N-O

NEAVERSON, Bob 1967-

PERSONAL: Born 1967.

ADDRESSES: Agent—c/o Author Mail, Peter Owen Publishers, Inc., 73 Kenway Rd., London SW5 0RE, England.

CAREER: Lecturer on film and media; writer. Has worked on film production.

WRITINGS:

The Beatles Movies, Cassell (New York, NY), 1997.
(With Denis O'Dell) *At the Apple's Core: The Beatles from the Inside,* Peter Owen (London, England), 2002.

SIDELIGHTS: Bob Neaverson was born during the era when the Beatles were at their height of popularity. As an adult Neaverson has studied the Beatles' films and other video creations and has written and lectured on the subject. His book *The Beatles Movies* takes a serious look at how the Beatles influenced mainstream cinema, and how each of their finished films inaugurated a new phase in their careers. A reviewer for *Sight and Sound* called Neaverson's production histories in *The Beatles Movies* "fascinating" and praised the author for his "concise, resonant writing."

While conducting his research for *The Beatles Movies,* Neaverson arranged an interview with Denis O'Dell, who produced or co-produced *A Hard Day's Night,* *How I Won the War, Magical Mystery Tour,* and *Let It Be.* O'Dell took a leading role in the Beatles' Apple, Inc., an umbrella company that created everything from records and movies to apparel. Although he was a longtime friend of the Beatles, O'Dell had rarely spoken or written about his relationship with them prior to meeting Neaverson. The two men got along well, and Neaverson helped O'Dell to write a memoir titled *At the Apple's Core: The Beatles from the Inside.* Neaverson's aim was to afford Beatles fans a glimpse of the group from the perspective of an insider who worked intimately with them for years.

At the Apple's Core contains never before published photographs of the Beatles, as well as O'Dell's reflections on the group, particularly in reference to their films and promotional videos. *Variety* correspondent Archie Thomas deemed the book "an entertaining if overfawning firsthand account of the pain and the pleasure of working at the core of Apple Corps in those heady years." Thomas felt that the strength of the memoir "lies in its portrayal of a day in the lives of the biggest band that ever was." A *Publishers Weekly* critic praised the work as "genteel yet engaging" and concluded that it "provides a welcome insight into a small but crucial part of the Beatles' artistic legacy."

BIOGRAPHICAL AND CRITICAL SOURCES:

PERIODICALS

Publishers Weekly, November 18, 2002, review of *At the Apple's Core: The Beatles from the Inside,* p. 54.

Sight and Sound, November, 1997, review of *The Beatles Movies,* p. 30.

Variety, October 21, 2002, Archie Thomas, "Foibles of Fab Four Enliven Insider Tale," p. 41.*

* * *

NEVILLE, Richard F. 1931-2004

OBITUARY NOTICE—See index for *CA* sketch: Born September 6, 1931, in Brooklyn, NY; died March 1, 2004, in Tacoma Park, MD. Educator, administrator, and author. Neville was a longtime professor of education, a dean, and a provost at the University of Maryland—Baltimore County. A graduate of Central Connecticut State College, where he earned a B.S. in 1953, he completed a master's degree at Columbia in 1957 and his Ph.D. at the University of Connecticut in 1963. He began his career in the 1950s as an elementary school teacher and high school basketball coach, then taught for two years at Central Connecticut State College, and spent another two years as an elementary school principal in Berlin, Connecticut before joining the University of Connecticut as an instructor in education in 1960. From 1964 to 1969 he was an associate professor for the University of Maryland at College Park, moving to the Baltimore faculty in 1969 as professor of education and head of the division of education. During the mid-1970s, Neville was the division's dean, rising through the ranks as acting dean of faculty in 1978, dean of faculty in 1979, and dean of arts and sciences from 1980 to 1989. Beginning in 1989, he also served as senior advisor to the university's president and was provost of the Biotechnology Institute from 1991 to 1994. When he retired in 1995, he was named dean emeritus. Neville coauthored the books *The Foundations of Elementary School Teaching* (1963), *The Faculty as Teachers: A Perspective of Evaluation* (1971), and *Instructional Supervision: A Behavior System* (1975; second edition, 1978).

OBITUARIES AND OTHER SOURCES:

ONLINE

University of Maryland—Baltimore County, http:// www.umbc.edu/ (May 20, 2004).

University of Maryland Biotechnology Institute, http:// www.umbi.umd.edu/ (April 16, 2004).

NORWOOD, Mandi 1963-

PERSONAL: Born October 9, 1963, in Oldham, Lancashire, England; married Martin Kelly, 1995; children: Rosie, Daisy. *Education:* Attended Darlington College of Technology and London College of Fashion.

ADDRESSES: Home—312 East 69th St., New York, NY 10021.

CAREER: Look Now (magazine), sub-editor and deputy chief sub-editor, 1986-87; *Clothes Show* (magazine), features editor, 1987; *More!* (magazine), deputy editor, 1987-89; *Looks* (magazine), editor, 1989-90; *Company* (magazine), editor, 1990-95; *Cosmopolitan,* editor, 1995-2000; *Mademoiselle,* New York, NY, editor-in-chief, 2000-01.

MEMBER: British Society of Magazine Editors, Periodical Publishers Association (member of editorial committee).

AWARDS, HONORS: Women's Magazine Editor of the Year Award, British Society of Magazine Editors, 1993, 1999.

WRITINGS:

Sex and the Married Girl, from Clicking to Climaxing: The Complete Truth about Modern Marriage, St. Martin's Press (New York, NY), 2003.

SIDELIGHTS: Mandi Norwood has been the editor of such prominent women's magazines as *Cosmopolitan* and *Mademoiselle,* and has twice won the Women's Magazine Editor of the Year Award from the British Society of Magazine Editors. She is also "fondly known for such headlines as 'Six Guys to Do before You Say *I Do*' and for unabashedly filling her magazines with sex and salaciousness," as Anna Kierstan reported in *Life Changing Books.* While editing *Company* magazine, Norwood included a graphically illustrated "penis supplement" to boost circulation. This same approach to sexuality is also found in Norwood's book *Sex and the Married Girl, from Clicking to Climaxing: The Complete Truth about Modern Marriage.*

"Norwood is a woman who knows what she wants and works her damnedest to get it," according to Claire Beale in *Campaign.* "And, if her track record is anything to go by, she usually succeeds." Norwood began her career by freelancing for various London fashion magazines before landing the editorship of *Looks* magazine at the age of twenty-five. During her tenureship at *Company,* Norwood increased the magazine's circulation by some forty percent. In 1997 she took the helm of the British edition of *Cosmopolitan,* "one of the most prestigious jobs in women's magazines," as Beale described it. As editor of *Cosmopolitan,* Norwood built "a reputation for sexing it up," as a writer for *MediaWeek* termed it. In 2000 Norwood came to America to take over the editorship of *Mademoiselle,* a venerable women's magazine suffering from sluggish circulation and declining advertising revenues. Norwood quickly changed the magazine's logo and gave it a new nickname ("Millie"). She also refocused the magazine's direction, "celebrating young women's unabashed passion for shopping, makeup, guys and work," as Lisa Granatstein noted in *MediaWeek.* Despite Norwood's efforts, by late 2001 the troubled *Mademoiselle* had folded. By mid-2003 she was busy developing a new magazine for Hearst.

In 2003 Norwood published *Sex and the Married Girl,* a title meant to echo Helen Gurley Brown's bestselling *Sex and the Single Girl* of the 1960s. To research her book, Norwood interviewed over 100 women in the United States and England about their married lives. "It dives into the marital bed head first," Rachel Cooke admitted in the London *Observer.* Kierstan found *Sex and the Married Girl* to be "a gloves-off look at modern marriage from the female perspective." The book is "plump with sisterly counsel," Cooke believed. "Norwood reveals a lot of truth here," David Leonhardt added in his review for the *Library Journal,* "and no matter how often readers find themselves agreeing one minute and disagreeing the next, she totally engages and will provoke important discussion."

BIOGRAPHICAL AND CRITICAL SOURCES:

PERIODICALS

Campaign, August 4, 1995, Claire Beale, "*Cosmo* Succumbs to Charms of Aggressive Career Woman: How Will Mandi Norwood's Pugnacious Style Go down at *Cosmo?,*" p. 19.

Library Journal, April 1, 2003, David Leonhardt, review of *Sex and the Married Girl, from Clicking to Climaxing: The Complete Truth about Modern Marriage,* pp. 116-117.

MediaWeek, September 6, 1999, "*Cosmo* Girl Now a *Mademoiselle,*" p. 5; June 26, 2000, Lisa Granatstein, "Millie's Makeover," p. 66.

Observer (London, England), June 8, 2003, Rachel Cooke, "Thoroughly Modern Mandi."

Women's Wear Daily, September 2, 1999, "Mandi Norwood Appointed New Editor of *Mademoiselle,*" p. 5; December 8, 2000, Lisa Lockwood, "Editors Give Sneak Preview," p. 4B.

ONLINE

Life Changing Books, http://pollux.jour.city.ac.uk/books/ (October 7, 2003), Anna Kierstan, "Girls on Top: Interview with Mandi Norwood."*

*   *   *

O'DONNELL, Edward T. 1963-

PERSONAL: Born 1963; married; wife's name Stephanie; children: Erin, Kelly, Michelle, Katherine. *Education:* Holy Cross College (Worcester, MA), B.A. (history), 1986; Columbia University, M.A. (history), 1989, M.Phil., 1991, Ph.D. (ethnic and urban history), 1995.

ADDRESSES: Home—Holden, MA. *Office*—Department of History, 1 College St., College of the Holy Cross, Worcester, MA 01610. *E-mail*—eodonnell@holycross.edu.

CAREER: Historian, educator, and author. Hunter College, City University of New York, associate professor of history, 1995-2001; Holy Cross College, Worcester, MA, associate professor of history, 2001—. Columbia University, visiting assistant summer-session professor, 1997—; Fordham University, visiting associate professor, 2001. Exhibit curator, lecturer, and tour guide. Commentator on television and radio; commentator on National Public Radio's *Morning Edition.* Alliance for New York City History, member of executive board, 1999-2001.

AWARDS, HONORS: Named New York City Centennial Historian, 1999.

WRITINGS:

1,001 Things Everyone Should Know about Irish American History, Broadway Books (New York, NY), 2002.

Ship Ablaze: The Tragedy of the Steamboat "General Slocum," Broadway Books (New York, NY), 2003.

Henry George for Mayor! Irish Nationalism, Labor Radicalism, and Independent Politics in Gilded-Age New York City, Columbia University Press (New York, NY), 2004.

(Coauthor) *Visions of America: A History of the United States,* Addison Wesley Longman (Reading MA), 2005.

Contributor to books, including *New York Walks,* Henry Holt, 1992; *The Hungry Stream: Emigration from Ireland during the Great Famine,* Institute of Irish Studies Press, 1997; *The Irish in America,* edited by Terry Golway, Hyperion Press, 1997; and *Encyclopedia of the Irish in America,* University of Notre Dame Press, 2000; contributor to periodicals, including *Journal of Urban History, New York Times,* and *American Journal of Economics and Sociology.* Author of column "Hibernian Chronicle," for *Irish Echo* (newspaper). Project editor, *Encyclopedia of New York,* Yale University Press, 1995.

WORK IN PROGRESS: The nonfiction books *The Ethnic Crucible: New York City's Lower East Side, 1820-2000* and *The Road Well Traveled: 101 Stories of Wisdom, Achievement, and Inspiration from the American Past.*

SIDELIGHTS: Historian and educator Edward T. O'Donnell has spent much of his career studying and popularizing the early history of the metropolitan New York area. Earning advanced degrees at New York City's Columbia University, and teaching at the city's Hunter College, he was also active in promoting local history by hosting walking tours of the city's ethnic neighborhoods and working to further other history-related projects. When the wreckage of the steamship *General Slocum* was discovered off the New Jersey coast in 2000, it served as inspiration for O'Donnell's

Ship Ablaze: The Tragedy of the Steamboat "General Slocum," an account of the greatest disaster to occur in New York City until surpassed by the events of September 11, 2001.

On June 15, 1904, 1,300 New Yorkers boarded the *General Slocum,* a steamship that transported passengers from the city's Lower East Side across Long Island Sound. Among those passengers, most were German-American families, members of a local East Side church, who planned to take a group picnic on Long Island. After a small fire broke out in a storage room, negligence on the part of the ship's owner, an untrained crew, rotting life preservers, the passengers' general lack of swimming ability, and the shortage of life boats resulted in the deaths of 1,000 passengers and the loss of the ship. The fire left behind another legacy, however; as O'Donnell explained to *Publishers Weekly* interviewer Dylan Foley, "Though the 'Little Germany' neighborhood on the Lower East Side was dissolving like most ethnic neighborhoods, the General Slocum disaster obliterated it from the ethnic map of New York." While made much of by the press for a time, the tragedy slipped from public memory, particularly after public sentiment turned heavily against Germans at the approach of World War I.

Writing in *Publishers Weekly,* a critic noted of *Ship Ablaze* that O'Donnell presents a compelling backdrop to the tragedy by explaining what life was like in the first years of the twentieth century and also shows how newspapers helped drum up public furor following the fire. Tales of heroism and stories of shady business dealings are told side by side, and the historian ends by putting the *General Slocum* tragedy into a context by which readers can compare it to the terrorist attacks on the city of almost a century later. "In O'Donnell's deft hands," the critic concluded, "the disaster becomes more than just a historical event—it's a fascinating window into an era, a community and the lives of ordinary people." *Booklist* contributor Gavin Quinn also praised the book, noting that *Ship Ablaze* "does not feel like printed history, but rather a terrible scene that has just unfolded in front of the reader." In *Ship Ablaze,* according to a reviewer for *Library Journal,* O'Donnell creates a "fascinating book, researched with care and written with sensitivity."

BIOGRAPHICAL AND CRITICAL SOURCES:

PERIODICALS

Booklist, May, 2003, Gavin Quinn, review of *Ship Ablaze: The Tragedy of the Steamboat "General Slocum."*

Kirkus Reviews, April 15, 2003, review of *Ship Ablaze,* p. 392.

Library Journal, May 15, 2003, review of *Ship Ablaze.*

New York Daily News, June 8, 2003, review of *Ship Ablaze.*

Publishers Weekly, May 5, 2004, Dylan Foley, interview with O'Donnell, p. 201, and review of *Ship Ablaze,* p. 211.

ONLINE

Edward T. O'Donnell Home Page, http://www.edwardtodonnell.com (June 15, 2004).

General Slocum Disaster Web site, http://www.general-slocum.com/ (May 20, 2004).

Holy Cross College Web site, http://www.holycross.edu/ (August 2, 2001), "Holy Cross Historian Is Expert on New York's Forgotten Disaster."*

*　　*　　*

OKIN, Susan Moller 1946-2004

OBITUARY NOTICE—See index for *CA* sketch: Born July 19, 1946, in Auckland, New Zealand; died March 3, 2004, in Lincoln, MA. Philosopher, educator, and author. Okin was a Stanford University professor well known as a feminist political philosopher. Her childhood life growing up among strong-willed women led her to question her professor's stance on women's issues while at the University of Auckland. Graduating there in 1967, she earned her B.Phil. in 1970 from Somerville College, Oxford, and her Ph.D. from Harvard in 1975. After a few visiting professor stints, she became an assistant professor of political theory at Brandeis University in 1976. Her first book, *Women in Western Political Thought* (1979), was based on her Ph.D. dissertation. After being promoted to full professor in 1989 at Brandeis, Okin accepted a position as Marta Sutton Weeks Professor of Ethics in Society at Stanford in 1990, where she was also director of the

ethics in society program. Throughout her career, she argued for more equity for women in society, politics, and business, declaring that the root of the imbalance in society that favored men found its basis in accepted family structures. One of her fervent positions was that the legal system was biased against women and that courts, in considering divorce cases, should take into greater consideration the fact that women have less income-earning power; furthermore, she brought attention to the injustice of courts considering the "cultural defense" argument as valid when male defendants among minorities from Asian and Middle Eastern origin tried to justify abuse of women as a part of their culture. Most recently, Okin worked in India with the Global Fund for Women to support women's rights. Among her other books are *Justice, Gender, and the Family* (1989) and *Is Multiculturalism Bad for Women?* (1999). Okin was working as a distinguished visiting professor at the Radcliffe Institute for Advanced Study at Harvard when she apparently died of natural causes.

OBITUARIES AND OTHER SOURCES:

PERIODICALS

Los Angeles Times, March 12, 2004, p. B14.

Washington Post, March 13, 2004, p. B6.

*　　*　　*

OSTLING, Joan K.

PERSONAL: Married Richard N. Ostling (an author); children: two. *Education:* University of California at Santa Cruz, B.A. (theater), 1979; University of Southern California, M.F.A., 1981; Greenwich University, Ph.D. (professional writing), 1993.

ADDRESSES: Home—Ridgewood, NJ. *Agent*—c/o Author Mail, HarperCollins, 7th Floor, 10 East 53rd St., New York, NY 10022.

CAREER: U.S. Information Agency, Washington, DC, former writer and editor; Press Publications (newspaper chain), Chicago, IL, former reporter; Nyack College, teacher of English and journalism.

WRITINGS:

(Editor, with Joe R. Christopher) *C. S. Lewis: An Annotated Checklist of Writings about Him and His Works,* Kent State University Press (Kent, OH), 1974.

(With husband, Richard N. Ostling) *Mormon America: The Power and the Promise,* HarperSanFrancisco (San Francisco, CA), 1999.

SIDELIGHTS: After honing her writing skills at the U.S. Information Agency and the Press Publications newspaper chain, Joan K. Ostling became a freelance writer and editor for various magazines and other publications. With Joe R. Christopher, she edited *C. S. Lewis: An Annotated Checklist of Writings about Him and His Works,* a sourcebook for scholars of the famed religious writer and novelist. In 1999, she teamed up with her husband, longtime *Time* magazine religion writer Richard Ostling, to explore a more controversial subject in *Mormon America: The Power and the Promise.*

With *Mormon America* the Ostlings describe the transformation of the small, detested new faith founded by Joseph Smith in the 1840s to the wealthy, eminently respectable, rapidly growing religion it is today. At the same time, they discuss polygamy, racist teachings—only in 1978 were blacks allowed full participation in the religion—and other controversial doctrines that have marginalized Mormons at various times in their history. "The Ostlings have presented, in a very ap-pealing, accessibly way, massive amounts of information. And as they promised, *Mormon America* isn't a polemic. Still, both insiders and outsiders will feel uneasy after reading it," concluded *Christian Science Monitor* reviewer Linda L. Giedl. For *Los Angeles Times Book Review* critic Kenneth Anderson "it is a scrupulous, fair-minded account, one that neither shies away from the controversies that have shaped the perception of Mormonism nor has any particular ax to grind about them."

BIOGRAPHICAL AND CRITICAL SOURCES:

PERIODICALS

Christianity Today, March 6, 2000, Richard J. Mouw, "Mormon Makeover."

Christian Science Monitor, December 23, 1999, Linda L. Giedl, review of *Mormon America: The Power and the Promise.*

Library Journal, November 1, 1999, David S. Azzolina, review of *Mormon America,* p. 90.

Los Angeles Times Book Review, November 28, 1999, Kenneth Anderson, review of *Mormon America,* p. 1.

New York Times Book Review, January 9, 2000, Timothy Egan, "Theocracy in the Desert."

Publishers Weekly, July 12, 1999, "An Appetite for Home-Grown Religion," p. 54; August 30, 1999, Michael Kress, "Richard & Joan Ostling."; October 11, 1999, Jana Riess, "Forecasts: Religion."

Times Literary Supplement, May 26, 2000, Patrick Allitt, "Chariots of Fire."*

P

PARKER, Gary E. 1953-

PERSONAL: Born June 24, 1953, in Spartanburg, SC; married Melody Worrell; children: Andrea, Ashley. *Education:* Furman University, B.A. (history), 1976; Southeastern Baptist Seminary, M.Div., 1979, Baylor University, Ph.D. (historical theology), 1984.

ADDRESSES: Home—Decatur, GA. *Agent*—c/o Author Mail, Bethany House Publishers, 11400 Hampshire Ave. South, Minneapolis, MN 55438.

CAREER: First Baptist Church, Denton, NC, associate pastor, 1976-79; Hilltop Lakes Chapel, Hilltop Lakes, TX, pastor 1979-82; Warrenton Baptist Church, Warrenton, NC, pastor, 1982-85; Grace Baptist Church, Sumter, SC, pastor, 1985-90; First Baptist Church, Jefferson City, MO, pastor, 1990-96; First Baptist Church of Decatur, Decatur, GA, 2001—. National consultant on theological education. Writer.

AWARDS, HONORS: Christy Award finalist, 2002, for *Highland Hopes.*

WRITINGS:

The Gift of Doubt: From Crisis to Authentic Faith, Harper & Row (San Francisco, CA), 1990.
Creative Tensions: Personal Growth through Stress, Broadman Press (Nashville, TN), 1991.
Principles Worth Protecting, Smyth & Helwys Publishing (Macon, GA), 1993.

Desert Water, Victor Books (Wheaton, IL), 1995.
Dark Road to Daylight, Thomas Nelson (Nashville, TN), 1996.
A Capital Offense, Thomas Nelson (Nashville, TN), 1998.
The Ephesus Fragment, Bethany House (Minneapolis, MN), 1999.
The Last Gift, Chariot Victor Publishers (Colorado Springs, CO), 1999.
The Wedding Dress, Victor (Colorado Springs, CO), 2001.

NOVELS

Beyond a Reasonable Doubt, Thomas Nelson (Nashville, TN), 1994.
Death Stalks a Holiday (sequel to *Beyond a Reasonable Doubt*), Thomas Nelson (Nashville, TN), 1996.
Highland Hopes (part of "Blue Ridge Legacy" series), Bethany House Publishers (Minneapolis, MN), 2001.
Highland Mercies (part of "Blue Ridge Legacy" series), Bethany House (Minneapolis, MN), 2002.
Highland Grace (part of "Blue Ridge Legacy" series), Bethany House Publishers (Minneapolis, MN), 2003.

SIDELIGHTS: In addition to being the senior pastor of the First Baptist Church in Decatur, Georgia, Gary E. Parker is the author of several novels, among them *Highland Hopes, Beyond a Reasonable Doubt, Dark Road to Daylight,* and *Highland Grace.* Parker also currently serves as a national consultant on theological education.

In *Highland Hopes,* the first installment in his Christian historical fiction series "Blue Ridge Legacy," Parker introduces the Porter family. The Porters have resided in Blue Springs, North Carolina, for generations. As the series opens in the early 1900s, the highland family is headed by Granny Abby, the book's narrator, who is over one hundred years old. As Abby recounts her story to her great-granddaughter, when she was born her mother died, and her father eventually remarried the comely Elsa Clack. A few years later, after losing a bet, Abby's father lost their family home and the family fragmented in the hard times that followed. Determined to pursue her own dreams of an education, Abby boldly leaves home, but winds up in a troubled married to a "city slicker." "Beautifully written passages describing the Blue Ridge Mountains will woo the reader, as will the charming dialect of the characters," commented a reviewer for *Publishers Weekly* in reviewing the first installment in Abby's life story. Donna Scanlon, reviewing *Highland Hopes* for *Rambles.net,* dubbed the book "a solid page-turner that creates anticipation for the next installment."

In *Highland Mercies* Parker picks up where *Highland Hopes* left off, and continues to tell the story of Granny Abby. As the novel opens Abby is facing the challenges of motherhood, while also weathering the challenges set before her as a result of the Great Depression. Meanwhile, her brother, Daniel Porter, has to deal with the deaths of several people close to him, while concurrently grappling with the consequences of mistakes he made in the past. As the years pass, readers find Abby and her brother Daniel with heightened worries once again, as they watch their sons head off to fight in World War II following the Pearl Harbor bombing. Picking up a continuing plotline from the first book, Parker also draws readers into the ongoing feud between the Porter family and the family of Elsa Clack sparked by the actions of Abby's father.

Drawing from his own family's history, Parker concludes the "Blue Ridge Legacy" trilogy with *Highland Grace,* in which he recounts the final decades in Granny Abby's life. After the end of World War II, Abby and her family undergo changes that threaten not only the Porters but all of Blue Springs. While the Clack and Porter families finally strike a peace, Ben Clack threatens to undo this progress. Meanwhile, Daniel Porter is struggling to reclaim the family's homestead lost years through his grandfather's gambling. "Once again, Parker combines well-rounded characters and compelling plot with a strong sense of place and mountain traditions," stated Wilda Williams in *Library Journal.* Focusing on the series as a whole, Scanlon noted that Parker's "supporting cast of characters are well drawn" and that the author's "writing brings the little town of Blue Springs to life in. . . . a sustained narrative with a strong but not overbearing inspirational message."

BIOGRAPHICAL AND CRITICAL SOURCES:

PERIODICALS

Booklist, September 15, 1994, John Mort, review of *Beyond a Reasonable Doubt,* p. 113.
Library Journal, November 1, 1994, Henry Carrigan, Jr., review of *Beyond a Reasonable Doubt,* p. 65; February 1, 1996, Henry Carrigan, Jr., review of *Death Stalks a Holiday,* p. 66; April 1, 1997, Melissa Hudak, review of *Dark Road to Daylight* and *A Capital Offense,* p. 78; April 1, 2003, Wilda Williams, review of *Highland Grace,* p. 84.
Publishers Weekly, July 2, 2001, review of *Highland Hopes,* p. 51.

ONLINE

Bethany House Web site, http://www.bethanyhouse. com/ (October 7, 2003).
Rambles.net, http://www.rambles.net/ (October 7, 2003), Donna Scanlon, review of "Blue Ridge Legacy" series.*

*   *   *

PARVIN, Manoucher 1934-

PERSONAL: Born 1934, in Tehran, Iran. *Ethnicity:* "Iranian/American." *Education:* University of Toledo, B.S.E.E., 1959; Columbia University, Ph.D., 1969. *Hobbies and other interests:* Chess, various sports, classical music, reading and composing poetry, reading science.

ADDRESSES: Home—4601 Ranchwood Rd, Akron, OH 44333. *E-mail*—mparvin@adelphia.net.

CAREER: Barnard School for Boys, New York, NY, chairman of math department, 1963-65; Columbia University, New York, NY, lecturer, 1967-69; City University of New York, Hunter College, New York, NY, assistant professor of economics, beginning 1969; Emory University, visiting professor of economics, 2000-03.

MEMBER: Society for Iranian Studies (president), Middle East Economic Association.

AWARDS, HONORS: Many academic awards and honors.

WRITINGS:

Cry for My Revolution, Iran, Mazda Publishers (Costa Mesa, CA), 1987.
(Coeditor with Hooshang Amirahmadi) *Post-Revolutionary Iran,* Westview Press (Boulder, CO), 1988.
Avicenna and I: The Journey of Spirits, Blind Owl Press (Costa Mesa, CA), 1996.
Dardedel: Rumi, Hafez and Love in New York, Permanent Press (Sag Harbor, NY), 2003.

Author of numerous scholarly works in all fields of social sciences.

WORK IN PROGRESS: A novel on brain/mind relation; a book of poems, *Cosmological Accent;* a novel, *Fear of Truth.*

SIDELIGHTS: In addition to his work as an economist and social scientist, Manoucher Parvin has written a number of works focusing on the history and literature of his country of origin, Iran. His *Cry for My Revolution, Iran* is a novelistic treatment of the tumultuous events that drove the Shah from power. Parvin focuses on three participants who first come together at Columbia University in a class taught by Professor Pirooz, an Iranian expatriate who yearns for a reform of the Shah's brutal, corrupt regime. Ali Keshavarz is the young radical who feels that Pirooz's reforms don't go nearly far enough. Eric Saunders is the young conservative who feels the professor is wrong, and even dangerous. And Sara Patrick, the object of desire for both Ali and Eric, is the journalistic observer,

interested but detached. Years later, the three wind up in Iran during the overthrow of the Shah, Ali as a revolutionary who will find the new regime as troublesome as the old, Eric as a CIA agent, and Sara as a reporter. "Parvin has written a novel that is worth the strong attention of concerned Americans," wrote *Choice* reviewer G. O. Carey. "Although the language engages in a polemic against despotism, it does so without sacrificing the artistic purpose of raising awareness about the higher implications of politics. This fervent and articulate book is essential to anyone who wishes to go beyond American newspaper and television accounts for a truer picture of the relations between the United States and Iran following World War II, for cliches do not explain that poisoned marriage," concluded *Literary Review* contributor Thomas Filbin. Val Moghadam wrote in the *Guardian,* "Manoucher Parvin has written a sensitive and passionate historical novel about Iran's revolution and revolutionaries. It will surely take its place among the best of third world political literature. *Cry for My Revolution, Iran* is a big book that treats a big subject in a highly readable and unforgettable way." Parvin has also coedited *Post-Revolutionary Iran,* a collection of academic pieces on the aftermath of the Iranian Revolution.

From the tumults of modern Iran, Parvin turned to the timeless wisdom of Ibn Sina, the medieval Persian philosopher known to Europeans as Avicenna. In *Avicenna and I: The Journey of Spirits,* Parvin tells the story of two troubled lovers who visit the ancient city of Hamadan, where Avicenna lies buried, and learn from him the secrets of mental and spiritual fulfillment. Even more whimsical is Parvin's *Dardedel: Rumi, Hafez, and Love in New York,* a novel-in-verse. It's the story of an unhappy Iranian academic named Pirooz (like the professor in *Cry for My Revolution, Iran*) who travels from New York to the Sonora Desert in Arizona in the vague hope of alleviating a despair that has crept into his soul by killing himself. There he encounters two cacti, the reincarnated forms of the famed Persian poets, wise Rumi and passionate Hafez. In a freewheeling, intimate heart-to heart (a "dardedel" in Persian) they talk Pirooz out of his depression, and he returns to New York. There he encounters Hafez again, this time as a curly-haired cabbie who gives him a ride, and Rumi, incarnated in various New Yorkers. Enchanted by his new surroundings, Hafez is unable to conform to some of its strictures and finds himself on trial for statutory rape when his 15-year-old girlfriend gets pregnant. The trial turns into a fanciful meditation on love in the face of society's laws. "Some of the meditative conversations fall flat, Parvin's dialogues are mostly entertaining, and the author wisely sticks to a lighthearted take on his two legendary reincarnations," concluded a *Publishers Weekly* reviewer. "A witty, insightful clash of cultural perspectives," concluded a *Kirkus Reviews* contributor.

BIOGRAPHICAL AND CRITICAL SOURCES:

PERIODICALS

Choice, December, 1988, G. O. Carey, review of *Cry for My Revolution, Iran,* p. 635.
Kirkus Reviews, December 1, 2002, review of *Dard-edel: Rumi, Hafez and Love in New York,* p. 1725.
Literary Review, fall, 1996, Thomas Filbin, "The Expatriate Memory: Four Iranian Writers in America," pp. 172-177.
Publishers Weekly, February 3, 2003, review of *Dard-edel,* p. 57.
West Coast Review of Books, 1988, Christine Watson, review of *Cry for My Revolution, Iran,* p. 43.

*   *   *

PATRICK, William 1948-

PERSONAL: Born December 28, 1948, in Houston, TX; son of Theodore Douglas (a bomber pilot for U.S. Air Force) and Bernice (Cooper) Patrick; married Kathleen Donohue (an actress), December 30, 1969; children: Ian Thomas. *Education:* University of Texas, B.A., 1969; attended Columbia University, 1970; University of Iowa, M.A., 1972.

ADDRESSES: Office—Henry Holt, 115 W. 18th. St., New York, NY 10011.

CAREER: Little, Brown & Co., Boston, MA, medical editor, 1973-78; Harvard University Press, Cambridge, MA, science and medicine editor, 1978-86; Addison-Wesley, Reading, MA, editor, 1986-94, vice president and editorial director, 1994-97; Henry Holt, New York, NY, senior executive editor, 1997—.

MEMBER: P.E.N.

WRITINGS:

Sprials, Houghton Mifflin (Boston, MA), 1983.
Blood Winter, Houghton Mifflin (Boston, MA), 1990.

Spirals has been translated into Spanish and Dutch.

SIDELIGHTS: William Patrick has led a distinguished career in the field of publishing. He is also the author of two thrillers, *Spirals* and *Blood Winter.*

Spirals is a medical thriller that takes place in the laboratories of Harvard University and the jungles of South America. Patrick McKusick is a scientist in the bioengineering department of Harvard; he has a three-year-old daughter, Kathleen, who is a product of science experimentation. After Kathleen falls ill, the two fly to South America where McKusick believes his daughter can be cured. William A. Nolen from *Book World* called the plot of *Sprials* "sheer silliness." Not all critics agreed with Nolen, however. A reviewer for *Publishers Weekly* wrote that "Patrick is sharp and good at his characterizations . . . and he keeps us guessing right up to the final page."

Patrick talked to Barbara A. Bannon of *Publishers Weekly* about his first novel, noting that "I began to imagine a story in which harm might come to a child, a kind of modern-day Abraham and Isaac story in which a man has to ask himself, 'Will you follow the great God science or . . . ?' Within three weeks I had outlined a plot involving recombinant DNA and spliced genes, and all the things that were actually going on around me in Cambridge."

Patrick's second book, *Blood Winter,* is another medical thriller; this time the action is set against the backdrop of World War I. British agents are on a mission to determine whether Germany is developing chemical weapons, specifically a deadly strain of an infectious disease. Christopher Walker from the *Observer* wrote, "The novel skilfully develops its sense of intrigue and duplicity." A reviewer from *Publishers Weekly* called *Blood Winter* a "well-done thriller" that "closes with an unexpected and properly dark surprise."

BIOGRAPHICAL AND CRITICAL SOURCES:

PERIODICALS

Book World, October 23, 1983, William A. Nolen, review of *Spirals,* p. 8.

Observer (London, England), June 9, 1991, Christopher Walker, review of *Blood Winter,* p. 59.

Publishers Weekly, August 19, 1983, Barbara A. Bannon, "A Trio of Medical Thrillers Will Chill the Fall Season," pp. 40-41; October 12, 1984, review of *Spirals,* p. 50; March 16, 1990, review of *Blood Winter,* p. 61.*

* * *

PEACHMENT, Christopher

PERSONAL: Male.

ADDRESSES: Home—Hoxton, London, England. *Agent*—St. Martin's Press, 175 Fifth Ave., New York, NY 10010.

CAREER: Novelist and journalist. Royal Court Theatre, London, England, former stage manager; *Time Out* (magazine), former film editor; *Times,* London, former deputy literary editor and arts editor.

WRITINGS:

Caravaggio, Picador (London, England), 2002, St. Martin's Press (New York, NY), 2003.
The Green and the Gold, Picador (London, England), 2003.

SIDELIGHTS: Christopher Peachment has written two novels featuring historical figures from the arts. In *Caravaggio* Peachment tells a fictionalized version of the life of Michelangelo Merisi da Caravaggio, an Italian artist who lived in the sixteenth century. *The Green and the Gold* is an account of seventeenth-century British poet Andrew Marvell's life. Both novels are written in the first person and rely less on historical fact than on Peachment's creative invention.

Caravaggio takes the larger-than-life story of the real artist and renders it with enthusiasm. According to Keith Miller in the *Times Literary Supplement,* Peachment "takes some bold leaps in the small matter of plot." In Peachment's story, the promiscuous and bisexual Caravaggio frequents prostitutes and taverns, drinking and brawling and even murdering a man.

While much of this story is consistent with the known facts of Caravaggio's tumultuous life, Peachment also creates entirely fictional incidents based on possibility rather than fact. The novelist asserts that in the 1580s Caravaggio had a love affair with Giordano Bruno, a fellow artist history does not record he ever met. Bruno's eventual execution by the Catholic Church for heresy, Peachment's novel alleges, led Caravaggio to a strong anti-clerical stance which spurred a conspiracy against him by church leaders. A critic for *Kirkus Reviews* dubbed Peachment's version of events a "crude and bumptious story of a true life treated with great liberty." Josh Cohen was even more enthusiastic in his review for *Library Journal,* writing that in *Caravaggio* Peachment "creates a lively character," while Miller concluded that "Peachment's story certainly inclines towards the swashbuckling."

The Green and the Gold is Peachment's fictionalized account of the life of Andrew Marvell, a British poet of the seventeenth century. As in *Caravaggio,* Peachment plays loose with the facts. While history records little about Marvell's personal life, it is known that he held a number of political positions during his career. Peachment's story of Marvell's life casts him as a government spy involved in secret behind-the-scenes machinations. "This may be because," Michael Caines noted in the *Times Literary Supplement,* "Peachment is more interested in espionage and the secret history of seventeenth-history England than poetry." In addition, Peachment employs a vocabulary often inappropriate for the time. Not only does Marvell use words not yet invented, he quotes authors born after his death. "The story," Richard Cavendish explained in *History Today,* "is told with sardonic humour from an openly present-day slant in prose laced with deliberate anachronisms. . . . Remarkably, it works." Similarly, John Mullan in the London *Guardian* concluded that "it is all absurd, yet oddly enjoyable. The novel is written with a careless, carefree gusto. It is really a kind of mock-historical novel—the Restoration seen through disrespectful eyes."

BIOGRAPHICAL AND CRITICAL SOURCES:

PERIODICALS

Guardian (London, England), April 26, 2003, John Mullan, review of *The Green and the Gold.*
History Today, May, 2003, Richard Cavendish, review of *The Green and the Gold,* p. 88.

Kirkus Reviews, March 1, 2003, review of *Caravaggio,* p. 340.

Library Journal, April 1, 2003, Josh Cohen, review of *Caravaggio,* p. 130.

Times Literary Supplement, February 22, 2002, Keith Miller, review of *Caravaggio,* p. 21; January 31, 2003, Michael Caines, review of *The Green and the Gold,* p. 22.*

*   *   *

PEDERSEN, Vernon L. 1955-

PERSONAL: Born December 2, 1955, in Shelby, MT; son of David (an auto mechanic) and Luella (McClouth) Pedersen; married Kay Kreider, May 28, 1976 (divorced, January, 1981); married Kate Hopkins (a registered nurse), October 28, 1983; children: Gwendelyn Louise, Jacob Morgan. *Education:* Indiana State University, B.S., 1985, M.A., 1987; Georgetown University, Ph.D., 1993. *Politics:* Republican. *Hobbies and other interests:* History of the American West, spy novels, movies, collecting art.

ADDRESSES: Home—942 Turner Ave., Shelby, MT 59474. *Office*—Great Falls College of Technology, Montana State University, 2100 16th Ave. S., Great Falls, MT 59406. *E-mail*—vkped@3rivers.net.

CAREER: Shepherd College, Shepherdstown, WV, adjunct professor of history, 1991-94; American University in Bulgaria, Blagoevgrad, Bulgaria, associate professor of history, 1994-2001, associate vice president for academic affairs and dean of faculty, 2001-03; Montana State University, Great Falls, associate dean of academic affairs and student services, 2003—.

WRITINGS:

The Communist Party of Maryland, 1919-1957, University of Illinois Press (Urbana, IL), 2001.

Underfunded, Understaffed, and Underground: The History of the San Francisco Bureau of the Pan-Pacific Trade Union Secretariat, Continuity, 2003.

Contributor to *Labor History, Journal of American Studies, Turkey,* and *American Studies Today.*

SIDELIGHTS: Vernon L. Pedersen is a scholar of American communism whose book *The Communist Party of Maryland, 1919-1957* draws on a wide range of sources, including Soviet archive documents, F.B.I. files, and interviews with former members, to present the history of the Maryland state organization of the Communist Party from its inception to its collapse. According to Myron I. Scholnick in the *Journal of Southern History,* "Pedersen's book is particularly important because the Maryland Communist Party was a microcosm of the national one." While admitting the party's role in the creation of unions and the push for civil rights, Pedersen also reveals "the duplicity of the Communists, who constantly followed their party agenda, used undemocratic methods, and considered the unions primarily 'political tools,'" Scholnick explained. Pedersen's book, Scholnick concluded, is a "wholly admirable study."

Pedersen told *CA:* "I write history from a desire to experience the lives of people in the past and to bring those lives vividly back to life so that my readers can appreciate the intensity and passions that filled the existence of so many almost forgotten individuals. I chose my primary subject, American Communism, because of initial ideological sympathy and because of the challenges involved in writing the history of a semi-concealed group. I still take great satisfaction in my research but nine years of living in a post-communist country (Bulgaria) and extensive access to the Communist party records in Moscow have convinced me of the bankruptcy of both communism and Marxism and placed me in the ranks of such anticommunists as John Haynes and Harvey Klehr."

BIOGRAPHICAL AND CRITICAL SOURCES:

PERIODICALS

Choice, July-August, 2001, R. J. Goldstein, review of *The Communist Party of Maryland, 1919-1957,* p. 2024.

Journal of American History, June, 2002, Edward P. Johanningsneier, review of *The Communist Party of Maryland, 1919-1957,* p. 268.

Journal of Southern History, August, 2002, Myron I. Scholnick, review of *The Communist Party of Maryland, 1919-1957,* p. 735.*

PEELER, Tim 1957-

PERSONAL: Born March 26, 1957, in Reidsville, NC; son of J. L. (a Lutheran minister) and Ethel (a teacher of mathematics; maiden name, Sloop) Peeler; married January 3, 1981; wife's name Penny (a program coordinator); children: Aaron Michael, Thomas Dylan. *Education:* East Carolina University, B.A., 1980; Appalachian State University, M.A., 1992. *Hobbies and other interests:* Competitive running.

ADDRESSES: Home—1665 Crafton Rd., Hickory, NC 28602. *Office*—Catawba Valley Community College, Highway 70 S.E., Hickory, NC 28602. *E-mail*—tpeeler@cvcc.edu.

CAREER: Catawba Valley Community College, Hickory, NC, instructor in English, 1992—.

MEMBER: National Association of Developmental Educators, North Carolina Association of Developmental Educators.

WRITINGS:

Touching All the Bases: Poems from Baseball, McFarland and Co. (Jefferson, NC), 2000.
Waiting for Godot's First Pitch (poetry), McFarland and Co. (Jefferson, NC), 2001.
Writers on the Storm (short stories and essays), 1st-Books Library (Bloomington, IN), 2001.

SIDELIGHTS: Tim Peeler told *CA:* "I write mostly for the same reason that I run—the horrible wonderful way it makes me feel while I'm doing it.

"Stylistically, my biggest influences are the late Connecticut poet Leo Conellan and the Florida poet Harry Brody. More recently I have been influenced by South Carolina poet Ron Rash. A wide variety of music also has an effect on my work, especially blues. I write most nights, staying up however long it takes to finish a first draft.

"Since much of my published work touches on the subject of baseball, I must acknowledge influence in that area from writers like Mike Shannon and W. P.

Kinsella, but also the wonderful radio announcers like Milo Hamilton and Ernie Johnson, who brought bright imagery to me on hot summer childhood nights."

BIOGRAPHICAL AND CRITICAL SOURCES:

PERIODICALS

Nine, fall, 2000, Matt Brennan, review of *Touching All the Bases: Poems from Baseball,* p. 123.

*   *   *

PETERS, Shawn Francis 1966-

PERSONAL: Born November 2, 1966, in Baltimore, MD; son of Eugene G. (an engineer) and Frances (a homemaker; maiden name, Mentrek) Peters; married Susan M. Crawford (an attorney), May 27, 2000; children: Margaret Karen. *Education:* Rutgers University, B.A. (with highest honors), 1988; University of New Hampshire, M.A. (English), 1991; University of Iowa, M.A. (American studies), 1995.

ADDRESSES: Home—1306 Eberhardt Ct., Madison, WI 53715. *E-mail*—shawn_peters@msn.com.

CAREER: W. H. Freeman (publisher), assistant project editor for Scientific American Books, 1988-89; *New Hampshire Premier,* political reporter, 1989-92; freelance journalist and editor, Des Moines, IA, 1995-96; Des Moines Art Center, Des Moines, IA, manager of grants and exhibition funds, 1996-97; University of Wisconsin—Madison, Madison, WI, student services coordinator for School of Journalism and Mass Communication, 1997-2001; freelance journalist, 2001—. University of New Hampshire, instructor, 1991-92; writing instructor for summer programs at Amherst College and University of Massachusetts—Amherst, 1991-95.

AWARDS, HONORS: Scribes Book Award, American Society of Writers on Legal Subjects, and Outstanding Achievement Award, Wisconsin Library Association, both 2001, and Pulitzer Prize nomination, history category, all for *Judging Jehovah's Witnesses: Religious Persecution and the Dawn of the Rights Revolution.*

WRITINGS:

Judging Jehovah's Witnesses: Religious Persecution and the Dawn of the Rights Revolution, University Press of Kansas (Lawrence, KS), 2000.
Defending the Faith: The Yoder Case and the First Amendment, University Press of Kansas (Lawrence, KS), 2003.

Contributor to periodicals, including *Vietnam Generation* and *Milwaukee Journal Sentinel.*

SIDELIGHTS: Shawn Francis Peters told *CA:* "I was drawn to writing about law after reading Anthony Lewis's *Gideon's Trumpet* and Richard Kluger's *Simple Justice* in the early 1990s. Those two classic works struck a chord with me because they examined relatively complex legal issues in an unusual way. Instead of providing dry analyses of judicial opinions, they focused on the struggles of unheralded people who battled for their rights in the courts. As a graduate student in nonfiction writing at the University of New Hampshire, I decided that I wanted to produce similarly engaging and accessible narratives—works that explored the genesis and development of significant legal cases primarily by telling the stories of the litigants.

"My first book, *Judging Jehovah's Witnesses: Religious Persecution and the Dawn of the Rights Revolution,* provided the first comprehensive account of the persecution of Jehovah's Witnesses in the United States during the World War II era and the victims' landmark campaign in the courts to secure judicial protections for their civil liberties. In *Judging,* I tried to weave together accounts of the Witnesses' suffering with analysis of the hundreds of cases they brought before state and federal courts in the early and mid-1940s. My second book also deals with religion and law, although its scope is somewhat narrower than that of my first work. *Defending the Faith: The Yoder Case and the First Amendment* focuses on a single landmark religious liberty case involving the Old Order Amish in Wisconsin. It too combines narrative with more traditional scholarly analysis.

"In both of my books, I've attempted to satisfy the interests of both scholars and general readers. Because of my background in journalism, my writing style is relatively straightforward; I've tried at all costs to avoid the jargon and tangled sentence structure that mars so much academic writing. At the same time, I haven't shied away from assessing complex jurisprudential issues. My books also reflect my interest in examining the lives of people who exist on the fringes of American culture. Folks like the Jehovah's Witnesses and the Amish have largely rejected mainstream life, yet their interactions with our legal system have produced landmark judicial opinions that benefit everyone. If there's a theme to my work, it lies in exploring that paradox.

"I always encourage aspiring writers to become obsessive readers. One of the best ways to learn how to write is by constantly reading the work of people who seem to have mastered the craft. I also counsel patience. It takes a long time—as well as a good deal of luck—to build even a modestly successful career as a writer."

BIOGRAPHICAL AND CRITICAL SOURCES:

PERIODICALS

American Historical Review, April, 2001, Merlin Owen Newton, review of *Judging Jehovah's Witnesses: Religious Persecution and the Dawn of the Rights Revolution,* p. 594.
Journal of American History, September, 2001, Charles R. Epp, review of *Judging Jehovah's Witnesses,* p. 702.
Journal of Church and State, winter, 2002, Chuck E. Smith, review of *Judging Jehovah's Witnesses,* p. 166.
Library Journal, April 1, 2000, Sandra Collins, review of *Judging Jehovah's Witnesses,* p. 107.

*   *   *

PICANO, Felice 1944-

PERSONAL: Born February 22, 1944, in New York, NY; son of Philip (a grocer) and Ann (Del Santo) Picano. *Education:* Queens College of the City University of New York, B.A., 1964.

ADDRESSES: Agent—Malaga Baldi, Malaga Baldi Agency, 204 West 84th St., Suite 3C, New York, NY 10024.

CAREER: New York City Department of Welfare, New York City, social worker, 1964-66; *Art Direction,* New York City, assistant editor, 1966-68; Doubleday Bookstore, New York City, assistant manager, 1969-70; free-lance writer, 1970-72; Rizzoli's Bookstore, New York City, assistant manager and buyer, 1972-74; writer, 1974—. Founder and publisher of the Sea Horse Press Ltd., 1977-94; co-founder and co-publisher of the Gay Presses of New York, 1980-94. Instructor of fiction writing classes, YMCA West Side Y Writers Voice Workshop, 1982-83.

MEMBER: Authors Guild, Writers Guild of America, PEN.

AWARDS, HONORS: PEN/Ernest Hemingway Award nomination, 1976, for *Smart as the Devil;* New York State Arts Council Grant, 1981; American Library Association Award, 1982, for *A True Likeness;* Jane Chambers Playwriting Award, 1985, for *One O'Clock Jump;* Chapbook award, Poetry Society of America, 1986; Short Story award, PEN, 1986; *Story* Magazine Award, 1994, for "Love and the She-Lion"; Lambda Literary Award nominations, 1995, for *Dryland's End,* 1996, for *Like People in History,* 1998, for *A House on the Ocean, a House on the Bay,* and 2000, for *The Book of Lies;* Ferro-Grumley Award, Le Figaro Litteraire Citation, top five foreign language books of the year, and *Gay Times of England* Award, all 1996, all for *Like People in History.*

WRITINGS:

Smart as the Devil (novel), Arbor House (New York, NY), 1975.
Eyes (novel), Arbor House (New York, NY), 1976.
The Mesmerist (novel), Delacorte (New York, NY), 1977.
The Deformity Lover and Other Poems, Sea Horse Press (New York, NY), 1978.
The Lure (novel), Delacorte (New York, NY), 1979, Alyson Books (Los Angeles, CA), 2002.
(Editor) *A True Likeness: An Anthology of Lesbian and Gay Writing Today,* Sea Horse Press (New York, NY), 1980.
An Asian Minor: The True Story of Ganymede (novella; also see below), Sea Horse Press (New York, NY), 1981.
Late in the Season (novel), Delacorte (New York, NY), 1981.

Slashed to Ribbons in Defense of Love and Other Stories (also see below), Gay Presses of New York (New York, NY), 1983.
House of Cards (novel), Delacorte (New York, NY), 1984.
Ambidextrous: The Secret Lives of Children (memoir), Gay Presses of New York (New York, NY), 1985, Harrington Park Press (New York, NY), 2003.
Window Elegies (poetry), Close Grip Press, 1986.
Immortal (play with music; based on Picano's novella *An Asian Minor: The True Story of Ganymede*), produced Off-Off Broadway, 1986.
One o'Clock (one-act play), produced Off-Off Broadway, 1986.
Men Who Loved Me: A Memoir in the Form of a Novel, New American Library (New York, NY), 1989, Harrington Park Press (New York, NY), 2003.
To the Seventh Power, William Morrow (New York, NY), 1990.
(With Charles Silverstein) *The New Joy of Gay Sex,* HarperPerennial (New York, NY), 1993.
Like People in History (novel), Viking (New York, NY), 1995.
Dryland's End, Masquerade Books, 1995, Harrington Park Press (New York, NY), 2004.
A House on the Ocean, a House on the Bay: A Memoir, Faber and Faber (Boston, MA), 1997.
Looking Glass Lives: A Novel, illustrated by F. Ronald Fowler, Alyson Books (Los Angeles, CA), 1998.
The Book of Lies (novel), Little Brown/Abacus (London, England), 2000.
The New York Years: Stories (contains *An Asian Minor* and *Slashed to Ribbons in Defense of Love*), Alyson Books (Los Angeles, CA), 2000.
Onyx (novel), Alyson Books (Los Angeles, CA), 2001.
The Bombay Trunk (play), produced in San Francisco, 2002.
Fred in Love (memoir), University of Wisconsin Press (Madison, WI), 2005.

Also author of the screenplay *Eyes,* based on the novel of the same title, 1986. Contributor of articles, poems, stories, and reviews to periodicals, including *Los Angeles Times, San Francisco Examiner, Advocate, Mandate, Washington Blade, Bay Windows, Genre, Harrington Gay Men's Fiction Quarterly, Lambda Book Report, Harvard Gay & Lesbian Review, Lexicon, Kindred Spirit, Global City Review, Story, Sodomite Invasion Review, OUT, Mouth of the Dragon, Islander, Cumberland Review, Connecticut Poetry Review, Cream City Review,* and *Soho Weekly News,* and to online periodicals, including *Vote.com—The Fifth Estate, Barnes & Noble.com,* and *Blithe House Quarterly. com.* Book editor, *New York Native,* 1980-83.

Contributor to anthologies, including *New Terrors, Number Two,* Pan Books, 1978; *Orgasms of Light,* Gay Sunshine, 1979; *Aphrodisiac: Fiction from Christopher Street,* Coward, 1980; *Getting from Here to There: Writing and Reading Poetry,* edited by F. Grossman, Boynton/Cook (Upper Montclair, NJ), 1982; *The Penguin Book of Homosexual Verse,* edited by Stephen Coote, Penguin, 1983; *The Male Muse, Number Two,* Crossing Press, 1983; *Not Love Alone,* edited by Martin Humphries, Gay Mens Press, 1985; *Men on Men,* volumes 1, 3, and 4, edited by George Stambolian, New American Library, 1986, 1990, 1992, and volume 7, Dutton, 1998; *Poets for Life,* edited by Michael Klein, Crown, 1989; *Scare Care,* edited by Graham Masterson, Putnam, 1989; *The Violet Quill Reader,* edited by David Bergman, St. Martin's Press (New York, NY), 1994; *The Badboy Book of Erotic Poetry,* edited by David Laurents, Masquerade Publishing, 1995; *The Best of The Harvard Gay & Lesbian Review,* edited by Richard Schneider, Jr., Temple University Press, 1997; *Gay Widowers,* edited by Michael Shernoff, Hayworth Press, 1997; *Gay Travels: A Literary Companion,* edited by Lucy Jane Bledsoe, Whereabouts Press, 1998; *The Mammoth Book of Gay Erotica,* edited by Lawrence Schimel, Carrol & Graf, 1998; *Gay Male Erotica, 1999,* edited by Richard Labonte, Cleis Press, 1999; *A Day for a Lay: A Century of Gay Poetry,* edited by Gavin Dillard, Barricade Books, 1999; *New York Sex,* edited by Jane de Lynn, Painted Leaf Press, 1999; *Hey Paesan!,* edited by Giovanna Capone, Denise Nico Leto, and Tommi Avicolli-Mecca, Three Guineas Press, 2000; *M2M: New Literary Fiction,* edited by Karl Woelz, AttaGirl Press, 2003; and *That Love that Dare Not Speak Its Name,* edited by Greg Wharton, Boheme Press.

ADAPTATIONS: An Asian Minor was adapted by Picano with Jerry Campbell for the stage as *Immortal!,* first produced in 1986.

SIDELIGHTS: Felice Picano is "a premier voice in gay letters," to quote Malcolm Boyd in the *Advocate.* A novelist, poet, memoirist, and pioneer in gay publishing, Picano was a founding member of New York City's Violet Quill Club, a group of intellectuals and artists who sought to promote gay writing.

Picano's own work has been praised for using "the history of gay culture as the subject for popular novels," according to *New York Times Book Review* correspondent Suzanne Berne. Robrt L. Pela in the *Advocate* maintained that, considering all of Picano's works—fiction, nonfiction, and poetry—"Picano's destiny . . . has been to lead the way for a generation of gay writers."

Timing was crucial to Picano's career. He began publishing mainstream novels in the mid-1970s and was earning a wide readership with them when he decided to write gay fiction instead. That decision led him to pen literate works with "well-constructed characters and settings," to quote *Library Journal* contributor Theodore R. Salvadori, while it also brought him friendships with other intellectual gay authors such as Edmund White and Andrew Holleran. Reflecting on his diverse career in an interview released by a recent publisher of his work, Picano said: "I've been accused of committing literary suicide several times over the years, because I keep on doing what I'm not supposed to do in my writing. I was enjoying a very successful mainstream career when I became one of the first openly gay writers. By the mid-eighties, I was writing gay literary novels and, after I had gathered a little bit of a reputation in gay literature, people told me I was making a mistake when I co-authored *The New Joy of Gay Sex.* I always seem to be doing something wrong. But I'm following a trajectory that I more or less understand."

The New Joy of Gay Sex was an updated version of the work that psychologist Charles Silverstein had originally created with Edmund White. The original version had not covered safety issues, as when it was first released, many of the safety issues related to sex had not yet been realized. The work that Silverstein and Picano put into the updated version made sure that safe-sex practices were included, as well as information reflecting the AIDS crisis and gay rights activism, making it a resource far more useful to a modern audience.

Picano has authored several memoirs, beginning with *Ambidextrous: The Secret Lives of Children* and continuing on in *Men Who Loved Me: A Memoir in the Form of a Novel.* The first volume tells the story of his childhood and the second continues on with his early adulthood, as he develops a better understanding of his identity, traveling through the United States and

Europe over the course of his story. The volumes, originally published in the mid and late eighties, were republished in 2003. In 1997, Picano released *A House on the Ocean, A House on the Bay,* in which he recalls the years of the 1960s and 1970s when he lived in Manhattan and partook of the pleasures of Fire Island, New York. "Picano is definitely gifted enough to ensure this book's popularity with lesbian and gay readers everywhere," declared Charles Harmon in *Booklist.* In the *Library Journal,* Richard Violette called Picano "a leading light in the gay literary world," adding that in *A House on the Ocean, a House on the Bay,* "his glints of flashing wit and subtle hints of dark decadence transcend cliches." In *Advocate,* Malcom Boyd wrote that the memoir "is exquisitely etched in finely honed detail."

Picano's novels have brought him at least as much critical success as his memoirs. In *Like People in History,* Picano wrote what he called a gay American epic. Set in 1991 with flashbacks to six periods of shared history going back to the fifties, *Like People In History* tells the story of cousins Roger Sansarc and Alistair Dodge. For Alistair's forty-fifth birthday, Roger brings him the present he had requested—pills that will end Alistair's life and stop his suffering from AIDS. Roger is a fairly untrustworthy narrator, telling his rememberances of events with definite evaluation of the situation; he does not tell it how it was, he tells it with commentary. According to Michael Bronski, writing in *Lambda Book Report,* "Roger is preening, self-involved, self-promoting, and self-indulgent. . . . The amazing thing about Picano's decision to portray Roger in this light—a daring decision that could easily have been the downfall of the book—is that it actually makes the novel work better. With Roger as the narrator, all the events, the trends, the cultural fads . . . take on a new beauty." Bronski continued that Roger's commentary "creates a context for actually evaluating the gay male culture that Picano describes in such detail. . . . Picano has provided a built-in bullshit detector." Even with the serious subject matter, reviewers referred to the title as less an epic than a beach book, but even those reviewers, including Charles Harmon of *Booklist,* felt that *Like People In History* "succeeds as a story that doesn't take itself too seriously." Though reviewers did not initially expect *Like People in History* to be a critical success, the epic won sevgeral awards in 1996, including a Lambda Literary Award nomination, the Ferro-Grumley Award, Le Figaro Litteraire Citation for the top five foreign language books of the year, and the *Gay Times of England* Award, earning it not only popular but also critical praise.

Published in 1998, *Looking Glass Lives* is a gothic romance dealing with reincarnation. The story takes place in two different times, during the Civil War Era as well as modern day. Narrator Roger Lynch and his wife, Karen, purchase a house that had belonged to spinster Amity Pritchard during the Civil War. As Roger and Karen work to restore the house, Roger's cousin and childhood lover Chas invites himself to come and stay with them. When Roger finds the diaries of Amity, he "discovers that the lives of Amity, her sister Constance, and Capt. Eugene Calder bear a strange parallel to Karen's, Chas's, and his own," according to Phillip Oliver in *Library Journal.* The story of the first love triangle is tragic and ends in murder; while Roger studies it, he sees that the events may be destined to happen again. Jaime Manrique wrote that Picano "succeeds in creating a smart, sexy page-turner full of thrills."

New York Times Book Review contributor David Lipsky called Picano "a word machine" who "approaches the page with a newcomer's joy." In his review of Picano's *The Book of Lies*—a *roman a clef* loosely about the Violet Quill Club (in the book, Picano renames the group the Purple Circle)—Lipsky noted that the characters are "outsize and the novel is written in a dishy, larger-than-life style. . . . The results are surprisingly entertaining." A *Publishers Weekly* correspondent, assessing the same work, concluded: "Picano is successful in his gossipy recreation of the group of gay literary innovators. In depicting the near future, his amusing assumptions demonstrate a keen tab on trends and the possible new technologies ahead. The surprises at the end keep the reader's head spinning." *The Book of Lies* is told by Ross Ohrenstedt; Picano commented about his narrator, "I've jokingly, but perhaps accurately, said that Ross Ohrenstedt in this book is the single most unreliable narrator in fiction since the governess in *The Turn of the Screw.*" With such an unreliable teller of the tale, the reality inside the novel is dubious. Ross is, depending on which time he tells it, a grad student, an assistant professor, and competing for tenure at UCLA. His research causes him to delve into the works and lives of the Purple Circle. When Ross discovers a mysterious manuscript, he latches onto it, determined that solving the mystery will be the key to his academic success. His investigation takes him across the country, meeting all the surviving members of the Purple Circle, who seem surprisingly tight lipped about the evidence he brings with him. He suspects consipracy, and this only urges him on to solve the mystery. Karl Woelz wrote in *Lambda Book Report,* "*Book of Lies* has something guaranteed to please just about everyone."

Talking about why he wrote *Book of Lies* to Greg Herren of *Lambda Book Report,* Picano explained, "I know I did want to write what no one else had done, i.e. a 'post modern' gay novel—composed of the apparatus of contemporary literature. . . . And the Violet Quill—which has been glorified and attacked in equal measure—was just waiting for its fictional deconstruction. It was too obvious a target for me to ignore."

With *Onyx,* which was released in 2001, Picano returned to a more traditional narrative, but took a chance in another direction; *Onyx* is an AIDS novel, published in an age when the common thought is that AIDS novels "don't sell anymore," wrote Greg Herren in a review for *Lambda Book Report.* But this did not seem to bother Picano; as Herren noted, "Taking chances is something that Felice Picano, in his long and varied career, has never shied away from." Ray Henriques and Jesse Moody, a long term New York couple and the main characters of *Onyx,* are facing the end of Jesse's life as he loses the battle against AIDS. Ray is HIV-negative, and Jesse encourages Ray to continue living his life. Ray finds himself in the middle of a new sexual awakening; while he is there to support Jesse, he begins a relationship with Mike, a married man confused about his own sexual desires. Jesse and Ray face the reality of love and loss, of life continuing even after the death of a loved one. Roger Durbin, writing a review for *Library Journal,* praised, "Picano is honest and excruciatingly descriptive." Drew Limsky, in a review for *Advocate,* called the book "an especially sensual work as well as a perceptive one." And Herren concluded, "The ultimate strength in *Onyx* lies in Ray's character, an ordinary gay man called upon to deal with incredible amounts of tragedy; a modern day Job."

Several of Picano's works have been translated into French, Japanese, Spanish, Dutch, Danish, German, Hebrew, Polish, and Portuguese. He described his writing in *CA:* "In my poetry I am keeping a sort of notebook of fragmentary experiences and understandings. In the past, this meant a polarization of subject matter: poems dealing either with perceptions gathered from the world of nature as revealed in Big Sur or Fire Island; or poems dealing with contemporary aspects of urban life and characters— portraits of epileptics, deformity lovers, obscene phone callers, etc. Of late, however, my poetry has become more autobiographical—though not at all confessional—integrating interior and exterior worlds. And forms have changed from lyric and monologic to more experimental structures such as self-interviews, imaginary dialogues, and letters to unknown persons.

"In fiction I write about the possible rather than the actual, and so, I suppose, 'Romances' in Hawthorne's sense of the word, even with 'realistic' settings, characters, and actions. My novels, novellas, and short stories deal with ordinary individuals who are suddenly thrust into extraordinary situations and relationships which test their very existence. Unusual perceptions and abilities, extrasensory powers, and psychological aberrations become tools and weapons in conflicts of mental and emotional control. Previous behavioral patterns are inadequate for such situations and must be changed to enable evolved awareness and survival, or they destroy their possessor. Thus, perspective is of the utmost importance in my fiction, both for structure and meaning. I am dedicated to experimenting with new and old points of view, which seem to have progressed very little since the pioneering work of Henry James and James Joyce."

Picano added that he also works in film and theater, starting with adaptations of previously written works: "These intensely collaborative efforts—apparently so very different than other solitary writing—have proven to be fascinating not only because I've learned the strengths and weaknesses in collaboration, but also because through experienced theater and film director's views of what the public requires, I've learned how completely idiosyncratic I and my perspective has been, is, and will probably continue to be. Few writing experiences can equal the intensity of theater rehearsals leading to opening night, and nothing can equal the simultaneous frustration and elation of having others speak the works you've written."

AUTOBIOGRAPHICAL ESSAY:

Felice Picano contributed the following autobiographical essay to *CA:*

My mother used to tell us stories. Growing up in eastern Queens during the fifties in the midst of a middle-class, television-age, melting-pot neighborhood, my mother used to tell us stories of growing up a generation before in New England.

Felice Picano, "the author as Angel," seven years old

Her storytelling was immediate and fully recalled—"That reminds me of the time I was working on Westminster Street when the hurricane hit," she'd begin, just like that. It was limpidly related, unbound by extraneous facts or irrelevant information, rising to a climax—"We had to stay in the building all night, without electricity, watching the Providence River rise above the tops of cars. We laughed and lit candles and sang. But were we scared!" Sometimes she ended with a moral, not always, but you always knew the end—"You can still see the high-water mark from the '38 hurricane on some downtown buildings!"

I knew some characters in her stories: my mother's mother was alive until 1955 and Grandpa outlived her by twenty years. My uncles Billy and George and Rudy visited with their wives and children, as did my mother's nephew Henry, oddly enough her age, who'd been her escort in adolescence. But they had minor roles: my mother's stories were about her boyfriend Bill, whom she always called "Sourpuss," and Clem-

my, short from Clementine. My mother had a nickname too—"Anna Banana"—because of the long, drooping curls she'd worn as a girl. And since her stories ranged willy-nilly, day to day, from her earliest years to just before she and my father married, we were sometimes confronted by confusions, mysteries.

How did our parents know each other? Visiting our grandparents in Thornton, Rhode Island, we could see from the second-floor bedrooms our other grandma's—Soscia's—chicken coops, vegetable garden, and, hidden in peach trees, her house. My mother sent us to our grandma Soscia's house, though she never went herself. We'd walk down State Street to Fletcher Avenue around the hill. Coming back we'd cut through the connecting gardens and climb the tall, grassy hill, under which lay an old Indian graveyard, where we'd hunt shards and shreds of anything in the least bit old.

We knew our grandparents—adjoining neighbors—weren't friendly. Knew that our parents' marriage was one (but not the only or the earliest) reason why not. That was one mystery.

We knew why Grandma's name was Soscia and not Picano: she'd remarried after her husband died of the Spanish flu in 1918, remarried and had three more children, Betty, Mike, and Little Tony—to distinguish him from Anthony Picano, known as Big Tony. But there was more mystery. My father's stories weren't about growing up in Rhode Island, but in New York: Ozone Park, though his siblings had grown up in Thornton and he'd once been my mother's classmate in an early grade. Why? My father's face would darken when he spoke of his stepfather, a man he hated with an intensity undiminished to this day. So my father's evil stepfather became another character in my mother's stories, with clever, gloomy, fortunate Sourpuss, and humorous, daring, social Clemmy.

When the Second World War was over and gasoline no longer rationed, we'd drive up to Thornton in a new, wooden-backed station wagon, along new highways spun like black ribbons through Connecticut's green hills, and we'd see and confirm places from my mother's stories—the trolley along Plainfield Street to funny-sounding Onleyville, Farmer Smith's fields stretching for miles, the orchards on the cliff above Atwood Avenue; in Providence itself, we'd play in Roger Williams Park, walk along Broadway, where a great-aunt lived in a huge Victorian house, or ascend Benefit Street on College Hill, where another aunt lived near Brown University, not far from where Poe and H. P. Lovecraft had resided. We'd drive to Barrington, where cousins lived on the waterside, or down to Bristol and Newport, or directly south to Rocky Point Amusement Park and Scarborough Beach, or further to Point Judith and Galilee. We'd even spend a July in a cottage in Petasquammscut, until it seemed we'd reclaimed all our mother's past and then some.

The more we reclaimed, the more the mysteries grew. Who was the boy in that old photo and why would no one speak of him? Who was that Air Force captain in that other photo? Why had we never heard of him? How come, if our mother was engaged to Sourpuss for so many years, she'd ended up marrying our father? Why was it some relatives hadn't spoken to each other in decades? Why was it our father had as a boy gone to live with Aunt Carrie and Uncle Recco? Why did we live not in Rhode Island, but in Queens? Not near my father's uncles and cousins, but an hour away, away from all relatives, at the city line?

I and my older brother and sister and cousins would pool rumors and data and try to figure it out, pushing into that treacherous, ultimately unknowable area of "what grown-ups do"—and why. We seldom came up with the answers.

Now, decades later, I've realized how those daily examples of my mother's storytelling and her sense of the importance of those stories have influenced me, perhaps decided me, to become a writer. Equally, unconsciously, influential for me in terms of *what* I'd write were my attempts to solve those mysteries in and between our parents' families—and our physical distance, even exile, from the rest of them.

*

I was born in New York City at midnight between the 22nd and 23rd of February in 1944, the third child of Phillip and Anne Picano. I have three birth certificates for two days giving three times. My mother was awake at my birth and said it was just before midnight, and I was the easiest birth of her children despite my size—ten-and-a-half pounds. With my father home asleep, she named me—after my paternal grandfather.

My father had also been Felice, son of Felice, son of Felice, etc., all the way back to mid-nineteenth-century Itria, a mountain town known for olive oil in the province of Roma. In Italy, Felice is a common male name, as I discovered when I lived there; one with literary connotations: poet Felice Romani wrote libretti to operas by Verdi, Bellini, and Donizetti that every Italian knows. My father didn't grow up in Italy, but here, and he'd often fought over his name—in effect over being Italian. He'd legally changed his name. He didn't want any child of his to suffer from the same prejudice.

For my mother, with her New England sense of tradition, a family name, no matter how odd or difficult to bear, must be passed to the next generation. She had a point: after my books were published in England, Argentina, and France, I received letters from Picanos there tracing their lines back to one or another Felice Picano from Itria. And an archeologist placed my family name with geographical exactitude. She'd come across it in a story in an Italian grade-school reader. More recently, in *Smithsonian Magazine,* I found a forebear—Giuseppe Picano. In an essay on Neapolitan wood sculpture in the eighteenth century, art critic Hilton Kramer wrote that Giuseppe had moved from Itria to Naples and for several decades dominated his field with crucifixions, *pietàs* and carved *baldachins,* some still extant in local churches.

I've never fought over my name: people have been befuddled by it, misspelled and mispronounced it (Fuh-leese is right); people have asked if I'm Spanish or Greek or if it's a *nom de plume.* Due to my name, I've been instantly unique from early on in life. Later I realized being special for a name wasn't enough: spoiled by the attention, I sought a way to solidly earn it.

For my generation, being Italian was limited to a name and a few guarded family recipes my grandma Soscia gave my mother, herself a fine cook with an international cuisine. Being Italian was reduced to biannual visits to my father's relatives in Ozone Park, where Italian was spoken by adults when they didn't want us to know something, and where Uncle Recco read Italian-language newspapers while the tantalizing odors of lemon and anise and hazelnut arose in the kitchen, preceding delicious confections served with tiny cups of *espresso,* candy-covered almonds, and doll-sized glasses of sherry. Catholic icons, calendars, and a cousin who became a nun completed the exoticism of these visits, and we never tired of correcting adults who referred to someone non-Italian as "American," saying, "We're American too. All of us!"

Until I was three years old, we lived in Richmond Hill, Queens, in an apartment above a supermarket my father and my uncle Tony owned and which flourished during the war, even when Tony went off to become a much-decorated hero in the Pacific theater, and despite the fact that (as my parents insisted) they thought black-market sales unpatriotic. When the city took over the block to build the Van Wyck Expressway, my father bought land for a store off one new service road, and a house further away, in eastern Queens.

My brother Bob and sister, Carol, two and three years older than me, recall the apartment and store and our neighbors on Liberty Avenue. They recall trolley cars on the street and weekly serial shows on the radio. I don't. My awareness begins later, on long blocks of single and attached houses with front and backyards, grass, bushes, trees, a neighborhood rife with kids on skates and bikes, plating in the street at all seasons of the year, or in furnished basements watching TV. This defines me as Post War, in the van of the largest baby boom in history that would change our country, and eventually the world.

I led a cushioned life until the fourth grade. There, one day, quite by accident, I had my first encounter with unreasoning prejudice, and met my first life enemy.

In the book titled *Ambidextrous: The Secret Lives of Children,* published in 1985, I wrote of this encounter in detail. It centered on my ambidexterity. I'd learned to read and write on my own, using my older siblings' schoolbooks and notebooks. I watched them write and taught myself that too. My mother—pregnant with my younger brother, Jerry—would correct me. By the age of four I read at first-grade level; when I entered kindergarten, I was reading third-grade books. One reason for my early success in any subject I was interested in was that I'd learned alone, forging my own methods. I used both hands to write and was very fluid in printing and script. I'd begin a sentence with my left hand and continue it with my right hand. In drawing, I'd shade and color-in using two crayons simultaneously.

"Carol, Bob, Jerry (in front), and me," about 1950

My fourth-grade teacher, a middle-aged man, opposed my ambidexterity, my creativity, anything in fact but using my right hand. He went further, he used me as an example of everything wrong with a child. The more intolerant he became, the more I resisted. My parents didn't believe me when I told them of his irrational behavior. His persecution worsened. I was appalled by the injustice of my situation, trapped, on my own for the first time in my life. No one, not even my God, seemed able to help me. I began to rebel, in school and out. An explosion between my teacher and me was inevitable and it occurred. I was ten years old. I'd been a perfectly behaved child at home and at school—but when our little war was over, I'd become a monster of egotism and suspicion, filled with hatred.

And I was forever left-handed.

I settled more warily into a new class with a new teacher and got through the next two years easily. Following some quite high IQ tests, I was offered a chance to enter a special program in junior high school: doubled science, music, art, social studies, two foreign languages, and tons of extracurricular activities. In recompense, we'd be socially and intellectually at the top of the school—and we'd skip the eighth grade!

I found I could learn at this advanced, subject-crammed, condensed level with only a bit more effort, since it depended so much upon autodidacticism, at which I was already a past master.

In *Ambidextrous,* I also wrote about my coming to sexuality, which happened between the ages of ten and thirteen, and involved several neighborhood girls and one boy. My third affair at the age of thirteen, recounted in the book, had more importance in that it led to my first piece of recognized writing, and my first artistic crisis.

The situation, briefly put, was that I realized one day that the surprising sexual relationship I'd been having with our ninth-grade class's "Ice Princess" had been completely set up and was being directed and watched by her father, an optics expert confined at home to a wheelchair by wounds suffered in the war. I ended the relationship.

Shortly later, when our English teacher had us write stories for a city-wide fiction contest, I wrote up what had happened with the girl and her father, greatly toning down the content, but not the situation nor its denouement. My story was much admired and picked to represent our grade in the contest. To my amazement, the story was sent back. The contest committee deemed it disrespectful of adults, in bad taste, overly mature, and even thought it was plagiarized. My teachers and even our dean weren't able to help me.

As a result, I became cynical and hard. It would be another decade and a half before I wrote fiction or showed it to anyone.

*

I had no special teacher in high school or college who intuited I had what it took to be a good writer and encouraged me.

Dr. Beringause conveyed his love for poetry: his clear, vivid analyses opened up the inner workings of poetry. Dr. Day's course in eighteenth-century British literature was sheer delight due to his legerdemain in making long-dead authors and their writings live again. James Wilhelm's seminar on Dante's work, life, and times was memorably comprehensive.

Though I was an art major—painting, sculpting, making collage—by my junior year I began to minor in cross-departmental literature using my alleged command of foreign tongues. I read six books a week, trying to keep plots and characters of Leskov and Genet apart from those in Henry James, William Faulkner, and Tolstoy.

Three students in most of my lit. courses were Steve, Barry, and Alan, who I joined during breaks between classes talking—arguing—in the "Little Caf," a small, older dining area favored by the bohemian elements on campus at Queens College, among which I suddenly found myself. But no matter how much Pinter or Proust that Alan or Barry or Steven read, they lived for, all but breathed, film. Not "movies," but film—experimental American film and any foreign-language one they could find. For them the novel was dead; literature completely moribund: film was the art form of the future. A few years younger and more restrained, I was less sure.

I had loved movies since I was two years old and awakened in a movie theater, stood on my mother's seat, being bottle-fed and watching Marlene Dietrich as a gypsy wrestle another actress for Gary Cooper in *Golden Earrings.* Now, living in lower Manhattan, I was closest to the cinemas that showed Resnais, Bergman, Fellini, and Mizoguchi: my apartment became a meeting place for the group—one teacher called us the "Hell Fire Club"—and my roommate Michael was also swept up in our cinema-madness.

Graduation neared and I still had no idea what I wanted to do with my life. I'd passed tests for the Peace Corps, but I wavered. The dean of the English department recommended me for a Woodrow Wilson Fellowship. That would mean more school: a masters and Ph.D. degree, then becoming a professor. I didn't think I wanted that. I'd written amusing and original term papers, so I'd been recommended for the Writing Workshop at the University of Iowa, and had been accepted. But Iowa looked so flat, so treeless, and I was so tired of going to school!

That spring, 1964, I'd accompanied my friend Ruth Reisiger when she'd applied for a job with the New York City Department of Social Services. I'd taken the tests and interviews too. Ruth had trained to be a social worker but I was less altruistic. Even so, when I discovered I'd be able to fulfill my military duty working for the Vista program—an American inner-cities version of the Peace Corps—I took the job.

At twenty, I was by no means a saint, but I'd been touched by several incidents bringing home our nation's social injustice. In 1962, the Black Muslim leader Malcolm X was to speak at Queens College. I knew he'd been a pimp and thief who'd become an eloquent speaker for Negro Rights (as it was called). One day before his appearance, the college administration cancelled it, calling Malcolm X "detrimental."

The uproar among students was immediate. The school had barred us from our First Amendment rights, although it insisted it was acting "in loco parentis"—in the place of a parent—protecting us.

In the sixties, Queens had as intellectual and liberal a faculty as any college in the country. They agreed it was a free-speech issue and joined our protest. When the administration failed to restore Malcolm X's speaking date, we organized a boycott of classes, marching around the campus's main quad with signs, chanting slogans, filling up the dean's office. The boycott spread to the rest of the City University system. We were assailed on all sides—our education was paid for by city taxes!—but we held firm, and the administration was embarrassed into letting Malcolm X speak. To my knowledge this was the first such student action in the country.

One result was that the implicit racism of the school, the city government, much of the public and the press was made explicit. The college's Student National Coordinating Committee chapter grew in size and activism. We organized sit-ins at lunch counters in the tri-state area where we heard of *de facto* segregation. I joined, was arrested, and experienced firsthand the oiled heat of bigotry. That summer and the next, SNCC sent students down South to enroll Black voters. I had to earn my living and didn't go. One pal and classmate, Andrew Goodman, did go—and paid with his life.

Despite this background, by the time my two year "hitch" as social worker was over, I'd become disillusioned: I could only see the program's lacks and failures. Oddly, others thought I did a great job: they wanted to promote me, to pay my tuition to get a graduate degree in social work.

This was also a time of personal crises—among them my need to investigate my sexuality more fully, which I knew would be difficult to do in the sexually repressive U.S. I quit work and went to Europe.

In the second volume of my memoirs, I've written in detail about this period and of my return. I merely note here that I returned to a new apartment in Greenwich Village, a new group of friends, mostly involved in the arts, and mostly homosexual. Nineteen sixty-six to 1971 were to be my years of experimentation: with different groups of people, life-styles, sexual and other relationships—and with psychedelic drugs.

Several people I met in this time influenced me greatly: among them the painter Jay Weiss, the writer Joseph Mathewson, the actor George Sampson, and Arnie Deerson. We—and others—were drawn by the charisma and generosity of Jan Rosenberry and formed a sort of group in 1968 and 1969. Jan was an advertising executive who tried to close the gap between the corporate world and rock music by befriending musicians and inviting them into TV commercials. Jan also opened his Manhattan flat to many people. It became a second home for some, an urban commune. His generosity toward me lay in his encouragement and his intelligent enthusiasm over any piece of writing—no matter how small or shallow—I showed him.

I'd written one story since the ill-fated one in junior high. In the "catalogue of my works," begun in 1974, it's listed as "Untitled: approx. 2,000 words, set in Cape Cod," with "artist from New York, and pre-teen local child" as characters. The subject is "betrayal." The entry reads: "August, 1966—MS missing. No typed copy." I.e. lost. I haven't a clue what it could be about.

As a social worker I'd written case histories, one of them complex enough to end up in the teaching manual. My next job was as a junior editor at a graphic-arts magazine. But there my writing was ephemeral, even the feature articles: not worth saving. My next job was at a bookstore. As was the next. At the latter store I wrote an introduction to an exhibit of

Jiri Mucha's works—and an interview with the Czech artist's son translated from the French, the only language we more or less shared.

My little catalog shows other works I'd deemed important: one-act comedies written in the summer of 1968, with titles like "The Persistence of Mal-En-tendu," and that fall, an unfinished novella that would become the seed upon which I built a career.

I was overqualified and overcompetent for any job I might land. It never failed—within months I'd be told I was the best employee, pushed into promotion, into pension plans and stock-sharing, my future in the company all laid out.

No way! I saw this period differently: as a time of testing and tasting and trying out. I would work as long as needed to save enough money to cover six to nine months of bills. Then I'd quit, giving as much advance warning as possible.

If asked, I'd say I was becoming a writer and needed time. And it's true that during these hiatuses from employment I taught myself the rudiments of poetry. I'd analyze, say, metaphor, then write a poem stressing metaphor—any topic would do—metaphor was what counted. Or I'd study form, say Spenserian Rhyme Royal, and use it to write a poem about my coffee cup or the first telephone call of the day—anything! Ditto with drama or comedy: I'd take any situation and turn it into a fifteen-page play. I'd even use authors I was reading, turn them into characters—with appalling results!

What I mostly did between stints of work was read, listen to music, go to movies and concerts, hang around with friends—anything but write. When a friend said it was an excuse for not working, for not tying myself to the "establishment," I couldn't deny it.

In the late winter of 1971, I was twenty-seven years old. I'd travelled, I'd had adventures, I'd lived in a variety of places among an assortment of people. A few months earlier I'd left the first bookstore I'd worked at, not only earlier than intended, but somewhat under a cloud, and with less savings than I would have liked. At the same time, a complicated and emotionally wrought romance with the late painter Ed

Armour had begun to distort into something even more incomprehensible and unsatisfactory: I saw no way out but to end the relationship.

It was in this state of virtually total life crisis that I decided to become a writer. I dared myself: I staked everything on it.

I looked through notebooks and diaries, read scraps of plays and stories and finally lit on the 1968 novel fragment. After some scrutiny it seemed to hold up. A bit of thought and I began to outline it more fully. Amazement! I found I had characters, a plot, scenes, everything! As pieces of the novel began to fall into place in my outline I became excited. Certain scenes played themselves out in my mind—I could hear what my characters were saying to each other, could feel as they did, could see, smell, taste, know what it was like to *be* them.

Halfway through the outline, I threw it away and bought a hardcover notebook. I recopied the opening pages of the fragment from years before, crossed it out and began again. It took ten tries but I finally found the first line I wanted, then the first paragraph, the first page, the first chapter.

I wrote continuously after that, daily, whenever I could, whenever I wanted to. Late into the night sometimes, playing Bach's *Well-Tempered Clavier* on the stereo, letting his sense of structure and rhythm and Wanda Landowska's style subconsciously influence my own. When Bach became too rigid or monochrome, I'd switch to Solomon playing Beethoven's piano sonatas, or to Cortot's Chopin mazurkas.

Keyboard music—because the protagonist of my novel was a pianist. He'd been a child prodigy before the turn of the century, the toast of Europe in short pants, playing for Paderewski, Brahms, Sauer, Liszt. Now, in his mid-twenties, living in New York, he'd returned to playing. A college acquaintance came to a recital and asked him to record for his new cylinder company. At the same time my protagonist had met a young European couple: a beautiful, charming, brilliant duo filled with extraordinary ideas, capable of anything!

My novel was unusual in other ways. It was set in New York of 1913, on the eve of the First World War. All that I'd read of that period's avant-garde convinced me that it was not too different than the late sixties I'd just gone through: bohemian life-styles, controversial art movements, experimentation with life-styles, sex, drugs. The young Hesse, Gide, and Ezra Pound seemed more my contemporaries than my grandparents—the half-century between their blossoming and my life a stupid waste filled with world wars.

It's not difficult to recall what writing that first novel was like for me: the same excitement, the same depth of concentration, the same trancelike, out-of-time sense that I'm on another plane of existence happens whenever I'm truly involved in writing. In an interview I once said that writing was one of the three physical/mental/emotional highs of my life—along with sexual climax and using LSD-25—and the only sustainable one.

One thrill in writing this first book was being in such full command of a fictional world that when I needed a minor character, one simply appeared at the tip of my pen, with her own personal quirks and demeanor, dress and history. I wondered how long this unexpectedly Olympian power could last.

Working at top speed to avoid its collapse, I completed a first draft in two months: a record I would never surpass, especially given that the ms. was 150,000 words long. I read it over, made notes for emendations, then typed a second draft over the next six weeks. On May 20 of 1971, 1 had two copies of a readable ms. in hand. I'd titled it *Narrative and Curse,* after the scene in Wagner's opera *Tristan and Isolde,* performed during the novel's climax.

I'd not told anyone what I was doing. Jan, Arnie, most of my friends from the Twelfth Street commune, had moved to California. I knew only one person with enough experience, savvy, and connections to help me if what I'd written was at all good. I'd met Jon Peterson a few years before through Jay Weiss. He was intelligent, clever, and sophisticated: he'd produced plays off-Broadway, and introduced the actor Al Pacino. I phoned Jon and said I'd written a novel and needed an agent.

Jon was cautious. He would read the ms. first. He warned me not to be surprised if the agent turned it down. He was right in trying to calm me. But Jon read

the novel quickly—and he loved it! He immediately got it to an agent friend, along with all of his enthusiasm. The agent read it and decided to represent my work.

In four months, I'd changed my life. Or so I thought.

*

By the time my savings ran out, my book still hadn't sold. I took part-time work and tightened my belt. As editor after editor turned it down, I saw I'd have to find a job. Through Dennis Sanders's recommendation I began work that fall at Rizzoli Bookstore.

Unlike the other bookstore I'd worked at, Rizzoli was unique. Truly international, its employees had to speak one or more foreign languages fluently. As a result our staff was unusual, many foreign-born, or Americans brought up abroad: many younger ones were biding their time while awaiting a break in their true careers as writers, painters, musicians—our manager had trained as a concert pianist. After I'd been there some months they seemed like a family—caring and close, but also emotional and irrational. Working at Rizzoli could be like a party where business also happened; at other times it was like being caught in the final act of some demented nineteenth-century opera.

After a year, my agent returned my ms. to me, unable to sell it. I was disappointed, but continued to work at the bookstore, and write.

Writing this novel had been creatively explosive: as though I'd been chock-filled with poems, stories, essays, plays, films, entire novels trying to get out. Among them would be my first published story, poem, and novel. But I'm getting ahead of myself.

For the next two-and-a-half years I continued at Rizzoli, moving steadily upward in its hierarchy—my usual course—and becoming steadily discouraged about finding a new agent or selling my novel. One poem I wrote in this time is titled "The Waiting Room," which pretty much sums up how I felt—on the brink of, but held back.

Our children's book manager, Alex Mehdevi, had written and published *Tales from Majorca,* folk stories from his homeland. When I told Alex of my frustration at being unpublished he was kind enough to have his own literary agent read my novel.

Jane Rotrosen phoned me before she'd even finished reading my ms. The title should be changed, she said, and she had other minor suggestions but she agreed to represent the book—even with its previous history! She spoke fast and made an appointment for us to meet.

The Kurt Hellmer Literary Agency office on Vanderbilt Avenue was a warren of small, dark rooms filled with manuscripts and shelves full of books. Jane and I went to the Pan Am Building, where we sat thirty floors above Park Avenue and she talked about my novel with all the detail, expertise, immediacy, and enthusiasm I could, hope for. As soon as I made those minor changes, she would send out the book. We sealed the deal with a handshake—and Jane has been my literary agent ever since.

Months went by, yet no editors seemed willing to take the ms. Jane couldn't get a fix on why not. Was it too new? Its combination of fictional world, characters, and style *too* different?

In February of 1974, Jane took me to dinner for my thirtieth birthday. My novel remained unsold. Meanwhile at Rizzoli, I'd been promoted to store manager and my boss had just explained the company's expansion plans, and my role in them. I'd said what I'd told each employer—I was a writer: the first book contract I got, I would leave. He and I knew the chances of this happening diminished daily. His offer included salaries and positions beyond my expectations. I told Jane this and of the decision I faced: I wanted to be a professional writer!

We returned to my apartment and Jane asked what was in the notebooks atop my nonworking fireplace. Unfinished works. She went through them, and stopped at the outline and opening chapters of a novel I'd titled *Who Is Christopher Darling?*

I'd begun it in the summer of 1972, basing it on the Greek myth of Phaeton—son of Apollo who'd driven his father's chariot across the heavens far too close to the sun, and who had to be destroyed. My updating retained the allegory with a sharp twist, and it was told as a psychological thriller. Its ideas reflected my interest in child prodigies and savants, and in the language and mores of Elizabethan and Jacobean England.

"At the studio apartment watched by woman voyeur!" age twenty-two

Jane thought it publishable. If I wrote up a fuller outline detailing characters and scenes, she'd get it to editors already intrigued with my work.

In a few weeks Don Fine, publisher of Arbor House, signed me to finish the novel. It was to be retitled *Smart as the Devil,* a more commercial title, he and Jane thought (I didn't). I'd receive an advance against royalties large enough to pay my bills while I left my job and wrote the book. My boss was surprised when I told him all this but the money involved was so small he gave me leave and agreed to keep all our future plans open.

From March through early October of 1974, I worked on the novel, moving out to Fire Island Pines that summer into a cottage I shared with Jon Peterson and two new friends, lovers named Nick Rock and Enno Poersch. As they all worked part-or full-time, I had the place to myself and was able to make real progress. I wrote two drafts, revised a bit after Jane had read it, and again after Don Fine read it.

Smart as the Devil was published by Arbor House on February 28, 1975, my mother's birthday. It wasn't given a large printing, and was not well advertised or promoted. It was excellently if not extensively reviewed, picked by the Mystery Guild book club, and paperback rights were sold to Dell, giving me somewhat more income. The book became one of five finalists for the Ernest Hemingway Award—for the best first novel of the year—partly due to the uniqueness of entire sections having been written in seventeenth-century English. It didn't get the award, but the nomination gave my reputation a boost.

I returned to Rizzoli after finishing the novel, but I had a new book I was eager to write, based on a personal experience. When I'd returned from Europe I'd moved into a studio apartment in the "Village," its two windows facing the street. One night, I got a phone call from a young woman. After a variety of questions and answers, it turned out I didn't know her.

She knew me, plenty about me, virtually everything about me! It took a while to figure it out; then I realized, she had binoculars—I was being watched! Whenever she phoned after that, I tried to elicit information from her—I'd lived in London too! I found out little. One night a young woman slept over with me. The next day my voyeur phoned: her words and tone of voice angry and bitter. I found that odd, given how flip she'd been about the many more young men who'd slept over. When I pointed this out, she said it was because she didn't take the men seriously as rivals.

Clearly this went beyond sport: she'd developed a fantasy life about me. I was flattered—and freaked! As a social worker I sought help for her. She refused and threatened blackmail. I said I didn't care who knew what I did in my own home. I warned her not to call anymore—it was harassment, a Federal offense. From then until I moved, I would flinch every time my phone rang—was it her?—even though I'd changed my phone number and it wasn't listed. I kept my window shades down, but I felt aware at all times that I was being watched—that I might be in danger.

But I wondered what would have happened if I'd been different: if I'd been a young man as needy of a relationship as she seemed to be. What if the relationship had bloomed, become complicated by hidden neuroses, even psychoses in her and by his growing determination to know who she was and to find her?

That was the basis *of Eyes,* which Jane, Don Fine, and Linda Grey, the editor at Dell who'd bought *Smart as the Devil,* all liked. I sold it on several chapters and an outline and wrote it during the summer and fall of 1975.

Eyes was published in 1976, following a falling out with my publisher. Editing my ms., he'd excised a short chapter describing a crucial secondary character. I deemed it necessary to give weight and color to this character, whose role was almost that of a fairy-tale witch in what was an otherwise minutely realistic narrative. When the book was published, I found out he'd not put back the chapter and I broke off relations. My editor at Dell agreed to replace the chapter and it first appeared in the paperback edition.

This second published novel was well received, sold better than my first, got more attention—reviews from several women's magazines—and earned higher book club, paperback, and foreign advances. As the book became read by more people, I realized that in attempting to investigate an incident in my own past, I'd come to symbolize in my female voyeur the questions so many young women were facing themselves—how they could be equal to men yet still feminine; how be sexual and emotional yet intelligent; how be themselves yet appropriate companions.

When the paperback was published in 1977, Peter Caras's artwork—a woman's hands in close-up, holding binoculars through which a half-naked man can be seen looking back—was stunning and appropriate. It helped the book become a best-seller, though word-of-mouth played an even larger role.

Eyes sold well here and in England until quite recently. It was translated into French, German, Spanish, Portuguese, and Japanese. Several television and filmmakers were interested in it, and it was under option for over a decade. Even so, the "unhappy" ending—the only realistic one for the story—kept it from being produced. That and the fact that a woman's p.o.v. is required to make it work. I'd suffered over that while writing the book: had to, in effect, become a mentally disturbed woman to have it come out without compromise or faked emotion.

Even before *Eyes* was published I'd begun another novel. Some years before, a friend, Nunzio D'Anarumo, avid collector of Cupids and haunter of antique stores, sent me a copy of a New York *Telegraph* from St. Patrick's Day, 1900. The paper was yellowing and cracked but one front page article couldn't fail to catch my attention, accompanied as it was by a dramatic drawing of a man shooting a pistol in a crowded court building.

"Prosecutor Shoots Defendant!" The headline was datelined the previous day from a large city in Nebraska. I read it with interest and found it strange yet very much of its time and place. I put the aged newspaper away and thought I'd forget it.

The story continued to haunt me. Partly because it was bizarre and sensational: it wasn't every day a noted lawyer attacked the man he was prosecuting for conspiracy and murder. Partly because of the characters: the defendant was shady. He'd once used hypnotism for "painless dentistry" in the poorer section of town but had become influential through his connection with a woman—beautiful, wealthy, and recently widowed under odd circumstances. As intriguing were minor characters: the dead husband; his housekeeper; the handsome con man's old assistant. I found it easy to assess the social and business classes of a Midwest boomtown; its mores and its amusements.

I mentioned it to my agent, who thought it had possibilities. I began to research the story and discovered it had been written up in many national papers of its day and in even greater detail in Midwestern ones. The more I read, the more bizarre the story, its major and minor characters and their relationships became. I was certain I had a classic American tale: one never told before. My plan was to go to Nebraska and research the book where it happened then write it up as a nonfiction novel, the form popularized by Truman Capote.

Almost immediately, I hit snags. The town hall with the trial records had burned down in 1910. No local and no state library had existed to keep copies. Only one newspaper of the time was still in business and its archives didn't go back that far. The state's Historical Society forwarded data to me—it was jejune: I wanted those aspects of character and motive I thought essential for a book. I tried contacting survivors of the families involved but they wrote back saying either they wouldn't help or knew nothing.

After a time, I was able to put together my own idea of what had happened in that Nebraska town three quarters of a century before; not only during the course of the trial, but in the years before—and after.

I knew it contained mystery and color and humanity—enough for a good novel! That's what I'd write. I pored over letters and diaries of the year for the spoken tongue, then medical journals for what was known about psychology and how it was discussed by those who practiced it—*crucial* to my story. I even consulted a specialist in Territorial and Early State Law at the A.L.A. to get the correct trial law.

I wrote the novel throughout 1976. *The Mesmerist* was published by Delacorte in September of 1977, with excellent cover art—again by Peter Caras—which also appeared on the paperback. My original title was "The Mesmerist and Mrs. Lane," which I still think superior. *The Mesmerist* was chosen as an Alternate Selection by the Literary Guild. It was better promoted and advertised than my previous books, more widely and better reviewed. It sold triple the earlier books in hardback but eventually less in paperback—*Eyes* was such a runaway seller. *The Mesmerist* was translated into six languages and published widely abroad. The biggest immediate change for me was that I'd sold hardcover and paperback rights to Delacorte/Dell and in England and come up with a big enough sum for me to quit work at Rizzoli, move into a larger flat, keep a summer place myself, travel, even invest.

By mid-1978, I was launched as a writer. Bookstores held fifty-unit displays of my recent books. Even so, my first novel languished in a drawer, unpublished, unread, and I couldn't understand why.

*

I was leading a double life—at least in publication, Since my return from Europe in the late sixties I'd been living in Greenwich Village: my associations predominantly gay men. After the Stonewall Riot of 1969, the Village became a mecca for lesbians and gays. Stonewall had begun as another police raid upon another Village gay bar. For many gays, fed up with outmoded laws and constant harassment, it was the last straw. Once word spread, the raid became a pitched battle on the streets in which police were outnumbered, overwhelmed, and humiliated. Riot squads were required to keep the peace in the area the

"At a publicity tour in downtown L.A.," 1979

entire following week. The true importance of the event became clear the day after the raid when a thousand gays—myself and my friends among them—gathered at Sheridan Square to protest the harassment. Protests continued, a political-action group formed—the Gay Liberation Front—and eventually splintered to include the more radical Gay Activists Alliance. Within weeks, a political agenda was devised. The GAA began to meet, ironically, in a former firehouse on Greene Street: a minority had begun to empower itself.

And to celebrate itself. If Black was Beautiful! as the slogan had it, then Gay was Proud! Weekly meetings at the Firehouse were attended by larger groups and ended in a dance, helping to attract, centralize, and allow people to celebrate themselves. Out of the Firehouse rose other, less political gay and lesbian clubs. The first totally gay dance club was the Tenth Floor, a

"private party" stressing Black and Latin Rock and Soul music in Manhattan's West Twenties, which attracted a crowd involved in music, design, and fashion. This same group had begun to transform Fire Island Pines into a stylish, unambiguously gay resort.

By 1975, a new gay social set had emerged, quite different from "Activists" with their academic and political background. Defined by membership in the arts, the media, recording and design professions, it was known as the "Pines-Flamingo Nexus," after the resort and the new discotheque with its five hundred members that had become its Manhattan center. This small, homogenous, sophisticated, self-conscious group began many trends in the next decade in fashion, music, and social behavior. Their imprint on gay life was instant, long-lasting, and ultimately international.

Some feared such "ghetto-ization," ergo the proliferation of more heterogenous clubs—among them Le Jardin, Twelve West, the Paradise Garage, Les Mouches, and Studio 54. The latter, Steve Rubell and Ian Schrager's glitzy club, caught the public's imagination, and soon designers, movie stars, and Social Register hopefuls were joining gays on its dance floor and in its lounges—and in summer, crowding the Botel and Sandpiper at Fire Island Pines. This same mixture of gays, jet setters, entertainers, personalities, and talent formed a highly creative social and artistic community that gave the seventies a distinctive high-gloss style, culminating in the "Beach" party of 1979, a charity drive at the Pines that commanded a full page of the "Society" section of the *New York Times* the following day.

I'd become a part of this group almost from its inception: in Manhattan as a member of the dance clubs, in the Pines as a full-time summer resident from 1975 on. Since others were offering their photography, music, sculpture, illustration, and design, I decided to offer my poetry and fiction.

Magazines of gay writing had begun: Andrew Bifrost's *Mouth of the Dragon* in New York, and Winston Leyland's *Gay Sunshine Press* in San Francisco. Even Manhattan's *Gaysweek* began a bi-monthly "Arts and Letters" section. Most of my earliest published poems and short stories appeared in these journals. Other gay magazines were *Fag Rag* and *Gay Community News* in Boston, *Body Politic* in Toronto, *New York City News, Christopher Street*, the *Native, Mandate, Stallion, Blueboy*, et al. in New York, the *Advocate* and *Drummer* in California. I wrote for them all—reviews, poems, stories, essays.

I—and other writers—began to give readings of poetry and fiction at the newly started lesbian/gay groups mushrooming on campuses at Hunter College, Columbia, Princeton, and Stanford universities.

A question now arose: I had a book of poetry, another volume of short stories, all written out of and addressing my experiences as a gay man: how could I get these books out where they could be read?

The answer, according to my agent Jane, my editor Linda, and my friend Susan Moldow, who also worked in book publishing, was that I couldn't! Few gay-themed books were published—and they had always

been special: Vidal's novel, Rechy's *City of Night*, Isherwood's *Single Man*, Baldwin's *Giovanni's Room*. No one could live off writing them, and no publisher would put out books by unknown gay writers, dramatists, or—heaven forbid!—poets. I was told to forget it, told to do what gay writers had done for years: keep them to myself, and continue writing nongay novels.

That struck me as unfair; worse, as usufructage; even a species of slavery. I'd begin my *own* publishing house and publish *nothing* but the work of gays. I'd hire, utilize, and work only with gays—artists, typesetters, printers, binders, distributors. I'd stock my books in lesbian/gay-owned bookstores. The company would be called the SeaHorse Press—named after the marine species in which the male bears and gives birth—and I felt it would work.

SeaHorse Press's first title was my *Deformity Lover and Other Poems*—chosen because the author didn't have to be paid. George Stavrinos's cover illustration and the high quality of all aspects of the book got it noticed. In the gay media, reviews were lengthy and laudatory—from its first line, the book *assumed* the reader and writer shared the gay experience and went on from there to detail and particularize that world. Critics also appreciated the book's range of styles and forms: lyric, epistle, ode, sonnet, dramatic monologue were all represented.

When the book was reviewed by nongay media, the reaction was far more mixed—some tried to but were unable to hide their prejudice. For others it was simply too different, too alien. One bright woman poet couldn't grasp why I would opt for rhythms that sounded to her like "popular music: phonograph songs!"—which was *exactly* what I wanted. The poet/translator Richard Howard encouraged me, and the late Howard Moss, poetry editor of the *New Yorker*, thought the work strong and asked to see new poems; but he could never bring himself to publish any of my gay work. Others invited me to send work to those many small poetry quarterlies that seem to define American verse today.

I continued to write poetry and many newer poems were published in magazines and anthologies—a high-school textbook published one I thought fairly gay, "Gym Shorts," to illustrate "image."

Gym Shorts

You really look good in those gym shorts
now that they're worn

and you're filled out to fit them
so manly.
You used to look good way back then, too.
Was it ten years ago?
That long?

Yes. I saw the games. I was watching.
Watching those gym shorts
grip muscled sides
as you dribbled and sped
playing king of the court.
Watched how the gold stripe you alone wore
marked you apart from the bodies rising
when you netted the ball
as if picking a rose.
How your shorts sort of fluttered
against trembling thighs
when you sprang to the floor
and ceiling spotlights stroked you.

You were sweat and smiles and modest lies
leaning on the railing
at halftime.
You shivered. So I loaned you my coat.
You thanked me.
Those gym shorts were new then,
shining blue
like childrens' Christmas wishes.

Three poems appeared in *The Oxford Book of Homo-sexual Verse.* I've only had one more book of poems published, a chapbook, *Window Elegies,* by the Close Grip Press at the University of Alabama in 1986, but I was pleased and honored to read it at the Poetry Society of America, a usually less adventuresome organization.

SeaHorse Press, however, was launched. Especially as my book went through four printings. The second title was *Two Plays by Doric Wilson,* the third, *Idols,* poems by the talented Dennis Cooper, then Kevin Esser's man-boy love novel *Streetboy Dreams.* Clark Henely's hilarious *Butch Manual* became a bestseller, and in 1980 I edited an anthology of poetry, drama, and fiction by lesbians and gay men, *A True Likeness.*

As the press continued to grow, so did its list—Alan Bowne's play *Forty-Deuce,* a collection of stories by Brad Gooch, *Jailbait* (cover photo by Robert Mapplethorpe), poetry by Robert Peters, Rudy Kikel, Gavin Dillard, and Mark Ameen, George Stambolian's

interviews, *Male Fantasies Gay Realities,* and a translation from the French of gay novelist Guy Hocquenghem's novel *Love in Relief.* Later on, I'd use the prestigious SeaHorse imprint on titles I would edit for Gay Presses of New York—our reprint of the 1933 Charles Henri Ford/Parker Tyler novel *The Young and Evil* and Martin Duberman's *About Time:Exploring the Gay Past.*

The SeaHorse Press turned out to be a great deal of work, fun, and a way to meet lesbian and gay authors all over. But it didn't solve the problem of writing gay material and getting it to a wide readership.

While writing *The Mesmerist,* I was approached by a film producer at Universal Studios who wanted me to write a gay-themed movie. His idea was for me to explore the darker side of gay life in Manhattan. He offered a single image which, while striking, ended up remaining unused. There was a basis to his idea. Arthur Bell, openly gay columnist for the *Village Voice,* had been writing a series on several bizarre and grisly murders of gay entrepreneurs. Bell was chasing leads and tying together clues when his life was threatened; he stopped the series.

Through my own contacts, I could go further: sex partners, acquaintances, and a close friend worked in the hierarchy of discos, bars, bathhouses, and private sex clubs which had sprung up in Chelsea. I began to ask questions and what I discovered began to intrigue me.

A former lover, the playwright Bob Herron, was a community leader in the Village through the Jane Street Block Association. He told me of an undercover unit of the New York City Police Department formed to investigate the seemingly related murders Bell had reported. I met a member of this unit who answered some of my questions. Shortly after, the unit was disbanded. It was supposed to be investigated itself, but that never happened.

I had more than enough material and some of it was very hot. But I knew that presenting as factual what I'd found out would lead to death threats or worse: I'd fictionalize it. I put together an outline and got it to the film producer.

He was horrified. It was so gay, so raw, so disturbing and violent he could barely read my outline. No doubt, he was being realistic about its chances of being filmed in a homophobic industry. Upon my return from California I mentioned the outline to my editor, Linda Grey, who read it and, bless her, said, "It'll be a terrific book!" I wrote a single, gripping, opening chapter and Delacorte bought it.

The Lure was my fourth published novel, my most controversial, and until recently the best known. Someone recently called it "pulp." Someone else "a cult classic," which seems pretentious yet in terms of sales and influence isn't inaccurate. The hardcover was well packaged, promoted, and advertised and it was the first gay-themed book sold by the Literary Guild: an Alternate Selection. It sold very well in hardcover and paperback and was translated into many languages. Its greatest foreign success was in Germany, where it sold steadily for a decade under the title *Gefangen in Babel*. "Warning: Explicit Sex and Violence," the ad read for the book club advertising *The Lure:* and it's true, I've never written anything quite like it again and have resisted all requests and demands for a sequel or to have it made into a film.

I wrote it in Manhattan and at Fire Island Pines throughout 1978. A long time, given how tightly plotted the book is and how fast it reads: many people told me they were up all night reading it. Author Edmund White called it "hallucinatory—as though one were drugged."

Some gays hated *The Lure*—and me—for its uncompromising portrait of the sleazier scenes that had arisen out of Gay Liberation, of which few political activists were proud. To them, I was washing dirty laundry in public. Worse, I was providing damaging confirmation to those opposing gay rights. At the least I was betraying the movement.

My intentions were different: I'd wanted the reader—gay or not, male or female, young or old—to share what it was like being gay in Manhattan: experiencing fear, doubt, the constant questioning of one's own and everyone else's motives, yet joy and camaraderie and love too; and always, motiveless bigotry and hatred.

Most nongay reviews (*The Lure* was reviewed widely) and the mail I received confirmed that I'd succeeded in that task. No matter how badly I portrayed some gays or some aspects of gay life in the novel, no mat-

With Andrew Holleran at "Gaywyck," New Jersey, 1980

ter how thin a slice of gay life I'd concentrated on, I'd drawn it richly, in the round, sympathetically, and without the usual knee-jerk judgementalism. And I'd portrayed those arrayed against gays worse: irrational, ruthless, often deadly. Years later when *The Lure* was being used in college courses about minorities or about psychology or even about urban life, I knew my critics had been wrong: I felt justified.

I'd also achieved something else. With *The Lure's* success I'd tied together that work I'd been publishing—classed as "commercial fiction" despite that Hemingway Award nomination—with my own private life and interests. It was the first time these two disparate, even opposing, forces would come together for me—and to date, the last!

I'd met Edmund White socially in 1976. He'd just published *The Joy of Gay Sex* with Charles Silverstein, but I admired more White's stories and his earlier novel, *Forgetting Elena*. I'd also met George Whitmore around this time, and we became friends. George told me of a remarkable novel he'd read in galleys. Titled *Dancer from the Dance,* the new book was about the Pines-Flamingo crowd by an unknown author—Andrew Holleran. I read it and confirmed for myself his talent and the book's truth, humor, and brilliance. A few weeks later, at a party at the Pines, I was introduced to Holleran: we've been good friends ever since.

Dancer was published in the autumn of 1978. My *Deformity Lover* had come out earlier that year, as had a fascinating nonfiction book, *After Midnight,* by Michael Grumley, author of *Hard Corps,* a study of the S/M leather scene. Michael's lover, Robert Ferro, had published a short enigmatic novel, *The Others,* in 1977. George Whitmore was writing poetry and articles. Edmund's lover, Chris Cox, was compiling an oral history of Key West. In the spring of 1979, White's *Nocturnes for the King of Naples* was published; that autumn my novel *The Lure.*

In the following months, we seven were constantly thrown together within the gay cultural scene and found out we shared many interests. I don't recall who suggested we meet on a regular basis to read and discuss our work. I know the first meeting was held at George's apartment on Washington Square. Casually, later on, we came up with a name—the Violet Quill Club—sometimes called the Lavender Quill Club.

No matter how light-hearted we were in talking about it, once together we were in earnest. We'd seen what happened to gay writers before us who'd not been able to write about the gay experience, forced to tailor their talent to the heterosexual majority—William Inge, Thornton Wilder, Tennessee Williams, Truman Capote, Edward Albee. Few of those who had succeeded in what Roger Austen called "Playing the Game" for the sake of their careers had escaped personal damage: alcoholism, psychosis, self-destruction, suicide. We refused to take that route, even though (especially for Edmund White and myself) a public coming out might well mean the destruction of our careers.

We knew not to expect our work to be critiqued fairly, even competently. The literarily powerful *New York Times* was virulently homophobic and reviews of gay-themed books were openly hostile, often written by "closeted" gay writers. But our books were sympathetically reviewed elsewhere, and other writers worked quietly in our cause.

Yet with public criticism on such a simplistic level, we lacked that dialogue we needed to grow in our work. The Violet Quill Club would provide it, as well as occasional technical aid in the niceties of prose fiction. We discovered we were all writing some sort of autobiography, but besides individual tales of growing up and "coming out" we hoped our gay-themed work could be enlarged to treat the "big" themes that have always attracted writers—love, death, how to live one's life.

Through appearances in *Christopher Street* and the *New York Native,* we became known as a group to other gay writers. As a group, we strengthened each other individually and began to wield influence. Those who admired our writing or our uncompromising stance called us the New York School, Those who felt excluded or threatened called us the Gay Literary Mafia. Many younger writers have told me that our work and our publicity lessened their own fear of ostracism and helped them define themselves as gay writers.

Our meetings were neither regular nor often: in all, no more than eight times over a year and a half. Like all groups with strong egos, the VQ Club eventually ended. With one exception, we all remained friends. In some cases even closer friends. In the years since, we would often meet together for "tea" or spend weekends at the Ferro family summer place on the Jersey shore, which we jokingly renamed "Gaywyck."

As of this writing—summer 1990—only three of us are still alive, and one of those three is infected: AIDS has taken and continues to take its toll. But the group's importance should continue to live on. The curators of the American Literature Collection at the Beinecke Library at Yale University believe the VQ Club to have been the key group in producing, popularizing, and legitimizing gay fiction in America: they are collecting our manuscripts and papers.

The VQ Club was responsible for an efflorescence of new books by its members, among them White's *Boy's Own Story* and *The Beautiful Room is Empty,* Ferro's *Family of Max Desir* and *The Blue Star,* Cox's *Key West,* Holleran's *Nights in Aruba,* Grumley's *Life-Drawing,* and Whitmore's *Confessions of Danny Slocum* and *Nebraska.* I'd completed my novel *Late in the Season* (1981) when we began to meet, but my

"Friends and Violet Quill Club members: George Stambolian, Robert Ferro (deceased), Michael Grumley (deceased), and me in front," Fire Island Pines, 1985

novella *An Asian Minor: The True Story of Ganymede* (1981), and several short stories which I eventually collected, were written or rewritten for VQ Club meetings. Our discussions gave me enough confidence to later write more autobiographical works.

Late in the Season was published by Delacorte, although with a tenth of the attention given *The Lure*—because it was a "smaller" book. It was in fact something new: an "idyll," a love story about two attractive, successful middle-class gay men during one late summer month as their "marriage" is tested by, among other things, one of them having an affair with a young woman.

I'd written the book from a double p.o.v. as I had in *Eyes,* and in a way, it's a companion piece to that book. Except that it's a series of prose poems: aquarelles, even. It opens like this:

It was a perfect day for composing. The morning mist had finally burned off the ocean, unfurling the blue sky like a huge banner of victory. Kites were fluttering at various levels of the warm, balmy air. From down the beach came the sweet-voiced distortions of children's cries in play—the last children of the season—adding extra vibrancy to their sounds, piercing the scrim of post-Labor-Day-weekend silence that had softly dropped a week ago. Already the first dying leaves of an autumn that came early to the seashore and would blaze madly for a mere month of picture-book beauty had flung themselves at the glass doors this morning. They had saddened Jonathan then, perched over his large mug of coffee, feeling the hot sun on his closed eyelids. But now the morning felt so clear and sunny, so absolutely cloudless, he felt he might strike it with the little glass pestle in the dining room bowl, and the day would ring back, echoing crystal, like a gamelan orchestra.

The novel's poetry has made it a lasting favorite among my readers. While it was sold to British and German publishers, *Late in the Season* attained a smaller, if more discriminating, readership than my earlier novels. It fell out of print at Dell and was reprinted in a trade paper edition by Gay Presses of New York, where it's been a steady seller.

As has been my gay short-story collection, *Slashed to Ribbons in Defense of Love,* published by GPNY in 1983, now in its third printing. I'd gathered all my stories from gay magazines, added the novella "And Baby Makes Three," and a final, autobiographical tale, "A Stroke." The book was published at a time when the short story was making one of its periodic comebacks. Besides fine reviews in the gay media, it was well received in general. *Writer's Digest* listed it along with collections by Barthelme, Carver, and Beattie as the best of the year.

Gay Presses of New York was put together in 1980 by myself, Larry Mitchell, who'd begun Calamus Press, and Terry Helbing, who'd begun the JH Press. Our idea was to combine administrative and overhead costs and to publish one new title per year. Our first book was a play in three parts the author wanted printed as one and produced in a single evening. Harvey Fierstein's *Torch Song Trilogy* still hadn't been produced as a trilogy when GPNY bought publication rights. The book came out in 1981, the play opened off-Broadway in 1982, where its successful run led it to Broadway, and it received the Tony Award in 1983.

The great success of *Torch Song Trilogy* allowed GPNY to flourish. We spread our net wide, pulling in lesbian authors, gay dramatists, nonfiction writers, novelists, etc. The 1985 catalogue showed seventy-five titles in print. I knew GPNY was secure when my partners bid for *my* new works along with commercial publishers. We continued to encounter bigotry: book clubs wouldn't purchase rights directly from us, a large distributor wouldn't do business with us. Prejudice dies hard.

Throughout, GPNY has been hard work with little or no profit, done as a challenge and as a service to the readers and writers of the lesbian/gay community.

When *Newsweek* ran a cover story on gay writing coming into the mainstream in 1989, it completely ignored GPNY and SeaHorse and Calamus, as well as other important lesbian/gay presses—Daughters Ink, Gay Sunshine Press—who were fully responsible for the inception and continued existence of a lesbian/gay literature.

I was happy enough for GPNY to publish my first book of memoirs. *Ambidextrous: The Secret Lives of Children* (1985) is a true story in the form of three novellas covering three years in my life, from the ages of eleven to thirteen. I began the first, "Basement Games," in the summer of 1983, driven by a need to deal with the most difficult problem I'd ever faced and the people involved. When I'd written it, I realized it was only one of three formative crises that had determined who I would become as a person and writer. I wrote "A Valentine" in the next few months, and spent the first third of 1984 writing the third and most complex section, "The Effect of 'Mirrors'."

The reception of *Ambidextrous* was strong enough for me to consider writing another volume. While I planned to be chronological, I didn't want a full sequential account. Like most lives, mine had gone through long fallow periods followed by sudden times of action: only those "highlights" would be my material.

I was impelled by more than memory and self-healing. I'd begun to feel increasingly limited and caged inside the novels I'd been writing. The tight, suspenseful plots and fully rendered p.o.v.s of characters required to drive my *House of Cards* (1984) and especially *To the Seventh Power* (1989) were making writing less "fun," more work. I tried other areas of writing: in 1985 and 1986 I worked on a screenplay of *Eyes* with director Frank Perry. I adapted my novella *An Asian Minor* at the request of director Jerry Campbell and it had a good off-Broadway run in 1986 as the play *Immortal!* That same summer my one-act play *One O'Clock Jump* was also produced off-Broadway.

Despite these distractions, I still wanted to use the individual "voice" I'd found in my poetry and short fiction and develop it into a more supple, varied, sophisticated prose. I was searching for new structures too, capable of the closest detail, yet open enough for sudden wide shifts in time, place, and character.

A short version of "The Most Golden Bulgari," the first part of the second book of my memoirs, appeared in George Stambolian's excellent anthology *Men on Men* in 1986. "A Most Imperfect Landing," the second part, was written in May 1987 and first published in a gay literary magazine, the *James White Review,* in 1989. I wrote the final part, "The Jane Street Girls," in the spring of 1988.

Gary Luke, editor of the Plume line at NAL, bought paper rights to *Ambidextrous* and hard/soft rights to *Men Who Loved Me*—as I'd cheekily titled the sequel. They were published together in the fall of 1989 and are the books I'm most proud of: they contain all I've learned so far of style, form, and technique in rendering the funny, tragic, sad, frustrating, incomprehensible, and ambiguous quotidian of our lives.

Not all reviewers grasped my purpose. While some found the books "distinguished" or "brilliant," others called them "bad jokes," "put on tell-alls." Unsurprisingly, complaints have been leveled at my prose for daring to mix "high" and "low" styles; also at the contents of the books for mixing the "popular" and "literary." Some British critics called the books flat-out lies, assuring their readers and me that children never have sex. But I'll continue to experiment with and develop this new style. At this time I'm utilizing it in a novel about the complex love-hate relationship of two gay friends over a busy, incident-filled, thirty-five-year period.

*

Looking over these pages, I see many deal not with myself, my life, my family, my friends, my work, but with larger issues: social and political forces—the Civil Rights and Student movements in the sixties, Gay Liberation and the world created by gays in the seventies. In a review of both memoirs in a Boston newspaper, Allan Smalling wrote: "Picano bids us to see his experiences as exemplary. . . . Whether good or bad, his life experiences virtually define what it meant to come of age in America in the 'Fifties and 'Sixties."

The seventies and eighties too—once I feel I'm able to write about those decades—not an easy or happy task and not one I look forward to or think myself

equal to. One example of the problem I face, think on this: two of my Fire Island Pines housemates and friends were among the first known American men to have been stricken with and died of AIDS. This past decade has been one in which I've watched my entire community, an era, an entire way of life—as rich and full as any I've known—swept away by disease as utterly as the Holocaust swept away European Jewry, and with about as little response from the rest of the world.

As those few friends left to me continue to sicken and suffer and die, I often wonder if that's the reason I lived through those times, knew those people, suffered those losses, became a writer, learned the value of storytelling from my mother—so that eventually I might bear witness to that era, those people, this great loss, and make it literature.

POSTSCRIPT: Felice Picano contributed the following update in 2004:

I'm reminded of the ambiguous Chinese toast that goes: "May you live in interesting times." I had already lived in very interesting times both for myself, the country, and the world when I wrote my autobiography for *Contemporary Authors,* but I had no idea how much more "interesting" they were about to become.

It's probably safe to say that most of what critics and academicians consider my major work has been published since July 1990, when I handed in that essay. Certainly my life has altered considerably since I wrote the autobiography. A few weeks after I'd mailed it, my partner and I went for HIV tests, as we'd been doing regularly. Having lived within the very heart of the maelstrom of the disease from before the time it even had a name, we naturally assumed it was only a matter of time until we were proven to test "positive" for and develop what was then still a life-ending illness.

That week, my partner tested positive, and astonishingly, I did not. (I haven't so far.) He'd already endured weeks of shingles, a neurological "marker" illness for AIDS. He soon developed other symptoms, and ten months later he was dead. No sooner was he cremated than my last close friend my age in Manhattan, the writer/critic George Stambolian, nearly crashed

Bob Lowe, 1989

a car he was driving, forcing me to take the wheel. His neuropathy worsened and two weeks later if was confirmed he too had AIDS. Three of us became his caretakers, and he died in January 1992.

I'd already lost ninety percent of my acquaintance to HIV, including my younger brother. In the next decade via AIDS, cancer, and car accidents, I would lose his wife, my older brother, his wife, both their children and my father who'd outlived my mother by sixteen years.

I operated in a constant state of crisis, trauma, and shock. But I kept writing, and, it's generally believed, I wrote better than before. Presciently, I'd written in the *CA* autobiography that I was supposed to witness and write of my times, and I certainly did that. I'd also written there that I planned to write a book about "The complex love-hate relationship between two gay friends over a busy, incident-filled, thirty-five year period." Those friends would become changed into second cousins, and that book would become *Like People in History,* my most popular book since *The Lure,* and the most honored to date.

In the midst of the panic and madness of Bob Lowe's illness, I met with Dr. Charles Silverstein who I'd known since the heady days of the Gay Activists Alliance right after the Stonewall Riots that established Gay Liberation politics back in 1968. Charles had helped persuade the American Psychiatric Association to remove the label of illness from people simply because they were homosexual. He's a formidable man, tall, stout, bearded, intelligent, and sensible.

Our discussion was about a complete overhaul of Silverstein and Edmund White's co-written path-breaking guide, *The Joy of Gay Sex.* Gay life had changed so much in fifteen years, Silverstein felt the book needed updating. Edmund White had been living in Paris for years, too distant to write it. Silverstein wanted me to join him as co-author, partly because he was uncertain of his own writing ability. My memoirs, *Ambidextrous* and *Men Who Loved Me,* had helped me acquire that elusive quality—literary cachet. But I'd also very much kept up with health issues. Bob and I (along with Edmund White) had been among the first to meet in 1980 to form a group of professionals that would soon become known as the Gay Men's Health Crisis, the first organization and the first real weapon against the spread of AIDS in the world.

Though published in 1976, the earlier book was in fact more of a Swinging Sixties text. "Being raped? Lay back and enjoy it?" Freaking out on drugs—"Everyone does sometimes." The world the book pictured was sunny, open, devil-may-care—and dangerously out of date. Drugs and alcohol were now known to be crutches and addictions; rape could now lead to a death sentence. So very much had changed, that ninety-nine percent of the book had to be rewritten, with many new entries brought in—even information about condoms hadn't been included in the first edition.

We sold the outline to HarperCollins editor-in-chief Susan Moldow, who let us package the book, including hiring the artist, Ron Fowler. I negotiated the contract from a pay phone in the Intensive Ward corridor where Bob lay dying. I wrote my half of the book in those first totally stunned months after his death: having a non-fiction project to do was very useful to me and kept me going during what must be counted the nadir of my existence. During our nationwide book tour in the summer of 1991, Silverstein had to return home when *his* partner began to die. But *The New Joy of Gay Sex* was well received, well publicized, sold well, and was later published in England, and translated into German, Japanese, Dutch, Scandinavian, and Hebrew. The guide was also the second most stolen book from libraries and bookstores in America, and gained the further dubious distinction of being the book with the most attempts of censorship against it in U.S. libraries and bookstores.

Silverstein had brought in his agent at William Morris to sell that title. My literary agent since the beginning said that was fine: she preferred not to be associated with the book. I thought nothing of this statement at the time.

A year later, I'd finished another big writing project I'd planned and worked on for years, a science fiction epic titled *Dryland's End*. This was the last of my books that Bob Lowe—who'd been my first reader for fifteen years—read in manuscript. I gave it to my agent, who returned it some weeks later saying she'd been unable to read more than a few pages: It was totally beyond her. In 1994, it was sold to a small New York press, right after my next novel, *Like People in History*, was sold to Viking-Penguin. My agent had been unable to get past much of the content in *that* book either, and had sent it back to me, requesting I instead write a best-seller. I insisted this book would be one. When we'd first met in 1974 and she'd told me she was interested in turning me into a "literary star," I'd reminded her that stars not only shine brightly, they also shine forever. Evidently she'd forgotten that last part. Her inability to follow me where I found myself going with my writing ended our professional relationship, although we've been able to pick up the personal end of it a bit lately. I sold the big novel to an old friend at Viking-Penguin.

These two biggest (in many ways) books of my career, *Dryland's End* and *Like People in History*, were published in the spring of 1995. Naturally, the mainstream book got all the attention. I went on a month-long book tour for it, extended as the hardcover went into four printings. Rights were sold to major publishers in England and Germany. In 1996, I went to London. When I arrived the book was number three on the best seller list. Without America's restrictive "gay/straight" labelling, my gay epic had become a national bestseller in the U.K. and Commonwealth overnight. I appeared on BBC radio and tv programs and gave readings at the Barbican Center; I was interviewed or featured in all the newspapers and my book went into double digit printings. The tabloids had a field day speculating which now British rock star I'd bedded. The novel sold almost as well in the U.S., tying for first place in sales at the Quality Book Club in 1996 with David Foster Wallace's *Infinite Jest*. It has since been published in Germany, France, and Canada, and a Spanish language edition is being prepared.

Like People in History, about two gay cousins who meet in a New York suburb at age eleven in 1955 and whose lives take them to Vietnam, Beverly Hills, San Francisco, Woodstock, Fire Island, and finally to Manhattan in the age of Act-Up, is the story of gay men *within* and *part of* American history; at that time a completely new and untold tale. The novel received good reviews in the *New York Times* and *Los Angeles Times, Guardian* (Manchester), *Le Figaro,* and *Le Monde,* where it was named best foreign language book of the year. It received five literary award nominations, and won three awards. I'm happy to say the book is dedicated to Bob Lowe's memory.

But literary honor counts little when a person has been as stricken, as surrounded by and eventually as utterly unmoored by so much death as I have been. No wonder I eagerly went on book tours and extended vacations, to Europe, all across the U.S. and Canada, and to Japan (1993). I even lived a summer in Berlin (1994), Germany, trying to help a friend write a difficult screenplay. But nowhere I went did I really feel comfortable. New York, my home for decades, had become a place of ghastly memories. Bicycling around Manhattan, it was all I could do to avoid many places, and finally entire neighborhoods that I couldn't stand to even see again. Although I made some new friends among young people there and worked as a volunteer in various charitable organizations, it wasn't the same as being with friends you'd grown to manhood with.

No surprise then that during a New Year's stopover for readings in Los Angeles, when my conductor/pianist host, Armen, offered to sublet me his apartment while he worked two years for the Paris Opera, I said yes. At the end of my 1995 book tour I moved to Los Angeles, mixing half my things with his in the spacious flat. I'd had a few friends in L.A. who I used to visit and I saw those people and even bought a car from one—an actor waiting for a part, working for an auto dealer. I also mixed with Armen's friends, and slowly developed a new social set. Again, it's not the same as those people you've grown up with, but on my sixtieth birthday recently, a large party was thrown for me, and over forty of these new friends showed up despite rain and bad weather, some driving from Santa Barbara and Palm Springs, other places I've grown familiar with in this area.

In the year before Bob had become so ill, he and I had flown out to Southern California. I'd lived here briefly several times in my life and I'd continued to want to relocate here. As a successful attorney in a partner-

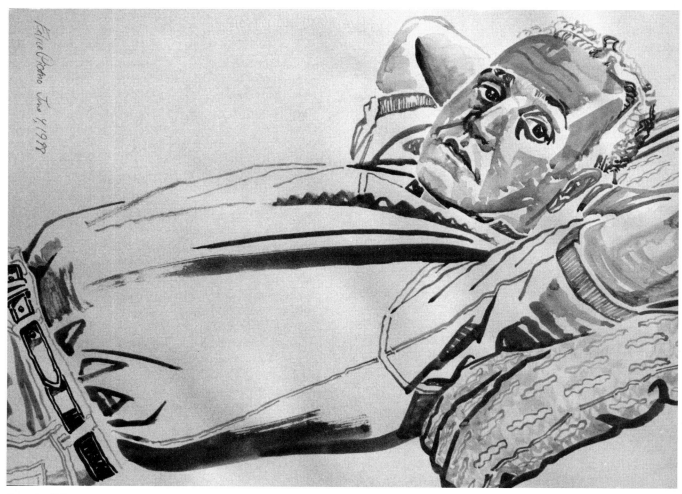

Portrait of Picano

ship, Bob could easily open an office and move. We had looked around both West Hollywood and the Hillcrest-Mission Heights area of San Diego as potential new homes.

After my L.A. sublet ended, I stayed another nine months in another flat in the same development, then a week before my father died, I moved the remainder of my possessions to Los Angeles, driving an overladen twenty-two-foot-long U-Haul truck across the U.S. during one of the hottest Augusts on record. I dodged or sat-out statewide thunderstorms in Ohio and Indiana and threaded through day-long tornadoes across Nebraska. The truck broke down once, at the New Mexico/Arizona state line. I was told to drive slowly and not very much per day the rest of the way. So I dawdled in Arizona, seeing sights like Canyon de Chelly and Meteor Crater, and I came to like the state as much as California.

A week after I'd moved, my father died and I flew back to New York to bury him. Six months earlier I'd closed out his home and put him into hospice care and I tried to ensure that he didn't suffer too much from the combined afflictions of heart disease and cancer. He was eighty-four years old.

Six months later, I moved into a small house high in the Hollywood Hills where I've lived ever since. Here I've found a modicum of the peace and quiet that escaped me for so long and in the process have become a dedicated flower, succulent, and vegetable gardener. Because of the proximity to so many hiking trails, I've also became a hiker, and so have kept in pretty physical good shape, to offset my aging, gray hair and beard.

Even so, my personal life never recovered. Bob had been my soul-mate, and the few men who interested me later on couldn't help but see his photos, and understand from my tone of voice in speaking of him the depth of our connection. Furthermore, the psychic damage caused by having this last prop of my very difficult life pulled out from under me more or less when I was at my most vulnerable, remains in place to this day. Anyone who gets too close to me is warned that people around me tend to die; their personal safety seems to lie in keeping a little distance. And while I may have acquired more than a little fame and reputation, especially in gay life and literature, when forced to, I have to compare myself to that extremely equivocal wedding gift in Henry James's late novel, *The Golden Bowl*—a seemingly perfect object with a hairline crack that makes it fragile and almost useless, perpetually flawed.

Here in the Hollywood Hills, I've also set up a point from which I've travelled more, exploring by car California and the American and Canadian West. Here too, I've written some of my best books, and revived one book from the past.

I'd written a first draft of *Looking Glass Lives* at my rental house in Fire Island Pines in 1979. I revised the short novel a year later. When I showed it to my literary agent she read it and found it too intellectual and philosophically challenging, and I'd put it away. The work had been revived by me in 1989, intended to become a publication of Gay Presses of New York, a company I'd co-founded with Terry Helbing and Larry Mitchell. A few years after Terry's death from AIDS, Larry's sight, which had been worsening due to macular degeneration, suddenly got much worse. Left alone to do all the work for all four presses, as well as to caretake my partner, family members and close friends, I was overwhelmed and forced to close down GPNY for good in 1992.

Five years later, I was approached by editor-in-chief Scott Brassart of Alyson Books in Hollywood to give him a book to publish, I decided to offer him *Looking Glass Lives,* which I felt was ready for publication. Alyson did use the illustrations that Provincetown-based artist Ron Fowler had done for the book over a period of two years and which GPNY had paid for. But alas they decided *not* to use his striking cover art. *Looking Glass Lives* was about a reincarnated love-triangle. Set in contemporary times and in the Civil War era, it is one of my most unusual and spiritual books, one of the few in which I explore some aspects

of the Eastern thought I've come to accept. The book was surprisingly popular, given that it was aimed directly into a gay male market, further confirming for me that the separation from my agent had been correct.

Meanwhile I'd been planning and working on a new novel. *The Book of Lies* was written as an academic mystery/high comedy, centering around a writing group similar to one I belonged to at the end of the 1970s—The Violet Quill Club. This group of friends, lovers (all writers) had met infrequently but had gained prestige early on from various newspaper articles and mostly because the books produced in our short time together formed a sort of early high water mark of modern gay male fiction. In 1994, poet/scholar/editor David Bergman published a volume of our work— stories, essays, excerpts from novels, letters—titled *The Violet Quill Reader,* containing the work of myself, Andrew Holleran, Edmund White, Christopher Cox, Robert Ferro, Michael Grumley, and George Whitmore. That book helped the group gain what has now become a kind of legendary stature. Bergman's scholarly study of the group's lives, loves and writing, *The Violet Hour,* in the works since then, was just published in 2004 and will doubtless continue to draw attention to our group's pivotal place in the formation of a contemporary Gay/Lesbian/Bisexual/Transgendered literature.

However if anyone goes to *my* novel to discover the truth about the group or its individuals, they'll find themselves trapped, led around by the nose, befuddled, addled and indeed as the title implies, lied to, in various ways. A completely post-modernist text, the novel consists of a first person story told by what one British reviewer called "the most unreliable narrator in literature since James' governess in *The Turn of the Screw.*" Interspersed with this less than candid Ph.D. student's narrative are a plethora of anecdotes, letters, phone-calls, faxes, e-mails, and contes trouves: an entire panoply of contemporary communication that further muddies rather than clarifying the truth. Originally published in England by Little Brown/ Abacus, *The Book of Lies* is one of my recent critical successes, if *not* one of my best sellers.

The third volume of my memoirs, *A House on the Ocean, A House on the Bay,* begun in 1989 and not finished till 1996, was published by Faber & Faber in 1996 and was another critical success. Like *The Book of Lies,* it was nominated for several awards. I'd lived almost half the year every year at Fire Island from 1975 to 1985, and this book was about that life, that place, and the people I had encountered and related to there—and also about how I became an author.

I had an odd experience writing it. The two novella-length halves were written separately, over a period of eight years, and when I came to do the book, I at times simply incorporated into one or another of these other pieces of writing I had sitting around on the subject. Oddly, this mishmash of "bleeding chunks" of prose, somehow fit together. And although I can see all the stitchings, readers often complimented me, saying the memoir is among my best structured and best written works.

In my fifties and because of Scott Brassart and Jay Quinn at Haworth Press, more of my earlier books were returned to print. *Late in the Season* was republished in 1994 as part of Stonewall Inn Classics out of St. Martin's Press and I wrote an afterward to it. Alyson put my 1981 novella *An Asian Minor* (*sans* David Martin's delicious artwork) with my 1983 story collection *Slashed to Ribbons in Defense of Love,* into a single volume that Brassart named *The New York Years*—so I wrote an introduction for that. And when Alyson reprinted *The Lure* in 2002, I wrote another intro, in effect explaining the gestation and history of these books. I then wrote three more introductions for Haworth Press's reissue of my three memoirs in a uniform edition in 2003.

One of my most difficult works, one that required three years to write on and off, was the novel, *Onyx,* published in 2001. The difficulty unquestionably arose because it was to be so personal a book for me. In effect, the novel explores the successful relationship of two mature gay men pulling apart as one of them sickens and dies, leaving the other as an unwilling survivor. For this novel, I abandoned my usual fun and games experimentation with novelistic structure and point of view for a straightforward third person exploration of character and action. What may be unusual is that in *Onyx* I follow the dying partner to the moment of his death. Another surprising aspect might be that he adjusts to his critical situation far better than his partner. And yet another startling aspect is that the men, rather than being the stereotypical gay party boys, are deeply embedded in family life, their home, their sister's children, etc.

Obviously autobiographical, *Onyx* was the best reviewed of my novels to date, and despite it's

altogether dark and tragic material, it was also one of my best selling books in the past decade. But shortly after publication, my editor left Alyson to pursue his own writing, in effect ending our excellent five-book streak.

Somewhat at sea again, I encountered opportunity in another area of writing, the stage. I already had a stage history. During the 1980s I'd transformed my novella *An Asian Minor* into a play with added music and dancing for Meridian Gay Theater, with the help of director Jerry Campbell who then put it on. An updating of the story of the Ganymede story from Ovid's *Metamorphoses* into contemporary times, *Immortal* ended up having a five month Off Broadway run and was a great deal of work and a lot of fun. Shortly after that, my one act play, *One O'clock Jump* was co-winner of the Jane Chambers playwriting award and I got to direct the black comedy for the Off-Broadway stage. It too went on to have a stage run of several months and was subsequently staged at The Seattle Rep and most recently at the Tennessee Wiliams Festival in New Orleans.

Around that same time as my second play closed, film writer and director, Frank Perry, (*David and Lisa, Mommy Dearest*) asked me to co-write with him an adaptation for film of my 1976 novel, *Eyes.* I'd already worked on a screen version of the book in 1978 in Los Angeles, with producer Milton Sperling, and subsequently a half dozen actors (Sissy Spacek, Lindsey Wagner, et al) and directors had optioned the novel and tried their hand at it, but the story continued to defy everyone's attempt to get it on screen. Perry and I had no better luck with it, but it was an excellent experience working with him, and it opened me up to future performing writing.

A year or so later I'd written what I thought might be a one act play, another black comedy I titled *The Bombay Trunk.* Acquaintances at the Perry Street Theater included it in a staged reading series, and other acquaintances did a good job of acting it. I'd originally hoped the play would be an accompaniment to *One O'Clock Jump,* making a full evening. Instead, it became painfully clear to all at the end of the reading that it was incomplete. One audience member asked what many were thinking, "Where's the second act?" After a short while I did write a second act. But my workload at Sea Horse Press and GPNY grew too burdensome, and too many people were sick and dying around me, calling for my attention, so I put the play away.

Picano at a Los Angeles writers gathering, 2002

Fourteen years later, in 2001, a friend from Los Angeles who'd moved to San Diego asked me to attend and be part of a staged reading of one of his plays for a group there known as Script Teasers. New plays would be read cold by the group members, either on stage or in someone's home, and then would be discussed. During our intermission someone asked if I had a new play for them to read. I remembered that I did, found it, made copies and a month later, Script Teasers presented it. To great effect. It got an altogether wonderful response. So much so that when a month later Ed Decker, the Artistic Director of San Francisco's New Conservatory Theater, asked to produce a play of mine, I had *The Bombay Trunk* cleaned up and ready for him.

The premiere in the fall of 2002 came at a very busy time for me. I drove to San Francisco, attended the dress rehearsal that night, had dinner and flew overnight to Sydney, Australia. I'd been asked to be the "International Author" honoree, part of the extensive Cultural Festival attached to the Gay Games in the antipodean city. I traveled along with hundreds of athletes and their partners, and quickly hooked up with several acquaintances from the East Coast who were in Sydney either to compete in the games or to report on the events. While there, I gave readings of my work, hosted a book launch, was interviewed on stage, on video and on the radio, judged a poetry slam and even emceed a talent contest. The weather was perfect, the city was lovely, the people were amazingly friendly, and the central area of Sydney—Hyde Park—was totally given over to the hundred thousand international attendees of the Gay Games. It was one of the great experiences of my life.

Since then I've gone back to work polishing and collecting published and unpublished short stories for two possible collections, keyboarding and gathering essays, reviews, and poems for more future books. I've also gone back to an unpublished novella from 1976 and turned it into a full length novel. Several years ago, a friend recommended that I collect, annotate, and present all of the material I had gathered and still had in storage from my days as publisher of Sea Horse Press and editor of Gay Presses of New York. I did so, and in 2002 I presented it at University of Southern California's ONE Institute, as an exhibit called *Early Gay Presses of New York.*

That exhibit went on to be shown at the Main Library in San Francisco and the Anderson Library at the University of Minnesota in Minneapolis, and I wrote lectures to accompany it for presentation at those places and at the Canadian National Archives in Ottawa, Ontario, when I spoke there this past February. As a result of the interest garnered, I'm planning future exhibitions of the work and I'm also writing a memoir, tentatively titled *Art & Death in Greenwich Village,* dealing with the fifteen or so years I was involved with these pathbreaking GLBT publishing companies.

In addition, in 2004, Haworth Press will republish my sci-fi gender-bender epic, *Dryland's End* in a proper manner. A small press production, it was swamped when it came out in 1995 by the success of *Like People in History,* put out by a major house. Also due out this autumn, from the University of Wisconsin Press, is a short autobiographical novel, *Fred in Love,* about me and my remarkable cat and friend, when we were two free-wheeling bachelors in Manhattan in the 1970s.

Living in Los Angeles, naturally enough I've acquired a show business manager and media agent and I am kept very busy writing and rewriting plays and original screenplays, and preparing film and tv treatments based on some of my published work. One of those scripts is science fiction, as is a recently written novella, *Ingoldsby,* a unique time-travel story told entirely in documents. As my epic is set up for two sequels, science fiction may well end up being my focus for the coming decade.

BIOGRAPHICAL AND CRITICAL SOURCES:

BOOKS

Bergman, David, editor, *The Violet Hour: The Violet Quill Club and the Making of Gay Culture,* Columbia University Press, 2003.

Bergman, David, editor, *The Violet Quill Reader,* St. Martin's Press, 1994.

Bouldry, Brian, editor, *Wrestling with the Angel,* Riverside Books, 1995.

Canning, Richard, *Gay Fiction Speaks: Twelve Interviews,* Columbia University Press, 2000.

Contemporary Authors Autobiography Series, Volume 13, Gale (Detroit), 1991.

Gay & Lesbian Literary Companion, Visible Ink Press, 1995.

Newman, Leslea, editor, *Bearing the Unbearable,* Crossing Press, 1995.

Picano, Felice, *Ambidextrous: The Secret Lives of Children,* Gay Presses of New York, 1985.

Picano, Felice, *Men Who Loved Me,* Dutton, 1989.

Picano, Felice, *A House on the Ocean, a House on the Bay: A Memoir,* Faber and Faber (Boston), 1997.

Schneider, Jr., Richard, editor, *The Best of The Harvard Gay & Lesbian Review,* Temple University Press, 1997.

Shernoff, Michael, editor, *Gay Widowers,* Hayworth Press, 1997.

PERIODICALS

A/B (special issue of *The Modern Language Association Quarterly*), fall, 2000, Kevin Stone Fries and Felice Picano, "Prelude to Process: Sources of Felice Picano's Lifewriting."

Advocate, April 15, 1997, Malcolm Boyd, review of *A House on the Ocean, a House on the Bay,* p. 53; September 15, 1998, Robrt L. Pela, "A Writer's Journey: Felice Picano Talks about His Latest Novel, a Tale of Love and Travel through Time," p. 64; December 21, 1999, Robrt L. Pela, review of *The Book of Lies,* p. 73; July 3, 2001, Drew Limsky, review of *Onyx,* p. 65.

Art & Understanding, November, 1999, Greg Herren, "Felice Picano: A Retrospective," and Kelly McQuain, "Lies and Lives: Interview with Felice Picano."

Bay Area Reporter, October 7, 1999, Deborah Peifer, "Purple Reign."

Booklist, July, 1995, Charles Harmon, review of *Like People in History,* p. 1860; April 15, 1997, Charles Harmon, review of *A House on the Ocean, a House on the Bay,* p. 1378; November 1, 1999, Whitney Scott, review of *The Book of Lies,* p. 509; April 1, 2001, Michael Spinella, review of *Onyx,* p. 1448.

Chiron Review, October, 2000, Robert Peters, "Felice Picano Featured and Interviewed."

Frontiers, October 15, 1999, Doug Sadownick, "Survivor: Felice Picano."

Gay and Lesbian Review Worldwide, November-December, 2001, Michael Wynne, "All the Satirized People," p. 42.

Gay and Lesbian Times of San Diego, November 18, 1999, Salvatore Sapienza, "Tales of a Founding Father."

Harvard Gay & Lesbian Review, fall, 1998.

James White Review, fall, 1999, "Telling the Truth in Fiction—Andrew Holleran and Felice Picano on the Violet Club and After."

Just out in Portland, October 15, 1999, Christopher Cuttone, "Look Back in Lavender," and Flora Sussely, "Talking to Felice Picano."

Lambda Book Report, July-August, 1995, Michael Bronski, review of *Like People in History,* p. 19; March, 1997, Walter Holland, review of *A House on the Ocean, a House on the Bay,* p. 11; October, 1998, Jaime Manrique, review of *Looking Glass Lives,* p. 17; April, 1999, David May, review of *Best Gay Erotica, 1999,* p. 23; October, 1999, Karl Woelz, review of *The Book of Lies,* p. 12; November, 1999, Greg Herren, "Felice Picano: Sex, Lies, and Manuscripts," p. 6; January, 2000, Felice Picano, "Letter to the Editor," p. 5; June, 2001, Greg Herren, "As I Lay Dying," p. 27.

Library Journal, February 15, 1989; November 1, 1989; June 1, 1997, Richard Violette, review of *A House on the Ocean, a House on the Bay,* p. 100; September 15, 1998, Phillip Oliver, review of *Looking Glass Lives,* p. 13; September 1, 1999, Theodore R. Salvadori, review of *The Book of Lies,* p. 235; April 1, 2001, Roger Durbin, review of *Onyx,* p. 134; May 1, 2003, Michael Rogers, review of *Ambidextrous* and *Men Who Loved Me,* p. 160; June 15, 2003, Martha Cornog, review of *The Joy of Gay Sex,* p. 11.

New York Times Book Review, December 2, 1979; July 16, 1995, Suzanne Berne, "Men in Love," p. 21; December 12, 1999, David Lipsky, review of *The Book of Lies,* p. 28.

Publishers Weekly, December 9, 1988; September 22, 1989; October 5, 1992, review of *The New Joy of Gay Sex,* p. 58; June 19, 1995, review of *Like People in History,* p. 51; March 17, 1997, review of *A House on the Ocean, a House on the Bay,* p. 70; August 17, 1998, review of *Looking Glass Lives,* p. 49; October 25, 1999, review of *The Book of Lies,* p. 49.

Village Voice, December 24, 1979.

ONLINE

Alyson Books, http://www.alyson.com/ (May 26, 2000).

*   *   *

PICKELL, David

PERSONAL: Male.

ADDRESSES: *Home*—Simi Valley, CA. *Agent*—c/o Author Mail, Tuttle Publishing, 153 Milk St., Boston, MA 02109.

CAREER: Writer, editor, and explorer.

WRITINGS:

(With Wally Slagian) *Diving Bali: A Guide to the World's Greatest Diving,* Tuttle Publishing (Boston, MA), 2000.

Kamoro: Between the Tides in Irian Jaya, photographs by Kal Muller, Aopao Productions (Jakarta, Indonesia), 2001.

Between the Tides: A Fascinating Journey among the Kamoro of New Guinea, photographs by Kal Muller, Periplus Editions: Tuttle Publishing (Boston, MA), 2003.

EDITOR

Borneo: Journey into the Tropical Rainforest, photographs by Kal Muller, Passport Books (Lincolnwood, IL), 1990.

East of Bali, from Lombok to Timor: Periplus Adventure Guide, photographs by Kal Muller, Passport Books (Lincolnwood, IL), 1991.

Kalimantan: Indonesian Borneo, text and photographs by Kal Muller, Periplus Editions (Singapore), 1996.

Maluku: Indonesian Spice Islands, text and photographs by Kal Muller, Periplus Editions (Singapore), 1997.

SIDELIGHTS: An explorer and travel writer, David Pickell has written or edited books about diving, exploration, and adventure in exotic locations around the world. With coauthor Wally Slagian, Pickell wrote *Diving Bali: A Guide to the World's Greatest Diving,* in which the authors provide detailed descriptions of some of the best places for exciting and visually rich diving off the Balinese coast. Pickell and Slagian explore the uniqueness of the sites they profile, and add informative background information on topics such as marine life, reef ecosystems, weather, tides, and more. The book also includes detailed maps and contact information for dive operations, transportation, and hotels.

In *Between the Tides: A Fascinating Journey among the Kamoro of New Guinea,* Pickell and photographer Kal Muller present a detailed profile of a culture once thought to be extinct. The Kamoro are a nomadic group numbering fewer than 20,000 who live in Irian Jaya, the Indonesian half of New Guinea. Long-term exposure to Dutch, Malay, and other Indonesian cultures was thought to have wiped out traditional Kamoro ways of life. However, when Muller chanced upon a Kamoro initiation ceremony, he recognized that the culture was still intact. *Between the Tides* documents Pickell and Muller's 1997 travels among the Kamoro as they documented cultural practices, ceremonies, social customs, and other unique aspects of Kamoro life, including ceremonies and practices being rediscovered or recreated. The book provides "both contemporary and historical views of this little-known culture," commented Lucille M. Boone in *Library Journal,* and includes material on the area's wildlife, geology, history, and plant life.

BIOGRAPHICAL AND CRITICAL SOURCES:

PERIODICALS

Booklist, September 15, 1996, review of *Borneo: Journey into the Tropical Rainforest,* p. 212.
Library Journal, May 1, 2003, Lucille M. Boone, review of *Between the Tides: A Fascinating Journey among the Kamoro of New Guinea,* p. 128.*

* * *

PIETRI, Pedro (Juan) 1943-2004

OBITUARY NOTICE—See index for *CA* sketch: Born March 21, 1943, in Ponce, PR; died of renal failure March 3, 2004, while on an airplane flight from Mexico to New York. Educator and author. Pietri was

a prominent Puerto Rican poet and playwright whose writings captured the experiences of Nuyoricans—Puerto Ricans who have settled in New York City. Encouraged as a boy by his aunt to write poems, he worked a variety of menial jobs in New York's garment district before being drafted into the U.S. Army. Seeing action in Vietnam proved to be a radicalizing experience for him, and upon returning to New York he pursued his art with greater vehemence. His most famous poem, "Puerto Rican Obituary," had its early day in the sun when Pietri read it in public in 1969 at the Methodist Church in East Harlem, which the Young Lords activist group had briefly taken over. The poem, first published around 1971, captures themes with which Pietri would be concerned throughout his life, such as the injustice of Puerto Rico's status as neither independent nation nor American state, and the struggles of Puerto Ricans to make a place for themselves in American society. Becoming a powerful voice for his people, Pietri later helped found the Nuyorican Poets Café on the Lower East Side, a venue that helped inspire other Latino poets and where Pietri performed such pieces as "The Spanglish National Anthem" and "El Puerto Rican Embassy." In the late-1960s and early 1970s, he also encouraged other poets as a creative writing instructor at the State University of New York at Buffalo, at the Cultural Council Foundation in New York, and as a conductor of children's workshops. Other poetry collections by Pietri include *The Blue and the Gray* (1975), *Uptown Train* (1980), and *Traffic Violations* (1983); he also penned plays and play collections, including *Dead Heroes Have No Feelings* (1978), *Jesus Is Leaving* (1978), and *Illusions of a Revolving Door: Plays* (1992).

OBITUARIES AND OTHER SOURCES:

PERIODICALS

Chicago Tribune, March 8, 2004, Section 4, p. 9.
New York Times, March 6, 2004, p. A25.

* * *

PIRARO, Dan 1958-

PERSONAL: Born 1958, in Kansas City, MO; son of Fred (a petroleum engineer) and Carol Lee (a secretary) Piraro; married Kalin Burke, 1980 (divorced, 1996), married Ashley Louise Smith, April 15, 2002; children: (first marriage) Katherine Killian, Kathryn Kaitlyn.

Education: Attended Washington University (St. Louis, MO). *Politics:* Liberal Democrat. *Hobbies and other interests:* Painting, animal rights and liberation, skiing/snowboarding, travel, stand-up comedy.

ADDRESSES: Home—11 John St., #800, New York, NY 10038. *Agent*—c/o Author Mail, King Features, 888 7th Ave., New York, NY 10019. *E-mail*—piraro@earthlink.net.

CAREER: Cartoonist, illustrator, creator of the comic strip "Bizarro." Worked variously as a store manager, display artist, rock musician, and designer of ads for Neiman Marcus and others.

MEMBER: National Cartoonists Society (New York Metro area chapter president).

AWARDS, HONORS: Reuben Award, National Cartoonists Society, 1999, 2000, and 2001, for best newspaper cartoon panel.

WRITINGS:

Bizarro, Chronicle Books (San Francisco, CA), 1986.
Too Bizarro, Chronicle Books (San Francisco, CA), 1988.
Mondo Bizarro, Chronicle Books (San Francisco, CA), 1989.
More Bizarro, Chronicle Books (San Francisco, CA), 1990.
Sumo Bizarro, Chronicle Books (San Francisco, CA), 1990.
Glasnost Bizarro, Chronicle Books (San Francisco, CA), 1990.
Post-Modern Bizarro, Chronicle Books (San Francisco, CA), 1991.
The Book of Lame Excuses, Chronicle Books (San Francisco, CA), 1991.
The Best of Bizarro, Chronicle Books (San Francisco, CA), 1992.
The Best of Bizarro, Volume II, Chronicle Books (San Francisco, CA), 1994.
Bizarro Number 9: A Collection of Bizarro Cartoons, Andrews and McMeel (Kansas City, MO), 1995.
Bizarro Number 10, Andrews and McMeel (Kansas City, MO), 1996.
Bizarro among the Savages: A Relatively Famous Guy's Experiences on the Road and in the Homes of Strangers, Andrews McMeel (Kansas City, MO), 1997.

Life Is Strange and So Are You, Andrews McMeel (Kansas City, MO), 2001.
The Three Little Pigs Buy the White House, Griffin (New York, NY), 2004.

SIDELIGHTS: Dan Piraro's long-running cartoon strip "Bizarro" was first syndicated with Chronicle Features in 1985, when it replaced Gary Larson's "Far Side," which had moved to Universal Press Syndicate. Ten years later, "Bizarro" moved to Universal as Larson retired. Piraro's strip is published in more than 200 daily and Sunday newspapers in the United States, Canada, and overseas, and he visits cities where it appears, starring in his own *The Bizarro Boloney Show.*

Piraro was born in Kansas City, Missouri. He spent his teen years in Tulsa, Oklahoma and attended college in St. Louis. Piraro was writing a science fiction strip in the early 1980s, and having no luck getting it published. When he saw how successful "Far Side" had become, he collected some of his own strange cartoons and sent them off to several syndicates. When Chronicle did have room for his strip, he didn't have a name for it. Managing editor Stuart Dodds picked "Bizarro" from a selection of names Piraro had solicited from friends.

When Piraro launched his collection, *Bizarro Number 9: A Collection of Bizarro Cartoons,* his publisher had no budget for a tour, and so he called on fans to finance one. He had collected email addresses through his Web site and sent out a plea for bed and board, meals, and plane tickets for his "The Bizarro 1995 Lap of Luxury Book Tour." He immediately began receiving invitations from families who said he could have a child's bed, and the more wealthy who could offer a room with a view of the pool. At one point he stayed in the skull-decorated apartment of a surfer. Piraro documents his adventure in *Bizarro among the Savages: A Relatively Famous Guy's Experiences on the Road and in the Homes of Strangers,* a running commentary on his couch-to-couch adventure in San Francisco, Los Angeles, Miami, Cleveland, Pittsburgh, Atlanta, Raleigh/Durham, and Portland.

A reviewer for *Whatzup* noted that upon arriving on the West Coast, Piraro realized that he and the person meeting him had not prearranged a way to identify each other. "Seeing a young man with a huge sign taped to his back that read 'Dan Piraro Your Fly Is Open,' Piraro figured that this was the guy. Like nearly everyone he met on his book tour, Piraro learned that his shy-biased fears of lunatics was unfounded, and he hit things off instantly with his host." The reviewer also noted that Piraro experienced a common phenomena, in that people shared with him the very intimate details of their lives. "Piraro thus heard over a dozen 'life stories' on his trip and began to crave them like a soap opera junkie. He was rarely disappointed and shares them with the reader." A *Publishers Weekly* contributor wrote that both fans of the strip "and those curious to encounter a colorful cast of real-life Americans will enjoy this offbeat twist on the travelogue/memoir."

BIOGRAPHICAL AND CRITICAL SOURCES:

BOOKS

Piraro, Dan, *Bizarro among the Savages: A Relatively Famous Guy's Experiences on the Road and in the Homes of Strangers,* Andrews McMeel (Kansas City, MO), 1997.

PERIODICALS

Editor & Publisher, August 9, 1986, David Astor, "How Dan Piraro came to draw 'Bizarro,'" pp. 32-33.
Publishers Weekly, October 13, 1997, review of *Bizarro among the Savages,* p. 68.

ONLINE

Dan Piraro Home Page, http://www.bizarro.com (January 9, 2004).
Planet Cartoonist, http://www.planetcartoonist.com/ (January 9, 2004), "Ten Stupid Questions" (interview with Piraro).
Whatzup http://www.whatzup.com/ (February, 1999), review of *Bizarro among the Savages.*

*   *   *

POHL-WEARY, Emily

PERSONAL: Female. *Hobbies and other interests:* Video games.

ADDRESSES: Home—Toronto, Ontario, Canada. *Agent*—Between the Lines Press, 720 Bathurst St., Suite 404, Toronto, Ontario M5S 2R4, Canada. *E-mail*—Emily@kissmachine.org.

CAREER: Writer, editor, and filmmaker. *Broken Pencil* magazine, coeditor; *Kiss Machine,* founder and editor.

AWARDS, HONORS: Hugo Award, and Toronto Book Awards finalist, 2003, both for *Better to Have Loved: The Life of Judith Merril.*

WRITINGS:

(With Judith Merril) *Better to Have Loved: The Life of Judith Merril,* Between the Lines (Toronto, Ontario, Canada), 2002.
Girls Who Bite Back: Witches, Mutants, Slayers, and Freaks, Sumach Press, 2004.

Contributor to periodicals, including *Shift, Lola, Taddle Creek, Fireweed, This,* and *Now.*

WORK IN PROGRESS: A novel titled *Sugar's Empty;* editing Tamara Faith Berger's novel *Messalina.*

SIDELIGHTS: Canadian writer and editor Emily Pohl-Weary is the founder and editor of the magazine *Kiss Machine,* as well as the coeditor of *Broken Pencil.* An avowed pop culture fanatic, Pohl-Weary also has literary roots in the avant-garde past through her grandmother, twentieth-century science-fiction writer Judith Merril. In 2002 Pohl-Weary explored those roots in *Better to Have Loved: The Life of Judith Merril.*

Merril, considered a pioneer of twentieth-century fiction, left her autobiography unfinished at her death in 1997, and willed the project to her granddaughter. In addition to complete instructions, Merril also left a number of taped interviews recorded by Pohl-Weary. In an interview with Michael Bryson for the *Danforth Review,* Pohl-Weary described Merril as "a science fiction writer and editor, feminist, cultural theorist and anti-war activist," and noted that the novels and short fiction Merril penned during the 1950s and 1960s "acted as catalysts that launched the careers of many important writers." Pohl-Weary also quoted writer J. G. Ballard: "Science fiction, I suspect, is now dead and probably died about the time that Judy closed her anthology and left to found her memorial library in the genre in Toronto. I remember my last sight of her, surrounded by her friends and all the books she loved, shouting me down whenever I tried to argue with her, the strongest woman in a genre for the most part created by timid and weak men."

Among Merril's works were *Daughters of Earth, That Only a Mother,* and *Shadow on the Hearth.* An American by birth, in 1968 she immigrated to Toronto, Canada, due to her objection to the Vietnam War. Work at Rochdale College and CBC Radio followed, as Merril developed a reputation as a respected cultural critic and celebrity, aided by her establishment of a science-fiction library in Toronto. Towards the end of her life Merril became increasingly pessimistic, viewing technology as an oppressor and arguing that those few who controlled it would control the entire world..

"At first, it was difficult to be surrounded by her voice and thoughts," Pohl-Weary noted to Bryson of her experience in completing her grandmother's life story, "because I missed and also had some mixed feelings toward her, due to unresolved family dynamics, but it got easier as time passed." Her work was received enthusiastically by reviewers, and in 2003 *Better to Have Loved* was honored with both a Hugo award and a Toronto Book Award nomination. In an online review for *SFRevu.com* Asta Sinusas called *Better to Have Loved* "a book about love—the passionate love Judith Merril had for particular moments and people in her life, of which this book is an expression, and the love of her granddaughter who completed the manuscript in her own expression of devotion."

A tireless editor who has founded several magazines of her own, Pohl-Weary has also embarked on a career as a fiction writer, beginning with the novel *Sugar's Empty.* A coming-of-age tale revolving around a young woman struggling to overcome the death of her boyfriend and take charge of her own life, the novel also deals with the corporate bombardment of advertising that promotes images of sex, drugs, and violence. In Pohl-Weary's hands, Sugar evolves from a vapid, self-conscious teen to a self-assured woman who takes control of her own destiny.

BIOGRAPHICAL AND CRITICAL SOURCES:

ONLINE

Danforth Review, http://www.danforthreview.com/ (October 7, 2003), interview with Pohl-Weary.

Kiss Machine Web Site, http://kissmachine.org/ (April 17, 2003).
SFRevu.com, http://www.sfrevu.com/ (February, 5, 2002), Asta Sinusas, review of *Better to Have Loved: The Life of Judith Merril.**

*   *   *

POLLACK, Kenneth M(ichael) 1966-

PERSONAL: Born 1966. *Education:* Yale University, B.A., 1988; Massachusetts Institute of Technology, Ph.D., 1996.

ADDRESSES: Office—Saban Center for Middle East Policy, The Brookings Institution, 1775 Massachusetts Ave. NW, Washington, DC 20036. *E-mail*—sabancenter@brookings.edu.

CAREER: Middle East policy analyst. Central Intelligence Agency, Washington, DC, Iran-Iraq military analyst, 1988-95; National Security Council, director for Near East and South Asian affairs, 1995-96, director for Persian Gulf affairs, 1999-2001; Council of Foreign Relations, director for national security studies, 2001-02; Saban Center for Middle East Policy, Brookings Institution, Washington, DC, director of research and senior fellow, Foreign Policy Studies. National Defense University, senior research professor, 1998-99, 2001.

WRITINGS:

Saudi Military Effectiveness in the 1990s, Washington Institute for Near East Policy (Washington, DC), 1999.
Arabs at War: Military Effectiveness, 1948-1991, University of Nebraska Press (Lincoln, NE), 2002.
The Threatening Storm: The Case for Invading Iraq, Random House (New York, NY), 2002.

Contributor to journals, including *International Security, Middle East Journal,* and *Foreign Affairs.* Author of studies for RAND Corporation.

SIDELIGHTS: Kenneth M. Pollack is an expert on Middle East policy who, in his positions at the Central Intelligence Agency during the 1980s and on the

National Security Council in more recent years, has maintained his view that the United States should invade Iraq and eliminate Iraqi dictator Saddam Hussein. In his 2002 book *The Threatening Storm: The Case for Invading Iraq* Pollack presents a detailed overview of the repressive regime of Hussein and marshals compelling evidence in support of his own "reluctantly arrived at" position that, as *Nation* contributor Ian S. Lustick explained, "only an American invasion, mounted to do the job even without help from Middle Eastern or European allies, can succeed" at eliminating the threat Hussein poses to not only the United States but Iraq's Middle East neighbors.

The Threatening Storm is the work of a man who "has spent virtually his entire professional life wrestling with the problem of Iraq," according to *Washington Monthly* contributor Joshua Micah Marshall. A timely volume that numbers close to 400 pages, Pollack's book presents readers with "a complete treatment of a critical question of national security policy," according to Marshall. Praising the book as "an indisputable success," Marshall went on to note that "Pollack manages to eschew the cant, stupidity, and obfuscation which are the common currency of much of the current public debate over Iraq policy and has produced one of the key books—probably the key book—for anyone trying to grapple with the Iraq question." That many were trying to grapple with that question was clear, and within months the U.S. government had followed Pollack's advice and ousted the Hussein regime as part of its ongoing war on terrorism waged in the wake of the September 11, 2001 attacks on the United States.

The Threatening Storm had as its genesis an article Pollack published in the March/April 2002 issue of *Foreign Affairs* in which he candidly addresses the question of war with Iraq. His well-substantiated argument is made within the context of rectifying the ineffective policy decisions of past administrations, most notably that of President Bill Clinton. "Thanks to Washington's own missed opportunities and others' shameful cynicism, there are no longer any good policy options toward Iraq," Pollack maintained in his article. "After the more immediate danger posed by Osama bin Laden's al Qaeda network has been dealt with. . . . The United States should invade Iraq, eliminate the present regime, and pave the way for a successor prepared to abide by its international commitments and live in peace with its neighbors." Options such as containment and deterrence are discussed

and rejected by Pollack, who goes on to provide a detailed, fact-based analysis of invasion strategies, timing, and the process of rebuilding Iraq in the war's aftermath. Pollack's 2002 book *Arabs at War: Military Effectiveness, 1948-1991* fuels the author's arguments for war by providing what *Library Journal* contributor Dale Ferris explained is "a highly specialized military history" of the Middle East nations, complete with an analysis of the "factors that have consistently hindered" their efforts at warfare and a "robust assessment of their strengths and weaknesses" in past battles.

Response to *The Threatening Storm* was overwhelmingly positive, although Pollack's arguments were closely critiqued by several critics. In the *Naval War College Review,* Preston C. Rodrigue noted that, although Pollack "argues his case well, going beyond the vituperative pronouncements of the [George W. Bush] administration to link operational objectives to national strategy, . . . he does not spend much time on the reconstruction of the country, which is, after all, the reason for invasion in the first place." Jack F. Matlock , Jr. questioned whether Pollack's comparisons of containment and deterrence to "the appeasement of Hitler in 1938" and in his *New York Times Book Review* article maintained that "such misplaced comparisons smack of hysteria, and damage Pollack's credibility." However, most critics agreed that *The Threatening Storm* should be required reading for U.S. citizens in the first months of 2003, as war loomed in the Middle East. As Richard Bernstein stated in the *New York Times,* "It's fair to say that whatever your feelings about the question of Iraq, you owe it to yourself to read Mr. Pollack's book, which is both hawkish and judicious."

BIOGRAPHICAL AND CRITICAL SOURCES:

PERIODICALS

Christian Century, December 18, 2002, David Heim, review of *The Threatening Storm: The Case for Invading Iraq,* p. 36.

Commentary, December, 2002, Frederick W. Kagan, review of *The Threatening Storm,* p. 69.

Economist, November 9, 2002, review of *The Threatening Storm.*

Foreign Affairs, March-April, 2002, Kenneth M. Pollack, "Next Stop Baghdad?," p. 32.

Library Journal, August, 2002, Dale Farris, review of *Arabs at War: Military Effectiveness,* p. 118.

Nation, March 24, 2003, Ian S. Lustick, "Storm Warnings for a Supply-Side War," p. 23.

Naval War College Review, winter, 2003, Preston C. Rodrigue, review of *The Threatening Storm,* p. 174.

Newsweek, February 17, 2003, Seth Mnookin, "On Iraq's Cockeyed Optimist" (interview), p. 66.

New York Review of Books, December 19, 2002, Brian Urquhart, "The Prospect of War," p. 16.

New York Times, October 22, 2002, Richard Bernstein, "Making a Case for a U.S. Invasion of Iraq," p. E5.

New York Times Book Review, October 20, 2002, Jack F. Matlock, Jr., "Deterring the Undeterrable," p. 11.

Publishers Weekly, August 5, 2002, p. 68; October 7, 2002, review of *The Threatening Storm,* p. 23.

Times Literary Supplement, January 31, 2003, Peter Baehr, "The Critical Path," p. 3.

Wall Street Journal, October 10, 2002, Asla Aydintasbas, "Yes, Change the Regime," p. D10.

Washington Monthly, November, 2002, Joshua Micah Marshall, "The Reluctant Hawk: The Skeptical Case for Regime Change in Iraq," pp. 43-47.

ONLINE

Brookings Institution Web site, http://www.brook.edu/ (April 16, 2003).*

*   *   *

PORTALES, Marco 1948-

PERSONAL: Born October 22, 1948, in Edinburg, TX; son of Toribio (a grocery store owner) and Carmen (Moya) Portales; married February 12, 1972; wife's name C. Rita; children: Carlos Antonio, Marie Christina. *Ethnicity:* "Mexican American." *Education:* University of Texas—Austin, B.A., 1970; State University of New York—Buffalo, Ph.D., 1974. *Religion:* Roman Catholic.

ADDRESSES: Home—3800 Chaucer Ct., Bryan, TX 77802. *Office*—Department of English, Texas A & M University, College Station, TX 77843; fax: 979-862-2292. *E-mail*—mportales@tamu.edu.

CAREER: University of California—Berkeley, assistant professor of English, 1974-79; University of Houston—Clear Lake, TX, associate professor of English, 1979-91; Texas A & M University, College Station, executive assistant to the president, 1996-97, and member of English faculty. Texas Southwest College, dean of arts and sciences, 1986-88. Public speaker.

MEMBER: Society for the Study of the Multi-Ethnic Literatures of the United States (president, 1992-94), Modern Language Association of America, Texas Association of Chicanos in Higher Education.

WRITINGS:

Youth and Age in American Literature, Peter Lang (New York, NY), 1989.

Crowding Out Latinos: Mexican Americans in the Public Consciousness, Temple University Press (Philadelphia, PA), 2000.

WORK IN PROGRESS: Quality Education for Latinos, Too, with wife, Rita Portales; *Latino Sun, Rising.*

SIDELIGHTS: Marco Portales told *CA:* "I write to help improve the lives of Latinos in the United States."

BIOGRAPHICAL AND CRITICAL SOURCES:

PERIODICALS

Library Journal, February 1, 2000, Gwen Gregory, review of *Crowding Out Latinos: Mexican Americans in the Public Consciousness,* p. 107.

MELUS, summer, 2001, John S. Christie, review of *Crowding Out Latinos,* p. 267.

*   *   *

POTVIN, Liza

PERSONAL: Born in France. *Education:* Attended University of Calgary and Queen's University; McMaster University, Ph.D., 1991.

ADDRESSES: Office—Department of English, Malaspina College, Nanaimo, 900 Fifth St., Nanaimo, British Columbia V9R 5S5, Canada. *E-mail*—potvin@mala.bc.ca.

CAREER: Educator and author. Malaspina College, Nanaimao, British Columbia, Canada, instructor, then professor in English.

WRITINGS:

White Lies for My Mother, NeWest Press (Edmonton, Alberta, Canada), 1992.
The Traveller's Hat, Raincoast Books (Vancouver, BC, Canada), 2003.

SIDELIGHTS: Canadian educator and author Liza Potvin has published two books: *White Lies for My Mother,* a memoir about the sexual abuse she suffered as a child, and *The Traveller's Hat,* a collection of short stories. According to Lisa Schmidt in *Quill & Quire,* Potvin's *White Lies for My Mother* "transforms her pain into strength and her anguish into hope." Speaking of *The Traveller's Hat,* Janet Forest in the *Link* stated that "Potvin's writing brings the reader into her world by brilliantly capturing the personality and texture of each character and setting."

BIOGRAPHICAL AND CRITICAL SOURCES:

PERIODICALS

Canadian Literature, fall, 1993, Marilyn Iwama, review of *White Lies for My Mother,* pp. 124-126.
Link, June 10, 2003, Janet Forest, review of *The Traveller's Hat.*
Quill & Quire, September, 1992, Lisa Schmidt, review of *White Lies for My Mother,* p. 64.*

*   *   *

PRICE, Hugh B(ernard) 1941-

PERSONAL: Born November 22, 1941, in Washington, DC; son of Kline Armond, Sr. (a physician), and Charlotte (a homemaker and career volunteer; maiden name, Schuster) Price; married Marilyn Lloyd, December 29, 1963; children: Traer, Janeen, Lauren. *Education:* Amherst College, B.A., 1963; Yale University Law School, LL.B., 1966.

ADDRESSES: Home—21 Trenor Drive, New Rochelle, NY 10804.

CAREER: Admitted to the Connecticut Bar, 1966; New Haven Legal Assistance Association, neighborhood attorney, 1966-68; Black Coalition of New Haven, executive director, 1968-70; Cogen, Holt & Associates, partner, 1970-76; City of New Haven, Human Resources Administration, director, 1977-78; *New York Times* Editorial Board, 1978-82; WNET/Thirteen TV, New York, NY, senior vice president, 1982-88; Rockefeller Foundation, vice president, 1988-94; National Urban League, president and chief executive officer, 1994-2003. Board of Directors, National Association for the Advancement of Colored People (NAACP) Legal Defense and Education Fund, 1986-88; assistant counsel, Urban Renewal Agency, New Haven Redevelopment Agency; served on board of Education Testing Service; member, boards of directors, Metropolitan Life Insurance Company, Verizon Wireless, Sears Roebuck, Mayo Clinic Foundation, Committee for Economic Development; keynote lecturer at National Press Club, Fortune 500 Forum, Detroit Economic Club, Los Angeles Urban League, others; guest on television shows, including *Crossfire, Meet the Press, NewsHour with Jim Lehrer, Charlie Rose,* and *Today Show.*

MEMBER: American Philosophical Society, NAACP, Council on Foreign Relations, Academy of Political Science, Century Association, Alpha Phi Alpha Fraternity, Rockefeller Brothers Fund of New York City (trustee, 1987-88), Municipal Art Society of New York City (trustee, 1990—), Public Development Corporation of New York City (trustee, 1991—), Boulé, Westchester Clubmen.

AWARDS, HONORS: Honorary degrees, Yale University, Amherst College, and others; Yale University Law School Medal of Honor; Hunter College President's Medal; Distinguished Service Award, Council of Chief State School Officers, 2000.

WRITINGS:

The Role of the Urban League Movement in Overcoming Inner-City Poverty: Challenges for the Twenty-first Century, William Monroe Trotter Institute

Occasional Paper, number 32, William Monroe Trotter Institute, University of Massachusetts (Boston, MA), 1995.

Education Accountability: Saving Schools—and Students, edited by Lee A. Daniels, National Urban League (Long Prairie, MN), 1999.

To Be Equal, edited by Lee A. Daniels, National Urban League (New York, NY), 1999, published as *To Be Equal: A Look at Our Nation,* 2001.

Destination: The American Dream, National Urban League (New York, NY), 2001.

Achievement Matters: Getting Your Child the Best Education Possible, Kensington Books (New York, NY), 2002.

Contributor to numerous magazines and periodicals, including *New York Times, Wall Street Journal, Education Week, Review of Black Political Economy, Los Angeles Times, San Francisco Chronicle, Phi Delta Kappan,* and *Chronicle of Higher Education.* Author of weekly syndicated column "To Be Equal" and of weekly radio commentary.

SIDELIGHTS: A lifelong advocate for the inner-city poor, for racial harmony, and for improved education and youth development, attorney Hugh B. Price served for nine years as president and chief executive officer of the National Urban League before resigning in 2003. In addition to numerous articles, speeches, and a weekly newspaper column, "To Be Equal," Price has written four books on the subjects of overcoming poverty and maximizing education for American children.

Price grew up in a middle-class family in Washington, D.C., where his father was a physician. He attended segregated schools until 1953, when his parents moved him to Georgetown Day School, along with other African American families who supported integration. The following year, Price was among the first black students to attend integrated schools in Washington, D.C. Throughout his high school and college career, he was one of only a handful of black students in his classes.

Price began working with teens in an antipoverty program while a law student at Yale University. After an early legal career in New Haven, Connecticut, he branched out into urban affairs and human resources before accepting a position as an editorial writer for the *New York Times,* where he wrote about education and domestic policy. In 1982, Price accepted a position at WNET/Thirteen, New York's public television station, and the nation's largest. In his six years as senior vice president, Price helped to bring about such notable programming as *American Masters, Childhood, The Mind,* and *Art of the Western World.* In 1984 he became director of national programming, helping to develop the series *Nature* and *Great Performances.*

In 1988, Price became vice president of the Rockefeller Foundation, where he helped to launch the successful National Guard Youth ChalleNGe Corps, the Coalition of Community Foundations for Youth, and the National Commission on Teaching and America's Future.

As president of the National Urban League, Price revived an ailing organization and reintroduced its mission to the nation. He helped to triple its endowment and reorganize its board of directors and staff. Price was also responsible for launching the Campaign for African-American Achievement; establishing the National Urban League Institute for Opportunity and Equality; reviving the league's magazine, *Opportunity;* and helping to set up its new headquarters on Wall Street in New York City. He also initiated the Achievement Matters public service campaign and the National Achievers Society for black students.

In a speech delivered early in his tenure with the National Urban League, Price established the new goals of ending separatism of African Americans and recognizing that poor schools, troubled young people, and high unemployment affect all races. He called on African Americans who could afford to, to donate money to help pay for programs for inner-city youth.

Speaking to the Detroit Economic Club in 1996, Price told the story of America's blue-collar urban workers whose employers moved factories overseas or replaced workers with technology, leaving once-prosperous families in poverty. He spoke about the so-called working homeless, who are left out of the loop in America's economic boom. He also spoke about welfare reform, which would put thousands of mothers and children on the streets because there are not enough jobs to go around. In a 1994 interview with Gayle Pollard Terry of the *Los Angeles Times,* Price said, "This country is in deep denial about whether or not we create enough jobs. The labor market in the inner city is broken." In the Detroit speech, Price recommended creating jobs by hiring the poor to make urban infrastructure improvements. He warned about the growing resentment of the underprivileged and the danger that the economic gap could undermine American democracy and civil society.

Price's main objectives in his work with the Urban League have been job training for the poor and better education and guidance for youth. Price has long been an advocate of better education, through parental involvement, teacher development and higher pay, after-school programs, and a national commitment to using public funds for public education. The Urban League's motto has been Our Children = Our Destiny. In an article for the *Phi Delta Kappan,* Mark F. Goldberg quoted Price as asking, "How can states hold children responsible for higher standards with a straight face if they can't guarantee the higher-quality education that must go with those standards?" In November 1990, according to the article, Price made the prescient statement that, "Some day, frustrated corporations, worried about where their workers will come from, and exasperated parents, fed up with unresponsive school systems, just might join forces on behalf of such truly radical reform [as vouchers]."

In his 2002 book, *Achievement Matters: Getting Your Child the Best Education Possible,* Price focuses on everyday working-class parents as their child's first teacher and on ways they can encourage children up to the third grade to value education as its own reward. The book instructs parents on ways to become involved with their child's teachers, administrators, and school system. Price lists benchmarks for achievement at each grade level and stresses the importance of enrolling in challenging classes. He also offers ideas for provision of the latest technology in schools and for after-school programs that shelter children from involvement with gangs and drugs. Price advocates parents' reading to their children each day as one of the most important activities for building the literacy skills they need. He also writes about reliance on "mother wit," or parental instinct in knowing what is best for a child. The philosophy in Price's book is based on the Urban League's Campaign for African-American Achievement.

Leroy Hommerding, in *Library Journal,* called *Achievement Matters* a "valuable resource" that educa-tors can use to help parents partner in their children's success. A *Publishers Weekly* contributor found that the book provides "a plan for parents to inspire their children to achieve."

In a "To Be Equal" column, Price wrote, "Education is the great equalizer of American society. It unlocks the doors to children's futures." In an article for *USA Today,* Tamara Henry quoted Price as saying, "If we allow our young people to grow up believing that academic achievement is above them, beneath them or beside the point, then we've failed them as parents and as a society. It's the mission in life of anyone who has created life to equip children for success through education."

BIOGRAPHICAL AND CRITICAL SOURCES:

BOOKS

African American Almanac, 8th edition, Gale (Detroit, MI), 1999.
LoDico, John, "Hugh B. Price," *Contemporary Black Biography,* Volume 9, Gale (Detroit, MI), 1995.

PERIODICALS

Emerge, December-January, 1997, Lottie L. Joiner, "Price Fixing," interview with Hugh B. Price, p. 36.
Fortune, August 4, 1997, Roy S. Johnson, "'There Is Opportunity and There Is Action,' conversation with Hugh Price of the National Urban League," p. 67.
Jet, June 13, 1994, "Hugh Price Named President and Chief Executive of National Urban League," p. 26.
Library Journal, October 1, 2002, Leroy Hommerding, review of *Achievement Matters: Getting Your Child the Best Education Possible,* p. 112.
Los Angeles Times, July 3, 1994, Gayle Pollard Terry, "Hugh Price: Rebuilding the Urban League and the Inner City, as Well," p. M3.
Phi Delta Kappan, April, 2000, Mark F. Goldberg, "Committed to High-Quality Education for All Children: An Interview with Hugh Price," p. 604.
Publishers Weekly, August 5, 2002, "American Parenting," review of *Achievement Matters: Getting Your Child the Best Education Possible,* p. 67.

Vital Speeches, January 15, 1995, Hugh B. Price, "Public Discourse: Our Very Fate as a Civil Society Is at Stake," p. 213; March 1, 1996, Hugh B. Price, "Cities: The Soul of America: Make America Work for All Americans," p. 293.

ONLINE

Council of Chief State School Officers, http://www. ccsso.org/ (October 27, 2000), Billie Rollins and Kathleen Seiler Neary, "Hugh B. Price to Receive the Council of Chief State School Officers' 2000 Distinguished Service Award."

Kansas City Call, Internet Edition, http://www.kccall. com/ (March 7, 2003), Hugh B. Price, column "To Be Equal: Voices from the Affirmative Action Front."

Kensingtonbooks.com, http://www.kensingtonbooks. com/ (May, 2003), description of *Achievement Matters: Getting Your Child the Best Education Possible.*

Los Angeles Urban League, http://www.laul.org/ (May 6, 2003), "Hugh B. Price, President and Chief Executive Officer."

National Urban League, http://www.nul.org/ (June 17, 2002), Hugh B. Price, "Our Necessary Credo: Achievement Matters"; (May 6, 2003), Rosario Peters, "About Us: Hugh B. Price, President and Chief Executive Officer"; (March 28, 2003), "American Express, Pitney Bowes and Bank of America Spearhead Farewell Tribute to National Urban League President Hugh B. Price."

USA Today Online, http://usatoday.com/ (August 21, 2002), Tamara Henry, "Play a Big Role in Education."*

Q-R

QUINN, Tara Taylor (a pseudonym)

PERSONAL: Born in Toledo, OH; married. *Education:* B.A. (English).

ADDRESSES: Agent—c/o Author Mail, Harlequin Enterprises, P.O. Box 5190, Buffalo, NY 14240-5190.

CAREER: Novelist. Also worked as a high school English teacher and a freelance reporter for *Dayton Daily News,* Dayton, OH.

AWARDS, HONORS: Rita Award nomination, Romance Writers of America, 1993, for *Yesterday's Secrets; Affaire de Coeur* Award, best contemporary novel, 2001, for *My Sister, Myself;* Rita Award nomination, 2002, for *The Secret Son.*

WRITINGS:

ROMANCE

Yesterday's Secrets, Harlequin Enterprises (Buffalo, NY), 1993.

McGillus V. Wright, Harlequin Enterprises (Buffalo, NY), 1994.

No Cure for Love, Harlequin Enterprises (Buffalo, NY), 1994.

Jacob's Girls, Harlequin Enterprises (Buffalo, NY), 1995.

The Birth Mother (also see below), Harlequin Enterprises (Buffalo, NY), 1996.

Shotgun Baby (also see below), Harlequin Enterprises (Buffalo, NY), 1997.

Another Man's Child (also see below), Harlequin Enterprises (Buffalo, NY), 1997.

The Heart of Christmas, Harlequin Enterprises (Buffalo, NY), 1998, published as *Christmas Wishes, Christmas Gifts,* 2002.

Father: Unknown, Harlequin Enterprises (Buffalo, NY), 1998, published as *Lost in the Night,,* 2002, published as *Yesterday's Memories,* 2003.

My Babies and Me, Harlequin Enterprises (Buffalo, NY), 1999.

Her Secret, His Child, Harlequin Enterprises (Buffalo, NY), 1999.

Tomorrow's Baby (Internet publication), Harlequin Enterprises (Buffalo, NY), 2000.

Cassidy's Kids, Harlequin Enterprises (Buffalo, NY), 2000.

Mother's Day Anthology (contains *Another Man's Child, The Birth Mother,* and *Shotgun Baby*), Harlequin Enterprises (Buffalo, NY), 2001.

His Brother's Bride, Harlequin Enterprises (Buffalo, NY), 2002.

The Secret Son, Harlequin Enterprises (Buffalo, NY), 2002.

The Rancher's Bride, Harlequin Enterprises (Buffalo, NY), 2002.

Trueblood Christmas: Beth, Harlequin Enterprises (Buffalo, NY), 2002.

For the Children, Harlequin Enterprises (Buffalo, NY), 2003.

Where the Road Ends, MIRA Books (Buffalo, NY), 2003.

Born in the Valley, Harlequin Enterprises (Buffalo, NY), 2003.

Yesterday's Memories, Harlequin Enterprises (Buffalo, NY), 2003.

High Stakes (tentative title), MIRA Books (Buffalo, NY), in press.

"SHELTER VALLEY STORY" SERIES

No Cure for Love, Harlequin Enterprises (Buffalo, NY), 2000.

My Sister, Myself, Harlequin Enterprises (Buffalo, NY), 2000.

White Picket Fences, Harlequin Enterprises (Buffalo, NY), 2000.

Just around the Corner, Harlequin Enterprises (Buffalo, NY), 2001.

Sheltered in His Arms, Harlequin Enterprises (Buffalo, NY), 2001.

The Sheriff of Shelter Valley, Harlequin Enterprises (Buffalo, NY), 2002.

Born in the Valley, Harlequin Enterprises (Buffalo, NY), 2003.

Nothing Sacred, Harlequin Enterprises (Buffalo, NY), 2004.

Work represented in anthologies, including *Valentine Babies Anthology,* Harlequin Enterprises (Buffalo, NY), 2000.

BIOGRAPHICAL AND CRITICAL SOURCES:

ONLINE

Tara Taylor Quinn, http://www.tarataylorquinn.com (December 28, 2003).

*   *   *

RADOVANOVIC, Ivan 1961-

PERSONAL: Born 1961, in Belgrade, Yugoslavia (now Serbia). *Education:* Belgrade University Law School, graduated.

ADDRESSES: Home—Serbia. *Agent*—c/o Author Mail, Palgrave Macmillan, 175 Fifth Ave., New York, NY 10010.

CAREER: Journalist and novelist. *Politica* (newspaper), writer; *Borba* (daily newspaper), war reporter; *Vreme* (newspaper), war reporter based in Sarajevo; *Dnevi Telegraf* (daily newspaper), reporter, 1996; *Evropljanin* (weekly journal), assistant chief editor, 1997-99; *Vecernje Novosti* (daily newspaper), Sarajevo, chief editor, beginning 1999. Media Center Belgrade, education coordinator, beginning 1999.

WRITINGS:

Nista, Stubovi kulture, 1999.

Kratka istorija zivota u mrtvom gradu, Stubovi kulture, 1999.

(With Dragan Bujosevic) *Peti October: dvadeset i cetiri sata prevrata,* Medija Centar (Belgrade, Serbia), 2001, translated by Dusica Vujic and Ivanka Grkovic as *October Fifth: A Twenty-four-Hour Coup,* Press Documents Edition (Belgrade, Serbia), 2001, published as *The Fall of Milosevic: The October Fifth Revolution,* Palgrave Macmillan (New York, NY), 2003.

SIDELIGHTS: Serbian journalist Ivan Radovanovic joined with colleague Dragan Bujosevic to write *The Fall of Milosevic: The October Fifth Revolution.* Written shortly after Serbian dictator and convicted war criminal Slobodan Milosevic fell from power following an attempt at rigging the nation's 2000 elections, Radovanovic and Bujosevic's effort presents a minute-by-minute of the overthrow of the Serbian government by the thousands of demonstrators who gathered in the city of Belgrade. Noting that the authors—both respected journalists—interviewed numerous individuals from both the old and new guard, Marcia L. Sprules wrote in *Library Journal* that "their vivid, fast-paced account gives a good sense of the chaos and excitement" of October 5, 2000. While an *Economist* critic found the work "fascinating but confusing" because of the lack of background material provided on Milosevic himself, in the *Times Literary Supplement* Mark Almond dubbed the British edition of *The Fall of Milosevic* a "remarkably enlightening first draft of a history of the fall" of the Serbian leader that "casts a shadow across the naive presentation of the Serbian revolution as simply the upheaval of a long-suffering people against their deluded tyrant."

BIOGRAPHICAL AND CRITICAL SOURCES:

PERIODICALS

Economist, March 10, 2001, review of *October Fifth: A Twenty-four-Hour Coup,* p. 86.

Library Journal, March 15, 2003, Marcia L. Sprules, review of *The Fall of Milosevic: The October Fifth Revolution,* p. 102.

Times Literary Supplement, September 7, 2001, Mark Almond, review of *October Fifth,* p. 28.

ONLINE

Serbian Unity Congress Web site, http://www.suc.org/ (October 7, 2003), "Ivan Radovanovic."*

* * *

RAVVEN, Heidi M(iriam Morrison) 1952-

PERSONAL: Born April 28, 1952, in Boston, MA; daughter of Robert M. (a psychoanalyst) and Lucille M. (a musician) Ravven; married Allen Manning (a consultant), April 17, 1988; children: Simha E. *Ethnicity:* "Jewish." *Education:* Attended Smith College, 1970-71; Brandeis University, B.A., M.A., 1974, Ph.D., 1984. *Politics:* Liberal Democrat. *Religion:* Jewish. *Hobbies and other interests:* Canoeing, collecting pens, hiking.

ADDRESSES: Home—Century House, 36 Albany St., Cazenovia, NY 13035. *Office*—Department of Religious Studies, Hamilton College, Clinton, NY 13323.

CAREER: Hamilton College, Clinton, NY, professor of religious studies, 1983—. University of Washington, Seattle, Stroum Visiting Professor of Modern Jewish Thought, 1997.

MEMBER: North American Spinoza Society, Society for Empirical Ethics (founding member), Academy of Jewish Philosophy, Society for Medieval and Renaissance Philosophy, Hegel Society of America, American Philosophical Association, American Academy of Religion, Association for Jewish Studies.

WRITINGS:

(Editor, with Lenn E. Goodman, and contributor) *Jewish Themes in Spinoza's Philosophy: A Collection of Essays,* State University of New York Press (Albany, NY), 2002.

(Editor, with Lenn E. Goodman, and contributor) *Spinoza and Judaism: A Collection of Essays,* State University of New York Press (Albany, NY), 2002.

Contributor to books, including *Rereading the Canon: Feminist Perspectives on Hegel,* edited by Patricia J. Mills, Pennsylvania State University Press (University Park, PA), 1995; *Spinoza,* edited by Yirmiahu Yovel and Gideon Segal, Ashgate Publishing (Aldershot, England), 2000; *The Jewish Philosophy Reader,* edited by Daniel H. Frank and Oliver Leaman, Routledge (New York, NY), 2000; *Women and Gender in Jewish Philosophy,* edited by Hava Tirosh-Samuelson, Indiana University Press (Bloomington, IN), 2003; and *Spinoza: Critical Assessments,* edited by Genevieve Lloyd, Routledge (New York, NY). Contributor to "Academic Companions Humor Column." Contributor of articles and reviews to periodicals, including *Journal of the Associates for Religion and Intellectual Life, Journal of Religious Studies, International Studies in Philosophy, Judaism: Quarterly Journal of Jewish Life and Thought, Iyyun: Jerusalem Philosophical Quarterly, Journal of the History of Philosophy, Animus, Philosophy and Theology, Owl of Minerva: Journal of the Hegel Society of America,* and *Studia Spinozana.*

BIOGRAPHICAL AND CRITICAL SOURCES:

PERIODICALS

Shofar, winter, 2003, review of *Jewish Themes in Spinoza's Philosophy: A Collection of Essays,* p. 200.

* * *

REHDER, Ben

PERSONAL: Born in Austin, TX; married, 1992; wife's name Beckie (a graphic artist). *Education:* University of Texas, B.A. *Hobbies and other interests:* Deer hunting.

ADDRESSES: Home and office—Austin, TX. *Agent*—c/o Author Mail, St. Martin's Press, 175 Fifth Ave., New York, NY 10010. *E-mail*—rehder@austin.rr.com.

CAREER: Professional copywriter and novelist. Copywriter at advertising agencies in Austin, TX; freelance writer, 1991—.

WRITINGS:

Buck Fever: A Blanco County, Texas Novel, Minotaur (New York, NY), 2002.
Bone Dry: A Blanco County, Texas Novel, Minotaur (New York, NY), 2003.

SIDELIGHTS: As a professional advertising copywriter, Austin, Texas native Ben Rehder decided that, after years of writing other people's prose, it was time to tackle something of his own. Inspired by the novels of Carl Hiassen, he drew on his love of Texas and his passion for deer hunting to pen his debut novel *Buck Fever: A Blanco County, Texas Novel.*

Cracking the cover of *Buck Fever,* readers meet Blanco County Game Warden John Marlin, whose circle of responsibility increases dramatically after a poaching discovered on a private game ranch turns out to be a dead man in a deer suit. Ranch owner Roy Swank, a man with political connections and a taste for the good life, is disgruntled to have the Circle S ranch filthy with police investigators as it is hampering his drug-trafficking business. While Marlin butts heads with the town sheriff, Swank gets a visit from his suppliers in South America, at which point both the murder investigation and Swank's peace of mind start to unravel in a novel a *Kirkus Reviews* critic praised as a "briskly, paced, amusing, . . . [and] altogether promising debut." Equally positive reactions were expressed by *Booklist* contributor Frank Sennett, who maintained that quirky characters, a fast-timing plot, and "some clever one-liners" place *Buck Fever* "within shooting distance of Hiassen." Particular note was given to Rehder's prose in *Publishers Weekly,* the reviewer there calling the writing "confident and vigorous" and the novelist's voice "quintessentially Texan and relentlessly wry."

BIOGRAPHICAL AND CRITICAL SOURCES:

PERIODICALS

Booklist, August, 2002, Frank Sennett, review of *Buck Fever: A Blanco County, Texas Novel,* p. 1933.

Kirkus Reviews, July 15, 2002, review of *Buck Fever,* p. 997; July 15, 2003, review of *Bone Dry: A Blanco County, Texas Novel,* p. 942.
Library Journal, September 1, 2002, Rex Klett, review of *Buck Fever,* p. 217.
Publishers Weekly, August 26, 2002, review of *Buck Fever,* p. 47; August 18, 2003, review of *Bone Dry,* p. 61.

ONLINE

Ben Rehder Home Page, http://www.benrehder.com (April 8, 2003).
Books'n'Bytes, http://www.booksnbytes.com/ (April 8, 2003), Harriet Klausner, review of *Buck Fever.*
Mystery Reader, http://www.themysteryreader.com/ (October 31, 2002), Cathy Sova, interview with Rehder.*

*   *   *

REICHERT, Tom

PERSONAL: Male. *Education:* University of Missouri, B.J., 1988; University of Arizona, M.A. (communications), 1993; University of Arizona, Ph.D. (communications), 1997.

ADDRESSES: Agent—c/o Author Mail, Prometheus Books, 59 John Glenn Dr., Amherst, NY 14228-2197.

CAREER: Educator and author. *Orange County Register,* salesperson; University of North Texas, former professor of advertising sales and promotion; University of Alabama, currently assistant professor of advertising and public relations. Also worked as a political consultant.

AWARDS, HONORS: J. Walter Thompson research grant.

WRITINGS:

(With Susan E. Morgan and Tyler R. Harrison) *From Numbers to Words: Reporting Statistical Results for the Social Sciences,* Allyn and Bacon (Boston, MA), 2002.

(Editor with Jacqueline Lambiase) *Sex in Advertising: Perspectives on the Erotic Appeal,* Lawrence Erlbaum Associates (Mahwah, NJ), 2003.

The Erotic History of Advertising, Prometheus Books (Amherst, NY), 2003.

Contributor to books, including *Encyclopedia of Advertising,* and to periodicals, including *Journal of Communication, Journal of Advertising, Journalism & Mass Communication Quarterly,* and *Sexuality & Culture,.*

SIDELIGHTS: Tom Reichert is an assistant professor of advertising and public relations at the University of Alabama, as well as the author of *The Erotic History of Advertising.* His first published book, the coauthored *From Numbers to Words: Reporting Statistical Results for the Social Sciences,* is a reference tool for students on quantitative experiments and investigations; he has also coedited *Sex in Advertising: Perspectives on the Erotic Appeal,* a book geared for an academic readership.

In *Sex in Advertising* Reichert and co-editor Jacqueline Lambiase combine fifteen essays by various well-respected scholars and popular writers that discuss sexuality in advertising, from the common physiological and psychological responses to such ads and issues of gender differences and representation to the inclusion of subliminal sexually oriented messages. The book proposes that about one-fifth of all forms of advertising utilize an obvious sex-driven approach to sell their products. The book brings together varying viewpoints and perspectives on the issue, providing readers with a well-rounded approach to the topic. A reviewer for *American Scientist* stated that some of the concepts presented in the book "offer a disturbing view of our cultural landscape. Whether or not one agrees with the authors' conclusions," the critic added, the essays included "provide interesting food for thought."

The Erotic History of Advertising picks up where *Sex in Advertising* leaves off, as Reichert delves further into the actual advertising process and the development of campaigns designed to promote products like beer, cars, and blue jeans that frequently utilize sex as a selling tool. Reichert traces such advertising strategies back 150 years, and argues that erotic imagery has been used in advertising to sell products for much longer than most consumers might think. He provides readers with examples of advertisements featuring semi-clad women posing with tobacco products as early as the late nineteenth century.

"Although Reichert doesn't delve fully into the social ramifications of the constant rise of and backlash against overt sexuality in advertising or how the ads are targeted differently at men and women, he provides a fun, accessible survey of a subject everyone's familiar with," commented a reviewer for *Publishers Weekly,* reflecting the view of several critics that *The Erotic History of Advertising* would serve general readers as a source of interesting browsing.

BIOGRAPHICAL AND CRITICAL SOURCES:

PERIODICALS

Adweek, January 27, 2003, Simon Butler, review of *The Erotic History of Advertising,* p. 5.

American Scientist, March-April, 2003, review of *Sex in Advertising: Perspectives on the Erotic Appeal,* p. 169.

Library Journal, March 15, 2003, Donna Marie Smith, review of *The Erotic History of Advertising,* p. 92.

Publishers Weekly, February 10, 2003, review of *The Erotic History of Advertising,* p. 176.

ONLINE

Prometheus Books Web site, http://www.prometheus books.com/ (October 10, 2003).*

*   *   *

RICHARDS, Amelia M. 1970-
(Amy Richards)

PERSONAL: Born February 9, 1970. *Education:* Barnard College, Columbia University, B.A. (art history; with honors), 1993.

ADDRESSES: *Agent*—c/o Author Mail, Farrar, Straus and Giroux, 19 Union Square West, New York, NY 10003.

CAREER: Cofounder of Third Wave Foundation, New York, NY, and, with Jennifer Baumgardner, Soapbox (lecture agency); Ms. Foundation, New York, consultant. Lecturer, author, and consultant. Member of the board, Third Wave, Choice USA, Planned Parenthood of New York City, and *Feminist.com.*

AWARDS, HONORS: Named one of "Twenty-one Great Women Leaders of the Twenty-first Century," Women's Enews, 2003.

WRITINGS:

UNDER NAME AMY RICHARDS

(With Jennifer Baumgardner) *Manifesta: Young Women, Feminism, and the Future,* Farrar, Straus (New York, NY), 2000.

Contributor to books, including *Listen Up!: Voices from the Next Feminist Generation,* 1994; *Adios, Barbie: Young Women Write about Body Image and Identity,* edited by Ophira Edut, Seal Press (Seattle, WA), 1998; *Letters of Intent: Women Cross the Generations to Talk about Family, Work, Sex, Love and the Future of Feminism,* edited by Anna Bondoc and Meg Daly, Free Press, 1999; *The BUST Guide to the New Girl Order,* edited by Marcelle Karp and Debbie Stoller, Penguin, 1999; and *Sisterhood Is Forever: The Women's Anthology for a New Millennium,* Washington Square Press, 2003; also a narrator on instructional video *Beyond Killing Us Softly: The Strength to Resist,* Cambridge Documentary Films, 2000. Contributor to periodicals, including *Ms., Los Angeles Times,* and *Nation.* Contributing editor to *Ms.* magazine. Author of "Ask Amy" Internet advice column for *Feminist. com.*

WORK IN PROGRESS: With Jennifer Baumgardner, *Recipe-tested: An Idea Bank for Activists.* A shopping guide on New York City for *Insight Guides.*

SIDELIGHTS: A primary architect of the so-called Third Wave in feminism, Amelia M. Richards has been a women's rights activist since she helped organize Freedom Summer '92, a cross-country voter registration drive. Shortly after that, she cofounded the Third Wave Foundation, which is designed to give younger women a voice in a movement dominated by Second Wave feminists such as Gloria Steinem and Betty Friedan. This is not a hostile relationship, and Richards' links to the Second Wave remain strong. She served for many years as a personal assistant to Steinem, and she remains a consultant for the Ms. Foundation. At the same time, she seeks to connect with younger women, some of whom are deeply disenchanted with the older feminist movement, through magazine articles, television appearances on such shows as *Oprah* and *The O'Reilly Factor,* and hundreds of public speaking engagements at universities throughout the country.

In 1998 Richards contributed to *Adios, Barbie: Young Women Write about Body Image and Identity,* a collection of pieces edited by Ophira Edut about body image from a wide array of young female writers, black and white, gay and straight, overweight and thin. The essayists describe an equally wide range of topics, from leg hair to transsexualism, and the complexities of many women's relationship with food. Eating disorders are a big part of the story of body image, and a number of authors recount their struggles with bulimia and anorexia. Others, such as a conflicted exotic dancer, confront their own ambiguous feelings toward sexuality and the way women are both empowered and oppressed by sexual attractiveness. "Although a few of the essays are weak when compared to the book's best pieces, the volume as a whole is a step forward in the discussion of how feminine attractiveness is viewed in American society," wrote a *Publishers Weekly* reviewer. All the authors share a conviction that body image and self-presentation are fundamental issues. As Richards put it in her own contribution to the collection, "For many women, our bodies have become the canvases upon which our struggles paint themselves. Body image, in fact, may be the pivotal third wave issue—the common struggle that mobilizes the current feminist generation."

To further mobilize that generation, Richards published *Manifesta: Young Women, Feminism, and the Future,* written with fellow *Ms.* editor Jennifer Baumgardner. "Their book is a colorful account of their own rising cohort and its concerns, as well as a program for an 'everyday feminism' suited for the world left to them by their ideological foremothers," explained *Commentary* reviewer Christine Stolba. As Richards and Baumgardner see it, the image of the grim, earnest, male-bashing feminist is a major stumbling block for many younger women, and the authors want to provide a new, more "Girlie" image with a broader appeal to the young. Not that they wish to exclude the women who paved the way. For them, feminism is a Big Tent. As *New Republic* contributor Christine Stansell noted, the authors "never fall into the smug self-regard that has long been a trademark of the youth manifesto, circling up the wagons into a cozy generational encampment. Exuberant and generous, *Manifesta* seeks to explain and to popularize, rather than to separate sleek insiders from dowdy outsiders. The book tries to forge an open-minded, big-hearted relationship between the Girlies and the women, the daughters and the mothers, the doubters and the zealots."

At the same time, some reviewers faulted the authors for a certain parochialism, noting their tendency to see well-educated, urban women like themselves as more representative than they really are. For "a book designed as an accessible primer on feminism for the masses, it seems disproportionately focused on an elite bunch of women, which, of course, is the longtime criticism of mainstream feminism," wrote *Washington Monthly* reviewer Patricia Simon. Others saluted these very qualities in the authors and other Third Wave feminists. "Savvy, conscientious, and ambitious, they represent, in many ways, exactly the bright, brash, and courageous heirs that the Steinem-era Second Wavers sought," noted *Progressive* contributor Laura Flanders. Still others saluted Richards and Baumgardner's attempt to reach beyond their immediate circle. According to *Women's Review of Books* contributor Anastasia Higginbotham, "They urge readers to put aside ego battles and rigid definitions of feminism and to stay in touch with women whose ideas may offend or confuse. They then hold themselves to this same standard throughout the book, criticizing, engaging, and finding the lessons embedded within any conflict. Their insights into the flaws of the girls' movement and their grasp of mental roadblocks that keep feminists distant from one another are right on."

BIOGRAPHICAL AND CRITICAL SOURCES:

PERIODICALS

Booklist, May 1, 1995, Whitney Scott, review of *Listen Up!: Voices from the Next Feminist Generation,* p. 1537; February 15, 1999, Ellie Barta-Moran, review of *Letters of Intent: Women Cross the Generations to Talk about Work, Family, Love, Sex, and the Future of Feminism,* p. 1013; May 15, 2001, review of *Beyond Killing Us Softly: The Strength to Resist* (video recording), Carol Holzberg, p. 1762; August, 2001, Vanessa Bush, review of *Listen Up: Voices from the Next Feminist Generation,* p. 2060; January 1, 2002, review of *Beyond Killing Us Softly,* p. 772.

Commentary, June, 2001, Christine Stolba, review of *Manifesta: Young Women, Feminism, and the Future,* p. 61.

Entertainment Weekly, January 8, 1999, review of *Adios, Barbie,* p. 62.

Feminist Studies, spring, 1997, Jennifer Drake, review of *Listen Up,* p. 97.

Herizons, spring, 2002, Lisa Rundle, review of *Manifesta,* p. 33.

Library Journal, July, 1999, Heather McCormack, review of *The BUST Guide to the New Girl Order,* p. 117; March 1, 2001, Harriet Edwards, review of *Beyond Killing Us Softly,* p. 148; March 15, 2003, Carolyn Kuebler, review of *Sisterhood Is Forever: The Women's Anthology for the New Millennium,* p. 104.

New Republic, January 15, 2001, Christine Stansell, "The Generational Progress of Feminism: Girlie Interrupted," p. 23.

Newsweek, August 23, 1999, Elizabeth Angell, "Welcome to the 'New Girl Order,'" p. 60.

New York Times Book Review, December 17, 2000, Ann Hulbert, "Unfinished Business."

Progressive, October, 2000, Laura Flanders, review of *Manifesta,* p. 42.

Publishers Weekly, March 27, 1995, review of *Listen Up!,* p. 81; May 8, 1995, Paul Nathan, "The New Feminism," p. 33; November 30, 1998, review of *Adios, Barbie,* p. 60; February 1, 1999, review of *Letters of Intent,* p. 70; June 28, 1999, review of *The BUST Guide to the New Girl Order,* p. 64; September 18, 2000, review of *Manifesta,* p. 96; July 23, 2001, "Women and Grrrls," p. 67; March 24, 2003, review of *Sisterhood Is Forever,* p. 73.

Signs, spring, 1998, Mary Celeste Kearney, review of *Listen Up!,* p. 844.

Washington Monthly, December, 2000, Patricia Simon, review of *Manifesta,* p. 57.

Women's Review of Books, June, 1995, Leora Tanenbaum, review of *Listen Up!,* p. 5; January, 1999, Meg Daly, review of *Adios, Barbie,* p. 10; April, 1999, Lisa Marcus, review of *Letters of Intent,* p. 6; November, 1999, Ameland Copeland, review of *The BUST Guide to the New Girl Order,* p. 24;

October, 2000, Anastasia Higginbotham, review of *Manifesta,* p. 1; September, 2003, Kathy Davis, "Sisterhood Is Forever," p. 8.*

* * *

RICHARDS, Amy
See RICHARDS, Amelia M.

* * *

RICHLER, Nancy 1957-

PERSONAL: Born 1957, in Montreal, Quebec, Canada; daughter of Meyer and Dianne Richler; partner of Vicki Trerise. *Ethnicity:* "Jewish." *Education:* Brandeis University, B.A. (history), 1979; Simmons College, M.S.W., 1981. *Religion:* Jewish.

ADDRESSES: Home—Vancouver, British Columbia, Canada. *Agent*—Dean Cooke, 278 Bloor St. E., #305, Toronto, Ontario, M4W 3M4, Canada. *E-mail*—richrise@telus.net.

CAREER: Novelist and author of short fiction.

MEMBER: Writers Union of Canada.

AWARDS, HONORS: Arthur Ellis Award for Best First Crime Novel shortlist, 1996, for *Throwaway Angels;* third prize, *Prairie Fire* Long Short Fiction Contest, 1999; Canadian Jewish Book Award for fiction, 2003, for *Your Mouth Is Lovely.*

WRITINGS:

Throwaway Angels, Press Gang (Vancouver, British Columbia, Canada), 1996.
Your Mouth Is Lovely, Ecco Press (New York, NY), 2002.

Contributor to literary journals. *Your Mouth Is Lovely* has been translated into six languages.

SIDELIGHTS: Canadian fiction writer Nancy Richler's second novel, *Your Mouth Is Lovely,* takes place in Siberia shortly after the Russian Revolution of 1905.

In the novel, the year is 1911, and twenty-three-year-old Russian Jew Miriam is incarcerated for life in a prison camp. As an escape from the confines where she has been for the past five years, she recalls her childhood in a small village as her country stood on the brink of the portentous change that would force an unwieldy Russia into the twentieth century. Unwanted by her parents—her mother committed suicide shortly after Miriam's birth—and disfigured as a child, Miriam has lived on the fringes of her impoverished, emotionally distant family, but has also been deeply influenced by the unconventional independence of her stepmother Tsila. Now she reflects not only on her distant past but also on the events that lead her to join Kiev's growing socialist movement. This decision ultimately results in Miriam's arrest as a revolutionary and condemns her to a bleak future as a political prisoner. Forced to give up her infant daughter Hayya and send the girl to live with an aunt in Canada, Miriam now writes down her reflections in the form of a letter to the child she will never know, and questions the meaning of her life.

A *Publishers Weekly* reviewer praised *Your Mouth Is Lovely* as "haunting," and Richler's characters as "unforgettable" and "deeply nuanced." In *Booklist,* contributor Kathleen Hughes dubbed it a "stunning novel that readers won't be able to put down." Recognizing the "admirable research" done by the author, a *Kirkus Reviews* critic commended in particular the "quietly assured detail" used to describe Miriam's childhood in Bellarus. Calling *Your Mouth Is Lovely* a "refreshing departure from most novels about revolution," *Maclean's* contributor Sue Ferguson concluded that in Richler's mix of historic fact and fiction "both story and texture leave a lasting impression." "Such is the power of her craft," *Library Journal* reviewer Edward Cone noted of Richler, "that Miriam's story transcends the mundane" and stands on a par with the revolution-era novels of Fyodor Dostoevsky.

Richler's first full-length novel, *Throwaway Angels,* was penned as a quasi-mystery. Her protagonist, a lesbian laundromat clerk in her thirties named Tova, sees the troubled lives of runaways from a safe distance, but is forced to leave the security of her quiet life after her friend Gina disappears. In trying to track down Gina, Tova is forced to truly understand her friend and, in the process, question her own life choices. In addition to working on novel-length works, Richler has penned a number of short stories that have appeared in literary magazines in both the United States and Canada.

BIOGRAPHICAL AND CRITICAL SOURCES:

PERIODICALS

Booklist, November 1, 2002, Kathleen Hughes, review of *Your Mouth Is Lovely,* p. 474.

Books in Canada, November, 1996, Eva Tihanyi, review of *Throwaway Angels,* p. 36.

Boston Globe, December 26, 2002, Judith Maas, review of *Your Mouth Is Lovely.*

Forward, January 31, 2003, Janet Burstein, review of *Your Mouth Is Lovely.*

Globe and Mail (Toronto, Ontario, Canada), October 5, 2002, Mark Frutkin, review of *Your Mouth Is Lovely.*

Jerusalem Report, February 24, 2003, Leah Eichler, review of *Your Mouth Is Lovely.*

Kirkus Reviews, September 15, 2002, review of *Your Mouth Is Lovely,* p. 1341.

Lambda Book Report, February, 1997, Judith Stelboum, review of *Throwaway Angels,* p. 23.

Library Journal, November 1, 1996, Rex E. Klett, review of *Throwaway Angels,* p. 111; October 15, 2002, Edward Cone, review of *Your Mouth Is Lovely,* p. 95.

Literary Review of Canada, December, 2002, Robin Roger, review of *Your Mouth Is Lovely.*

Los Angeles Times, December 13, 2002, Mark Rozzo, review of *Your Mouth Is Lovely.*

Maclean's, December 2, 2002, Sue Ferguson, review of *Your Mouth Is Lovely,* p. 64.

Montreal Gazette, September 21, 2002, Donna Bailey Nurse, review of *Your Mouth Is Lovely.*

National Post (Toronto, Ontario, Canada), October 12, 2002, Robin Roger, review of *Your Mouth Is Lovely.*

New Yorker, December 2, 2002, review of *Your Mouth Is Lovely.*

Publishers Weekly, October 7, 2002, review of *Your Mouth Is Lovely,* p. 50.

Quill & Quire, October, 1996, Maureen Phillips, review of *Throwaway Angels,* p. 31.

Vancouver Sun, September 21, 2003, Sara Dowse, review of *Your Mouth Is Lovely.*

Winnipeg Free Press, September 29, 2002, Sharon Chisvin, review of *Your Mouth Is Lovely.*

ONLINE

Bookreporter.com, http://www.bookreporter.com/ (April 8, 2003), Sarah Rachel Egelman, review of *Your Mouth Is Lovely.*

RIESSMAN, Frank 1924-2004

OBITUARY NOTICE—See index for *CA* sketch: Born April 9, 1924, in Manhattan, NY; died March 1, 2004, in New York, NY. Psychologist, educator, and author. Riessman was a social psychologist who championed self-help social programs for the poor and who was a founder of the journal *Social Policy.* Completing his undergraduate work in 1944 at what is now the City College of the City University of New York, Riessman attended graduate school at Columbia University, where he received his Ph.D. in 1955. He then joined the faculty at Bard College as associate professor of psychology and chair of the department. In the 1960s, he taught at Yeshiva University and then New York University. Always concerned with the problem of the poor, Riessman concluded that the best way to help them was through social programs that would help teach the poor how to help themselves. The journal he helped found in 1970, *Social Policy,* reflected this belief, and he encouraged governments to create jobs in the human services and environmental conservation fields that would be geared to hiring the unemployed; this approach, he averred, would be cheaper than paying for welfare programs. In 1971, he became a professor of education at Queens College of the City University of New York. It was during the 1970s, too, that Riessman founded the Self-Help Clearinghouse, which developed self-help programs for the poor to fight disease, crime, addiction, and unemployment. Riessman, who later also worked at the Graduate School and University Center of the City University of New York, succumbed to Parkinson's disease and diabetes in recent years and was at a nursing home at the time of his death. He was the author of such books as *Helping the Disadvantaged Pupil to Learn More Easily* (1966), *Strategies against Poverty* (1968), *The Inner City Child* (1976), and *HELP—A Working Guide to Self-Help Groups* (1979); he also coauthored *Self-Help in the Human Services* (1977) with Alan Gartner, and *Redefining Self-Help: Policies and Practice* (1995).

OBITUARIES AND OTHER SOURCES:

PERIODICALS

Los Angeles Times, March 15, 2004, p. B9.
New York Times, March 14, 2004, p. A25.

RILEY, Helene M. 1939-
(Helene M. Kastinger Riley)

PERSONAL: Born March 11, 1939, in Vienna, Austria; naturalized U.S. citizen; daughter of Josef (a machinist) and Helene (a photographer; maiden name, Friedl) Kastinger; married Edward R. Riley (deceased); married Darius G. Ornston (a physician), May 11, 1983; children: Schatzi, John, Jesse, Michael. *Education:* Attended business college in Vienna, Austria, 1953-55; University of North Texas, B.A. (magna cum laude), 1970; Rice University, M.A., 1973, Ph.D., 1975. *Politics:* Democrat. *Religion:* Southern Baptist. *Hobbies and other interests:* Reading, singing, painting, needlecraft.

ADDRESSES: Home—133 Whittington Dr., Greenville, SC 29615-2623. *Office*—Department of Languages, Clemson University, 510 Strode Tower, Clemson, SC 29631. *E-mail*—hmriley@earthlink.net and rhelene@clemson.edu.

CAREER: Rice University, Houston, TX, instructor, 1971; Yale University, New Haven, CT, assistant professor, 1975-78, associate professor, beginning 1979, head of Summer Language Institute, 1979-81, and fellow of Davenport College; Washington State University, Pullman, WA, associate professor, between 1979 and 1985, chair of Department of Foreign Languages, beginning 1981; Clemson University, Clemson, SC, associate professor, prior to 1985, professor of German, 1985-95, Alumni Distinguished Professor of German, 1995—, head of Department of Languages, 1985-86. Middlebury College, guest professor, 1976; guest speaker at other institutions, including Appalachian State University, McMaster University, Newberry Lutheran College, Cambridge University, University of Hawaii, University of New Hampshire, State University of New York—Stony Brook, Princeton University, University of Pennsylvania, and University of Alberta. Also worked for Kemper Insurance in Dallas, TX, 1971. *Exhibitions:* Producer and director of the traveling exhibit "Cultural Contributions of German-Speaking Settlers in South Carolina," 1996-2000.

MEMBER: Modern Language Association of America, American Association of Teachers of German, Society for German-American Studies, American Association of University Professors (president, 1988-89), Verwertungsgesellschaft WORT, South Atlantic Modern Language Association, SCFLT, MIFLC, Alpha Chi.

AWARDS, HONORS: Griswold grant, 1975-76; grants from Hilles Fund, 1979, 1982, German Academic Exchange Service, 1979, Holland Fund, 1982, Deutsche Forschungsgemeinschaft, 1982, and National Endowment for the Humanities, 1986, 1989, 1995; FRG Friendship Award, 1989; grants from Museum of Early Southern Decorative Arts, 1993, 1996, and South Carolina Humanities Council, 1996, 1997; award from German Friendly Society of Charleston, 1999.

WRITINGS:

Idee und Gestaltung. Das konfigurative Strukturprinzip in der Kurzprosa Achim von Arnims, Lang (Bern, Switzerland), 1977.

Ludwig Achim von Arnims Jugend-und-Reisejahre. Ein Beitrag zur Biographie, Bouvier (Bonn, West Germany), 1978.

Achim von Arnim in Selbstzeugnissen und Bilddokumenten, Rowohlt (Hamburg, West Germany), 1979, revised edition, 1994.

Romain Rolland, Colloquium (Berlin, Germany), 1979.

Das Bild der Antike in der deutschen Romantik, Benjamins (Amsterdam, Netherlands), 1981.

Virginia Wolf, Colloquium (Berlin, Germany), 1983.

Clemens Brentano, Metzler (Stuttgart, West Germany), 1985.

Die weibliche Muse. Sechs Essays über künstlerisch schaffende Frauen der Goethezeit, Camden House (Columbia, SC), 1986.

Ludwig Achim von Arnim. Kritische Schriften. Erstdrucke und Unbekanntes, Whittington (Greenville, SC), 1988.

Max Weber, Colloquium (Berlin, Germany), 1991.

Michael Kalteisen: Ein Deutscher in South Carolina, M. Fink (Merklingen, Germany), 1995.

Hildegard von Bingen, Rowohlt (Reinbek, Germany), 1997, revised edition, 1998.

Clemson University, Arcadia Publishing (Charleston, SC), 2002.

Author of pamphlets. Other writings including scripts for the videotapes "Journey to Freedom," 1992, "Heritage of Faith," 1994, and "Art and the Artisan: South Carolina German-American Artists of the 18th and 19th Centuries," released by Action Video, 1997. Work represented in anthologies, including *In Her Mother's Tongue,* edited by Lisa Kahn, Emerson (Denver, CO), 1983; *Stefan Zweig: The World of Yesterday's Humanist Today,* State University of New York Press (Albany, NY), 1983; *Critical Survey of Drama,* edited by Frank N. Magill, Salem Press (Englewood Cliffs, NJ), 1986; and *Romanticism and Beyond,* Peter Lang (New York, NY), 1996. Contributor of poetry, articles, and reviews to periodicals in the United States and abroad, including *Modern Language Review, Comparatist, Anglia, Journal of Early Southern Decorative Arts, Austrian Studies Newsletter, South Carolina Historical, Journal of English and Germanic Philology, German Quarterly, Modern Language Quarterly,* and *Antiques.* Some writings appear under the name Helene M. Kastinger Riley.

SIDELIGHTS: Helene M. Riley told *CA:* "I am a professional writer. When I was eleven years old, I wrote a short story about my dog and sent it to the editor of the 'children's page' of a newspaper in Vienna, Austria—my birthplace. The story was printed, and I had caught the fever.

"While raising my children as a single mother, I had little leisure for writing, but I did write letters to the local newspaper and poems (most were published in anthologies) and a novel, all in the hour before going to work at Kemper Insurance. That hour between the time the car pool dropped me off and my work hours started was prime and quiet time for writing.

"My most productive time as a writer commenced with the beginning of my professional life as a professor of German and a teacher. Initially my writing was related to my discipline—literary criticism. Soon, however, European publishers began asking me to produce high-quality, well-researched trade books for which there was a perceived spot on the market. Thus began my work for publishers that are market-oriented and which produce income for me.

"Over time I have learned to write in a disciplined fashion: four manuscript pages per day until the job is done. I always meet my deadlines, usually with time to spare.

"I enjoy writing and choose my subjects carefully, keeping in mind that, as I learn new and interesting things about the chosen topic, my view of the world in

which I live is ever-expanding and changing. That's why I love to write. There is so much to be learned while researching the subject, and so much to be cherished during the analytical process of writing."

BIOGRAPHICAL AND CRITICAL SOURCES:

PERIODICALS

German Quarterly, fall, 1987, review of *Die weibliche Muse. Sechs Essays über künstlerisch schaffende Frauen der Goethezeit,* pp. 666-668.
German Studies Review, February, 1987, review of *Die weibliche Muse,* pp. 171-172.
South Atlantic Review, November, 1987, review of *Die weibliche Muse,* pp. 135-137.
Virginia 2, March, 1987, B. R. Erdle, review of *Die weibliche Muse,* p. 15.

* * *

RILEY, Helene M. Kastinger
See RILEY, Helene M.

* * *

RITTER, Lawrence S(tanley) 1922-2004

OBITUARY NOTICE—See index for *CA* sketch: Born May 23, 1922, in New York, NY; died February 15, 2004, in New York, NY. Educator and author. An economist and New York University professor, as a writer Ritter was actually best remembered for his baseball book *The Glory of Their Times: The Story of the Early Days of Baseball Told by the Men Who Played It* (1966; revised edition, 1985). Earning his bachelor's degree from Indiana University in 1942, he served in the U.S. Navy during World War II as a lieutenant junior grade. After the war, Ritter completed his doctorate at the University of Wisconsin in 1951. His first teaching job was at Michigan State University during the early 1950s. This was followed by five years as an economist for the Federal Reserve Bank of New York, after which time he joined New York University's Graduate School of Business Administration as a professor of finance in 1960. Ritter chaired his department from 1961 to 1969 and again from

1972 to 1980, eventually retiring in 1991. Although his professional background was in economics, Ritter always fostered a love of baseball that had been with him since childhood. His father had taken him to places like Ebbets Field and Yankee Stadium, and when he passed away in 1961 he decided to honor his father by writing a baseball book about the early days of the game. He traveled around the country, interviewing former players who had been around since the 1890s. He then compiled the interviews into *The Glory of Their Times,* which has been widely praised by critics and has become a bestselling sports book. Ritter wrote a number of baseball books afterwards, including *The Story of Baseball* (1983), *Leagues Apart: The Men and Times of the Negro Baseball Leagues* (1995), and *The Babe: The Game that Ruth Built* (1997); he was also the author of books about economics and finance, including *Money and Economic Activity* (1952; third edition, 1967), *Principles of Money, Banking, and Financial Markets* (1974; fifth edition, 1986), and *The Flow of Funds Accounts: A Framework for Financial Analysis* (1998).

OBITUARIES AND OTHER SOURCES:

PERIODICALS

Los Angeles Times, February 20, 2004, p. B10.
New York Times, February 17, 2004, p. A21.

*   *   *

ROSCO, Jerry 1953-

PERSONAL: Born January 6, 1953, in New York, NY; son of Mario (an engineer) and Amelia (Young) Rosco. *Ethnicity:* "Italian-American." *Education:* Iona College, B.A. *Politics:* "Anti-war and ACT UP activist." *Religion:* "Agnostic." *Hobbies and other interests:* Animal protection organizations.

ADDRESSES: Home—51 Bond St., New York, NY 10012. *E-mail*—jerry_rosco@hotmail.com.

CAREER: Gannett Newspapers, worked as reporter; editor and copywriter for legal, business, and educational publishers; Mavety Magazines, New York, NY, associate editor, 1989-94; freelance writer and editor, 1994—.

WRITINGS:

(Editor, with Robert Phelps) *Continual Lessons: The Journals of Glenway Wescott, 1937-1955,* Farrar, Straus & Giroux (New York, NY), 1990.
Glenway Wescott Personally: A Biography, University of Wisconsin Press (Madison, WI), 2002.

Work represented in anthologies. Contributor to periodicals, including *Chicago Review, Literary Review, Sequoia, Lost Generation Journal,* and *James White Review.*

WORK IN PROGRESS: Editing *A Visit to Priapus and Other Stories,* the unpublished stories of Glenway Wescott, completion expected in 2004; editing Wescott's final journals.

SIDELIGHTS: Jerry Rosco told *CA:* "My personal talent is for articles, essays, and short stories, but also for editorial and biographical work—especially, of course, for Glenway Wescott. I was lucky to know Wescott in the last twelve or so years of his life and was greatly influenced by his love of and dedication to literature. As for Wescott's talent, there has been debate on whether he was a major or minor writer, based on his productivity. But there is little debate about the fact that he was one of America's great prose stylists. I am pleased to dedicate so much research and writing to this extraordinary man. As for my own work, some more stories and a political novel are what I'd like to accomplish."

BIOGRAPHICAL AND CRITICAL SOURCES:

PERIODICALS

Booklist, April 1, 2002, Donna Seaman, review of *Glenway Wescott Personally: A Biography,* p. 1300.
Library Journal, February 15, 2002, Charles C. Nash, review of *Glenway Wescott Personally,* p. 144.
Publishers Weekly, November 16, 1990, Genevieve Stuttaford, review of *Continual Lessons: The Journals of Glenway Wescott, 1937-1955,* p. 48.

*   *   *

ROSE, David 1959-

PERSONAL: Born 1959.

ADDRESSES: Office—*Observer,* 119 Farringdon Rd., London EC1R 3ER, England.

CAREER: Journalist, author. *Observer,* London England, home affairs correspondent.

WRITINGS:

(With Richard Gregson) *Beneath the Mountains: Exploring the Deep Caves of Asturias,* Hodder and Stoughton (London, England), 1987.

Climate of Fear: Blakelock Murder and the Tottenham Three, Bloomsbury Publishing (London, England), 1992.

In the Name of the Law: The Collapse of Criminal Justice, Jonathan Cape (London, England), 1996, revised edition, Vintage (London, England), 1996.

Guildford and District ("Memory Lane" series), Breedon (Derby, England), 2000.

(With Ed Douglas) *Regions of the Heart: The Triumph and Tragedy of Alison Hargreaves,* National Geographic Society (Washington, DC), 2000.

The Poupart Family in the Borough of Twickenham, 1874-1936, Borough of Twickenham Local History Society (Twickenham, England), 2002.

SIDELIGHTS: David Rose is a British journalist and outdoorsman whose books include *Beneath the Mountains: Exploring the Deep Caves of Asturias.* Rose and coauthor Richard Gregson, along with other cavers, were the first to explore the incredible limestone caves of the Picos de Europa mountains in the Asturia province of northern Spain. They descended using ropes and pitons and lived far below the surface of the earth for days at a time. What they discovered were subterranean rivers and waterfalls equal to those found aboveground, chambers as vast as cathedrals, and huge formations of stalactites and stalagmites. The group discovered the Sistema del Xitu, a network of caves, tunnels, and shafts that extend 4,000 feet deep. It eventually took six years to completely map the system, and the book contains many of these maps, plus an eight-page color photo insert.

Climate of Fear: Blakelock Murder and the Tottenham Three is Rose's account of the murder of police constable Keith Blakelock, who was stabbed forty times, slashed with a machete, and left to die on a patch of grass. The murder was never solved, and the sentences of three who were convicted were later dropped and the accused released. Blakelock was murdered as a result of mob violence after a local

woman suffered a fatal heart attack when police raided her home on October 5, 1985. The climate was already volatile, and after Blakelock's death, police arrested dozens of young men and boys, including some who were mentally retarded, and treated them inhumanely as they attempted to extract confessions from them.

Brian Raymond reviewed the history in the London *Observer,* calling it a "meticulous catalogue of police wickedness," and wrote that "this excellent book is not a story of purposive malevolence, or pure racism, but of a system placed under such pressure that it abandoned any pretense of justifiable methods of investigation."

In the Name of the Law: The Collapse of Criminal Justice is Rose's study of the British system and its failure to convict the guilty and acquit the innocent. Rose, who makes his points by using real cases, accompanied police over the course of six months observing procedures. Radmilla May remarked in *Contemporary Review* that Rose "writes with passion and eloquence" and called his style "gripping. . . . On the whole, the police come out well in this book. Mr. Rose does not shrink from describing recent cases of appalling misconduct, but he sees great changes in the police's present attitudes, a real desire to move away from old unsatisfactory methods of policing to methods which will restore greater public confidence."

Rose emphasizes that while the crime rate is up, convictions are down. He looks at the effectiveness, or ineffectiveness, of the Crown Prosecution Service (CPS), reforms necessary to improve the jury system, and the fears of citizens for their safety. Richard Stern commented in the *Spectator* that the CPS "enjoys few fans. Prosecutors vary alarmingly in competence. Some mumble into their notes, some leave out elementary 'facts,' and some speak in elusively Equatorial versions of English. David Rose believes that the CPS is cost-driven to discontinue too many cases, before or after they reach the courts. The CPS's own criterion for pursuing a case, a 'realistic' chance of conviction, is turning into an insistence on watertight certainty. In 1994 the CPS discontinued eleven percent of prosecutions. Is this excessive?"

Paul Barker commented in the *Times Literary Supplement* that "if neither the public nor the police can expect a reasonable chance that the guilty will be convicted, what happens to the bargain between citizen and state?" Rose looks at the rights of the noncriminal and how under the Criminal Justice Act of 1988, certain crimes have been downgraded. For example, theft of a car was changed to "taking without the owner's consent." Barker called *In the Name of the Law* "a recipe for having to think uncomfortable thoughts."

Rose and Ed Douglas wrote *Regions of the Heart: The Triumph and Tragedy of Alison Hargreaves,* a biography called "fiercely lyrical" by a *Publishers Weekly* contributor. In addition to relating the events of their subject's life and death in 1995, they explain the intricacies and dangers of climbing and the accomplishments of other women climbers. Hargreaves had an impressive history. She was the first woman to climb the North face of the Matterhorn, and she conquered Mount Everest, without supplemental oxygen, just two weeks before her solo attempt to climb K2, the world's second highest peak, again without oxygen. She succeeded, but on her descent, Hargreaves crashed against the mountain's side during hurricane-force winds; her body remains there. Her achievement was noted in the press, but obscured by stories of her foolhardiness in making the attempt, considering that she was the mother of two small children.

The story that Rose and Douglas tell reveals more about Hargreaves's life than had previously been known. She made the climb hoping to achieve financial independence, so that she could leave her husband, Jim Ballard, and gain custody of their children. The authors have used her diaries to reconstruct Hargreaves's fears and hopes and to show that she was caught in an abusive relationship. Sixteen years younger than Ballard, she skipped college to marry, and she was able to climb because he then had a successful climbing shop. They lost everything in the recession of the 1990s, however, and Hargreaves soloed six Alpine summits in 1993, looking for a sponsor. According to the book, Ballard pushed her to succeed.

In reviewing the book for *UC Climbing* online, Charles Arthur stated that Hargreaves "never told her side of her unhappy marriage and what it drove her to do. 'Better to live one day as a tiger than a thousand years as a sheep,' Ballard said at the news of her death. Thinking like that gets you killed on mountains. In

truth, it's better to live. But a lioness will die defending its young. So, it seems did Hargreaves."

BIOGRAPHICAL AND CRITICAL SOURCES:

PERIODICALS

Booklist, June 1, 2000, Vanessa Bush, review of *Regions of the Heart: The Triumph and Tragedy of Alison Hargreaves,* p. 1834.
Contemporary Review, June, 1996, Radmilla May, review of *In the Name of the Law: The Collapse of Criminal Justice,* p. 325.
Economist, March 16, 1996, review of *In the Name of the Law,* p. S3.
Library Journal, June 15, 2000, Robert E. Greenfield, review of *Regions of the Heart,* p. 92.
Observer (London, England), May 17, 1992, Brian Raymond, review of *Climate of Fear: Blakelock Murder and the Tottenham Three,* p. 54.
Publishers Weekly, May 29, 2000, review of *Regions of the Heart,* p. 63.
Spectator, February 10, 1996, Richard Stern, review of *In the Name of the Law,* pp. 27-28.
Times Literary Supplement, April 12, 1996, Paul Barker, review of *In the Name of the Law,* p. 26; January 7, 2000, Kathleen Jamie, review of *Regions of the Heart,* p. 25.

ONLINE

UK Climbing, http://www.ukclimbing.com/ (June 7, 2003), Charles Arthur, review of *Regions of the Heart.**

*   *   *

ROSENFELD, Stephanie

PERSONAL: Born in New York, NY; children: one daughter. *Education:* Wesleyan University, B.A.; University of Massachussetts, M.F.A.

ADDRESSES: Home—81 N St., Salt Lake City, UT 84103.

CAREER: Author. Worked as a printmaker and pastry chef; formerly with the Institute for Food and Development Policy, San Francisco.

AWARDS, HONORS: Named to the *Missouri Review*'s "Ten Fiction Writers to Watch" list.

WRITINGS:

(With Walden Bello) *Dragons in Distress: Asia's Miracle Economies in Crisis,* Institute for Food and Development Policy (San Francisco, CA), 1990.
What About the Love Part?, Ballantine Books (New York, NY), 2002.
Massachussetts, California, Timbuktu, Ballantine Books (New York, NY), 2003.

Contributor to *Missouri Review, Northwest Review, Massachussetts Review, Bellingham Review, Willow Review, Other Voices,* and *Creative City Review.*

SIDELIGHTS: Stephanie Rosenfeld is an author with an eclectic background. She has been variously a pastry chef, printmaker, novelist, and coauthor of an analysis of Asian economies. In *Dragons in Distress: Asia's Miracle Economies in Crisis,* her first published work, she and coauthor Walden Bello examine contemporary views of the "emerging" capitalist economies of South Korea, Taiwan, Hong Kong, and Singapore.

Warning against placing too much faith in the economic progress of Asian Newly Industrialized Countries, or NICs, Bello and Rosenfeld point to human rights abuses, authoritarian governments, and poor environmental policy in these nations as signs of instability. According to the authors, "Such is the cunning of history that at the very moment that the economists and technocrats have enshrined the NIC model as the new orthodoxy, that very strategy is running out of steam . . . the troublesome truth is that the external conditions that made the NIC's export successes possible are fast disappearing, while the long-suppressed costs of high-speed growth are catching up with these economies."

In the *Monthly Review,* Martin Hart-Landsberg thought Bello and Rosenfeld "convincingly argued" their point. He observed, "Bello and Rosenfeld's discussion of the different strategies pursued by the three states offers valuable material for those who want to learn more about the efficiency and techniques of social regulation of economic activity." James B. Goodno, writing in *Technology Review,* was more skeptical of the book's recommendations, but valued its non-standard approach: "Though sketchy, their proposals deserve consideration. Unlike schemes that place growth above all other considerations, Bello and Rosenfeld's recommendations give priority to environmental well-being and social justice concerns that need addressing for sustainable development."

Rosenfeld next turned to writing creative works of fiction with her début collection of short stories, *What about the Love Part?* Centered around the dysfunctional romantic life of one woman, Abby Hillman, Rosenfeld's book explores bad relationships and why some people accept them. A contributor to *Kirkus Reviews* observed, "Although the jacket copy would have us believe that our protagonist, Abby Hillman, is a smart woman who just chooses the wrong guys, there's little in the collection to prove she's anything but average. But it's Rosenfeld's decision to make her average—as opposed to the more common diamond-in-the-rough type—that lends interest to this intermittently impressive volume." The reviewer observed that the stories were best taken together as a whole, "Together they form a quick, seamless arc."

Rosenfeld followed up her collection of short stories with the novel *Massachussetts, California, Timbuktu.* Once again writing about a woman who pursues unhealthy relationships, she this time chose as her protagonist the woman's adolescent daughter, who must deal with the upheaval in her life that results from her mother's poor decisions. In an interview with the *Boox Review* Rosenfeld discussed her development of the novel. "What I think I learned to do," she stated, "was to listen to and observe my characters and to stay consistent with their individual realities—their voices, their actions, their patterns of thinking." Some critics also remarked upon the individual voice of her protagonist Justine Hawley. Writing in *Booklist,* Elsa Gaztambide predicted that "teen girls in particular will feel for wise-beyond-her-years Justine." A contributor to *Publishers Weekly* commented favorably on the epistolary structure of the novel, noting that "Rosenfeld's decision to intercut the story with ongoing excerpts from Justine's pioneer diary . . . is a clever device."

In an interview with Christy Karras of the *Salt Lake Tribune* Rosenfeld expressed her regret that serious critical attention is seldom payed to popular women's fiction. "I get sick of that whole division between 'chick lit'—stuff that women talk about, worry about, and that to a certain eye doesn't have much to do with the larger world—and 'real' writing," she related. "It took a long time to realize I don't have to spend so much of my energy worrying about pleasing the audience." She has been named to the *Missouri Review*'s list of "Ten Fiction Writers to Watch."

BIOGRAPHICAL AND CRITICAL SOURCES:

PERIODICALS

Booklist, May 15, 2003, Elsa Gaztambide, review of *Massachussetts, California, Timbuktu,* p. 1645; October 1, 2003, Barbara Baskin, review of *Massachusetts, California, Timbuktu,* p. 340.

Far Eastern Review, April 18, 1991, Rigoberto Tiglao, review of *Dragons in Distress: Asia's Miracle Economies in Crisis,* p. 56.

Journal of Contemporary Asia, December, 1992, Joseph Halevi, review of *Dragons in Distress,* pp. 546-548.

Kirkus Reviews, April 1, 2002, review of *What About the Love Part?,* pp. 448-449.

Management Today, May, 1992, Dick Wilson, review of *Dragons in Distress,* p. 113.

Monthly Review, September, 1991, Martin Hart-Landsberg, review of *Dragons in Distress,* pp. 57-63.

O, June, 2003, Cathleen Medwick, "I am 16, going on 40: the cracked joy and pain of adolescence," review of *Massachusetts, California, Timbuktu,* p. 124.

Publishers Weekly, March 18, 2002, review of *What About the Love Part?,* p. 72; April 28, 2003, review of *Massachussetts, California, Timbuktu,* p. 49.

Race and Class, October-December, 1992, S.B. Isabirye, review of *Dragons in Distress,* pp. 105-106.

Salt Lake Tribune, May 11, 2003, interview with the author.

School Library Journal, October, 2003, Kathy Tewell, review of *Massachusetts, California, Timbuktu,* p. 208.

Technology Review, February-March 1991, review of *Dragons in Distress.*

Utne Reader, March-April, 1991, Doug Henwood, review of *Dragons in Distress,* p. 152.

ONLINE

Boox Review, http://www.booxreview.com/ (July 27, 2004), interview with the author.*

* * *

RUNKEL, Sylvan T(homas) 1906-1995

PERSONAL: Born August 30, 1906 in Jacksonville, IL; died, 1995; son of C. A. and Myrtie Annabelle (Barnett) Runkel; married Beulah Skeie, 1930 (deceased, 1949); married Bernadine Neff, 1952; children: four sons, two daughters. *Education:* Iowa State College (now Iowa State University), B.S., 1933.

CAREER: Writer, forester, soil scientist, lecturer, and conservationist. Civilian Conservation Corps, camp superintendent, 1933; United States Soil Conservation Service, forester technician, 1934-39, forester and conservationist, 1939-1943, soil conservationist, forester, and biologist, 1947-52, Iowa state biologist, 1952-72. Appointed to Iowa State Preserves Board, 1969-1979 (served two years as chairman). Developed wildlife programming for Iowa Public Television Network. *Military service:* United States Army Air Corps, 1943-47; served as glider pilot; received Purple Heart, Air Medal, Bronze Arrowhead, and Presidential Unit Citation.

MEMBER: Soil Conservation Society of America (president of Iowa chapter), Wildlife Society, Boy Scouts of America, Society of American Foresters, Iowa Academy of Science (board of directors, two years), Des Moines Audubon Society.

AWARDS, HONORS: Federal Civil Servant of the Year, 1965; Frudden Award, Iowa Society of American Foresters, 1967; Iowa Conservation Hall of Fame, 1973; Soil Conservation Society of America fellow, 1974; Iowa Academy of Science fellow, 1977; Oak Leaf Award, Nature Conservancy, 1977; State Conservationist of the Year, 1987. An Iowa state nature preserve was named after Runkel in 1996.

WRITINGS:

(With Alvin F. Bull) *Wildflowers of Illinois Woodlands,* Wallace Homestead Book Co. (Des Moines, IA), 1979.

(With Alvin F. Bull) *Wildflowers of Indiana Woodlands,* Wallace Homestead Book Co. (Des Moines, IA), 1979.

(With Alvin F. Bull) *Wildflowers of Iowa Woodlands,* Wallace Homestead Book Co. (Des Moines, IA), 1979.

(With Dean M. Roosa) *Wildflowers of the Tallgrass Prairie: The Upper Midwest,* foreword by John Madson, Iowa State University Press (Ames, IA), 1989.

(With Dean M. Roosa) *Wildflowers and Other Plants of Iowa Wetlands,* Iowa State University Press (Ames, IA), 1999.

SIDELIGHTS: Conservationist, forester, and naturalist Sylvan T. Runkel dedicated his life to the preservation and maintenance of wetlands, wildlife, and other natural resources throughout Iowa and other areas in the United States. He began his career in forestry and conservation in the mid-1920s, and became superintendent of Iowa's first Civilian Conservation Corps camp in 1933. In 1934 he joined the United States Soil Conservation Service (SCS). After fighting for his country and becoming a decorated Air Force glider pilot during World War II, he returned to the SCS, where he remained until retiring in 1972. Runkel also served terms as the Iowa state biologist and as a member of the Iowa State Preserves Board.

Education was the primary tool in Runkel's conservation repertoire. He conducted hundreds of lectures, field trips, demonstrations, and workshops. "Many people were first introduced to the woodlands by taking a walk with Runkel and listening to him describe the natural community as a living entity," observed a reviewer on the *Prarie du Chien Area* Web site.

After retiring from government service, Runkel extended his educational mission to writing books focusing on the wildflowers, plants, trees, and other flora in the Midwestern states of Indiana, Illinois, and Iowa. *Wildflowers and Other Plants of Iowa Wetlands* covers 149 species of wetland plants found in Iowa and other areas of the United States and Canada. The mostly common species include ninety-five terrestrial flowering herbs, twenty-five aquatic flowering herbs, and sixteen types of trees, vines, and shrubs. "The text discusses distribution, morphology, ecology, and uses by wildlife, Native Americans, and other peoples," noted R. Schmid in *Choice.* "As wetlands decline in

size and abundance, there is a need for greater awareness of the economic and ecological value of wetlands," remarked Julie Stundins in a review of the book on the *Chicago Botanic Garden* Web site. "This book is a step in the right direction in its description of different types of wetlands and the value of these basic habitats."

Runkel died in 1995, but left a lasting legacy of respect for the environment and natural world. The Sylvan Runkel State Preserve in Iowa bears his name and sets aside 330 acres of unique Loess Hills prairie land that is native to Iowa. A biography, *Sylvan T. Runkel: Citizen of the Natural World,* was published by Runkel's colleagues, hawk researcher and conservationist Jon W. Stravers and outdoor writer and photographer Larry A. Stone. Runkel "turned out to be an incredible teacher," Stravers commented on the *Prarie du Chien Area* Web site. "He was very personable, kids had an immediate respect for him, and he had a great enthusiasm for knowledge." The man considered Iowa's foremost naturalist "was kind of famous among conservationists," Stravers remarked. "He was like a walking legend."

BIOGRAPHICAL AND CRITICAL SOURCES:

BOOKS

Stone, Larry, and Jon W. Stravers, *Sylvan T. Runkel: Citizen of the Natural World,* Larry A. Stone (Elkader, IA), 2004.

PERIODICALS

AB Bookman's Weekly, June 5, 1989, Kevin Kiddoo, review of *Wildflowers of the Tallgrass Prairie: The Upper Midwest,* pp. 2510-2511.
Appraisal: Science Books for Young People, winter, 1995, Sharon Rizzo, pp. 123-124.
Choice, January, 2000, R. Schmid, review of *Wildflowers and Other Plants of Iowa Wetlands.*

ONLINE

Chicago Botanic Garden, http://www.chicago-botanic.org/ (April 2, 2004), Julie Stundins, review of *Wildflowers and Other Plants of Iowa Wetlands.*

Iowa Association of Naturalists, http://www.ianpage.
20m.com/ (April 2, 2004), profile of Sylvan
Runkel.

Prairie du Chien Area, http://www.prairieduchienarea.
com/ (April 2, 2004), review of *Sylvan T. Runkel:
Citizen of the Natural World.**

* * *

RUSSELL, H(elen) Diane 1936-2004

OBITUARY NOTICE—See index for *CA* sketch: Born
April 8, 1936, in Kansas City, MO (one source says
Paola, KS); died of cancer March 4, 2004, in Falls
Church, VA. Museum curator, educator, and author.
Russell was a former curator at the National Gallery
of Art. After earning a B.A. in 1958 from Vassar College, she worked as a research assistant for the Smithsonian Institution from 1960 to 1961, and in 1964 was
hired by the National Gallery of Art as a museum
curator. Completing her Ph.D. in art history at Johns
Hopkins University in 1970, she remained at the
Washington, D.C., museum throughout her career,
becoming curator and head of Old Master prints from
1990 until her 1998 retirement. Russell was also a
lecturer at American University intermittently during
the late 1960s and 1970s, and was a member of the
Institute for Advanced Study from 1980 to 1981.
Involved in several organizations, she was a member
of the Renaissance Society of America, the Print
Council of America, and the College Art Association
of America. Russell published several exhibition
catalogs during her career, such as *Jacque Callot:
Prints and Related Drawings* (1975) and *Claude Lorraine, 1600-1682* (1982). For her service to the art
community, in 1984 she was presented with the Award
of Merit from the American Association of Museums
and the Alfred H. Barr Jr. Award from the College Art
Association of America.

OBITUARIES AND OTHER SOURCES:

PERIODICALS

Washington Post, March 10, 2004, p. B5.

S

SABATO, Haim

PERSONAL: Name sometimes transliterated as "Hayim"; born in Egypt.

ADDRESSES: Home—Israel. *Agent*—c/o Author Mail, Toby Press, P.O. Box 8531, New Milford, CT 06776-8531.

CAREER: Rabbi and novelist; head of yeshiva near Jerusalem, Israel. *Military service:* Israeli Tank Corps, gunner during Yom Kippur War, 1973.

AWARDS, HONORS: Sadeh Prize (Israel); Sapir Prize (Israel), 2000, for *Te'um Kavanot.*

WRITINGS:

Minhat Aharon: me'asaf Torani le-zikhro shel ha-Rav, [Jerusalem, Israel], 1980.
Emet me-erets titsmah/Truth Shall Spring from the Earth, Sifre ha-gag (Tel Aviv, Israel), 1997.
Ahavat Torah/Love of Torah, Yedi'ot aharonot (Tel Aviv, Israel), 2000.
Te'um Kavanot, Sifre ha-gag (Tel Aviv, Israel), 1999, translated by Hillel Halkin as *Adjusting Sights,* Toby Press (New Milford, CT), 2003.

SIDELIGHTS: Haim Sabato was born in Egypt, a descendent of several generations of rabbis living in Aleppo, Syria. When he was six years old, Sabato and his family moved to Israel, and in 1973 he served as a gunner in the Israeli Tank Corps during the Yom Kippur War. Now a rabbi leading a yeshiva, or Jewish seminary, near the city of Jerusalem, Sabato is also the author of several books. His second book *Adjusting Sights,* which won Israel's Sapir prize following its 1999 publication, is a fictionalized biography of Sabato's own account of war.

Adjusting Sights is not a commentary on religion or politics, and it does not proclaim to either condemn or condone acts of war. Rather it is the story of a nineteen-year-old young man and his personal accounts of the Yom Kippur War of 1973. Sabato shares his first name with main character Haim, who works as a tank gunner. Haim describes the first harrowing days of warfare, interspersing these descriptions with memories from his childhood and reflections on his current circumstances. Haim is not alone in his journey however; he is lucky enough to have his childhood friend Dov around to keep him company. While growing up, the two boys were scholarly and took their religion very seriously; now, in the midst of war, Haim finds that prayer and Talmudic passages gives him the courage to face another day and the challenges yet before him. While traveling through the rolling hills of the Golan Heights Haim eventually loses contact with Dov, unaware of his friend's fate until the novel's end. The novel's title, *Adjusting Sights,* not only refers to Haim's technical skill in deflecting the blinding sunlight that often interferes with his ability to properly aim his tank's guns, but also his growing faculty for comprehending the meaning of loss and tragedy.

Joan Cantor, in the *KBI Book Review,* commented of *Adjusting Sights* that in his novel Rabbi Sabato "presents the Torah as a living, breathing document that can lead one through difficult decisions, even in the midst of bloody battle." Molly Abramowitz also enjoyed the novel and appreciated Sabato's ability to present the war as multifacteted. "Other characters retell the battlefield story, adding dimension to this delicate, poignant story," Abramowitz wrote in *Library Journal,* adding that the "classical Hebrew is artfully translated" by Hillel Halkin.

BIOGRAPHICAL AND CRITICAL SOURCES:

PERIODICALS

Library Journal, April 1, 2003, Molly Abramowitz, review of *Adjusting Sights,* p. 130.

ONLINE

KBI Book Review, http://users.erols.com/kbi6300/KBI_Book_Review.html (October 10, 2003), Joan Cantor, review of *Adjusting Sites.*
Toby Press Web site, http://www.tobypyress.com/ (May 15, 2004), "Haim Sabato."*

*   *   *

SACK, John 1930-2004

OBITUARY NOTICE—See index for *CA* sketch: Born March 24, 1930, in New York, NY; died of complications from a bone marrow transplant to treat myelodysplasia (one source says the cause was prostate cancer) March 27, 2004, in San Francisco, CA. Journalist and author. A reporter numbered among those in the school of New Journalism, Sack was best known as a war correspondent who covered conflicts ranging from the Korean and Vietnam wars to the battles in Yugoslavia and Afghanistan. Beginning his vocation at a young age, Sack got his start as a stringer for the *Mamaroneck Daily Times* when he was just fifteen years old. Completing his bachelor's degree at Harvard in 1951, he joined the army and became a war correspondent for the U.S. military's publications *Stars and Stripes,* covering the Korean War from 1952 to 1953; he also wrote for *Esquire* and *Harper's* magazines while in Korea, and worked for the United

Press in the early Fifties. Becoming a freelance journalist, Sack contributed regularly to the *New Yorker* from 1953 to 1961, when he accepted a job with CBS News as a writer and documentary producer. With America's increasing involvement in Vietnam, Sack next became an *Esquire* correspondent in Asia, out of which came his books *M* (1967) and *Lieutenant Calley: His Own Story* (1971). From 1978 to 1986, Sack was a contributing editor to *Playboy,* and during the early 1980s he became involved in television again as a writer for the series *That's Incredible!* and as a writer and producer for KCBS-TV in Los Angeles. He returned to *Esquire* in 1991, reporting on the conflicts in Iraq, Kuwait, and Bosnia. It was also in the early 1990s that Sack received criticism for his book *An Eye for an Eye* (1993) in which he reported that German internment prisoners were tormented by Polish Communist Jews after World War II. Among his other books are *The Butcher: The Ascent of Yerupaja* (1952), *The Man-Eating Machine* (1973), *Fingerprint* (1983), *Company C: The Real War in Iraq* (1995), and *The Dragonhead: The True Story of the Godfather of Chinese Crime—His Rise and Fall* (2001).

OBITUARIES AND OTHER SOURCES:

BOOKS

Dictionary of Literary Biography, Volume 185: *American Literary Journalists, 1945-1995,* Gale (Detroit, MI), 1997.

PERIODICALS

Los Angeles Times, March 31, 2004, p. B10.
New York Times, March 31, 2004, p. C13.
Washington Post, April 2, 2004, p. B9.

*   *   *

SACKS, Steven 1968-

PERSONAL: Born January 3, 1968, in Bronx, NY; son of Allan and Elaine Sacks. *Education:* State University of New York—Buffalo, B.S., 1992; Fordham University, M.B.A., 1995.

ADDRESSES: Office—Mate Map Enterprises, 1289 N. Fordham Blvd., Suite 349, Chapel Hill, NC 27514. E-mail—steven@matemap.com

CAREER: Entrepreneur; Founder of Mate Map Enterprises; Relationship coach; Writer.

MEMBER: Publishers Marketing Association.

WRITINGS:

The Mate Map: The Right Tool for Choosing the Right Mate, Banner Publishing (New York, NY), 2002.

SIDELIGHTS: A relationship coach and entrepreneur, Steven Sacks is primarily known as creator of the Mate Map, a method for finding long-term relationship partners. The genesis of this method is described on the Mate Map Web site: "After several years of struggling to find the right person for him, Steven thought to himself 'there's got to be a better way.' So he looked for a book that would offer him help. But after searching the bookstores, the libraries and the internet, he didn't find anything that he was confident would work. . . . Since a tangible method didn't exist, the only way he was going to get what he wanted was if he created such a system himself. And that's exactly what he set out to do." Sacks drew on his ten years as a business strategist to come up with an analytical framework for judging both the emotional and practical aspects of any relationship, and for predicting the prospects of long-term success. Pleased with the results in his own life, he began sharing his method, then testing it under the supervision of a trained psychologist and statistician. In 2002, he published The Mate Map: The Right Tool for Choosing the Right Mate to give his method a wider audience. Library Journal reviewer Douglas Lord found it "Illustrative, informative, and not as wacky as it sounds." Suzie Housley, a contributor to the My-Shelf Web site, went further, calling the book "a must read for anyone seeking expert advice on how to find 'Mr./Ms. Right.' Do yourself a favor; set sail on an exciting adventure-ensure you make reading the Mate Map a top priority!"

Steven Sacks told CA: "The reason why so many relationships don't last is because the two people were never compatible enough in the first place. Therefore we need to do a thorough assessment of a potential mate before making a lifetime commitment."

BIOGRAPHICAL AND CRITICAL SOURCES:

PERIODICALS

Library Journal, September 15, 2002, review of The Mate Map, p. 81.

ONLINE

Mate Map Web site, http://www.matemap.com (accessed June 12, 2003), "The Story of the Mate Map."
My Shelf Web site, http://myshelf.com/ (accessed September 30, 2003), Suzie Housley, review of The Mate Map.*

*   *   *

SARKODIE-MENSAH, Kwasi 1955-

PERSONAL: Born June 13, 1955, in Ejisu-Ashanti, Ghana; naturalized U.S. citizen; son of Thomas Kwaku (an educator) and Margaret (Barnieh) Mensah; married Elizabeth Oppong (a librarian and anthropologist), September 21, 1980. Ethnicity: "Ghanaian/Black." Education: National University of the Ivory Coast, certificate in French, 1978; Universidad de Complutense, Madrid, Spain, diploma in Spanish, 1978; University of Ghana, B.A. (with honors), 1979; Clarion University, M.S.L.S., 1983; University of Illinois—Urbana-Champaign, Ph.D., 1988. Politics: Republican. Religion: Roman Catholic.

ADDRESSES: Home—3 Westwood St., Burlington, MA 01803. Office—312 O'Neill Library, Boston College, Chestnut Hill, MA 02467; fax: 617-552-8828. E-mail—sarkodiek@bc.edu.

CAREER: Teacher of French and English at secondary schools in Kumasi, Ghana, 1979-80, and Ipetumodu, Nigeria, 1980-82; Frontiers in Human Resources, Knoxville, PA, trainee aide, 1983-84; Xavier University of Louisiana, New Orleans, LA, head of public services, 1986-89, acting director of university library, 1987, and instructor in French; Northeastern University, Boston, MA, library instruction coordinator, 1989-92; Boston College, Chestnut Hill, MA, chief reference librarian at O'Neill Library, 1992-95, manager of instructional services, 1992—, Benjamin E. Mayes Mentor, 1995—, faculty member at College of Advancing Studies, 1996—. Southern University, New Orleans, LA, French teacher, summers, 1988-89; lecturer at other institutions, including Simmons College; speaker at many public schools on Africa and on growing up in Ghana. French Teachers Movement of Louisiana, member, 1986-89; Massachusetts Faculty Development Advisory Committee, member, 1992-97; New England Bibliographic Instruction Committee, chair, 1994-97. Multicultural Network of Winchester, MA, member, 1992-99; Archdiocese of Boston, board member of African Pastoral Center, 1997-2001. Redco Co., translator and interpreter, 1979; consultant in Ghanaian language to U.S. Customs and to state superior courts.

MEMBER: American Library Association (member of Black Caucus, 1991-97), Association of College and Research Libraries, Library Instruction Round Table, Beta Phi Mu.

AWARDS, HONORS: French government scholar in Ivory Coast, 1977-78; Spanish and Ghanaian government scholar in Spain, 1978; certificate of outstanding achievement in multi-cultural education, Arts in Progress, Boston, 1993; Boston College, Bill Day Award, 1995, Reverend John R. Trzaska Award, 2001, and Community Service Award, 2001.

WRITINGS:

(With Brendan Rapple) *Research in the Electronic Age: How to Distinguish between Good and Bad Data,* Boston College (Chestnut Hill, MA), 1999.
(Editor) *Reference Services for the Adult Learner: Challenging Issues for the Traditional and Technological Era,* Haworth Press (Binghamton, NY), 2000.
Helping the Difficult Library Patron: New Approaches to Examining and Resolving a Long-standing and Ongoing Problem, Haworth Press (Binghamton, NY), 2002.

Contributor to books, including *Recommended Videos for School: 1992,* American Bibliographical Center-Clio Press (Santa Barbara, CA), 1992; *Diversity and Multiculturalism in Libraries,* edited by Katherine

Hoover Hill, JAI Press (Greenwich, CT), 1994; and *Teaching the New Library to Today's Users: Reaching International, Minority, Senior Citizens, Gay/Lesbian, First Generation, At-risk, Graduate and Returning Students, and Distance Learners,* edited by Trudi E. Jacobson and Helene C. Williams, Neal-Schuman Publishers (New York, NY), 2000. Work represented in anthologies, including *World Treasury of Great Poems,* 1989. Contributor of articles and reviews to periodicals, including *Catholic Library World, Journal of Education for Library and Information Science, Library Mosaics, Journal of Academic Librarianship, College Teaching, College and Research Libraries News, University Teaching in the South,* and *Reference Librarian.* Editor, *LIRT Newsletter,* 1991-92.

SIDELIGHTS: Kwasi Sarkodie-Mensah told *CA:* "My primary motivation for writing is to share my knowledge and expertise with people in my profession and in the area of education. I feel a moral responsibility to be the voice of the under-served in libraries and on college campuses. Having come to the United States as a foreign student is an inspiration for me to write about issues that others may not initially find important because they have never had to live with the experience that international students go through.

"My writing process varies. I can compose in my head, scribble continuously on paper, or write in an outline format, and then take time to polish up things. I do a lot of thinking when I am on the treadmill or playing tennis in the gym each morning. It is not uncommon for me mentally to 'tread' my writing in the middle of my exercise routine.

"International students, adult learners, students with disabilities have not always been popular topics. It may be because people feel so remotely removed from them. When I walk across campus, walk in the library, interact with different students, a variety of ideas crops up in my mind. I think I can continue to raise awareness on how we should pay attention to our special populations on our campuses."

BIOGRAPHICAL AND CRITICAL SOURCES:

PERIODICALS

American Libraries, May, 2001, Cathleen Bourdon, review of *Reference Services for the Adult Learner: Challenging Issues for the Traditional and Technological Era,* p. 88.

SAVAN, Glenn 1953-2003

PERSONAL: Born December 28, 1953; died of a heart attack or stroke at his home, April 14, 2003, in Shrewsbury, MO; son of Sidney Savan (a former advertising executive; teacher at the University of Missouri). *Education:* Attended Webster University (St. Louis, MO) and Southern Illinois University at Carbondale; University of Iowa Writer's Workshop, M.F.A., 1982. *Hobbies and other interests:* Gem and mineral collecting.

CAREER: Novelist. Worked for his father at the Savan Company (an advertising agency); waited tables.

WRITINGS:

White Palace (novel), Bantam Books (New York, NY), 1987.
Goldman's Anatomy (novel), Doubleday (New York, NY), 1993.

ADAPTATIONS: White Palace was adapted into a motion picture starring James Spader and Susan Sarandon, Universal Pictures, 1990. Excerpts from *White Palace* were read by Savan for audio cassette, American Audio Prose Library, 1989; an abridged version of *Goldman's Anatomy* was adapted for audio cassette, read by Barry Williams, The Publishing Mills, 1993.

SIDELIGHTS: Glenn Savan quit a job at his father's advertising agency to wait tables and write his first novel, the best-selling *White Palace.* Published in 1987, the book became the first title in a Bantam paperback line of fiction by young authors. The success of the novel helped it make the transition to the silver screen, with a critically acclaimed production starring James Spader and Susan Sarandon. A second book, *Goldman's Anatomy,* also earned strong reviews, but Savan would not live to complete his third novel. He died in 2003 after suffering from poor health much of his life. Savan had a degenerative joint condition as well as Parkinson's disease, a neurological condition causing tremors and a progressive weakening of the muscles; for a period during his childhood, he used a wheelchair and crutches. Experimental neurosurgery performed in 2001 was not successful; Savan died of a heart attack or stroke at the age of forty-nine.

White Palace revolves around the love affair between a handsome, young, widowed advertising man named Max and an older, rather uncouth waitress, Nora. They cross paths twice; the second time they are both on their way to getting drunk at a bar, and despite Max's thinly veiled contempt for the aggressive Nora, they wind up in bed together. The story that follows explores whether Max can finally overcome his grief over his departed wife and if love and lust can keep together two people with very different interests, habits, and social backgrounds. While Max would appear to be quite a catch for any woman and someone who could "improve" Nora in a Professor Higgins-Eliza Doolittle type of relationship (a reference to Bernard Shaw's 1916 classic tale *Pygmalion*), Max comes to see Nora's influence over him as a powerful means of freeing him from himself.

The *Pygmalion*-like story appealed to many critics. In the *Los Angeles Times,* Tom Jenks called *White Palace* "a surprising, mid-American love song," noting it is "an unusually good, fast read" and that Savan was deft at writing "wrought-up explicit sex, which can't be quoted in a newspaper." According to Jonathan Yardley in *The Washington Post,* the book contains "occasional infelicities of prose and a tendency toward didacticism" but nevertheless is "a serious entertainment, and a far cut above the run of contemporary 'yuppie fiction.'" *Chicago Tribune* writer John Blades observed that the "surefire" plot resembles that of Somerset Maugham's *In Human Bondage* and advised that "Savan is such a brashly assured writer and *White Palace* is such a model of energetic, fast-forward storytelling that this first novel is compulsive reading." A dissenting opinion was voiced in *Mademoiselle* by Joyce Maynard, who commented, "There's something almost insufferably insulting about the way Savan portrays [Nora]. . . . In the end he never takes her seriously enough to show her experiencing any believable sensations besides orgasms."

When *White Palace* was made into a film in 1990, reviews indicated that it benefited from the performances of Spader and Sarandon, but that the story lost something in the adaptation. *Los Angeles Times* critic Sheila Benson described the film as "searingly well-acted" but found that the relationship between Max and Nora seemed more implausible on screen, having shed important details from the novel. In *National Review* John Simon remarked that "the film could have been interesting but for the simple-mindedness Hollywood exacts from its so-called 'adult' movies," referring to a neat romanticism he found imposed on the story.

Savan's second novel, *Goldman's Anatomy,* is the story of a threesome of misfits who are both attracted and aggravated by each other's physical and mental frailties. The central character, Arnie Goldman, is a reclusive, arthritic gem dealer who is surprised by the appearance of a high school friend who has dropped out of college. Arnie invites Redso and his girlfriend Billy to stay with him while Redso is writing a play. Arnie is strongly attracted to Billy, who has devoted herself to taking care of the manic-depressive Redso. Arnie eventually wants to leave the destructive triangle, but cannot bring himself to act.

The story is told, according to Savan, in a consciously film-like manner. He told *Chicago Tribune* writer Steve Rhodes, "I do write scenically, not in order to make my stuff easily translatable to the screen but maybe because movies have been almost as influential on my imagination as books have." Reviewers again admired the author's storytelling ability. A *Publishers Weekly* critic remarked that "Savan's brisk pacing allows for energetic dialogue if less than full-blooded characterizations." In a review for the *Chicago Tribune,* Bill Mahin reflected, "a book based on three such characters . . . has all the ingredients of lurid, sensational trash. But *Goldman's Anatomy* is, rather, a book about people coming to terms with physical and mental afflictions, often with a certain amount of insight." Donna Levin expressed her pleasure at finding another novel by Savan, and wrote in the *Los Angeles Times* that the book is "even more assured, and fulfills the promise of the first without covering the same territory." She called the book "a fascinating study of [Arnie's] paralysis; of madness and codependency, but mostly of love."

BIOGRAPHICAL AND CRITICAL SOURCES:

PERIODICALS

Chicago Tribune, June 28, 1987, John Blades, "First Novelists Deliver on the Paperback Route," p. 3; June 18, 1993, Bill Mahin, "A Confederacy of Cripples Struggling to Adjust," p. 3; July 19, 1993, Steve Rhodes, "Sick Thoughts *White Palace* Author Muses about Illness, Physical and Otherwise," p. 3.

Los Angeles Times, August 2, 1987, Tom Jenks, "Literature as Life Style," p. 1; October 19, 1990, Sheila Benson, "Prime Sarandon on *White Palace* Menu," p. 1; May 30, 1993, Donna Levin, "Victims of Love," p. 5.

Mademoiselle, November, 1987, Joyce Maynard, "Soon to Be a Major Motion Picture," pp. 116, 118-119.

National Review, December 31, 1990, John Simon, "Odd Couples."

Publishers Weekly, March 15, 1993, review of *Goldman's Anatomy,* p. 68.

Washington Post, June 24, 1987, Jonathan Yardley, "Love and Fate in Dogtown," p. D2.

OBITUARIES:

PERIODICALS

New York Times, April 17, 2003, p. C13.

Post-Dispatch (St. Louis, MO), April 15, 2003, p. B1.*

*   *   *

SCARTH, Alwyn

PERSONAL: Male.

ADDRESSES: Agent—c/o Author Mail, Oxford University Press, 2001 Evans Rd., Cary, NC 27513.

CAREER: Geologist, author, and educator. Former lecturer in geography, University of Dundee, Scotland.

WRITINGS:

Volcanoes: An Introduction, Texas A&M University Press (College Station, TX), 1994.

(With Jean-Claude Tanguy) *Vulcan's Fury: Man against the Volcano,* Yale University Press (New Haven, CT), 1999.

Volcanoes of Europe, Oxford University Press (New York, NY), 2001.

La Catastrophe: The Eruption of Mount Pelee, the Worst Volcanic Eruption of the Twentieth Century, Oxford University Press (New York, NY), 2002.

Savage Earth: The Dramatic Story of Volcanoes and Earthquakes, Harpercollins (New York, NY), 2002.

SIDELIGHTS: A noted volcanologist, Alwyn Scarth has written several books about one of the nature's most spectacular and devastating displays: volcanic eruptions. In his first book, *Volcanoes: An Introduction,* Scarth writes about volcanoes for a general audience, emphasizing both geography and geomorphology—that is, a volcano's characteristics, configuration, and evolution. The book includes historical accounts of various volcanic eruptions and the consequences that they had on the societies of the time. Scarth discusses the geographical location of volcanoes (most lie beneath the oceans), the process of creating magma (molten rock), and various categories of volcanic landforms.

In *Nature,* reviewer Peter Francis commented that *Volcanoes: An Introduction* revisits too much ground about volcanoes already detailed by other writers. He also believed that Scarth sometimes oversimplifies his explanations, which could mislead the reader. Nevertheless, he noted, "Such reservations apart, the book has much to offer." Writing in *American Scientist,* James B. Garvin noted, "In general, the author has produced a very readable and admirable short discussion of a selected set of volcanoes and volcanic eruptions from around the world."

In *Vulcan's Fury: Man against the Volcano,* the author turns from a scientific discussion of how volcanoes work to focus on the history of volcanoes, describing fifteen historic eruptions that occurred around the world. Much of the work is based on original sources in Latin, French, Spanish, and English. The author also includes numerous eyewitness accounts of volcanic eruptions, from the eruption of Mount Vesuvius overlooking the Bay of Naples in A.D. 79 to 1981's eruption of Mount St. Helens and the Mount Pinatubo eruption in the Philippines a decade later. Scarth uses details from these accounts to provide a full picture of disasters, their origins, and their aftermaths. The chapters are chronologically arranged, and Scarth includes a discussion on how scientists can now predict and prepare for large volcanic eruptions such as Mount Pinatubo. Although Mount Pinatubo's eruption potentially could have killed a half-million people, early warnings to evacuate kept the death toll to around a thousand people. The book also includes maps and numerous illustrations.

"Alwyn Scarth has done what many of us aspire to do," wrote geologist Sally Newcomb in a review of *Vulcan's Fury: Man against the Volcano* in *Isis.* "He has taken a huge subject, best described in highly technical terms, and has written a gripping, highly readable history about it." She went on to note, "This story is a true intersection of science and society from which we all can learn." In *Geographical Review,* reviewer Michael Ort commented that his initial reaction to the book was "mixed" but concluded, "Overall, though, I found myself greatly impressed by a well-written account of the effects that volcanoes have had on society."

In his 2002 book *La Catastrophe: The Eruption of Mount Pelee, the Worst Volcanic Eruption of the Twentieth Century,* Scarth provides a definitive study of the 1902 eruption of Mount Pelee in Martinique. The eruption killed more than 27,000 people in the town of Saint-Pierre, leveling the island's capital in less than two minutes. Once again, Scarth relies heavily on eyewitness reports to describe in detail the worst volcanic eruption since the eruption of Mount Vesuvius buried the city of Pompeii nearly 2,000 years earlier. In addition to discussing the natural events that led up to eruption, his account also explores the tragic aftermath of Mount Pelee's eruption and its wide-ranging political implications.

Writing in *National Geographic Adventure,* a reviewer called *La Catastrophe* "spectacularly detailed and heartbreakingly vivid." In a review in the *Library Journal,* Jean E. Crampon noted that she found that Scarth's "meticulous detail sometimes detracts from the smoothness of the reading." However, Crampon praised Scarth's "heavy emphasis on the political commentary, which will help readers understand the implications of the volcano in light of its time." Writing in *Publishers Weekly,* another reviewer praised Scarth for providing a "much-needed sociological dimension to the natural tragedy." The reviewer also noted that "Scarth maintains the reader's interest without watering down his formidable knowledge of how volcanoes actually work."

BIOGRAPHICAL AND CRITICAL SOURCES:

PERIODICALS

American Scientist, November-December, 1995, James B. Garvin, review of *Volcanoes: An Introduction,* pp. 574-576.

Discover, October, 1999, Robert Kunzig, review of *Vulcan's Fury: Man against the Volcano,* p. 108.

Geographical Review, April, 2000, Michael Ort, review of *Vulcan's Fury,* pp. 297-298.

Isis, September, 2002, Sally Newcomb, review of *Vulcan's Fury,* pp. 465-466.

Library Journal, September 1, 1999, Jean E. Crampon, review of *Vulcan's Fury,* p. 230; June 1, 2002, review of *La Catastrophe: The Eruption of Mount Pelee, the Worst Volcanic Eruption of the Twentieth Century,* p. 184.

National Geographic Adventurer, August, 2002, review of *La Catastrophe,* p. 42.

Nature, October 13, 1994, Peter Francis, review of *Volcanoes,* p. 569.

New York Times, February 29, 2000, "A Brief History of Beauty, Terror and Trial by Fire," p. F5.

Publishers Weekly, August 30, 1999, review of *Vulcan's Fury,* p. 63; May 20, 2002, review of *La Catastrophe,* p. 57.

Science News, September 11, 1999, Cait Anthony, review of *Vulcan's Fury,* p. 163.

Sciences, January-February, 2000, Laurence A. Marschall, review of *Vulcan's Fury,* p. 45.*

*   *   *

SCHAIN, Richard J. 1930-

PERSONAL: Born October 16, 1930, in New York, NY; son of Maurice and Beatrice (Gaier) Schain; married, 1952; married Melanie Dreisbach, August 15, 1980; children: two. *Education:* New York University, A.B., 1950, M.D., 1954.

ADDRESSES: Home—Box 517, Glen Ellen, CA 95442. *E-mail*—rjschain@lycos.com.

CAREER: Yale University School of Medicine, resident in pediatrics, 1957-59; University of Nebraska, assistant professor to associate professor of neurology and psychiatry, 1962-66; University of California—Los Angeles, associate professor of pediatrics, 1967-77, professor of pediatrics, neurology, and psychiatry, 1977-80, adjunct professor of pediatrics, neurology, and psychiatry, 1980—; neurological consultant at a California state hospital, 1980—. *Military service:* U.S. Air Force, 1955-57, captain.

MEMBER: American Academy of Neurology, American Association for Mental Deficiency, American Academy of Pediatrics, Society for Research in Child Development, Society for Pediatric Research.

AWARDS, HONORS: Fellowships in neurology, 1959-60, 1961-62, fellowship in physiology and pharmacology, 1960-61, National Institute for Medical Research, London, England.

WRITINGS:

The Neurology of Childhood Learning Disorders, Williams & Wilkins (Baltimore, MD), 1972, 2nd edition, 1977.

Affirmations of Reality, Garric Press (Glen Ellen, CA), 1982.

Philosophical Artwork and Other Writings, Garric Press (Glen Ellen, CA), 1983.

Sententiae, Garric Press (Glen Ellen, CA), 1984.

A Fanatic of the Mind, Garric Press (Glen Ellen, CA), 1987.

Souls Exist, Garric Press (Berkeley, CA), 1989.

The Legend of Nietzsche's Syphilis, Contributions in Medical Studies, no. 46, Greenwood Press (Westport, CT), 2001.

Radical Metaphysics, self-published through Xlibris (Olde City, PA), 2003.

SIDELIGHTS: A professor of child neurology, pediatrics, and psychiatry, Richard J. Schain wrote his first book, *The Neurology of Childhood Learning Disorders,* in the early 1970s. He was the first child neurologist to write about the subject of minimal brain dysfunction (MBD)—or specific learning disability (SLD)—syndrome and related neurocognitive developmental disorders. His book received praise from R. D. Becker, in the *Journal of Learning Disabilities,* as an "important and instructive little volume" on the subject of "the inner-conflicted cognitive, affective, experiential, intersensory and neurological realities" of children who appear to have MBD, which, says Schain, is a clinical diagnosis that is widely abused. Schain discusses the many diagnostic terms that have come in and out of vogue to describe the same set of learning, perceptual, visual, emotional, and behavioral symptoms. He stresses the importance of using systematic approaches to the complicated issue of diagnosis, acknowledging the existence of neuropathologic disorders that can mimic MBD in early stages. Schain gives clinical descriptions of such degenerative pediatric problems as Huntington's Chorea, Wilson's Disease, Speilmeyer-Vogt Disease, and Friedreich's Ataxia in his book. According to Becker, Schain's volume is "a lucid, systematic, and cogently instructive view of an increasingly important area of clinical pediatric and neurological concern."

Schain's book, *The Legend of Nietzsche's Syphilis,* is an assessment of the great German philosopher's life from a neurological and psychological viewpoint. Schain strives to put to rest the legend that Nietzsche's degenerative mental disorder was the result of general paresis, or syphilis of the brain. Doctors diagnosed him with the advanced stages of syphilis, and commentary was that he had acquired the sexually transmitted disease while in college. However, Schain contends that Nietzsche's lifelong symptoms actually point toward a manic-depressive psychosis that later developed into chronic schizophrenia. Nietzsche sustained a nervous breakdown at age forty-four and died at age fifty-six after his condition slowly deteriorated to paralysis. Schain finds that the philosopher's childhood illnesses, the slow progression of his disease, and the absence of certain neurological symptoms common to late-stage syphilis indicate that syphilis was not the cause of his illness and death.

In a review of *The Legend of Nietzsche's Syphilis* for the *Times Literary Supplement,* Brian Leiter called Schain's theory plausible and noted that he "makes a compelling case" for it. "Indeed," Leiter wrote, "Schain must surely be right that the 'lucid and vigorous thought content . . . and usual masterful prose' of Nietzsche's last work, *Ecce Homo,* is simply not compatible with syphilitic damage to the brain." G. Eknoyan, reviewing the book for *Choice,* called it "an informed and insightful summary account" of Nietzsche's illness and suffering.

BIOGRAPHICAL AND CRITICAL SOURCES:

BOOKS

American Men & Women of Science, 12th, 13th, 15th, and 16th editions, Gale (Detroit, MI).

PERIODICALS

Choice, March, 2002, G. Eknoyan, review of *The Legend of Nietzsche's Syphilis,* p. 1272.

Journal of Learning Disabilities, May, 1975, R. D. Becker, review of *The Neurology of Childhood Learning Disorders,* pp. 70-71.
Reference & Research Book News, November, 2001, review of *The Legend of Nietzsche's Syphilis,* p. 239.
Times Literary Supplement, October 18, 2002, Brian Leiter, "The Fate of Genius" (review of *The Legend of Nietzsche's Syphilis* and others), pp. 12-13.

ONLINE

Radical Metaphysics of Richard Schain, http://rschain1.tripod.com/index.html (September 25, 2003).*

*   *   *

SCHATZKIN, Paul

PERSONAL: Born in New York, NY; married, wife's name Ann. *Education:* Antioch College, B.A.

ADDRESSES: Home—Pegram, TN. *Office*—c/o Author Mail, TeamCom, Inc., P.O. Box 1251, Burtonsville, MD 20866.

CAREER: Worked as videotape editor for television, including American Broadcasting Company (ABC)-TV series *Barney Miller;* writer.

AWARDS, HONORS: Emmy Award nomination for editing work on *Barney Miller.*

WRITINGS:

The Boy Who Invented Television: A Story of Inspiration, Persistence, and Quiet Passion, TeamCom Books (Burtonsville, MD), 2002.

Contributor to *Encyclopedia Britannica.*

SIDELIGHTS: The year 2002 marked the seventy-fifth anniversary of the first demonstration of television. The inventor of the medium, Philo T. Farnsworth, was twenty-one years old when he devised the invention in 1927. Like many other inventors, Farnsworth was a self-educated genius whose strengths lay in visionary thinking, not in the day-to-day corporate machinations that inevitably accompany any new technology. Although awarded the first patent for television, Farnsworth found himself embroiled in litigation with the giant Radio Corporation of America (RCA). Eventually he faded into obscurity, anonymously pursuing research into cold fusion.

Former television editor Paul Schatzkin became interested in Farnsworth more than a quarter century ago while working in Hollywood. Schatzkin's timing was good. He was able to interview some of Farnsworth's associates and Farnsworth's widow, Pem. Schatzkin's book, *The Boy Who Invented Television: A Story of Inspiration, Persistence, and Quiet Passion,* charts Farnsworth's life from his burst of inspiration while working in a farm field at age fourteen to his unheralded death amidst unfinished research many years later.

Schatzkin's book is part of a resurgence of interest in Farnsworth and his scientific contributions that began at the turn of the twenty-first century. In *Booklist,* Mark Knoblauch praised *The Boy Who Invented Television* as "a readable . . . biography of the man whose invention truly revolutionized the world." In his online review for *The Onion A. V. Club,* Noel Murray commented: "Schatzkin's exhaustive research is impressive, and he has a purposeful sense of structure, which pushes the Farnsworth story toward one inevitable, all-but-irrefutable conclusion." *Library Journal* contributor David M. Lisa concluded that the book is "a great biography of a gifted inventor."

BIOGRAPHICAL AND CRITICAL SOURCES:

PERIODICALS

Booklist, September 1, 2002, Mark Knoblauch, review of *The Boy Who Invented Television: A Story of Inspiration, Persistence, and Quiet Passion,* p. 34.
Library Journal, September 15, 2002, David M. Lisa, review of *The Boy Who Invented Television,* p. 66.

ONLINE

Farnovision, http://www.farnovision.com/ (June 12, 2003), information about Farnsworth, Schatzkin, and *The Boy Who Invented Television.*

Onion A. V. Club, http://www.theonionavclub.com/ (June 12, 2003), review of *The Boy Who Invented Television.**

* * *

SCHEESE, Don 1954-

PERSONAL: Born March 11, 1954, in Coaldale, PA; son of Leonard (a coal miner and construction worker) and Mary (a homemaker; maiden name, Gavornik) Scheese; married Petty Butzer (a clothing designer), 1982. *Ethnicity:* "White." *Education:* Temple University, B.A., 1976; University of Idaho, M.A., 1982; University of Iowa, Ph.D., 1991. *Politics:* Independent. *Religion:* "Transcendental pagan." *Hobbies and other interests:* Hiking, canoeing, cross-country skiing, snowshoeing, birdwatching.

ADDRESSES: Home—1936 Waterford Lane, Chaska, MN 55318. *Office*—Department of English, Gustavus Adolphus College, St. Peter, MN 56082. *E-mail*—dscheese@gac.edu.

CAREER: Gustavus Adolphus College, St. Peter, MN, associate professor of English, 1992—, director of Environmental Studies Program, 1997—. Guest lecturer at Carleton College, Northfield, MN, 1994, and Northland College, Ashland, WI, 2000. Worked as a fire lookout in Idaho for more than ten years; public speaker on the work of a fire lookout and on environmental topics.

MEMBER: Association for the Study of Literature and the Environment (member of executive council, 1994-98), American Society of Environmental History, Thoreau Society, Western Literature Association (member of executive council, 2000-02), Phi Beta Kappa.

AWARDS, HONORS: Grants from National Endowment for the Humanities, 1993, 2000; citation for "outstanding academic book," *Choice,* 1997, for *Nature Writing: The Pastoral Impulse in America.*

WRITINGS:

Nature Writing: The Pastoral Impulse in America, Twayne (New York, NY), 1996.

Mountains of Memory: A Fire Lookout's Life in the River of No Return Wilderness, University of Iowa Press (Iowa City, IA), 2001.

Contributor to books, including *Take This Exit: Rediscovering the Iowa Landscape,* edited by Robert F. Sayre, Iowa State University Press (Ames, IA), 1989; *Mapping American Culture,* edited by Wayne Franklin and Michael Steiner, University of Iowa Press (Iowa City, IA), 1992; *The Ecocriticism Reader: Landmarks in Literary Ecology,* edited by Cheryll Glotfelty and Harold Fromm, University of Georgia Press (Athens, GA), 1996; *Go Tell It on the Mountain,* edited by Jackie Johnson Maughan, Stackpole (Mechanicsburg, PA), 1996; and *Violence in America: An Encyclopedia,* edited by Ronald Gottesman and Richard Maxwell Brown, Scribner (New York, NY), 1999. Contributor of articles and reviews to periodicals, including *Forest and Conservation History.* Coeditor of special issue, *North Dakota Quarterly,* 1991; member of editorial board, *ISLE: Interdisciplinary Studies in Literature and Environment,* 1995—.

WORK IN PROGRESS: Stories of Stone: Representations of the Anasazi in Art and Literature, completion expected in 2005.

SIDELIGHTS: Don Scheese told *CA:* "I write to answer questions and solve problems. I write because I have been inspired by others to write. I write because I cannot *not* write: it's become a daily habit.

"Most of all, I am influenced by the great presence of the nonhuman environment, and by writers who have written on the same subject. There is no more important or worthwhile or urgent subject.

"My writing process involved copious journal writing, research, and reading of background materials, followed by lots of thinking, teaching, and rewriting over the years. *Mountains of Memory: A Fire Lookout's Life in the River of No Return Wilderness* was twenty years in the making.

"My writing is inspired by great places and great writers: the River of No Return Wilderness in central Idaho, the canyon behind our house in southern Minnesota, the desert Southwest, the Boundary Waters Canoe Area Wilderness, and many other places where I have lived or visited."

BIOGRAPHICAL AND CRITICAL SOURCES:

PERIODICALS

Choice, March, 2002, M. J. Zwolinski, review of *Mountains of Memory: A Fire Lookout's Life in the River of No Return Wilderness,* p. 1260.
Library Journal, November 15, 2001, Tim Markus, review of *Mountains of Memory,* p. 95.

*   *   *

SCOTT, Manda

PERSONAL: Born in Glasgow, Scotland. *Education:* Attended Glasgow University Veterinary School. *Hobbies and other interests:* Rock climbing, running her dogs, riding.

ADDRESSES: Home—Suffolk, England. *Agent*—c/o Author Mail, Delacorte, Dell Publishing, 1540 Broadway, New York, NY 10036. *E-mail*—manda@ mandascott.co.uk.

CAREER: Veterinary surgeon, equine neonatologist, anaesthetist, and fiction writer. Worked as a veterinarian in Newmarket, England, late 1980s.

AWARDS, HONORS: Orange Prize shortlist, 1997, for *Hen's Teeth.*

WRITINGS:

Hen's Teeth, Women's Press (London, England), 1996.
Night Mares, Viking (New York, NY), 1998.
Stronger than Death, Hodder Headline (London, England), 1999.
No Good Deed, Hodder Headline (London, England), 2001, Bantam (New York, NY), 2002.
Boudica: Dreaming the Eagle, Delacorte Press (New York, NY), 2003.
Boudica II: Dreaming the Bull, Delacorte Press (New York, NY), 2004.

WORK IN PROGRESS: Absolution, the sequel to *No Good Deed.*

SIDELIGHTS: Scottish veterinarian Manda Scott was born and raised in Glasgow, where as a child she loved animals and dreamed of becoming a farmer. Attending Glasgow University, she eventually became a veterinary surgeon and specialized in horses. After many sleep-deprived years Scott finally decided to change careers, becoming a professional writer instead. Today she resides in Suffolk, England and has several contemporary crime thrillers to her credit, among them the thrillers *No Good Deed* and *Hen's Teeth* and the historical novels *Boudica: Dreaming the Eagle* and *Boudica II: Dreaming the Bull.* Praising Scott's debut novel *Hen's Teeth, Books'n'Bytes* reviewer Harriet Klausner called it "a fabulous medical thriller" that "deserves much reader attention."

Published in 2002, *No Good Deed* opens with a deadly shoot-out as a police sting in Glasgow goes terribly wrong. Special Branch agent Orla McLeod is left standing alongside nine-year-old Jamie Buchanan, while Orla's lover and the young boy's prostitute mother are brutally murdered by Tord Svenson, the violent criminal McLeod and her unit were attempting to catch. Her cover now blown, McLeod takes the wounded boy to her mother's secluded cabin in the snowy Scottish highlands, where she hopes to remain safe while the boy recovers from his injuries. However, McLeod begins to wonder whether she can trust the friends to whom she has confided her situation; one of them appears to secretly be working for the other side. When Jamie is kidnaped at gunpoint, it is up to McLeod to get him back safely, while continuing to track down the villainous Svenson.

"Besides exposing the gristle and bone of human violence, Scott astutely probes the aftermath of crime—the loss of moral certitude that truly shatters the soul," stated Marilyn Stasio in the *New York Times Book Review.* While Carrie Bissey in a *Booklist* review maintained that "the obviously close-knit relationships between Orla and her partners are never fully explained," the critic went on to compliment *No Good Deed* as "an unflinching portrayal of police work at its dirties" with a protagonist who's life story "lends authenticity to her tough yet vulnerable personal." Jane Judd, writing in *Publishers Weekly,* commented that "Scott's prose suits her tough yet sensitive heroine and her storytelling is equally unflinching. Graphic violence contrasts with wilderness beauty in a thriller that has plenty of touching moments."

Boudica: Dreaming the Eagle is the first book in a projected series of four novels that relates the life and times of Breaca nic Graine—later named Boudica—the queen warrior and legendary leader of the Eceni, who led the revolt against Rome in 61 AD. While little factual detail is actually known about Breaca and her times, Scott manages to create a thoroughly detailed environment. The story begins with the slaying of Breaca's pregnant mother, after which young Breaca is sent to live with another family and develops a relationship with her half brother Ban. In the Eceni tribe members are shown their destiny by the gods in dreams which lead them to become dreamers or warriors; while Breaca hopes to be a dreamer, her dreams reveal her to be a strong warrior. Breaca's brother Bán, a dreamer, returns to Britain after escaping a rival tribes ambush, where he joins Breaca in attempting to ward off invading Roman forces. Laurel Bliss, writing in the *Library Journal,* praised the "Boudica" series, noting that "Scott weaves the stories of Breaca and Bán into a complicated and satisfying pattern. Definitely not a tired old retelling of a legend, this novel is beautifully written and lovingly told, filled with drama and passion."

Scott's series continues with *Boudica II: Dreaming the Bull,* as Breaca and Bán find themselves on opposite sides of a terrible war for their country: Bán as part of the Roman cavalry and Breaca defending her tribe. When Breaca's lover, Caradoc, is caught by the Romans and faced with death, Bán is forced to rethink his loyalties and confront his heritage. Other books in the "Boudica" series include *Dreaming the Wren* and *Dreaming the Hare,* which were scheduled to be published in 2006.

BIOGRAPHICAL AND CRITICAL SOURCES:

PERIODICALS

Booklist, March 15, 2002, Carrie Bissey, review of *No Good Deed,* p. 1216.
Globe & Mail (Toronto, Ontario, Canada), December 18, 1999, Margaret Cannon, review of *Stronger than Death,* p. D25.
Kirkus Reviews, February 15, 2002, review of *No Good Deed,* p. 216; May 1, 2003, review of *Dreaming the Eagle,* p. 639.
Library Journal, May 1, 2003, Laurel Bliss, review of *Dreaming the Eagle,* p.157.
New York Times Book Review, May 19, 2002, Marilyn Stasio, review of *No Good Deed,* p.44.
Publishers Weekly, March 11, 2002, review of *No Good Deed,* p.52.

ONLINE

Books'n'Bytes, http://www.booksnbytes.com/ (October 12, 2003), Harriet Klausner, review of *Hen's Teeth.*

Manda Scott Web site, http://www.mandascott.co.uk (May 15, 2004).

Mystery Reader Web site, http://www.themystery readers.com/ (August 13, 2000), Wendy Crutcher, review of *Stronger than Death.*

Time Warner Books Web site, http://www.twbooks.co.uk/ (October 12, 2003), "Manda Scott."*

*   *   *

SEARS, Richard

PERSONAL: Immigrated to London, England, late 1970s; married; children: one son.

ADDRESSES: Home—Buenos Aires, Argentina; and Long Island, NY. *Agent*—c/o Tom Doherty Associates/Forge, 175 Fifth Ave., New York, NY 10010.

CAREER: Former psychiatric counselor and investigative journalist.

WRITINGS:

First Born (novel), Forge (New York, NY), 2000.
Last Day (novel), Forge (New York, NY), 2001.

SIDELIGHTS: Richard Sears drew inspiration from his long-standing interest in the paranormal and aliens when he began writing thrillers. His debut novel, *First Born,* features an unnaturally precocious baby boy who appears to have been conceived through a close encounter with an alien. However, the boy's mother's only memory of his conception is of seeing a bright light. Combined with the boy's unnatural healing powers, this is enough to convince some people that Christ's Second Coming has arrived. Others, particularly the super-secret cabal that is running the world, fear the boy and want to kill him. Although some critics found the plot far-fetched, many reviewers felt that the tale's fast action would keep readers hooked.

School Library Journal critic Carol DeAngelo also felt that *First Born* would appeal to young readers because of its "nonstop action, suspense, and strange doings."

Sears's second novel, *Last Day,* "starts as a straight thriller, then takes its protagonist into increasingly occult territory," a critic explained in *Kirkus Reviews.* Jack Lamb is an undercover police officer who finds himself in over his head while investigating Ray Sasso, the leader of the Sons of Fire Motorcycle Club and a big-time drug dealer. In order to keep up his cover as a methamphetamine dealer, Lamb (going by the name "Charlie Wolf") starts taking the drug himself and soon finds himself addicted to it. When the police botch a raid on Sasso, Lamb is shot in the head. He survives, but the bullet lodges in his brain and, combined with methamphetamine withdrawal, starts giving him what may be supernatural premonitions or what may simply be psychotic episodes. The author "writes some of the hardest-edged crime going," a *Publishers Weekly* reviewer commented, "and his characters are viscerally real."

BIOGRAPHICAL AND CRITICAL SOURCES:

PERIODICALS

Booklist, January 1, 2000, Budd Arthur, review of *First Born,* p. 885; December 1, 2001, David Pitt, review of *Last Day,* p. 634.

Kirkus Reviews, October 15, 2001, review of *Last Day,* p. 1449.

Publishers Weekly, December 13, 1999, review of *First Born,* p. 66; November 19, 2001, review of *Last Day,* p. 49.

School Library Journal, June, 2000, Carol DeAngelo, review of *First Born,* p. 174.

ONLINE

eReader.com, http://www.palmdigitalmedia.com/ (January 27, 2004), "Author: Richard Sears."*

*   *   *

SHAKOORI, Ali 1962-

PERSONAL: Born February 27, 1962, in Marand, Iran; married Maryam Taremi, 2001. *Ethnicity:* "Asian." *Education:* Earned M.A. degree; University of York, Ph.D., 1998. *Hobbies and other interests:* Football, classical music, travel.

ADDRESSES: Home—225 Shahid Nouri, Tehran 13577, Iran. *Office*—Department of Cooperative and Social Welfare, University of Tehran, Ghisha Bridge, P.O. Box 14395/773, Tehran, Iran; fax: 0098-21-801-2524. *E-mail*—shakoori@chamran.ut.ac.ir.

CAREER: University of Tehran, Tehran, Iran, assistant professor, 2001—, and director of Department of Cooperative and Social Welfare.

WRITINGS:

The State and Rural Development in Post-Revolutionary Iran, Palgrave (New York, NY), 2001.

Contributor to Persian-language journals.

WORK IN PROGRESS: A comparative study of agricultural policies in pre-and post-revolutionary Iran.

SIDELIGHTS: Ali Shakoori told *CA:* "When I began to study for my master's degree in sociology, I was interested in such issues as poverty, development, and rural poverty and development, particularly in third-world countries. The underdevelopment of these countries, particularly Iran, which had a considerable capacity for development, became my preoccupation. Then, when I started my doctoral work at the University of York, I chose to research rural development and problems of the state in Iran after the victory of the revolution in 1979. When I completed my thesis and submitted it, and defended it successfully, Professors Haleh Afshar and Adrian Leftwich recommended and encouraged me to publish it."

BIOGRAPHICAL AND CRITICAL SOURCES:

PERIODICALS

Middle East Journal, spring, 2002, Vahid Nowshirvani, A. William Samii, and Michael P. Zirinsky, review of *The State and Rural Development in Post-Revolutionary Iran,* p. 336.

*   *   *

SHALANT, Phyllis 1949-

PERSONAL: Born July 22, 1949, in Brooklyn, NY; daughter of Edward Jushpy (a salesman) and Anne Jushpy Scherwin (a homemaker); married Herbert Shalant (an orthotist and prosthetist); children: Emily Kate, Jennifer Melissa. *Education:* University of California at Berkeley, 1967-69; Brooklyn College (now Brooklyn College of the City University of New York), B.A., 1971; Manhattanville College, M.A., 1997. *Politics:* Liberal. *Religion:* Jewish. *Hobbies and other interests:* Reading, gardening, observing nature, art, music, travel.

ADDRESSES: Agent—c/o author correspondence, Dutton Children's Books, 345 Hudson St., New York, NY 10014. *E-mail*—phyllis@phyllisshalant.com.

CAREER: Writer. Professor of children's writing, Manhattanville College, NY. Conducts writing workshops for adults and for children as part of school visitations.

MEMBER: Authors Guild, Society of Children's Book Writers and Illustrators.

AWARDS, HONORS: Texas Bluebonnet Award Master List, 1997, for *Beware of Kissing Lizard Lips;* Florida Sunshine State Young Readers Award Master List, 1997, for *The Great Eye;* "best book" citation from New York Public Library, 2000, and Washington Irving Children's Choice Honor Book, 2002, both for *Bartleby of the Mighty Mississippi;* "best children's book" citation, Bank Street College of Education, 2002, for *When Pirates Came to Brooklyn.*

WRITINGS:

FICTION

The Rock Star, The Rooster, & Me, The Reporter, Dutton Children's Books (New York, NY), 1990.
The Transformation of Faith Futterman, Dutton Children's Books (New York, NY), 1990.
Shalom, Geneva Peace, Dutton Children's Books (New York, NY), 1992.
Beware of Kissing Lizard Lips, Dutton Children's Books (New York, NY), 1995.
The Great Eye, Dutton Children's Books (New York, NY), 1996.
Bartleby of the Mighty Mississippi, Dutton Children's Books (New York, NY), 2000.
When Pirates Came to Brooklyn, Dutton Children's Books (New York, NY), 2002.

NONFICTION

Look What We've Brought You from Vietnam: Crafts, Games, Recipes, Stories and Other Cultural Activities from Vietnamese Americans, Silver Burdett Press, 1988, reprinted, 1998.

Look What We've Brought You from Korea: Crafts, Games, Recipes, Stories and Other Cultural Activities from Korean-Americans, Silver Burdett Press, 1994.

Look What We've Brought You from India: Crafts, Games, Recipes, Stories and Other Cultural Activities from Indian Americans, Silver Burdett Press, 1997.

Look What We've Brought You from the Caribbean: Crafts, Games, Recipes, Stories, and Other Cultural Activities, Silver Burdett Press, 1998.

Look What We've Brought You from Mexico: Crafts, Games, Recipes, Stories and Other Cultural Activities from Mexican Americans, Silver Burdett Press, 1998.

Contributor of short story, "Pinch-Hitting," to anthology, *With All My Heart, With All My Mind,* 2000.

WORK IN PROGRESS: Bartleby of the Big, Bad Bayou, a novel for publication in 2005; a new series, "The Society of Secret Superheroes," for Dutton, a series of books about a group of fourth-grade boys who form a secret club in order to perform superhero feats.

SIDELIGHTS: Phyllis Shalant once commented: "My earliest memories of storytelling begin long before I could read or write. I can clearly remember sitting under the kitchen table in my parents' apartment and using my dolls and stuffed animals to act out the tales I created.

"My stories all come from real life experiences—even *Bartleby of the Mighty Mississippi,* which has a red-eared turtle as its main character. *When Pirates Came to Brooklyn* is an autobiographical novel. Main characters Lee and Polly imagine a wondrous world where shipwrecks occur in the attic, pirates hover over Brooklyn in a cloudship galleon, and it might just be possible for a kid to fly. But in Brooklyn, 1960, the girls' closed-minded mothers put religious differences above friendship—and the two steadfast and spirited friends must use their minds and hearts to fly above the bigotry."

Shalant has been credited with "understanding the ways preteens think, act, and talk," to quote a *Kirkus Reviews* critic. Through a series of young adult novels—some humorous, some serious—Shalant has allowed her young protagonists to work through their own problems and to understand their strengths and weaknesses better by seeing them through the eyes of others. Zach, the hero of *Beware of Kissing Lizard Lips,* has a problem common to sixth-grade boys: he's puny, and some of the girls in his class tower over him. At the same time, to his dismay, Zach finds he is taking new interest in some of the girls in his class, including Nikki Lee, his tae kwon do teacher. Hazel Rochman in *Booklist* called the novel "a laugh-out-loud story about growing up male."

In *The Great Eye,* Lucy seeks consolation for her parents' breakup from her close friend Calvin and from her computer, on which she composes thoughtful poetry. When Lucy gets an opportunity to train a puppy for use as a seeing-eye dog, her relationship with the animal helps her to come to terms with her absent father. In *Booklist* Hazel Rochman praised Shalant for creating a novel that offers an "honest treatment of love that hurts."

Two of Shalant's novels revolve around Jewish characters and themes. In *Shalom, Geneva Peace,* eighth grader Andi Applebaum learns important lessons about the shallow veneer of sophistication when she befriends Geneva Peace, a girl her age who seems to have so much more maturity and opportunities. Roger Sutton in the *Bulletin of the Center for Chilren's Books* liked the Hebrew school setting Shalant uses in *Shalom, Geneva Peace,* concluding that it "brings a fresh and welcome reality to teen fiction." Religion proves a point of contention in *When Pirates Came to Brooklyn.* Lonely Lee finds happiness and adventure in a new friendship with Polly Burke, whose active imagination conjures Peter Pan and pirates in her Brooklyn attic. Troubles arise when the girls' mothers discover their friendship—Polly's mother tries to convert Lee to Catholicism and Lee's mother forbids Lee to see Polly. "Place and time are exceptionally well defined in this perceptive story," noted Julie Cummins in *Booklist*. A *Publishers Weekly* reviewer called *When Pirates Came to Brooklyn* a "tender novel" that "achieves a delicate balance between heart-wrenching events and uplifting scenes."

When Shalant was a little girl she had a pet red-eared turtle who lived in a bowl in her Brooklyn apartment. Bartleby, the hero of *Bartleby of the Mighty Mississippi,* is not so coincidentally a red-eared turtle living in a bowl at the outset of his adventures. When one of Bartleby's young owners throws him into a pond for a swim, the previously pampered pet must learn a whole new way of life, one that includes danger and adventure. Having seen a television show about the Mississippi River from his bowl, Bartleby sets out in search of it, helped along the way by friends but also accompanied by another ex-pet, Seezer, an alligator who just might get hungry for a turtle. Bartleby's friendly nature and quick wits endear him to readers who will find him "tiny, tough, loyal, and canny," to quote John Peters in *Booklist*. Judith Everitt in *School Library Journal* called *Bartleby of the Mighty Mississippi* "a gentle story with an ethical and likable main character dealing with his own uniqueness."

BIOGRAPHICAL AND CRITICAL SOURCES:

PERIODICALS

Booklist, May 15, 1995, Hazel Rochman, review of *Beware of Kissing Lizard Lips,* p. 1674; November 1, 1996, Hazel Rochman, review of *The Great Eye,* p. 501; May 15, 2000, John Peters, review of *Bartleby of the Mighty Mississippi,* p. 1744; October 15, 2002, Julie Cummins, review of *When Pirates Came to Brooklyn,* p. 407.

Bulletin of the Center for Children's Books, September, 1992, Roger Sutton, review of *Shalom, Geneva Peace,* p. 23.

Kirkus Reviews, June 1, 1995, review of *Beware of Kissing Lizard Lips,* p. 786; August 1, 2002, review of *When Pirates Came to Brooklyn,* p. 1142.

Publishers Weekly, June 15, 1992, review of *Shalom, Geneva Peace,* p. 104; November 18, 1996, review of *The Great Eye,* p. 76; August 12, 2002, review of *When Pirates Came to Brooklyn,* p. 301.

School Library Journal, August, 2000, Judith Everitt, review of *Bartleby of the Mighty Mississippi,* p. 189; October, 2002, Farida S. Dowler, review of *When Pirates Came to Brooklyn,* p. 170.

ONLINE

Phyllis Shalant Home Page, http://www.phyllisshalant.com (October 1, 2003).

*   *   *

SHANAHAN, Michael Edward 1952-
(Mike Shanahan)

PERSONAL: Born August 24, 1952 in Oak Park, IL; married; wife's name Peggy; children: Kyle, Krystal. *Education:* Eastern Illinois University, earned bachelor's and master's degrees.

ADDRESSES: Agent—c/o Author Mail, HarperBusiness, 10 East 53rd St., New York, NY 10022.

CAREER: Professional football coach and writer.

AWARDS, HONORS: Victor Award for professional football coach, 1999.

WRITINGS:

(Under the name Mike Shanahan, with Adam Schefter) *Think Like a Champion,* HarperBusiness (New York, NY), 1999.

SIDELIGHTS: Mike Shanahan is a successful National Football League (NFL) coach who has guided the Denver Broncos to several Super Bowl appearances, including two Super Bowl wins. An outstanding high school athlete during his days at Leyden High School in Franklin Park, Illinois, Shanahan earned early honors in the athletic fields of both football and track. He earned a football scholarship to Eastern Illinois University (EIU), where he played quarterback. A hard tackle during the spring game of his junior year at

EIU left Shanahan with a split kidney that was removed during emergency surgery. The near-fatal injury put Shanahan into intensive care for five days, but the resilient player was lifting weights within days of his discharge from the hospital, wrote Michael Silver in *Sports Illustrated*. The injury took Shanahan off the field, and he soon began his coaching career.

Shanahan took his first coaching job with the Oklahoma Sooners in 1975, and helped to lead them to a national championship in his first year. Many years of college-level coaching followed at schools such as Northern Arizona University, the University of Florida, and Shanahan's alma mater, Eastern Illinois University.

In his early NFL career, Shanahan experienced some surprising setbacks. He was fired from the Oakland Raiders in 1989, and was dismissed from the Denver Broncos in 1991 by head coach Dan Reeves, amid accusations that he went around Reeves to work on strategy with quarterback John Elway. Despite these defeats, Shanahan persisted as the offensive coordinator of the San Francisco 49ers from 1992 to 1994 before returning as head coach of the Denver Broncos in 1995. Since then, Shanahan "has quietly emerged as the most powerful presence in his profession," wrote Silver, earning comparisons to legendary coaches such as Chuck Noll, Don Shula, and Vince Lombardi.

In *Think Like a Champion*, Shanahan brings his winning philosophy from the gridiron to the living rooms and boardrooms of everyday life. Part pep-talk and part insider's look at the NFL, Shanahan offers "aphoristic advice with anecdotes from practice and from big games," wrote a *Publishers Weekly* reviewer. Other reviewers, such as Mark Bodenrader in *Sport* and Wes Lukowsky in *Booklist*, criticized the "strained metaphors" (in Bodenrader's words) and "familiar homilies" (noted Lukowsky) used throughout the book. But Shanahan also offers straightforward stories of his experiences with football players and team administrators, creating a book that the *Publishers Weekly* reviewer called "less interesting for its motivational truisms than for its dishy NFL gossip."

BIOGRAPHICAL AND CRITICAL SOURCES:

PERIODICALS

Booklist, September 1, 1999, Wes Lukowsky, review of *Think Like a Champion*, p. 63.

Entrepreneur, September, 1999, review of *Think Like a Champion*, p. 154.

Publishers Weekly, August 9, 1999, review of *Think Like a Champion*, p. 335.

Sport, December, 1999, Mark Bodenrader, review of *Think Like a Champion*, p. 100.

Sporting News, July 24, 1995, Michael Knisley, profile of Mike Shanahan, pp. 36-38.

Sports Illustrated, November 17, 1997, Michael Silver, "Master Mind," profile of Mike Shanahan, pp. 48-52.

ONLINE

Denver Broncos Web site, http://www.denverbroncos.com/ (November 21, 2003), biography of Mike Shanahan.*

*   *   *

SHANAHAN, Mike
See SHANAHAN, Michael Edward

*   *   *

SHAPIRO, Henry D(avid). 1937-2004

OBITUARY NOTICE—See index for *CA* sketch: Born May 7, 1937, in New York, NY; died of complications from lung cancer January 21, 2004, in York, PA. Historian, educator, and author. Shapiro was a history professor noted for his interest in Appalachia that led to his book *Appalachia on Our Mind: The Southern Mountains and Mountaineers in the American Consciousness, 1870-1920* (1978). Earning his bachelor's from Columbia University in 1958, his master's from Cornell University in 1960, and his doctorate from Rutgers University in 1966, he began his career at Rutgers as an assistant instructor in 1960. A brief stint at the Manhattan School of Music in 1963 was followed by three years at Ohio State University. In 1966, Shapiro joined the University of Cincinnati faculty, becoming a full professor of history in 1979 and retiring in 1988. Specializing in American history, he won the W. D. Weatherford Prize in 1979 for his *Appalachia on Our Mind*, which remains a standard reference on the subject; he was also the author of *Confiscation of Confederate Property in the North* (1962) and coauthor of *Clifton: Neighborhood and Community in an Urban Setting* (1976), as well as editor and contributor to other works. With an interest in literature, as well, Shapiro served for a time as vice chair of the Cleveland Arts Prize.

OBITUARIES AND OTHER SOURCES:

PERIODICALS

Chronicle of Higher Education, February 13, 2004, p. A44.
Enquirer (Cincinnati, OH), January 26, 2004.
Plain Dealer (Cleveland, OH), January 27, 2004, p. B7.

*   *   *

SHAY, Jonathan 1941-

PERSONAL: Born 1941. *Education:* M.D., Ph.D. (neuroscience).

ADDRESSES: Office—c/o Department of Veterans' Services, 239 Causeway St., Ste. 100, Boston, MA 02114

CAREER: Clinical psychiatrist, Department of Psychiatry, Tufts Medical School; psychiatrist with Department of Veteran Affairs Veterans' Improvement Program, at the Boston Veterans' Administration Hospital and at the Department of Veteran Affairs Outpatient Clinic, Boston, MA. Visiting scholar-at-large, U.S. Naval War College, 2001; public speaker.

WRITINGS:

Achilles in Vietnam: Combat Trauma and the Undoing of Character, Atheneum (New York, NY), 1994.
Odysseus in America: Combat Trauma and the Trials of Homecoming, foreword by Max Cleland and John McCain, Scribner (New York, NY), 2002.

SIDELIGHTS: Dr. Jonathan Shay is a clinical psychiatrist who works with U.S. Vietnam War veterans with long-term symptoms of posttraumatic stress disorder (PTSD). He is the author of two books on the subject, *Achilles in Vietnam: Combat Trauma and the Undoing of Character* and *Odysseus in America: Combat Trauma and the Trials of Homecoming,* in which he finds parallels between the classical Greek Homerian epics and the experiences of modern-day soldiers, both on the battlefield and on their return home.

In *Achilles in Vietnam,* Shay compares passages from Homer's *Iliad* to combat stories of Vietnam veterans. In the first chapter, "Betrayal of 'What's Right,'" Shay shows how the moral betrayal of Achilles by his commander Agamemnon also occurred among units in Vietnam and how that betrayal—from the murder of civilians to deaths by so-called friendly fire to the unfair safety of officers on the battlefield, commanders in high places, or politicians in Washington, D.C.—leaves a permanent mark on the psyche of soldiers. Shay later shows how the important bonds formed between a soldier and his closest comrades-in-arms are shattered when a comrade is killed and how the lack of time to mourn for the dead contributes to the rage and the need for revenge, as experienced by Achilles on the death of his close friend Patroklos. Shay tells how in ancient Greek times, bodies of the fallen stayed with their units longer and battle was suspended at night, giving soldiers time to mourn the dead.

The trauma of betrayal and the loss of comrades, says Shay, can lead to personal guilt over surviving battle and to extreme rage, or berserk behavior, for the surviving warrior. Achilles displayed this berserk state when he sought horrible revenge on Patroklos's killers, and many Vietnam veterans show it through PTSD, in which they are potentially violent and perpetually mobilized to defend themselves, often waking from nightmares reaching for a weapon. Shay explains that some 250,000 Vietnam veterans suffer from this disorder, as well as despair and isolation that can lead to drug or alcohol abuse or even suicide. He also says they lack the capacity for participating in a democratic society because they no longer believe in the existence of a meaningful future. In short, he writes, "fighting for one's country can render one unfit to be its citizen." Shay advocates above all the prevention of war, but in the absence of prevention he stresses that soldiers should be trained differently and should be allowed to mourn lost comrades.

Sallie Goetsch, in a review of for the *Bryn Mawr Classical Review,* praised the book, saying it is "clearly written and a marvel of organization," with easy access to "particular aspects of the comparison between the wrath of Achilles and the berserk rage of Vietnam veterans." She concluded, "Shay's purpose is not to offer a definitive treatment of Greek ethics or Homeric vocabulary or even ancient warfare. His aim is to discuss the persistence of combat trauma and the soldier's experience through thousands of years of warfare, and he does that superbly well." In the *New York Times,* Herbert Mitgang wrote, "Even where allowances must be made to take into account the differences between chariots and B-52 bombers, the reader follows the parallels between the Greek classic and the Vietnam veterans' recollections with admiration for what Dr. Shay has achieved."

Vince Gotera, writing in the *Journal of Popular Culture,* called the book "one of the most important texts to appear recently on the already immense bookshelf of analytic works on the Vietnam war; it's very difficult at this point to say anything *new* about 'Vietnam,' but Shay does."

In a review for the *Journal of the American Medical Association,* Richard Dayringer wrote, "I found this book to be original, humane, powerful, and even terrifying. . . . I think the book should be required reading for all mental health professionals who work with veterans of any war." William Beatty, of *Booklist,* concluded, "This is a profoundly human book and a strong, realistic argument against modern warfare." A contributor to *Publishers Weekly* commented that "Shay's ideas merit attention by soldiers and scholars alike."

Irwin L. Kutash, writing in the *Journal of Criminal Justice and Popular Culture,* commented that Shay makes "a painstaking and noble attempt to teach the psychologically damaging results of war in a desire to prevent future war. . . . As historians have long promulgated, he who does not learn from history is bound to repeat it."

Shay's second book about Vietnam veterans is *Odysseus in America,* which parallels the story of Homer's *Odyssey* with the returning home of Vietnam veterans

and the difficulties they have faced in rejoining American society. Shay writes in this book, "The most fervent wish of the veterans I serve is that future kids not be wrecked the way they were wrecked. . . . The most effective prevention lies almost entirely with better military practices." *Odysseus in America* is divided into three parts: "Unhealed Wounds, Restoration," and "Prevention." In the first, Shay parallels the long and arduous journey that Odysseus and his men took home, much like the experiences that Vietnam veterans encounter with alcohol and drugs and family problems. In the second part, Shay discusses problems that come with attempts to restore veterans to society, detailing his work with veterans and their emotional experiences in retelling their stories and coming to terms with the war. He also outlines a three-step program for stopping dangerous behaviors, grieving, and learning to trust again. Although he would prefer that war be prevented altogether, in part three Shay outlines a plan for improving the outcome for soldiers who do have to fight. He advocates their being kept together as a unit throughout training, battle, and the return home, instead of replacing individual soldiers like parts in a machine. William Beatty, of *Booklist,* commented on this theory, saying that readers "will perceive . . . the wisdom of replacing whole units rather than individual soldiers at the front." Shay also emphasizes new training that involves not only the body but the mind, emotions, and character as well. And Shay stresses the importance of choosing officers who have the character to lead, instead of, like Odysseus, a self-serving nature.

Edwin B. Burgess, writing in *Library Journal,* called *Odysseus in America* "a mandatory purchase" for libraries serving military families and for professionals working with PTSD patients. He also called it "a fresh take on a literary classic." A *Publishers Weekly* contributor found the book to have "an intriguing argument" but thought the tone was sometimes "hectoring or stridently didactic."

Tim Trask, in a review for the *Massasoit Community College Web site,* wrote: "Shay's patients and their fellow combat veterans around the world are Odysseuses, wrecked on our Phaeacian shore, who are trying through their stories to help us understand just what it means to have risked their all for us. . . . One of the values of Shay's book is that he shows us how to listen and how to make things better for future soldiers. That is work that we as a society have to do."

BIOGRAPHICAL AND CRITICAL SOURCES:

PERIODICALS

Booklist, April 1, 1994, William Beatty, review of *Achilles in Vietnam: Combat Trauma and the Undoing of Character,* p. 1415; October 1, 2002, William Beatty, review of *Odysseus in America: Combat Trauma and the Trials of Homecoming,* p. 294.

Bryn Mawr Classical Review, March 21, 1994, Sallie Goetsch, review of *Achilles in Vietnam,* p. 246.

Journal of Criminal Justice and Popular Culture, volume 2, number 5 (1994), Irwin L. Kutash, "What We Haven't Learned about War We Have Repeated: Warriors as Victims," pp. 122-124.

Journal of Popular Culture, fall, 1994, Vince Gotera, review of *Achilles in Vietnam,* pp. 229-231.

Journal of the American Medical Association, June 12, 1996, Richard Dayringer, review of *Achilles in Vietnam,* p. 1769.

Library Journal, October 1, 2002, Edwin B. Burgess, review of *Odysseus in America,* p. 114.

New York Times, June 13, 1994, Herbert Mitgang, "Vietnam War as Ling to Battles of Antiquity," p. C15.

Publishers Weekly, March 7, 1994, review of *Achilles in Vietnam,* p. 58; September 9, 2002, review of *Odysseus in America* and *Achilles in Vietnam,* p. 50.

ONLINE

American Repertory Theatre Web site, http://www.amrep.org/ (January 26, 2003), Jonathan Shay, excerpt from *Odysseus in America.*

Massasoit Community College Web site, http://www.massasoit.mass.edu/ (January, 2003), Tim Trask, "Wrecked on the Phaeacian Shore."*

*   *   *

SHERROD, Blackie 1919-

PERSONAL: Given name, William Forrest Sherrod; born November 9, 1919, in Belton, TX; son of Marvin (a barber) and Leola (a music teacher; maiden name, Forrest) Sherrod. *Education:* Howard Payne College, B.A., 1941; attended Baylor University.

ADDRESSES: Office—Dallas Morning News, 508 Young St., Dallas, TX 75202-4808. *Agent*—c/o Author Mail, Eakin Press, P.O. Drawer 90159, Austin, TX 78709-0159; fax: 512-288-1813.

CAREER: Journalist, editor, columnist, and sportswriter. *Temple Daily Telegram,* Temple, TX, reporter, 1941-42 and 1946; *Fort Worth Press,* Fort Worth, TX, reporter, sportswriter, and sports editor, 1946-58; *Dallas Times Herald,* Dallas, TX, sports editor, sports columnist, and assistant managing editor, 1958-85; *Dallas Morning News,* Dallas, TX, sports and general columnist, 1985-2003. *Military service:* United States Navy, 1941-45; served as a torpedo plane gunner.

AWARDS, HONORS: Texas Headliners Club, annual award for science writing, 1969, for coverage of *Apollo 11* mission; Red Smith Award for lifetime achievement; sixteen-time winner, Texas Sportswriter of the Year Award; inducted into National Sportscaster-Sportswriter Hall of Fame.

WRITINGS:

(With Darrell Royal) *Darrell Royal Talks Football,* Prentice-Hall (Englewood Cliffs, NJ), 1963.

(With Freddie Steinmark) *I Play to Win,* Little, Brown (Boston, MA), 1971.

Scattershooting, Strode Publishers (Huntsville, AL), 1975.

The Blackie Sherrod Collection (sports columns), introduction by Dan Jenkins, Taylor Publishing Co. (Dallas, TX), 1988.

Blackie Sherrod at Large (columns), Eakin Press (Austin, TX), 2003.

Work frequently appeared in *Best Sports Stories* of the year collections throughout the 1950s, 1960s, and 1970s. Contributor to *Our Navy* magazine during World War II.

SIDELIGHTS: The locker room and the newsroom were equally home to sportswriter Blackie Sherrod during a career that spanned more than sixty years of writing columns—over 10,000 of them—covering minor games and major events in sports throughout Texas and the entire United States. Sherrod's career began at the *Temple Daily Telegram,* in Temple, Texas, where he worked as a reporter both before and after serving in the U.S. Navy during World War II. He spent twelve years at the *Fort Worth Press,* from 1946 to 1958, followed by twenty-seven years at the *Dallas Times Herald,* then eighteen years at the *Dallas Morning News,* where he retired in 2003 at the age of eighty-three. But retirement did not come easily to the active, tenacious, mock-irascible Sherrod. When asked what retirement was like, he likened it to a steam bath, noted Gary Cartwright in *Texas Monthly.* "Once you get used to it," Sherrod said, "it's not so hot."

Deeply professional, dedicated to his craft, Sherrod "draws on a code of old-fashioned decency and professionalism that applies to athletes as well as journalists," commented Kevin Kerrane in *Dictionary of Literary Biography.* "Showcasing the same values, Sherrod's style is modest, even self-deprecatory," Kerrane observed. "His prose, though elegant, conveys the persona of a common man: folksy, weathered (with such identifying tags as 'old buster' and 'our aging hero'), and street-smart rather than book-smart." But there is great precision and sophistication to his style as well, Kerrane noted. "His style is also marked by precise images and fresh metaphors, guided by a reportorial style that can break a moment of sports action into a striking series of still scenes."

Part of his mission was to pass on his knowledge and sense of professionalism to another generation. While working as a writer and editor for the *Fort Worth Press,* Sherrod served as mentor to a "Who's Who" of storied sportswriters, including Dan Jenkins, Bud Shrake, and Gary Cartwright. "In his own tough, erudite way, he taught us to break the mold, to take chances," Cartwright wrote in *Texas Monthly.* "News stories had to transcend facts, stretching instead for style and analysis. He had no patience for pretense and no stomach for grandstanding, but he had a true and abiding love of language, of the intoxicating dance of words carefully selected and arranged." When Sherrod moved to the *Dallas Times Herald,* his students and comrades—known as "Blackie's Boys"—went with him. "Working for Blackie required wit and will," Cartwright observed. Still, for Cartwright and his peers, Sherrod's "sarcasm and his above-the-fray attitude shaped us as young writers; he made us appreciate that sportswriting, done correctly, was a noble pursuit."

The Blackie Sherrod Collection contains a selection of Sherrod's best sportswriting from twelve years in Dallas. Sherrod's "writing is consistently energetic and entertaining, with the hard edge of a no-nonsense 'good old boy' from the Southwest," commented Thomas J. Reigstad in *Library Journal.* The collection concentrates on college and professional football, including the Dallas Cowboys, although it also highlights Sherrod's humor and wit in writing. These attributes compliment the "perspective and insight that are the soul of a successful column," observed Douglas S. Looney in *Sports Illustrated.* "In this," Looney concluded, "Sherrod is topped by no one."

Similarly, *Blackie Sherrod at Large* includes a selection of columns from the *Dallas Morning News.* *Library Journal* reviewer Susan M. Colowick called Sherrod a "shrewd observer of personalities and events," and noted that "each piece holds up well as a standalone commentary" on the events covered and on athletics in general.

"However great the influence of Sherrod the editor, Sherrod won fans for three generations with his writing," Kerrane commented. "His range as a reporter, his storytelling skill, his evocation of character, and his writing voice—regional and yet universal—all have made an enduring mark on American sportswriting."

BIOGRAPHICAL AND CRITICAL SOURCES:

BOOKS

Cartwright, Gary, *Confessions of a Washed-up Sportswriter,* Texas Monthly Press (Austin, TX), 1983.
Dictionary of Literary Biography, Volume 241: *American Sportswriters and Writers on Sports,* Gale (Detroit, MI), 2001.
MacCambridge, Mark, *The Franchise: A History of Sports Illustrated Magazine,* Hyperion Press (New York, NY), 1998.

PERIODICALS

Continental, November, 1985, David Gaines, "Blackie Sherrod," pp. 42-43.
Dallas Free Press, November, 1991, Chris Thomas, "Blackie Sherrod: Sportswriter, Artist, and Part American Indian," pp. 15, 18.

Dallas Morning News, November 11, 1999, Kevin Sherrington, "Still a Prose Pro," pp. D1, D5.

Editor & Publisher, June 15, 1985, Jim Haughton, "The Richest Sportswriter in the Business," pp. 20-21.

Houston Chronicle, January 12, 2003, Mickey Herskowitz, "Retirement Claims Sherrod, But He Leaves Mark," p. 5.

Journalism Quarterly, winter, 1988, review of *The Blackie Sherrod Collection,* p. 1015.

Library Journal, June 1, 1988, Thomas J. Reigstad, review of *The Blackie Sherrod Collection,* p. 134; May 1, 2003, Susan M. Colowick, review of *Blackie Sherrod at Large,* pp. 130-131.

Los Angeles Times, July 27, 1981, "Sports Columnists Have Their Own Little Corner, So to Speak," pp. 1, 7-8.

Men's Journal, February, 1998, Bob Drury, "The Sportswriter's Apocalypse," pp. 69-71, 102.

Newsweek, December 26, 1983, Charles Kaiser and Tessa Namuth, "Losing the Two-Front War," pp. 51-52.

Southern Living, April, 1978, "A Philosopher in Newsprint," pp. 142, 145.

Sports Illustrated, December 24, 1984, Jerry Kirshebaum, "Traffic Stopper," p. 11; June 13, 1988, Douglas S. Looney, "Collections by Four All-Prose," review of *The Blackie Sherrod Collection,* p. 11.

Texas Monthly, April, 2003, Gary Cartwright, "-30-: The Very Best Columnist Ever to Grace the Pages of a Texas Newspaper Has Called It Quits—But Please Don't Tell Blackie Sherrod I Mentioned It," profile of Blackie Sherrod, pp. 58-60.

ONLINE

Associated Press Sports Editors Web site, http://apse.dallasnews.com/ (February, 2003), Kevin Sherrington, "Texas Legend," profile of Blackie Sherrod.

*   *   *

SHIFF, Richard

PERSONAL: Male. *Education:* Harvard College, B.A., 1965; Yale Graduate School, M.A., 1969, Ph.D., 1973.

ADDRESSES: Office—University of Texas at Austin, Fine Arts Doty Fine Arts Building (DFA) 2.4, 23rd Street and Trinity Street, Austin, TX 78712-0340. *E-mail*—rshiff@mail.utexas.edu.

CAREER: Writer, historian, painter, and educator. University of Texas at Austin, Effie Marie Cain Regents Chair in art and director of the Center for the Study of Modernism.

AWARDS, HONORS: University of Pennsylvania, Mellon Fellow in Humanities, 1979-80; John Simon Guggenheim Fellowship, 1985-86; National Humanities Center Fellow, 1986; Getty Senior Research Grant, 1996-97.

WRITINGS:

Cézanne and the End of Impressionism: A Study of the Theory, Technique, and Critical Evaluation of Modern Art, University of Chicago Press (Chicago, IL), 1984.

(Author of introduction) *Joachim Gasquet's Cézanne: A Memoir with Conversations,* translated by Christopher Pemberton, preface by John Rewald, Thames and Hudson (London, England), 1991.

Paul Cézanne, Rizzoli International (New York, NY), 1994.

(Editor, with Robert S. Nelson) *Critical Terms for Art History* (essay collection), University of Chicago Press (Chicago, IL), 1996, 2nd expanded edition, University of Chicago Press (Chicago, IL), 2003.

(Author of introduction) *Solomon's Temple: The European Building-Crafts Legacy,* edited by James Alinder, photographs by Laura Volkerding, Center for Creative Photography, University of Arizona (Tucson, AZ), 1996.

Contributor to volumes such as *Foirades/Fizzles: Echo and Allusion in the Art of Jasper Johns,* The Grunwald Center for the Graphic Arts, Wight Art Gallery, University of California, Los Angeles (Los Angeles, CA), 1989; *Willem de Kooning: Paintings* (exhibition catalogue), National Gallery of Art (Washington, DC), 1994; *In Visible Touch: Modernism and Masculinity,* edited by Terry Smith, University of Chicago Press (Chicago, IL), 1997; *Robert Mangold,* Phaidon (London, England), 2000; *Chuck Close: Recent Paintings: March 17-April 29, 2000* (exhibition catalogue), Pace Wildenstein (New York, NY), 2000; *Donald Judd: Late Work: October 27-November 25, 2000* (exhibition catalogue), Pace Wildenstein (New York, NY), 2000; *Impossible Presence: The Work of Art in the Age of Replication,* edited by Terry Smith, University of Chicago Press (Chicago, IL), 2001; and *Barnett Newman,* edited by Ann Temkin, Philadelphia Museum of Art (Philadelphia, PA), 2002.

Articles and criticism have appeared in publications such as *Burlington Magazine, Artforum,* and *Parkett.*

SIDELIGHTS: Art historian and scholar Richard Shiff has spent much of his career as an educator and an academic, and many of his works are particularly useful for the art history student as well as established scholars in the field. He is the editor, along with Robert S. Nelson, of the book *Critical Terms for Art History,* which provides more than thirty essays on prominent subjects and important terms in the field of art history. Included are essays by art history and cultural studies scholars such as Paul Wood, Richard Meyer, and Ivan Gaskell, who delve in-depth into the history and meaning of terms such as "Performance," "Body," "Memory/Monument," "Originality," "Representation," and "Visual Culture/Visual Studies." *Critical Terms for Art History* "thoroughly examines the variable meanings and historic usage of each term or concept selected for inclusion," commented Savannah Schroll in *Library Journal,* who also noted that the essays "are carefully conceived and thoroughly accessible." The "erudite essays" in the book are "intended to promote research and debate," noted Joan Levin in a *Library Journal* review of the first edition of the book. *Art Journal* reviewer David Carrier commented, "There is in this book almost always a good balance between exposition of theory and presentation of examples; forced to be relatively brief, the contributors are mostly highly engaging."

Shiff has also been a contributor of introductions, essays, commentaries, and other material to volumes on a variety of art styles and artists. *Willem de Kooning: Paintings* is an exhibition catalog that offers a retrospective of the lengthy career of abstract expressionist painter de Kooning. Shiff, along with coauthors David Sylvester and Marla Prather, examines various periods of de Kooning's work, from the 1930s through the 1980s. De Kooning himself "was a restless and quixotic painter of many moods whose art, over the course of a very long life, kept shifting in significant ways," commented Mark Stevens in *New Republic.* De

Kooning "never moved toward a summary style or image," Stevens remarked. "No single moment can represent him the way, for example, the 'poured' or 'drip' paintings can represent Pollock." Shiff provides "a carefully researched essay . . . on the great constant in de Kooning, which is change," Stevens wrote. Shiff's contribution "provocatively explores de Kooning's preoccupation with certain recurring body features," noted a *Publishers Weekly* reviewer, including facial features such as the mouth and eyes, extremities such as the feet, and more intimate body parts, such as the breasts and genitals. Deidre Robson, writing in *Art History,* noted that Shiff's "discussion of the body in de Kooning's art brings out two main themes: that of the importance of the artist's coming to terms with the physicality of his own body, and the contemporaneity of favored figural references such as lipsticked lips, feet, and shoes, which Shiff traces to de Kooning's background as a commercial artist."

The book *Barnett Newman,* a study of expressionist and minimalist abstract painter, sculptor, and printmaker Newman, offers a "magnificent account of Newman's art production and its influence on late modern Western culture," noted R. W. Liscombe in *Choice.* Shiff contributes "a thoughtful assessment" of Newman's role and his impact in associated areas of art and the New York school of transatlantic modernism, Liscombe noted.

Shiff, himself a painter, is also the author of scholarly studies. In *Cézanne and the End of Impressionism: A Study of the Theory, Technique, and Critical Evaluation of Modern Art,* Shiff looks closely at the works of Paul Cézanne in the context of the last years of Impressionism, the French school of painting marked by its emphasis on mood and impressions, and the "broader spectrum of creative activities in 19th-century France," noted R. Dittman in *Choice.* "Concentrating on the years after about 1880, Shiff attempts to home in on Cézanne's aims and achievements, by close analysis of selected paintings, discussion of the artist's remarks and writings, and by studying the early critics' comments," commented Richard Thomson in *Burlington Magazine.* He shows how "an artist's self-understanding, his contemporary reputation, and the dominant trends of criticism in his wake come together," noted Alexander Gelley in *Library Journal.* Shiff's "impressive familiarity with essays and monographs is manifested by the endnotes which occupy seventy-five pages," Dittman observed. "Richard

Shiff's rich volume on Cézanne is a dense, cerebral text, which will no doubt bear regular rereading in years to come," Thomson remarked. Although Shiff "covers familiar ground," Thomson observed, "he has added great intensity and depth to the notional foundations of Cézanne scholarship."

BIOGRAPHICAL AND CRITICAL SOURCES:

PERIODICALS

Art History, June, 1995, Deirdre Robson, review of *Willem de Kooning: Paintings,* pp. 311-312.

Art Journal, summer, 1997, David Carrier, review of *Critical Terms for Art History,* pp. 93-95.

Burlington Magazine, April, 1986, Richard Thomson, review of *Cézanne and the End of Impressionism: A Study of the Theory, Technique, and Critical Evaluation of Modern Art,* pp. 297-298.

Chicago Tribune August 4, 1991, Alan G. Artner, "More than Picture Books: A Crop of Summer Editions Provides Fine Reading amid the Masters," p. 18.

Choice, February, 1985, R. Dittman, review of *Cézanne and the End of Impressionism,* p. 806; November, 2002, R. W. Liscombe, review of *Barnett Newman,* p. 460.

Library Journal, June 15, 1984, Alexander Gelley, review of *Cézanne and the End of Impressionism,* p. 1234; August, 1996, Joan Levin, review of *Critical Terms for Art History,* p. 67; May 1, 2003, Savannah Schroll, review of *Critical Terms for Art History,* p. 128.

New Republic, July 4, 1994, Mark Stevens, review of *Willem de Kooning,* pp. 28-33.

New York Review of Books, February 2, 1989, William Gass, review of *Foirades-Fizzles: Echo and Allusion in the Art of Jasper Johns,* pp. 22-27.

New York Times, July 28, 1991, John Russel, "The Poet Who Kick-started a Stalled Cézanne," p. H27.

Publishers Weekly, May 23, 1994, review of *Willem de Kooning,* p. 74.

ONLINE

University of Chicago Press Web site, http://www.pres.uchicago.edu/ (April 2, 2004).

University of Texas at Austin Web site, http://www.utexas.edu/ (April 2, 2004), biography of Richard Shiff.

SIBUM, Norm 1947-

PERSONAL: Born July 2, 1947, in Oberammergau, Germany. *Ethnicity:* "Caucasian." *Education:* "Self-educated." *Politics:* "Vaguely liberal."

ADDRESSES: Home—6077 Sherbrooke St. W., No. 202, Montreal, Quebec, Canada H4A 1Y2. *E-mail*—sibum@videotron.ca.

CAREER: Poet.

WRITINGS:

POETRY

Among Other Howls in the Storm, Pulp Press (Vancouver, British Columbia, Canada), 1982.

Cafe Poems, Oberon Press (Ottawa, Ontario, Canada), 1988.

Narratives and Continuations, Oberon Press (Ottawa, Ontario, Canada), 1990.

In Laban's Field, Carcanet Press (Manchester, England), 1993.

The November Propertius, Carcanet Press (Manchester, England), 1998.

Girls and Handsome Dogs, Porcupine's Quill Press (Erin, Ontario, Canada), 2002.

Intimations of a Realm in Jeopardy, Porcupine's Quill Press (Erin, Ontario, Canada), in press.

WORK IN PROGRESS: Gardens of the Interregnum, poetry.

SIDELIGHTS: Norm Sibum told *CA:* "My primary motivation for writing is that I don't know how to do anything else. My work is influenced by many writers, but mostly the 'classical' canon. I still have no idea what inspires me to write."

*   *   *

SIMS, Elizabeth

PERSONAL: Female. *Education:* Michigan State University, degree in English literature; Wayne State University, degree in English composition.

ADDRESSES: Home—136 East 8th St., #242, Port Angeles, WA 98362-6129. *E-mail*—esims@ elizabethsims.com.

CAREER: Worked as a reporter, corporate trainer, executive, and writing coach; has also worked for Borders for ten years as a bookseller and manager.

AWARDS, HONORS: Tompkins Award for Fiction, Wayne State University; Lambda Literary Award finalist, for *Damn Straight.*

WRITINGS:

"LILLIAN BYRD CRIME STORY" SERIES

Holy Hell, Alyson Books (Los Angeles, CA), 2002.
Damn Straight, Alyson Books (Los Angeles, CA), 2003.
Lucky Stiff, Alyson Books (Los Angeles, CA), 2004.

Work represented in anthologies, including *A Woman's Touch: New Lesbian Love Stories,* edited by Valerie Reed, Alyson Books (Los Angeles, CA), 2003, and *Best Lesbian Love Stories,* edited by Angela Brown, Alyson Books (Los Angeles, CA), 2003, 2004; contributor to periodicals, including *Moving Out, LOGOS: Journal of the World Book Community,* and *Smudge.*

SIDELIGHTS: Before becoming a novelist, Elizabeth Sims wrote newspaper articles, technical manuals, training videos, press releases, book reviews, and poems and stories. She has found success recently with her series of books featuring reporter Lillian Byrd. Byrd is introduced in *Holy Hell,* which is set in Detroit. In this debut, the protagonist has just experienced a breakup with her lover and is fired for stabbing the boss's obnoxious son, who has been sexually harassing her, in the buttocks. She picks up a freelance assignment to cover the same story she was working on at the newspaper concerning the disappearance of women. As Byrd delves deeper into the facts of the crimes, she becomes pursued by the criminals who perpetrated them.

The sequel, *Damn Straight,* is set in California during the Dinah Shore Weekend in Palm Springs. Lillian leaves dreary Detroit when her friend Truby calls, asking for advice on how to be a lesbian, which she suspects she must be because none of her heterosexual relationships have worked out. To entice Lillian, she mentions that she has passes to the LPGA tournament. Lillian, a golf enthusiast, arrives in sunny Los Angeles, where she hooks up with top-ranked Genie Maychild, who she soon discovers is being stalked by someone who wants to prevent her from winning the championship.

Lillian makes a quick trip to Genie's Midwestern hometown, where she pretends to be a reporter for *Sports Illustrated* in order to delve into Genie's past, hoping she can find a clue to the current dilemma. When she returns to the tournament with new knowledge, Genie's caddy is killed in an accident, and Lillian steps in to help out. Genie's failure to observe anything beyond her own game puts a damper on their relationship, however, and Truby, who finally has sex with a woman, finds that it is no more fulfilling than her previous relationships. She is damn straight, as the title suggests. Other characters include Coco Nash, the rookie who threatens to overcome Genie, and a rabbit named Todd.

"Though the plot's a tad thin," commented a *Kirkus Reviews* contributor, "the Dinah and sports celebrities are well-handled, and there's much charm and deprecating humor in Lillian's instructions to Truby." Lynne Maxwell reviewed Sims's second novel in *Lambda Book Report,* in which she wrote: "Intrinsically decent heroine Lillian Byrd exemplifies the qualities we all like to think we display. Not only is she the kind of person we would like to be, but she is also the kind of friend and/or lover we would like to have. Lillian, though, is far from perfect; she is also endearingly human, which means that she, like all of us, makes her share of mistakes." *Booklist* contributor Whitney Scott concluded that *Damn Straight* is "a sassy, smart, ultimately thoughtful thriller."

BIOGRAPHICAL AND CRITICAL SOURCES:

PERIODICALS

A Look at Books, March, 2002, Teresa DeCrescenzo, review of *Holy Hell.*
Booklist, May 1, 2003, Whitney Scott, review of *Damn Straight,* p. 1554.

Kirkus Reviews, March 15, 2003, review of *Damn Straight,* p. 432.

Lambda Book Report, August-September, 2003, Michele Spring-Moore, review of *Best Lesbian Love Stories 2003,* p. 25, Lynne Maxwell, review of *Damn Straight,* p. 30.

Library Journal, May 1, 2003, Rex Klett, review of *Damn Straight,* p. 159.

ONLINE

Alyson.com, http://www.alyson.com/ (March 20, 2004), interview with Elizabeth Sims.

Elizabeth Sims Home Page, http://www.elizabethsims. com (March 20, 2004).

Planetout.com, http://www.planetout.com/ (March 20, 2004), interview with Elizabeth Sims.

*   *   *

SIRLIN, Rhoda 1949-

PERSONAL: Born April 1, 1949, in New York, NY; daughter of Irving (in business) and Lottie (a secretary; maiden name, Kaplan) Sirlin. *Ethnicity:* "White." *Education:* Brooklyn College of the City University of New York, B.A., 1971; Pennsylvania State University, M.A., 1974; Graduate School of the City University of New York, Ph.D., 1989. *Politics:* Democrat.

ADDRESSES: Office—Queens College of the City University of New York, Flushing, NY 11367. *E-mail*—bklynheights@hotmail.com.

CAREER: Liveright Publishing, New York, NY, literary editor, 1971-72; Brooklyn College of the City University of New York, Brooklyn, NY, lecturer, 1974-76; Queens College of the City University of New York, Flushing, NY, lecturer, 1976-89; New School for Social Research, New York, NY, lecturer, 1989-90; Queens College of the City University of New York, adjunct assistant professor, 1990—. New York University, adjunct assistant professor, 1990-92; New York City Technical College, adjunct assistant professor, 1990—; Pratt Institute, visiting assistant professor, 1998-99; Polytechnic University, adjunct assistant professor, 2000—; guest speaker at other institutions, including State University of New York—Albany, Winthrop College, and Hollins University; public speaker.

MEMBER: Modern Language Association of America, American Culture Association, Conference on College Composition and Communication, Continuing Education Association, Northeast Modern Language Association, Mid-Atlantic Popular Culture Association.

WRITINGS:

William Styron's Sophie's Choice: Crime and Self Punishment, foreword by William Styron, UMI Research Press (Ann Arbor, MI), 1990.

Author of instructor's manuals. Contributor to books, including *Modern Critical Interpretations: William Styron's Sophie's Choice,* edited by Harold Bloom, Chelsea House Publishers (Philadelphia, PA), 2002. Contributor of articles and reviews to periodicals, including *Studies in American Jewish Literature* and *Southern Literary Journal.*

*   *   *

SNYDER, Brad M. 1972-

PERSONAL: Born June 28, 1972, in Potomac, MD. *Education:* Duke University, graduated 1994; Yale Law School, graduated 1999.

ADDRESSES: Agent—c/o Miranda Shafer, McGraw-Hill Co., 130 East Randolph St., Suite 900, Chicago, IL 60601. *E-mail*—snyder@beyondtheshadow.com.

CAREER: Baltimore Sun, Baltimore, MD, sportswriter, 1994-96; worked as a researcher for John Feinstein (*Hart Courts* and *Play Ball*); Williams & Connally, Washington, DC, attorney.

AWARDS, HONORS: Research grant and William P. Laprade Prize, Duke University; Robert Peterson Recognition Award from Society of American Baseball Negro League Committee Research, Casey Award finalist from *Spitball* magazine, for one of the year's ten best baseball books, and Dave Moore Award finalist from *Elysian Fields Quarterly: The Baseball Review,* for one of the year's best baseball books, all 2003, all for *Beyond the Shadow of the Senators: The Untold Story of the Homestead Grays and the Integration of Baseball.*

WRITINGS:

Beyond the Shadow of the Senators: The Untold Story of the Homestead Grays and the Integration of Baseball, Contemporary Books (Chicago, IL), 2003.

Contributor of sports-related stories to periodicals, including the *Washington Post, Basketball America,* and *Raleigh News and Observer,* and to law reviews, including *Yale Law Journal, Rutgers Law Review,* and *Vermont Law Review.*

WORK IN PROGRESS: Research of *Flood v. Kuhn,* the 1972 Supreme Court case in which Curt Flood filed an antitrust suit against major league baseball.

SIDELIGHTS: Brad M. Snyder is an attorney who defends civil litigation cases, but he has also had a great deal of experience as a journalist, particularly as a sportswriter. In 1993 Snyder received a research grant from Duke University's Center for Documentary Studies to interview Negro League players and black sports fans who remembered Homestead Grays games at Griffith Stadium. His research and interviews developed into his senior honors thesis. From 1994 to 1996, Snyder was a baseball reporter for the *Baltimore Sun,* covering the Baltimore Orioles during Cal Ripkin's run to break Lou Gehrig's record for consecutive games played. His interviews with owner Peter Angelos, also a plaintiff lawyer, led to Snyder's abandoning of journalism to study law.

Snyder's thesis eventually became his first book, *Beyond the Shadow of the Senators: The Untold Story of the Homestead Grays and the Integration of Baseball,* which he completed in nine months after his graduation from Yale Law School. Snyder studies the period from the mid 1920s to mid 1940s, which he calls the "lost era between the Babe [Ruth] and Jackie [Robinson]." It was during these years that the Negro Leagues grew teams like the Homestead Grays, who began in 1910 to play near the steel mills in Homestead, Pennsylvania, near Pittsburg, as well as the Kansas City Monarchs, whose roots were also in Homestead. The Grays boasted some of the finest ballplayers in the country, including sluggers like catcher Josh Gibson, dubbed the "black Babe Ruth," and the equally talented first baseman Buck Leonard, who is often referred to as the "black Lou Gehrig." From 1937 to 1945, the Grays won eight of nine Negro National League titles.

The book also mirrors the history of the white Washington team, the Senators, and owner Clark Griffith, who owned Griffith Stadium near Howard University. The Grays moved from Pennsylvania in 1940, and Griffith rented out the stadium to them when the Senators were on the road, charging high fees. The Grays games became more well-attended than those of the Senators, in spite of the fact that black support was slow to come because many blacks felt an allegiance to the Senators, who were, in fact, a worse team. In 1943 Gibson hit more home runs in the stadium than all of the Senators combined. Snyder also writes how the shrewd Cum Posey, black owner of the Grays, attracted the top talents with decent pay and a chance to play ball in the evolving black Washington community.

Snyder, furthermore, profiles Sam Lacy, a black journalist who worked tirelessly for the integration of baseball, and Wendell Smith, another black Hall of Fame sportswriter. Griffith opposed integration on not only racist grounds but also because he would lose the fees he collected from the Grays if segregation ended. And when it did, white owners—Branch Rickey in particular—snapped up the best black players, offering them low pay and no contracts. Robinson was the first to break the color barrier when he was signed by the Brooklyn Dodgers in 1947. The Senators moved to Minnesota in 1961, and the Washington team that replaced them failed, leaving Washington teamless.

"Snyder suggests that had Griffith signed one of the great black players, the Senators might still be playing in Washington today," commented Brent Kendall in the *Christian Science Monitor.* "While that's anyone's guess (Jackie Robinson's Dodgers did leave Brooklyn, after all), Snyder offers up another wrong that is more easily righted. Washington, the city of monuments, has no plaque or statue to commemorate the Grays' legacy." *Booklist* contributor Wes Lukowsky called *Beyond the Shadow of the Senators* "a textured account of a time when baseball symbolized the nation at large and when those with vision understood the implications of integrating an experience shared by so many Americans."

BIOGRAPHICAL AND CRITICAL SOURCES:

PERIODICALS

Booklist, February 15, 2003, Wes Lukowsky, review of *Beyond the Shadow of the Senators: The Untold*

Story of the Homestead Grays and the Integration of Baseball, p. 1042.

Choice, September, 2003, R. Browning, review of *Beyond the Shadow of the Senators.*

Christian Science Monitor, March 20, 2003, Brent Kendall, review of *Beyond the Shadow of the Senators,* p. 18.

New York Times Book Review, May 25, 2003, Roberto Gonzalez Echevarria, review of *Beyond the Shadow of the Senators,* p. 10.

Publishers Weekly, February 17, 2003, review of *Beyond the Shadow of the Senators,* p. 68.

ONLINE

Africana.com, http://www.africana.com/ (April 29, 2003), Tracy Grant, review of *Beyond the Shadow of the Senators.*

Brad Snyder Home Page, http://www.beyondtheshadow.com/ (March 20, 2004).*

*   *   *

SOROUSH, Abdolkarim 1945-

PERSONAL: Born 1945, in Tehran, Iran. *Education:* Earned a degree in pharmacy in Iran; graduated from University of London (analytical chemistry); attended Chelsea College (history, philosophy of science).

ADDRESSES: Agent—c/o Author Mail, Oxford University Press, 198 Madison Ave., New York, NY 10016.

CAREER: Educator, Iranian scholar. Laboratory for Food Products, Toiletries, and Sanitary Materials, Bushehr, Iran, director; Teacher Training College, Tehran, Iran, director of Islamic Culture Group; Institute for Cultural Studies, researcher; Tehran Academy of Philosophy, professor of ethics. Imam Sadeq Mosque, Tehran, lecturer; Tehran University, instructor; Harvard University, visiting professor. *Military service:* Served two years in the Iranian army..

WRITINGS:

Reason, Freedom, and Democracy in Islam: Essential Writings of Abdolkarim Soroush, translated and edited by Mahmoud Sadri and Ahmad Sadri, Oxford University Press (New York, NY), 2000.

Other writings, including lecture series, have been published in Persian.

SIDELIGHTS: Islamic scholar and revisionist thinker Abdolkarim Soroush was described by *Los Angeles Times* writer Robin Wright as a "gentle man [who is] shaking the foundations of a faith that claims a billion followers, nearly one out of every five people on Earth. Both supporters and critics now call him the Martin Luther of Islam—a man whose ideas on religion and democracy could bridge the chasm between Muslim societies and the outside world."

Soroush's philosophical beliefs began forming when as a student in London he was active in the Muslim Youth Association during the prerevolutionary years. He lectured at the imam-barah which was the center of their activities, and many of these talks were produced as pamphlets. He returned to Iran during the revolution and was charged with weakening the Marxist thought that had infiltrated Iranian politics. The plan was to keep the universities closed for at least twenty years, in which time fundamental reforms would have been established.

It was this experience that led Soroush to question the rigid interpretation of Islam and the establishment that used religion as a front for their politics and their economic aspirations. He championed democracy, and his ideas were published in columns in a magazine called *Kiyan* (title means "Source or Soul"), which was created just for this purpose. Because of his challenges to the prevailing ideology, Soroush was harassed and exiled. He returned to Iran following the 1997 election of reformist President Muhammad Khatami and gained a strong following with many Iranian students and some of the mullahs.

Reason, Freedom, and Democracy in Islam: Essential Writings of Abdolkarim Soroush is a collection of eleven of Soroush's seminal essays, originally published in Persian between 1985 and 1994. The editors have provided not only the translations but also an insightful interview that affords a better understanding of Soroush's life and philosophy. L. Carl Brown noted in *Foreign Affairs* that Soroush "cites the likes of Jalal al-Din Rumi, Muhammad Iqbal, Jorgen Habermas, and Alexis de Tocqueville as often as the Quran and the Prophet Muhammad."

Soroush does not get involved in politics, but rather affirms that the leaders of the Islamic religion should not also be the leaders of governments—in other words, a separation of church and state. "As did the Reformation," noted Wright, "Soroush's argument establishes the rights of individuals—in their relationship both with government and with God. And like democracy anywhere, the beliefs and will of the majority at the bottom define the ideal Islamic state. It can't be imposed from the top or by an elite."

Ali Ansari wrote in the *Times Literary Supplement* that "in his critique of the intellectual activities of the ulema, Soroush is in many ways continuing a tradition established by Jamal al Din al Afghani and, later, Ali Shariati. But whereas the latter were rebels with a cause, often eclectic and ambiguous in their pronunciations, Soroush is more exacting, seeking in precise ways to redefine the parameters of Iranian political and philosophical debate." In a *Middle East Journal* review, Mehrzad Boroujerdi said that the essays in this book "make abundantly clear why his admirers consider Soroush and innovative thinker while the clerical officialdom in Iran regards him as an enfant terrible."

BIOGRAPHICAL AND CRITICAL SOURCES:

PERIODICALS

Foreign Affairs, September-October, 2000, L. Carl Brown, review of *Reason, Freedom, and Democracy in Islam: Essential Writings of Abdolkarim Soroush,* p. 148.

Los Angeles Times, January 27, 1995, Robin Wright, "Islamist's Theory of Relativity," pp. A1, A10-A11.

Middle East Journal, summer, 2001, Mehrzad Boroujerdi, review of *Reason, Freedom, and Democracy in Islam,* p. 519.

Times Literary Supplement, May 24, 2002, Ali Ansari, review of *Reason, Freedom, and Democracy in Islam,* p. 26.

ONLINE

Middle East Institute, http://www.mideasti.org/ (January 8, 2003), Romain Fremont, "Policy Briefs: Islamic Democracy and Islamic Governance."*

SPIEGELMAN, Annie

PERSONAL: Married; husband's name, Bill; children: Jack.

ADDRESSES: Home—Northern California. *Agent*—c/o Author Mail, Seal Press, 300 Queen Anne Ave. N., #375, Seattle, WA 98109.

CAREER: Film director and author. Assistant director for television series *Midnight Caller,* 1988, for television movies, including *Babies,* 1990, *Long Road Home,* 1991, *Shadow of a Doubt,* 1991, *They,* 1993, and *My Very Best Friend,* 1996; and for films, including *True Believer,* 1989, *My Blue Heaven,* 1990, *The Doors,* 1991, *Raising Cain,* 1992, *When a Man Loves a Woman,* 1994, *Nine Months,* 1995, *Bee Season,* 2003, and *Twisted,* 2003.

MEMBER: Director's Guild of America.

WRITINGS:

Annie's Garden Journal: Reflections on Roses, Weeds, Men, and Life, Carol Publishing (Secaucus, NJ), 1996.

Dear Jack—I'll Be with You When the Sky Is Full of Colors, Wildcat Canyon Press (Berkeley, CA), 2001, published as *Growing Seasons: Half-baked Garden Tips, Cheap Advice on Marriage, and Questionable Theories on Motherhood,* Seal Press (New York, NY), 2003.

SIDELIGHTS: Annie Spiegelman is an assistant film and television director whose writings chronicle the many changes in her life as she moves from New York City to northern California, gets married, has a child, and deals with her mother's illness. Connecting her thoughts about life and her first forays into starting a garden by using gardening as a metaphor, her first book, *Annie's Garden Journal: Reflections on Roses, Weeds, Men, and Life,* relates her frustrations with planting and maintaining her garden as she deals with her emotions of an impending marriage to Bill and her relationship with her divorced parents. All of this is done, as several critics have noted, with a sense of humor aided by the colorful characters in her life, such as the sisters who were largely responsible for raising her. The author, according to a *Publishers Weekly* contributor, "writes knowingly of the travails of responsible adulthood in a way that is appealing to women." "Annie's sassy, cynical veneer," added *Booklist* reviewer Alice Joyce, "scarcely conceals a fervent enthusiasm for life's most essential elements."

Similar in some ways to *Annie's Garden Journal,* Spiegelman's *Growing Seasons: Half-baked Garden Tips, Cheap Advice on Marriage, and Questionable Theories on Motherhood* is written as a series of diary entries to her toddler son, Jack. Here, Spiegelman struggles to balance motherhood, caring for her sick mother, and her ambition to become a master gardener. Because the author directs her book to her son, however, *Library Journal* critics Rachel Collins and Mirela Roncevic felt that "it's hard for the reader to feel any connection with the text." On the other hand, Alice Joyce, writing again in *Booklist,* asserted that "readers will find the refreshingly zany writing to be compelling."

BIOGRAPHICAL AND CRITICAL SOURCES:

PERIODICALS

Booklist, October 1, 1996, Alice Joyce, review of *Annie's Garden Journal: Reflections on Roses, Weeds, and Life,* p. 317; June 1, 2003, Alice Joyce, review of *Growing Seasons: Half-baked Garden Tips, Cheap Advice on Marriage, and Questionable Theories on Motherhood,* p. 1729.
Library Journal, May 1, 2003, Rachel Collins and Mirela Roncevic, "What to Expect: Six Books Discuss the Art of Mothering," p. 142.
Publishers Weekly, September 9, 1996, review of *Annie's Garden Journal,* p. 75.

*   *   *

STATEN, Vince 1947-

PERSONAL: Born 1947.

ADDRESSES: Agent—c/o Author Mail, Simon & Schuster, 1230 Avenue of the Americas, New York, NY 10020.

CAREER: Writer.

WRITINGS:

The Real Elvis: Good Old Boy, Media Ventures (Dayton, OH), 1978.
Golly Wally: The Story of "Leave It to Beaver," Crown (New York, NY), 1984.
(With Greg Johnson) *Real Barbecue,* Perennial Library (New York, NY), 1988.
Unauthorized America: A Travel Guide to the Places the Chamber of Commerce Won't Tell You About, Perennial Library (New York, NY), 1990.
Jack Daniel's Old Time Barbecue Cookbook, Sulgrave Press (Louisville, KY), 1991.
Ol' Diz: A Biography of Dizzy Dean, HarperCollins (New York, NY), 1992.
Can You Trust a Tomato in January?: Everything You Wanted to Know (and a Few Things You Didn't) about Food in the Grocery Store, Simon & Schuster (New York, NY), 1993.
Did Monkeys Invent the Monkey Wrench?: Hardware Stores and Hardware Stories, Simon & Schuster (New York, NY), 1996.
Do Pharmacists Sell Farms?: A Trip inside the Corner Drugstore, Simon & Schuster (New York, NY), 1998.
Do Bald Men Get Half-price Haircuts?: In Search of America's Great Barbershops, Simon & Schuster (New York, NY), 2001.
Kentucky Curiosities: Quirky Characters, Roadside Oddities, and Other Offbeat Stuff, Globe Pequot Press (Guilford, CT), 2003.
Why Is the Foul Pole Fair?; or, Answers to the Baseball Questions Your Dad Hoped You'd Never Ask, Simon & Schuster (New York, NY), 2003.

SIDELIGHTS: Writer Vince Staten specializes in books of trivia, offbeat history, amusing anecdotes, and nostalgic memories, all presented in what Mike Tribby, writing in *Booklist,* called "a warm, chuckling tone." Among Staten's works are: *Unauthorized America: A Travel Guide to the Places the Chamber of Commerce Won't Tell You About; Ol' Diz: A Biography of Dizzy Dean; Can You Trust a Tomato in January?: Everything You Wanted to Know (and a Few Things You Didn't) about Food in the Grocery Store; Did Monkeys Invent the Monkey Wrench?: Hardware Stores and Hardware Stories; Do Pharmacists Sell Farms?: A Trip inside the Corner Drugstore;* and *Why Is the Foul Pole Fair?; or, Answers to the Baseball Questions Your Dad Hoped You'd Never Ask.*

Staten has written two books concerned with baseball. In *Ol' Diz* he presents the life story of one of the sport's greatest legends. Dizzy Dean pitched for the St. Louis Cardinals in the 1930s, one of the "Gas House Gang" which included Leo Durocher and Pepper Martin. Sidelined by an arm injury, Dean retired from baseball in 1941 to become a popular radio and television commentator. Because Dean was adept at mythologizing himself, even his full name and date and place of birth are still matters of contention. He was also prone to verbal gaffs. Hit in the head by a baseball, he explained to reporters that the doctors had X-rayed his head "and found nothing." Staten's account of Dean's colorful life is "a scrupulously documented, well-rounded portrait of an American original," a *Kirkus Reviews* critic concluded. In *Why Is the Foul Pole Fair?* Staten presents not so much baseball trivia as trivia about the "the accoutrements of baseball," as Ed Zotti put it in the *New York Times Book Review.* Staten talks about turnstiles, beer sales, team nicknames, scoreboards, radar guns, baseball equipment, and much else, providing little-known facts even devoted fans may not know. "Staten provides good, trivia-packed reading," Morey Berger wrote in the *Library Journal.*

Staten's *Unauthorized America* is a guide to locations around the country where offbeat history occurred. Among the items listed are the stretch of road where actress Jayne Mansfield had her fatal car accident, the place Richard Nixon's dog Checkers is buried, Michael Jordan's high school in North Carolina, and the New York hotel suite where Marilyn Monroe met with John F. Kennedy. Under the chapter title "Historic Battle Sites" are listed the places where celebrities like Frank Sinatra and Sean Penn got into fistfights with reporters. "Here you will be guided to places where modern history was made," Clarence Petersen explained in Chicago's *Tribune Books.* As Thomas Swick stated in the *New York Times Book Review,* "With this book, you can get in touch with Elvis's doctor or the Rev. Al Sharpton's hairdresser. What traveler should be without it?"

Several of Staten's books take the reader behind the scenes of a familiar retail industry. *Can You Trust a Tomato in January?* is a look at the food sold in grocery stores, telling the behind-the-scenes stories of how the various products are made and delivered to the grocer's shelf. Winter tomatoes, for example, are picked still green off the vine in Mexico and take seven days to arrive at American stores. Laurie Graham in the *New York Times Book Review* described the book as a "lighthearted look at the origins, development and distribution of the foods Americans love," while a critic for *Publishers Weekly* dubbed *Can You Trust a Tomato in January?* "an entertaining social history of the supermarket and its contents."

The hardware store is the focus of Staten's *Did Monkeys Invent the Monkey Wrench?* Staten's father owned a hardware store in Tennessee and the author worked there as a boy. Staten draws on this experience while discussing the modern hardware store in an "aisle-by-aisle" manner, arranging his chapters by typical hardware store departments. Under each department, the reader learns the "anecdotal histories of nearly everything you can find," Tribby wrote. Along the way, Staten also explains that the hardware store not only sells products but gives advice on how to use those products. In this sense, customers go to a hardware store to find solutions to their problems. "A reader will come away with new respect for hardware men, along with a lot of fascinating trivia," Gregory M. Lamb noted in the *Christian Science Monitor.* Chris Goodrich in the *Los Angeles Times Book Review* admitted: "I'm a sucker for this kind of book, and Vince Staten has produced a good one."

Staten turns his attention to the corner drugstore in *Do Pharmacists Sell Farms?,* which takes the reader on a tour of the average drugstore and gives behind-the-scenes stories of the products found there. Staten also provides offbeat histories of some of the terms and practices of the business. "This is charming, nostalgic history," a critic for *Publishers Weekly* wrote. In *Kirkus Reviews* a contributor also praised the work, finding *Do Pharmacists Sell Farms?* to be "full of entertaining if trivial facts presented with good humor."

BIOGRAPHICAL AND CRITICAL SOURCES:

PERIODICALS

Booklist, February 15, 1984, Martin A. Brady, review of *Golly Wally: The Story of "Leave It to Beaver,"* p. 838; February 15, 1992, Barbara Jacobs, review of *Ol' Diz: A Biography of Dizzy Dean,* p. 1081; June 1, 1993, Barbara Jacobs, review of *Can You Trust a Tomato in January?: Everything You*

Wanted to Know (and a Few Things You Didn't) about Food in the Grocery Store, p. 1760; June 1, 1996, Mike Tribby, review of *Did Monkeys Invent the Monkey Wrench?: Hardware Stores and Hardware Stories,* p. 1650; June 1, 1998, Mike Tribby, review of *Do Pharmacists Sell Farms?: A Trip inside the Corner Drugstore,* p. 1686.

Christian Science Monitor, October 2, 1996, Gregory M. Lamb, review of *Did Monkeys Invent the Monkey Wrench?,* p. 15.

Harper's, May, 1989, Frank Gannon, review of *Real Barbecue,* p. 55.

Kirkus Reviews, December 1, 1991, review of *Ol' Diz,* p. 1522; May 15, 1998, review of *Do Pharmacists Sell Farms?,* p. 725.

Library Journal, March 15, 1984, Annie Davis, review of *Golly Wally,* p. 581; February 1, 1992, Morey Berger, review of *Ol' Diz,* p. 96; July, 1993, Linda Chopra, review of *Can You Trust a Tomato in January?,* p. 108; May 1, 1996, Jonathan N. Hershey, review of *Did Monkeys Invent the Monkey Wrench?,* p. 126; March 15, 2003, Morey Berger, review of *Why Is the Foul Pole Fair?: or, Answers to the Baseball Questions Your Dad Hoped You'd Never Ask,* p. 90.

Los Angeles Times Book Review, March 29, 1992, Dick Roraback, review of *Ol' Diz,* p. 6; May 19, 1996, Chris Goodrich, review of *Did Monkeys Invent the Monkey Wrench?,* p. 10.

New York Times Book Review, June 5, 1988, Florence Fabricant, review of *Real Barbecue,* p. 15; June 10, 1990, Thomas Swick, review of *Unauthorized America: A Travel Guide to the Places the Chamber of Commerce Won't Tell You About,* p. 49; April 5, 1992, Maria Gallagher, review of *Ol' Diz,* p. 21; August 22, 1993, Laurie Graham, review of *Can You Trust a Tomato in January?,* p. 12; May 25, 2003, Ed Zotti, review of *Why Is the Foul Pole Fair?,* p. 18.

Publishers Weekly, January 20, 1984, review of *Golly Wally,* p. 87; December 6, 1991, review of *Ol' Diz,* p. 66; June 28, 1993, review of *Can You Trust a Tomato in January?,* p. 73; April 22, 1996, review of *Did Monkeys Invent the Monkey Wrench?,* p. 55; May 4, 1998, review of *Do Pharmacists Sell Farms?,* p. 197.

Sporting News, April 6, 1992, Steve Gietschier, review of *Ol' Diz,* p. 43.

Tribune Books (Chicago, IL), June 24, 1990, Clarence Petersen, review of *Unauthorized America,* p. 8.

U.S. News and World Report, April 8, 1991, James Popkin, review of *Unauthorized America,* p. 68.*

STAVITSKY, Gail 1954-

PERSONAL: Born May 13, 1954, in Cleveland, OH; daughter of Abraham (a scientist and immunologist) and Ruth (a homemaker; maiden name, Okney) Stavitsky; married Richard Sheinaus (a graphic designer), April 4, 1993; children: Anna. *Ethnicity:* "Jewish." *Education:* University of Michigan, A.B. (with high honors), 1976; New York University, M.A., 1978, Ph. D., 1990.

ADDRESSES: Home—23 Macopin Ave., Montclair, NJ 07043. *Office*—Montclair Art Museum, 3 South Mountain Ave., Montclair, NJ 07042; fax: 973-746-0920. *E-mail*—gail@montclair-art.org.

CAREER: Carnegie Museum of Art, assistant curator of fine arts, 1981-83; Montclair Art Museum, Montclair, NJ, curator of collections and exhibitions, 1994-98, chief curator, 1998—. Museum of Modern Art, instructor, beginning 1986; guest speaker at schools and museums, including New York University and Metropolitan Museum of Art.

MEMBER: American Association of Museums, College Art Association of America, Phi Beta Kappa.

WRITINGS:

(With others) *Precisionism in America: Reordering Reality, 1915-1941,* Harry N. Abrams (New York, NY), 1994.

(With others) *Paris 1900: The "American School" at the Universal Exposition,* Rutgers University Press (Piscataway, NJ), 1999.

(With others) *Will Barnet: A Timeless World,* Rutgers University Press (Piscataway, NJ), 2000.

(With others) *Montclair Art Museum: Selected Works,* Marquand Books (Seattle, WA), 2002.

Author of exhibition catalogs for Montclair Art Museum. Contributor to exhibition catalogs and books, including *Conversion to Modernism: The Early Works of Man Ray,* edited by Francis M. Naumann, Rutgers University Press (Piscataway, NJ), 2003.

WORK IN PROGRESS: Creating exhibitions of modern American art.

SIDELIGHTS: Gail Stavitsky told *CA:* "My primary motivation for writing is to complement and provide a fuller context for the subjects of the exhibitions that I curate. I am fascinated with relatively unknown, unappreciated, and under-recognized aspects of American art, and these inspire my writings and shows. My writing style and process are scholarly and academic, yet I always aim for clarity and accessibility."

BIOGRAPHICAL AND CRITICAL SOURCES:

PERIODICALS

Choice, January, 2001, C. Stroh, review of *Will Barnet: A Timeless World,* p. 8.

*   *   *

STEINER, Kurt 1912-2003

OBITUARY NOTICE—See index for *CA* sketch: Born June 10, 1912, in Vienna, Austria; died of pancreatic cancer October 20, 2003, in Stanford, CA. Educator, linguist, political advisor, and author. Steiner was a longtime professor of political science at Stanford University who, early in his career, was involved in the war crimes trials in Japan after World War II, as well as in helping to frame Japan's post-war constitution. After earning a law degree from the University of Vienna in 1935, he practiced law and published anti-Nazi articles. Being Jewish, in addition to having protested against the Nazis, led to his wise decision to flee Austria in 1938. Arriving in the United States, he worked various odd jobs until his gift for languages led him to direct Berlitz schools in Pittsburgh and Cleveland during the early 1940s. Enlisting in the U.S. Army in 1944, Steiner learned to speak Japanese and was sent to the Pacific, where he served in the U.S. military government that was organized in Japan after the war. He was instrumental in assisting with the war crime trials there, translating German documents that were used as evidence against Japanese leaders who had destroyed their own documentation. Leaving the army in 1948, Steiner remained in Japan as chief of the Civil Affairs and Civil Liberties Branch of the Legislative and Justice Division, where he helped to write the new Japanese constitution. It was Steiner who wrote many of the liberal laws into the constitution that granted substantially more freedom to Japan's citizenry than had previously existed. Finally leaving Japan in 1951, he went back to school to earn a doctorate in political science from Stanford University in 1955. He then joined Stanford's faculty as an assistant professor, becoming a full professor in 1962 and retiring in 1977. While associated with Stanford, Steiner was a founding faculty member of the university's center near Stuttgart, Germany, and was the director there in 1961. He also helped establish a campus at Semmering, Austria, and directed the Stanford Center for Japanese Studies in 1962. A recognized authority on both Japan and Austria, Steiner wrote, edited, and contributed to a number of books on these subjects, including *Local Government in Japan* (1965), *Politics in Austria* (1972), and *Tradition and Innovation in Contemporary Austria* (1982). At the time of his death, he had been working on a history of the Japanese war-crime trials, which is expected to be published posthumously.

OBITUARIES AND OTHER SOURCES:

ONLINE

Palo Alto Weekly Online, http://www.paloaltoonline.com/ (January 21, 2004).
Stanford University News Service, http://www.stanford.edu/dept/news/ (January 14, 2004).

*   *   *

STEPANIANTS, Marietta 1935-

PERSONAL: Born October 16, 1935, in Moscow, U.S.S.R. (now Russia); daughter of Tigran (an economist) and Asya (a teacher; maiden name, Bahchinian) Stepaniants; married Alexander Syrodeev (a diplomat), June 15, 1961; children: Asya. *Ethnicity:* "Armenian." *Education:* Degrees from Moscow State Institute of International Affairs, 1959 and 1963, D.Phil., 1974, professor, 1983. *Politics:* Democrat. *Religion:* "Agnostic." *Hobbies and other interests:* Literature, music, gardening.

ADDRESSES: Home—1/2 Krasnopresnenskay nal., Apt. 60, Moscow, Russia 123100. *Office*—Institute of Philosophy, Russian Academy of Sciences, 14 Volhonka St., Moscow, Russia 119842. *E-mail*—mstepani@iph.ras.ru.

CAREER: Russian Academy of Sciences, Institute of Philosophy, Moscow, fellow and researcher, 1959-80, director of Center for the Study of Oriental Philosophies, 1980—. Diplomatic Academy of the U.S.S.R., professor, 1980-94; Academy of Humanities Research, member, beginning 1995; State University of Humanities, Moscow, chair of Oriental philosophical and political thought, 1996—; guest speaker at other institutions, including University of Hawaii, Villanova University, Columbia University, New School for Social Research, State University of New York at Stony Brook, and Juniata College; director of international conferences.

MEMBER: Russian Philosophical Association.

AWARDS, HONORS: Sarasvati Samana Award, 1996; Ashraf, an award of the state of Tajikstan, Russia, 1999; annual lecturer award, Indian Council for Philosophical Research, 2001; named Honored Scholar of the Russian Federation, 2002.

WRITINGS:

Pakistan: Philosophy and Sociology, Nauka (Moscow, U.S.S.R.), 1971, People's Publishing House (Lahore, Pakistan), 1972.

(Editor) *Muslim Philosophy in Soviet Studies,* Sterling Publishing House (New Delhi, India), 1988.

The Philosophical Aspects of Sufism, Ajanta Publications (New Delhi, India), 1989.

Islamic Philosophy and Social Thought (XIX-XX Centuries), People's Publishing House (Lahore, Pakistan), 1989.

Sufi Wisdom, State University of New York Press (Albany, NY), 1994.

(Editor, with Ron Bontekoe) *Justice and Democracy: Crosscultural Perspectives,* University Press of Hawaii (Honolulu, NI), 1997.

Gandhi and the World Today: A Russian Perspective, Rajendra Prasad Academy (New Delhi, India), 1998.

Introduction to Eastern Thought, AltaMira Press (Walnut Creek, CA), 2002.

(Editor, with Peter Hershock and Roger T. Ames) *Technology and Cultural Values: On the Edge of the Third Millennium,* University Press of Hawaii (Honolulu, HI), 2003.

Editor of *History of Indian Philosophy: A Russian Viewpoint,* Indian Council of Philosophical Research (New Delhi, India). Author or editor of several books in Russian. Editor in chief of book series on Eastern philosophy and comparative philosophy, Nauka (Moscow, Russia). Contributor of articles and reviews to Russian and English-language periodicals, including *Philosophy East and West, Social Sciences, Muslim World,* and *Central Asian Review.*

Stepaniants's work has also been published in Arabic.

WORK IN PROGRESS: Editing *Religion and Identities in Russia;* coediting an Italian edition on Sufism in the dialogue between cultures and religions.

*   *   *

STERLING, Robert
   See CASIL, Amy Sterling

*   *   *

STEWART, Mary Anne 1831-1911
   (Mary Anne Barker, Lady Barker, Lady Broome)

PERSONAL: Born in 1831, in Jamaica; died on March 6, 1911; daughter of Walter George Stewart (island secretary of Jamaica); married Captain George Barker, 1852 (died 1861); married Frederick Napier Broome (sheep farmer, colonial secretary, and poet) in 1865; children (with Barker): two sons, including Walter George; children (with Broome): Guy, Louis.

CAREER: Travel writer, 1870-1904.

WRITINGS:

Station Life in New Zealand, Macmillan (London, England and New York, NY), 1870, Lent (New York, NY), 1872.

Stories About:—, Macmillan (London, England and New York, NY), 1871.

A Christmas Cake in Four Quarters, Macmillan (London, England and New York, NY), 1871.

Spring Comedies, Macmillan (London, England and New York, NY), 1871.

Travelling About over New and Old Ground, Routledge (London, England), 1872.

Ribbon Stories, Macmillan (London, England and New York, NY), 1872.

Station Amusements in New Zealand, Hunt (London, England), 1873.

Holiday Stories for Boys and Girls, Routledge (London, England), 1873.

Boys, Routledge (London, England), 1874.

First Lessons in the Principles of Cooking, Macmillan (London, England and New York, NY), 1874.

Sybil's Book, Macmillan (London, England and New York, NY), 1874.

This Troublesome World; or, "Bet of Stow", Hatchards (London, England), 1875.

Houses and Housekeeping: A Fireside Gossip upon Home and Its Comforts, Hunt (London, England), 1876.

A Year's Housekeeping in South Africa, Macmillan (London, England and New York, NY), 1877, republished as *Life in South Africa,* Lippincott (Philadelphia, PA), 1877.

The Bedroom and Boudoir, Macmillan (London, England and New York, NY), 1878.

The White Rat, and Some Other Stories, Macmillan (London, England and New York, NY), 1880.

Letters to Guy, Macmillan (London, England and New York, NY), 1885.

(As Lady Broome) *Harry Treverton, His Tramps and Troubles Told by Himself,* Routledge (London, England), 1889.

Colonial Memories, Smith, Elder (London, England), 1904.

OTHER

(Editor as Mary Anne Broome) Lady Annie Brassey, *The Last Voyage,* Longmans, Green (London, England), 1889.

Contributor to periodical publication *Macmillan's Magazine.*

SIDELIGHTS: Mary Anne Stewart, better-known as Lady Mary Anne Barker, is best remembered for her travel writing, in which she describes the landscape of the British colonies from a colonist's perspective. Some of Barker's writing was successful as children's literature; but as Carol Huebscher Rhoades noted in *Dictionary of Literary Biography:* "Many of [Barker's] stories derive from her travel experiences, and those books, even if written ostensibly for children, were aimed also at adult readers in the British leisured classes." Barker's writing tends to depict the colonial life—sheep farming, local customs—in stories that glorify British colonialism, offering some useful information along with much patriotic cooing. In *Travelling about over New and Old Ground,* for example, she exclaims, "It is exactly like England! That is the highest praise the exile can bestow on any place."

Barker was born Mary Anne Stewart in 1831. Her father, Walter George Stewart, was a British gentleman serving as island secretary in Jamaica, where Barker was born. Barker grew up between England and its colonies; though she was raised in Jamaica, she was educated in England. In many ways, Barker's early history set a pattern for her future efforts: throughout Barker's life, she seems always to have attempted to bring English culture to the colonies while translating the colonies' culture to a British audience. At the age of twenty-one, Barker married her first husband, Captain George Barker (later Sir Barker); she raised her two sons in England while her husband worked in India until his death in 1861.

By 1865, Barker had met and married her second husband, Frederick Napier Broome (later Sir Broome). She left her two children in England and set out for New Zealand with Broome; together, the couple planned to run a sheep farm. The farm failed, and Barker and her young husband returned to England. They supported themselves by writing: he as a poet and journalist, she as a travel writer. Barker's first book, *Station Life in New Zealand,* is based on the letters Barker wrote to her sister while in New Zealand. Rhoades explained, "Barker's book synthesizes two opposing messages. On one hand, she stresses the opportunities in New Zealand for hardworking, progressive settlers who can make the most of the abundant resources the country has. Echoing one theme of earlier colonial literature such as Butler's *First Year in Canterbury Settlement,* Barker discourages the colonial settlement dreams of educated gentlemen who have money but lack fitness or desire for work. On the other hand, her narrative describes, for the most part, the leisured life of people who spend mornings reading and writing and who then divert themselves with horse riding, pig hunting, fishing, and picnics."

Station Life in New Zealand, which became Barker's most popular book, offers a view of the British "domestication" of New Zealand—for Barker, this "domestication" is an unmitigated good. Barker describes her efforts to spread her method of Christian worship to the native New Zealanders, as well as her effort to reinforce the old-world habits of the British colonizers living in New Zealand. She is particularly careful to describe how she and her husband developed Anglican services in the bush, and how they would try to share religious literature with shepherds in the area. As Rhoades suggested: "Barker's . . . New Zealand stories are intended not simply to amuse and inform but to reassure readers at home that the colonies are nurturing and, most of all, maintaining the sacred bonds of British domesticity. The close, colonial ties to England and the queen."

Since *Station Life* became a hit with the British audience back home, Barker followed it with another such work, *Station Amusements in New Zealand.* In it, Barker relates her attempts to bring British habits to the new land; in one section, she describes a day of whipping down hills on a toboggan following a New Zealand snowstorm—for her, the new landscape brings new zest to an old pastime. Barker suggests that though the rough climate offers challenges to those wishing to cling to their British ways, it offers excitement and a sense of mission as well. Reviewers were generally pleased by the work, and by Barker's later collections of children's stories, such as *Spring Comedies, A Christmas Cake in Four Quarters, Stories About:—, Ribbon Stories, Holiday Stories for Boys and Girls, Boys,* and *Sybil's Book.* In each of these collections, Barker describes the process of domestication: in the stories, settlers are found domesticating foreign lands, domesticating children, and domesticating themselves as they learn to live without servants, making British comfort with their own hands. During this period, Barker also spent time in England as a cooking school teacher and as an editor, teaching others to follow British traditions in London as well as abroad.

Barker continued to write in this mode—teaching English domestic traditions—after a brief stay in Natal, where her husband was posted as colonial secretary. In 1877, she published *A Year's Housekeeping in South Africa,* in which she described her efforts to make a British life in her husband's new land. But the book reveals the kind of ideas at the heart of Barker's colonial writing. In it, she describes the African people in truly crass and derogatory language—so much so that even her British reviewers were discomfited. Rhoades pointed out: "Her political and social naiveté is particularly galling in view of her wide travels and her position as the wife of a government official: 'it is not any one's business to laugh at people suffering under the injustice of English officials' [a review in the *Westminster and Foreign Quarterly Review*]."

Barker's books, throughout her life, attempt to suggest the benefits of bringing English beliefs and customs to the colonies, and her books consistently depict the importance and life-affirming potential of colonialism. For that reason, Barker often evades some of the more troubling events that disturbed her travels. Rhoades noted: "Barker portrays the colony in idealistic terms: it is, like New Zealand, a better England. Unpleasantries such as the burning of Governor Broome in effigy midway through his term and the question of the place of the Aborigines within the new society are glossed over or, more often, not discussed at all. . . . Barker is uncritical of the treatment the Aborigines receive from the whites . . . she excellently describes the lives and perspectives of middle-and upper-middle class British colonialists, and she ignores or stereotypes other social groups."

Barker's work suggests much about the perspective of those working to turn the colonies into a "better England." A taste for adventure, a steadfast belief in English values, and a certain blindness characterizes Barker's narratives of domestication, but through them the reader is offered a more complex picture of the colonialist's mission. She died on March 6, 1911—a world traveler who, in some ways, never left home.

BIOGRAPHICAL AND CRITICAL SOURCES:

BOOKS

Dictionary of Literary Biography, Volume 166: *British Travel Writers, 1837-1875,* Gale (Detroit, MI), 1996.

Gross, Konrad and Wolfgang Klooss, *English Literature of the Dominions: Writings on Australia, Canada and New Zealand,* Koenigshausen & Neumann (Wurzburg, Germany), 1981.*

STRAUSS, David Levi

PERSONAL: Male. *Education:* Goddard College, received degree.

ADDRESSES: Agent—c/o Author Mail, Aperture's Book Center, 20 East 23rd St., New York, NY 10010.

CAREER: Center for Curatorial Studies, Bard College, Annandale-on-Hudson, New York, NY, faculty member of Avery Graduate School of the Arts; has worked as an art curator.

AWARDS, HONORS: Visiting scholar research fellowship, Center for Creative Photography; Logan grant; Guggenheim fellowship; three Artspace grants.

WRITINGS:

(With Daniel J. Martinze and others) *The Things You See when You Don't Have a Grenade!,* Smart Art Press (Santa Monica, CA), 1996.
Miguel Rio Branco (essay), Aperture (New York, NY), 1998.
Between Dog & Wolf: Essays on Art & Politics, Autonomedia, 1999.
Jorge Zeno: Semilla Abierta/Open Seed (exhibit catalog), Museo de Arte de Ponce (Ponce, Puerto Rico), 2000.
Between the Eyes: Essays on Photography and Politics, introduction by John Berger, Aperture (New York, NY), 2003.

Also author of poetry. Contributor to books, including *Points of Entry—Three Rivers Arts Festival,* by Mary J. Jacob and others, edited by Michelle Illuminato, Ram Publications, 1997; *Francesca Woodman,* by Francesca Woodman, translated by Rana Dasgupta, Scalo Verlag, 1998; *Cecilia Vicuna: Cloud-Net,* by Cecilia Vicuna, translated by Rosa Alcala, Art in General, 2000; *The Book of 101 Books: Seminal Photographic Books of the Twentieth Century,* edited by Andrew Roth, Roth Horowitz, 2001; *Imaging Her Erotics: Essays, Interviews, Projects,* by Carolee Schneeman, MIT Press, 2001; and *Hannah Villiger,* edited by Jolanda Bucher, Scalo Verlag, 2001. Contributor to periodicals, including *Art Forum, Aperture, Art in*

America, Exposure, Artscribe, Arena, Art Issues, Afterimage, Artes de Mexico, Nation, and *Edinburgh Review. Miguel Rio Branco* has been translated into Spanish.

WORK IN PROGRESS: Several books, including *Odile & Odette, Artists and Photography, Beuys in Ireland: 7000 Oaks on the Hill of Uisneach,* and *Nine Latin American Photographers.*

SIDELIGHTS: David Levi Strauss is an author, poet, and art critic who often writes about art and photography as it pertains to politics and modern culture. In his art criticism book *Between Dog & Wolf: Essays on Art & Politics,* he "attributes much of the emphasis on the body in recent art to a struggle for control over this immediately political domain," according to *Afterimage* contributor Alan Gilbert. In Strauss's view, much of modern art is created in support of the status quo, and thus its aesthetics do not delve into the root of the issues that ail society but only present images that support a "return to normalcy or stasis." "The implicit argument running through these essays," according to Gilbert, "is that art will never be able to [make use of the power of imagery] . . . on its own, whether in theory or practice. Instead, Strauss foresees a strategy of constant contextualization, both on the part of the artist and the critic, thereby creating a web of relations between art, culture and history." The critic concluded that *Between Dog & Wolf* "is an impassioned and lucid attempt to articulate a radical aesthetics in opposition to widespread anaesthetic visual culture."

With *Between the Eyes: Essays on Photography and Politics,* Strauss has written a work that has often been compared by critics to Susan Sontag's *Regarding the Pain of Others,* in which Sontag avers that the efforts of photographers to make their pictures of horrifying world events into some type of art has resulted in distancing audiences from their subject and making them, therefore, largely indifferent to it. Strauss, in contrast, asserts that "it is both possible and desirable for a photograph to have a political as well as an aesthetic dimension," according to Peter Wollen in the *Nation.* As an example, Strauss defends the work of Sebastiao Salgado, whom Sontag accuses of trying to add beauty to despairing subjects, saying that it is the artistry of Salgado's work that leads to discussion among audiences about his subjects. Nevertheless, Strauss echoes Sontag's concerns about the state of modern photojournalism, saying that images of distant wars, disease, and poverty can lead to a sense of "distance and superiority in consumers while providing them with vicarious thrills," according to Talya Halkin in the *Jerusalem Post*. While at times, Halkin felt, the author fails to draw a convincing "connection between photography and politics," his book helps show "how contemporary artists can subvert the way we look at photography." *Between the Eyes,* concluded *Library Journal* contributor Shauna Frischkorn, is a "compelling" work with a "writing style [that is] intellectual but accessible."

BIOGRAPHICAL AND CRITICAL SOURCES:

PERIODICALS

Afterimage, March, 2001, Alan Gilbert, "A(na)esthetics," p. 20.
Jerusalem Post, August 29, 2003, Talya Halkin, "An Open-and-closed (Shutter) Case," p. B13.
Library Journal, June 15, 2003, Shauna Frischkorn, review of *Between the Eyes: Essays on Photography and Politics,* p. 69.
Nation, October 6, 2003, Peter Wollen, "Shooting Wars," p. 26.
Publishers Weekly, May 12, 2003, review of *Between the Eyes,* p. 57.

ONLINE

College of the Atlantic, http://www.coa.edu/ (April 13, 2004), "David Levi Strauss, Author and Critic, to Speak at College of the Atlantic."*

*   *   *

SUMMER, Lauralee 1976-

PERSONAL: Born 1976, in CA; daughter of Elizabeth Summer. *Education:* Harvard University, B.A. (children's studies), 1998; University of California, Berkeley, graduate study (education).

ADDRESSES: *Agent*—c/o Author Mail, Simon & Schuster, 1230 Avenue of the Americas, New York, NY 10020.

CAREER: Student and author.

WRITINGS:

Learning Joy from Dogs without Collars: A Memoir, Simon & Schuster (New York, NY), 2003.

SIDELIGHTS: Lauralee Summer was raised by a peripatetic but loving mother who moved from state to state, and lived cheaply—sometimes even making a temporary home in a shelter. Living on welfare in order to be able to spend as much time with her daughter as possible, Elizabeth Summer passed along her love of books, as well as "cultivating her daughter's sense of wonder and interest in the world," according to *Boston Globe* contributor Jan Gardner. With no car, no stable home, no father that Lauralee knew, and little money, the girl learned to be resilient, open to new experiences, and self-reliant, although she also felt periods of anger and frustration as poverty and class differences made her feel inadequate among her peers. Due in part to a dedicated teacher at Massachusetts' Quincy High School, Summer finally got her first taste of what consistent, long-term effort could achieve—and gained the first inkling that her life was somewhat out of the ordinary—when she won a wrestling scholarship to Harvard University as a member of the boys' team. When armies of reporters began showing up, begging for interviews, and Summer was asked to appear on television interviews, she realized that it was important for people to realize that she did not feel deprived by her unusual childhood. Her book *Learning Joy from Dogs without Collars,* written during her college career, is her attempt to set the record straight.

Calling the book "part mother-daughter road trip, part antimaterialist manifesto complete with low-budget decorating ideas, and part meditation on the challenges of being the first woman on the varsity wrestling team at Harvard," Gardner commented that *Learning Joy from Dogs without Collars* serves as a "tribute to mothers who—often with little more than sheer determination—make a better life for their offspring." While finding Summers' story compelling, *Pittsburgh Post-Gazette* reviewer Ruth Hammond noted that the author's "approach is a bit uneven. The intellectual analysis she imposes on her story [due to her college studies in child development and education] does not always graft well. . . . The mother of the girl's early years is such a well-drawn character that it's a shame the reader doesn't get a chance to know her better." In *Publishers Weekly* a reviewer praised the book as a "memorable" work in which the author "writes frankly about poverty, shame and class distinctions." a *Kirkus* contributor found Summer's memoir "both forgiving and perceptive," while in *Library Journal* Dale Farris found *Learning Joy from Dogs without Collars* a "sophisticated, literary" book in which both teen and adult readers will "admire the author's determination not to dwell on disappointment or live with anger."

BIOGRAPHICAL AND CRITICAL SOURCES:

PERIODICALS

Booklist, May 1, 2003, Hazel Rochman, review of *Learning Joy from Dogs without Collars: A Memoir,* p. 1560.
Boston Globe, August 4, 2003, Jan Gardner, "A Mother-Daughter Journey through Homelessness," p. B10.
Kirkus Reviews, April 15, 2003, review of *Learning Joy from Dogs without Collars,* p. 598.
Library Journal, April 15, 2003, Dale Farris, review of *Learning Joy from Dogs without Collars,* p. 98.
Post-Gazette (Pittsburgh, PA), June 20, 3004, Ruth Hammond, review of *Learning Joy from Dogs without Collars.*
Publishers Weekly, May 12, 2003, review of *Learning Joy from dogs without Collars,* p. 57.
USA Today, July 14, 2003, Kathy Balog, "From Homeless to Harvard and the World Beyond."

ONLINE

BookPage.com, http://www.bookpage.com/ (October 12, 2003), Alison Hood, "A Nomad Finds a Home at Last."*

*   *   *

SVENVOLD, Mark 1958-

PERSONAL: Born 1958, in Seattle, WA. *Education:* University of Iowa Writers' Workshop, M.F.A.

ADDRESSES: Agent—c/o Author Mail, HarperCollins, 10 E. 53rd St., 7th Floor, New York, NY 10022.

CAREER: Writer, poet. Fordham University, New York, NY, poet in residence.

AWARDS, HONORS: Vassar Miller prize and Discovery/*Nation* award, both for *Soul Data.*

WRITINGS:

Soul Data: Poems, University of North Texas Press (Denton, TX), 1998.
Elmer McCurdy: The Misadventures in Life and Afterlife of an American Outlaw, Basic Books (New York, NY), 2002.

Contributor to periodicals, including *Harper's Bazaar, Ploughshares, Virginia Quarterly Review, Atlantic Monthly, Gettysburg Review,* and *Nation.*

SIDELIGHTS: Mark Svenvold's poetry is collected in his prize-winning *Soul Data,* featuring the long poem, "Death of the Cabaret Hegel," about a Seattle performance space that is sacrificed for a freeway. A *Kirkus Reviews* contributor wrote that "the scene . . . boasts the glories of mixed zoning and thrift-shop hunting." The writer commented that three poems have as their subject Thelonious Monk, but added that Svenvold "seems more at home with the 1960s nihilism of the Doors." In other poems, Svenvold focuses on his job working in a garage and the deaths of his parents.

Svenvold's *Elmer McCurdy: The Misadventures in Life and Afterlife of an American Outlaw* is a biography of the man, and later the mummy, who was, and is, Elmer McCurdy. T. W. H. Miller began his review for the *St. Louis Post-Dispatch Online* with an old-timey spiel, saying, "Step right up folks, and we will amaze you, yes, even astonish you, with the life and times of one of the West's last outlaws. . . . The true saga of this inept train robber has been faithfully recorded by the talented Mark Svenvold, who has let no obstacle stand in his way in his resolve to bring you the truth. Not only does Svenvold offer you the lurid details of Elmer's misspent life, but we positively guarantee that you will be appalled and fascinated when our author cleverly plays out the cards of this drama."

"Svenvold works hard to set his main character in a larger context," wrote Adam Woog in the *Seattle Times.* "Many disparate strands of Americana come into play, with the McCurdy mummy as their unwitting nexus. We're thus treated to potted histories of, among other things, cadaver preservation, the Osage Indians, exploitation film making, grave snatchers, and carnivals."

Elmer the mummy was discovered in 1976 in a Long Beach, California fun house during the shooting of an episode of *The Six Million Dollar Man.* When a technician moved what seemed to be a dummy, hanging overhead from a noose, one arm fell off, and the horrified crew discovered that the dummy was, in fact, a mummy. It was Elmer McCurdy, embalmed with generous amounts of arsenic, a method of preservation that ended around 1920. The copper jacket of the bullet that had killed him was also discovered, and it was determined to be of a type that ceased to be manufactured before World War II. Additional clues to the mummy's identity were found in his mouth—a rusted 1924 penny and ticket stubs, one of which read "Louis Soney's Museum of Crime," along with a Los Angeles address.

Born in Maine in 1880 to an unwed teenager, McCurdy left the home of the aunt and uncle who raised him and traveled west, where he worked as a miner, plumber, and soldier. It is said that he may have learned about explosives from Douglas MacArthur while at Fort Leavenworth. Investigators discovered that McCurdy had been killed by a posse in 1911, in a shootout in an outlaw refuge in the Osage Hills of Oklahoma following a failed train robbery, during which the thieves found only a few dollars. That Elmer had picked the wrong train was indicative of the life he led, filled with mistakes and drunken misdeeds. He was a man who couldn't find success, even in crime. *Booklist*'s George Cohen felt that Svenvold "has done a first-rate job in documenting the story of a second-rate felon."

The undertaker who handled McCurdy's body was unable to find someone willing to pay for his work, so he used enough arsenic to preserve the corpse and charged five cents a viewing to see "The Bandit Who Wouldn't Give Up." In 1916, a carnival owner claimed the body, saying that he would return it to McCurdy's mother, but in fact, he saw an opportunity to cash in. McCurdy traded hands many times. He traveled with the Museum of Crime, was sold to Craft's Carnival Circus, and then was featured as "The One Thousand-Year-Old Man" in a Long Beach wax museum. Mc-

Curdy was used as a prop for the film *Narcotic,* by Dwain Esper, who was also responsible for the cult film, *Reefer Madness.*

McCurdy was rejected for a spot in the Mount Rushmore Haunted House, because he had become too stiff, and it was then that the owner of the Nu-Pike Amusement Park in Long Beach, who thought he was a prop, decided to cover him with paint that glowed in the dark under ultraviolet light. After the 1976 discovery, McCurdy was finally laid to rest in a boot hill in Guthrie, Oklahoma, where he became a tourist attraction and the headliner in a local bed and breakfast's murder mystery weekends.

David Traxel noted in the *New York Times Book Review* that the story of Elmer McCurdy has been retold in poems, a play, another book, and in a documentary film, but said that "what Svenvold brings to the party, aside from jaunty prose and a keen eye for the incongruous but telling detail, is a willingness to ramble with his subject through the decades and across the country, using him as a line upon which to string odd facts and insights about the lower reaches of American culture."

BIOGRAPHICAL AND CRITICAL SOURCES:

PERIODICALS

Booklist, October 15, 2002, George Cohen, review of *Elmer McCurdy: The Misadventures in Life and After-Life of an American Outlaw,* p. 368.
Kirkus Reviews, May 15, 1998, review of *Soul Data,* p. 695; September 15, 2002, review of *Elmer McCurdy,* p. 1373.
New York Times Book Review, January 26, 2003, David Traxel, review of *Elmer McCurdy,* p. 17.
Philadelphia Inquirer, November 20, 2002, Rusty Pray, review of *Elmer McCurdy.*
Publishers Weekly, September 23, 2002, review of *Elmer McCurdy,* p. 61.
Seattle Times, November 29, 2002, Adam Woog, review of *Elmer McCurdy.*

ONLINE

BookPage, http://www.bookpage.com/ (August 27, 2003), Lynn Hamilton, review of *Elmer McCurdy.*
Kansas City Star Online, http://www.kansascity.com/ (November 19, 2002), John Mark Eberhart, review of *Elmer McCurdy.*
St. Louis Post-Dispatch Online, http://www.stltoday.com/ (December 15, 2002), T. W. H. Miller, review of *Elmer McCurdy.**

T

TALLIS, Frank

PERSONAL: Male. *Education:* University of London, B.S., M.S., Ph.D.

ADDRESSES: Office—Florence Nightingale Hospital, 11-19 Lisson Grove, London, NW1 6SH, England.

CAREER: Clinical psychologist, neuroscientist. Worked in the record industry; Florence Nightingale Hospital (formerly Charter Nightingale Hospital), London, England, clinical psychologist.

AWARDS, HONORS: New London Writers award, London Arts Board, for *Killing Time.*

WRITINGS:

How to Stop Worrying, Sheldon (London, England), 1990.
Understanding Obsessions and Compulsions: A Self-Help Manual, Sheldon (London, England), 1992.
(Editor, with Graham C. L. Davey) *Worrying: Perspectives on Theory, Assessment, and Treatment,* John Wiley & Sons (New York, NY), 1994.
(With Steven Jones) *Coping with Schizophrenia,* Sheldon (London, England), 1994.
Obsessive Compulsive Disorder: A Cognitive and Neuropsychological Perspective, John Wiley (New York, NY), 1995.
(With Sophie Hodgson and Graham C. L. Davey) *Worried Sick: The Relationship between Worrying and Psychological and Physical Health Status,* University of Sussex (Sussex, England), 1997.

Changing Minds: The History of Psychotherapy as an Answer to Human Suffering, Cassell (New York, NY), 1998.
Killing Time (novel), Hamish Hamilton (London, England), 1999.
Sensing Others (novel), Penguin (London, England), 2001.
Hidden Minds: A History of the Unconscious, Arcade Publishing (New York, NY), 2002.

SIDELIGHTS: Frank Tallis has written a number of books that evolved from his work as a clinical psychologist and one of Britain's leading experts on obsessive-compulsive behavior. Several of them, including *Understanding Obsessions and Compulsions: A Self-Help Manual,* are written for the lay audience.

David Richards reviewed the manual for *Nursing Times,* indicating that it is a book he would recommend to his patients. He remarked that the volume is "easy to read and makes self-treatment straightforward to follow." Richards acknowledged Tallis as an expert in this field and concluded by saying that the book "fits well with the consumerist approach to health care."

Tallis is also a novelist, and his *Killing Time* and *Sensing Others* mix science fiction with the psychological thriller genre. The protagonist of *Killing Time* is Tom, a mathematician, whose best friend Dave is a molecular biologist, and who falls in love with Anna, a cellist. The plot revolves around a trans-temporal camera developed by Dave and the disappearance of Anna.

Tallis spent some time working in the commercial recording industry, and the main character of *Sensing Others* is Nick, a rock keyboardist who makes money on the side participating in the testing trials of a drug that is being developed for intelligence purposes. Naloxl enables Nick to read people's minds, but when he senses that an at-large S&M killer is coming closer, he isn't sure whether his intuitions are correct or whether his sensing of the murderer is a side effect of the drug. Added to the cast are Nick's friend Eric, a former rock star turned ecoterrorist, the other members of Nick's band, and his lover.

William Field, who reviewed *Sensing Others* for *Crime Time* online, called it "amusing, weird, and occasionally erotic," noting that "Hendrix, prog rock, hippy chick Cairo, and rare vinyl all fuel a mixture of paranoia and nostalgia."

In *Hidden Minds: A History of the Unconscious,* Tallis gives a considerable amount of space to Freud and his psychoanalytic theory. He notes that Freud believed his "discovery" of the unconscious was equal to Copernicus's discovery of the heliocentric universe and Darwin's theory of evolution. Of course, Freud did not discover the unconscious, and Tallis begins his study with the ideas of St. Augustine, who wrote, "I cannot grasp all that I am," and continues with Wilhelm Leibniz's rebuttal to John Locke's "Essay Concerning Human Understanding."

Tallis recounts the findings of nineteenth-century French philosophy teacher Pierre Janet, whose research demonstrated that physical ailments could have psychological causes. Tallis points out that Freud never gave credit to the work he appropriated from Janet, who was alive at the time. Peter B. Raabe wrote for *Metaphsychology Online* that "this is one of many glimpses the author gives his readers into the fierce competitive mind set of some of the most famous names in history." *Booklist*'s William Beatty called Tallis's treatment of Janet "outstanding."

Tallis covers the cocaine-addicted Freud becoming his own patient, his relationship with Josef Breuer, their use of hypnosis to treat hysteria, and their split over Freud's insistence that the primary cause of mental illness was unconscious sexual desire. Tallis writes of hypnotist Franz Mesmer, whose name generated the word mesmerized, and notes the way in which advertisers manipulate the unconscious in their attempts to convince us to buy their products. Raabe noted that "the fifth chapter deals with the power struggles between Freud and his followers (notably Adler and Jung), Freud's success in the United States, the adoption of Freudian language and imagery of the unconscious into literature, art, and film, and how the notion of repressed sexuality became less important to psychotherapists as they began to turn their attention away from the unconscious to the role of social relationships in the formation of symptoms."

The study of the unconscious returned to favor toward the end of the twentieth century. A *Publishers Weekly* contributor commented that the book "is strongest when reporting the post-Freudian research that has built a new understanding of unconscious processes."

A *Kirkus Reviews* contributor wrote that "now, Tallis observes, the dominant metaphor for the 'automatic, unconscious processes operating in the brain' is borrowed from the world of computer processing, with the workings of the brain likened to the functioning of complex software."

New Statesman's Lavinia Greenlaw commented that Tallis "is a psychologist and neuroscientist, and so this history concentrates on managing and mending. His conclusive analogy is that 'identity is to the brain what the shape of a wave is to sea water.'" Greenlaw wrote that "Freud's claim to have made the 'third blow' to mankind, after Copernicus and Darwin, frames the book. Now, evolutionary theory, neuroscience, psychology, and artificial intelligence research have reinforced the dominance of the unconscious, and Freud's reputation is being dusted off. Tallis warns of the 'narcissism of exaggerating our mystery,' but he also acknowledges that what we need now, as with quantum mechanics, is a philosophical response."

In reviewing *Hidden Minds* for *New Scientist.com,* Roy Herbert wrote that this book "is enthralling, even exciting, bedizened with anecdote and of remarkable scope." *Library Journal*'s David Valencia noted, "Highly readable and possessing a surprising degree of depth, this book manages to be both entertaining and informative."

BIOGRAPHICAL AND CRITICAL SOURCES:

PERIODICALS

Booklist, September 1, 2002, William Beatty, review of *Hidden Minds: A History of the Unconscious,* p. 22.

Kirkus Reviews, August 1, 2002, review of *Hidden Minds,* p. 1113.

Library Journal, September 15, 2002, David Valencia, review of *Hidden Minds,* p. 79.

New Statesman, February 11, 2002, Lavinia Greenlaw, review of *Hidden Minds,* p. 49.

Nursing Times, June 16, 1993, David Richards, review of *Understanding Obsessions and Compulsions: A Self-Help Manual,* p. 53.

Publishers Weekly, August 26, 2002, review of *Hidden Minds,* p. 61.

ONLINE

Crime Time, http://www.crimetime.co.uk/ (August 28, 2003), William Field, review of *Sensing Others.*

Metapsychology Online, http://mentalhelp.net/books/ (March 24, 2002), Peter B. Raabe, review of *Hidden Minds.*

New Scientist.com, http://www.newscientist.com/ August 29, 2003, Roy Herbert, review of *Hidden Minds.*

SF Site, http://www.sfsite.com/ (August 28, 2003), Georges T. Dodds, reviews of *Killing Time* and *Sensing Others.**

*   *   *

TAUBER, Peter 1947-2004

OBITUARY NOTICE—See index for *CA* sketch: Born May 19, 1947, in the Bronx, NY; died March 12, 2004, in Park City, UT. Journalist and author. A freelance journalist, Tauber was best known for his 1971 book *The Sunshine Soldiers.* A graduate of Hobart College, where he earned a B.A. in 1968, his first reporting job was with the *Geneva Times* in New York. From 1968 to 1970, he was on staff at the *New York Times,* before setting out on his own as a freelance writer. At the same time, Tauber avoided service in Vietnam by enlisting in the U.S. Army Reserve in 1969. He remained in the reserve until 1975, drawing on his experiences at the Fort Bliss, Texas, boot camp for his first book, *The Sunshine Soldiers;* meanwhile, he combined journalism with a career in comedy, appearing in nightclubs and on television in the 1970s and, during the late 1970s, contributing to the popular *Saturday Night Live* television comedy series. In 1978, he also published the novel *The Last Best Hope,* which

received critical praise but not to the same extent as his first book. For the remainder of his career, Tauber continued freelancing, contributing to the *New York Times* and other magazines and newspapers. While on a skiing vacation in Utah in 2004, he suddenly collapsed and died at the scene.

OBITUARIES AND OTHER SOURCES:

PERIODICALS

Chicago Tribune, March 20, 2004, Section 2, p. 10.

New York Times, March 19, 2004, p. C13.

*   *   *

TAUBMAN, Philip 1948-

PERSONAL: Born 1948; married Felicity Barringer; children: Michael, Gregory. *Education:* Stanford University, graduated 1971.

ADDRESSES: *Office*—New York Times News Bureau, 1627 I St. NW, Washington, DC 20006.

CAREER: *New York Times,* New York, NY, journalist and editor, 1979—, Moscow correspondent and bureau chief 1985-88, deputy Washington bureau chief, 1989-92, deputy national editor, 1993-94, assistant editorial page editor, 1994-2001; editorial page foreign policy commentary coordinator, 1995—, deputy editorial page editor, 2001-2003; Washington bureau chief, 2003—. Served on Stanford University Board of Trustees, 1978-82.

AWARDS, HONORS: George Polk Award, 1981, for a series of stories with Seymour Hersh and Jeff Gerth on rogue CIA agents, and 1983, for foreign policy reporting on Central America.

WRITINGS:

Secret Empire: Eisenhower, the CIA, and the Hidden Story of America's Space Espionage, Simon & Schuster (New York, NY), 2003.

SIDELIGHTS: Journalist Philip Taubman has been a *New York Times* reporter, editor, and bureau chief since joining the paper in 1979. While serving as chief of the paper's Moscow bureau, Taubman spent time in areas once spied on by planes and satellites of the U.S. overhead reconnaissance program described in detail in his book, *Secret Empire: Eisenhower, the CIA, and the Hidden Story of America's Space Espionage.*

United States history shows that intelligence gathering—spying—has long been a major weapon in the arsenal against threats by foreign powers. The fall of the Soviet Union brought to light many documents once thought to be permanently unavailable. U.S. security agencies entered a prolonged period of declassification after the end of the Cold War in 1991. "Many of the agencies that run or use spy satellites—the Central Intelligence Agency, National Security Agency, National Reconnaissance Office, and Naval Research Laboratory—were suddenly eager to have formerly secret stories told once their budgets were no longer guaranteed by the Soviet menace," observed Gregg Herken in the *Boston Globe.*

Taubman delves deeply into these newly declassified documents—along with oral histories and interviews with participants—and emerges with the in-depth story of the development of the airborne and spaceborne observation systems that have equalized the worldwide balance of power since the Cold War. In the 1950s, America had little hard knowledge about the offensive capabilities of the Soviet Union. "Bison bombers flew circles around Moscow to inflate the estimates of Western air attaches of their numbers; Nikita Krushchev rattled rockets to add to the noise," noted Frank C. Mahncke in *Naval War College Review.* The Soviets had atomic weapons and the means to use them, but America was uncertain of the Soviet Union's true abilities and intentions.

Determined to improve the country's knowledge and defensive position, President Dwight Eisenhower authorized the creation of the U2 spy plane. The U2 could soar high into the atmosphere and take crisply detailed photographs of objects on the ground. The U2 flew only two dozen missions before the infamous downing of pilot Francis Gary Powers in 1960, but by then the truth was clear. "It proved that the missile gap was a myth, that the dreaded Soviet Bison bombers were scarce, and that we faced no imminent threat," related Nicholas Thompson in *Washington Monthly.* Eisenhower also authorized the equally innovative Corona reconnaissance satellite, "designed to take photographs from orbit and then eject film canisters that would withstand atmospheric reentry and literally parachute down to an American recovery team," Thompson remarked. In use from 1960 to 1972, the Corona created a comprehensive photographic record of Soviet military power.

Taubman's tale presents detailed portraits of the scientists and engineers who brought the U2 and Corona projects into existence. "Taubman paints these men unreservedly as patriots, putting their considerable technical skills and imagination at their country's service. That they were," Mahncke commented. "More importantly, they grasped the need for hard strategic intelligence and had the perspective to see the promise of new technologies and their application to the problem of strategic reconnaissance." "This book functions marvelously as a history of science, detailing the research, engineering, and policy decisions behind the U2 and Corona, but it's also an excellent social history," wrote a *Publishers Weekly* reviewer. The work demonstrates Taubman's "impressive skills at writing crackling prose while juggling numerous details," noted Ed Goedeken in *Library Journal.* And a *Kirkus Reviews* critic concluded that the book is "absorbing throughout, and meaty stuff for intelligence and aviation buffs."

BIOGRAPHICAL AND CRITICAL SOURCES:

PERIODICALS

Booklist, February 15, 2003, Gilbert Taylor, review of *Secret Empire: Eisenhower, the CIA, and the Hidden Story of America's Space Espionage,* p. 1023.
Boston Globe, April 6, 2003, Gregg Herken, "*Secret Empire* Details the History of U.S. Spy Planes and Satellites, as Well as the Innovators Behind Them Eyes in the Sky," p. C8.
Chicago Tribune, August 27, 2003, Ray Jenkins, "Ike and CIA: Men Who Built Our Eyes in Skies," p. 4.
International Herald Tribune, April 19, 2003, Jeff Stein, review of *Secret Empire,* p. 20.
Kirkus Reviews, December 15, 2002, review of *Secret Empire,* p. 1834.

Library Journal, February 1, 2003, Ed Goedeken, review of *Secret Empire,* p. 103.

Naval War College Review, winter, 2004, Frank C. Mahncke, review of *Secret Empire,* pp. 152-153.

New York Times Book Review, March 30, 2003, review of *Secret Empire,* p. 18.

Nieman Reports, summer, 1997, "When Couples Work on the Same Paper," pp. 28-31.

Publishers Weekly, February 17, 2003, review of *Secret Empire,* p. 65.

Quill, October, 2001, pp. 41-42; September, 2003, "Philip Taubman, Deputy Editor of the Editorial Page at *The New York Times,* Has Been Named the Newspaper's Washington Bureau Chief," p. 58.

Science News, March 29, 2003, review of *Secret Empire,* p. 207.

Washington Monthly, May, 2003, Nicholas Thompson, "Space Balls," pp. 52-54.

ONLINE

Secret Empire Book, http://www.secretempirethebook. com/ (April 3, 2004).

Tantor Media, http://www.tantor.com/ (April 3, 2004), biography of Philip Taubman.

Washingtonian Online, http://www.washingtonian.com/ (April 6, 2003), Harry Jaffee, "Philip Taubman Named NYT's Washington Bureau Chief."*

*   *   *

TAYLOR, Anne-Marie 1964-

PERSONAL: Born April 24, 1964, in New York, NY; daughter of Robert Edward (a professor of French) and Olga (a homemaker; maiden name, Zazuliak) Taylor. *Education:* University of Massachusetts—Amherst, B.A. (summa cum laude), 1986, M.A. (French), 1989, M.A. (history), 1993, Ph.D. (with distinction), 1999. *Hobbies and other interests:* Piano, drawing.

ADDRESSES: Office—c/o Department of French, University of Massachusetts—Amherst, Amherst, MA 01003.

CAREER: Substitute high school teacher, Amherst, MA, 1987; Université de Bordeaux III, Bordeaux, France, lectrice, 1989-90; Université François Rabe-lais, Tours, France, lectrice, 2990-91; Greenfield Community College, adjunct instructor in French, 2002; University of Massachusetts—Amherst, Amherst, MA, lecturer in French, 2002—. Mount Holyoke College, visiting assistant professor, 2001—.

MEMBER: American Historical Association, Organization of American Historians, Modern Language Association of America, Massachusetts Historical Society (member of library), Phi Beta Kappa, Phi Kappa Phi.

WRITINGS:

Young Charles Sumner and the Legacy of the American Enlightenment, 1811-1851, University of Massachusetts Press (Amherst, MA), 2001.

WORK IN PROGRESS: Continuing research on Charles Sumner; research on early Gothic architecture.

SIDELIGHTS: Anne-Marie Taylor told *CA:* "I like to consider myself a student of human nature. I am fascinated by why people feel and act as they do, what motivates them, what inspires them, what holds them back, and how they confront it. Thus I love biography—not the kind of biography that tells merely what and when, but the kind that seeks to understand life from its subject's point of view. I want to live the subject's life with him between the covers of the book and, by extension, during the research toward anything I write.

"In writing *Young Charles Sumner and the Legacy of the American Enlightenment, 1811-1851,* I was urged on also by a deep sense of the wrong committed by scholars when they write biographies rooted in the trends of the moment, or in the received opinions of their own time. The experiences and accomplishments of a person's life may have lessons or consequences for other times, but they happen in the framework of that person's own life and time. As a nationally recognized advocate against slavery, Sumner was glorified or vilified by others according to their political opinions, and so he has been ever since—his own humanity, his own personal story being largely forgotten in the ongoing controversy over slavery and race. Whenever this is done in biography, the essential and universal truths of human nature are overlooked as well.

"My background, after all, was in literature before history. I cannot accept the twentieth-century fashion of trying to turn history into a science; it is the story of men's lives, of their minds and hearts, and to me that makes it clearly one of the humanities. And though some biographies have influenced me, such as David Cecil's deeply insightful and moving *Melbourne,* I find my principal inspiration in literature, in the painful humanity of a François Villon or the humanistic and artistic élan of a Victor Hugo. My background was also in France before the United States, through both my French studies and a lifelong tie to France and French culture, and so it seems impossible to me to see one country's history, whether artistic or political, in isolation."

*   *   *

TERRIO, Susan J. 1950-

PERSONAL: Born November 24, 1950 in PA; daughter of Marvin (a civil engineer) and Helen (a teacher; maiden name, Millington) Hoy; married Stephen Terrio (a businessman), December 27, 1969; children: Kristin Terrio DeLeonardis, Stephanie Millington Singer. *Education:* Colby College, B.A. (cum laude with distinction in major), 1972; Pennsylvania State University, M.A. (French civilization and applied linguistics), 1975; New York University, M.A. (French studies), 1987; New York University, Ph.D., 1987. *Politics:* Democrat. *Religion:* Protestant. *Hobbies and other interests:* Theater, cooking, wine, riding.

ADDRESSES: Home—17401 Kirstin Ct., Olney, MD 20832. *Office*—ICC 417, Georgetown University, Washington, DC 20047. *E-mail*—terrios@georgetown. edu.

CAREER: Writer and educator. Elizabethtown College, instructor in French, 1980-86; Georgetown University, visiting assistant professor of French, 1993-94, assistant professor of French civilization, adjunct assistant professor of anthropology, sociology department and Edmund Walsh School of Foreign Service, 1994—, associate professor of French, 2000—, associate professor of French and anthropology, department of French, Edmund Walsh School of Foreign Service, chair, culture and politics program, Edmund Walsh School of Foreign Service, 2001—.

MEMBER: Bayonne Académie du Chocolat, (France), American Ethnological Society, Society for Urban Anthropology, Association for French Cultural Studies, Society for the Anthropology of Europe, American Anthropology Association, Society for the Anthropology of Work, Council for European Studies, American Association of the Teachers of French.

AWARDS, HONORS: John Frederick Steinman Award for Teaching Excellence, Elizabethtown College, 1985; New York University Fellowship, 1986-1988; French Government Study Fellowship, 1988-89; French Government Chateaubriand Research Fellowship, 1989-90; Social Science Research Council Dissertation Fellowship, 1990-91; National Science Foundation Dissertation Improvement Award, 1990-91; Georgetown University FLL summer research grant, 1995, 1996, and 1997; American Council of Learned Societies Travel Grant, 1996; Georgetown University Andrew Mellon Junior Faculty Fellowship, 1997; Georgetown College Award for Teaching Excellence, 2001; National Endowment of the Humanities summer research grant, 2001.

WRITINGS:

Crafting the Culture and History of French Chocolate, University of California Press (Berkeley, CA), 2000.

Contributor to journals, including *American Ethnologist, Anthropological Quarterly, Comparative Literature Studies, American Anthropologist,* and *Comparative Studies in Society and History.*

Referee for journals, including *Anthropological Quarterly,* 1997—, *American Anthropologist,* 1995—, *Journal of Cultural Anthropology,* 2002—, and *Journal of Law and Social Inquiry,* 2002—; book review editor for *Anthropological Quarterly,* 1997-2000.

WORK IN PROGRESS: Comparative study of treatment of juvenile delinquency in France and the United States.

SIDELIGHTS: The veneer of French chocolate may be luxurious and sweet, but beneath the dignified surface of the hand-made French chocolate industry are social and ethnographic truths darker than the richest confections. In her book, *Crafting the Culture and History of French Chocolate,* writer and anthropologist Susan J. Terrio critically examines the cultural, economic, geographic, and social aspects of the manufacture and sale of fine chocolates in the Bayonne region of France. Her "examination of entrepreneurship in the Bayonnais region serves as both narrative and metaphor for understanding artisanship and fieldwork in the context of modern cultural transformations," wrote Kristin Selinder in *Geographical Review.*

Despite the renaissance of cuisine, cognac, and pastries introduced to the world by the French, little attention has been paid to the history, development, and importance of chocolate houses to French society and food culture. In her book, Terrio "details this culture-defining artisanship in an attempt to separate myth from reality in the manufacture and sale of fine French chocolate," Selinder remarked.

Evolving from Terrio's doctoral thesis and based on five extended research visits conducted throughout the 1990s, *Crafting the Culture and History of French Chocolate* details the chocolate industry in Bayonne, in southwestern France, where superior hand-made chocolates have been created for generations. "On the surface, the life of the chocolatier may appear idyllic, marked by self-employment, family involvement, and success," Selinder remarked. However, the opposite is often true. Terrio's "detailed interviews with the owners of various chocolate houses and their workers show than one may expect protracted apprenticeships for little or no remuneration, long hours, demanding customers, scant opportunities for career advancement, little social standing, and few, if any, benefits."

As with other forms of French industry, "artisans have built highly structured organizations both to train workers and to regulate the craft trades," Selinder wrote. "Crucially, the domain of chocolate artisanship has traditionally been one of family and filial duty." Men are considered the most capable of actually making the chocolates, while women are expected to run the shops. "The hierarchical structure of the chocolate manufacturing houses is rigid and sexist," wrote a reviewer in *Economist.* In more recent times, "these family businesses employed salaried workers and in fact had little in common with romanticized workshops through employing sometimes as many as 50 workers," wrote Robert C. Ulin in *French Politics, Culture,*

and Society. Relations between shop owners and workers were also sometimes strained; in some shops, salaried workers "referred to the owner as a singe (monkey), a metaphor that unfortunately is not unpacked by Terrio," Ulin commented.

As a writer, Terrio's motivations are her "career in research and university teaching" and her "interest in social and cultural processes," she told *CA.* Her influences are a variety of "social and cultural theorists and experiments in ethnographic writing." Her writing process itself, however, is "long, slow, & arduous," she told *CA.* She will "start with ideas, get them all out on paper, then sift, sort, develop," she said. "I write and rewrite; even as [an] academic author, style and story line [are] very important."

Crafting the Culture and History of French Chocolate, is "a fascinating account of the multiple historical connections and significations that are associated with chocolate making as perhaps illustrative of commodities more generally," Ulin wrote. "Terrio's book is an important contribution to the historical anthropology of Europe and the culture of late capitalism." Ulin concluded, "Terrio has written an outstanding ethnographic and historical account of the making of an elite commodity that is likely to interest readers with diverse intellectual interests."

BIOGRAPHICAL AND CRITICAL SOURCES:

PERIODICALS

Economist, October 21, 2000, "Culinary History-Black and Bitter," review of *Crafting the Culture and History of French Chocolate,* p. 99.

French Politics, Culture and Society, summer, 2001, Robert C. Ulin, review of *Crafting the Culture and History of French Chocolate,* p. 132.

Geographical Review, July, 2001, Kristin Selinder, review of *Crafting the Culture and History of French Chocolate,* pp. 608-610.

ONLINE

Susan J. Terrio Home Page http://www.georgetown. edu/ (October 27, 2003).*

THEIS, Paul A(nthony) 1923-2004

OBITUARY NOTICE—See index for *CA* sketch: Born February 14, 1923, in Fort Wayne, IN; died of complications after heart valve surgery, March 24, 2004, in Washington, DC. Journalist, government administrator, consultant, and author. Theis was a journalist whose writing skills led to a career in political speechwriting for President Gerald Ford and congressional leaders. Serving in the U.S. Army Air Forces during World War II, he was a war hero who piloted a B-17 in Italy and was awarded an Air Medal and the European Theater Ribbon with six battle stars. After the war, he obtained a B.A. from the University of Notre Dame in 1948 and a B.S. from Georgetown University the next year; he also remained in the Air Force Reserve, where he eventually attained the rank of major. Theis began his career shortly after graduating with reporting and correspondent jobs in Washington, D.C., at the *Army Times,* Fairchild Publications, and then *Newsweek.* In 1955 he was hired as an executive assistant for the U.S. Congress, which led to a position as director of public relations for the Republican Congressional Committee, a job he held from 1957 to 1974, when President Ford put him in charge of his administration's editorial department. After Ford left office in 1976, Theis remained in government as deputy undersecretary of agriculture for congressional and public affairs at the U.S. Department of Agriculture. He left a year later to become a consultant for the House of Representatives, and when Ronald Reagan took office he was on the transition team for the Agriculture Department. In 1981, Theis founded his own speechwriting and editorial company, Headliner Editorial Service, which catered to both government and private businesses concerns. Theis's published works include coediting *Who's Who in American Politics* during the late 1960s, cowriting, with William Steponkus, the book *All about Politics* (1972), and penning a novel, *Devil in the House* (2004).

OBITUARIES AND OTHER SOURCES:

PERIODICALS

Washington Post, March 29, 2004, p. B4.
Washington Times, April 8, 2004, p. B2.

THEODORE, Wayne 1958-

PERSONAL: Born 1958, in MA; married; wife's name, Laura; children: five daughters, one son. *Hobbies and other interests:* Boating, snowmobiling, riding his Harley Davidson motorcycle.

ADDRESSES: Home—New Hampshire. *Agent*—c/o Author Mail, Harbor Press, P.O. Box 1656, Gig Harbor, WA 98335.

CAREER: Business owner and writer. Coach of local little league team. Has appeared on television talk shows, including *Sally.*

WRITINGS:

(With Leslie A. Horvitz)*Wayne: An Abused Child's Story of Courage, Survival, and Hope,* Harbor Press (Gig Harbor, WA), 2003.

SIDELIGHTS: Born in northern Massachusetts in the late 1950s, Wayne Theodore and his eleven siblings were raised in a home where their abusive father beat his children daily, unopposed by his passive wife, and regularly subjected his offspring to starvation, torture, and humiliation. Theodore's father denied his son an education after the eighth grade, and then farmed the young teen out to a series of menial jobs, confiscating all his wages. After running away from home, Theodore's problems didn't end: he battled teen drug addiction, suicide, and had difficulty with close relationships due to his own abusive tendencies until he finally confronted his abusive past and turned his life around. Hoping to help others who have been raised in similar situations, he collaborated with New York City-based writer Leslie A. Horvitz and penned his autobiography *Wayne: An Abused Child's Story of Courage, Survival, and Hope.*

Praising Theodore's book for not veering into the sensational, Dale Ferris added in his *Library Journal* review of *Wayne* that the "heartbreaking account" will "stun readers with it s astonishing details of unimaginable abuse and neglect." Noting that some of Theodore's story may be "too graphic and disturbing for some readers"—Theodore's father almost killed him at age six—*Booklist* contributor Vanessa Bush nonetheless praised *Wayne* as a "powerful memoir" and an "inspiring look at surviving child abuse."

BIOGRAPHICAL AND CRITICAL SOURCES:

BOOKS

Theodore, Wayne, *Wayne: An Abused Child's Story of Courage, Survival, and Hope,* Harbor Press (Gig Harbor, WA), 2003.

PERIODICALS

Booklist, April 1, 2003, Vanessa Bush, review of *Wayne: An Abused Child's Story of Courage, Survival, and Hope,* p. 1361.
Library Journal, March 15, 2003, Dale Farris, review of *Wayne,* p. 103.

ONLINE

Wayne Theodore Web site, http://www.waynetheodore. com/ (May 18, 2004).*

*   *   *

THIRLWELL, Adam 1978-

PERSONAL: Born 1978. *Education:* New College; fellow of All Soul's College, Oxford University, 2003.

ADDRESSES: Office—c/o All Souls College, Oxford, OX1 4AL England. *E-mail*—adam.thirlwell@all-souls. ox.ac.uk; adam.thirlwell@new.ox.ac.uk.

CAREER: Scholar, assistant editor of *Areté* Magazine.

AWARDS, HONORS: Seven-year fellowship, All Soul's College, Oxford University; *Granta* magazine Best of Young British Novelists list, 2003, for *Politics.*

WRITINGS:

Politics, Fourth Estate (New York, NY), 2003.

"The Art of Fellatio," extract from *Politics,* was published in *Areté,* 2003.

SIDELIGHTS: At age twenty-five, English scholar, magazine editor, and new novelist Adam Thirlwell was named to *Granta* magazine's Best of Young British Novelists list, 2003, for his first novel, *Politics,* which had not yet been published at the time. Only a twelve-page extract, titled "The Art of Fellatio," had made a debut, in the Oxford literary magazine "Areté," for which Thirlwell serves as assistant editor. Thirlwell was the youngest honoree named to the *Granta* list for 2003.

Politics is a humorous novel about sexual manners within a youthful North London ménage à trois. The story opens with a sex scene between the main character, Moshe, and his girlfriend, Nana. Moshe is shy and underconfident and is trying hard to please Nana, as the two explore the technique of "rimming," with Nana fastened to the bedposts with pink handcuffs that are too large for her slender wrists. Later in the story, a lesbian character, Anjali, enters the picture, having fallen for Nana.

Thirlwell describes his sex scenes in minute detail, using a realist approach. Yet the real story is behind the scenes, in what the characters are thinking during sex. Small distractions, such as noticing a particular table lamp, serve to set their minds wandering, and from there the musings continue on to what *Bookseller* contributor Benedicte Page called "cheeky digressions into the domestic lives of Stalin, Hitler and Chairman Mao."

In a *Bookseller* interview, Thirlwell explained, "I thought how often with sex, the feelings one has during it are not particularly sexual. They could easily be psychological, or ethical, or just worrying about not having bought something. So it's a book that looks as though it were obscene, but actually it's deeply innocent." Page remarked, "The reader is more likely to come away . . . with a sense of the characters' simple kindness and awkward good intentions."

Emma Brockes, in a review for the *Guardian,* also commented on the distraction from sex, saying the author "leaves the sex scenes for interludes to quote Stendhal, muse on the universality of perversion and speculate about the sexual appetites of Adolf Hitler." She found the novel to be "quite saucy."

BIOGRAPHICAL AND CRITICAL SOURCES:

PERIODICALS

Booklist, September 15, 2003, John Green, review of *Politics,* p. 213.

Bookseller, June 6, 2003, Benedicte Page, "How to Be Good in Bed: Adam Thirlwell's Debut Novel Explores the Complications of a Youthful Menage a Trois," p. 28.

Guardian, January 6, 2003, Fiachra Gibbons, "Obscure Unpublished Novelist Joins the Elite"; January 7, 2003, Emma Brockes, "Going Down in the Anals of Literature."

Kirkus Reviews, August 1, 2003, review of *Politics,* p. 991.

New Statesman (1996), August 25, 2003, Phil Whitaker, review of *Politics,* p. 39.

Publishers Weekly, September 29, 2003, review of *Politics,* p. 28.

Spectator, September 6, 2003, G. E. Armitage, review of *Politics,* p. 42.

Times Literary Supplement, August 29, 2003, Christopher Tayler, "Gilongirl, hopefully," p. 20.

ONLINE

All Souls College Web site, http://www.all-souls.ox.ac.uk/ (September 12, 2003).

Contemporary Writers.com, http://www.contemporarywriters.com/ (May 21, 2003), "Adam Thirlwell."

Mostlyfiction.com, http://www.mostlyfiction.com/ (March 21, 2004), review of *Politics.*

Observer Online (London, England), http://www.observer.co.uk/ (May 21, 2003), "The Granta List 2003."

Sydney Morning Herald, http://www.smh.com.au/ (January 7, 2003), "Best of British."*

*　　*　　*

THOMAS, Chantal

PERSONAL: Female.

ADDRESSES: Agent—c/o Author Mail, George Braziller, Inc., 171 Madison Ave., New York, NY 10016; fax: 212-689-5405.

CAREER: Writer, educator, historian, and researcher. Centre National de la Recherche Scientifique, France, director of research. Has taught literature in New York, NY, and Tucson, AZ.

AWARDS, HONORS: Prix Femina, for *Les Adieux a la Reine.*

WRITINGS:

Sade, l'oeil de la lettre, Payot (Paris, France), 1978.

Casanova: Un voyage libertin, Denoël (Paris, France), 1985.

(With Claude Bonnange) *Don Juan ou Pavlov: essai sur la communication publicitaire,* Seuil (Paris, France), 1987.

La reine scélérate: Marie-Antoinette dans les pamphlets, Seuil (Paris, France), 1989, translated by Julie Rose as *The Wicked Queen: The Origins of the Myth of Marie-Antoinette,* Zone Books (New York, NY), 1999.

Thomas Bernhard, Seuil (Paris, France), 1990.

Sade, Seuil (Paris, France), 1994.

La vie réele des petites filles, Gallimard (Paris, France), 1995.

(With Jean-Marie Abgrall) *Healing or Stealing? Medical Charlatans in the New Age,* Algora Publishing (New York, NY), 2000.

Coping with Freedom: Reflexions on Ephemeral Happiness, translated by Andrea L. Secara, Algora Publishing (New York, NY), 2001.

Lettres de Madame du Deffand, Mercure de France (Paris, France), 2002.

Les adieux à la reine (novel), Seuil (Paris, France), 2002, translated by Moishe Black as *Farewell, My Queen,* G. Braziller (New York, NY), 2003.

La lectrice-adjointe: Suivi de Marie-Antoinette de le théâtre, Mercure de France (Paris, France), 2003.

(With Denis Reynaud, Charlotte Burel, and others) *Le régent: entre fable et histoire,* CNRSéditions (Paris, France), 2003.

SIDELIGHTS: In both a nonfiction book and a novel, Chantal Thomas, an expert in eighteenth-century literature, explores the life and the myth of celebrated French queen Marie-Antoinette. *The Wicked Queen: The Origins of the Myth of Marie-Antoinette* is a detailed study of the attacks made upon Marie-Antoinette in the pamphlets and popular media of the late-eighteenth century. Thomas offers a "lively examination of the extensive defamatory, and often pornographic pamphlet literature directed against the queen," noted Elizabeth Colwill in *Canadian Journal of History.* In the pamphlets, Marie-Antoinette was characterized as a monster, accused of base depravities, and denigrated without mercy. In lurid, inflammatory accounts, she was accused of being "a treacherous tribade [lesbian], incestuous mother, and bloodthirsty Austrian wolf," Colwill stated. Over time, the pamphleteers "were forced to cast their target in ever more unfavorable ways to increase their sales and perpetuate the culture of shock that they had created," commented Jason T. Kuznicki in *Journal of Women's History.*

These pamphlets succeeded in their mission of "undermining the monarchy," stated Jay Freeman in *Booklist.* Further, the image of the queen that they perpetrated was a lasting one. "Thomas shows how deadly media attacks could be in the late eighteenth century, effective enough for the image of a frivolous queen to have lasted for two centuries," commented Angelica Goodden in the *Times Literary Supplement.* Thomas "rightly refuses to gloss the pornographic content of the pamphlets and transcribes seven pamphlets in full, invoking the catalogue of charges against Marie-Antoinette in colorful prose that lays bare the dual tasks of gratification and condemnation that the literature performs," Colwill observed. Freeman called the book "an unusual and interesting examination of a primitive but quite effective effort at mass political indoctrination."

Farewell, My Queen is Thomas's fictionalized account of Marie-Antoinette's last days at Versailles before the eruption of violence of the French Revolution and the queen's last gasp on the guillotine. "Marie-Antoinette is the subject of hundreds of biographies and novels, but perhaps none of them brings the reader quite so close to her as *Farewell, My Queen,*" commented Hilary Mantel in the *New Statesman.* "And there are very few historical novels that create, as this one does, a shiver of uncertainty in the reader."

Farewell, My Queen is told from the point of view of Madam Agathe-Sidonie Laborde, the queen's designated reader. More than twenty years have passed since the fall of the Bastille and the destruction of Louis XVI's court at Versailles, and it is Agathe's intention to set down the story of her queen as she saw it, as both observer and participant. She describes in detail the three days between the storming of the Bastille by revolutionaries and the panic-stricken flight of the residents of Versailles. When word of the fall of the Bastille reached Versailles, courtiers gathered what belongings they could carry and fled, leaving behind possessions and children alike. Finally, Agathe fled. Louis, racked with indecision, remained behind, as did Marie-Antoinette; both would die in the revolution.

A *Publishers Weekly* reviewer called *Farewell, My Queen* a "graceful, exquisitely detailed novel." Thomas's "imaginative fluency and her close acquaintance with every detail are astonishing; her writing is delicate, aerial, precise," Mantel observed. The book "is an object lesson in how quickly the end can come when those in power believe so much in their own glory that they are the last to smell the stench of their own corruption," commented Helen Falconer in the *Guardian.* And *Washington Post Book World* reviewer Zofia Smardz declared: "*Farewell, My Queen* is no ordinary historical novel. It's a bravura glimpse into a time past and a dreamlike life that seemed to have nowhere to go but oblivion."

BIOGRAPHICAL AND CRITICAL SOURCES:

PERIODICALS

Biography, summer, 2003, Philippe-Jean Catinchi, "Orleans, Phillipe, Duc D', Regent de France," pp. 547-548.

Booklist, April 1, 1999, Jay Freeman, review of *The Wicked Queen: The Origins of the Myth of Marie-Antoinette,* p. 1384; May 15, 2003, Karen Jenkins Holt, review of *Farewell, My Queen,* p. 1640.

Canadian Journal of History, April, 2001, Elizabeth Colwill, review of *The Wicked Queen,* p. 131.

Choice, November, 1999, T. J. Schaeper, review of *The Wicked Queen.*

Guardian (Manchester, England), January 10, 2004, Helen Falconer, "The Rats of Versaille: Helen Falconer Eavesdrops on a Fictionalised Marie-Antoinette," p. 26.

Journal of Women's History, spring, 2000, Jason T. Kuznicki, review of *The Wicked Queen,* p. 234.

Kirkus Reviews, April 15, 2003, review of *Farewell, My Queen,* p. 567.

Library Journal, March 15, 1999, Jean E. S. Storrs, review of *The Wicked Queen,* p. 95; July, 2003, Jo Manning, review of *Farewell, My Queen,* p. 126.

New Orleans Times-Picayune, August 31, 2003, Julia Kamysz, "Allons, Enfants; Maybe Not. *Farewell, My Queen* Is a French Revolution Tale Minus the Suspense of the Event," p. 7.

New Statesman, January 19, 2004, Hilary Mantel, "The Real Princess: Marie-Antoinette Has Been the Subject of Countless Biographies, but None Brings Her to Life More Fully Than Chantal Thomas's Vivid Historical Novel," pp. 50-51.

New York Times Book Review, August 31, 2003, Alan Riding, "Late Lunch with Late King," p. 18.

Publishers Weekly, June 9, 2003, review of *Farewell, My Queen,* p. 37.

Times Literary Supplement, February 4, 2000, Angelica Goodden, "Social History"; January 16, 2004, David Coward, "Last Days at Versailles."

Washington Post Book World, August 24, 2003, Zofia Smardz, "Lady in Waiting," p. T07.*

*   *   *

TINSLEY, Kevin (M.)

PERSONAL: Male. *Education:* Virginia Commonwealth University, B.F.A. 1986; Kubert School of Cartoon and Graphic Art, diploma, 1989; studied at the School of Visual Arts and New School University.

ADDRESSES: Office—Stickman Graphics, 141 16th St., Brooklyn, NY 11215. *E-mail*—stick@stickmangraphics.com.

CAREER: Writer, colorist, publisher, prepress and desktop production consultant. Clients have included Marvel Entertainment Group, Dark Horse Comics, Prentice Hall, Inc., the New York Cotton Exchange, Warner Lambert Corporation, Unicorn Publishing, Pig Run Press, and others.

WRITINGS:

Digital Prepress for Comic Books: The Definitive Desktop Production Guide, Stickman Graphics (Brooklyn, NY), 1999.

(Writer, colorist) *The Festering Season* (graphic novel), illustrated by Tim Smith 3, edited by Deborah S. Creighton, Stickman Graphics (Brooklyn, NY), 2002.

SIDELIGHTS: As a consultant, Kevin Tinsley lent his prepress and production expertise to many projects before publishing his own writing through his company Stickman Graphics. During a four-year stint at Marvel Comics, he led the team that transformed the production department from all analog/cut and paste to an all-digital environment. This experience led him to write *Digital Prepress for Comic Books: The Definitive Desktop Production Guide,* a guide compiled from methods learned from two decades of experience.

Tinsley also wrote and published, with illustrator Tim Smith 3, the graphic novel *The Festering Season,* which is set in New York, parodies real people and incidents, and has a diverse cast of villains and heroes. *New York Times* critic George Gene Gustines noted that "recognizable settings include the Washington Arch, a backdrop for a buy-and-bust operation, and Tony Rosenthal's steel cube sculpture 'Alamo' on Lafayette Street."

The protagonist, Rene DuBoise, leaves Haiti and her study of voodoo and returns to New York City following the killing of her mother. She comes back to a city ready to explode from a combination of a heat wave, political corruption, volatile race relations, and the upcoming trial of a group of police officers. Among the characters are a cultural anthropologist from New York University, who is working for the police, and a black minister who seems to be patterned after Al Sharpton. Rene soon finds herself fighting a crime lord who would control the city through magical means with her own brand of powers, drawn from the Caribbean and African spirituality of her religion.

A *Publishers Weekly* reviewer called the story "an engaging, fast-paced action drama" and concluded by saying that "Tinsley's script has an urgent subtext commenting on the illegal police brutality endured by many black and Latino New Yorkers."

Randy Lander and Don MacPherson reviewed the novel for *FourthRail.com.* MacPherson remarked that "what struck me most about this script is its anger. Tinsley has clearly built his plot around the nastier side of New York City's past. . . . In the wake of September 11, 2001, it's become remarkably easy for us to forget about the sociological and political blemishes that characterized the city in the world's eyes. I think it's great that police officers and other emergency-response professionals are now held in high regard, but Tinsley reminds us how easy it is for the power we've entrusted them with to corrupt."

Scott Woods reviewed *The Festering Season* for *Comic World News* online, calling it "a strong story set with real characters, good pacing, and some engaging art, especially with its daring two-tone presentation (tan and gray). That the book was designed as a novel and not a series allows it to unfold in a natural, nonrepetitive way that's refreshing, even at 227 pages. Check it out. The company's got the Motts, and if they keep their editorial chops up, they're set to release some really stunning work in the future."

BIOGRAPHICAL AND CRITICAL SOURCES:

PERIODICALS

Comic Buyer's Guide, August 9, 2002, Maggie Thompson, review of *The Festering Season.*

New York Times, November 3, 2002, George Gene Gustines, review of *The Festering Season.*

Publishers Weekly, September 23, 2002, review of *The Festering Season,* p. 51.

ONLINE

Comic World News, http://www.comicworldnews.com/ (March 7, 2003), Scott Woods, review of *The Festering Season.*

FourthRail.com, http://www.thefourthrail.com/ (November 2, 2002), Randy Lander and Don MacPherson, review of *The Festering Season.*

Stickman Graphics, http://www.stickmangraphics.com/ (March 20, 2004).*

*   *   *

TODD, Pamela A. 1950-

PERSONAL: Born February 22, 1950. *Education:* Degree in English (first class); M.A. (art history).

ADDRESSES: Agent—c/o Author Mail, Watson-Guptil Publications, 770 Broadway, New York, NY 10003. *E-mail*—pamtodd5@comcast.net.

CAREER: Creative writing teacher. *Punch* magazine, London, England, former art exhibit and restaurant reviewer. Has also worked as a literary agent for ten years.

AWARDS, HONORS: Illinois Arts Council grant.

WRITINGS:

(Compiler and designer, with David Fordham) *Private Tucker's Boer War Diary: The Transvaal War of 1899, 1900, 1901, & 1902 with Natal Field Forces,* Elm Tree Books (London, England), 1980.

Forget-Me-Not: A Floral Treasury: Sentiments and Plant Lore from the Language of Flowers, illustrated by Ian Penney, Little, Brown (Boston, MA), 1993.

The Little Book of Daffodils: A Garden of Poetry, History, Lore, and Floriculture, illustrated by Ian Penney, Little, Brown (Boston, MA), 1994.

The Little Book of Tulips: A Garden of Poetry, History, Lore, and Floriculture, illustrated by Ian Penney, Little, Brown (Boston, MA), 1994.

Celebrating the Impressionist Table: A Celebration of Regional French Foods through the Palettes of the Great Impressionists, recipes by Louise Pickford, Stewart, Tabori & Chang (New York, NY), 1997.

Pig and the Shrink (young adult novel), Delacorte Press (New York, NY), 1999.

Bloomsbury at Home, H. N. Abrams (New York, NY), 1999.

Pre-Raphaelites at Home, Watson-Guptill Publications (New York, NY), 2001.

The Arts and Crafts Companion, Bullfinch (Boston, MA), 2004.

Contributor to *The Historical Encyclopedia of Chicago Women,* and to periodicals, including *Chicago Tribune Magazine* and *Writer.*

EDITOR

William Morris, *The Sweet Days Die,* Pavilion Books (London, England), 1996.

William Wordsworth, *Trailing Clouds of Glory,* Pavilion Books (London, England), 1996.

W. B. Yeats, *Heaven's Embroidered Cloths: Poems by W. B. Yeats,* Pavilion Books (London, England), 1996.

SIDELIGHTS: As a columnist at England's *Punch* magazine, Pamela A. Todd specialized in reviewing both art exhibits and restaurants. This interest in high art and fine dining has played out in many of her books, including *Celebrating the Impressionists' Table: A Celebration of Regional French Foods through the Palettes of the Great Impressionists, Bloomsbury at Home,* and *The Pre-Raphaelites at Home.* In addition, Todd has edited a number of poetry collections, compiled a couple of miscellanies on flowers, and written a children's book; and she has worked as a literary agent and creative writing instructor at numerous workshops, including teaching journal writing at a women's prison.

In three unusual art books, Pamela Todd focuses on the day-to-day lives of some of the great names in art and literature, revealing the more homey aspects of their lives. *Celebrating the Impressionists' Table* turns the reader's attention from the studios where the masterpieces were created to the kitchens where these artists relaxed and indulged other tastes. "Here, the human (and occasionally, humane) side of these masters stands out," explained *Booklist* reviewer Barbara Jacobs, such as Monet's fascination with gadgets, including an ice cream machine, Renoir's insistence on Parisian brie over other varieties, and Gauguin's love of cooking. In addition, the book provides over one hundred classic French recipes. In *Bloomsbury at Home* Todd "focuses upon the districts and houses where the artists and writers of the Bloomsbury group chose to live and how these places reflected their ideas on art and life," observed *Library Journal* reviewer Sandra Rothenberg. Todd drew on a huge number of photographs, diaries, letters, as well as the preserved houses themselves, to convey the curious mixture of middle-class conventionality and bohemian lifestyle that marked the group, and she "makes judicious use of the vast amount of material available," according to *Booklist* reviewer Donna Seaman. In addition, her use of the many drawings and paintings done by Bloomsbury members reveals that this was as much an artistic as a literary circle. *Birmingham Post* contributor Ross Reyburn observed that Todd "skillfully intermingles quotations and anecdotes with her narrative to provide a wonderful insight into the group, whose artistic and literary talents prospered in an atmosphere of liberalism and sexual freedom that outraged the more conventional world." Similarly, in *Pre-Raphaelites at Home,* Todd draws on numerous letters and diary quotations to show how artists such as Dante Gabriel Rossetti, Edward Burne-Jones, and William Morris "worked together to shape the day-to-day world according to their aesthetic ideals," as *Victoria* contributor Laura Hannett wrote.

In addition to her studies of poetry and artistic movements, Todd has produced a novel of her own, a story for middle-school readers titled *Pig and the Shrink.* This "humorous first novel," in the words of a *Publishers Weekly* reviewer, tells the story of Tucker Harrison, who decides to help his friend Angelo "Pig" Pighetti lose weight as part of a science project. The son of a neurosurgeon and a psychologist, Tucker is determined to win first place at the science fair, and he throws himself into the project of "saving" his friend, reading up on diet and fiber, and the psychology of overeating. The only problem is, Angelo actually likes himself as he is, and the fact that Angelo's family runs a pizza parlor is not helping Tucker's plan. Gradually, of course, it is Tucker who must change, as he realizes that his project has blinded him to his friend's wishes and feelings. While noting that some of the characters were too generic, *Booklist* reviewer Carolyn Phelan found that the story "rolls along ... sparked by humorous situations and witty dialogue." Told through Tucker's voice, it is a story of true friendship and "what readers will enjoy most is the mellow commentary Tucker gives and the mellower person he learns to become," commented Mary Harris Russell in a review for the *Chicago Tribune.* Similarly, a *Kirkus Reviews* contributor concluded that "Readers will be laughing as they comprehend the subtle but strong message about looking beyond outward appearances."

BIOGRAPHICAL AND CRITICAL SOURCES:

PERIODICALS

Birmingham Post, October 21, 2001, Ross Reyburn, review of *Bloomsbury at Home,* p. 53.

Booklist, May 15, 1997, Barbara Jacobs, review of *Celebrating the Impressionist Table: A Celebration of Regional French Foods through the Palettes of the Great Impressionists,* p. 1554; October 1, 1999, Carolyn Phelan, review of *Pig and the Shrink,* p. 358; March 1, 2000, Donna Seaman, review of *Bloomsbury at Home,* p. 1186.

Book Report, November-December, 1999, review of *Pig and Shrink.*

Chicago Tribune, January 23, 2000, Mary Harris Russell, review of *Pig and the Shrink,* p. 4.

Kirkus Reviews, June 1, 1999, review of *Pig and the Shrink,* p. 890.

Library Journal, April 1, 2000, Sandra Rothenberg, review of *Bloomsbury at Home,* p. 100.

New York Times, May 18, 2000, Eve Kahn, "Around the World with Artists and Happy Campers."

New York Times Book Review, May 21, 2000, Jillian Dunham, "Books in Brief: Nonfiction; Bloomsberries."

Publishers Weekly, August 2, 1999, review of *Pig and the Shrink,* p. 85.

Victoria, February, 2000, Laura Hannett, review of *Pre-Raphaelites at Home,* p. 30.*

*   *   *

TOURNEY, Leonard D(on) 1942-

PERSONAL: Born June 10, 1942 in Long Beach, CA; son of Leonard Raymond (a soldier) and Katherine McMillan (a homemaker) Tourney; married Martha Evelyn Barnard (a homemaker), April 6, 1966; children: Anne, Megan. *Education:* Brigham Young University, B.A., 1963; University of California at Santa Barbara, M.A., 1966, Ph.D., 1972. *Religion:* Latter-Day Saints (Mormon).

ADDRESSES: Office—Writing Program, University of California, Santa Barbara, Santa Barbara, CA 93106. *E-mail*—tourney@writing.ucsb.edu.

CAREER: Western Illinois University, Macomb, instructor in English, 1966-68; University of Tulsa, Tulsa, Oklahoma, associate professor of English, 1970-85; University of California, Santa Barbara, lecturer in the writing program, 1985—. *Military service:* U.S. Naval Reserve, petty officer 3rd class; served in Southeast Asia aboard destroyer USS Ernest G. Small, 1964-66.

MEMBER: Modern Language Association of America, Spenser Society, Rhetoric Society of America.

WRITINGS:

Joseph Hall, Twayne (Boston, MA), 1979.
Time's Fool: A Mystery of Shakespeare, Forge (New York, NY), 2004.

"CONSTABLE STOCK" SERIES

The Players' Boy Is Dead, St. Martin's (New York, NY), 1980.
Low Treason, St. Martin's (New York, NY), 1982.

Familiar Spirits, St. Martin's (New York, NY), 1984.
The Bartholomew Fair Murders, St. Martin's (New York, NY), 1986.
Old Saxon Blood, St. Martin's (New York, NY), 1988.
Knaves Templar, St. Martin's (New York, NY), 1991.
Witness of Bones, St. Martin's (New York, NY), 1992.
Frobisher's Savage, St. Martin's (New York, NY), 1994.

Also contributor of scholarly articles to *Studies in Philology, Papers on Language & Literature, Essays in Literature,* and *The Rhetoric Society Quarterly.*

SIDELIGHTS: Leonard D. Tourney is a lecturer in the writing program at the University of California in Santa Barbara. A professional academic who has published many scholarly articles, Tourney is also a prolific writer of fiction. He once told *CA:* "I view my career as a teacher of English (Shakespeare, English language, writing) and my avocation as a fiction writer as highly compatible activities. I continue to do scholarship, but find myself spending more and more time on fiction." The fiction Tourney refers to is his popular "Constable Stock" mystery series which features a medieval couple, Matthew, a small town constable and clothier, and Joan Stock. The series is noted for its authentic Elizabethan detail as all the novels are set in the final few years of the reign of Elizabeth I. According to an essayist for the *St. James Guide to Crime and Mystery Writers,* "What Tourney does do very well indeed is to construct intricate and fascinating plots, which he then fills with characters that are usually well-drawn, lively, even appropriately raw and pungent.... His other excellences, especially his sharp and ingenious plotting, are likely to win over all but the most particular and critical readers."

The first installation of the "Constable Stock" series is *The Players' Boy Is Dead.* A fourteen-year-old boy who plays women in a strolling theater company is murdered on the estate of a lord who is also the local magistrate. Matthew Stock is ordered by the magistrate to find the killer but Stock soon finds himself in a dilemma; the murderer is the magistrate so how can Stock "bring justice to him who administers it?" Jean M. White from *Bookworld* found *The Players' Boy Is Dead* to be "a gorgeous period piece. Tourney weaves a rich tapestry of Elizabethan life." A reviewer from the *New Yorker* commended the novel, noting that Tourney "gives us just enough of sixteenth-century culture to establish appropriate tone, and the story he has to tell us is a good one."

Tourney's fourth book in the "Constable Stock" series is *The Bartholomew Fair Murders*. Queen Elizabeth decides to attend the St. Bartholomew Fair, a place full of "horrid smells, boozing, stalls, violent characters—and murders, which demand the attention of Matthew Stock," remarked Callendar. However, the queen's arrival depends upon Stock capturing Gabriel Stubs, a religious fanatic who declares himself to be a slayer of the ungodly and, with his gullible accomplice Rose, is killing people at the fair. Callendar continued, "Though the period is some 400 years removed, *Bartholomew Fair* is a traditional mystery, well worked out, expertly written and full of information about a great generation in England." The Toronto *Globe & Mail*'s Margaret Cannon observed that the plot was slow paced and "muddy" but also called the book a "joyful recreation of Elizabethan life and times, replete with bear-baiting and sectarian religious snits."

The next book in Tourney's series, *Old Saxon Blood*, features the Stock couple traveling to London to receive a commission from Queen Elizabeth I. Matthew and Joan are placed as chief steward and housekeeper at a country castle where the lord knight has been murdered. A reviewer for *Publishers Weekly* commended Tourney on the "colorful Elizabethan phrases and period detail [that] pepper the novel."

For the sixth novel of the "Constable Stock" series, the Stocks, after the investigation at the country castle, are asked by the queen's adviser, Robert Cecil, to stay in London in service to the queen. In *Knaves Templar*, three law students have died in unconvincingly suicidal circumstances. Matthew is sent to the Middle Temple of the Inns of Court to investigate, posing as a prospective student's father. Joan is banned from entering the grounds because of her sex so she disguises herself as a young man and tracks the students. And it is Joan who, upon entering a notorious riverside tavern, sets the tale in motion. The *Los Angeles Times Book Review*'s Charles Champlin found that "the Stocks are as warmly likable a couple as can be found in all crime fiction. Tourney's plotting is expert." A reviewer for *Publishers Weekly* noted that "Tourney skillfully interjects observations that have contemporary relevance, about the morality of lawyers and the souls of women."

Witness of Bones is the seventh book in the series. In this novel, the Stocks are called back to London by Cecil to investigate a Catholic martyr who has suppos-edly risen from the grave and, Cecil fears, may be leading a papist political insurrection. Before long, Matthew is framed and imprisoned for the murder of a minister and Joan is forced to solve the mystery on her own. Champlin called *Witness of Bones* "quite possibly the best in his series about Matthew Stock . . . the intrigues are engrossing, and as always the Stocks are a wonderfully attractive pair." A *Publishers Weekly* reviewer praised the book as "far superior to the usual intrigue-behind-court-walls saga," noting that "Tourney neither belabors nor neglects his setting, and although his puzzle's solution isn't very gripping, the Stocks make wonderful guides to a world quite different from our own, yet sometimes shockingly familiar."

Tourney's 1994 "Constable Stock" novel is *Forbisher's Savage*. Adam Nemo is a servant accused of killing his employers and their two children; the other suspect in the crime is that employer's deaf and dumb son, Nicholas. The Stocks are given custody of the defenseless pair and the hunt for the real killers begin. A critic for *Publishers Weekly* wrote that "fraud, vigilantes and a chase by a posse in a snowstorm move the story along smartly."

In 2004 Tourney released a new historical mystery set in the Elizabethan age, *Time's Fool: A Mystery of Shakespeare*. After a meeting with the Dark Lady of his romantic sonnets, William Shakespeare finds that his old lover now suffers from syphilis and threatens to tell his wife about their long-ago relationship. When the Dark Lady dies in a suspicious fire, and one of Shakespeare's proteges is found dead, the famous bard is suspected of murder. With the help of his wife, Anne Hathaway, Shakespeare must solve the mystery and clear his name. Harriet Klausner, reviewing the novel for *AllReaders.com,* found that Shakespeare "comes across as a fascinating, multifaceted figure." The critic for *Publishers Weekly* described *Time's Fool* as both "literate and entertaining" and believed that "Shakespeare fans will delight in this witty caper."

Tourney once told *CA:* "I take great pains with the period detail, sometimes beyond all reason; but my greatest concern is with the validity of motives, depth of characterization, and what I like to call the atmospheric resuscitiation of the Elizabethan age. Of course I like to tell a good story too, but perhaps that goes without saying."

BIOGRAPHICAL AND CRITICAL SOURCES:

BOOKS

St. James Guide to Crime and Mystery Writers, 4th edition, St. James Press (Detroit, MI), 1996.

PERIODICALS

Bookworld, December 21, 1980, Jean M. White, review of *The Players' Boy Is Dead.*

Globe & Mail (Toronto, Ontario, Canada), July 5, 1986, Margaret Cannon, review of *The Players' Boy Is Dead.*

Kirkus Reviews, May 1, 2004, review of *Time's Fool,* p. 426.

Los Angeles Times Book Review, March 10, 1991, Charles Champlin, review of *Knaves Templar,* p.7; October 11, 1992, Charles Champlin, review of *Witness of Bones,* p. 13.

New Yorker, January 19, 1981, review of *The Players' Boy Is Dead,* p. 115.

New York Times Book Review, January 11, 1981, Newgate Callendar, review of *The Players' Boy Is Dead,* p. 22; August 31, 1986, Newgate Callendar, review of *The Bartholomew Fair Murders,* p.14; September 18, 1988, Marilyn Stasio, review of *Old Saxon Blood,* p. 46; March 10, 1991, Marilyn Stasio, review of *Knaves Templar,* p. 21.

Publishers Weekly, October 10, 1980, review of *The Players' Boy Is Dead,* p. 69; May 23, 1986, review of *The Bartholomew Fair Murders,* p. 92; June 17, 1988, review of *Old Saxon Blood,* p. 60.; January 11, 1991, review of *Knaves Templar,* p. 93; August 31, 1992, review of *Witness of Bones,* p. 67; October 3, 1994, review of *Frobisher's Savage,* p. 55; May 3, 2004, review of *Time's Fool,* p. 174.

ONLINE

AllReaders.com, http://www.allreaders.com/ (August 16, 2004), Harriet Klausner, review of *Time's Fool.*

University of California Santa Barbara Writing Program Web site, http://www.writing.ucsb.edu/ (September 17, 2003), Leonard Tourney Faculty page.*

TRANEL, Virginia

PERSONAL: Born in Dubuque, IA; married Ned Tranel, January, 1957; children: five girls and five boys. *Education:* Clark College, B.A. (English and Spanish), 1955. *Religion:* Catholic.

ADDRESSES: Home—Billings, MT. *Agent*—c/o Author Mail, Knopf Publishing, 1745 Broadway, New York, NY 10019.

CAREER: Author.

WRITINGS:

Ten Circles upon the Pond: Reflections of a Prodigal Mother (memoir), Knopf (New York, NY), 2003.

Essays published in magazines and anthologies, including the Notre Dame Press anthology *Family.*

SIDELIGHTS: Virginia Tranel is the author of *Ten Circles upon the Pond: Reflections of a Prodigal Mother,* a memoir about her experiences raising ten children, who were born between 1957 and 1978. The book recalls Tranel's enjoyment of her children as well as the anxieties she experienced and the outright criticisms she faced. Following her first child's birth in 1957, she entered a hectic but rewarding existence filled with frequent moves, the inevitable childhood illnesses (at one point she simultaneously nursed seven cases of chicken pox), and the making of homemade items like bread, butter, and even prom dresses. In the late 1960s, Tranel began to receive negative comments about having such a large family, which then numbered seven children. Each of the book's chapters is devoted to one child, tracing how he or she developed into an adult. Tranel, while pointing out that the "culture" of a large family is not for everyone, celebrates in the book the joys she found as a mother of ten and how she feels personally enriched by the experience.

The author's honesty and skill as a writer were commended by reviewers. *Library Journal*'s Rachel Collins and Mirela Roncevic found that Tranel used "simple and poetic prose" while revealing how she "opened herself to new experiences rather than closing herself off, which is the usual perception." In *Publish-*

ers Weekly, a critic remarked on Tranel's "overextended but always levelheaded musings" and exceptionally "frank discussions" of the criticism she faced. According to Joanne Wilkinson in *Booklist,* the memoir is "steeped in nostalgia, yet it could not be more timely." She noted that the author's "abiding faith in the power of family and human connection" will comfort readers. A *Kirkus Reviews* critic called the book "intelligent and candid, crafted in fine prose."

BIOGRAPHICAL AND CRITICAL SOURCES:

BOOKS

Tranel, Virginia, *Ten Circles upon the Pond: Reflections of a Prodigal Mother,* Knopf (New York, NY), 2003.

PERIODICALS

Booklist, April 15, 2003, Joanne Wilkinson, review of *Ten Circles upon the Pond: Reflections of a Prodigal Mother,* p. 1434.
Daily Herald (Arlington Heights, IL), January 8, 2004, Pam DeFiglio, "Mom of Ten Fends Off Criticism of Big Families," p. 4.
Kirkus Reviews, March 15, 2003, review of *Ten Circles upon the Pond,* p. 450.
Library Journal, May 1, 2003, Rachel Collins and Mirela Roncevic, review of *Ten Circles upon the Pond,* p. 142.
Publishers Weekly, May 12, 2003, review of *Ten Circles upon the Pond,* p. 60.*

*　　*　　*

TRASK, Larry 1944-2004
(R. L. Trask)

OBITUARY NOTICE—See index for *CA* sketch: Born November 10, 1944, in Olean, NY; died of a motor neurone disease March 27, 2004, in Brighton, England. Linguist, chemist, educator, and author. Trask was a recognized authority on the Basque language. Originally trained as a chemist, during the 1960s he earned

a B.S. in the subject from Rensseleaer Polytechnic and an M.S. from Brandeis University. Abandoning his Ph.D. studies, he joined the Peace Corps as a chemistry instructor and found himself teaching at the Middle East Technical University in Ankara, Turkey. He left Turkey in 1970 and moved to London, where he met his first wife, Esther Barrutia. Barrutia was a chemist from the Basque region of Spain, and Trask, who was already interested in languages at the time, became fascinated by the unique Basque tongue. This led him, in turn, to earn a Ph.D. in linguistics from the School of Oriental and African Studies at London University in 1983. By this time he was already Liverpool University. He moved on to the University of Sussex in 1988, becoming a full professor in 1998. Trask's intense study of the Basque language led him to conclude, unlike his colleagues, that Basque was uniquely unrelated to any other languages and that it had somehow evolved independently, a position he defended in his 1997 book, *The History of Basque.* The scholar was also unique in his arguments against the famous linguist Noam Chomsky, contending, contrary to Chomsky's position, that language is not somehow "hard-wired" into the human brain, compelling humans to follow basic rules of a universal grammar. Considered an entertaining and lucid writer, especially considering his difficult subject matter, Trask was also the author of such textbooks and scholarly works as *Language Change* (1994), *A Dictionary of Phonetics and Phonology* (1996), *Historical Linguistics* (1996), *The Dictionary of Historical and Comparative Linguistics* (2000), and *Mind the Gaffe: The Penguin Guide to Common Errors in English* (2001).

OBITUARIES AND OTHER SOURCES:

PERIODICALS

Guardian (London, England), April 8, 2004, p. 27.
Independent (London, England), April 7, 2004, p. 34.
Times (London, England), May 28, 2004, p. 44.

*　　*　　*

TRASK, R. L.
See TRASK, Larry

U-V

USTINOV, Peter (Alexander) 1921-2004

OBITUARY NOTICE—See index for *CA* sketch: Born April 16, 1921, in London, England; died of heart failure March 28, 2004, in Bursins, Switzerland. Actor, director, producer, and author. The versatile Ustinov was an award-winning novelist, playwright, and actor who was a regular feature of stage and screen for more than five decades. A descendant of a prominent czarist Russia family, he was born and raised in London, where he quickly demonstrated his love and talent in the theater. After attending private school, he studied acting with Michel Saint-Denis at the London Theater Studio from 1937 to 1939. By 1941, he was appearing on stage and writing plays, and his *The Bishop of Limpopoland* was produced in London in 1939; the first play he ever wrote, *House of Regrets,* which he penned while still in his teens, was produced in 1942 to positive reviews. During World War II, Ustinov served as a private in the Sussex Regiment and was assigned to the Royal Army Ordnance Corps, the Kinematograph Service, and the Directorate of Army Psychiatry; he was not promoted due to his superiors' fears of putting such a puckish man, who once said he liked being in a tank because he could engage in battle while sitting down, in charge of troops. After the war, he returned to play writing and the stage, and he began making film appearances, developing a reputation as a character actor. In the 1960s he won two Academy Awards, one in 1960 for a role in *Spartacus,* and one in 1964 for his part as a jewel thief in *Topkapi;* as an actor on television, Ustinov earned Emmy Awards for *The Life of Samuel Johnson* in 1958, *Barefoot in Athens* in 1966, and *Storm in Summer* in 1970. Other memorable roles came in *We're No Angels* (1955), *Billy Budd* (1962), for which he wrote the screenplay, produced, and directed, *Viva Max!* (1969), *The Last Remake of Beau Geste* (1977), and *Charlie Chan and the Curse of the Dragon Queen* (1981); many fans especially remember Ustinov's portrayal of Agatha Christie's Belgian detective, Hercule Poirot, in the films *Death on the Nile* (1978), *Evil under the Sun* (1982), and *Appointment with Death* (1988). His original plays, too, were winning awards, such as a 1953 New York Drama Critics Circle Award for *The Love of Four Colonels* and the 1956 British Critics' Best Play for *Romanoff and Juliet,* which was also earned the *Evening Standard* Drama Award and was nominated for a Tony. In no way a snob about his acting work, Ustinov narrated the children's album *Peter and the Wolf,* receiving a Grammy for it in 1959, and he even voiced the character of Prince John in Disney's animated feature *Robin Hood.* Among his artistic pursuits, though, Ustinov numbered his favorite as writing novels, short stories, and plays, which he found to be the most satisfying creatively, while he found his work as a director and producer the least satisfying. He was the author of novels such as *The Loser* (1960), *Krumnagel* (1971), and *The Old Man and Mr. Smith* (1990), essays and articles collected in works like *My Russia* (1983) and *The Quotable Ustinov* (1995), and the autobiography *Dear Me* (1977). In more recent years, Ustinov's health was plagued by diabetes and heart trouble, which made it difficult for him to stand; he nevertheless remained as active as possible, appearing in 1990s movies such as *Lorenzo's Oil* (1992) and a 1999 version of *Alice in Wonderland,* in which he played the Walrus. Perhaps because he was so prolific and involved in all types of art forms, some critics of Ustinov's work felt that he spread himself too thin and could not realize his full potential in any single field; more often, however, critics and audiences appreciated his wit, humor, talent, and literate and intelligent style. Furthermore, Ustinov was a humanitarian, establishing the Peter Ustinov Foundation, which fought against prejudice and disease around the world, and working as a pro bono ambassador for the United Nation's Children's Fund. For his many humanitarian and artistic contributions, Ustinov was made a Commander of the Order of the British Empire in 1975 and knighted in 1990; he also received numerous honorary degrees and other honors.

OBITUARIES AND OTHER SOURCES:

BOOKS

Contemporary Dramatists, sixth edition, St. James Press (Detroit, MI), 1999.
Contemporary Theatre, Film, and Television, Volume 28, Gale (Detroit, MI), 2000.

PERIODICALS

Chicago Tribune, March 30, 2004, Section 3, p. 11.
Los Angeles Times, March 30, 2004, p. B10.
New York Times, March 30, 2004, p. C14.
Times (London, England), March 30, 2004, p. 29.
Washington Post, March 30, 2004, p. B7.

*   *   *

VANIER, Jean 1928-

PERSONAL: Born September 10, 1928, in Geneva, Switzerland; son of George Vanier (a diplomat and politician). *Education:* Attended Dartmouth Royal Naval College; Institute Catholique de Paris, Ph.D. (philosophy), 1962. *Religion:* Roman Catholic.

ADDRESSES: Home—Trosly-Breuil, France. *Office*—L'Arche International, 10 Rue Fenoux, 75015 Paris, France.

CAREER: Educator and advocate of the disadvantaged. St. Michael's University, Toronto, Ontario, Canada, instructor in philosophy, c. 1963; L'Arch (network of faith-based communities), Trosly-Breuil, France, founder, 1964-80; Faith and Light, founder. *Military*

service: British Royal Navy, 1941-49; Canadian Navy, 1948-50; officer on battleship *Vanguard* during World War II; officer on aircraft carrier *Magnificent* until 1950.

AWARDS, HONORS: Named companion, Order of Canada, 1989; Paul VI International Prize for lay ministry work, 1997; Gordon Montador Award, 1998, for *Becoming Human.*

WRITINGS:

In Weakness, Strength; The Spiritual Sources of Georges P. Vanier, Nineteenth Governor-General of Canada, Griffin House (Toronto, Ontario, Canada), 1969.
Tears of Silence, Griffin House (Toronto, Ontario, Canada), 1970.
Eruption to Hope, Griffin House (Toronto, Ontario, Canada), 1971.
Be Not Afraid, Paulist Press (New York, NY), 1975.
Diciple de Jésus, Fleurus (Paris, France), 1977, translated as *Followers of Jesus,* Paulist Press (New York, NY), 1996.
La communauté, lieu du pardon et de la fête, translated by Ann Shearer as *Community and Growth: Our Pilgrimage Together,* Paulist Press (New York, NY), 1979, revised edition, St. Paul Publications (Bombay, India), 1991.
(Author of introduction and afterword) *The Challenge of l'Arche,* Darton, Longman, and Todd (London, England), 1982.
Homme et femme Il les fit, translation published as *Man and Woman He Made Them,* Paulist Press (Mahwah, NJ), 1985.
Ouvre mes bras, Fleurus (Paris, France), 1993.
Jesus, the Gift of Love, Crossroad (New York, NY), 1994.
A Network of Friends: The Letters of Jean Vanier to the Friends and Communities of l'Arche, 3 volumes, edited by John Sumarah, Lancelot Press (Hantsport, Nova Scotia, Canada), 1994-1997.
Toute personne est une histoire sacré, Plon (Paris, France), 1994, translated by Maggie Parham as *Our Journey Home: Rediscovering a Common Humanity beyond Our Differences,* Orbis (Maryknoll, NJ), 1994.
L'histoire de l'Arche, translated as *An Ark for the Poor: The Story of l'Arche,* Novalis (Ottawa, Ontario, Canada), 1995.

The Heart of l'Arche: A Spirituality for Every Day, Crossroad (New York, NY), 1995.

Becoming Human (Massey Lectures; broadcast on CBC Radio, 1998), House of Anansi Press (Toronto, Ontario, Canada), 1997, Paulist Press (New York, NY), 1998.

The Scandal of Service: Jesus Washes Our Feet, Continuum (New York, NY), 1998.

Le goût du bonheur: au fondement de la morale avec Aristote, Presses de la Renaissance (Paris, France), 2000, translated by Kathryn Spink as *Made for Happiness: Discovering the Meaning of Life with Aristotle,* House of Anansi Press (Toronto, Ontario, Canada), 2001, translation published as *Happiness: A Guide to a Good Life: Aristotle for the New Century,* Arcade (New York, NY), 2002.

Seeing beyond Depression, Paulist Press (New York, NY), 2002.

Finding Peace, House of Anansi Press (Toronto, Ontario, Canada), 2003.

Also author of published lectures, including *From Brokenness to Community,* 1992.

Vanier's works have been translated into numerous languages, including Armenian.

SIDELIGHTS: When author and activist Jean Vanier traveled from his home in rural France to the Canadian capital city of Ottawa to be honored as a companion of the Order of Canada, he brought with him an entourage: 150 mentally-disabled adults who represent the thousands who have been helped by Vanier through his establishment, in August of 1964, of l'Arche. Consisting of small communities designed to serve the mentally impaired, l'Arche has grown from one home in France to a network of over one hundred communities, and has become world-wide in its scope. Although retiring from his official position in l'Arche in 1980, Vanier has continued to dedicate himself to the underprivileged, and has also published a number of books that spread the Christian-based philosophy underlying his organization. As he was quoted by a *Maclean's* contributor, Vanier believes that the mentally handicapped "are the weakest and the most fragile, and they have much to teach us."

Joining the British Royal Navy in 1941 at age thirteen, Vanier remained in military service during and following World War II, moving to the Canadian Navy in 1948. In 1950, after rethinking his military career, he resigned his Navy post and moved to Paris, France, to earn his Ph.D. in philosophy. Initially intending to become a teacher at a Toronto university, Vanier's life plans changed after he met Father Thomas Philippe, who worked with a small group of mentally retarded men in rural France. A visit to Father Thomas's retreat convinced the aspiring philosophy professor that he could do more good outside the classroom; in August of 1964 he bought a farmhouse in Trosly-Breuil, France, and invited two mentally impaired men to live with him. This was the beginning of the first l'Arche community—named after Noah's Ark—as nearby houses were bought and refurbished, and soon hundreds of handicapped individuals worked together to support and sustain their fledgling community. Vanier's ability to promote his work attracted the funding necessary to build a network of such communities, and by 2000 l'Arche outposts could be found in many European nations, within the United States and Canada, Latin America, Japan, India, Africa, Scandinavia, the Philippines, and the Caribbean.

In his 1994 work, *Our Journey Home: Rediscovering a Common Humanity beyond Our Differences,* Vanier employs his characteristic "simple and spare" prose to set forth the philosophy underlying the l'Arche communities; as *America* contributor Michael Downey explained, Vanier esteems "relationship, covenant, forgiveness, respect for the wounded and the weak and the celebration of the fragility of life." Praising *Our Journey Home* as "an inspirational and humanist tract," *Utopian Studies* contributor Jeanne M. Wolfe added: "This is not a scholarly book, nor is it real autobiography, but rather offers the reader a devotional guide, and tantalizing anecdotes."

In 1998 Vanier appeared on the Canadian Broadcasting Corporation radio program *Ideas* and presented his Massey Lectures in a series of five talks. The transcript of these lectures was edited and published in book form as *Becoming Human.* In a further exploration of spirituality undergirded by Vanier's strong Roman Catholic faith, he maintains in *Becoming Human* that the modern focus on the individual has weakened rather than strengthened society. As a *Maclean's* contributor noted, Vanier "stresses that the loneliness and pain experienced by so many is actually created and stimulated by individualism and the competition it implies," and "the resulting hard-heartedness" results in the rising divorce rate, materialism and greed, and a host of environmental issues. Praising *Becoming Human* as a work useful for guiding readers through difficult passages in life, Diane Torres Velasquez wrote in *Phi Delta Kappan:* "In only 163 pages, Vanier profoundly crafts an anthropological model for spiritual growth that includes a growth toward freedom, an opening up of our hearts to others, and a discovering of our common humanity."

In 1997 Vanier was awarded the Vatican's Paul VI International Prize for his formation of l'Arche. With the financial award accompanying that prize, he set to work expanding l'Arche into formerly communist eastern Europe. Calling Vanier "by any standard, one of the most remarkable people in contemporary Catholicism," *National Catholic Reporter* contributor John L. Allen, Jr. added: "Like Mother Teresa before him, he carries the rare burden of being both a public figure and someone widely flagged as a saint in his own lifetime."

BIOGRAPHICAL AND CRITICAL SOURCES:

BOOKS

Clarke, Bill, *Enough Room for Joy,* 1974.

PERIODICALS

America, April 13, 1985, Jean Grigsby, interview with Vanier, pp. 302-305; April. 18, 1992, Martin E. O'Malley, interview with Vanier, pp. 319-321; November 1, 1997, Michael Downey, review of *Our Journey Home: Rediscovering a Common Humanity beyond Our Differences,* p. 31.
Canadian Book Review Annual, 1997, Les Harding, review of *A Network of Friends,* p. 101.
Catholic Library World, June, 1999, Arnold Rzepecki, review of *The Scandal of Service,* p. 56.
Commonweal, September 10, 1982, Mary Gerhart, review of *The Challenge of l'Arche,* p. 477.
Library Journal, November 15, 1985, Elise Chase, review of *Man and Woman He Made Them,* p. 104; November 15, 2002, David Gordon, review of *Happiness: A Guide to a Good Life,* p. 75.
Maclean's, December 31, 1990, "Communities Built on Love," p. 34; November 30, 1998, review of *Becoming Human,* p. 82; September 4, 2000, "The Caregiver: Jean Vanier," p. 33.

National Catholic Reporter, September 27, 1985, pp. 9-10; September 9, 1988, p. 12; November 17, 2000, Gerry McCarthy, "Simple Relationships Are Key," p. 20; November 1, 2002, John L. Allen, Jr., "L'Arche Founder Reveals Face of Christ," p. 14.
Phi Delta Kappan, June, 2000, Diane Torres Velasquez, review of *Becoming Human,* p. 782.
Publishers Weekly, February 14, 1994, p. 65.
Quill & Quire, December, 2001, Marina Glogovac, review of *Made for Happiness,* p. 17.
Religious Studies Review, October, 1981, Karen McCarthy Brown, review of *Community and Growth,* p. 342.
Sojourners, January-February, 2002, Wayne A. Holst, review of *Seeing Beyond Depression,* p. 58.
Utopian Studies, winter, 1999, Jeanne M. Wolfe, review of *Our Journey Home,* p. 293.*

*   *   *

Van LOON, Karel Glastra 1962-

PERSONAL: Born December 24, 1962, in Amsterdam, The Netherlands

ADDRESSES: Home—Amsterdam, The Netherlands. *Agent*—c/o Author Mail, Canongate Books, 14 High St., Edinburgh EH1 1E Scotland; fax: 44131-557-5211. *E-mail*—info@canongate.co.uk.

CAREER: Writer, filmmaker, television producer, and educator. Elsevier Science, desk editor, 1983-84; VNU Magazine Publishers, editor, 1984-85; *Nieuwe Revu,* reporter, 1985-90, staff editor, 1990; freelance journalist, 1991—. University of Michigan, Ann Arbor, MI, writer in residence. Researcher and producer for television programs such as *Lolapaloeza, Karel, Political Broadcasts Socialist Party, Het laatste woord,* and *Lopende Zaken,*

AWARDS, HONORS: ECI Prijs voor Schrijvers van Nu (ECI Prize) shortlist, 1998, for *Vannacht is de wereld gek geworden;* Generale Banke Literatuur Prijs (Generale Bank Literature Prize), 1999, for *De Passievrucht.*

WRITINGS:

FICTION

(With Tiziana Alings) *De Beuk Erin* (for children), illustrated by Olivier Saive, BSO, 1992.

Vannacht is de Wereld gek Geworden (title means "Tonight the World Has Gone Crazy"), L. J. Veen (Amsterdam, The Netherlands), 1997.

De Passievrucht (novel), L. J. Veen (Amsterdam, The Netherlands), 1999, translated by Sam Garrett as *A Father's Affair,* Canongate Books (Edinburgh, Scotland), 2002, revised edition, 2003.

Lisa's Adem (novel; title means "Lisa's Breath"), L. J. Veen (Amsterdam, The Netherlands), 2001.

De Onzichtbaren (novel; title means "The Invisible Ones"), L. J. Veen (Amsterdam, The Netherlands), 2003.

NONFICTION

De Poppe-methode: Milieu-activist Remi Poppe Ontmaskert de Grote Vervuilers, Jan van Arkel (Utrecht, The Netherlands), 1993.

(With Karin Kuiper) *Herman: De Biografie van een Genetisch Gemanipuleerde Stier* (title means "Herman: The Biography of a Genetically Engineered Bull"), L. J. Veen (Amsterdam, The Netherlands), 1995.

(With Nico Schouten) *Atlas van de Macht,* Papieren Tijger (Utrecht, The Netherlands), 1998.

(With Jan Marijnissen) *De Laatste Oorlog: Gesprekken over de nieuwe wereldorde* (title means "The Last War"), L. J. Veen (Amsterdam, The Netherlands), 2000.

Contributor to periodicals, including *Cosmopolitan, Marie Claire, Vrii Nederland, Volkskrant,* and *Hollands Maandblad.* Van Loon's works have been translated into twenty-nine languages.

ADAPTATIONS: *De Passievrucht* was adapted as a film, 2003.

SIDELIGHTS: Dutch writer Karel Glastra Van Loon's books have been bestsellers in his native Netherlands. *De Passievrucht,* which was translated into English as *A Father's Affair,* has sold more than 300,000 copies there, which in proportion to the country's population "is the equivalent of 10 million copies in the U.S.," noted a writer for *ArborWeb.* In *A Father's Affair,* widower Armin Minderhout and his thirteen-year-old son, Bo, live a quiet but affectionate life together after the death of Monika, Bo's mother and the love of Armin's life, ten years earlier. Armin's job as a freelance proofreader for scientific publications does not pay spectacularly, but they get by, watching movies, talking late into the night, and spending time together. When Armin's girlfriend, Ellen, moves in, they decide that a new baby would make their family complete. Despite repeated attempts, however, Ellen does not get pregnant. A series of medical tests reveals that Armin is sterile, and has been so for his entire life.

The news is devastating to Armin, for the tests mean that he is not and could not be Bo's biological father. Why would Monika, with whom he was deeply and happily in love, betray him? And the most obvious question looms large: if he is not Bo's genetic father, then who is? "Armin is appalled to find himself brooding on the biology of a child he has loved wholeheartedly since birth," wrote Brian Bethune in *Maclean's.* "But he can't help himself." Faced with a maddening, even humiliating mystery, Armin sets out to discover who fathered the son he thought was his own. Several possible suspects are considered: Monika's doctor; her former boyfriend, Robbert Hubeek; and one of her friends, Nike Neerinckx. The questions are finally and "spectacularly answered," noted Amy Benfer in the *New York Times Book Review,* but the solution brings an even more shocking surprise to the bewildered Armin.

"The first half of Karel Van Loon's absorbing novel is a beautifully crafted lament for lost love, and a tender paean to a particular kind of parenthood," commented a reviewer in the London *Times.* "But the shock revelation about the protagonist's faulty chromosomes turns *A Father's Affair* into a full-on psychological thriller, in which the search for whoever impregnated his dead girlfriend almost drives Armin mad." Benfer remarked that "The novel gains the speed of a good mystery as Armin dutifully gumshoes his way through his former girlfriend's life, seeing her potential lovers at every turn." A *Publishers Weekly* reviewer stated that "the inventive storyline and the stunning ending combine to make this book a winner." Although Bethune found the conclusion of the novel "slightly ridiculous," he concluded that "the journey there is exhilarating."

BIOGRAPHICAL AND CRITICAL SOURCES:

PERIODICALS

Guardian (Manchester, England), July 26, 2003, Josh Lacey, review of *A Father's Affair,* p. 24.

Kirkus Reviews, February 1, 2003, review of *A Father's Affair,* pp. 177-178.

Maclean's, June 16, 2003, Brian Bethune, "Voices from Far Away," p. 89.

New York Times Book Review, May 4, 2003, Amy Benfer, review of *A Father's Affair,* p. 24.

New Zealand Herald, July 9, 2003, Robin Arthur, review of *A Father's Affair.*

Publishers Weekly, March 31, 2003, review of *A Father's Affair,* p. 41.

Times (London, England), August 10, 2002, review of *A Father's Affair,* p. 19; June 14, 2003, review of *A Father's Affair,* p. 14.

ONLINE

ArborWeb, http://www.arborweb.com/ (April 5, 2004), biography of Karel Glastra Van Loon.

Canongate Books, http://www.canongate.net/ (April 5, 2004), biography of Karel Glastra Van Loon.

International Network for Cultural Diversity, http://www.incd.net/ (April 5, 2004), biography of Karel Glastra Van Loon.

Susijn Agency, http://www.thesusijnagency.com/ (April 5, 2004).*

*　　*　　*

Van NATTA, Don, Jr. 1964-

PERSONAL: Born July 22, 1964; married Lizette Alvarez (a journalist); children: Isabel, Sofia. *Education:* College of Communication, Boston University, B.A., 1986.

ADDRESSES: Agent—c/o Author Mail, PublicAffairs, 250 West 57th St., Suite 1321, New York, NY 10107.

CAREER: Miami Herald, Miami, FL, reporter, 1987-95; *New York Times,* metropolitan reporter, 1995-97, reporter in Washington bureau, 1997—.

AWARDS, HONORS: Pulitzer Prize co-winner, 1993, for coverage of Hurricane Andrew, 1999, for stories exposing the sale of U.S. military technology to China, and 2004, for reports on terrorism; distinguished Alumnus Award, Boston University College of Communication, 2000.

WRITINGS:

First Off the Tee: Presidential Hackers, Duffers, and Cheaters, from Taft to Bush, PublicAffairs (New York, NY), 2003.

SIDELIGHTS: Pulitzer Prize-winning journalist Don Van Natta, Jr., is acclaimed for his investigative journalism into such issues as the government's sale of military technology to the Chinese and the fight against international terrorism. But Van Natta, who currently writes about affairs in Washington, D.C., for the *New York Times,* offers an unexpected view of the White House with his first book, *First Off the Tee: Presidential Hackers, Duffers, and Cheaters, from Taft to Bush.* Drawing on historical research and his own personal experiences—he has competed on the links with President Bill Clinton—Van Natta proposes that one can learn a lot about an American president's character by watching his behavior on a golf course. With the exception of Herbert Hoover, Harry Truman, and Jimmy Carter, the reporter notes, all the presidents since Howard Taft have been avid golfers, even those, such as Woodrow Wilson and Calvin Coolidge, who have been abominable players. "Almost everything is revealed on a golf course," according to Van Natta—"a player's shortcomings and strengths, most of all, but other subtleties of personality and foibles of character that you may never see across a desk."

Among the revelations and insights Van Natta offers are how President Taft's preference for golf was characteristic of his lax attitude toward his presidential responsibilities; how Lyndon Johnson used his time on the links to persuade congressmen to support the Civil Rights Act of 1964; and how the cheating tendencies of presidents Nixon and Clinton were very revealing of their personal character in office. One of Van Natta's favorite anecdotes, in fact, involves the time he played golf with Clinton. The president was liberal with his use of "mulligans"—or "practice shots"—and with the end of the game declared he shot a low score. When Van Natta later wrote a story about it in the newspaper, Clinton, according to the reporter, was furious. As he recalled in an *American Intelligence Wire* interview by Brit Hume and Tony Snow, "I said wait a minute . . . I've written stories about Bill Clinton and Monica Lewinsky, and about the Lincoln bedroom. He said those things bothered him too but this is different. The president takes his golf game very seriously." *First Off the Tee* concludes with Van Natta comparing the golf games of Presidents George H. W. and George W. Bush. For the Bushes, the game is all about speed, and the score is never as important as keeping the ball in the air. After the September 11, 2001, terrorist attacks, Van Natta also relates, George W. Bush's words on the golf course were rather revealing: "I call upon all nations to do everything they can to stop these terrorist killers. Thank you. Now watch this drive."

Van Natta summarized his conclusions about presidents and their golf games, and why golf appeals to our leaders, in an interview for National Public Radio's *Morning Edition:* "I think it's a mind game, camaraderie. They love being out away from the pressures of the Oval Office. And it's a prism into their characters. It's really a way for us to see how they really will behave under pressure, whether they have a short fuse or a long fuse." Some critics of *First Off the Tee* did not completely buy into the author's thesis, but many still found it a fun read. "While the book's central thesis may be a little overstated," according to Jamie Malanowski in the *Washington Monthly,* "it's still entertaining for all the cool presidential golf trivia it includes." Lynda Cardwell, writing in the *New York Times,* felt that *First Off the Tee* "is an easy, engaging book, and not such a bad history lesson." On the other hand, *Library Journal* reviewer John Maxymuk concluded that Van Natta's book is more a biography than a book about golf or politics, "This is a niche item but is very well done."

BIOGRAPHICAL AND CRITICAL SOURCES:

PERIODICALS

American Spectator, June-July, 2003, "Hail to the Cheat!"
America's Intelligence Wire, July 4, 2003, Brit Hume and Tony Snow, "Interview with Don Van Natta."
Booklist, April 15, 2003, Gilbert Taylor, review of *First Off the Tee: Presidential Hackers, Duffers, and Cheaters, from Taft to Bush,* p. 1442.
B.U. Bridge (Boston University), May 14, 1999, Hope Green, "Pulitzer Hat Trick fro COM Alumni."
Daily Free Press (Boston University), March 5, 2004, Scott Brooks, "Training for the *Times.*"
Library Journal, May 1, 2003, John Maxymuk, review of *First Off the Tee,* p. 126.

New York Times, May 9, 2003, Lynda Cardwell, "Books of the Times; Sure You Shot a 79, Mr. President. Of Course You Did," p. E44.
New York Times Book Review, April 20, 2003, Bradley S. Klein, "Bunker Mentality," p. 14.
Presidential Studies Quarterly, December, 2003, David Gray Adler, review of *First Off the Tee,* p. 947.
Times Literary Supplement, September 26, 2003, Daniel Crewe, review of *First Off the Tee.*
Washington Monthly, June, 2003, Jamie Malanowski, "Ball Boys: Why Golf Is the Driving Obsession of Middle-Age Alpha Males."

OTHER

Morning Edition (National Public Radio program transcript), May 1, 2003, "Interview: Don Van Natta Jr. on His New Book, *First Off the Tee.*"*

*   *   *

VERMA, Nirmal 1929-

PERSONAL: Born April 3, 1929 in Simla, India. *Education:* Attended St. Stephen's College; attended Oriental Institute, Prague, Czechoslovakia; Delhi University, M.A.

ADDRESSES: Agent—c/o Author Mail, Rājkamal Prakasan, 1B Netaji Subhas Marg, New Delhi, 110 002 India.

CAREER: Writer, journalist, and educator. Worked as a correspondent for *Times of India* until 1972.

AWARDS, HONORS: Sahitya Akademi Award, 1985, for *Kavve aura Kālā Pānī;* Jnanpith Award, 1999, for outstanding contribution to the enrichment of Indian literature; International Institute for Asian Studies fellow; Indian Institute for Advanced Studies fellow.

WRITINGS:

Parinde, Rājkamal (New Delhi, India) 1958, translation published as *The Hill Station and Other Stories,* Writers Workshop (Calcutta, India), 1973.

Ve din, Rājkamal (New Delhi, India), 1964, translation by Krisna Baldev Vaid published as *Days of Longing,* Hind Pocket Books (New Delhi, India), 1972.

Māyā-darpan, Bhārtīy Jnānpīth (Benares, India), 1967, translation published as *Maya Darpan and Other Stories,* Oxford University Press (New York, NY), 1986.

Lāl Tin Kī Chat, Rājkamal (New Delhi, India), 1974, translation by Kuldip Singh published as *The Red Tin Roof,* Ravi Dayal Publisher (New Delhi, India), 1997.

Kavve Aura Kālā Pānī, Rajakamala (New Delhi, India), 1983, translation by Kuldip Singh and Jai Ratan published as *The Crows of Deliverance,* Readers International (London, England), 1991.

Word and Memory, Vagdevi Prakashan (Bikaner, India), 1988.

The World Elsewhere and Other Stories, Readers International (London, England), 1988.

Dark Dispatches, translated by Alok Bhalla, Indus (New Delhi, India), 1993.

A Rag Called Happiness, translated by Kuldip Singh, Penguin Books India (New Delhi, India), 1993.

Such a Big Yearning & Other Stories, Indus (New Delhi, India), 1995.

India and Europe: Selected Essays, edited by Alok Bhalla, Centre for the Study of Indian Civilization and Indian Institute of Advanced Study (Shimla, India), 2000.

Indian Errant: Selected Stories of Nirmal Verma, translated by Prasenjit Gupta, Indialog Publications (Delhi, India), 2002.

The Last Wilderness, Indigo Publishing (Delhi, India), 2002.

WORKS IN HINDI

Cirō Par Cadnī (travelogue; title means "Moonlit Pines"),Rājkamal (New Delhi, India), 1962.

Jaltī Jhārī, Rājkamal (New Delhi, India), 1964.

Itne bare Dhabbe (title means "Such Large Stains") Rādhākrsna (New Delhi, India) 1966.

Pichlī Garmiyō Mē (title means "Last Summer"), Rajakamala Prakasana (New Delhi, India), 1968.

Merī Priy Kahāniya, (title means "My Favorite Stories"), Rajpal & Sons (New Delhi, India), 1970.

Har B&aamacr;riś Mē (title means "With Every Rain"), Rādhākrsna (New Delhi, India), 1970.

Bic Bahas Mē (title means "Discussions"), Sambhavna (Hapur, India), 1971.

Hara Barisamem, 1973.

Bica Bahasa Mem, 1973.

Śabd Aur Smrti, Rajakamala Prakasana (New Delhi, India), 1976, translation published as *Word and Memory,* Vagdevi (Bikaner, India), 1988.

Tīn Ekānt, (play; title means "Three Solitudes"), Rājkamal (New Delhi, India), 1976.

Dusrī Duniyā (title means "The Other World: Collected Essays"), Sambhavana Prakasana (Hapura, India), 1978.

Ek Cithrā Sukha (title means "A Patch of Happiness"), Rajakamala Prakasana (New Delhi, India), 1979.

Kālā Ka Jokhima, Rajakamala (New Delhi, India), 1981.

Meri Kahaniya (title means "My Stories"), Disa (Delhi, India), 1985.

Dhalāna se utarate hue, Rajakamala Prakasana (New Delhi, India), 1985.

Pratinidhi Kahāniya (title means "Representative Stories") Rajakamala Prakasana (New Delhi, India), 1988.

Rāta Kāa riportara (title means "Night Reporter") Rajakamala Prakasana (New Delhi, India), 1989.

Tina Ekanta, Rajakamala Prakasana (New Delhi, India), 1990.

India aur Europe, Rājkamal (New Delhi, India), 1991.

Itihās, Smrti, Akānkśhā, National Publishing House (New Delhi, India), 1992.

Dhunda se uthatī Dhuna: Dāyāri, Notsa, y Atra-Samsmarana, Rajakamala Prakasana (New Delhi, India), 1997.

Gyaraha Lambi Kahaniyam (short stories), Bharatiya Jnapitha (New Delhi, India), 2000.

Adi, Anta Aura Arambha, Rajakamala Prakasana (New Delhi, India), 2001.

Lekhaka ki Astha: Sahityika Nibanda, Vagdevi Prakasana (Bikanera, India), 2001.

SIDELIGHTS: A prominent figure in Hindi literature, Nirmal Verma first drew attention in the late 1950s with his short story collection, *Parinde* (published in English as *The Hill Station and Other Stories*). Verma's early work coincided with the growth of the "New Story" movement in Hindi literature. Although some critics have called Verma a pioneer of the New Story style, "he stands almost alone in the light and shade-play of language, reflective and self-reflexive mode of narration, metaphorical and imagistic composition, and sonorous yet deeply disturbing voice," wrote Girdhar Rathi in *Contemporary World Writers.* Verma acknowledges himself to be a writer of "poetic prose," Rathi remarked.

In college, Verma was a member of the Communist Party and subscribed to a Marxist ideology, wrote Rajes Ranjan in an interview with Verma on the *Literate World* Web site. But his literary influences were found in writers such as Anton Chekhov, T. S. Eliot, Ivan Turgenev, Ranier Maria Rilke, and Paul Eluard, Rathi wrote. "A long stay at Prague enabled Verma to settle accounts with his early Marxist leanings," Rathi commented, and by 1968 Verma had moved away from his Marxist influences.

Although Verma studied the English language as part of his education in India, he deliberately chose to write the bulk of his works in Hindi. "Hindi happens to be my mother tongue," Verma said in the interview with Ranjan. "I studied in English medium schools, but when I took to writing I knew I would not write in any other language except my own." He wrote some freelance articles, book reviews, and essays in English, "but I stuck to Hindi when it came to creative writing," Verma said.

"Among the contemporary Hindi writers, perhaps the most important figure is Nirmal Verma, whose novels and short stories try to grapple with the modern Indian sensibility, and whose essays amplify his vision through his critical observations," wrote Satish C. Aikant in *World Literature Today*. Akshaya Kumar, in a review of *India and Europe: Selected Essays* commented that "Nirmal Verma is an exceptional Hindi writer whose fictional works, both novels and short stories, do not easily fit into the stereotypes normally associated with Hindi fiction. There is no sentimentalism of rural poverty, nor is there any invocation of India as a pure and pristine cultural space." Instead, his work addresses "existential experiences of a native in the alien ambience of the western world." But even while embracing the healing power of modern experience, Verma does not forget his origins and the origins of his country. "If in his novels and short stories Verma is obsessed with the themes of loneliness, angst, and vacuity in human life, in his essays he emerges almost a fierce, if not rabid, advocate of India's sacred past," Kumar wrote.

Verma spent a considerable amount of time abroad, in England and in Czechoslovakia, where his novel *Days of Longing* and the travelogue *Cirō Par Cadnī* were published. These volumes "established him as an internationalist-modernist writer," Rathi commented. However, he did not find all international contact favorable, and in particular he was displeased with British colonialism. "For Verma, India's contact with the West was not a meeting among equals," Aikant wrote, but instead was considered by Verma a "violent culture rupture" affecting all aspects of Indian ways of life. The worst effects of colonialism were found in the "Indian psyche," and in order to recover from those ill effects, "this self needed to be decolonized not by harking back to a mythical past but by embracing qualified modernity," Aikant observed.

In *The Crows of Deliverance,* a collection of six short stories translated from Hindi, Verma presents stories of "human experience that crosses cultural boundaries into universality, while still affording the Western reader a glimpse at the particulars of life in the author's homeland," wrote Michael Cain in *MultiCultural Review.* In "Last Summer" an Indian architectural student finds he has to resist the cultural customs of his homeland. He has met and fallen in love with a fellow student in Vienna. But while visiting India during the last summer before returning to Vienna and marrying his beloved there, his parents attempt to arrange a marriage to a local girl. In "Morning Walk," which Susheela N. Rao called "a tragic story of loneliness in life" in a *World Literature Today* review, an old man faces the prospect of life alone after his son goes abroad, and makes the only choice he can. The title character of "The Visitor" is an academic who travels widely, and who becomes almost a stranger, an unwelcome visitor, to his wife and daughter in England. In *Deliverance,* the story which gives the collection its name, a man travels to a crow-infested mountain town in search of his brother, a holy man who has renounced the material world. The self-exiled brother's signature is required on a business document, a secular need at odds with the holy brother's retreat from the world. "The crows in the story are symbolic of a deliverance not quite delivered, with a lingering touch of the memory of *Samsara,* or worldly life," Rao observed. A *Kirkus Reviews* critic remarked on the "clear and deceptively simple prose" of the work.

Aamer Hussein, reviewing *The Crows of Deliverance* in *Times Literary Supplement,* noted the difficulties in translating Verma's Hindi works into English. "His mastery of succinct detail, controlled epiphany, and impressionistic evocation of setting is, however, virtually impossible to emmulate; it is equally difficult to convey in another language the careful cadences of his imagistic prose," Hussein observed.

Another of Verma's collections of short stories, *The World Elsewhere and Other Stories,* fared better in translation, having been "translated with intuition and sensitivity," wrote Maria Couto in *Times Literary Supplement.* The book "brings to the Western reader a glimpse of the variety of Indian literature, whose vibrant, multilingual profusion is virtually unknown outside the subcontinent." Navtej Sarna had similar remarks about Verma's novel, *The Last Wilderness,* writing in *Times Literary Supplement* that the book "points the way to the immense treasure that lies hidden in the literature of the Indian languages, awaiting a wider audience." The novel's narrator arrives in a sleepy mountain town to serve as secretary to civil servant Mehra Sahib. He was hired by Sahib's wife, Diva, to help the aging Sahib. The narrator strikes up a fledgling relationship with Tiya, Sahib's daughter by his first wife. However, tragedy befalls the community when Diva is stricken by cancer, leaving the narrator feeling like "a parasite whose very existence was contingent upon the extinction of another," Verma wrote. The grief of Diva's death is surpassed only when Sahib himself dies. "The novel itself becomes a gripping examination of the time before death: how memories jostle for space, how internal dialogue of the sprit take place, how man himself becomes fragmented into different time-spaces," Sarna wrote, until it becomes, Verma observed, "impossible to tell which is the last and final copy."

BIOGRAPHICAL AND CRITICAL SOURCES:

BOOKS

Contemporary World Writers, Girdhar Rathi, biography of Nirmal Verma, St. James Press (Detroit, MI), 1993.

PERIODICALS

Kirkus Reviews, July 15, 1991, review of *The Crows of Deliverance,* p. 889.

MultiCultural Review, July, 1992, Michael Cain, review of *The Crows of Deliverance,* p. 54.

New York Times Book Review, August 21, 1988, Carolyn See, "Shame in Simla," review of *The World Elsewhere and Other Stories,* p. 35.

Publishers Weekly, August 9, 1991, review of *The Crows of Deliverance,* p. 53.

Times Literary Supplement, October 28, 1988, Maria Couto, "Threads and Shards," review of *The World Elsewhere and Other Stories,* p. 1212; October 11, 1991, Aamer Hussein, "Vision of India, Voices of Exile," review of *The Crows of Deliverance,* p. 22; October 25, 2002, Navtej Sarna, "Under a Sequined Sky," review of *The Last Wilderness,* p. 22.

World Literature Today, spring, 1992, Susheela N. Rao, review of *The Crows of Deliverance,* pp. 405-406; winter, 1997, Susheela N. Rao, review of *Such a Big Yearing & Other Stories,* p. 227; summer, 1998, A. L. McLeod, *The Red Tin Roof,* p. 688; winter, 2000, Prasenjit Gupta, "Refusing the Gaze: Identity and Translation in Nirmal Verma's Fiction,", critical essay on Nirmal Verma, p 53; winter, 2001, Satish C. Aikant, review of *India and Europe: Selected Essays,* p. 106.

ONLINE

Literate World Web site, http://www.literateworld.com/ (July 11, 2003), Rajesh Ranjan, interview with Nirmal Verma.

South Asian Literary Recordings Project, http://www.loc.gov/acq/ovop/delhi/salrp/ (July 11, 2003), biography of Nirmal Verma.

Tribune Web site (India), http://www.tribuneindia.com/ (July 8, 2001), Akshaya Kumar, "Reviving Indian Identity," review of *India and Europe: Selected Essays.* *

*   *   *

VOIGT, Stefan 1962-

PERSONAL: Born August 19, 1962, in Hamburg, West Germany (now Germany); son of Karl Heinz (a pastor) and Marlene (Viet) Voigt. *Education:* Attended University of Strasbourg, 1983-84; University of Freiburg, Dr.rer.pol. (summa cum laude), 1988; attended University of Jena, 1997.

ADDRESSES: Home—Am Comeniusplatz 4, D-10243 Berlin, Germany. *Office*—Department of Economics, Ruhr-University Bochum, Universitätsstraße 150, 44780 Bochum, Germany. *E-mail*—stefanvoigt@lycos.de.

CAREER: Bremer Nachrichten (daily newspaper), Bremen, West Germany (now Germany), intern, 1982; parish worker at a home for the aged in Bremen and at a hospital in Strasbourg, France, between 1983 and 1984; *Frankfurter Rundschau* (daily newspaper), Frankfurt, West Germany (now Germany), intern, 1985; La Seda de Barcelona (textile company), Barcelona, Spain, intern, 1986; HOECHST, Milan, Italy, intern, 1987; McKinsey and Co., summer associate, 1990; University of Freiburg, Freiburg, Germany, assistant professor, 1993-94; Max Planck Institute for Research into Economic Systems, Jena, Germany, research fellow, 1993-98; University of Freiburg, professor of economic policy, 1998-99; Institute for Advanced Study, Berlin, Germany, fellow, 1999-2000; European University Viadrina, Frankfurt, Germany, associate professor, 2000-01; Ruhr-University Bochum, Bochum, Germany, professor of economic policy, 2001—. George Mason University, visiting scholar at Center for the Study of Public Choice, 1992; University of Maryland—College Park, visiting scholar, 1994. Radio Bremen (public radio station), member of board of directors, 1982-85, intern, 1986.

MEMBER: European Center of Comparative Government and Public Policy (corresponding member), European Public Choice Society, European Association of Law and Economics, Verein für Socialpolitik, American Economic Association, American Law and Economics Association.

AWARDS, HONORS: Walter-Eucken-Prize, Stifterverband der Deutschen Wissenschaft, 1994, for contributions to the theory of order; Herbert Quandt-Förderpreis, Herbert Quandt-Stiftung, c. 1997, for *Explaining Constitutional Change: A Positive Economics Approach.*

WRITINGS:

Die Welthandelsordnung zwischen Konflikt und Stabilität: Konfliktpotentiale und Konfliktlösungsmechanismen (title means "The World Trade Order between Conflict and Stability: Conflict Potential and Conflict Resolution Mechanisms"), Haufe (Freiburg, Germany), 1992.

(Editor, with Manfred E. Streit) *Europa reformieren: Vorschläge von Ökonomen und Juristen zur zukünftigen Verfaßtheit Europas* (title means "Reforming Europe: Proposals from Economists and Lawyers concerning the Future Constitution of Europe"), Nomos (Baden-Baden, Germany), 1996.

Explaining Constitutional Change: A Positive Economics Approach, Edward Elgar Publishing (Northampton, MA), 1999.

(Editor) *Constitutional Political Economy,* Edward Elgar Publishing (Northampton, MA), 2002.

(Editor, with H.-J. Wagener) *Constitutions, Markets, and the Law: Recent Experiences in Transition Economics,* Edward Elgar Publishing (Northampton, MA), 2002.

Also author (with others) of *Konsequenzen der Globalisierung für die Wettbewerbspolitik* (title means "Consequences of Globalization for Antitrust Policy"), Peter Lang (Frankfurt, Germany). Contributor to books, including *Conflict Resolution in International Trade,* edited by D. Friedmann and E. J. Mestmäcker, Nomos (Baden-Baden, Germany), 1993; *Stability in East Central Europe?,* edited by E. Jahn and R. Wildenmann, Nomos (Baden-Baden, Germany), 1995; *Constitutional Law and Economics of the European Union,* edited by Dieter Schmidtchen and Robert Cooter, Edward Elgar Publishing (Northampton, MA), 1997; and *Constitutional political Economy in a Public Choice Perspective,* edited by Charles K. Rowley, Kluwer Publishing (Dordrecht, Netherlands), 1997. Contributor of articles and reviews to academic journals and newspapers in Germany and elsewhere, including *Theoretical Inquiries into Law, European Journal of Law and Economics, Cato Journal, International Review of Law and Economics, Public Choice,* and *Kyklos.* Associate editor, *Review of Austrian Economics;* member of editorial board, *Constitutional Political Economy,* 2002—; member of scientific committee, *Journal des Economistes et des Études Humaines,* 2002—; member of editorial committee, *Schmollers Jahrbuch.*

W

WADDINGTON, Miriam 1917-2004
(E. B. Merritt)

OBITUARY NOTICE—See index for *CA* sketch: Born December 23, 1917, in Winnipeg, Manitoba, Canada; died March 3, 2004, in Vancouver, British Columbia, Canada. Social worker, educator, and author. Waddington was a prize-winning poet who, as part of the "first generation" movement, helped steer Canada literature away from its European influences. Completing her undergraduate work at the University of Toronto in 1939, she earned a diploma in social work there in 1942, followed by a master's in 1945; she would later return to the University of Toronto to receive an M.A. in 1968. Waddington's career began in the 1940s as a social worker, first as assistant director for the Jewish Child Welfare Bureau in Montreal, then as an instructor at McGill University's School of Social Work. In the early 1950s, she was on staff at Montreal Children's Hospital for two years, followed by three years at the John Howard Society and three more years at the Jewish Family Bureau in Montreal. After working as a casework supervisor for North York Family Service in Toronto from 1960 to 1962, Waddington's success as a writer led her to York University, where she taught English and Canadian literature from 1964 until her retirement as professor emerita in 1983. As a poet, Waddington drew on her Russian-Jewish family background and her experiences growing up on the Canadian prairies. Her interest in social work also influenced her subject matter, and she wrote on subjects ranging from poverty to motherhood. But it was her exploration of themes about the Canadian experience that lent her verses distinction, making them an important part of Canada's search for its own literary voice. She published twelve poetry collections in her lifetime, including *Green World* (1945), *The Glass Trumpet* (1966), *The Price of Gold* (1976), and *The Last Landscape* (1992); *Driving Home: Poems New and Selected* (1972) and *Collected Poems* (1986) both received the J. I Segal award. Waddington also penned short stories and was the editor or author of a number of essay, criticism, and story collections; some of her writings were published under the pseudonym E. B. Merritt. Her poetic skills received another honor when a stanza from her "Jacques Cartier" was selected to be reproduced on Canada's one hundred dollar bill.

OBITUARIES AND OTHER SOURCES:

BOOKS

Contemporary Poets, seventh edition, St. James Press (Detroit, MI), 2001.

PERIODICALS

Globe & Mail, March 6, 2004.

ONLINE

BC Book World, http://www.abcbookworld.com/ (May 28, 2004).

* * *

WALDMAN, Ayelet 1964-

PERSONAL: Given name pronounced "eye-*yell*-it"; born 1964, in Israel; daughter of Leonard (a fund raiser) and Ricki (a public health administrator) Waldman; married Michael Chabon (an author), 1993;

children: Sophie, Abraham, Zeke, Ida-Rose. *Education:* Wesleyan University, graduated; Harvard University, earned law degree, 1991.

ADDRESSES: Home—Berkeley, CA. *Agent*—c/o Author Mail, Berkley Books Publicity, 375 Hudson St., New York, NY 10014.

CAREER: Attorney for a law firm in New York, NY, c. 1991-92; worked for public defender's office in Orange County and Los Angeles, CA, c. 1992-96; Boalt Hall School of Law, University of California at Berkeley, currently adjunct professor of law.

WRITINGS:

Nursery Crimes (part of "Mommy Track" mystery series), Berkley Prime Crime (New York, NY), 2000.

The Big Nap (part of "Mommy Track" mystery series), Berkley Prime Crime (New York, NY), 2001.

A Playdate with Death (part of "Mommy Track" mystery series), Berkley Prime Crime (New York, NY), 2002.

Death Gets a Time-Out (part of "Mommy Track" mystery series), Berkley Prime Crime (New York, NY), 2003.

Daughter's Keeper (novel), Sourcebooks (Naperville, IL), 2003.

Murder Plays House (part of "Mommy Track" mystery series), Berkley Books (New York, NY), 2004.

WORK IN PROGRESS: A second mainstream novel, *The Bloom Girls,* a story that is set in 1920s Montreal, Canada; more "Mommy Track" mysteries.

SIDELIGHTS: Ayelet Waldman's career intentions had always been to work as a public defender. Even after she married Pulitzer Prize-winning novelist Michael Chabon, she never thought being an author herself might be something she would want to pursue. But events in her life conspired to turn her path from law to literature so that now she is a best-selling mystery author of the "Mommy Track" mysteries, as well as of the well-received mainstream novel *Daughter's Keeper.*

The daughter of ardent Zionist parents, Waldman came from a liberal background that led to her initial career in law. "My parents were good liberals," she told Heidi

Benson in the *San Francisco Chronicle,* "and they trained me that you have to give back. And being a criminal defense lawyer was the perfect combination of theatrics—because I really wanted to be an actress, but I was too short—and doing good." After graduating from Harvard Law School in 1991, she joined a law firm in New York City. Not too long after that, she met her future husband, Michael Chabon, and the couple moved to the Los Angeles area. Here, Waldman became a public defender, working primarily on drug cases. But after Waldman and Chabon were married and she began having children, life as an attorney became increasingly impractical. A combination of guilt over neglecting her children and frustration about what she felt were ridiculously overzealous laws against petty drug dealers led Waldman to quit. "I thought, 'I just can't do this anymore, be part of this system sending people to jail,'" she told Michael J. Ybarra in the *Los Angeles Times.* "I loved what I was doing, but the drug sentences were so insane it nearly killed me. I don't like to lose; I lost all the time. The prosecutors have all the power."

Waldman decided she would be better off focusing on motherhood. She left her job in 1996 but found that being a full-time mom was not without its problems. She had felt guilty over "being a crappy mother," as she told Benson, but she was also upset over leaving her job: "It was actually sort of heartbreaking, because this was the job I'd always wanted." Feeling she might find a happy compromise, Waldman got the idea of teaching law part time. In order to do this, however, she thought she should beef up her resume by publishing a couple of articles in law reviews. While at the library, ostensibly researching her article, Waldman began scribbling down the first pages of a novel instead, a story featuring a lawyer and mother named Juliet Applebaum. After writing the first fifty pages, she showed her efforts to her novelist husband, who encouraged her to continue and helped get her debut novel, *Nursery Crimes,* published in 2000.

Nursery Crimes became the first in a series of lighthearted mystery novels in the "Mommy Track" series. In these books, Applebaum quits her job as a federal public defender to become a full-time mother, yet she finds herself repeatedly drawn into murder investigations and becomes a private investigator. Her first case involves the death of a nursery school owner, yet most of the fun involves Applebaum's struggles with domestic life as she simultaneously tries to solve the crime. *Nursery Crimes* was followed by several more books in the series, including *The Big Nap, A Playdate with Death, Death Gets a Time-Out,* and *Murder Plays House,* many of which have received positive reviews. *Booklist* reviewer Barbara Bibel called *The Big Nap,* the story of the suspicious disappearance of Applebaum's baby sitter, "an entertaining mystery with a satirical tone." And in a review of *A Playdate with Death,* in which Applebaum suspects foul play is involved in her personal trainer's "suicide," a *Kirkus Reviews* contributor enjoyed the "funny tidbits about bringing up toddlers and the liberal mom's dilemma over giving her kids toy guns to play with." A *Publishers Weekly* critic added that this novel provides a "swift and engaging plot" that is ideal for "those with a taste for lighter mystery fare." *Death Gets a Time-Out,* a tangled mystery involving a film star, rape, murder, and a large cast of suspects, received similar praise for Waldman's blend of crime solving and domestic troubles. While a *Publishers Weekly* reviewer complimented the way the author "skillfully unravels the intertwined relationships between all [the] . . . characters to reveal a cunning plot," a *Kirkus Reviews* writer said "Waldman is at her witty best when dealing with children, carpooling, and first-trimester woes."

In 2003, Waldman began to explore writing novels outside of the "Mommy Track" series, and published *Daughter's Keeper.* While the plot still involves crime, the focus of the story is really the relationship between a mother, drug store owner Elaine Goodman, and her daughter, Olivia. Drawing on her outrage over how the legal system relentlessly pursues and punishes those who are even remotely involved in drug crimes, Waldman tells the story of Olivia's unfortunate involvement with her boyfriend, a Mexican immigrant named Jorge. Jorge, frustrated that he cannot earn a decent income because he is an illegal immigrant, turns to drug dealing. When Olivia, against her better judgment, passes along a message about a deal to him, she is implicated in a crime that gets her sentenced to ten years in prison. This happens just as Olivia discovers she is pregnant, and she implores her mother to raise the child until she can be released. Although mother and daughter have had a strained relationship, Elaine eventually agrees to put off her own plans to help her daughter, and her personal sacrifices help melt their long frosty relationship.

Many critics noted Waldman's focus on drug policies in America, with *People* reviewer Ting Yu stating that she "offers a compelling portrait of the unintended victims of the American legal system." "Olivia's final statement at her sentencing," a *Kirkus Reviews* writer further noted, "is a no-holds-barred indictment of the evils of mandatory minimum and the absurdity of the current drug laws." Other reviewers were also complimentary about Waldman's portrayal of her characters. For example, *School Library Journal* writer Francisca Goldsmith said, "The two women and the men in their lives are fully realized, with both their sympathetic and shameful motivations clearly limned." Although Suzan Sherman, writing in the *New York Times Book Review,* felt that "not everything here works" in terms of plot, she called Waldman's depiction of the character of Elaine an "incisive portrayal." *Booklist* contributor Deborah Donovan also appreciated the author's "perceptive digging into a tenuous mother-daughter relationship pushed to unexpected limits."

BIOGRAPHICAL AND CRITICAL SOURCES:

PERIODICALS

Booklist, May 1, 2001, Barbara Bibel, review of *The Big Nap,* p. 1642; May 15, 2002, review of *A Playdate with Death,* p. 1580; September 1, 2003, Deborah Donovan, review of *Daughter's Keeper,* p. 63.

Chicago Sun-Times, August 25, 2002, Delia O'Hara, "Author and Mommy Gets Her Life on the Right Track," p. 13; November 12, 2003, Delia O'Hara, "Every Parent's Nightmare," p. 62.

Contra Costa Times (Walnut Creek, CA), January 14, 2004, "Heading Off Track: Author Ayelet Waldman Explores New Writing Path."

Kirkus Reviews, April 15, 2002, review of *A Playdate with Death,* p. 532; May 1, 2003, review of *Death Gets a Time-Out,* p. 648; August 15, 2003, review of *Daughter's Keeper,* p. 1044.

Library Journal, June 1, 2000, Rex E. Klett, review of *Nursery Crimes,* p. 208; September 1, 2003, Nancy Pearl, review of *Daughter's Keeper,* p. 211.

Los Angeles Times, October 5, 2003, Michael J. Ybarra, "Style & Culture; Taking on the Law; Ayelet Waldman Lashes Out at Drug Sentencing in Her New Novel," p. E4.

New York Times Book Review, July 7, 2002, Marilyn Stasio, "Crime," Section 7, p. 16; September 28, 2003, Suzan Sherman, "Books in Brief: Fiction," Section 7, p. 28.

People, December 16, 2002, Galina Espinoza, "Author, Author: She Writes. He Writes. And Both Ayelet Waldman and Michael Chabon Raise Kids," p. 151; October 27, 2003, Ting Yu, review of *Daughter's Keeper,* p. 47.

Publishers Weekly, May 21, 2001, review of *The Big Nap,* p. 83; May 13, 2002, Tim Peters, "PW Talks with Ayelet Waldman," p. 54, and review of *A Playdate with Death,* p. 54; June 9, 2003, review of *Death Gets a Time-Out,* p. 40; July 7, 2003, review of *Daughter's Keeper,* p. 48.

San Francisco Chronicle, October 22, 2003, Heidi Benson, "Profile: Ayelet Waldman," p. D1.

School Library Journal, November, 2003, Francisca Goldsmith, review of *Daughter's Keeper,* p. 172.

U.S. News & World Report, June 23, 2003, Beth Brophy, "Clues You Can Use," p. D4.

Washington Post, December 22, 2003, "Mandatory Madness," p. C2.

ONLINE

Ayelet Waldman Home Page, http://www.ayeletwaldman.com (April 14, 2004).

OTHER

All Things Considered (National Public Radio transcript), June 29, 2002, "Interview: Ayelet Waldman Discusses Her Book *A Playdate with Death.*"*

*   *   *

WANG, Wallace E. 1961-

PERSONAL: Born September 26, 1961, in Birmingham, MI; married, 1993. *Education:* Michigan State University, B.A. (material engineering), 1983; M.S. (computer science).

ADDRESSES: Home—San Diego, CA. *Agent*—c/o Author Mail, No Starch Press, 555 De Haro St., Suite 250, San Francisco, CA 94107. *E-mail*—bothecat@cox.net.

CAREER: Comedian and freelance writer. Worked as a technical writer for General Dynamics, 1983-85; *ComputorEdge* (magazine), San Diego, CA, editor and writer, 1985-87. Founder, with Patrick DeGuire, Top Bananas Entertainment; has appeared on A&E's *Evening at the Improv;* also makes regular stand-up appearances at the Riviera Hotel Comedy Club, Las Vegas, NV. Visiting professor of computer science, University of Zimbabwe, 1989.

WRITINGS:

(With John Mueller), *Illustrated Ready, Set, Go! 4.5,* Wordware Publishing (Plano, TX), 1989.

(With John Mueller) *Illustrated VP-Expert,* Wordware Publishing (Plano, TX), 1989.

The Best Free Time-saving Utilities for the PC, edited by Tina Berke, Computer Publishing Enterprises, 1989.

(With Scott Millard) *Simple Computer Maintenance and Repair,* edited by Gretchen Lingham, Computer Publishing Enterprises, 1990.

101 Computer Business Ideas, edited by Tina Berke, Computer Publishing Enterprises, 1990.

(With John Mueller) *Illustrated Microsoft Word 5.0,* Wordware Publishing (Plano, TX), 1990.

(With John Mueller) *Illustrated PFS: First Publisher,* Wordware Publishing (Plano, TX), 1990, second edition published as *Illustrated PFS: First Publisher: For Versions 2.0 and 3.0,* 1991.

(With John Mueller) *Microsoft Macro Assembler 5.1: Programming in the 80386 Environment,* Windcrest Books (Blue Ridge Summit, PA), 1990.

(With Joe Kraynak) *The First Book of Personal Computing,* H. W. Sams (Carmel, IN), 1990, fourth edition, with Kraynak, Jennifer Flynn, and Stephen R. Poland, Alpha Books (Carmel, IN), 1993.

(With John Mueller) *The Ultimate DOS Programmer's Manual,* Windcrest (Blue Ridge Summit, PA), 1991.

(With Kenneth Bibb) *Illustrated Turbo C++,* Wordware Publishing (Plano, TX), 1991.

Software Buying Secrets, second edition, Computer Publishing Enterprises (San Diego, CA), 1991.

(With Dan Gookin and Chris Van Buren) *Illustrated Computer Dictionary for Dummies,* IDG Books Worldwide (San Mateo, CA), 1993, second edition, IDG Books Worldwide (Foster City, CA), 1995.

Learn Quicken in a Day, Wordware Publishing (Plano, TX), 1993.

Build Your Own Green PC, illustrated by Rick Wilkins, Windcrest/McGraw-Hill (New York, NY), 1994.

CompuServe for Dummies, IDG Books (San Mateo, CA), 1994, third edition, IDG Books Worldwide (Foster City, CA), 1996.

More WordPerfect 6 for DOS for Dummies, edited by Dan Gookin, IDG Books (San Mateo, CA), 1994.

ProComm Plus 2 for Windows for Dummies, IDG Books (Foster City, CA), 1994.

Visual Basic 3 for Dummies, IDG Books Worldwide (San Mateo, CA), 1994.

(With John Paul Mueller) *OLE for Dummies,* IDG Books Worldwide (Foster City, CA), 1995.

Visual Basic 4 for Windows for Dummies, IDG Books Worldwide (Foster City, CA), 1995.

(With John Mueller) *Dummies 101. Visual Basic Programming,* IDG Books Worldwide (Foster City, CA), 1996.

(With Roger C. Parker) *Microsoft Office 97 for Windows for Dummies,* IDG Books Worldwide (Foster City, CA), 1996.

More Microsoft Office for Windows 95 for Dummies, IDG Books Worldwide (Foster City, CA), 1996.

More Visual Basic 4 for Windows for Dummies, IDG Books Worldwide (Foster City, CA), 1996.

Surfing the Microsoft Network, Prentice Hall PTR (Upper Saddle River, NJ), 1996.

(With John Mueller) *Dummies 101. Visual Basic 5 Programming,* IDG Books Worldwide (Foster City, CA), 1997.

More Microsoft Office 97 for Windows for Dummies, IDG Books Worldwide (Foster City, CA), 1997.

Visual Basic 5 for Windows for Dummies, IDG Books Worldwide (Foster City, CA), 1997.

More Visual Basic 5 for Windows for Dummies, IDG Books Worldwide (Foster City, CA), 1997.

Steal This Computer Book, No Starch Press (San Francisco, CA), 1998, third edition published as *Steal This Computer Book 3: What They Won't Tell You about the Internet,* 2003.

Visual Basic 6 for Dummies, IDG Books Worldwide (Foster City, CA), 1998.

Visual Basic 6 for Dummies Deluxe Compiler Kit (includes CD-ROM), 1999.

Beginning Programming for Dummies, IDG Books Worldwide (Foster City, CA), 1999, third edition, Wiley (Hoboken, NJ), 2004.

(With Roger C. Parker) *Microsoft Office 2000 for Windows for Dummies,* IDG Books Worldwide (Foster City, CA), 1999.

More Microsoft Office 2000 for Windows for Dummies, IDG Books Worldwide (Foster City, CA), 1999.

(With Richard Hing) *Print Shop Deluxe for Dummies,* IDG Books Worldwide (Foster City, CA), 2000.

Office XP for Dummies, Hungry Minds (New York, NY), 2001.

Web Cams for Dummies, IDG Books Worldwide (Foster City, CA), 2001.

(With Larry Garrison) *Breaking into Acting for Dummies,* Wiley (New York, NY), 2002.

Visual Basic .NET for Dummies, Hungry Minds (New York, NY), 2002.

Totally Tasteless Photoshop Elements, McGraw-Hill/Osborne (New York, NY), 2003.

Office 2003 for Dummies, Wiley (Indianapolis, IN), 2003.

Start! The No Nonsense Guide to Windows XP (Consumer), McGraw-Hill/Osborne (New York, NY), 2003.

(With William Pollock) *The Book of Nero 6,* No Starch Press (San Francisco, CA), 2004.

Former author of column "Notes from the Underground" for *Boardwatch Magazine,* 1995—.

WORK IN PROGRESS: Steal this File-Sharing Book.

SIDELIGHTS: Wallace E. Wang is a study in contradictions. An engineering graduate with a distaste for computer technology, he has made a career out of writing books about PCs and software. He has also been an editor of a computer magazine and taught computer science at the University of Zimbabwe. It was while in Zimbabwe that he was first inspired to pursue another type of career entirely: stand-up comedy. As he related to Lisa Ferguson in a *Las Vegas Sun* interview, one night while staying in his hotel room, he became "so bored . . . I just started babbling to myself, and then I started laughing and I thought, 'This is actually kind of funny.'" When he returned home, a friend encouraged him to try comedy for a living. At first, Wang felt he had some success on stage, but he struggled in the entertainment field to make a living. So, having worked as a technical writer for General Dynamics, and having studied writing in college, Wang decided to make a go of it as a freelance writer. Combining his sense of humor with his empathy for computer neophytes, Wang has written or cowritten numerous guides explaining operating systems and software for beginners, particularly with his contributions to the "For Dummies" series. As Wang explained to Ferguson, it is his goal to reassure typical computer users that they are not idiots; the problem with computers is that "they're designed so poorly" that they are hard for the average person to understand.

In addition to his empathy for his readers, Wang has an advantage over other computer book writers in that, as he confessed to Ferguson, he often accepts assignments to write computer guides before he has even used the software: "[Typically,] I have never used the program, and when they give me the contract, I'm like, 'I've gotta figure out how to use it.' That's how I can write to the beginners' attitude, because I'm writing the book essentially for myself." With the "For Dummies" books, which typically include witty cartoons and asides, Wang can also indulge his natural comedic talent. But he has also written a number of books outside the "Dummies" series, the most successful of which has been his *Steal This Computer Book,* first published in 1998 and now in its third edition as *Steal This Computer Book 3: What They Won't Tell You about the Internet. Library Journal* reviewer Rachel Singer Gordon described the third edition as "an odd but fascinating compendium of resources, recommendations, and philosophical musings."

While still continuing to write about computer technology, Wang has more recently published *Breaking into Acting for Dummies,* which he wrote with Larry Garrison. Elias Stimac, writing in *Back Stage,* said "the easy-to-read formula of the 'Dummies' series, and the sly sense of humor that the writers sneak in every once in a while, make this book both informative and enjoyable." Wang, who has had several non-speaking roles in films, is himself aspiring to break his way into acting one day and especially hopes to make it on television. As a comic, his goal is to elevate America's taste in humor to a more sophisticated level that does not rely on foul language for a laugh. As he revealed to Ferguson: "I don't want people to laugh at that. I want people to get used to a higher standard of comedy . . . I want to get audiences smarter."

Wang told *CA:* "What first got me interested in writing computer books was my desire to use a computer for word processing. Like most people, I found computers were poorly designed and their accompanying manuals horribly written that I knew I could explain technical issues much clearer and simpler."

BIOGRAPHICAL AND CRITICAL SOURCES:

PERIODICALS

Back Stage, April 18, 2003, Elias Stimac, "The ABC-DEFs of Acting."
Computer Shopper, February, 1995, Christopher O'Malley, review of *Build Your Own Green PC,* p. 451.
Database Magazine, April-May, 1995, Judith A. Copler, "Hardcopy."
Library Journal, May 1, 2003, review of *Start! The No Nonsense Guide to Mac OS X Jaguar;* October 1, 2003, Rachel Singer Gordon, review of *Steal This Computer Book 3: What They Won't Tell You about the Internet,* p. 109.
Quill & Quire, May, 1997, review of *Microsoft Office 97 for Windows for Dummies,* pp. 28-29.

ONLINE

Las Vegas Sun, http://www.lasvegassun.com/ (January 23, 2004), Lisa Ferguson, "Columnist Lisa Ferguson: Wang Prefers Practicing Comedy, Computer Basics."

*   *   *

WARBURTON, Nigel 1962-

PERSONAL: Born 1962, in England. *Education:* University of Bristol, B.A.; Cambridge University, Ph.D. (philosophy), 1989.

ADDRESSES: Office—Department of Philosophy, Faculty of Arts, Open University, Walton Hall, Milton Keynes MK7 6AA, England. *E-mail*—N.Warburton@ open.ac.uk.

CAREER: Educator and author. Nottingham University, Nottingham, England, former lecturer in philosophy; Open University, Milton Keynes, England, senior lecturer in philosophy, 1994—.

WRITINGS:

Philosophy: The Basics, Routledge (New York, NY), 1992, third edition, 1999.
(Editor) *Bill Brandt: Selected Texts and Bibliography,* G. K. Hall (New York, NY), 1993.

Thinking from A to Z, Routledge (New York, NY), 1996, second edition, 2000.

Philosophy: The Classics, Routledge (New York, NY), 1998, second edition, 2001.

(Author of text, with Bill Jay) *Brandt: The Photography of Bill Brandt,* introduction by David Hockney, Harry M. Abrams (New York, NY), 1999.

Philosophy: The Basic Readings, Routledge (New York, NY), 1999.

Freedom: An Introduction with Readings, Routledge (New York, NY), 2000.

(With Derek Maltravers and Jonathan Pike) *Reading Political Philosophy: Machiavelli to Mill,* Routledge (New York, NY), 2001.

The Art Question, Routledge (New York, NY), 2003.

Ernö Goldfinger: The Life of an Architect, Routledge (New York, NY), 2004.

SIDELIGHTS: Although his interest in aesthetics has prompted a biography of architect Ernö Goldfinger and several books that focus on the photography of artist Bill Brandt, British educator Nigel Warburton has concentrated much of his writing efforts on aiding college students in grappling with theoretical rather than visual complexities. He has authored several books that, while written to provide college students an introduction to the work of the world's major philosophers, have also been praised by critics as excellent resources for more general readers. *Philosophy: The Basics* presents the topics, vocabulary, and thinkers that figure most prominently in the study of philosophy, and its author was praised by *Philosopher* reviewer Ashley Frank for his ability to present challenging material "with a remarkable lucidity, enhanced by exemplary presentation of arguments and a thoroughly engaging style." Noting that Warburton encourages readers toward independent conclusions in such areas as Politics, Science, God, and the concepts of Right and Wrong. Individual philosophers from Aristotle and Rene Descartes to Sjoren Kierkegaard and Jean-Paul Sartre are represented in *Philosophy: The Classics,* which includes excerpts, critical summaries, and brief backgrounds on the twenty philosophers included, while *Thinking from A to Z* is a dictionary of key terms used in the discussion of philosophic concepts, and includes definitions of such things as informal fallacies, circular and other types of arguments, paradoxes, and Ockham's Razor.

While *Philosophy: The Classics* allows readers to follow the development of intellectual thought up to the present, *Philosophy: Basic Readings* focuses primarily on contemporary works that present new views of the concepts that have occupied philosophers for centuries, god, the meaning of existence, morality, and the imperatives of human society among them. In its organization, it serves as an effective companion volume to the third edition of *Philosophy: The Basics.* Writing in the *Times Educational Supplement,* Julian Baggini noted that while Warburton avoids organizing his text around the four classic philosophical centers—metaphysics, logic, epistemology, and language—these "elements . . . are not so much missing as concealed—lurking in the background of much of the text. Warburton has chosen not to put the spotlight on them, perhaps," Baggini supposed, "so as not to frighten the reader." Noting the difficulties inherent in compiling a collection of representative readings for beginning philosophy students, the critic added that *Philosophy: Basic Readings* is of such quality that it is "surely sufficient to silence the doubters who continue to believe philosophy cannot be popularised without being deformed." Warburton's "well-edited" book, Baggini added, "can be recommended without caveat or qualification."

BIOGRAPHICAL AND CRITICAL SOURCES:

BOOKS

New British Philosophy, Routledge (London, England), 2002.

PERIODICALS

American Reference Book Annual, 1998, John P. Stierman, review of *Thinking from A to Z,* p. 584.

Choice, January, 1993, P. K. Moser, review of *Philosophy: The Basics,* p. 813.

Contemporary Review, June, 1999, review of *Philosophy: The Classics,* p. 335.

Library Journal, February 15, 2000, David Bryant, review of *Brandt: The Photography of Bill Brandt,* p. 154; March 15, 2003, David A. Berona, review of *The Art Question,* p. 81.

Philosophy in Review, December, 2000, Brian Richardson, review of *Philosophy: Basic Readings,* pp. 446-447.

Times Educational Supplement, June 18, 1999, Julian Baggini, review of *Philosophy: Basic Readings,* p. 12.

Times Literary Supplement, April 18, 1997, A. C. Grayling, review of *Philosophy: The Basics,* pp. 10-11.

ONLINE

Open University Web site, http://www.open.ac.uk/ (April 15, 2004), "Nigel Warburton."
Philosopher Online, http://www.atschool.eduweb.co. uk/cite/staff/philosopher/ (October 13, 2003), Ashley Frank, review of *Philosophy: The Basics.**

* * *

WARNER, Elizabeth (Ann) 1940-

PERSONAL: Born 1940. *Education:* M.A., Ph.D.

ADDRESSES: Office—c/o University of Durham School of Modern Languages, Elvet Riverside, New Elvet, Durham DH1 3JT, England.

CAREER: University of Durham, professor of Russian, head of Department of Slavonic Studies, director of Ustinov Institute for the Study of Central and Eastern Europe, emerita professor of Russian.

AWARDS, HONORS: Sir James Knott Fellowship, University of Durham Department of Russian, 1995.

WRITINGS:

The Russian Folk Theatre ("Slavistic Printings and Reprintings" series, number 104), Mouton (The Hague, Netherlands), 1977.
Heroes, Monsters and Other Worlds from Russian Mythology, illustrated by Alexander Koshkin (part of "Schocken World Mythology" series), Schocken Books (New York, NY), 1985.
(With Evgenii S. Kustovskii) *Russian Traditional Folk Song* (with sound recording), Hull University Press (Hull, England), 1990.
Russian Myths (part of "The Legendary Past" series), University of Texas Press (Austin, TX), 2002.

SIDELIGHTS: A longtime professor of Russian at England's Durham University, Elizabeth Warner is the author of many scholarly articles as well as four books. Her first book deals with the Russian folk theater. In her second she turns to the subject of Russian folk music. *Russian Traditional Folk Song* is divided into three parts and includes a cassette sound recording. The book has two essays, the first "Some Distinguishing Musical Features of Russian Folk Song," written by Warner's coauthor, the Russian ethnomusicologist Evgennii S. Kustovskii, and the second, "The Russian Folk Song and Village Life," written by Warner. A third section of the book contains the text of the twenty-seven songs in the sound recording, transcribed in Russian by Kustovskii and translated, with commentaries, by Warner. The songs are divided into two main categories—ritual songs and nonritual songs—and then arranged by genre, such as *Calendar Songs, Wedding Songs and Laments,* and *Keening.*

Margarita Mazo, in a review of the book for *Ethnomusicology,* pointed out the absence of a discussion and examples of Russian epic songs. Nor are folksongs that have been created since the eighteenth century included in the work. About this omission, Mazo commented, "I still think that the notion that Russian folksong in its wholeness can be presented through old village songs exclusively is symptomatic of a negative attitude towards processes in real life." Still, Mazo praised the work as "a much awaited and welcome endeavor" and described Kustovskii's selection of songs for the recording as "a parade of gems." In a review for *Choice,* M. Forry commented that musicology specialists "will be disappointed with the lack of musical detail and sociohistorical context" and noted that the sound recording was the book's strongest feature. Mazo found Warner's "choice of topics and research for discussion . . . very effective" and the book "a credible source of ethnographic information in an area where so little is available for those who do not speak the language." Mazo also remarked that the cassette is "simply indispensable for anyone interested in Russian culture."

Warner's third book is *Heroes, Monsters and Other Worlds from Russian Mythology.* Illustrated in black and white and color by Alexander Koshkin, the book contains peasant stories of supernatural encounters (*bylichkas*), tales of wonder (*skazkas*), and accounts of ancient heroes (*bylinas*). It includes tales of the witch Baba Yaga, Prince Ivan, the Firebird, Koshchei the Deathless, Vasilisa, and many more, from the traditional Afanas'ev and Potebnya collections, among others. Warner has also included a discussion of the historical and social background within which these tales developed, from Pagan times. She has added an appendix with the origins of ancient symbols and their relation to the Russian alphabet.

Libby K. White, in a review of *Heroes, Monsters and Other Worlds* for *School Library Journal,* called it "memorable" and described the illustrations as "exquisite," "intelligent," and "witty." However, she thought the dense text made for "a monotonous, uninviting appearance." Denise A. Anton, also reviewing the book for *School Library Journal,* found the stories "well-researched" and the drawings "luxurious in eerie detail." Michael Dirda, in a review for *Book World,* praised the illustrations, saying they "dazzle with their animal vitality." He said the book is "Very Russian yes, but universal too." Hazel Rochman, of *Booklist,* called the book "an excellent resource" for those studying Russian history and culture.

Warner's 2002 book is *Russian Myths,* which explores the ancient, pre-Christian Russian beliefs in gods and goddesses of the natural world, witchcraft, and the cult of the dead, some of which have survived into modern times. She uses narratives, legends, songs, folk religion, and folktales—what the *University of Texas Press* called "a rich variety of sources"—to place Russian myths into the context of world mythology. Although Katherine Kaigler-Koenig, writing in *Library Journal,* wrote that she thought a glossary would have helped readers keep track of the many Russian terms, she found the book "invaluable to understanding the primary sources."

BIOGRAPHICAL AND CRITICAL SOURCES:

PERIODICALS

Booklist, May 15, 1996, Hazel Rochman, review of *Heroes, Monsters and Other Worlds from Russian Mythology,* p. 1581.

Book World (*Washington Post*), January 12, 1986, Michael Dirda, "Of Time Travel, Poetry, Cossacks, and Boats," p. 8.

Choice, April, 1991, M. Forry, review of *Russian Traditional Folk Song,* p. 1321.

Ethnomusicology, fall, 1992, Margarita Mazo, review of *Russian Traditional Folk Song,* pp. 429-432.

Folklore, December, 2003, W. F. Ryan, review of *Russian Myths,* p. 440.

Library Journal, October 1, 2002, Katherine Kaigler-Koenig, review of *Russian Myths,* p. 106.

School Library Journal, September, 1986, Denise A. Anton, review of *Heroes, Monsters and Other Worlds from Russian Mythology,* p. 147; May, 1996, Libby K. White, review of *Heroes, Monsters and Other Worlds from Russian Mythology,* p. 144.

ONLINE

University of Durham Web site, http://www.dur.ac.uk/ (September 14, 2003), "Department of Russian, Research Report 1995"; (July 13, 1998), "The Ustinov Route to Opportunities in Central and Eastern Europe"; (September 14, 2003), "Professors Emeriti."*

* * *

WATSON, Sterling

PERSONAL: Male. *Education:* University of Florida, M.A.

ADDRESSES: Office—Eckerd College, 4200 54th Ave. South, St. Petersburg, FL 33711.

CAREER: Eckerd College, St. Petersburg, FL, professor of literature and creative writing, director of writing workshop. Taught English and fiction writing at Raiford Prison, Raiford, FL.

AWARDS, HONORS: Four Florida Arts Council grants.

WRITINGS:

Weep No More, My Brother, Morrow (New York, NY), 1978.

The Calling, Peachtree Publishers (Atlanta, GA), 1986.

Blind Tongues, Dell Publishing (New York, NY), 1989.

Deadly Sweet, Pocket Books (New York, NY), 1994.

Sweet Dream Baby, Sourcebooks Landmark (Napierville, IL), 2002.

Author, with Dennis Lehane, of *Bad Blood* (screenplay). Former fiction editor, *Florida Quarterly.*

SIDELIGHTS: Sterling Watson has taught creative writing at the university level and to prisoners incarcerated in north Florida. The facility at Raiford is also the setting for his debut novel, *Weep No More, My Brother,* in which an English professor volunteers to teach inmates in hopes of finding a way to avenge his older brother. The man who killed him is now serving time at Raiford, and the teacher makes a deal with two other inmates who can assist him, but at a terrible cost.

Bruce Allen critiqued the novel in *Sewanee Review,* commenting on what he saw as problems in this first novel, but added that Watson "handles his demanding past/present structure skillfully and writes good graphic prose."

A *Publishers Weekly* reviewer called the story "taut, hard, imaginative . . . a portrait of prison and of a man who willfully becomes enmeshed in its life and its psychology."

In *The Calling,* young Blackford "Toad" Turlow leaves the family farm to work in a convenience store and writes in his cheap rented room. He then moves on to attend college and study under Eldon Odom, a famous Southern novelist. The story is one of the writing class and the students who are changed by their relationship to their instructor. They are not all young and innocent like Toad. They include a Vietnam veteran, an acne-scarred bodybuilder, a salesman of sex toys, and a waitress Odom draws into a relationship. Toad eventually finds Odom's self-destructive lifestyle, rife with booze, drugs, and aberrant sexual behavior, so repugnant that he returns to the farm and his sweetheart.

A *Publishers Weekly* contributor wrote that Watson "deftly fuses sardonic wit and graphic realism to portray Toad's growing maturity and his depraved idol's downfall."

Art Gardner reviewed *The Calling* for *West Coast Review of Books,* saying that Watson "has a true ability to establish a mood or an attitude with a few words or lines of dialogue. Here he is at his best."

A *Kirkus Reviews* critic called *Blind Tongues* "a fine, affecting story about a strong woman who learns to make choices the hard way: with her soft heart." In

Watson's third novel, set in 1973, his heroine, Merelene Durham, struggles in a small Florida town, where she raises her two sons—Bull, who is serving in Vietnam, and Roland, a young man brain-damaged since early childhood. Merelene was abandoned by her husband, Mayfield, years earlier and was befriended by Enos Sawyer, a lawyer from a prominent family who returned scarred and disfigured from World War II. Enos wants to marry Merelene and help her retain custody of her son when the state threatens to place him in a closed facility, but Merelene finds herself torn when her husband suddenly reappears after sixteen years, now wealthy and successful, but dying and remorseful.

As the story continues to unfold, it is revealed that the reason Mayfield had originally come to Swinford was that it was all Enos could talk about when they served together during the war—Enos as a pilot and Mayfield as a mechanic. The accident that so damaged Enos was blamed on Mayfield, who was then assigned to dig corpses out of the mud. When the war ended, he hoped to find peace in the small Southern town he had heard so much about. He wooed and married the beautiful young girl the somewhat reclusive Enos had always loved from afar and started a family. Mayfield abandoned them, unable to cope with his son's affliction and still suffering from his humiliation during the war.

In a *Los Angeles Times Book Review,* Stewart Lindh called *Blind Tongues* "remarkable" and added that "what is apparent in the Southern novel is a wondrous ceiling—of history, of legend, of event, transforming the South itself into an extended family whose dark secrets are known only to its members."

"It is not the plot but the poetry of Sterling Watson's prose and the depth of his attention to human connectedness that keep you reading *Blind Tongues,*" wrote Judith Paterson in *Washington Post Book World.*

Library Journal's Rex E. Klett wrote that Watson's *Deadly Sweet* "contains all the elements of a good historical mystery without recreating a distant past." In Watson's fourth novel, former football player and attorney, and now a boat salesman, Eddie Priest is approached by beautiful Corey Darrow, whose knowledge of an agribusiness scam has put her life in jeopardy. Eddie dismisses her fears, but Corey is found dead the next day. Her equally lovely sister, Sawnie, entreats Eddie to assist her in finding the killer. Guilty because of his refusal to believe Corey, he agrees to help Sawnie, who has political aspirations and motives of her own.

A *Publishers Weekly* reviewer called *Deadly Sweet* "a stunning, intricate bit of Florida noir. . . . It's hair-raising fun to watch the colorful characters work their own agendas."

In a *Booklist* review, Wes Lukowsky remarked that if Watson "continues to produce work of this quality, he'll soon be the standard with which others are compared."

A *Kirkus Reviews* contributor wrote that *Sweet Dream Baby* has "all the elements of a classic southern horror tale." It is a coming-of-age-story set in the 1950s South. Twelve-year-old Travis leaves Omaha, Nebraska to spend the summer with his grandparents in Widow Rock, Florida while his mother recovers from a nervous breakdown. There he finds a soul mate in his wild sixteen-year-old Aunt Delia, a beauty who is desired by all the boys in town. Delia shares her secrets with Travis, introduces him to rock 'n' roll, and takes him cruising in her Chevy.

Annette Clifford reviewed the novel for *Florida Today Online,* writing that Travis, "innocent upon his arrival, is thrust into the fires of incestuous desire, murderous rage, and rank hypocrisy. His transformation from passive child to man of action is brutal."

A *Publishers Weekly* contributor felt that Watson "portrays the rich relationship between Travis and Delia with convincing psychological detail" and added that "he proves himself a first-rate storyteller."

BIOGRAPHICAL AND CRITICAL SOURCES:

PERIODICALS

Booklist, September 15, 1994, Wes Lukowsky, review of *Deadly Sweet,* p. 117; October 1, 2002, Meredith Parets, review of *Sweet Dream Baby,* p. 302.

Kirkus Reviews, February 15, 1986, review of *The Calling,* p. 250; December 15, 1988, review of *Blind Tongues,* pp. 1771-1772; July 15, 1994, review of *Deadly Sweet,* p. 947; August 1, 2002, review of *Sweet Dream Baby,* p. 1074.

Library Journal, April 1, 1978, Henri C. Veit, review of *Weep No More, My Brother,* p. 779; February 1, 1989, Thomas L. Kilpatrick, review of *Blind Tongues,* p. 84; September 1, 1994, Rex E. Klett, review of *Deadly Sweet,* p. 219.

Los Angeles Times Book Review, Stewart Lindh, review of *Blind Tongues,* p. 13.

Publishers Weekly, April 10, 1978, review of *Weep No More, My Brother,* p. 67; February 28, 1986, review of *The Calling,* p. 114; July 25, 1994, review of *Deadly Sweet,* p. 36; September 30, 2002, review of *Sweet Dream Baby,* p. 45.

Sewanee Review, fall, 1978, Bruce Allen, review of *Weep No More, My Brother,* pp. 609-617.

Washington Post Book World, February 5, 1989, Judith Paterson, review of *Blind Tongues,* p. 6.

West Coast Review of Books, Volume 1, issue 1, 1986, Art Gardner, review of *The Calling,* p. 23.

ONLINE

Florida Today Online, http://www.floridatoday.com/ (October 16, 2002), Annette Clifford, review of *Sweet Dream Baby.**

*   *   *

WEIGLEY, Russell F(rank) 1930-2004

OBITUARY NOTICE—See index for *CA* sketch: Born July 2, 1930, in Reading, PA; died of a heart attack March 3, 2004, in Philadelphia, PA. Educator and author. Weigley was an award-winning author of military history books and a professor emeritus at Temple University. After earning his bachelor's at Albright College in 1952, he completed a master's and doctorate in history at the University of Pennsylvania in 1953 and 1956 respectively. Weigley, who was inspired to study American history by a childhood visit to the Gettysburg battlefield, then embarked on a teaching career, first at the University of Pennsylvania, where he taught from 1956 to 1958, then at the Drexel Institute of Technology in Philadelphia. In 1962, he joined the Temple University faculty as an associate professor, rising to the position of distinguished university professor of history in 1985, and retiring as professor emeritus in 1998. Although he never glorified war in any way, Weigley was fascinated by military history, penning several award winning books including *Eisenhower's Lieutenants: The Campaign of France and Germany, 1944-1945* (1981), which won the Atheneum of Philadelphia Special Award and was nominated for an American Book Award, *The Age of Battles: The Quest for Decisive Warfare from Breitenfeld to Waterloo* (1991), which won the Samuel Eliot Morison Award from the American Military Institute and the Outstanding Book Award for non-American history from the Society for Military History, and *A Great Civil War: A Military and Political History, 1861-1865* (2000), which received the prestigious Lincoln Prize. Weigley also earned critical praise for such books as *History of the United States Army* (1967; enlarged edition, 1984) and *The American Way of War: A History of American Military Strategy and Policy* (1973). A former president of the American Military Institute, Weigley was also a member of many other history organizations, such as the Organization of American Historians, the Society of Military History, the Society of American Historians, and the Pennsylvania Historical Association. Most recently, he had been on an advisory board to help design the National World War II Memorial in Washington, D.C.

OBITUARIES AND OTHER SOURCES:

PERIODICALS

Los Angeles Times, March 11, 2004, p. B13.
New York Times, March 12, 2004, p. C12.
Washington Post, March 10, 2004, p. B6.

*   *   *

WEINTRAUB, Karl Joachim 1924-2004

OBITUARY NOTICE—See index for *CA* sketch: Born December 31, 1924, in Darmstadt, Germany; died of a brain tumor March 25, 2004, in Chicago, IL. Educator and author. A celebrated professor at the University of Chicago, Weintraub was famous for his highly popular course on Western civilization. The son of a Jewish father and Christian mother, he was forced to hide in

Holland when the Nazis came to power in Germany. With the aid of a Quaker organization, he made his way to the United States, where he became a student at the University of Chicago. There, he attended undergraduate and graduate school, completing his Ph.D. in 1957. Weintraub was destined to make the university his home, joining the faculty in 1955 and becoming Thomas E. Donnelly Professor of History in 1970. Also serving as dean of humanities from 1973 to 1983, he retired as professor emeritus in 2001. By all counts a remarkable teacher, Weintraub was so popular at the university that students would sleep on the campus's quadrangle the night before registration in order to sign up for his course. Also recognized by the university for his teaching skills, he was honored on numerous occasions, receiving the Quantrell Award for Excellence in Undergraduate Teaching from the University of Chicago in 1960 and again in 1986, the E. Harris Harbison Award for Distinguished Teaching from the Danforth Foundation in 1967, the Award for Distinguished Contributions to Undergraduate Teaching from the Amoco Foundation in 1995, and the Norman Maclean Alumni Award in 2001. Even in retirement, Weintraub continued to teach until 2002, when ill health prevented him from going to class. He did this without pay as a way of protesting changing teaching practices at the university with which he did not agree. Weintraub was the author of two books, *Visions of Culture* (1966) and *The Value of the Individual: Self and Circumstance in Autobiography* (1978).

OBITUARIES AND OTHER SOURCES:

PERIODICALS

Chicago Tribune, March 27, 2004, Section 2, p. 11.
St. Louis Post-Dispatch, March 28, 2004, p. C11.

ONLINE

University of Chicago News Office, http://www-news. uchicago.edu/ (March 26, 2004).

*   *   *

WEISSMAN, Karen

PERSONAL: Born in United States; married. *Education:* Princeton University, Ph.D. *Religion:* Jewish.

ADDRESSES: Home—Greenwich Village, New York, NY. *Agent*—c/o Author Mail, Red Wheel/Weiser, P.O. Box 612, York Beach, ME 03910-0612. *E-mail*—info@spiritualchicks.com

CAREER: Research scientist; engineering consultant; vice president of corporate development; certified Concept-Therapy instructor; author.

WRITINGS:

(With Tami Coyne) *The Spiritual Chicks Question Everything: Learn to Risk, Release, and Soar,* Red Wheel/Weiser, (York Beach, ME), 2002.

SIDELIGHTS: Karen Weissman began her career as an engineer and research scientist studying noise and vibration concerns. She eventually became an engineering consultant, then a vice president of corporate development for a technology startup company. However, delving into metaphysics and spirituality changed all that. After meeting Tami Coyne, coauthor of her book, *The Spiritual Chicks Question Everything: Learn to Risk, Release, and Soar,* and discovering they had similar spiritual philosophies, the two women began writing articles for a webzine on metaphysics and spirituality, which culminated in their book. Weissman left her engineering career and now teaches Concept Therapy seminars.

Weismann's educational path led her to the study of physical phenomenon. Her career path led her to investigate vibration and noise problems in consumer products and during space shuttle launches. Just before completing her doctorate, however, she became ill with mononucleosis, then developed an infection that put her in hospital. Her illnesses put her on a path that ultimately led to the study of metaphysics and spirituality and her new career as a Concept Therapy instructor.

After becoming ill, Weismann took a serious look at her life and her philosophies. A writer for *Princeton Alumni Weekly* said Weismann—a self-confessed health food snob at the time—realized she was focusing on "not getting sick rather than maintaining a healthy diet and lifestyle." Weismann therefore decided to pay less attention to what she put into her body and more to what she enjoyed—like interests and friends. She also decided to redirect her beliefs and energy.

The more she studied the physical phenomenon, the more convinced she became that the same energy drives everything in the universe. So, in 1994, she enrolled in a "Concept Therapy," course in Brooklyn, New York, investigating the underlying similarity between spirituality and science. In that large New York metropolis, at one of those very small seminars, she met Coyne. The two women discovered not only did they have a similar interest in metaphysics, they lived just a block from each other in Greenwich Village. They also discovered during long sidewalk conversations that they had similar philosophies to life and the concept of spirituality.

As their friendship developed, so did their future. In 1999 they began collaborating on articles for a webzine site and, being self-confirmed spiritual women, called themselves "The Spiritual Chicks." After the Web site's demise, the women collected their articles and sent them to Red Wheel as a book proposal. The proposal was accepted, but more material was necessary to make their work book length. In the process of writing additional essays and articles, they started their own Web site, *SpiritualChicks.com,* to field test their new material. The book was written with the deliberate intent of relating to the real-life experiences of its audience.

While the women come from entirely different backgrounds and admit to having entirely different personalities—Weismann is left-brained and analytical; Coyne is right-brained and passionate and a French literature major—they declare their writing styles are similar and collaboration has been a positive experience.

The basis of *The Spiritual Chicks Question Everything* is the "One Life Principle," the idea that a single universal power manifests in all things and holds the universe together at the same time. Coyne and Weismann formatted their book in a question-and-answer style, with short essays on real-life experiences wherever they felt it necessary to bring an answer to life. Those essays may be hard hitting, or humorous, just as real-life experiences are. Many answers, however, have no corresponding essay, the reason being—according to the authors—that readers need the opportunity to apply their own life experiences rather than just reading those of the authors. "Otherwise it would just read like the 'Tami and Karen show!'" the authors commented on an Internet interview for *girlposse.com.*

In her review in *Awareness Magazine,* Maryel McKinley described their work as "a refreshing, if not mind-blowing, book that will open your heart and help you dispose of junk thoughts one might be holding onto unnecessarily." Leslie Gilbert Elman, in *Healing Retreats and Spas Magazine,* called the book "savvy, affirming and enjoyable," and Trixie for *girlposse.com* called it "Sassy, saucy and completely insightful." Jan Suzukawa in *Science of Mind* magazine, said this is a "delightful and irreverent book" that counsels its readers to "(1) question everything; (2) condemn nothing; (3) and then, align ourselves with what we want."

In their online interview with *girlposse.com,* the authors wrote: "Spirituality is such a loaded word. Many people think it's just for goodie-goodies, the really desperate, or people who otherwise don't have a life. We wrote this book to dispel the myth that we have to be something other than who we already are to be spiritual. This book is for everyone, because everyone is already spiritual. We hope that when people read it they recognize this aspect in themselves."

BIOGRAPHICAL AND CRITICAL SOURCES:

PERIODICALS

Healing Retreats and Spas Magazine, November-December, 2002, review of *The Spiritual Chicks Question Everything: Learn to Risk, Release, and Soar.*
Publishers Weekly, September 30, 2002, review of *The Spiritual Chicks Question Everything,* p. 66.
Science of Mind Magazine, February, 2003, Jan Suzukawa, review of *The Spiritual Chicks Question Everything.*

ONLINE

girlposse.com, http://www.girlposse.com/ (May 8, 2003), Trixie, review of "A Spiritual Chick Questions Everything," (December 18, 2002).
Spiritualchicks.com, http://www.spiritualchicks.com/ (May 8, 2003), detailed biographies.*

*   *   *

WELLISCH, Hans H(anan) 1920-2004

OBITUARY NOTICE—See index for *CA* sketch: Born April 25, 1920, in Vienna, Austria; died of complications from diabetes February 6, 2004, in Rockville, WA. Librarian, educator, and author. Wellisch was widely regarded as an authority on indexing methods and the Universal Decimal Classification system. As a Jewish youth in Vienna, he was sent to the Dachau concentration camp by the Nazis, but managed to be released when he obtained a visa from Sweden. From 1939 to 1949, he remained in that country, where he received training in farming and became a library assistant, carpenter, and newsletter editor. With the founding of Israel, Wellisch and his wife moved to the new country, and he joined the Israeli Army's Signal Corps as a librarian. It was here that Wellisch first learned the Universal Decimal Classification system, a method for indexing technical and scientific publications. A study grant from the United Nations permitted Wellisch to visit the University of Maryland in 1967; two years later, the university invited him to join the School of Library Science as a visiting lecturer. He remained in Maryland for the rest of his career. Here he attended graduate school, earning an M.L.S. in 1972 and a Ph.D. in 1975, and was named a Distinguished Scholar by the division of human and community resources in 1983, before becoming a full professor in 1987; he retired the next year. Wellisch was a prolific writer and researcher, with eighteen books and pamphlets to his name. His most acclaimed work is *Indexing from A to Z* (1991; revised edition, 1995), which is widely regarded as a classic in the field. Among his many other works are *The Conversion of Scripts: Its Nature, History, and Utilization* (1978), *Indexing and Abstracting, 1977-1981: An International Bibliography* (1984), and *Guidelines for Alphabetical Arrangement of Letters and Sorting of Numerals and Other Symbols* (1999).

OBITUARIES AND OTHER SOURCES:

PERIODICALS

Washington Post, February 12, 2004, p. B6.

ONLINE

College of Information Science, http://www.clis.umd.edu/ (February 13, 2004).

*   *   *

WELLS, Simon 1961-

PERSONAL: Born 1961.

ADDRESSES: Office—Enteraction TV, 8 Park Place, Lawn Lane, Vauxhall, London, SW8 1UD England.

CAREER: Director. Films include *An American Tail: Fievel Goes West,* Universal City Studios, 1991; *We're Back!: A Dinosaur's Story,* Universal City Studios, 1993; *Balto,* Universal City Studios, 1995; *The Prince of Egypt,* Dreamworks SKG, 1998; *The Time Machine,* DreamWorks Pictures, 2002. WCRS, London, England, former board member; Enteraction TV, London, England, head of branded programming division, 2002—.

WRITINGS:

(With Ali Catterall) *Your Face Here: British Cult Movies since the Sixties,* Fourth Estate (London, England), 2001.

SIDELIGHTS: Simon Wells, the great-grandson of famous author H. G. Wells, worked in the film industry for many years before writing his first book, *Your Face Here: British Cult Movies since the Sixties.* After directing several animated features, Wells made his live-action directing debut with a film adaptation of his great-grandfather's novel *The Time Machine* in 2002. This was not Wells's first experience with time-traveling motion pictures: he was inspired to make movies after seeing the first *Back to the Future* film, and then he actually worked on the sequels, *Back to the Future Part II* and *Back to the Future Part III.*

Your Face Here is a book for people who are already devotees of the cult classics it covers, including, among others, *A Hard Day's Night, A Clockwork Orange,* and *Trainspotting.* Although the book does include plot summaries of the movies, the bulk of it is "an enjoyable and largely uncritical homage to the selling power of the cult movie and patriotic spirit," Michael Caines remarked in the *Times Literary Supplement.* Wells and his coauthor, Ali Catterall, made pilgrimages to the places where the movies were shot and collected anecdotes about the filming process from the actors and others who were involved. Wells and Catterall "clearly loved doing this book," a reviewer noted in the *Guardian.* "It shows on every page."

BIOGRAPHICAL AND CRITICAL SOURCES:

BOOKS

Singer, Michael, *Michael Singer's Film Directors,* Lone Eagle Publishing (Los Angeles, CA), 1992.

Wallflower Critical Guide to Contemporary North American Directors, Wallflower Press (London, England), 2000.

PERIODICALS

Campaign, June 7, 2002, "Simon Wells Joins Enteraction TV," p. 3.

Daily Variety, March 8, 2002, Todd McCarthy, review of *The Time Machine,* pp. 12-13.

Esquire, March, 2002, interview with Simon Wells, p. 64.

Film Journal International, April, 2002, Doris Toumarkine, review of *The Time Machine,* pp. 32-33.

Guardian, September 28, 2002, review of *Your Face Here: British Cult Movies since the Sixties.*

Hollywood Reporter, March 8, 2002, Kirk Honeycutt, review of *The Time Machine,* pp. 12-13.

M2 Best Books, March 15, 2002, review of *The Time Machine.*

Nation, January 11, 1999, Stuart Klawans, review of *The Prince of Egypt,* p. 35; April 1, 2002, Stuart Klawans, review of *The Time Machine,* p. 44.

New Media Age, June 6, 2002, "Enteraction TV Opens Branded Content Arm," p. 12.

New York Times, November 22, 1991, Stephen Holden, review of *An American Tail: Fievel Goes West,* pp. B10, C21; April 5, 1996, review of *Balto,* pp. B14, D17; December 18, 1998, Janet Maslin, review of *The Prince of Egypt,* p. E17; March 3, 2002, Lewis Beale, review of *The Time Machine,* p. AR18; March 8, 2002, Elvis Mitchell, review of *The Time Machine,* pp. B14, E12; March 15, 2002, Peter M. Nichols, review of *The Time Machine,* pp. B10, E8.

Parabola, spring, 1999, Shanti Fader, review of *The Prince of Egypt,* p. 135.

Premiere, March, 2002, Anna David, review of *The Time Machine,* pp. 60-62.

Sight and Sound, January, 1992, Kim Newman, review of *An American Tail: Fievel Goes West,* p. 40.

Times Literary Supplement, April 12, 2002, review of *Your Face Here,* pp. 30-31.

US Weekly, March 18, 2002, Andrew Johnston, review of *The Time Machine,* p. 69.

Variety, November 25, 1991, Joseph McBride, review of *An American Tale: Fievel Goes West,* p. 40; January 1, 1996, review of *Balto,* p. 83; December 14, 1998, Glenn Lovell, review of *The Prince of Egypt,* p. 130; March 11, 2002, Todd McCarthy, review of *The Time Machine,* pp. 31-32.

Wall Street Journal, March 8, 2002, Joe Morganstern, review of *The Time Machine,* p. W1.

ONLINE

About.com, http://www.about.com/ (September 9, 2002), "Exclusive Simon Wells Interview."

Canoe, http://www.canoe.ca/ (May 11, 2001), "Director Too Ill to Finish 'Time Machine.'"

Filmforce, http://filmforce.ign.com/ (July 25, 2001), "Simon Wells Talks *Time Machine.*"

IFilm, http://www.ifilm.com/ (September 9, 2002).

Internet Movie Database, http://www.imdb.com/ (December 10, 2002).

Northern Rivers Echo (Lismore, New South Wales, Australia), http://www.echonews.com/ (September 9, 2002), Evelyn Gough, review of *The Time Machine.**

* * *

WIDDECOMBE, Ann (Noreen) 1947-

PERSONAL: Born October 4, 1947 in Bath, Somerset, England; daughter of James Murray (CB/OBE, Head of Naval Supplies and Transport, Ministry of Defense) and Rita Noreen (Plummer) Widdecombe. *Education:* Birmingham University, B.A. (honors Latin), Oxford University, B.A. (honors in Politics, Philosophy, and Economics), Lady Margaret Hall, M.A., 1976. *Politics:* Conservative. *Religion:* Catholic. *Hobbies and other interests:* Reading, researching Charles II's escape.

ADDRESSES: Home—Kloof Cottage, Sutton Valence, Maidstone, Kent, England. *Office*—House of Commons, London, SW1A 0AA, England.

CAREER: British politician. Unilever, marketing department, 1973-75; London University, senior administrator, 1975-87; member of parliament for Maidstone (later Maidstone and The Weald), 1987—; under secretary of State Department of Employment, 1993; minister of State Department of Employment, 1994; minister of State Home Office, 1995; member of Standards and Privileges Committee of the House of Commons, 1997; Shadow Health Secretary, 1998; Shadow Home Secretary, 1999.

WRITINGS:

Layman's Guide to Defence, 1984.
Inspired and Outspoken, 1999.

The Clematis Tree, Weidenfeld and Nicholson (London, England), 2000.

Right From the Beginning, Politico's Publishing Limited (London, England), 2001.

An Act of Treachery Weidenfeld and Nicolson (London, England), 2003.

ADAPTATIONS: The Clematis Tree was adapted for audiocassette, Chivers Audio Books (London, England), 2001; *An Act of Treachery* was adapted for audiocassette, BBC Audiobooks America.

WORK IN PROGRESS: A third novel.

SIDELIGHTS: Ann Widdecombe is a member of parliament representing a constituency in Kent, is also a former Conservative minister, and one of several British politicians to turn novelist in recent years. She has published two novels that explore issues of morality, *The Clematis Tree* and *An Act of Treachery.* Widdecombe's books have been closely examined for political import, but at the time of her first novel's release she told *Books Magazine* that she was not attempting to press her political agenda. She also explained that she has always loved writing. After winning essay prizes at school, she wrote a novel, now lost, during her college years.

The Clematis Tree chronicles how a couple's rocky marriage is further challenged when their son is brain-damaged after being run over by a car. While Claire and Mark Wellings struggle with caring for the boy at home, his aunt, a member of parliament, is working on a euthanasia bill. Reviews of the novel concentrated on the author's political reputation and on the book's literary merits. In *Guardian Unlimited Books* Stephen Moss sorted through several reviews and noted "the most pointedly (and personal) knocking review came from Miss Widdecombe's former Conservative colleague, Edwina Currie," who is also a novelist. He quoted Curried as calling the style "almost dottily old-fashioned." But Moss explained that while "The cynic in me expected Ann Widdecombe's debut novel . . . to be universally panned. . . . others were ready to take the novel seriously."

Reviews included criticism on stylistic matters and commendations for tackling a complex theme. In *New Statesman,* Rowan Pelling called the book a "a thinly disguised moral tract" in which "the hallmark of Widdecombe's writing is the neat correlation of cause and effect. . . . The author has precious little time for cruel Fate; tragedy in her fiction is a direct result of breaching middle-class mores." The *Spectator*'s D. J. Taylor judged that "this novel would not have been published did its author not double up as shadow home secretary." Taylor noted, however, "on the plus side, it is a well-meaning book about a serious subject . . . written with great sympathy and compassion." Writing for the *Times Literary Supplement,* Rupert Shortt also felt that the author "should be saluted for raising an important moral conundrum," while remarking that the novel had "the breezy style and two-dimensional characters of airport fiction, but scarcely a trace of either sex or shopping."

Widdecombe's next novel, *An Act of Treachery,* is primarily set in World War II's German occupation of France. The protagonist is Catherine Dessin, a schoolgirl who lives in Paris. As a teenager, she falls in love with a married German officer, Klaus, who is also much older and has children. When she is eighteen they have an affair, despite her family's disapproval and conflict with her Catholic upbringing. Catherine sees how Klaus struggles to do good at the same time that he cannot overtly turn against the Nazi regime. Klaus is killed in the war, leaving Catherine pregnant with his child.

A *Kirkus Reviews* writer described the book as "unconvincing" and "more queasy-making than heart-rending; Catherine is worse than just a fool for love." In a review for the *Times Literary Supplement,* Sarah Curtis noted that Widdecombe's "plot has ingenious twists which surprise the reader and her prose has pace." However, she concluded, "Both characters seem constructed to illustrate moral conflicts. At the end it is suggested that all love is an act of treachery because it involves submersion of the self, a dubious assertion which it would take a more subtle book than this to uphold." In *Reformer* magazine, Lindsay Moore called the novel "commendable" and remarked that Widdecombe "handles her chosen subject with a skill and insight that many . . . would not immediately consider her capable of, given her parliamentary reputation."

BIOGRAPHICAL AND CRITICAL SOURCES:

PERIODICALS

Books Magazine, spring, 2000, Liz Thomson, "Widdecombe Set Fair," p. 16.

Kirkus Reviews, November 15, 2002, review of *An Act of Treachery,* p. 1655.
New Statesman, May 1, 2000, Rowan Pelling, "Back to Basics," p. 54.
Spectator April 22, 2000, D. J. Taylor, review of *The Clematis Tree,* pp. 33-34.
Times Literary Supplement June 23, 2000, Rupert Shortt, review of *The Clematis Tree,* p. 33; July 19, 2002, Sarah Curtis, review of *An Act of Treachery,* p. 23.

ONLINE

Guardian Unlimited Books, http://books.guardian.co. uk/ (April 20, 2000), Stephen Moss, article about *The Clematis Tree.*
Reformer, http://www.trg.org.uk/reformer/2002autumn/ (Autumn, 2002), Lindsay Moore, review of *An Act of Treachery.*
Widdy Web (Ann Widdecombe Home Page), http:// political.co.uk/annwiddecombe (February 13, 2004),*

* * *

WIESEN, S. Jonathan 1968-

PERSONAL: Born June 26, 1968, in Cambridge, MA; son of David S. (a classicist and professor) and Ellen E. (Cohen) Wiesen; married Natasha P. Zaretsky, July 15, 2001; children: Daniel Zaretsky. *Education:* Attended University of Sussex, 1988-89; University of California—Berkeley, B.A. (with highest distinction), 1990; Brown University, M.A., 1991, Ph.D., 1998.

ADDRESSES: Home—506 West Pecan St., Carbondale, IL 62901. *Office*—Department of History, Southern Illinois University, Carbondale, IL 62901; fax: 618-453-5440. *E-mail*—jwiesen@siu.edu.

CAREER: Colgate University, Hamilton, NY, visiting assistant professor, 1997-98; Southern Illinois University, Carbondale, IL, assistant professor, 1998-2003, associate professor of history, 2003—. Guest teacher at Massachusetts Institute of Technology and Florida Atlantic University, 2002; conference and workshop presenter; public lecturer in the United States and Germany; guest on radio programs; media consultant on topics in German history.

MEMBER: American Historical Association, German Studies Association, Business History Conference, Working Group on Big Business and National Socialism (Germany), Working Group for the Critical History of Business and Industry (Germany), Phi Beta Kappa.

AWARDS, HONORS: Grants from German Academic Exchange Service, 1992, for Goethe Institute in Germany, and 2000; ORDA special research fellowship, 1999-2001; J. Walter Thompson research fellow, John W. Hartman Center for Sales, Advertising, and Marketing, Duke University, 2000; Hagley Museum Prize, best book in business history, 2002, for *West German Industry and the Challenge of the Nazi Past, 1945-1955.*

WRITINGS:

West German Industry and the Challenge of the Nazi Past, 1945-1955, University of North Carolina Press (Chapel Hill, NC), 2001.

Contributor to books, including *The German Chemical Industry in the Twentieth Century,* edited by John E. Lesch, Kluwer Academic Publishers (Dordrecht, Netherlands), 2000; *The Work of Memory: New Directions in the Study of German Society and Culture,* edited by Alon Confino and Peter Fritzsche, University of Illinois Press (Urbana, IL), 2002; *Consuming Germany in the Cold War: Consumption and National Identity in East and West Germany, 1949-1989,* edited by David F. Crew, Berg Publishers (New York, NY), 2003; and *Coping with the Nazi Past: West German Debates on Nazism and Generational Conflict, 1955-1975,* edited by Alan Steinweis and Philipp Gassert, Berghahn Books (New York, NY), in press. Contributor of articles and reviews to periodicals, including *Journal of Holocaust Education, Journal of Contemporary History, Dimensions: Journal of Holocaust Studies,* and *Central European History.*

WORK IN PROGRESS: The Nazi Marketplace: Public Relations and Capitalism in the Third Reich, completion expected in 2005; research on the history of public relations, fears of "the masses" in modern Europe, and historical memory.

WIKTOROWICZ, Quintan 1970-

PERSONAL: Born August 23, 1970, in Boston, MA; son of Hank Wiktorowicz and Pamela Westendorf Hill; married Debra Geraghty, June 21, 1997; children: Aidan, Nora. *Education:* Cornell University, B.A. (government), 1992, American University, Ph.D. (political science), 1998.

ADDRESSES: Office—Department of International Studies, Rhodes College, 2000 North Parkway, Memphis, TN 38112-1690. *E-mail*—Wiktorowiczq@ rhodes.edu.

CAREER: Educator. American Enterprise Institute for Public Policy Research, Washington, DC, research assistant on Nuclear and Ballistic Missile Proliferation Research Project, 1991; Shippensburg University, Shippensburg, PA, assistant professor of political science, 1998-2000; Rhodes College, Memphis, TN, assistant professor of international studies, 2001—. Visiting assistant professor of government, Dartmouth College, 2000-01. Lecturer and presenter at conferences and workshops.

AWARDS, HONORS: American Center for Oriental Studies grant to Jordan, 1996-97; Fulbright grant to Jordan, 1996-97; American Sociological Association/ National Science Foundation grant (co-recipient), 2002; Rhodes College faculty development grant, 2002, 2003; *Foreward* magazine's Book of the Year in audio book category, 2002.

WRITINGS:

The Management of Islamic Activism: Salafis, the Muslim Brotherhood, and State Power in Jordan, State University of New York Press (Albany, NY), 2001.
Global Jihad: Understanding September 11 (audiobook), In Audio (Falls Church, VA), 2002.
(Editor and contributor) *Islamic Activism: A Social Movement Theory,* Indiana University Press (Bloomington, IN), 2003.

Contributor to books, including *Everyday Experiences in the Muslim Middle East,* second edition, Indiana University Press, 2001, *In the Service of al-Qaeda:*

Radical Islamic Movements, New York University Press, 2003, and *Muslim Networks: Metaphor and Meaning,* University of North Carolina Press, 2003. Contributor of articles and reviews to periodicals, including *Mediterranean Politics, World Development, International Journal of Middle-East Studies, International Review of Social History, International Journal of Comparative Sociology, al-Jadid Magazine, Middle East Policy, Arab Studies Quarterly, Journal of Church and State,* and *Comparative Politics.*

SIDELIGHTS: Quintan Wiktorowicz is an assistant professor of international studies at Rhodes College and the author of a number of books that contribute to American readers' understanding of Middle Eastern culture and politics. In *The Management of Islamic Activism: Salafis, the Muslim Brotherhood, and State Power in Jordan,* Wiktorowicz explores the reason why Islamic activist groups endure in the Middle East. While informal networking between activist "cells" in remote areas would seem to be a preferred method of operations for such extremist groups, Wiktorowicz shows that, in Jordan, this approach has certain drawbacks. Citing the radical Salafi movement, he shows that their strength results from a traditional informal network and interpersonal ties. For the less-radical Muslim Brotherhood, however, Jordan's encouragement of a system of non-governmental organizations (NGO's) to carry on social service reforms has created what *American Journal of Sociology* contributor Nader Sohrabi characterized as "a critical site for the activity of Islamic groups and a potential locus from which delegitimating attacks may be launched" against the Jordanian government. By moderating its activities and following the rules appropriate to NGO's, the Muslim Brotherhood has actually increased its membership. Still, Wiktorowicz continues, the Jordanian government itself is not the democratic institution many in the West believe. Although it has democratized much of its policies and practices, it continues to allow a latitude of surveillance capability that, coupled with authoritarian administrative policies, serve to repress unwanted activism.

Reviewing *The Management of Islamic Activism* in the *Journal of Church and State,* Linda Adams praised Wiktorowicz's "thorough" fieldwork and research and dubbed the book "an important contribution to the study of state-civil society relations in the post-1989 political liberalization environment . . . of Jordan."

Mark Lynch also voiced appreciation in his *Middle East Journal* review, noting: "With a solid application of social movement theory, a healthy skepticism about the claims made for democracy and civil society in the Arab world, and a solid empirical base, *The Management of Islamic Activism* makes a useful contribution to the literature on Islamic movements in the Arab world." In the *American Journal of Sociology,* Sohrabi commented that Wiktorowicz' book "signals the growing maturity and theoretical sophistication of sociological investigations of politics in the Middle East."

BIOGRAPHICAL AND CRITICAL SOURCES:

PERIODICALS

American Journal of Sociology, March, 2002, Nader Sohrabi, review of *The Management of Islamic Activism: Salafis, the Muslim Brotherhood, and State Power in Jordan,* p. 1350.
Journal of Church and State, summer, 2001, Linda Adams, review of *The Management of Islamic Activism,* p. 605.
Middle East Journal, summer, 2001, Mark Lynch, review of *The Management of Islamic Activism,* p. 504.

*   *   *

WILKINS, Sally (E.D.)

PERSONAL: Female.

ADDRESSES: Agent—c/o Author Mail, Greenwood Publishing Group, Inc., 88 Post Rd. W., Westport, CT 06881.

CAREER: Freelance writer.

WRITINGS:

Deserts, Bridgestone Books (Mankato, MN), 2000.
Grasslands, Bridgestone Books (Mankato, MN), 2000.
Temperate Forests, Bridgestone Books (Mankato, MN), 2000.
Sports and Games of Medieval Cultures, Greenwood Press (Westport, CT), 2002.

Contributor to *The Louisa May Alcott Encyclopedia,* Greenwood Press (Westport, CT).

SIDELIGHTS: Sally Wilkins's book *Sports and Games of Medieval Cultures* surveys the pastimes of peoples around the world during the Middle Ages. These pastimes range from simple board games to team sports to children's outdoor play. While familiar activities like chess, tennis, and swimming are covered, Wilkins also describes such unfamiliar activities as tsoro yematatu, an African version of tick-tack-toe, and tako-no kiri-ai, an Asian game involving kite fighting. S. A. Reiss in *Choice* noted that Wilkins is careful to "trace each game's development, describe the rules of play, and explain how the necessary equipment was made." In cases where existing information is scanty, the author attempts "to stay true to the games while avoiding too much conjecture," according to Craig Shufelt in the *Reference and User Services Quarterly.*

BIOGRAPHICAL AND CRITICAL SOURCES:

PERIODICALS

Booklist, November 1, 2002, review of *Sports and Games of Medieval Cultures,* p. 542.
Choice, February, 2003, S. A. Riess, review of *Sports and Games of Medieval Cultures,* p. 1020.
Reference and User Services Quarterly, winter, 2002, Craig Shufelt, review of *Sports and Games of Medieval Cultures,* p. 177.*

*   *   *

WILLIAMSON, Marilyn L. 1927-

PERSONAL: Born September 6, 1927, in Chicago, IL; daughter of Raymond (a manufacturer) and Edith (Eisenbies) Lammert; married Robert W. Williamson, October 28, 1950 (divorced April 15, 1974); married James H. McKay, August 15, 1974; children: (first marriage) Timothy L. *Ethnicity:* "White, Anglo-Saxon Protestant." *Education:* Vassar College, B.A., 1949; University of Wisconsin—Madison, M.A., 1951; attended Duke University, 1956. *Politics:* Democrat. *Hobbies and other interests:* Gardening, boating, volunteer work.

ADDRESSES: Home—2275 Oakway, West Bloomfield, MI 48324; fax: 248-332-2206. *E-mail*—ae9109@ wayne.edu.

CAREER: Duke University, Durham, NC, instructor, 1955-56; North Carolina State University, Raleigh, NC, lecturer, 1957-58; Duke University, Durham, NC, instructor, 1958-59; North Carolina State University, Raleigh, NC, lecturer, 1961-62; Oakland University, Rochester, MI, began as assistant professor, became professor, 1965-72; Wayne State University, Detroit, MI, began as professor, became distinguished professor, 1972-2000; retired, 2000. Michigan Academy, president, 1978-79; Michigan Humanities Council, board chair, 1988-2001; Federation of State Humanities Councils, chair, 1994-2001.

MEMBER: Modern Language association of America (member of executive council, 1977-80), Renaissance Society of America, League of Women Voters of Rochester (president, 1963-65).

AWARDS, HONORS: Detroit Service Award, 1986.

WRITINGS:

(Editor) *Female Poets of Great Britain,* Wayne State University Press (Detroit, MI), 1981.
The Patriarchy of Shakespeare's Comedies, Wayne State University Press (Detroit, MI), 1986.
English Women Poets, 1640-1740, Wayne State University Press (Detroit, MI), 1990.
Shakespeare Studies: The Middle Comedies, Pegasus Press (Fairview, NC), 2003.

Contributor to *Renaissance Drama.*

WORK IN PROGRESS: Research on the tragedies of John Webster.

*   *   *

WINNER, Lauren F. 1975?-

PERSONAL: Born c. 1975, in Asheville, NC; daughter of Dennis Winner. *Education:* Columbia University, B.A., work toward Ph.D. (history of religion); Clare College, Cambridge, M.A.

ADDRESSES: Home—Lives in Charlotte, VA. *Office*—c/o Christianity Today, 465 Gundersen Drive, Carol Stream, IL 60188.

CAREER: Writer and editor. *Christianity Today,* senior writer; *Beliefnet.com,* former book review editor.

WRITINGS:

(With Randall Balmer) *Protestantism in America,* Columbia University Press (New York, NY), 2002.
Girl Meets God: On the Path to a Spiritual Life, Algonquin Books of Chapel Hill (Chapel Hill, NC), 2002.
Mudhouse Sabbath, Paraclete Press (Brewster, MA), 2002.

Contributor to periodicals, including *New York Times Book Review, Publishers Weekly,* and *Washington Post.*

SIDELIGHTS: As a teen, Lauren F. Winner so enthusiastically embraced the Orthodox Jewish faith to which she was exposed by her Reformed Jewish/lapsed Southern Baptist parents that it came as no surprise when she announced her conversion to Orthodox Judaism upon her arrival at Columbia University as a freshman. It *was* a surprise when, four years later, she announced her second conversion to evangelical Christianity. Fully embracing the Episcopalian faith while a graduate student at Cambridge University, Winner has chronicled her spiritual journey in *Girl Meets God: On the Path to a Spiritual Life.* In her book she explains: "What draws me to a religion is the beliefs, the theologies, the books, the incantations, the recipes to get to God, and I like to imagine that they work in the abstract, that they are enough, that they exist, somewhere, pure and distinct from the people who enact them."

Reviewers found much to enjoy in Winner's autobiographical excursion. As Andrea Jeyaveeran pointed out in her *Sojourners* review, one of the compelling aspects of *Girl Meets God* is Winner's "quirkiness," a characteristic Jeyaveeran maintained "shines through in anecdotes that infuse the book with much of its appeal." Related the reviewer, prior to Winner's conversion, the young woman "has an epic dream about being kidnapped by a band of mermaids and taken to live for a year under the sea. The dream culminates with her rescue by a Daniel Day-Lewis–like hero who she realizes upon waking, with absolute certainty, is Jesus." The clincher was a reading of Jan Karon's novel *At Home in Mitford* the summer of her senior year at Columbia University. In reviewing the book for the *New York Times Book Review,* Reeve Lindbergh felt much the same as Jeyaveeran, commenting that "The sheer energy of [Winner's] . . . quest, combined with her refreshing honesty and flashes of wild humor, give her story its edge."

Praising Winner's book as "learned and discerning" *Wilson Quarterly* contributor C. Michael Curtis noted that *Girl Meets God* is "neither a repudiation of Orthodox Judaism nor a celebration of Protestantism's putatively unique virtues." In the *Christian Century* Mark Oppenheimer viewed the work from two levels—as a spiritual memoir and as literature, and noted that while Winner's *Girl Meets God* succeeds on the second level, "as a spiritual memoir her book is a failure in the ways that spiritual memoirs almost have to be: communion with God, like falling in love, is almost impossible to describe convincingly to the uninitiated." Joyce Smothers had a different take on the book, describing it in her *Library Journal* review as a "sexually frank portrait of a deeply engaged faith shopper" that provides readers with a new "perspective on the ways religion relates to the lives of Gen Xers."

Winner's spiritual memoir is only one aspect of her career as a writer. A staff writer for the magazine *Christianity Today,* she has also collaborated with coauthor Randall Balmer on the volume *Protestantism in America,* part of the "Columbia Contemporary American Religions" series. The volume provides an historical overview of the growth of Protestant denominations in the New World, drawing on recent scholarship in their discussion of both evangelical and liberal Protestant theologies and how they deal with such issues as feminism, homosexuality, and other contemporary social issues. While praising the book for its coverage of Lutheranism, Calvinism, and other faiths, Richard Wightman Fox took issue with the book overall in his *Christian Century* review, questioning whether "such a thing as 'Protestantism' really exists." Drawing on the writings of such theologians as H. Richard Niebuhr, Fox noted that, for many modern theorists, "the only thing Protestants ever had in common . . . was anti-Catholicism."

BIOGRAPHICAL AND CRITICAL SOURCES:

BOOKS

Winner, Lauren F., *Girl Meets God: On the Path to a Spiritual Life,* Algonquin Books of Chapel Hill (Chapel Hill, NC), 2002.

PERIODICALS

Booklist, October 1, 2002, Ilene Cooper, review of *Girl Meets God: On the Path to a Spiritual Life,* p. 292.
Books and Culture, November-December, 2002, Betty Smartt Carter, "Twice Chosen: A Young Convert to Orthodox Judaism Converts to Christianity," p. 9.
Christian Century, October 9, 2002, Mark Oppenheimer, review of *Girl Meets God,* p. 23; October 23, 2002, Richard Wightman Fox, review of *Protestantism in America,* p. 40.
Kirkus Reviews, August 1, 2002, review of *Girl Meets God,* p. 1115.
Library Journal, August, 2002, Jan Blodgett, review of *Protestantism in America,* p. 102; November 1, 2002, Joyce Smothers, review of *Girl Meets God,* p. 97.
New York Times Book Review, December 15, 2002, Reeve Lindbergh, "Born Again . . . and Again," p. 24.
Publishers Weekly, August 12, 2002, review of *Girl Meets God,* p. 293.
Sojourners, November-December, 2002, Andrea Jeyaveeran, "Reinventing a Religious Self," p. 50.
Wall Street Journal, October 4, 2002, Susan Lee, "No Ordinary Path," p. W27.
Wilson Quarterly, winter, 2003, C. Michael Curtis, review of *Girl Meets God,* p. 122.*

*   *   *

WOOD, Gaby

PERSONAL: Female. *Education:* Attended Cambridge University.

ADDRESSES: Office—*Observer,* 119 Farringdon Rd., London EC1R 3ER, England.

CAREER: Journalist and author. *Observer,* London, England, staff writer.

WRITINGS:

The Smallest of All Persons Mentioned in the Record of Littleness, Profile Books (London, England), 1998.
Edison's Eve: A Magical History of the Quest for Mechanical Life, Knopf (New York, NY), 2002, published in England as *Living Dolls: A Magical History of the Quest for Mechanical Life,* Faber and Faber (London, England), 2002.

Contributor to *London Review of Books* and *Guardian.*

SIDELIGHTS: British journalist Gaby Wood's first book, *The Smallest of All Persons Mentioned in the Record of Littleness,* documents the life and career of Caroline Crachami, a twenty-inch-tall girl born at the beginning of the nineteenth century who was exhibited as the "Sicilian Fairy." She died before she turned nine, and it was then that her history became known. Her father, Emmanuel Crachami, was a Sicilian musician who played at the Theatre Royal in Dublin, and who went by the name of Lewis Fogle. When Fogle consulted with a Dr. Gilligan about his daughter's health, the doctor was granted permission to bring her to London from Sicily for exhibition, the profits from which would pay the medical bills.

Unknown to Fogle, Gilligan had made a financial deal with the Royal College of Surgeons, in which he agreed that if she died, he would deliver her body for dissection and experimentation. When the child did pass away, Fogle came for her remains, only to find that dissection had already begun. Caroline Crachami's skeleton is displayed to this day in the Hunterian Museum of the Royal College of Surgeons, alongside that of Irish giant Charles Byrne.

Roy Porter wrote in the London *Observer,* "Was the Fairy fascinating mainly because she was what Leslie Fiedler has called a 'scale freak'? Or did she, Gaby Wood wonders, owe her allure to her erotic ambivalence, a baby-like near-adolescent, packaged as that archetypal male fantasy, the living doll?" He concluded, "Here is a little book that raises big issues."

Edison's Eve: A Magical History of the Quest for Mechanical Life, published in England as *Living Dolls: A Magical History of the Quest for Mechanical Life,* discusses the history of mechanical dolls. *New Statesman* contributor Edward Platt wrote that "Wood believes that contemporary attempts to devise robots capable of thought or feeling should be understood in the context of a long history of similar attempts, and she begins her account of the 'quest for mechanical life' during the Enlightenment—the golden age of the philosophical toy, when the 'ambitions of the necromancers were revived in the well-respected name of science.'"

The title chapter is a history of one of Thomas Edison's least successful inventions, a mass-produced talking doll fitted with a tiny phonograph-like device. The manufacture of each doll required 250 production workers. Brian Aldiss noted in *Times Literary Supplement* that "the dolls recited 'Mary had a little lamb,' much as HAL, in the later Kubrick film, was to recite 'Daisy, Daisy,' to similar chilling effect, one imagines."

Wood describes the Swiss clockwork dolls of Pierre Jacquet-Droz, dolls that could pick up a quill and write with it. She suggests that Mary Shelley might have been inspired by these lifelike dolls to write about a creature assembled from human parts lifted from graveyards. Hungarian Wolfgang von Kempelen created a chess player, the wooden "Automatic Turk" that moved the pieces and rolled its eyes, although it was known to be controlled by a person hidden in its workings. It was later learned that Kempelen and later owners of the contraption had hired the greatest chess masters of the time to direct its movements. It beat Napoleon Bonaparte, and in a match with Catherine the Great, she was disqualified for cheating. The outcome of a match against Benjamin Franklin is undocumented.

It ends with a chapter about the Schneiders, who billed themselves as the Doll Family. They were dwarfs who toured with the Ringling Brothers Circus during the 1920s and later appeared in *The Wizard of Oz,* but they did nothing to dissuade audiences from believing that they were mechanical—like the inventions Wood discusses in the book. They were thought by most observers to be sophisticated mechanical dolls. At the time of the book's publication, thirty-nine-inch tall Tiny Doll, the surviving member, was in her late eighties and living in Florida.

An *Economist* reviewer noted that the techniques used to develop these inventions were a precursor to the industrial revolution, and said that "the men who made them, as Gaby Wood relates . . . were driven by the desire to play God." Wood describes her visit to a Japanese robotics laboratory, drawing comparisons between the present-day obsession with mechanical life and its counterpart centuries ago. A *Kirkus Reviews* contributor noted that although these mechanical marvels that could tell fortunes, play chess, and write poetry are very unlike the computer-driven robots of the present, "Wood finds the sentiments of compulsion and fascination . . . to be a constant passed from tinkerer to cyberneticist." *New York Times Book Review* contributor Miranda Seymour concluded by calling *Edison's Eve* "a lively, elegant, and surprising book, packed with curious details and enticing anecdotes."

BIOGRAPHICAL AND CRITICAL SOURCES:

PERIODICALS

Choice, February, 2003, J. Y. Cheung, review of *Edison's Eve: A Magical History of the Quest for Mechanical Life,* p. 1002.

Economist (US), March 9, 2002, review of *Living Dolls: A Magical History of the Quest for Mechanical Life.*

Forbes FYI, September 16, 2002, John Glassie, review of *Edison's Eve,* p. 120.

Kirkus Reviews, June 15, 2002, review of *Edison's Eve,* p. 871.

London Review of Books, May 9, 2002, Jonathan Rée, review of *Living Dolls,* pp. 16-18.

New Statesman, March 4, 2002, Edward Platt, review of *Living Dolls,* pp. 50-51.

New York Review of Books, February 13, 2003, Jennifer Schuessler, review of *Edison's Eve,* pp. 29-31.

New York Times Book Review, August 25, 2002, Miranda Seymour, review of *Edison's Eve,* p. 14.

Observer (London, England), June 28, 1998, Roy Porter, review of *The Smallest of All Persons Mentioned in the Record of Littleness,* p. 17.

Publishers Weekly, June 17, 2002, review of *Edison's Eve,* p. 52.

Spectator, March 2, 2002, Raymond Keene, review of *Living Dolls,* pp. 41-42.

Times Literary Supplement, May 3, 2002, Brian Aldiss, review of *Living Dolls,* p. 33.

ONLINE

Complete Review, http://www.complete-review.com/ (January 8, 2003), review of *Living Dolls.*

Guardian, http://books.guardian.co.uk/ (February 16, 2002), excerpt from *Living Dolls.*

Star Tribune, http://www.startribune.com/ (September 22, 2002), John Freeman, review of *Edison's Eve.**

*   *   *

WORTHEN, John

PERSONAL: Male. *Education:* Cambridge Univerisity, B.A.; Kent University, M.A. and Ph.D.

ADDRESSES: Office—School of English Studies, the University of Nottingham, University Park, Nottingham NG7 2RD, England.

CAREER: University of Nottingham, professor of D.H. Lawernce Studies.

WRITINGS:

D. H. Lawrence and the Idea of the Novel, Rowman and Littlefield (Totowa, NJ), 1979.

D. H. Lawrence: A Literary Life, St. Martin's Press (New York, NY), 1989.

D. H. Lawrence, E. Arnold (London, England), 1991.

D. H. Lawrence, the Early Years, 1885-1912, Cambridge University Press (New York, NY), 1991.

(Editor, with Paul Eggert) *Lawrence and Comedy,* Cambridge University Press (New York, NY), 1996.

The Gang: Coleridge, the Hutchinsons and Wordsworths in 1802, Yale University Press (New Haven, CT), 2001.

(Editor, with Ezra Greenspan and Lindeth Vasey) *Studies in Classic American Literature/D.H. Lawrence,* Cambridge University Press (New York, NY), 2003.

EDITOR OF BOOKS BY D. H. LAWRENCE

The Lost Girl, Cambridge University (New York, NY), 1981, revised edition, Penguin (New York, NY) 1995.

The Rainbow, Penguin (New York, NY), 1981.

The Prussian Officer and Other Stories, Cambridge University Press (New York, NY), 1983, revised edition, Penguin (New York, NY), 1995.

Love Among the Haystacks and Other Stories, Cambridge University Press (New York, NY), 1987, revised edition, Penguin (New York, NY), 1996.

(With David Farmer and Lindeth Vasey) *Women in Love,* Penguin Books (New York, NY), 1995.

(With Lindeth Vasey) *The First 'Women in Love',* Cambridge University Press (New York, NY), 1998.

(With Hans-Wilhelm Schwarze) *The Plays,* Cambridge University Press (New York, NY), 1999.

Contributed "The Life of D. H. Lawrence" biography section to *D. H. Lawrence: A Reference Companion,* Paul Poplawski, Greenwood Press (Westport, CT), 1996.

SIDELIGHTS: Since the late 1970s, University of Nottingham professor John Worthen has built a reputation as one of today's leading D. H. Lawrence scholars. He's published three biographies of Lawrence and edited more than half a dozen editions of Lawrence's works.

The first of Worthen's books to receive widespread critical and mainstream attention was 1989's *D. H. Lawrence: A Literary Life,* which focused on Lawrence as a professional writer and examined how his finances and the marketplace influenced his writing. Paul Delany of the *London Review of Books* stated that "Worthen argues convincingly that economic necessity directly affected Lawrence's style and choice of subjects." Charles Rossman, in *Modern Fiction Studies,* notes that the author "is interested in the tension that Lawrence felt during his entire writing life between 'earning a living with his pen' and 'saying exactly what he wanted.'" *Choice's* M. Tucker praised Worthen's "novel and fascinating approach to a writer's biography," and declared *D. H. Lawrence: A Literary Life* "An impressive summary of DHL's career."

In 1991 Worthen penned the first volume of the Cambridge University Press's three-volume biography of Lawrence. *D. H. Lawrence, the Early Years, 1885-1912* covered how the author's childhood in Eastland and the Midlands, the role of class in his upbringing, his teaching stint in London, and his early relationships laid the groundwork for his later writing. Daniel J. Schneider, in the *Modern Language Review,* felt that "Worthen . . . has seen Lawrence's early life freshly, penetratingly, and with remarkable objectivity." James Fenton, in the *New York Review of Books,* found that "Worthen is particularly good on the background—the nuances of class, what was poverty, what was a respectable income." Karen McLeod of the *Review of English Studies* praised how "Worthen ingeniously manages to combine Lawrentian fluidity and a coherent structure" to create a "subtle and humane biography."

For *Lawrence and Comedy* Worthen teamed with Paul Eggert to edit a collection of writings illuminating Lawrence's oft-ignored humor. Mara Kalnins of *Notes and Queries* appreciated the effort, stating, "It is a tribute to Eggert, Worthen and their contributors to this fine volume that they have redressed the imbalance of received critical opinion on Lawrence and revealed not only the gaiety and sense of fun that characterized [Lawrence] . . . but also the energetic wordplay, wit, humour, and laughter . . . that informs his art."

In 2001 Worthen expanded his circle from Lawrence to address another of his literary interests: Wordsworth and Coleridge. *The Gang: Coleridge, the Hutchinsons and Wordsworths in 1802* looks at the tight group that formed around the two Romantic poets during an intense six-month period in 1802, a "gang" that included Wordsworth's sister Dorothy and the Hutchinson sisters Sara and Mary. The book explores the dynamics of the group's relationships leading up to Wordsworth's marriage to Mary Hutchinson in October of 1802, and examines how the social situation created a fertile environment for Coleridge and Wordsworth to pen some of their most important poems. A contributor to *Publishers Weekly* stated that "Worthen does a fine job balancing the personal with the critical and offers those who idolize one or both of the poets much to consider."

BIOGRAPHICAL AND CRITICAL SOURCES:

PERIODICALS

Choice, April, 1990, M. Tucker, review of *D. H. Lawrence: A Literary Life,* p. 1326; June, 1999, J. E. Steiner, review of *The First 'Women in Love',* p. 1787.

English Language Notes, December 12, 1997, Mark Spilka, review of *Lawrence and Comedy,* pp. 74-79.

English Literature in Transition 1880-1920, spring, 2000, Peter Balbert, review of *The First 'Women in Love',* pp. 236-239; winter, 2001, J. P. Wearing, review of *The Plays,* pp. 122-125.

Essays in Criticism, October 10, 1988, Charles L. Ross, review of *Women in Love,* pp. 342-351.

Library Journal, March 1, 2001, Scott Hightower, review of *The Gang: Coleridge, the Hutchinsons and Wordsworths in 1802,* p. 93.

London Review of Books, January 24, 1991, Paul Delany, "Keeping Up the Fight," review of *D.H. Lawrence: A Literary Life,* pp. 22-23.

Modern Fiction Studies, winter, 1990, Charles Rossman, review of *D. H. Lawrence: A Literary Life,* pp. 604-608.

Modern Language Review, April, 1993, Daniel J. Schneider, review of *D. H. Lawrence, the Early Years, 1885-1912,* pp. 433-435.

National Review, May 27, 1988, Jeffrey Meyers, review of *Women in Love,* p. 54.

New York Review of Books, October 22, 1998, James Fenton, "Men, Women & Beasts," review of *D.H. Lawrence, the Early Years, 1885-1912,* pp. 51-58.

Notes and Queries, June, 1993, Mara Kalnins, review of *D. H. Lawrence, the Early Years, 1885-1912,* pp. 261-263; September, 1998, Mara Kalnins, review of *Lawrence and Comedy,* pp. 402-404; December 12, 1999, Mara Kalnins, review of *The First 'Women in Love',* pp. 553-554.

Publishers Weekly, August 2, 1991, review of *D. H. Lawrence, the Early Years, 1885-1912,* p. 56; February 26, 2001, review of *The Gang,* p. 75.

Review of English Studies, February, 1993, Karen McLeod, review of *D. H. Lawrence, the Early Years, 1885-1912,* p. 142.*

*   *   *

WYLIE, Diana 1948-

PERSONAL: Born January 1, 1948, in Woodbury, CT; daughter of Andrew Duncan and Jeanne (Sands) Wylie. *Education:* Goucher College, B.A., 1969, University of Edinburgh, M.Litt., 1974, Yale University, Ph.D. (history), 1984.

ADDRESSES: Home—22 Phillips St., Boston, MA 02114. *Office*—Department of History, Boston University, Boston, MA 02215. *E-mail*—dwylie@bu.edu.

CAREER: Educator and historian. University of Oran, Algeria, instructor in history, 1975-76; Vassar College, Poughkeepsie, NY, instructor in history, 1978-79; Mount Holyoke College, South Hadley, MA, assistant professor of history, 1982, 1985; Yale University, New Haven, CT, assistant professor, 1985-91, associate professor of history, 1991-94, associate director of Southern African research program, 1985-94, member of advisory committee on Yale Educational Initiatives in South Africa, 1986-87; Boston University, Boston, MA, associate professor, 1994-2003, professor of history, 2003—. Visiting professor at Harvard University, 1999-2000; presenter at numerous conferences. Peace Corps volunteer in Kenya, 1970-71; editor for Holmes & Meier, Publishers, New York, NY, 1974-82.

AWARDS, HONORS: Yale University Morse Junior Faculty fellowship, 1988-89; Senior Faculty fellowship, 1992-93; Social Science Research Council midcareer fellowship, 2000; Marion and Jasper Whiting fellowship, 2001; Boston University Humanities Foundation senior fellow, 2002-03; Metcalf Award for Excellence in Teaching, Boston University, 2002; Melville J. Herskovits Award, African Studies Association, and *Choice* Outstanding Academic Book designation, both 2002, both for *Starving on a Full Stomach.*

WRITINGS:

A Little God: The Twilight of Patriarchy in a Southern African Chiefdom, Wesleyan University Press (Middletown, CT), 1990.
Starving on a Full Stomach: Hunger and the Triumph of Cultural Racism in Modern South Africa, University Press of Virginia (Charlottesville, VA), 2001.

Contributor to books, including *Oxford History of the British Empire,* 1999, *Multi-Cultural Space and Fabric in the Eastern Mediterranean,* edited by Maurice Cerasi and Stefan Weber, 2004, and *Dictionary of Labour Biography.* Contributor to periodicals, including *Past and Present, Journal of African History, Journal of Imperial and Commonwealth History,* and *Yale Review.* Member of editorial board, *International Journal of African Historical Studies,* 1998—.

WORK IN PROGRESS: A biography of South African artist T. H. Mnyele; research into the history of architecture and city planning in Rabat, Morocco.

SIDELIGHTS: Historian and educator Diana Wylie has focused primarily on the history of southern Africa in both her academic career and in her writing. The author of two books on the recent history of South Africa and nearby regions, Wylie has conducted extensive research in Botswana and South Africa, in archives as well as by interviewing the region's inhabitants.

Based on Wylie's Ph.D. dissertation at Yale University, *A Little God: The Twilight of Patriarchy in a Southern African Chiefdom* delves into the nineteenth-and early twentieth-century social structures of Southern Africa's Tswana society as local cultures changed with the advent of colonial rule. Focusing in particular on the Ngwato chiefdom, she shows how the growth of the region's diamond and gold mining industries transformed the traditional chief, Tshekedi Khama, into both and adversary and an agent of the colonial government, while the chief's traditional patriarchal roles were both strengthened and weakened by colonial courts and governments. Calling Wylie's book "well-written" and "interesting to read" due to its wealth of factual detail, *Africa Today* contributor Mohamed H. Abucar nonetheless took issue with the author's "modernization approach," which Abucar contended "undermines understanding the effect structural changes have on the value system" of the Tswana. In *African Affairs* Neil Parsons viewed Wylie's work more favorably, noting that in *A Little God* Wylie "deftly weaves the pattern of events" and highlights issues centrally important to the region's rural past.

Starvation has become linked in many minds with the African continent, and Wylie examines the implications of this connection in *Starving on a Full Stomach: Hunger and the Triumph of Cultural Racism in Modern South Africa.* In this 2002 book she presents what *Isis* contributor Keith Snedegar referred to as "an impressive yet accessible work on nutritional science as failed mediator between European and African food cultures." In African food culture the quantity of food formerly varied with the seasons, and so people prized plenty, while in the European's view the preparation and variety of foodstuffs marked class distinctions. From these roots, many South African whites evolved a theory of cultural racism: they justified white supremacy by explaining that Africans, who were hungry for political and economic reasons, were, rather, ignorant or science and, thus, not eligible for inclusion in the modern state. In the *Journal of Social*

History Clifton Crais praised Wylie's book for presenting readers with "many useful insights on the politics of poverty over nearly two centuries of historical change." Snedegar also praised Wylie's efforts by noting that in *Starving on a Full Stomach* she "exhibits a breadth of scholarship and clarity of style that will make it rewarding for a wide audience."

Wylie told *CA:* "I often say to my students 'Writing is thinking,' and so it follows logically that one reason why I write is to figure things out.

"Because I am an historian of Africa, that task entails imagining myself into a time and place far removed from my New England roots. Further, because my audience may be similarly removed from Africa's past, I try to express my insights in the least arcane prose possible. I want to avoid abstruse academic writing, tangled up in excessively complex theory: it distances most readers from the tangible realities of the continent. At a time when the news out of Africa has become a litany of disaster and despair, I would like to help people—those who read—to apply to Africa the same analytical concepts they bring to bear on other continents. And I would like to render Africa less exotic for them by making vivid the simple details of daily life: the markets that work and the ones that don't; the feasts as well as the hunger; the graffiti and the humor and the songs.

"The data I have collected during my field trips have *made* me tell certain stories. I have learned that the historian is as much a conduit for the story the past wants to tell as a storyteller in her own right. What I strive hardest to express is a holistic view of the past, that is, the integration of the political with the material with the cultural aspects of people's lives."

BIOGRAPHICAL AND CRITICAL SOURCES:

PERIODICALS

African Affairs, April, 1993, Neil Parsons, review of *A Little God: The Twilight of Patriarchy in a Southern African Chiefdom,* p. 304.

Africa Today, winter, 1993, Mohamed H. Abucar, review of *A Little God,* p. 74.

Isis, March, 2003, Keith Snedegar, review of *Starving on a Full Stomach: Hunger and the Triumph of Cultural Racism in Modern South Africa,* p. 196.

Journal of African History, July, 2002, Bill Freund, review of *Starving on a Full Stomach,* p. 341.

Journal of Social History, spring, 2003, Clifton Crais, review of *Starving on a Full Stomach,* p. 802.